PHILIP'S

Green ROAD

Contents

II **Britain's road transport** – what's the damage?
III **Emissions** – what goes in must come out
IV **Choosing to go Green** – what you need to know about cars, emissions and fuel
V **ETA Car Buyers' Guide**
VI **Making a difference** – the ETA's green tips for drivers
VIII **The bigger picture**

X **Route planning maps** with list of restricted motorway junctions
XVI **Distance table**

1 **Key to road map pages**
2 **Road maps at 3 miles to 1 inch**

177 **Town plans and urban area maps**

- 177 Aberdeen, Bath, Birmingham
- 178 Birmingham *approaches*
- 180 Blackpool, Bournemouth, Bradford, Brighton
- 192 Bradford *approaches*
- 181 Bristol, Cambridge, Canterbury
- 182 Bristol *approaches*
- 183 Cardiff *approaches*
- 184 Cardiff, Cheltenham, Chester
- 185 Colchester, Coventry, Derby, Durham
- 186 Edinburgh *approaches*
- 187 Edinburgh, Glasgow
- 188 Glasgow *approaches*
- 190 Exeter, Gloucester, Hull, Ipswich
- 191 Leeds, Lancaster, Leicester
- 193 Leeds *approaches*
- 194 Liverpool, Lincoln, Middlesbrough
- 195 Liverpool *approaches*
- 196 London
- 198 London *approaches*
- 206 Manchester, Milton Keynes, Northampton
- 207 Manchester *approaches*
- 208 Newcastle, Norwich, Oxford
- 209 Newcastle *approaches*
- 210 Nottingham, Plymouth, Portsmouth, Preston
- 211 Nottingham *approaches*
- 212 Reading, Salisbury, Sheffield
- 213 Sheffield *approaches*
- 214 Scarborough, Southampton, Stoke-on-Trent (Hanley), Stratford upon Avon
- 215 Sunderland, Swansea, Telford, Torquay
- 216 Winchester, Windsor, Worcester, York

217 **M25 and routes into London**
218 **M60 and routes into Manchester and Liverpool**

219 **Airport and port plans**

- 219 Heathrow, Gatwick, Manchester
- 220 Dover, Felixstowe, Portsmouth, Southampton

221 **The Channel**

- 221 Boulogne and Calais town plans and area map
- 222 Cross-Channel ferry map

224 **Index** to road maps of Great Britain

Britain's road transport – what's the damage?

Britain now has almost 250,000 miles of roads. That's about the distance from the Earth to the Moon. In the course of a single year it's estimated that the vehicles using these roads – motorbikes, cars, vans, lorries, buses – travel a staggering 310 billion miles, the equivalent of well over one million journeys to the Moon. Along the way, these vehicles consume about 38 million tons of petroleum. Add in the petroleum used by other forms of transport and that figure is closer to 53 million tons.

When petrol is combusted as fuel, harmful by-products are emitted, including greenhouse gases, which clog up the atmosphere and prevent all of the heat from the sun bouncing right back into space (for a comprehensive breakdown of different emissions, see opposite). If greenhouse gases didn't exist at all, Earth would be too cold to sustain life, but emissions produced by human activities have pushed the levels of greenhouse gases in the atmosphere to record levels, and they continue to rise. And as they rise, the world heats up.

In 2000, road transport in Britain generated some 32 million tons of one of the most damaging greenhouse gases, carbon dioxide, classified as such because of the length of time it takes to be broken down in the atmosphere. That figure is rising all the time and is predicted to reach 34 million tons by 2015. That is still under a quarter of the total projected CO_2 emissions, but by comparison, other forms of transport are expected to generate only 2.6 million tons in the same period. The figures for other greenhouse gases are more severe: road transport produces some 88% of Britain's total carbon monoxide emissions; 48% of nitrogen oxides; and 37% of hydrocarbons.

Speculation about the long-term effects of these emissions (which, of course, are only a fraction of the world's total) range in severity from the anxious to the apocalyptic. But other than a questionably motivated few, no-one now doubts the truth of global warming. It is again only those few that doubt the critical need to rein in our emissions and start reducing them as soon as possible. With road emissions constituting such a large proportion of the overall totals, it is one area where radical, lasting change is not merely desirable but imperative.

The global picture

The Intergovernmental Panel on Climate Change estimates that by 2100, the mean world temperature will have increased by between 1.4°C and 5.8°C, though the change could be even greater; the actual figure depends upon human activity during that period. Most scientists would agree that a 6°C average rise in temperature would be nothing short of catastrophic; the general consensus is that 2°C represents the ceiling above which the situation would start to be untenable.

All the good intentions in the world would not bring about an overnight halt to the rise in emissions and temperatures; and in any case, amongst the world's powers there are still those that are somewhat lacking in good intentions. Some governments are rejecting the demands for cuts in their emissions because of the restrictive effect that would have on their economy.

Those organisations and governments that wholeheartedly accept the need for rapid change have, by and large, recognised the 2°C threshold, and have agreed to set targets to ensure that it is never transgressed. The Kyoto Treaty was one of the milestones in this process, though it has been blighted by uncooperative countries and others that have failed to meet their promises.

Road transport: what's being done?

The British government recognises the acuteness of the situation and accepts the need for swift action. And with road transport responsible for a significant proportion of overall emissions, naturally that is one of the areas being targeted via new regulations and taxes.

In 1998 a White Paper published by the government set out plans for what it called an 'integrated transport policy'. Its overall goal was to present a transport strategy that would improve the health, safety, and economic wealth of the British people and their environment. A key component of this strategy was to be a regime of taxation that took stock of the damage caused to the environment by transport.

The most significant change in taxation so far has been the redefinition of car tax (technically Vehicle Excise Duty, 'VED') categories according to the emissions levels of each individual vehicle. Cars registered before 1 March 2001 are taxed according to their engine size, but newer vehicles are charged according to their levels of CO_2 emissions. The greenest vehicles can currently expect reductions of up to 100% off the standard fee, while the most harmful vehicles will be taxed at a rate 110% higher than the standard fee.

Road charging

The ETA (Environmental Transport Association) approves of the government's general notion of an integrated transport policy, but believes that the environment would benefit more if road transport was funded not by distributed taxes, but by charges levied at the point of consumption. In other words, those who use the roads more should pay as they use the roads, and in direct proportion to their use. To an extent this system is already in place via fuel tax; but the ETA believes that fuel tax is an outmoded system and that we can go even further.

In early 2007 the government's controversial 'Road User Charging' ('RUC' aka 'pay as you drive') plans made the headlines after a petition of protest garnered over one million signatures on the government's website. Objections included the argument that RUC was a 'stealth tax' to be levied on top of existing taxes, leaving people increasingly out of pocket. Another significant objection relates to concerns about the 'big brother' implications of a system where charges are calculated via a satellite tracking system that monitors each journey.

The ETA believes that the online petition drastically misrepresented the philosophy and possibilities of RUC. Firstly, it is not a 'stealth tax'. In fact, it is not a system of taxation at all, but a system of charges, whereby the consumer pays directly in exchange for a service. What's more, these charges could be a replacement for current taxes, not supplementary. Secondly, because the charges would be linked directly to congestion, the scheme would help free up busy roads and ultimately benefit all motorists. Charges would be levied in congested areas; so a car travelling along a free-flowing motorway might pay nothing at all, and rural drivers would pay the least. Thirdly, the satellite tracking system would not supply any more information to supposedly Machiavellian authorities than is already available via the tracking of mobile phones.

In some guise Road User Charging is, in the ETA's opinion, the only scheme to offer a significant long-term benefit to the environment. Fuel tax and VED could be phased out as RUC is phased in. The only tax advocated by the ETA is a duty on fuel at the point of production or import (ie paid by the fossil fuel producers). This 'carbon tax' would be calculated based on the prospective emissions of the fuel. Individual consumers would not be affected by this tax.

And what can I do?

It's not just the actions of governments which will help to bring emissions and global warming under control. Every individual has the power to supplement these big decisions with their own positive actions. Over the next four pages you will find information about how you, as a driver, can do your best to help the environment. Then on pages VIII-IX we explain how those attitudes can be put in a wider context, with a guide to calculating your personal carbon footprint. There is also more information about all these subjects on the ETA website: **www.eta.co.uk**

Emissions – what goes in must come out

Cars emit a complex cocktail of exhaust gases, many of which cause damage to our bodies and to the planet. The ETA cites the following list as the major pollutants and gives some of their harmful effects.

Benzene – C_6H_6

This naturally occurring hydrocarbon is found in crude oil, and therefore petrol, but is also produced during its refinement and combustion. Although typical atmospheric levels of Benzene are thought not to be harmful, benzene is carcinogenic, so high levels of inhalation are a serious threat to health.

Cadmium – Cd

This metal occurs naturally in the Earth's crust, and is released into the air in the form of various cadmium compounds on the combustion of petrol and other fossil fuels. Cadmium oxide, one of the main by-products of combustion, is damaging to the lungs and kidneys if inhaled or ingested, and is thought to be carcinogenic.

Carbon Dioxide – CO_2

Although CO_2 is not harmful at normal atmospheric concentrations, it is the principal agent of climate change today, and arguably the most dangerous pollutant of all. Transportation is the fastest growing source of CO_2 emissions, with road transport accounting for between a fifth and a quarter of Britain's emissions.

The main way to cut these emissions is through reducing our use of fuel, and this can be done by (a) driving less, and (b) using cars with higher fuel efficiency. You can also help offset the emissions you do create by making your driving carbon neutral. For more information, see pages IV-IX

Carbon Monoxide – CO

This is a toxic, colourless and odourless gas, produced by the incomplete combustion of fossil fuels such as coal, oil, petrol and gas. In Britain, road traffic is responsible for over 70% of CO emissions. CO reduces the oxygen carrying capacity of the blood, and its inhalation can cause headaches, nausea, fatigue, and at high concentrations, coma and death. CO also adds to ground-level ozone concentrations, combining with other pollutants to form photochemical smog, and is one of the minor anthropogenic gases contributing to climate change.

Nitrogen Oxides – NOx

There are a number of nitrogen oxides, all of which are produced by the combustion of fossil fuels. Not only do they aggravate asthmatic conditions by reacting with oxygen in the air to form the irritant ozone, they are also one of the key causal agents of acid rain. Atmospheric moisture becomes acidified upon reaction with NOx; when this moisture subsequently falls as rain it inhibits the growth of plants, is damaging to freshwater and soil life, and even buildings. Nitrogen oxides also contribute to photochemical smog. They irritate the lungs, and increase susceptibility to viral infections. In Britain, 44% of NOx emissions come from road vehicles.

Particulates

Diesel engines emit particulates (soot), which are increasingly being linked with asthma. Although car manufacturers are attempting to make these particulates smaller (as is now legally required), the new micro-particulates now penetrate even further into the lungs resulting in less obvious, but longer-term damage. Some estimates have suggested that particulates are responsible for up to 10,000 premature deaths per year in Britain alone. Some 25% of particulates come from road transport. The black, smoky exhaust of a badly maintained diesel vehicle contains dangerously high levels of soot and should be reported to the Smoky Vehicle hotline on 0870 60 60 440.

Sulphur Dioxide – SO_2

This is a colourless gas with a smell akin to burnt matches, and is emitted by both petrol and diesel engines. Along with nitrogen oxides, SO_2 contributes to acid rain. The gas can also cause breathing problems, aggravate asthma, and worsen both respiratory and cardiovascular disease. It also precipitates the formation of acid aerosols, which are detrimental to health and contribute further to climate change.

Further information

For more information go to **www.eta.co.uk**

Choosing to go Green – what you need to know about cars, emissions and fuel

Making a difference

With road transport responsible for 88% of Britain's carbon monoxide emissions and almost a fifth of its carbon dioxide emissions, the best thing for the environment would be the total elimination of petrol-based vehicles; or better still, of road transport altogether. But this is sheer fantasy: road transport is inextricably linked to our economy and culture; modern society would collapse without it. If we want to halt the damage that our vehicles are inflicting on the environment, we must settle for the next best strategy: to get a hold on that damage, and then minimise or neutralise it as best we can.

The power to curb the damage lies not only with governments and multinational organisations, but also with road users themselves. It's only through the collective, positive efforts of individual drivers and passengers that the large-scale damage limitation our planet acutely requires will be achieved.

For any individual, the first step along this road is, of course, the simple but conscious acceptance of the need to act. In more scientific terms, that means deciding to reduce or neutralise our 'carbon footprint' (see page VIII for a detailed explanation). And one of the most effective ways for any road user to do this is by opting to drive a greener vehicle.

What car?

If only it were as simple as investing in a petrol-free car and just getting on with it. Yet the question of which vehicle to choose defies a straightforward answer. The first consideration is the debate over buying new vs buying second-hand. On the one hand, emissions standards are improving all the time, so the newest vehicles are the least damaging. On the other hand, it's estimated that the manufacturing process of any given vehicle generates up to 20% of its lifetime emissions; so the continued, unchecked manufacture of new vehicles is in itself environmentally unsound. If you can, buy a near-new second-hand car, though ultimately the question of whether you choose new or second-hand is secondary to the more important issue of which vehicle you buy. Your usage habits are also very significant, and on pages VI–VII we offer advice about how best to use (and indeed not use!) your car to minimise its harmfulness.

What to consider when buying a car

Definitive environmental information about a specific make and model of car is not always easy to obtain, particularly with older cars. But a car's environmental impact is invariably related to a few key factors.

Size

Consider both the size of the engine and the size of the car overall as both affect the emissions. A car weighs on average around 1,500kg and a human less than 70kg, which means that a car's weight is about twenty times that of a person. Therefore twenty times as much energy is required to move the car than the person in it. Likewise twenty times as much pollution is caused by the weight of the car than the weight of the driver. A simple rule is to buy the smallest that is practical for you.

Age

Over the past few decades there has been a broad trend amongst car manufacturers towards reducing emissions. As a rule of thumb, a newer car will be cleaner than an older car of a similar

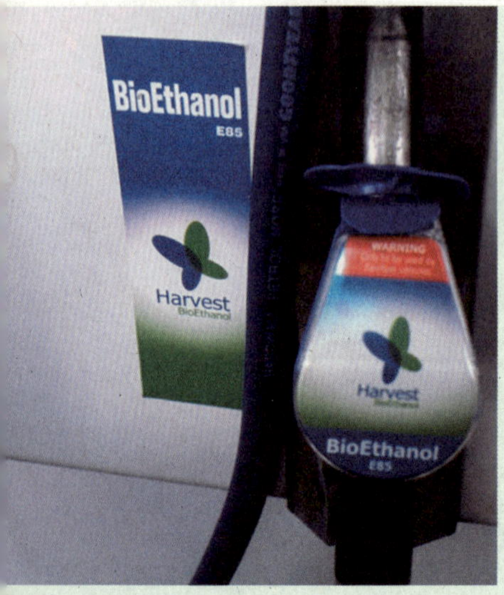

Alternative fuels

Some of the earliest cars were designed to run on non-fossil fuels. The Model T Ford, first produced in 1908, was originally designed to use ethanol, while Rudolf Diesel's demonstration engine ran on peanut oil in 1912. But petroleum-based engines rapidly became the norm because of the ready availability and low cost of the fuel.

Concerns about the environmental impact of conventional fuels have led to extensive research into, and development of, new forms of fuel during recent years; and though none yet rivals the combination of convenience and cost offered by the older fuels, technologies continue to improve.

This quick-reference guide to alternative fuels will help the environmentally conscious car buyer to understand the relative merits of the different fuel options available, and offers practical information about their availability in Britain.

Compressed natural gas – CNG

This is the fuel used in most homes. Though still a finite resource, CNG emits less carbon dioxide (and other harmful substances) per mile than the other fossil fuels (though the methane offsets this to a degree; the overall impact is comparable to that of diesel). CNG engines are also quieter than conventional engines.

Existing petrol and diesel engines can be converted to run on CNG; the procedure costs between £1,500 and £2,500. Filling stations supplying CNG are still limited, but it is also possible to refuel your vehicle from home using a 'trickle charge' system. This involves a slow-fill compressor unit that charges over a period of 5-6 hours.

Liquified Petroleum Gas – LPG

Though as a by-product of the refinement of crude oil or natural gas, LPG is still a fossil fuel, when used as a car fuel it has significantly lower emissions than conventional fuels. Indeed, levels are around 80% of the nitrogen oxides and 85% of the carbon dioxide generated by a petrol engine.

Regular petrol and diesel engines can be converted to run LPG at a cost of between £1,200 and £2,000. LPG is so far the only 'alternative' fuel with a sufficiently large distribution network. The Energy Saving Trust (www.energysavingtrust.org.uk) maintains an up-to-date list of refuelling points.

www.eta.co.uk/page.asp?p=287

Biofuels

Because they derive from organic matter, biofuels are by definition a renewable resource. More importantly, the plants grown to produce biofuels absorb the same amount of carbon dioxide as is released when the fuels are burned. Because of this their emissions levels are far lower than those of conventional fuels. We currently lack the infrastructure to deliver biofuels widely to road users, but there are also reservations over their long-term viability. It's estimated that 90% of the world's current agricultural land would be required to produce enough biofuel to satisfy our current petroleum-based needs.

At present, biofuels are predominantly available mixed in small measure with conventional fuels. Conventional engines can usually accept these fuels without modification. More concentrated biofuel options, or pure biofuel, usually necessitate an engine conversion.

Biodiesel – Diesel alternative

B5 (a blend of 5% biodiesel and 95% diesel) is sold in some filling stations across the country. Stronger blends and 100% biodiesel are mainly sold by specialist retailers.

Bioethanol – Petrol alternative

A lot of petrol sold in Britain already contains 5% bioethanol, although it is rarely labelled. A few filling stations in East Anglia and Somerset sell E85 (85% bioethanol).

Pure plant oil – Diesel alternative

Requires engine conversion (cost around £500). Available from specialist suppliers only.

Car Buyers' Guide

First published in 1992, the annual ETA Car Buyers' Guide now provides information on over 2,500 models, evaluating the greenest vehicles in every category. Published entirely on-line, in keeping with the ETA's environmental remit, the guide presents a table of detailed information for each vehicle. In addition, a combined score is calculated using statistics including emissions rates, fuel consumption, power to size ratio, plus data relating to noise, safety, etc.

size, but a poorly maintained newer car can be far worse than a well-maintained older one. VCA Car Fuel Data (www.vcacarfueldata.org.uk) has estimated that it would take eighty new cars to produce the same emissions per mile as a single vehicle made in 1970.

There have been two major environmental milestones in road legislation over the past decade. Cars sold in the EU after 1 January 2001 had to comply with emissions limits specified in a directive commonly called EURO III; those sold after 1 January 2007 must comply with an even stricter set of guidelines, EURO IV.

Fuel and engine type

It used to be a simple decision of petrol or diesel. Nowadays the first fuel choice any car buyer must make is still binary, but it has diversified into the choice between conventional or 'new' fuel. The majority of road vehicles still use the conventional fossil fuels, but these, though readily available and economical for drivers in the short term, are by far the most detrimental to the environment.

If you decide that conventional is your only option, it's worth remembering that diesel cars emit less carbon dioxide, carbon monoxide and hydrocarbons per mile than equivalent petrol cars. Nevertheless, their emissions of nitrogen oxides and particulates are higher.

A raft of alternative energy options has emerged over the last two decades; see our guide to these 'new' fuels (left). None of them is without its environmental consequences, but in general they provide a significantly greener alternative to conventional petrol and diesel.

Electric cars and hybrid engines

One 'new' option – which it could be argued is a third alternative altogether to conventional and 'new' fuels – is the battery-powered engine. Battery-powered cars offer, in principle, one of the most environmentally friendly solutions, since it's theoretically possible to recharge them using electricity generated from renewable sources (even if, in practice, this is hard to guarantee). The problem is that at present they cannot compete with conventionally-fuelled vehicles for either range or top speed.

However, those who require the speed and power of a conventional engine could consider using a hybrid engine. A hybrid engine supplements its battery power with energy from conventional fuel – but only when it is needed. This fuel can simultaneously be used to recharge the battery.

More detailed information about these topics, and about specific vehicles and their emissions, can be found in the ETA's annual Car Buyers' Guide (see right).

In 2007 the Honda Civic Hybrid was the best performer for the second year running, winning the overall award as well as the Small Family Car category.

An Innovation Award was introduced in 2007 to applaud a manufacturer that has demonstrated environmental concern through a new product or project, or in its production processes. The first winner was Saab, which has developed the first production car to run on E85 bio fuel.

Overall top five winners

1. Honda Civic Hybrid 1.41 IMA ES
2. Vauxhall Corsa 1.3 CDTi 16V
3. Toyota Yaris 1.4 D-4D Manual
4. Renault Modus 1.2 16V VVT
5. Daihatsu Sirion M300 1.0 EFi

Overall top five worst performers

1. Lamborghini Diablo Roadster L144
2. Lamborghini Murciélago 147 Roadster
3. Ferrari 575 Superamerica
4. Ferrari 612 Scagliatti
5. Bentley Azure

Winners and losers in specific categories

City – Tiny car with four seats or less

Winner	REVA G-Wiz	electric
Worst overall	Ford Ka 1.6 Duratec Sportka	petrol manual

Supermini – small car but roomier interior

Winner	VAUXHALL Corsa 1.3 CDTi 16V	diesel manual
Worst overall	Mini R52 Cooper S	petrol auto

Small family – the most popular category of car, suitable for most families

Winner	HONDA Civic Hybrid1.4 IMA ES	petrol/electric hybrid
Worst overall	Audi A3 Sportback S line 3.2 V6 Quattro	petrol manual

Large family – suitable for larger families or if you need that extra leg room/ storage space

Winner	MAZDA 6 2.0 TD 4/5 Door 121 PS & 143 PS	diesel manual
Worst overall	BMW 3 Series E46 M3 Convertible SMG MY2005	petrol manual

Small MPV – high-roofed vehicle with flexible seating/storage and high driving position for enhanced visibility

Winner	RENAULT Modus 1.2 16V VVT	petrol auto
Worst overall	Mercedes-Benz Viano 3.5 Low Roof	petrol auto

Executive – high quality features and premium comfort for long-distance driving, often used as company car

Winner	MERCEDES-BENZ E Class E320 CDI 225 W211	diesel auto
Worst overall	BMW 5 Series E60/E61 M5	petrol manual

MPV – people carrier up to seven seats with high roof, lots of storage space/ flexible seating and high driving position for enhanced visibility

Winner	SKODA Roomster 1.4 TDI PD (70bhp)	diesel manual
Worst overall	Cadillac SRX 3.6 V6	petrol auto

Off-road – off-road vehicle for country living

Winner	TOYOTA RAV4 2.2 D-4D 180 5 Door	diesel manual
Worst overall	Porsche Cayenne S 6-speed	petrol auto

Luxury – all the mod-cons, no expenses spared, gas guzzling status symbol

Winner	JAGUAR XJ 2.7	diesel auto
Worst overall	Bentley Azure	petrol auto

Sports – high speed, high risk, high emission often fuel-thirsty coupés, roadsters and sport vehicles

Winner	VAUXHALL Tigra 1.3 CDTi 16V 2 Door	diesel manual
Worst overall	Lamborghini Diablo Roadster L144	petrol manual

Innovation Winner

Winner	SAAB Bio Power Flex-Fuel Technology
Runner-up	MAZDA Paint Process

The full list of winners, losers and runners-up can be found in this year's Car Buyers' Guide, on-line at **www.eta.co.uk**

Making a difference – the ETA's green tips for drivers

Whatever your choice of vehicle – be it the smallest, battery-powered city runaround, or the largest, gas-guzzling, emissions-spluttering off-roader – there are countless steps you can take to reduce your environmental impact when you're on the road. With the tips and advice offered in this comprehensive guide, the overriding lesson is to remember that every little helps. So while it may seem a little over the top to have to take your golf clubs out of the car every time you've used them, or to switch off your engine when stationary for just a couple of minutes, don't be dissuaded. Be conscientious; be principled. Follow as much of this advice as often as you can – however trivial it may at first appear – and you can be confident that you are making a difference to the fortunes of the planet. Even better, broadcast this information far and wide; offer family and friends tips on how they too can reduce their impact on the road. It's not difficult to understand: a small change, made by many people, over a long period of time, equals a much bigger change. And that's just what the planet needs!

Car preparation

Reduce the weight of your car

The lighter your car, the less fuel required to propel it, and the less emissions released. Remove unnecessary items from your car if not needed for a particular journey – buggies, golf clubs, and tools to name but a few examples.

Remove roof-racks

If it's not needed, remove it, and reattach only when required. The wind resistance incurred by roof-racks dramatically increases fuel consumption.

Keep your tyres inflated

Check regularly that your tyres are inflated to the correct pressure. For every 6psi a tyre is under-inflated, fuel consumption increases by around 1%.

Maintain your car

Check that your engine is properly tuned, as this improves performance and limits fuel consumption. Have your car serviced at least once a year.

Refuelling

Avoid overfilling the tank; spilled fuel evaporates and releases harmful emissions.

Check your windows and lights

Ensuring that your windows are clean and your lights are working will make your journey safer.

Green products

When buying components and accessories for your car, buy products from environmentally conscious companies wherever possible. Good examples of greener products include fuel-saving tyres from Firestone (www.firestone-eu.com), Varta batteries for electric cars (www.varta-automotive.co.uk), and Zymol cleaning wax, for use with all road vehicles, which has no harsh chemical solvents, is water-based and blended without hydrocarbons (www.zymol.com).

Personal preparation

Rest

A well-rested driver is an alert driver and has better control. Even this can have its environmental benefits, because better control means more efficient driving, and ultimately less emissions.

Eyesight

Have your eyes tested regularly. Again, better control means more efficient driving and less harm to the environment.

Footwear

Even something as seemingly unimportant as your choice of shoes can affect the environmental impact of your driving. Footwear that is light and less bulky ensures a more sensitive control over the accelerator, thereby reducing emissions. Consider driving without shoes or purchasing driving shoes. Softer, lightweight shoes can easily be kept in the car for a quick change before you step on the accelerator.

Journey preparation

Consider planning as many jobs as possible in one trip

Get as much as you can out of each journey: five jobs achieved in one trip is better for the environment than five trips. Think ahead.

Never use a car for short journeys

If your journey is less than two miles, walk or cycle.

Avoid congested areas to reduce travel time

The less time you're in the car, the less harm you do to the environment. Avoid travel in the rush hour unless you absolutely have to.

Time shift your journey

Be conscious of traffic patterns, follow traffic reports, and think intelligently about the timing of every journey. Even a ten-minute delay can make all the difference to the amount of time spent in the car, especially in built-up areas.

◀ *Stationary rush-hour traffic on the M25*

Share cars

Don't be coy about sharing cars and journeys with friends and family. The average British commuting car has 1.2 passengers. If two car drivers shared a car they would reduce their overall pollution by 60 per cent. Not only would this benefit the environment by lowering emissions, it could also give you more time for other activities. Sharing the school-run, for example, with a roster of parents reduces congestion and fuel.

During the journey

Close the windows

Where possible, drive with the windows up to reduce drag and make your fuel consumption more efficient.

Don't hurry

Stressed driving can be erratic and thereby uneconomical. Try to relax and enjoy the trip.

Don't try to beat the lights

The chances are that if you hit a red light and then try to beat all the following lights, you will rush but miss them anyway. If you drive at a more considered speed you will often find that by the time you reach the next light it will have turned green again.

Be sparing with air-con

Try to use air conditioning only when strictly necessary, as it consumes more fuel.

Switch off the engine

If you think you will be stationary for more than two minutes, turn the engine off.

Optimum speed

A speed of between 50 and 60mph typically generates the lowest emissions. Travelling at less than 15mph creates the most pollution; as your speed increases up to 60mph the rate of pollution decreases. Over 70mph emissions increase again rapidly, indeed you can use up to 25% more fuel by driving at 70mph compared with 50mph. Control your speed at all times: not too fast and not too slow.

Don't rev the engine

Calm down! The revving and idling of the engine uses unnecessary fuel.

Drive smoothly

Harsh acceleration and braking can use up to 30% more fuel and can cause increased wear and tear on the vehicle. A car's fuel consumption is always at its least economical in the first second after a standing start. Always try to keep moving, even in congested traffic and also try to anticipate the speed of the vehicle in front.

Intelligent motorway driving

Careful driving on motorways improves safety and traffic flow. The concertina effect caused by one motorist braking sharply often results in traffic slowing to a near stop due to the delayed reaction of drivers behind. This is inconvenient, potentially unsafe, and bad for the environment. Try to observe the car three or four ahead and give yourself plenty of distance from the car immediately in front, that way you'll be better placed to anticipate changes in speed early and to respond smoothly. When you see a car braking up ahead, ease off the accelerator; by the time you get close to the car in front the chances are that it will have increased its speed

ETA Case study...

Caroline Marx,

Businesswoman, West London

I am freaked out by the whole subject of global warming. I recycle and have always turned off the electricity in empty rooms, but I never felt that was enough, so in late 2005 I decided to take another positive step towards conserving the environment by purchasing a G-Wiz electric car. The 7th July bombings in London were the catalyst for my decision. I had become very nervous about travelling to work on the bus or tube. But then someone told me about the car; I did some research and had a test drive and quickly realised there were just so many advantages to it that I couldn't carry on without one.

I think it's the best thing in the world. I live in west London with my husband and two teenage daughters and run my own specialist trimmings business, Barnett Lawson, which is based in the centre of town, just behind Oxford Circus. I drive to work in my G-Wiz every day and park in Cavendish Square car park for just £200 per year [cost of annual parking permit for any of the 13 MasterParks in Westminster that operate the scheme]. I also use the car for all my errands. Parking in general is a doddle. Parking tickets are not an issue because in the boroughs of Westminster and City of London parking is free for electric cars on meters, as long as you move off within the allotted time (usually four hours). Also, I'm exempt from the congestion charge, car tax is free and the insurance cost is very low.

Maintenance is very straightforward. *Goingreen* service the car at your home every six months for £300 or so, and all you have to do is remember to charge it up whenever the battery is low. Much like your mobile phone, really. A full charge takes eight hours, so as I have off-street parking, I just plug it into the socket that I had wired to the outside of the house (with a safety-control switch indoors) with an ordinary three-pin plug. I do it overnight. The other end of the charge cable fits into a socket where the petrol cap would normally be. You also need to fill the batteries with distilled water every three to four weeks, but if you forget, a light comes on to remind you. It only takes a few minutes and it's easy to get distilled water on the high street.

The maximum speed is 45mph, but this is almost never an issue, as you can't do much more than 20mph on most busy London roads. I'm very laid back about other cars cutting me up because I've never been a speed freak having always driven small cars in the past. I also love the attention the car gets. It's lilac with purple bumpers and people just wave and laugh. I wave back. Taxi and lorry drivers might get impatient but they're mainly intrigued by the car and its colour and I've had many a jokey conversation with them at the lights.

I can't extol the virtues of the G-Wiz enough. The only time I can't use it is when I take my elderly mother to Gatwick for her annual Italian holiday, as the range of the car is only around 35 miles without recharging. For that journey I still have to borrow my husband's Lexus, but apart from that it's solved so many problems. It has given me a new way to travel that's cheap, convenient, safe and environmentally friendly all in one.

The bigger picture

The advice already offered about greener driving habits and choosing a vehicle will help you minimise the environmental effects of your motoring. But even following these tips to the letter, you'll continue to produce some harmful emissions, especially carbon dioxide. By putting your driving within the broader context of a more environmentally conscious lifestyle, you can help to reduce or offset these even further.

Don't drive if you can help it!

Obvious though it may sound, carbon emissions would be drastically reduced if people simply chose alternative methods of transport, especially for shorter journeys. At least half of all journeys undertaken in Britain are under two miles long, a distance which can be cycled or walked quite comfortably. If car use for all such journeys was eliminated, the overall mileage travelled by cars would be reduced by one sixth – a very significant proportion.

For journeys of this length, cycling can even be quicker than driving, especially in built-up and congested areas. Yet cycle usage comprises only 4% of the total journeys made in London; compare this with Hanover in Germany, where the figure is 20%, and in Groningen and Delft in the Netherlands, where it's touching 50%.

Not only is cycling beneficial to health, there is no fuel to pay for, no car tax, no licensing and no parking costs! A bike typically costs no more than £50 per year to run, in comparison with the hundreds or thousands of pounds incurred by a motor vehicle. And despite prejudices about the relative safety of cycling, any risks can be hugely reduced by observing a few straightforward precautions:

- **Know the Highway Code, be legal and observe the rules of the road**
- **Use your ears as well as your eyes**
- **Cycle assertively and not passively or aggressively**
- **Be visible, wearing reflective clothing and using lights at night**

Follow these guidelines, ensuring that you are alert, cautious and unhurried at all times, and cycling need not be a danger to you or other road users.

Furthermore, in cases where walking and cycling would be impractical, the use of public transport as an alternative to driving can cut effective emissions by up to 95%. Trains, in particular, have amongst the lowest carbon emission levels of any means of transport. So if you can, leave your car at home!

ETA Case study...

Tony Bosworth and Sandra Bell

Campaigners for Friends of the Earth, Bradford, West Yorkshire

Our work for Friends of the Earth involves inspiring people to act together to make our environment a good place for us all to live. Part of this involves getting the Government to make it cheaper and easier for people to help protect the environment, but these issues are very important to us on a personal, as well as professional, level. We are very worried about climate change: it is the biggest threat the world faces. Having a young child – two-year-old Danny – makes these concerns all the more real: what will the world be like when he grows up?

We try to make a difference in as many areas as possible: we eat locally-sourced, organic food if we can, and try to buy from local shops – we are lucky to have good options. We belong to a local cooperative which delivers a number of essential items of food and supplies, so that we don't have to source them from further away. We minimise our domestic waste and recycle as much as we can, and we're trying to improve the energy-efficiency of our home, for instance by replacing our old boiler, using better insulation, and buying more efficient appliances.

Our attitude to transport is that prevention is better than cure. In other words, we feel that 'carbon offsetting' is not so much a solution as a diversion, and that it's better to do your best not to produce emissions in the first place, so we try to drive as little as possible. When we lived in London we found it easy to survive without a car at all, but when we moved to Yorkshire seven years ago, we decided it would be useful to have one – so we could go walking in the Dales more easily, for example. But we were determined that it would not compromise our commitment to the environment, so we looked for a small, fuel-efficient, second-hand car. We considered a number of options and got a good deal on a Nissan Micra. We've now had it for four years and it serves us well. We joined the ETA as we wanted breakdown cover from an organisation that supported sustainable transport.

Nevertheless, we use the car very sparingly, around 3,000 miles per year. We try to restrict its use to essential trips only, such as transporting bulky items. Being part of a food co-op and having good local shops really helps to cut down the need to shop by car but we do occasionally use it for shopping at DIY stores and garden centres.

We walk a lot – an hour a day helps to keep fitness levels up. We take it in turns to walk to nursery with Danny on our way to the station. When he goes to primary school we will be able to do the same as its between our house and the nearest station. We have good secondary schools locally so Danny will either take the bus or walk depending on where he goes.

As a rule, we both take the train to work though Tony sometimes cycles, if the weather's fair and, as we're buying a child seat for the bike, we plan to cycle more. We use local buses, for example, we take Danny on the bus to the nearby town of Shipley for toddler music group – he loves going on the bus so it makes it part of the outing for him. We also use the bus to go into Bradford socially when we can get a babysitter, but use the train more as we have really good local train services.

When travelling to London or further afield on work trips we always go by train. Despite the bad press, public transport really is a viable alternative to driving, even when you have a small child. It is always worth thinking ahead – buying rail tickets in advance is often cheaper. If you do have children with you just make sure you remember to bring games and toys to keep them entertained.

Offsetting your remaining emissions

The ETA, along with other environmentally conscious organisations, recognises that the elimination of carbon-emitting road transport altogether is unfeasible; our economy and lifestyles are too dependent upon it. In any case, transport is not the only activity that creates emissions, so even a decision to abandon motorised transport altogether (whether by road, rail or air) would not mean the total elimination of your carbon footprint.

The use of energy in the home (from conventional sources, at least) for heating, light, washing, or anything else at all, will crank up your carbon footprint. In addition, many staple consumer habits have their own implicit carbon cost. Buying food is the most obvious, and the term 'food miles' has come to denote the distance that goods have travelled before consumption, and by implication the carbon emissions generated by their transport.

Switching to a renewable energy source (see www.good-energy.co.uk) and buying local, seasonal produce which hasn't travelled far (instead of mass-produced, imported goods) are ways to drive down your carbon footprint. But some carbon emission is inevitable, and most environmental organisations, like the ETA, accept the reality of this. That's why, having first done everything possible to minimise our actual emissions, we then need to find further ways of offsetting those which remain, if we are to become truly 'carbon neutral'.

Climate neutral projects

One simple way to offset our emissions is to invest directly in projects designed specifically for that purpose. It may seem unreasonable to have to spend more money after taking conscious action to improve our motoring and consumption habits, but the global problem is so severe that individuals really do need to take personal responsibility for attaining carbon neutrality – whatever the cost.

The ETA prides itself on being a carbon neutral organisation. As a roadside rescue service, it naturally has a carbon footprint of its own but works in partnership with Climate Care, an organisation which is dedicated to projects which offset carbon emissions.

You can invest directly in these projects via the ETA. They include providing stoves that run on crop waste, distributing energy-saving bulbs to small communities in Honduras, funding renewable energy projects in India, and, with the remaining funds, restoring rainforests in Uganda, which crucially serve to remove carbon dioxide from the atmosphere. All these projects aim to neutralize CO_2 emissions, are permanent and would not happen if they weren't funded. Find more details of how you can offset your specific carbon emissions online at **www.eta.co.uk**

▼ *The glaciers of the Himalayas are the greatest store of fresh water outside the polar ice caps. They supply seven major Asian rivers but are threatened by global warming.*

Green Transport Week

The ETA organised the first Green Transport Week in June 1992 to promote awareness of the need for greener transport. During the week, people are encouraged to use alternative forms of transport and to think more seriously about ways in which they can do more to help. Overall, road use and pollution levels continue to increase, and Green Transport Week plays a crucial role in helping campaigns for traffic calming, more cycle paths, better buses, and a unified rail network, and against more and more roads. See the ETA website at **www.eta.co.uk** for dates of the next Green Transport Week, and how you can get involved.

Greystones
Wicklow
Holyhead
Holy I.
Anglesey
Llangefni
Bangor
Caernarfon
Llandudno
Colwyn Bay
Conwy
Prestatyn
Rhyl
Birkenhead
Widnes
Warrington
Runcorn
Ellesmere Port
Northwich
Macclesfield
MANCHESTER
Bethesda
Llanrwst
Denbigh
Flint
Mold
Chester
Sandbach
Congleton
Crewe
Penygroes
Betws-y-Coed
Ruthin
Wrexham
Nantwich
Newcastle-Under-Lyme
STOKE-TRENT
Nefyn
Porthmadog
Blaenau Ffestiniog
Llangollen
Whitchurch
Pwllheli
Abersoch
Bala
Oswestry
Stone
Eccleshall
Llanbedr
L. Vyrnwy
Newport
Barmouth
Dolgellau
Llwyngwril
Mallwyd
Welshpool
Shrewsbury
Telford
Tywyn
Machynlleth
Church Stretton
WOLVERHAMPTON
West Bromwich
Bridgnorth
Dudley
Talybont
Caersws
Newtown
Aberystwyth
Llangurig
Kidderminster
Knighton
Ludlow
Stourport-on-Severn
Rhayader
Aberaeron
Tregaron
Llandrindod Wells
Kington
Leominster
Worcester
Builth Wells
Lampeter
Cardigan
ROSSLARE
Goodwick
Newcastle Emlyn
Hay-on-Wye
Hereford
Great Malvern
Ledbury
Fishguard
Llandovery
Brecon
Tewkesbury
St. David's
Llandissilio
Llandeilo
Llangadog
Ross-on-Wye
Gloucester
Carmarthen
Haverfordwest
Abergavenny
Milford Haven
Merthyr Tydfil
Ebbw Vale
Monmouth
Stroud
Pembroke
Tenby
Llanelli
Neath
Rhondda
Pontypool
Cwmbran
Lydney
Swansea
Port Talbot
Pontypridd
Caerphilly
Chepstow
Newport
Tetbury
Port Eynon
Bridgend
CARDIFF
Yate
Porthcawl
Penarth
BRISTOL
Bath
Barry
Bristol Channel
Severn
Weston-super-Mare
Melksham
Radstock
Trowbridge
Ilfracombe
Lynton
Minehead
Wells
Frome
Warminster
Glastonbury
Barnstaple
Bridgwater
Bideford
Great Torrington
Taunton
Wincanton
Mere
Shaftesbury
Wellington
Henstridge
Tiverton
Chard
Ilminster
Yeovil
Blandford Forum
Bude
Holsworthy
Hatherleigh
Crediton
Honiton
Beaminster
Cerne Abbas
Wimborne Minster
Okehampton
Exeter
Lyme Regis
Bridport
Dorchester
Poole
Launceston
Exmouth
Weymouth
Tavistock
Teignmouth
Easton
Newquay
Bodmin
Liskeard
Newton Abbot
Torquay
GUERNSEY JERSEY ST. MALO
Fowey
PLYMOUTH
Totnes
Paignton
Brixham
St. Austell
Dartmouth
Redruth
Truro
St. Ives
Camborne
ROSCOFF SANTANDER
Salcombe
Penzance
Helston
Falmouth
Lizard
ENGLISH

Worksop
Retford
Sutton-on-Sea
Lincoln
Alford
Chesterfield
Bolsover
Horncastle
Skegness
Bakewell
Matlock
Mansfield
Stickney
Newark-on-Trent
Ashbourne
Ripley
Sleaford
Thornham
Cromer
Ilkeston
NOTTINGHAM
Boston
Wells-next-the-Sea
Holt
DERBY
Grantham
North Walsham
Uttoxeter
Dersingham
Fakenham
Burton Upon Trent
Ashby de-la-Zouch
Loughborough
Melton Mowbray
Spalding
Holbeach
Long Sutton
King's Lynn
East Dereham
Rugeley
Bourne
Norwich
Lichfield
Oakham
Stamford
Wisbech
Swaffham
Great Yarmouth
Tamworth
LEICESTER
Rutland Water
Downham Market
Watton
Walsall
Hinckley
Peterborough
Attleborough
Lowestoft
Nuneaton
Market Harborough
Corby
Chatteris
Littleport
Bungay
Beccles
COVENTRY
Kettering
Ely
Thetford
Diss
Rugby
Huntingdon
Stretham
Southwold
Warwick
Royal Leamington Spa
Daventry
Rushden
Grafham Water
St. Neots
Bury St. Edmunds
Saxmundham
Northampton
Cambridge
Newmarket
Stowmarket
Aldeburgh
Stratford-Upon-Avon
Towcester
Newport Pagnell
Bedford
Haverhill
Ipswich
Evesham
Banbury
Brackley
Buckingham
Milton Keynes
Sudbury
Felixstowe
Stow-on-the-Wold
Chipping Norton
Hitchin
Baldock
Halstead
Harwich
Stevenage
STANSTED
Braintree
Colchester
Cheltenham
Bicester
Luton
Bishop's Stortford
ESBJERG
HOEK VAN HOLLAND
Woodstock
Dunstable
LUTON
Hertford
Aylesbury
Harlow
Witham
Clacton-on-Sea
Burford
Oxford
Hemel Hempstead
St. Albans
Hatfield
Chelmsford
Cirencester
Lechlade-on-Thames
Thame
Cheshunt
Maldon
Abingdon
High Wycombe
Amersham
Barnet
Enfield
Brentwood
Rayleigh
Watford
Harrow
Swindon
Wantage
Marlow
Maidenhead
Ealing
LONDON
Dagenham
Basildon
Southend-on-Sea
Henley-on-Thames
Slough
CITY
Canvey
Thames Estuary
Windsor
HEATHROW
Tilbury
Sheerness
Reading
Dartford
Gravesend
Herne Bay
Margate
Marlborough
Staines
Kingston
Rochester
Broadstairs
Newbury
Wokingham
Sittingbourne
Ramsgate
Devizes
Esher
Croydon
OOSTENDE
Burbage
Epsom
Canterbury
Woking
Leatherhead
Sandwich
Basingstoke
Maidstone
Aldershot
Guildford
Sevenoaks
Reigate
Tonbridge
Andover
Farnham
GATWICK
East Grinstead
Ashford
Amesbury
Crawley
Dover
Alton
Royal Tunbridge Wells
Folkestone
Winchester
Haslemere
Horsham
CALAIS
DUNKERQUE
Hythe
Salisbury
Billingshurst
Haywards Heath
Crowborough
Hawkhurst
Strait of Dover
Calais
Romsey
Petersfield
Eastleigh
Midhurst
Burgess Hill
Uckfield
Battle
Rye
SOUTHAMPTON
Havant
Lewes
Ringwood
Fareham
Chichester
Brighton
Hastings
Gosport
Portsmouth
Worthing
Hove
Bexhill
Lymington
Cowes
Ryde
Bognor Regis
Newhaven
Eastbourne
Boulogne-sur-Mer
Christchurch
Bournemouth
Totland
Newport
Sandown
Ventnor
Swanage
DIEPPE
LE HAVRE
Le Touquet-Paris-Plage
GUERNSEY
JERSEY
ST. MALO
CHERBOURG
BILBAO
CAEN
CHERBOURG
LE HAVRE
ST.MALO
GUERNSEY
JERSEY
C H A N N E L
Motorway
Motorway Junction (full/restricted access)
Motorway Service Area (full/restricted access)
Primary Route (dual)
Primary Route (Single)
A Road
National Boundary
Car Ferry
Major Airport
Town or City with Park & Ride Scheme
Scale: approx 20 miles to 1 inch
0 10 20 30 40 50 60 miles
0 20 40 60 80 100 km

Helensburgh
Dunfermline
Cowdenbeath
Burntisland
North Berwick
Colintraive
Dunoon
Gourock
Greenock
Kilsyth
Falkirk
EDINBURGH
Haddington
Port Askaig
Feolin Ferry
Islay
Bridgend
Tarbert
Rothesay
Port Glasgow
Clydebank
Cumbernauld
Airdrie
Livingston
Bonnyrigg
Penicuik
Glasgow
Largs
Paisley
GLASGOW
Hamilton
Leadburn
Portnahaven
Port Ellen
Tayinloan
Lochranza
East Kilbride
Stewarton
Carnwath
Lauder
Peebles
Arran
Ardrossan
Irvine
Lanark
Galashiels
Brodick
Troon
Kilmarnock
Biggar
Blackwaterfoot
Prestwick
Selkirk
Kilchenzie
Campbeltown
Ayr
Mauchline
Cumnock
Hawick
Firth of Clyde
Turnberry
Maybole
Dalmellington
Sanquhar
Moffat
Ballintoy
Ballycastle
L. Doon
Thornhill
Coleraine
Carsphairn
Ballymoney
Glenariff
Ballantrae
Barrhill
Lockerbie
NORTH CHANNEL
New Galloway
Dumfries
Kielder Res.
Glenarm
Kirkcolm
Cairnryan
Newton Stewart
Crocketford
Longtown
Swatragh
Gretna
Ballymena
Broughshane
Stranraer
Castle Douglas
Dalbeattie
Carlisle
Brampton
Larne
Glenluce
Wigtown
Caulkerbush
FLEETWOOD
Portpatrick
Kirkcudbright
Magherafelt
Ballyclare
Dundrennan
High Hesket
Antrim
Carrickfergus
Solway Firth
Moneymore
BELFAST
Newtownabbey
Bangor
Drummore
Whithorn
Maryport
Bothel
Lough Neagh
BELFAST
Newtownards
LIVERPOOL DOUGLAS
Cockermouth
Penrith
Workington
Lisburn
Keswick
Whitehaven
Portadown
Lurgan
Saintfield
Strangford Lough
Shap
Egremont
Ballynahinch
Portaferry
Isle of Man
Ambleside
Armagh
Banbridge
Bride
Coniston
Windermere
Downpatrick
Ramsey
Ballaugh
Kendal
Sedbergh
Ardglass
Kilcoo
Bootle
Peel
Laxey
Newry
Newcastle
Whicham
Warrenpoint
Annalong
Douglas
Ulverston
Cullaville
Barrow-in-Furness
Kilkeel
Port Erin
Castletown
Morecambe
Dundalk
Heysham
Lancaster
LIVERPOOL
BELFAST
Ardee
LARNE
Fleetwood
DUBLIN
Drogheda
Blackpool
IRISH SEA
Lytham St. Anne's
Preston
Balbriggan
Southport
Chorley
Ormskirk
BELFAST DOUGLAS DUBLIN
Wigan
Dunshaughlin
DUBLIN
Malahide
Kirkby
DOUGLAS LIVERPOOL
LIVERPOOL
St. Helens
Wallasey
Bootle
Amlwch
DUBLIN
Widnes
Warrington
Dun Laoghaire
Holyhead
Anglesey
Llandudno
Colwyn Bay
Prestatyn
Birkenhead
Runcorn
Llangefni
Rhyl
Ellesmere Port
Bray
Bangor
Conwy
Northwich
Flint
Greystones
Bethesda
Denbigh
Hollywood
Mold
Chester
Caernarfon
Llanrwst
Betws-y-Coed
Ruthin
Crewe
Penygroes
Wrexham
Nantwich
Wicklow
Blaenau Ffestiniog
Whitchurch
Nefyn
Porthmadog
Llangollen
Pwllheli
Bala
Arklow
Abersoch
Oswestry
Llanbedr
L. Vyrnwy
Barmouth
Dolgellau
Gorey
Cardigan Bay
Llwyngwril
Mallwyd
Welshpool
Shrewsbury
Camolin
Telford
Enniscorthy
Tywyn
Machynlleth
Church Stretton

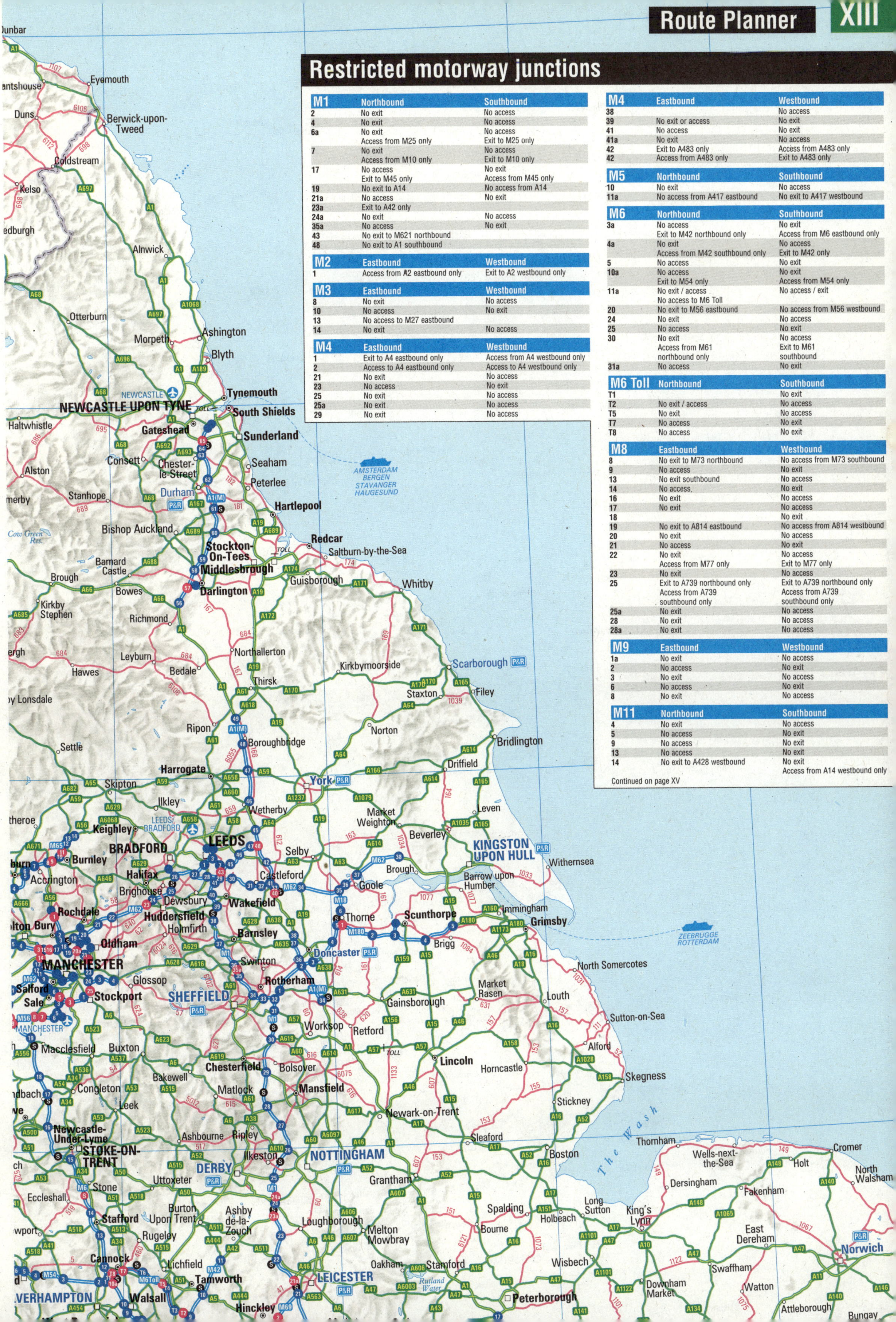

Restricted motorway junctions

M1	Northbound	Southbound
2	No exit	No access
4	No exit	No access
6a	No exit Access from M25 only	No access Exit to M25 only
7	No exit Access from M10 only	No access Exit to M10 only
17	No access Exit to M45 only	No exit Access from M45 only
19	No exit to A14	No access from A14
21a	No access	No exit
23a	Exit to A42 only	
24a	No exit	No access
35a	No access	No exit
43	No exit to M621 northbound	
48	No exit to A1 southbound	

M2	Eastbound	Westbound
1	Access from A2 eastbound only	Exit to A2 westbound only

M3	Eastbound	Westbound
8	No exit	No access
10	No access	No exit
13	No access to M27 eastbound	
14	No exit	No access

M4	Eastbound	Westbound
1	Exit to A4 eastbound only	Access from A4 westbound only
2	Access to A4 eastbound only	Access to A4 westbound only
21	No exit	No access
23	No access	No exit
25	No exit	No access
25a	No exit	No access
29	No exit	No access
38		No access
39	No exit or access	No exit
41	No access	No exit
41a	No exit	No access
42	Exit to A483 only	Access from A483 only
42	Access from A483 only	Exit to A483 only

M5	Northbound	Southbound
10	No exit	No access
11a	No access from A417 eastbound	No exit to A417 westbound

M6	Northbound	Southbound
3a	No access Exit to M42 northbound only	No exit Access from M6 eastbound only
4a	No exit Access from M42 southbound only	No access Exit to M42 only
5	No access	No exit
10a	No access Exit to M54 only	No exit Access from M54 only
11a	No exit / access No access to M6 Toll	No access / exit
20	No exit to M56 eastbound	No access from M56 westbound
24	No exit	No access
25	No access	No exit
30	No exit Access from M61 northbound only	No access Exit to M61 southbound
31a	No access	No exit

M6 Toll	Northbound	Southbound
T1		No exit
T2	No exit / access	No access
T5	No exit	No access
T7	No access	No exit
T8	No access	No exit

M8	Eastbound	Westbound
8	No exit to M73 northbound	No access from M73 southbound
9	No access	No exit
13	No exit southbound	No access
14	No access.	No exit
16	No exit	No access
17	No exit	No access
18		No exit
19	No exit to A814 eastbound	No access from A814 westbound
20	No exit	No access
21	No access	No exit
22	No exit Access from M77 only	No access Exit to M77 only
23	No exit	No access
25	Exit to A739 northbound only Access from A739 southbound only	Exit to A739 northbound only Access from A739 southbound only
25a	No exit	No access
28	No exit	No access
28a	No exit	No access

M9	Eastbound	Westbound
1a	No exit	No access
2	No access	No exit
3	No exit	No access
6	No access	No exit
8	No exit	No access

M11	Northbound	Southbound
4	No exit	No access
5	No access	No exit
9	No access	No exit
13	No access	No exit
14	No exit to A428 westbound	No exit Access from A14 westbound only

Continued on page XV

Pentland Firth
Stromness
John o' Groats
Scrabster
Thurso
Durness
Melvich
Tongue
Eriboll
Dalhalvaig
Mybster
Wick
Laxford Bridge
Kylestrome
Kinloch
Altnaharra
Kinbrace
Latheron
Lochinver
Inchnadamph
Helmsdale
Ledmore
Loch Shin
Lairg
Brora
Rosehall
Inveran
Ullapool
Dornoch
Kincardine
Tain
Moray Firth
Aultbea
Ardessie
Braemore
Fionn L.
Gairloch
L. Maree
Invergordon
Cromarty
Lossiemouth
Elgin
Achnasheen
Garve
Dingwall
Nairn
Forres
Shieldaig
Muir of Ord
Inverness
Ferness
Rothes
L. Monar
Dufftown
Lochcarron
Drumnadrochit
Tomatin
Grantown-on-Spey
Kyle of Lochalsh
Loch Ness
Shiel Bridge
Invermoriston
Aviemore
Strathdon
Broadford
Armadale
L. Quoich
Fort Augustus
Mallaig
L. Garry
L. Lochy
Newtonmore
Braemar
L. Arkaig
Spean Bridge
Dalwhinnie
Lochailort
Spittal of Glenshee
Fort William
L. Treig
L. Ericht
Acharacle
Strontian
Onich
Glencoe
L. Rannoch
Blair Atholl
Pitlochry
Kirriemuir
L. Tummel
Tobermory
Lochaline
Aberfeldy
Blairgowrie
Coupar Angus
Salen
Mull
Bridge of Orchy
Lawers
L. Tay
Connel
Killin
Amulree
Oban
Tyndrum
Perth
Newburgh
Fionnphort
Dalmally
Crianlarich
St. Fillans
Crieff
Firth of Lorn
L. Earn
Strathyre
Auchtermuchty
Loch Awe
Kilmelford
Inveraray
L. Katrine
Greenloaning
Glenrothes
Furnace
Strachur
Tarbet
Aberfoyle
Loch Lomond
Dunblane
Kilmartin
Stirling
Alloa
Kirkcaldy
Cowdenbeath
Ardlussa
Lochgilphead
Garelochhead
Dunfermline
Burntisland
Helensburgh
Kilsyth
Falkirk
Gourock
Greenock
EDINBURGH
Jura
Port Askaig
Feolin Ferry
Tarbert
Colintraive
Dunoon
Port Glasgow
Clydebank
Cumbernauld
Islay
Bridgend
Rothesay
GLASGOW
Paisley
Airdrie
Livingston
Bonnyrigg
Penicuik
Largs
Hamilton
East Kilbride
Leadburn
Portnahaven
Port Ellen
Lochranza
Tayinloan
Stewarton
Carnwath
Arran
Ardrossan
Lanark
Peebles
Irvine
Brodick
Kilmarnock
Biggar
Troon
Blackwaterfoot
Prestwick
Mauchline
Kilchenzie
Ayr
Cumnock
Campbeltown
Firth of Clyde
Larne
Sanquhar
Moffat
Turnberry
Maybole
Dalmellington
Ballintoy
Port Nis
Barabhas
Stornoway
Port Nan Giuran
Lewis
Outer Hebrides
North Minch
Tairbeart (Tarbert)
Roghadal
Little Minch
Kilmaluag
North Uist
Loch nam Madadh (Lochmaddy)
Clachan na Luib
Uig
Dunvegan
Skye
Carbost
Portree
Tobha Mor
South Uist
Sligachan
Loch Baghasdail (Lochboisdale)
Bagh a Chaisteil (Castlebay)
Inner Hebrides

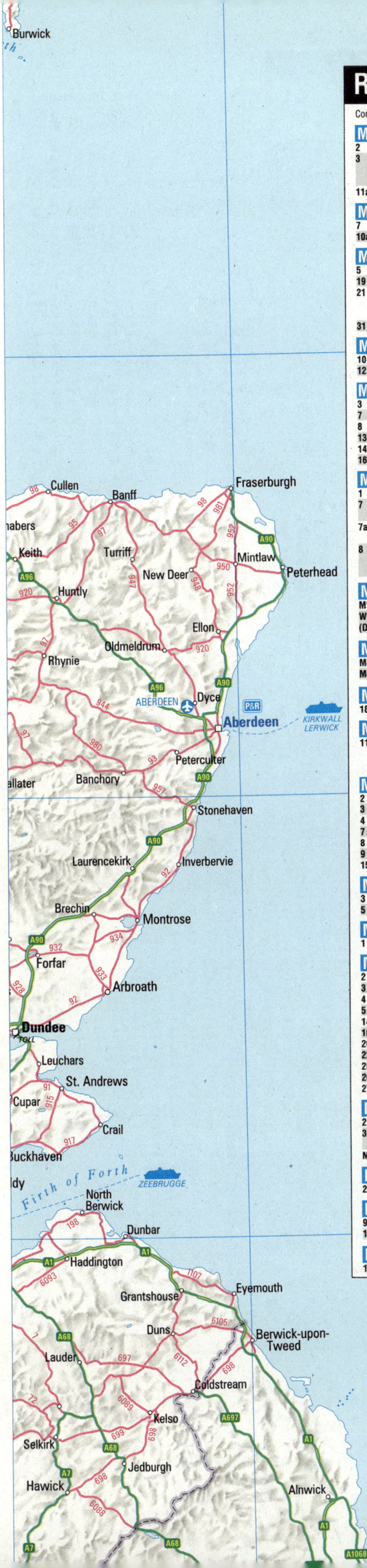

Restricted motorway junctions

Continuation from page XIII

M20	Eastbound	Westbound
2	No access	No exit
3	No exit Access from M26 eastbound only	No access Exit to M26 westbound only
11a	No access	No exit

M23	Northbound	Southbound
7	No exit to A23 southbound	No access from A23 northbound
10a	No exit	No access

M25	Clockwise	Anticlockwise
5	No exit to M26 eastbound	No access from M26 westbound
19	No access	No exit
21	No exit to M1 southbound Access from M1 southbound only	No exit to M1 southbound Access from M1 southbound only
31	No exit	No access

M27	Eastbound	Westbound
10	No exit	No access
12	No access	No exit

M40	Eastbound	Westbound
3	No exit	No access
7	No exit	No access
8	No exit	No access
13	No exit	No access
14	No access	No exit
16	No access	No exit

M42	Northbound	Southbound
1	No exit	No access
7	No access Exit to M6 northbound only	No exit Access from M6 northbound only
7a	No access Exit to M6 only	No exit Access from M6 northbound only
8	No exit Access from M6 southbound only	Exit to M6 northbound Access from M6 southbound only

M45	Eastbound	Westbound
M1 junc 17	Access to M1 southbound only	No access from M1 southbound
With A45 (Dunchurch)	No access	No exit

M48	Eastbound	Westbound
M4 junc 21	No exit to M4 westbound	No access from M4 eastbound
M4 junc 23	No access from M4 westbound	No exit to M4 eastbound

M49	Southbound
18a	No exit to M5 northbound

M53	Northbound	Southbound
11	Exit to M56 eastbound only Access from M56 westbound only	Exit to M56 eastbound only Access from M56 westbound only

M56	Eastbound	Westbound
2	No exit	No access
3	No access	No exit
4	No exit	No access
7		No access
8	No exit or access	No exit
9	No access from M6 northbound	No access to M6 southbound
15	No exit to M53	No access from M53 northbound

M57	Northbound	Southbound
3	No exit	No access
5	No exit	No access

M58	Eastbound	Westbound
1	No exit	No access

M60	Clockwise	Anticlockwise
2	No exit	No access
3	No exit to A34 northbound	No exit to A34 northbound
4	No access to M56	No exit to M56
5	No exit to A5103 southbound	No exit to A5103 northbound
14	No exit to A580	No access from A580
16	No exit	No access
20	No access	No exit
22		No access
25	No access	
26		No exit or access
27	No exit	No access

M61	Northbound	Southbound
2	No access from A580 eastbound	No exit to A580 westbound
3	No access from A580 eastbound No access from A666 southbound	No exit to A580 westbound
M6 junc 30	No exit to M6 southbound	No access from M6 northbound

M62	Eastbound	Westbound
23	No access	No exit

M65	Eastbound	Westbound
9	No access	No exit
11	No exit	No access

M66	Northbound	Southbound
1	No access	No exit

M67	Eastbound	Westbound
1a	No access	No exit
2	No exit	No access

M69	Northbound	Southbound
2	No exit	No access

M73	Northbound	Southbound
2	No access from M8 or A89 eastbound No exit to A89	No exit to M8 or A89 westbound No access from A89
3	Exit to A80 northbound only	Access from A80 southbound only

M74	Northbound	Southbound
2	No access	No exit
3	No exit	No access
7	No exit	No access
9	No exit or access	No access
10		No exit
11	No exit	No access
12	No access	No exit

M77	Northbound	Southbound
4	No exit	No access
6	No exit	No access
7	No exit or access	
8	No access	No access
M8 junc 22	Exit to M8 eastbound only	Access from M8 westbound only

M80	Northbound	Southbound
3	No access	No exit
5	No access from M876	No exit to M876

M90	Northbound	Southbound
2a	No access	No exit
7	No exit	No access
8	No access	No exit
10	No access from A912	No exit to A912

M180	Northbound	Southbound
1	No access	No exit

M621	Eastbound	Westbound
2a	No exit	No access
4	No exit or access	
5	No exit	No access
6	No access	No exit

M876	Northbound	Southbound
2	No access	No exit

A1(M)	Northbound	Southbound
2	No access	No exit
3		No access
5	No exit	No access
40	No access	No exit
44	No exit, access from M1 only	Exit to M1 only
57	No access	No exit
65	No access	No exit

A3(M)	Northbound	Southbound
1		No access
4	No access	No exit

A38(M)	Northbound	Southbound
With Victoria Road (Park Circus) Birmingham	No exit	No access

A48(M)	Northbound	Southbound
M4 Junc 29	Exit to M4 eastbound only	Access from M4 westbound only
29a	Access from A48 eastbound only	Exit to A48 westbound only

A57(M)	Eastbound	Westbound
With A5103	No access	No exit
With A34	No access	No exit

A58(M)	Southbound
With Park Lane and Westgate, Leeds	No access

A64(M)	Eastbound	Westbound
With A58 Clay Pit Lane, Leeds	No access	No exit
With Regent Street, Leeds	No access	No access

A74(M)	Northbound	Southbound
18	No access	No exit
22	No access	No exit

A167(M)	Northbound	Southbound
With Camden St, Newcastle	No exit	No exit or access

A194(M)	Northbound	Southbound
A1(M) junc 65 Gateshead Western Bypass	Access from A1(M) northbound only	Exit to A1(M) southbound only

Distance table

How to use this table

Distances are shown in miles and kilometres with estimated journey times in hours and minutes.

For example: the distance between Dover and Fishguard is 331 miles or 533 kilometres with an estimated journey time of 6 hours, 20 minutes.

Estimated driving times are based on an average speed of 60mph on Motorways and 40mph on other roads. Drivers should allow extra time when driving at peak periods or through areas likely to be congested.

Dover					
Dundee					523 / 842 / 9:10
Edinburgh				56 / 90 / 1:30	462 / 744 / 8:10
Exeter			450 / 724 / 8:00	518 / 834 / 9:10	248 / 399 / 4:40
Fishguard		230 / 370 / 4:30	399 / 642 / 7:30	460 / 740 / 8:30	331 / 533 / 6:20
Fort William	486 / 782 / 9:30	560 / 901 / 10:20	144 / 232 / 3:30	127 / 204 / 3:10	596 / 959 / 11:00

London																																																
Aberdeen																																																517 / 832 / 11:20
Aberystwyth																																															445 / 716 / 8:40	211 / 340 / 4:40
Ayr																																														317 / 510 / 6:10	183 / 295 / 4:20	394 / 634 / 7:20
Berwick-upon-Tweed																																													134 / 216 / 3:00	311 / 501 / 6:20	182 / 293 / 4:40	352 / 567 / 7:30
Birmingham																																												274 / 441 / 5:30	289 / 465 / 5:30	114 / 183 / 2:50	420 / 676 / 8:30	117 / 188 / 2:50
Blackpool																																											123 / 198 / 2:40	181 / 291 / 3:50	180 / 290 / 3:30	153 / 246 / 3:20	308 / 496 / 6:20	226 / 364 / 4:30
Bournemouth																																										270 / 435 / 5:00	147 / 237 / 3:10	412 / 663 / 7:50	436 / 702 / 8:00	207 / 333 / 4:30	564 / 908 / 10:20	107 / 172 / 2:40
Braemar																																									524 / 843 / 9:30	281 / 452 / 5:20	385 / 620 / 7:10	148 / 238 / 3:20	143 / 230 / 3:00	405 / 652 / 7:50	59 / 95 / 1:30	482 / 776 / 10:30
Brighton																																								534 / 859 / 9:40	92 / 148 / 2:10	286 / 460 / 5:20	163 / 262 / 3:20	409 / 658 / 7:40	446 / 718 / 8:00	253 / 407 / 5:10	573 / 922 / 10:30	52 / 84 / 1:50
Bristol																																							147 / 237 / 4:10	477 / 768 / 8:40	82 / 132 / 2:30	204 / 328 / 3:50	81 / 130 / 2:00	362 / 583 / 6:50	370 / 595 / 6:40	125 / 201 / 3:00	493 / 793 / 9:10	122 / 196 / 2:50
Cambridge																																						169 / 272 / 3:10	116 / 187 / 2:20	438 / 705 / 7:50	154 / 248 / 3:00	208 / 335 / 3:50	100 / 161 / 2:10	306 / 493 / 5:40	357 / 575 / 6:20	214 / 344 / 4:20	471 / 758 / 10:00	54 / 87 / 1:30
Cardiff																																					190 / 306 / 3:30	45 / 72 / 1:20	182 / 293 / 3:40	483 / 778 / 8:40	117 / 188 / 3:00	209 / 336 / 4:00	103 / 166 / 2:20	368 / 592 / 7:00	382 / 615 / 7:00	105 / 169 / 2:40	505 / 813 / 9:20	157 / 253 / 3:20
Carlisle																																				289 / 465 / 5:20	264 / 425 / 4:40	277 / 446 / 5:00	370 / 596 / 6:40	196 / 316 / 3:50	343 / 552 / 6:20	87 / 140 / 1:50	196 / 315 / 3:50	87 / 140 / 2:10	93 / 150 / 2:00	224 / 360 / 4:30	221 / 356 / 4:30	301 / 484 / 5:40
Doncaster																																			142 / 229 / 3:00	209 / 336 / 4:00	116 / 187 / 2:10	175 / 282 / 3:20	236 / 380 / 4:30	310 / 499 / 5:40	235 / 378 / 4:20	94 / 151 / 1:50	94 / 151 / 2:00	184 / 296 / 3:50	235 / 378 / 4:20	176 / 283 / 3:40	344 / 554 / 6:50	171 / 275 / 3:30
Dover																																		242 / 390 / 4:30	389 / 626 / 7:00	238 / 383 / 4:30	125 / 201 / 2:30	202 / 325 / 3:50	82 / 132 / 2:20	553 / 890 / 9:50	174 / 280 / 4:30	312 / 502 / 5:40	194 / 312 / 3:50	424 / 683 / 7:50	478 / 769 / 8:30	297 / 478 / 5:50	588 / 947 / 10:40	71 / 114 / 2:00
Dundee																																	523 / 842 / 9:10	275 / 443 / 5:00	152 / 245 / 3:00	441 / 710 / 8:00	406 / 654 / 7:10	430 / 692 / 7:40	517 / 832 / 9:10	52 / 84 / 1:20	495 / 797 / 8:50	239 / 385 / 4:30	349 / 562 / 6:20	113 / 182 / 2:40	117 / 188 / 2:30	376 / 605 / 7:10	67 / 108 / 1:50	448 / 721 / 8:40
Edinburgh																																56 / 90 / 1:30	462 / 744 / 8:10	219 / 352 / 4:00	96 / 154 / 2:00	385 / 620 / 7:00	345 / 555 / 6:10	373 / 600 / 6:50	456 / 734 / 8:20	91 / 146 / 2:10	439 / 707 / 8:00	183 / 295 / 3:30	292 / 470 / 5:30	57 / 92 / 1:40	73 / 117 / 1:50	320 / 515 / 6:20	125 / 201 / 3:10	390 / 628 / 7:20
Exeter																															450 / 724 / 8:00	518 / 834 / 9:10	248 / 399 / 4:40	251 / 404 / 4:30	353 / 568 / 6:20	121 / 195 / 2:30	249 / 401 / 4:30	76 / 122 / 1:40	184 / 296 / 5:00	550 / 885 / 9:40	82 / 132 / 2:20	282 / 454 / 5:10	157 / 253 / 3:10	428 / 689 / 7:50	446 / 718 / 7:50	201 / 323 / 4:10	569 / 916 / 10:20	181 / 291 / 3:40
Fishguard																														230 / 370 / 4:30	399 / 642 / 7:30	460 / 740 / 8:30	331 / 533 / 6:20	247 / 398 / 4:50	297 / 478 / 5:40	112 / 180 / 2:40	270 / 435 / 5:10	154 / 248 / 3:20	291 / 468 / 5:40	493 / 794 / 9:10	222 / 357 / 4:40	209 / 336 / 4:10	170 / 274 / 3:40	371 / 597 / 7:20	373 / 600 / 7:00	56 / 90 / 1:30	504 / 811 / 10:10	260 / 418 / 5:20
Fort William																													486 / 782 / 9:30	560 / 901 / 10:20	144 / 232 / 3:30	127 / 204 / 3:10	596 / 959 / 11:00	357 / 575 / 7:00	206 / 332 / 4:30	485 / 781 / 9:10	479 / 771 / 9:00	486 / 782 / 9:10	575 / 926 / 10:50	125 / 201 / 3:10	539 / 867 / 10:10	296 / 476 / 6:00	392 / 631 / 7:40	190 / 306 / 4:40	133 / 214 / 3:20	430 / 692 / 8:40	149 / 240 / 3:50	510 / 821 / 9:50
Glasgow																												101 / 163 / 2:50	376 / 605 / 7:10	449 / 723 / 8:00	44 / 71 / 1:20	83 / 134 / 2:00	488 / 786 / 8:40	249 / 401 / 4:40	96 / 154 / 2:10	385 / 620 / 7:00	372 / 599 / 6:40	373 / 600 / 6:50	468 / 753 / 8:30	110 / 177 / 2:30	439 / 707 / 8:00	183 / 295 / 3:40	292 / 470 / 5:30	101 / 163 / 2:40	33 / 53 / 1:10	320 / 515 / 6:20	145 / 233 / 3:30	397 / 639 / 7:30
Gloucester																											346 / 557 / 6:10	454 / 731 / 8:30	153 / 246 / 3:10	111 / 179 / 2:10	349 / 562 / 6:10	410 / 660 / 7:10	191 / 307 / 3:30	150 / 241 / 2:50	247 / 398 / 4:20	56 / 90 / 1:20	123 / 198 / 2:20	35 / 56 / 1:00	159 / 256 / 3:10	443 / 713 / 8:00	99 / 159 / 2:40	174 / 280 / 3:10	56 / 90 / 1:20	318 / 512 / 6:00	330 / 531 / 5:50	102 / 164 / 2:30	468 / 753 / 8:30	109 / 175 / 2:30
Great Yarmouth																										225 / 362 / 4:40	419 / 674 / 8:00	527 / 848 / 10:20	366 / 589 / 7:20	335 / 539 / 6:30	386 / 621 / 7:30	484 / 779 / 9:00	185 / 298 / 4:00	167 / 269 / 3:40	320 / 515 / 6:20	284 / 457 / 5:50	82 / 132 / 2:10	275 / 443 / 5:40	180 / 290 / 4:10	477 / 768 / 9:10	240 / 386 / 5:00	252 / 406 / 5:10	180 / 290 / 4:10	345 / 555 / 7:00	402 / 647 / 7:40	294 / 473 / 6:20	517 / 832 / 10:50	128 / 206 / 3:40
Harwich																									82 / 132 / 2:10	196 / 316 / 4:00	432 / 695 / 8:10	543 / 874 / 10:30	337 / 542 / 6:40	279 / 449 / 5:20	413 / 665 / 7:40	469 / 755 / 8:40	125 / 201 / 2:50	194 / 312 / 4:00	336 / 541 / 6:20	246 / 396 / 5:00	67 / 108 / 1:50	217 / 349 / 4:30	128 / 206 / 3:00	504 / 811 / 9:20	187 / 301 / 4:00	275 / 443 / 5:20	167 / 269 / 3:40	372 / 599 / 7:20	425 / 684 / 8:00	281 / 452 / 5:50	535 / 861 / 11:20	76 / 122 / 2:20
Holyhead																								349 / 562 / 7:10	334 / 538 / 7:00	191 / 307 / 4:00	330 / 531 / 6:40	438 / 705 / 8:50	167 / 269 / 4:00	282 / 454 / 5:40	333 / 536 / 6:40	394 / 634 / 7:30	360 / 580 / 7:00	181 / 291 / 3:50	231 / 372 / 4:50	216 / 348 / 5:40	270 / 435 / 5:20	206 / 332 / 4:30	334 / 538 / 6:40	426 / 686 / 8:20	288 / 463 / 5:50	141 / 227 / 3:20	148 / 238 / 3:30	311 / 501 / 6:30	305 / 491 / 6:10	111 / 179 / 2:50	439 / 707 / 8:40	269 / 433 / 5:40
Inverness																							474 / 763 / 9:40	569 / 916 / 11:00	553 / 890 / 11:00	504 / 811 / 9:30	166 / 267 / 4:00	66 / 106 / 1:40	542 / 872 / 10:30	618 / 995 / 11:30	158 / 254 / 3:50	132 / 212 / 3:20	622 / 1001 / 11:30	383 / 617 / 7:30	262 / 422 / 5:30	549 / 884 / 10:20	505 / 813 / 9:30	539 / 867 / 10:10	617 / 993 / 11:30	75 / 121 / 2:00	597 / 961 / 11:20	348 / 560 / 7:00	458 / 737 / 9:00	215 / 346 / 5:10	199 / 320 / 4:30	486 / 782 / 9:40	105 / 169 / 2:50	550 / 885 / 10:40
John o' Groats																						129 / 208 / 3:20	603 / 970 / 12:40	693 / 1116 / 14:00	677 / 1090 / 14:00	628 / 1011 / 12:30	295 / 475 / 7:10	195 / 314 / 5:00	671 / 1080 / 13:40	744 / 1197 / 14:30	285 / 459 / 7:00	259 / 417 / 6:30	746 / 1201 / 14:40	507 / 816 / 10:30	391 / 629 / 8:40	680 / 1094 / 13:30	630 / 1014 / 12:30	668 / 1075 / 13:20	741 / 1193 / 14:40	202 / 325 / 5:00	724 / 1165 / 14:20	478 / 769 / 10:00	574 / 924 / 11:50	342 / 550 / 8:10	328 / 528 / 7:40	601 / 967 / 12:40	232 / 373 / 5:50	663 / 1067 / 13:30
Kingston upon Hull																					518 / 834 / 10:50	394 / 634 / 7:50	231 / 372 / 4:50	196 / 316 / 4:10	207 / 333 / 5:20	169 / 272 / 3:10	254 / 409 / 4:50	369 / 594 / 7:20	280 / 451 / 5:30	309 / 497 / 5:40	234 / 377 / 4:30	295 / 475 / 5:30	256 / 412 / 4:50	47 / 76 / 1:10	158 / 254 / 3:00	244 / 393 / 4:40	139 / 224 / 3:10	233 / 375 / 4:20	245 / 394 / 4:40	327 / 526 / 6:10	264 / 425 / 5:00	127 / 204 / 2:30	134 / 216 / 2:50	185 / 298 / 3:50	251 / 404 / 4:40	223 / 359 / 4:40	364 / 586 / 7:20	184 / 296 / 3:50
Kyle of Lochalsh																				445 / 716 / 9:00	189 / 304 / 4:40	84 / 135 / 2:10	514 / 827 / 10:40	611 / 983 / 12:10	602 / 969 / 12:10	528 / 850 / 10:20	179 / 288 / 4:40	79 / 127 / 2:00	567 / 913 / 11:20	628 / 1011 / 12:00	216 / 348 / 5:20	186 / 299 / 4:40	671 / 1080 / 12:50	432 / 695 / 8:40	275 / 443 / 6:10	564 / 908 / 11:10	555 / 893 / 10:50	552 / 888 / 10:50	651 / 1048 / 12:40	159 / 256 / 4:00	618 / 995 / 12:10	372 / 599 / 7:50	471 / 758 / 9:40	263 / 423 / 6:20	212 / 341 / 5:10	499 / 803 / 10:20	189 / 304 / 4:50	586 / 943 / 11:40
Land's End																			763 / 1228 / 15:10	421 / 678 / 8:20	868 / 1397 / 17:20	741 / 1193 / 14:20	405 / 652 / 8:30	390 / 628 / 8:00	446 / 718 / 9:10	235 / 378 / 5:00	573 / 922 / 10:50	686 / 1104 / 13:20	353 / 568 / 7:20	123 / 198 / 3:20	574 / 924 / 10:50	642 / 1033 / 12:00	381 / 613 / 7:40	374 / 602 / 7:20	477 / 768 / 9:10	245 / 394 / 5:20	374 / 602 / 7:20	200 / 322 / 4:40	308 / 496 / 7:50	665 / 1070 / 12:30	205 / 330 / 5:20	405 / 652 / 8:00	281 / 452 / 6:00	552 / 888 / 10:40	570 / 917 / 10:50	313 / 504 / 6:50	692 / 1114 / 13:10	297 / 478 / 6:30
Leeds																		405 / 652 / 8:00	394 / 634 / 8:20	55 / 89 / 1:30	487 / 784 / 10:20	360 / 579 / 7:10	176 / 283 / 4:00	223 / 359 / 4:30	196 / 315 / 4:20	174 / 280 / 3:20	215 / 346 / 4:10	329 / 530 / 6:40	237 / 381 / 4:40	270 / 435 / 5:00	202 / 325 / 4:00	258 / 415 / 4:50	260 / 418 / 4:50	29 / 47 / 0:50	119 / 192 / 2:30	232 / 373 / 4:20	145 / 233 / 2:50	194 / 312 / 3:50	260 / 419 / 5:00	293 / 472 / 5:30	255 / 410 / 4:50	72 / 116 / 1:40	113 / 182 / 2:30	156 / 251 / 3:20	212 / 341 / 4:00	169 / 272 / 3:40	327 / 526 / 6:50	189 / 304 / 3:50
Leicester																	95 / 153 / 2:00	320 / 515 / 6:30	500 / 805 / 9:50	102 / 164 / 2:10	588 / 947 / 11:50	461 / 742 / 8:50	190 / 306 / 4:00	147 / 237 / 3:10	140 / 225 / 3:20	85 / 137 / 1:40	314 / 505 / 5:40	422 / 679 / 8:00	209 / 336 / 4:10	196 / 315 / 3:40	296 / 476 / 5:20	349 / 562 / 6:20	185 / 298 / 3:30	74 / 119 / 1:30	206 / 332 / 3:50	154 / 248 / 3:00	68 / 109 / 1:20	120 / 193 / 2:30	166 / 267 / 3:20	389 / 626 / 7:00	158 / 254 / 3:10	140 / 225 / 2:40	39 / 63 / 1:10	252 / 406 / 5:00	299 / 481 / 5:20	153 / 246 / 3:20	414 / 666 / 7:40	97 / 156 / 2:20
Lincoln																51 / 82 / 1:20	68 / 109 / 1:50	371 / 597 / 7:30	476 / 766 / 9:40	44 / 71 / 1:20	554 / 892 / 11:30	427 / 687 / 8:30	216 / 348 / 4:40	155 / 249 / 3:30	128 / 206 / 3:20	159 / 256 / 3:10	291 / 468 / 5:30	399 / 642 / 7:50	272 / 438 / 5:30	247 / 398 / 4:40	258 / 415 / 5:00	314 / 505 / 5:50	202 / 325 / 4:00	39 / 63 / 1:10	191 / 307 / 3:40	208 / 335 / 4:10	85 / 137 / 2:20	183 / 295 / 3:40	197 / 317 / 4:00	357 / 575 / 6:40	209 / 336 / 4:10	128 / 206 / 2:40	90 / 145 / 2:10	224 / 360 / 4:40	274 / 441 / 5:10	199 / 320 / 4:20	383 / 616 / 7:20	131 / 211 / 3:10
Liverpool															129 / 208 / 2:50	130 / 209 / 2:40	75 / 121 / 1:50	361 / 581 / 7:20	407 / 655 / 8:30	130 / 209 / 2:40	511 / 822 / 10:40	382 / 615 / 7:40	102 / 164 / 2:40	265 / 427 / 5:20	240 / 386 / 5:00	140 / 225 / 2:40	216 / 348 / 4:10	329 / 530 / 6:40	160 / 257 / 3:30	237 / 381 / 4:30	216 / 348 / 4:10	286 / 460 / 5:20	299 / 481 / 5:30	86 / 138 / 1:50	120 / 193 / 2:30	169 / 272 / 3:20	194 / 312 / 3:40	161 / 259 / 3:10	272 / 438 / 5:10	318 / 512 / 6:00	234 / 377 / 4:30	49 / 79 / 1:20	93 / 150 / 2:10	219 / 352 / 4:30	213 / 343 / 4:10	104 / 167 / 2:40	341 / 549 / 6:40	202 / 325 / 4:10
Manchester														35 / 56 / 1:10	84 / 135 / 2:00	92 / 148 / 2:00	40 / 64 / 1:10	361 / 581 / 7:20	406 / 654 / 8:30	95 / 153 / 2:10	500 / 805 / 10:30	373 / 600 / 7:30	124 / 200 / 3:00	228 / 367 / 4:40	212 / 341 / 4:30	126 / 203 / 2:30	215 / 346 / 4:10	329 / 530 / 6:40	197 / 317 / 4:00	236 / 380 / 4:20	215 / 346 / 4:10	285 / 459 / 5:20	276 / 444 / 5:10	61 / 98 / 1:30	119 / 192 / 2:30	183 / 295 / 3:40	165 / 266 / 3:10	161 / 259 / 3:10	257 / 414 / 4:50	318 / 512 / 6:00	227 / 365 / 4:20	48 / 77 / 1:20	80 / 129 / 2:00	196 / 315 / 4:00	212 / 341 / 4:00	129 / 208 / 3:00	340 / 547 / 6:30	185 / 298 / 3:50
Newcastle upon Tyne													132 / 212 / 2:50	168 / 270 / 3:20	159 / 256 / 3:20	187 / 301 / 3:40	92 / 148 / 2:10	498 / 802 / 9:40	318 / 512 / 7:00	132 / 212 / 2:50	395 / 636 / 8:50	268 / 431 / 5:40	272 / 438 / 5:40	308 / 496 / 6:00	281 / 452 / 5:40	266 / 428 / 4:50	148 / 238 / 3:10	253 / 407 / 5:20	329 / 529 / 6:20	364 / 586 / 6:30	110 / 177 / 2:20	166 / 267 / 3:20	358 / 576 / 6:30	114 / 183 / 2:20	57 / 92 / 1:50	325 / 523 / 6:00	241 / 388 / 4:20	299 / 481 / 5:30	352 / 567 / 6:30	201 / 323 / 4:00	347 / 558 / 6:30	129 / 208 / 2:40	207 / 333 / 4:10	64 / 103 / 1:50	149 / 240 / 3:00	257 / 414 / 5:20	235 / 378 / 4:50	286 / 460 / 5:40
Norwich												264 / 425 / 5:20	185 / 298 / 4:30	220 / 354 / 4:40	105 / 169 / 2:50	119 / 192 / 3:20	176 / 283 / 3:50	421 / 678 / 8:40	582 / 937 / 11:50	149 / 240 / 4:00	654 / 1053 / 13:30	529 / 852 / 10:30	311 / 501 / 6:40	73 / 117 / 2:00	20 / 32 / 0:40	204 / 328 / 4:10	385 / 620 / 9:00	504 / 811 / 10:00	343 / 552 / 7:00	308 / 496 / 6:00	366 / 589 / 7:00	422 / 679 / 8:00	174 / 280 / 3:50	147 / 237 / 3:20	289 / 465 / 5:40	262 / 422 / 5:20	62 / 100 / 1:50	252 / 406 / 5:10	175 / 282 / 4:00	457 / 735 / 8:40	214 / 344 / 4:40	232 / 373 / 4:50	166 / 267 / 3:50	328 / 528 / 6:40	382 / 615 / 7:20	276 / 444 / 6:00	496 / 798 / 9:40	114 / 183 / 3:30
Nottingham											130 / 209 / 3:40	157 / 253 / 3:10	73 / 118 / 1:40	98 / 158 / 2:10	35 / 56 / 1:10	25 / 40 / 0:50	70 / 113 / 1:40	345 / 555 / 7:00	479 / 771 / 9:40	90 / 145 / 2:00	557 / 896 / 11:30	430 / 692 / 8:20	185 / 298 / 4:00	150 / 241 / 3:20	153 / 246 / 3:30	110 / 177 / 2:10	293 / 472 / 5:30	401 / 646 / 7:50	220 / 354 / 4:30	221 / 356 / 4:10	262 / 422 / 4:50	328 / 528 / 6:00	205 / 330 / 3:50	43 / 69 / 1:10	194 / 312 / 3:40	172 / 277 / 3:20	83 / 134 / 1:40	145 / 233 / 3:00	193 / 311 / 3:50	353 / 568 / 6:30	183 / 295 / 3:40	111 / 179 / 2:20	50 / 80 / 1:20	221 / 356 / 4:30	274 / 441 / 5:10	164 / 264 / 3:40	393 / 633 / 7:30	122 / 196 / 2:40
Oban										390 / 628 / 7:30	492 / 792 / 9:40	233 / 375 / 4:50	307 / 494 / 6:00	308 / 496 / 6:10	387 / 623 / 7:30	419 / 674 / 7:50	307 / 494 / 6:00	665 / 1070 / 12:50	128 / 206 / 3:10	346 / 557 / 6:40	244 / 393 / 6:10	117 / 188 / 3:00	427 / 687 / 8:30	524 / 843 / 10:00	515 / 829 / 10:00	441 / 710 / 8:10	92 / 148 / 2:30	49 / 79 / 1:20	481 / 774 / 9:10	549 / 884 / 10:00	123 / 198 / 3:00	117 / 188 / 2:50	585 / 942 / 10:40	346 / 557 / 6:40	188 / 303 / 4:00	477 / 768 / 9:00	468 / 753 / 8:40	465 / 748 / 8:40	565 / 910 / 10:30	141 / 227 / 3:30	530 / 853 / 9:50	285 / 459 / 5:40	384 / 618 / 7:30	180 / 290 / 4:20	94 / 151 / 2:20	412 / 663 / 8:10	178 / 286 / 4:20	499 / 803 / 9:30
Oxford									462 / 744 / 8:30	109 / 175 / 2:10	145 / 233 / 3:50	260 / 418 / 4:50	144 / 232 / 2:50	172 / 277 / 3:20	137 / 221 / 2:50	73 / 117 / 1:30	168 / 270 / 3:10	274 / 441 / 5:40	550 / 885 / 10:40	192 / 309 / 3:40	656 / 1056 / 13:00	532 / 856 / 10:00	238 / 383 / 4:50	145 / 233 / 3:10	200 / 322 / 4:20	52 / 84 / 1:30	356 / 573 / 6:30	472 / 760 / 9:00	205 / 330 / 4:10	156 / 251 / 3:00	372 / 599 / 6:40	433 / 697 / 7:40	141 / 227 / 2:50	145 / 233 / 2:40	260 / 418 / 4:40	108 / 174 / 2:20	83 / 134 / 1:40	74 / 119 / 1:40	108 / 174 / 2:20	465 / 749 / 8:20	90 / 145 / 2:00	187 / 301 / 3:30	64 / 103 / 1:30	324 / 521 / 6:10	353 / 568 / 6:20	154 / 248 / 3:20	483 / 777 / 8:50	57 / 92 / 1:40
Plymouth								199 / 320 / 4:00	587 / 945 / 11:00	267 / 430 / 5:10	343 / 552 / 7:00	410 / 660 / 7:40	283 / 455 / 5:30	283 / 455 / 5:30	293 / 472 / 5:50	242 / 389 / 4:40	316 / 509 / 6:00	89 / 143 / 2:20	674 / 1085 / 13:10	355 / 571 / 6:40	790 / 1271 / 15:40	664 / 1069 / 12:30	328 / 528 / 6:40	309 / 497 / 6:10	365 / 588 / 7:20	157 / 253 / 3:20	495 / 797 / 9:10	595 / 958 / 11:20	264 / 425 / 5:30	46 / 74 / 1:30	496 / 798 / 9:00	552 / 888 / 10:00	300 / 483 / 5:50	297 / 478 / 5:40	399 / 642 / 7:20	167 / 269 / 3:40	293 / 472 / 5:30	122 / 196 / 2:50	224 / 361 / 6:00	587 / 945 / 10:40	128 / 206 / 3:30	328 / 528 / 6:10	203 / 327 / 4:20	474 / 763 / 9:00	492 / 792 / 9:00	237 / 382 / 5:10	615 / 990 / 11:20	218 / 351 / 4:40
Portsmouth							176 / 283 / 4:50	77 / 124 / 1:40	545 / 877 / 10:00	191 / 307 / 3:40	207 / 333 / 4:20	337 / 542 / 6:10	236 / 380 / 4:30	254 / 409 / 4:50	201 / 323 / 4:00	162 / 261 / 3:10	257 / 414 / 4:50	259 / 417 / 5:40	633 / 1019 / 12:10	269 / 433 / 5:00	737 / 1186 / 14:30	613 / 987 / 11:30	311 / 501 / 6:10	166 / 267 / 3:40	221 / 356 / 4:40	119 / 192 / 3:00	448 / 721 / 8:10	555 / 893 / 10:20	251 / 404 / 5:00	135 / 217 / 2:40	453 / 729 / 8:10	514 / 827 / 9:00	130 / 209 / 2:50	234 / 377 / 4:20	348 / 560 / 6:10	142 / 229 / 3:00	144 / 232 / 2:50	97 / 156 / 2:10	48 / 77 / 1:40	547 / 881 / 9:50	52 / 84 / 1:30	264 / 425 / 4:50	141 / 227 / 3:00	401 / 645 / 7:30	430 / 692 / 7:40	222 / 357 / 4:40	560 / 901 / 10:10	70 / 113 / 2:00
Sheffield						230 / 370 / 4:20	283 / 455 / 5:30	135 / 217 / 2:40	339 / 546 / 6:30	37 / 60 / 1:00	146 / 235 / 3:20	125 / 201 / 2:40	38 / 61 / 1:00	72 / 116 / 1:40	46 / 74 / 1:20	62 / 100 / 1:20	33 / 53 / 1:00	361 / 581 / 7:10	427 / 687 / 8:40	65 / 105 / 1:30	520 / 837 / 10:50	393 / 632 / 7:40	168 / 270 / 3:40	187 / 301 / 3:50	166 / 267 / 3:40	126 / 203 / 2:20	248 / 399 / 4:40	348 / 560 / 6:50	215 / 346 / 4:20	237 / 381 / 4:20	235 / 378 / 4:20	291 / 468 / 5:20	245 / 394 / 4:30	18 / 29 / 0:40	152 / 245 / 3:00	194 / 312 / 3:40	120 / 193 / 2:20	161 / 259 / 3:10	226 / 364 / 4:20	320 / 515 / 6:00	216 / 348 / 4:10	86 / 138 / 1:50	76 / 122 / 1:50	190 / 306 / 4:00	245 / 394 / 4:30	159 / 256 / 3:30	360 / 579 / 6:50	159 / 256 / 3:20
Shrewsbury					82 / 132 / 2:10	207 / 333 / 3:50	225 / 362 / 4:40	106 / 171 / 2:10	364 / 586 / 7:00	93 / 150 / 2:00	205 / 330 / 4:20	201 / 323 / 3:50	69 / 111 / 1:40	58 / 93 / 1:50	133 / 214 / 2:50	84 / 135 / 1:40	109 / 175 / 2:20	303 / 488 / 6:10	451 / 726 / 9:00	169 / 272 / 3:10	567 / 912 / 11:30	438 / 705 / 8:20	113 / 182 / 2:50	240 / 386 / 4:40	225 / 362 / 4:40	77 / 124 / 1:30	272 / 438 / 5:00	382 / 615 / 7:20	145 / 233 / 3:10	179 / 288 / 3:20	274 / 441 / 5:00	330 / 531 / 6:00	251 / 404 / 4:30	109 / 175 / 2:10	176 / 283 / 3:20	111 / 179 / 2:20	159 / 256 / 3:00	103 / 166 / 2:50	226 / 364 / 4:20	371 / 597 / 6:50	185 / 298 / 3:40	98 / 158 / 2:00	45 / 72 / 1:20	265 / 426 / 5:10	269 / 433 / 5:00	77 / 124 / 2:10	399 / 642 / 7:30	160 / 258 / 3:20
Southampton				185 / 298 / 4:10	199 / 320 / 3:40	21 / 34 / 0:50	151 / 243 / 4:10	64 / 103 / 1:30	530 / 853 / 9:40	176 / 283 / 3:20	206 / 332 / 4:20	324 / 521 / 5:50	221 / 356 / 4:10	239 / 385 / 4:30	204 / 328 / 4:00	137 / 220 / 2:40	232 / 373 / 4:20	228 / 367 / 5:00	618 / 995 / 12:00	256 / 412 / 4:40	723 / 1164 / 14:10	598 / 963 / 11:10	293 / 472 / 5:50	164 / 264 / 3:30	220 / 354 / 4:40	105 / 169 / 2:40	433 / 697 / 7:40	541 / 871 / 10:00	233 / 375 / 4:40	105 / 169 / 3:00	438 / 705 / 7:50	500 / 805 / 8:50	143 / 230 / 2:50	209 / 336 / 3:50	324 / 521 / 5:50	121 / 195 / 2:30	148 / 238 / 2:50	76 / 122 / 2:20	61 / 98 / 1:50	532 / 856 / 9:30	31 / 50 / 1:00	251 / 404 / 4:40	128 / 206 / 2:40	388 / 624 / 7:10	417 / 671 / 7:30	201 / 323 / 4:10	547 / 880 / 10:00	77 / 124 / 2:00
Stranraer			445 / 716 / 8:20	277 / 446 / 5:30	263 / 423 / 5:20	461 / 742 / 8:40	500 / 805 / 9:40	379 / 610 / 7:10	148 / 238 / 3:40	290 / 467 / 5:50	403 / 649 / 8:10	158 / 254 / 3:40	220 / 354 / 4:40	221 / 356 / 4:40	298 / 480 / 6:00	330 / 531 / 6:20	220 / 354 / 4:40	585 / 942 / 11:30	263 / 423 / 6:30	259 / 417 / 5:20	379 / 610 / 9:00	262 / 422 / 6:00	338 / 544 / 7:00	410 / 660 / 8:10	426 / 686 / 8:40	343 / 552 / 6:30	84 / 135 / 2:30	195 / 314 / 4:50	392 / 631 / 7:50	454 / 731 / 8:30	124 / 200 / 3:00	167 / 269 / 3:40	496 / 798 / 9:10	257 / 414 / 5:10	101 / 163 / 2:40	390 / 628 / 7:30	379 / 610 / 7:10	378 / 608 / 7:20	475 / 765 / 9:00	194 / 312 / 4:20	444 / 715 / 8:30	188 / 303 / 4:00	297 / 478 / 6:00	170 / 274 / 4:10	51 / 82 / 1:20	325 / 523 / 6:50	228 / 367 / 5:10	402 / 647 / 7:50
Swansea		417 / 671 / 7:50	161 / 259 / 3:00	118 / 190 / 2:20	217 / 349 / 4:00	182 / 293 / 3:30	206 / 332 / 4:10	141 / 227 / 2:40	506 / 815 / 9:20	192 / 309 / 3:40	301 / 485 / 6:00	347 / 559 / 6:20	187 / 301 / 3:30	195 / 314 / 3:40	233 / 375 / 4:30	177 / 285 / 3:20	248 / 399 / 4:40	285 / 459 / 6:00	594 / 956 / 11:30	264 / 425 / 4:50	696 / 1120 / 13:40	572 / 921 / 10:40	184 / 296 / 4:50	267 / 430 / 5:10	329 / 530 / 6:30	89 / 143 / 1:50	409 / 658 / 7:20	496 / 798 / 9:20	67 / 108 / 1:50	161 / 259 / 3:00	412 / 663 / 7:20	473 / 761 / 8:20	274 / 441 / 5:00	232 / 373 / 4:10	309 / 497 / 5:30	41 / 66 / 1:10	227 / 365 / 4:10	85 / 137 / 1:50	222 / 357 / 4:20	505 / 813 / 9:00	167 / 269 / 3:20	216 / 348 / 4:00	119 / 192 / 2:30	383 / 616 / 7:10	379 / 610 / 6:50	73 / 117 / 2:00	507 / 816 / 9:20	194 / 312 / 4:00
York	272 / 438 / 5:10	222 / 357 / 4:40	258 / 415 / 5:10	133 / 214 / 2:40	52 / 84 / 1:20	278 / 448 / 5:10	333 / 536 / 6:20	181 / 291 / 3:20	309 / 497 / 6:00	77 / 124 / 1:40	181 / 291 / 4:20	84 / 135 / 2:20	64 / 103 / 1:30	99 / 159 / 2:10	75 / 121 / 1:50	108 / 174 / 2:10	24 / 39 / 0:50	411 / 661 / 8:00	407 / 655 / 8:20	37 / 60 / 1:10	479 / 771 / 10:10	352 / 566 / 7:00	204 / 328 / 4:20	228 / 367 / 4:40	201 / 323 / 4:20	189 / 304 / 3:30	217 / 349 / 4:10	330 / 531 / 6:30	261 / 420 / 5:10	287 / 462 / 5:10	194 / 312 / 3:40	250 / 402 / 4:40	282 / 454 / 5:10	34 / 55 / 1:00	121 / 195 / 2:30	244 / 393 / 4:40	165 / 266 / 3:10	222 / 357 / 4:10	275 / 443 / 5:10	285 / 459 / 5:20	269 / 433 / 5:00	96 / 154 / 2:00	130 / 209 / 2:40	148 / 238 / 3:10	214 / 344 / 4:00	195 / 314 / 4:10	319 / 513 / 6:10	207 / 333 / 4:10

Key to 3-mile map pages

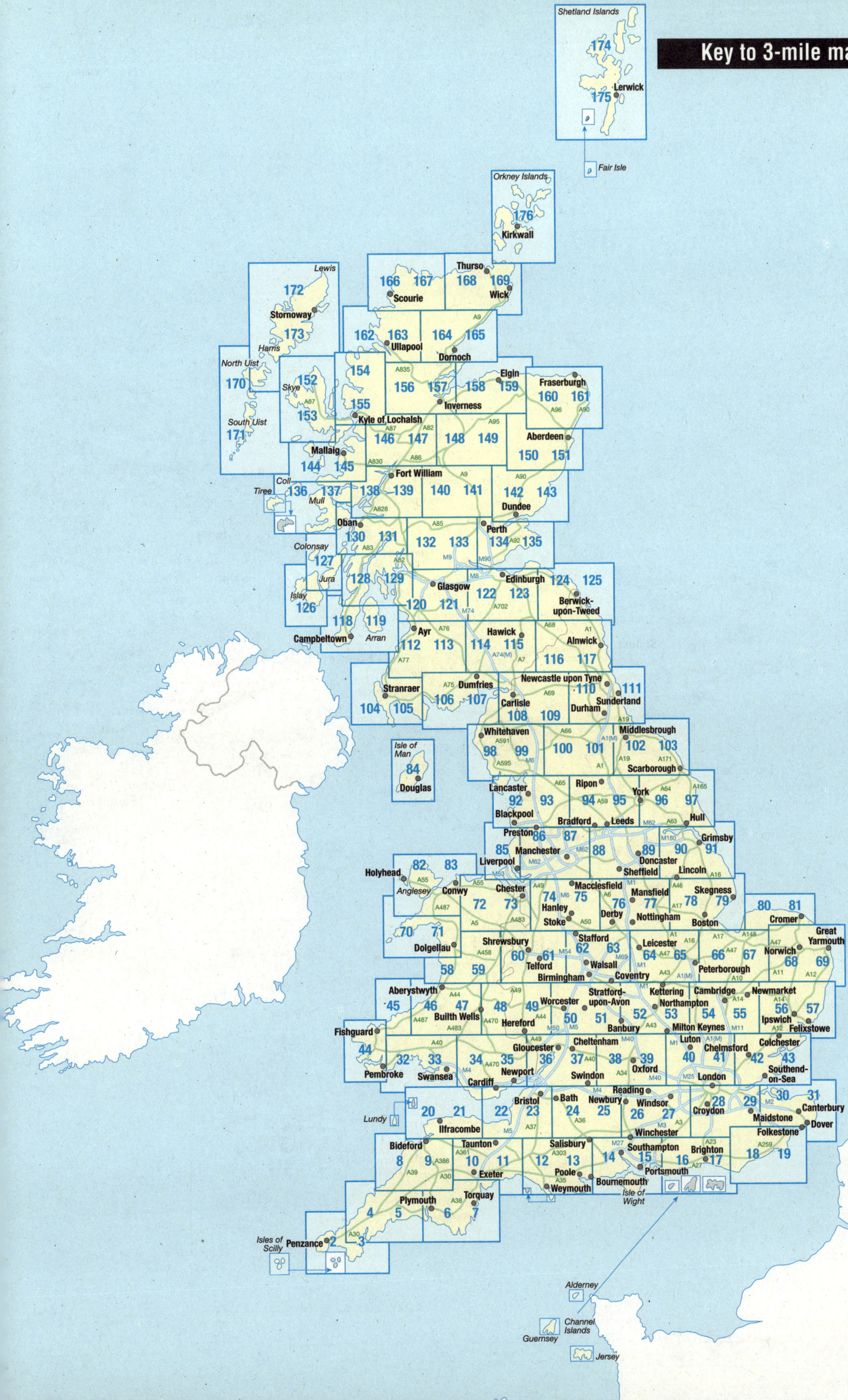

CORNWALL
SW
St Ives
Carbis Bay
Hayle
Penzance
Newlyn
St Just
Porthleven
LAND'S END
Godrevy Island
Godrevy Pt.
Navax Pt.
The Carracks
Clodgy Pt.
The Island
St Ives Bay
TATE ST IVES
BARBARA HEPWORTH MUSEUM
SOUTH WEST COAST PATH
Gwithian
Kehelland
Roseworthy
TREVITHICK COTTAGE
TEHIDY
Phillack
Connor Downs
Copperhouse
Barripper
Carnhell Green
Praze-an-Beeble
Gurnard's Head
Zennor
Towednack
Halsetown
Lelant
PARADISE PARK
Porthmeor
WAYSIDE FOLK MUSEUM
Cripplesease
Nancledra
Canonstown
St Erth
Praze
Fraddam
Crowan
Leedstown
Drym
Townshend
Nancegollan
Godolphin Cross
GODOLPHIN HOUSE
Trescowe
Relubbus
St Hilary
Goldsithney
Crowntown
Marazion
ST. MICHAEL'S MOUNT
Perranuthnoe
Germoe
Ashton
Sithney
Breage
Praa Sands
Rinsey
Cudden Pt.
Trewavas Hd.
The Loe
Porthleven Sands
MOUNT'S BAY
Morvah
Bojewyan
Pendeen
GEEVOR TIN MINE MUSEUM
Trewellard
Higher Boscaswell
CHYSAUSTER ANCIENT VILLAGE
Newmill
Botallack
Carnyorth
Cape Cornwall
PENZANCE HELIPORT
Ludgvan
Crowlas
Gulval
Madron
TRENGWAINTON
Newbridge
Heamoor
PENZANCE
Chyandour
The Bisons
BALLOWALL BARROW
LAND'S END
Bosavern
Kelynack
Sancreed
CARN EUNY VILLAGE
Brane
Tredavoe
Lower Drift
Res.
TRINITY HOUSE NATIONAL LIGHTHOUSE CENTRE
NEWLYN ART GALLERY
Whitesand Bay
Sennen Cove
Sennen
Longships
Crows-an-wra
Catchall
Kerris
Paul
Mousehole
St Buryan
Trewoofe
St Clement's Island
Lamorna
Polgigga
Porthcurno
Treen
Boskenna
TREGIFFIAN BURIAL CHAMBER
Lamorna Cove
St Levan
MINACK OPEN AIR THEATRE
Gwennap Hd.
Runnel Stone
ISLES OF SCILLY 2:40 (Apr-Nov)
A30
A394
A3071
A3074
B3306
B3311
B3309
B3318
B3283
B3315
B3301
B3302
B3280
B3303
B3304
Isles of Scilly
White Island
St Helens
KING CHARLES CASTLE
St Martin's
Higher Town
Bryher
CROMWELL'S CASTLE
New Grimsby
Tresco
TRESCO ABBEY GARDENS
Samson
Crow Sound
Eastern Isles
BANT'S CARN
INNISIDGEN CAIRNS
North West Passage
The Road
Newford
Maypole
LONGSTONE HERITAGE CEN.
St Mary's
Hugh Town
A3110
ST.MARY'S
GARRISON WALLS
Old Town
Broad Sound
Smith Sound
St Mary's Sound
Annet
St Agnes
Gugh
PENZANCE 2:40 (Apr-Nov)
0 1 2 3 4 5 6 miles
0 1 2 3 4 5 6 7 8 9 10km

5
6
7
8
9
A
B
C
D
E
F
SW
CORNWALL
Penhale Pt.
Holywell
HOLYWELL BAY FUN PARK
Carines
Ligger or Perran Bay
Penhale Sands
Cubert
Rejerrah
Mount
SOUTH WEST COAST PATH
Rose
PERRAN ROUND
Perranporth
PERRANPORTH
Goonhavern
WORLD IN MINIATURE
Bolingey
Perranzabuloe
St Agnes Hd.
Trevellas
Zelah
St Agnes
Mithian
LEISURE PA
Callestick
CORNISH CYDER FARM
Goonbell
Marazanvose
St Allen
Trispen
St Erme
Ladock
Grampound Road
Sticker
Polgooth
Porthpean
Allet
Mount Hawke
Porthtowan
Three Burrows
Blackwater
Shortlanesend
Tresillian
Probus
PROBUS GDNS
Grampound
TREWITHEN
Creed
St Ewe
THE LOST GARDENS OF HELIGAN
Kestle
Mevagissey
WORLD OF MODEL RAILWAYS
Portreath
Mawla
TOLGUS TIN
CORNISH GOLD
Scorrier
Chacewater
Truro
Threemilestone
ROYAL CORNWALL MUS.
Kenwyn
CATHEDRAL
Merther
Tresawle
Tregony
Polmassick
Portmellon
Chapel Pt.
Illogan
Baldhu
Kea
St Clement
Ruan Lanihorne
Trevarrick
Gorran Churchtown
Gorran Haven
St Michael Caerhays
Redruth
St Day
Twelve Heads
Malpas
Bissoe
Playing Place
Old Kea
St Michael Penkevil
Lamorran
Portholland
Boswinger
BOSWINGER
Penare
Dodman Pt.
Veryan Bay
Roscroggan
Pool
Tuckingmill
Carnbrea
Carnkie
GWENNAP PIT
Carharrack
Gwennap
Carnon Downs
Trelissick
Philleigh
Treworga
Camborne
CAMBORNE
SHIRE HORSE FARM
Troon
Lanner
Four Lanes
Perranarworthal
Penpol
Devoran
Feock
TRELISSICK
Treworlas
Veryan
Portloe
SOUTH WEST COAST PATH
Carne
Gerrans Bay
Nare Hd.
Ponsanooth
Penhalvaen
Stithians
Stithians Res.
Burnthouse
Mylor Bridge
St Just in Roseland
Trewithian
Gerrans
Portscatho
Penmarth
Burras
Carnkie
Penryn
Flushing
Carrick Roads
St Mawes
Greeb Pt.
Rame
Longdowns
Mabe Burnthouse
Falmouth
NATIONAL MARITIME
ART GALLERY
Releath
Porkellis
POLDARK MINE
Budock Water
PENDENNIS CASTLE
Pendennis Pt.
Bohortha
Zone Pt.
Wendron
Seworgan
Treverva
Penjerrick
Falmouth Bay
Constantine
Mawnan Smith
SOUTH WEST COAST PATH
Rosemullion Hd.
Trewennack
Porth Navas
GLENDURGAN
Helford Passage
TREBAH
Mawnan
Helston
Helford River
Gweek
NATIONAL SEAL SANCTUARY
FLAMBARDS EXPERIENCE
Helford
St Anthony
Nare Pt.
Mawgan
Manaccan
Garras
St Martins
HALLIGGYE FOGOU
TRELOWARREN
Newtown
Porthallow
Berepper
Tregidden
Gunwalloe
Porthoustock
Cury
Cross Lanes
St Keverne
Manacle Pt.
The Manacles
GOONHILLY SATELLITE EARTH STATION
Traboe
Lowland Pt.
Goonhilly Downs
Mullion
Penhale
THE LIZARD
Trelan
Coverack
COVERACK
Mullion Cove
Mullion Island
Gwenter
Chynhalls Pt.
Kuggar
Black Hd.
Predannack Wollas
St Ruan
Ruan Minor
Vellan Hd.
Cadgwith
Grade
SOUTH WEST COAST PATH
Kynance Cove
Lizard
Landewednock
Hot Pt.
LIZARD POINT
LIZARD
Kestle Mill
St Columb Road
Indian Queens
Trezaise
Bugle
DAIRYLAND FARM WORLD
Fraddon
Penhale
St Dennis
Whitemoor
Hensbarrow Downs
Stenalees
Penwithick
TRERICE
St Newlyn East
Gummow's Shop
St Enoder
Retew
Treviscoe
Nanpean
Carthew
Trethurgy
St Blaze
LAPPA VALLEY STEAM RAILWAY
Summercourt
Foxhole
WHEAL MARTYN CHINA CLAY HER. CENTRE
EDEN PROJECT
Newlyn Downs
Mitchell
Brighton
Trethosa
Carclaze
Tregoppa
Carland Cross
Trelassick
St Stephen
High Street
St Austell
Trewoon
Holmbush
SHIPWRECK & HERITAGE CE
New Mills
Coombe
St Mewan
Charlestown
ST AUSTELL BREWERY
Hewas Water
TORTOISE GARDEN
Trenarren
Black Hd.
Pentewan
Mevagissey Bay
Fal
Truro
A30
A39
A390
A394
A3083
A3078
A3075
A3076
A3058
A3047
B3284
B3285
B3277
B3298
B3300
B3297
B3280
B3282
B3289
B3287
B3275
B3279
B3274
B3273
B3293
B3294
B3296
B3297

CORNWALL
Tintagel Hd.
POST OFFICE
TINTAGEL
CASTLE
Start Pt.
SOUTH WEST COAST PATH
Port Isaac Bay
Port Isaac
Port Quin Bay
Port Quin
Port Gaverne
Pendoggett
Pentire Pt.
New Polzeath
Padstow Bay
Polzeath
LONG CROSS
Trelights
St Endellion
Trelill
Gulland Rock
Trebetherick
St Minver
Gunver Hd.
TREVOSE HEAD
Trewethern
St Kew
St Kew Highway
Chapel Amble
Pityme
Crugmeer
PRIDEAUX PLACE
Trevone
Rock
TREYARNON BAY
Constantine Bay
Treyarnon
St Merryn
Padstow
NATIONAL LOBSTER HATCHERY
Camel
Bodieve
St Mabyn
Trevanson
Wadebridge
SOUTH WEST COAST PATH
Shop
Porthcothan
Little Petherick
Whitecross
St Breock
Egloshayle
PENCARROW HOUSE
Park Hd.
Penrose
St Ervan
Rumford
St Issey
Tredinnick
Burlawn
Washaway
RARE BREEDS CENTRE
St Jidgey
CREALY GREAT ADVENTURE PARK
ST.BREOCK DOWNS MONOLITH
St Eval
Trenance
Nanstallon
Berryl's Pt.
Trevarrian
St Mawgan
CORNISH BIRDS OF PREY CENTRE
SPIRIT OF THE WEST
Rosenannon
Rutherbridge
St Lawrence
WATERGATE BAY
Talskiddy
Withiel
Tregurrian
St Wenn
NEWQUAY
St Columb Major
Tregonetha
Lanivet
Towan Hd.
Newquay Bay
Fistral Bay
Porth
St Columb Minor
Trebudannon
CASTLE AN DINAS
Belowda
Victoria
Pentire
ANIMAL WORLD
SPRINGFIELDS FUN PARK & PONY CENTRE
Lockengate
Kelsey Hd.
SEA LIFE CENTRE
Newquay
Quintrell Downs
Colan
Mountjoy
Ruthvoes
Tregoss
West Pentire
Crantock
GOSS MOOR
Roche
Bilberry
Lane
Kestle Mill
St Columb Road
Trevarren
Indian Queens
Penhale Pt.
HOLYWELL BAY FUN PARK
Fraddon
Trezaise
Bugle
Holywell
Carines
DAIRYLAND FARM WORLD
Penhale
St Dennis
Hensbarrow Downs
Cubert
TRERICE
Gummow's Shop
St Enoder
Retew
Whitemoor
Stenalees
Ligger or Perran Bay
Penhale Sands
St Newlyn East
Treviscoe
Nanpean
Penwithick
SOUTH WEST COAST PATH
Mount
Rejerrah
LAPPA VALLEY STEAM RAILWAY
Summercourt
Carthew
Trethurgy
Rose
PERRAN ROUND
Newlyn Downs
Mitchell
Brighton
Trethosa
Foxhole
WHEAL MARTYN CHINA CLAY HER. CENTRE
EDEN PROJECT
Perranporth
PERRANPORTH
Goonhavern
WORLD IN MINIATURE
Carland Cross
High Street
Carclaze
Boscoppa
Bolingey
Trelassick
St Stephen
St Austell
Holmbush
Perranzabuloe
Zelah
Trewoon
St Agnes Hd.
Trevellas
New Mills
Coombe
St Mewan
Charlestown
St Agnes
Mithian
St Allen
St Erme
Trispen
Ladock
Grampound Road
Polgooth
ST AUSTELL BREWERY
LEISURE PARK
Callestick
Porthpean
CORNISH CYDER FARM
Marazanvose
Sticker
Goonhavern
Hewas Water
TORTOISE GARDEN
Allet
Trenarren
Porthtowan
Mount Hawke
Shortlanesend
Probus
Grampound
Black Hd.
TREWITHEN
PROBUS GDNS
Creed
THE LOST GARDENS OF HELIGAN
Pentewan
Three Burrows
Blackwater
Tresillian
St Ewe
Mevagissey Bay
Portreath
Mawla
Truro
Kenwyn
Tresawle
Polmassick
Kestle
WORLD OF MODEL RAILWAYS
PORTREATH
TOLGUS TIN
CORNISH GOLD
Scorrier
Threemilestone
CATHEDRAL
Merther
Mevagissey
Illogan
Chacewater
ROYAL CORNWALL MUS.
Fal
Tregony
Portmellon
CORNISH MINES & ENGINES
St Day
Baldhu
Kea
St Clement
Trevarrick
Chapel Pt.
Redruth
Twelve Heads
Ruan Lanihorne
Gorran Churchtown
Pool
Cambrea
Carharrack
Bissoe
Malpas
St Michael Penkevil
Lamorran
St Michael Caerhays
Gorran Haven
Tuckingmill
Carnkie
GWENNAP PIT
Playing Place
Old Kea
Carnon Downs
Treworga
Portholland
Boswinger
BOSWINGER
Penare
CAMBORNE
Gwennap
Lanner
Perranarworthal
Penpol
Trelissick
Philleigh
SHIRE HORSE FARM
Four Lanes
TRELISSICK
Feock
Devoran
Treworlas
Veryan Bay
Veryan
Portloe
Dodman Pt.
Troon
Ponsanooth
SOUTH WEST COAST PATH
Carne
Penhalvaen
Stithians
Burnthouse
Gerrans Bay
Stithians Res.
Trewithian
Nare Hd.
Penmarth
Mylor Bridge
St Just in Roseland
Crowan
Burras
Carnkie
Carrick Roads
Gerrans
Portscatho
Penryn
Flushing
Relea
Falmouth
St Mawes
Greeb Pt.
NATIONAL MARITIME
Bohortha
Nancegollan
PENDENNIS CASTLE
Wendron
Seworgan
Treverva
Pendennis Pt.
Zone Pt.
Crowntown
0 1 2 3 4 5 6 miles
0 1 2 3 4 5 6 7 8 9 10 km
A30
A39
A390
A392
A3058
A3059
A3075
A3076
A3078
A389
A391
A393
A394
A3047
B3274
B3276
B3279
B3285
B3284
B3275
B3287
B3289
B3292
B3297
B3298
B3301
B3303
B3314
B3267
B3277
B3280
B3273
SW
A
B
C
D
E
F
1
2
3
4
5

Bossiney
Tintagel
Treknow
Trewarmett
Trebarwith
Treligga
Delabole
Valley Truckle
Camelford
Helstone
St Teath
Treveighan
Michaelstow
St Tudy
St Breward
Row
Wenfordbridge
Blisland
Helland
Camel
Bodmin Forest
Bodmin
BODMIN AND WENFORD RAILWAY
LANHYDROCK HOUSE
Trebyan
Sweethouse
Redmoor
Lostwithiel
Lanlivery
Luxulyan
Penpillick
St Blazey
Tywardreath
Par
Polkerris
Menabilly
Fowey
SHIPWRECK & HERITAGE CENTRE
ST. CATHERINE'S CASTLE
ST. AUSTELL BAY
Gribbin Hd.
Polruan
Bodinnick
Pencarrow Hd.
SOUTH WEST COAST PATH
Lansallos
Lanteglos Highway
Trenewan
St Veep
Penpoll
Golant
GOLANT
Milltown
Lerryn
Couch's Mill
RESTORMEL CASTLE
Braddock
West Taphouse
East Taphouse
Doublebois
Dobwalls
St Pinnock
Bocaddon
Lanreath
LANREATH FOLK FARM MUS
Herodsfoot
Muchlarnick
Pelynt
Polperro
SMUGGLERS MUSEUM
Talland Bay
Porthallow
West Looe
Looe
East Looe
CORNISH MUSEUM
Looe Bay
St George's or Looe I.
St Martin
Morval
Sandplace
Duloe
Trewidland
St Keyne
MUSIC MACHINES
Liskeard
Merrymeet
Pengover Green
Menheniot
Widegates
Hessenford
Downderry
Seaton
Portwrinkle
Polbathic
Treruie Foot
Tideford Cross
Tideford
Landrake
St Germans
Sheviock
Crafthole
Antony
St John
Torpoint
Devonport
Cremyll
Millbrook
Freathy
Whitsand Bay
Kingsand
Cawsand
Rame
Rame Hd.
Penlee Pt.
ROSCOFF 6:00
SANTANDER 18:00
(Mar-Nov)
Saltash
Trematon
St Erney
St Stephens
MARY NEWMAN'S COTTAGE
ANTONY HOUSE
St Germans R.
Botusfleming
Hatt
Landulph
SALTASH SERVICES
Cargreen
Pillaton
St Mellion
Newbridge
Blunts
Quethiock
St Ive
Gang
Pensilva
Trevigro
Haye
Callington
Kelly Bray
KIT HILL
DUPATH WELL HOUSE
Harrowbarrow
COTEHELE
St Dominick
Bere Alston
TAMAR VALLEY
Weir Quay
Calstock
MORWELLHAM QUAY
Albaston
Drakewalls
Gunnislake
St Ann's Chapel
Chilsworthy
Gulworthy
Latchley
Luckett
Downgate
Stoke Climsland
Horsebridge
Sydenham Damerel
Dunterton
Rezare
Trekenner
Lezant
Treburley
Trebullett
Coad's Green
Bray Shop
Linkinhorne
South Hill
Golberdon
Rilla Mill
Bathpool
Upton Cross
CARADON HILL
Minions
THE HURLERS STONE CIRCLE
Siblyback Lake
Darite
TRETHEVY QUOIT
Tremar
Commonmoor
GOLITHA FALLS
KING DONIERT'S STONE
St Cleer
DOBWALLS ADVENTURE PARK
CARNGLAZE SLATE CAVERNS
Ley
St Neot
Warleggan
Mount
Cardinham
Millpool
Maidenwell
Temple
COLLIFORD LAKE
Colliford Lake
Dozmary Pool
BODMIN MOOR
Bolventor
MUSEUM OF SMUGGLING
Codda
GARROW TOR
BROWN WILLY
High Moor
Crowdy Res.
Davidstow Moor
Davidstow
Trewassa
Tremail
Hallworthy
Treneglos
Tremaine
Tresmeer
Tregeare
Cold Northcott
St Clether
Laneast
Altarnun
Trewint
Polyphant
Trewen
Lewannick
Congdon's Shop
Trebartha
North Hill
Henwood
KILMAR TOR
Inny
Piper's Pool
HIDDEN VALLEY DISCOVERY PARK
TRETHORNE LEISURE FARM
Tregadillett
Launceston
LAUNCESTON STEAM RAILWAY
CASTLE
Daw's House
South Petherwin
St Stephen's
Egloskerry
Langore
Yeolmbridge
North Petherwin
Bridgetown
Werrington
Dutson
Ottery
Lawhitton
Tamar
Kelly
Bradstone
Milton Abbot
Liftondown
Lifton
Tinhay
Broadwoodwidger
Cross Green
Stowford
DINGLE'S STEAM VILLAGE
Portgate
Thrushelton
Lewdown
Chillaton
Lamerton
THE ARTHURIAN CENTRE
BRITISH CYCLING MUS.
A30
A38
A39
A388
A390
A395
A374
A387
A3082
B3266
B3262
B3263
B3314
B3267
B3254
B3257
B3362
B3268
B3269
B3359
B3252
B3251
B3253
B3247
B3249
B3271
SX
Cornwall

DARTMOOR
DARTMOOR
NATIONAL
FOREST
PARK
D
e
v
SX
TAMAR
VALLEY
Tavistock
Plymouth
Plymouth
Saltash
Torpoint
Devonport
Plymstock
Plympton
Ivybridge
Kingsbridge
Salcombe
Buckfastleigh
Yelverton
Horrabridge
Princetown
Two Bridges
Broadwoodwidger
Cross Green
Bridestowe
Bridestowe and Sourton Common
BLACK-A-TOR COPSE
621 HIGH WILLHAYS
Gidleigh
Murchington
Sandypark
Easton
Chagford
Teigncombe
Frenchbeer
Lettaford
North Bovey
Thrushelton
Stowford
DINGLE'S STEAM VILLAGE
Lewdown
Portgate
Lewtrenchard
Lydford
LYDFORD
LYDFORD GORGE
Coryton
Shortacombe
OKEMENT HILL
HANGINGSTONE HILL
CUT HILL
SITTAFORD TOR
Dutson
LAUNCESTON STEAM RAILWAY
Liftondown
Lifton
Tinhay
Lawhitton
Kelly
Bradstone
Chillaton
North Brentor
Black Down
Willsworthy
GRIMSPOUND
HAMELDOWN TOR
Milton Abbot
Dunterton
Mary Tavy
Horndon
Cudliptown
ROUGH TOR
Postbridge
HOUND TOR
Trekenner
Rezare
Peter Tavy
Bellever
BELLEVER (Dartmoor)
WISTMAN'S WOOD
Widecombe in the Moor
Bonehill
Sydenham Damerel
Lamerton
Wilminstone
GT. MIS TOR
Merrivale
PREHISTORIC SETTLEMENT
Rundlestone
RIPPON TOR
Stoke Climsland
Horsebridge
Luckett
Latchley
HIGH MOORLAND VISITOR CENTRE
W. Dart
E. Dart
Ponsworthy
Dartmeet
Buckland in the Moor
Downgate
Chilsworthy
Gunnislake
Gulworthy
Whitchurch
Grenofen
Sampford Spiney
Hexworthy
Poundsgate
Kelly Bray
KIT HILL
TOLL
St Ann's Chapel
Drakewalls
Higher Walreddon
Whiteworks
RIVER DART ADVENTURES
Golberdon
Haye
Callington
Albaston
MORWELLHAM QUAY
Walkhampton
Harrowbarrow
DUPATH WELL HOUSE
COTEHELE
Calstock
Buckland Monachorum
GARDEN HOUSE
PAPERWEIGHT CENTRE
Dousland
Burrator Res.
Sheepstor
RYDER'S HILL
Holne
BUCKFAST ABBEY
Buckfast
St Dominick
BUCKLAND ABBEY
Crapstone
Meavy
UPPER PLYM VALLEY
Newbridge
Bere Alston
Milton Combe
Clearbrook
St Mellion
Weir Quay
Lopwell
Dean
PENNYWELL FARM
Pillaton
Bere Ferrers
Shaugh Prior
SHELL TOP
Ugborough Moor
Dean Prior
Cargreen
Bickleigh
DENDLES WOOD
Didworthy
Hatt
Landulph
Roborough
Wotter
Lee Moor
Botusfleming
Tamerton Foliot
SALTASH SERVICES
P&R
PLYMOUTH CITY
CROWNHILL FORT
Rattery
Landrake
Crownhill
Plym
Forest
Drakeland Corner
Lutton
Cornwood
Harford
South Brent
Tideford
Trematon
UGBOROUGH BEACON
Cheston
Lincombe
St Erney
St Stephens
MARY NEWMAN'S COTTAGE
St Budeaux
Eggbuckland
PLYM VALLEY RAILWAY
Sparkwell
Bittaford
Avonwick
St Germans
ANTONY HOUSE
MERCHANT'S HOUSE
Diptford
Polbathic
Lee Mill
North Huish
St Germans R.
Sheviock
Ugborough
Ferry
Antony
SALTRAM
Crafthole
Cremyll
ROYAL CITADEL
Elburton
Westlake
Curtisknowle
Portwrinkle
St John
MOUNT EDGCUMBE
Brixton
Yealmpton
Ermington
Brownston
SOUTH WEST COAST PATH
Freathy
Millbrook
Drake's I.
Hooe
Yealm
Modbury
Whitsand Bay
Kingsand
The Sound
Staddiscombe
Holbeton
Cawsand
Bovisand Bay
Down Thomas
Luson
Rame
Knighton
Penlee Pt.
Heybrook Bay
Wembury
Newton Ferrers
Battisborough Cross
Loddiswell
Woodleigh
Rame Hd.
Wembury Bay
Mothecombe
St Ann's Chapel
Aveton Gifford
Great Mew Stone
Worswell
Noss Mayo
Kingston
SORLEY TUNNEL ADVENTURE WORLDS
SOUTH WEST COAST PATH
Ringmore
Bigbury
Churchstow
Stoke Pt.
West Alvington
Bigbury on Sea
Burgh I.
BIGBURY BAY
Bantham
Buckland
Thurlestone
South Milton
Woolston
ROSCOFF 6:00
SANTANDER 18:00
(Mar-Nov)
Galmpton
Hope
Bolt Tail
Malborough
Bolberry
East Portlemouth
Soar
SALCOMBE
OVERBECKS MUSEUM AND GARDEN
Bolt Hd.
SOUTH
Avon
Erme
Tamar
Tavy
A30
A386
A388
A390
A38
A374
A379
A3121
A381
A385
B3362
B3357
B3212
B3257
B3212
B3387
B3206
B3249
B3247
B3413
B3373
B3432
B3417
B3186
B3392
B3196
B3213
B3271
0 1 2 3 4 5 6 miles
0 1 2 3 4 5 6 7 8 9 10km

Dunsford
Steps Bridge (Dartmoor)
Bridfordmills
Shillingford St George
Alphington
Exeter
P&R
Topsham
Clyst St George
Woodbury Salterton
Newton Poppleford
Sidmouth
Doccombe
Moretonhampstead
Bridford
Doddiscombsleigh
Exminster
Ebford
Exton
Woodbury
Colaton Raleigh
Cotmaton
Christow
Higher Ashton
Kennford
Kenn
Bicton Park
Yettington
Otterton
Ladram Bay
Lower Ashton
Powderham
River Exe
Lympstone
A La Ronde
East Budleigh
Otterton Mill
Powderham Castle
Kenton
Withycombe Raleigh
Knowle
South West Coast Path
Canonteign Falls
Trusham
Devon & Exeter
Starcross
Budleigh Salterton
Danger Pt.
Lustleigh
Manaton
Water
Hennock
Cockwood
Littleham
World of Country Life
Fairlynch Arts Centre and Museum
Exmouth
Dawlish Warren
Exmouth Model Railway
Straight Pt.
Ashcombe
East Dartmoor Woods & Heaths
Bovey Tracey
Chudleigh
Chudleigh Knighton
Craft Centre
Brimley
Haytor Vale
Ilsington
Heathfield
Ideford
Luton
Little Haldon
Dawlish
Liverton
Stover
Trago Mills
Coldeast
Preston
Teigngrace
Holcombe
Bishopsteignton
Sigford
Teignmouth
Kingsteignton
Teign
Shaldon
Shaldon Wildlife Trust
Bickington
Highweek
Newton Abbot
Combeinteignhead
South West Coast Path
Netherton
Stokeinteignhead
West Ogwell
Bradley
Wolborough
Plant World
Ashburton
East Ogwell
Prickly Ball Hedgehog Hospital
Babbacombe Bay
Woodland
Denbury
Abbotskerswell
Coffinswell
Maidencombe
Forder Grn.
Kingskerswell
Barton
Torbryan
Ipplepen
North Whilborough
Watcombe
Landscove
Broadhempston
Model Village
Babbacombe
SX
SY
Butterfly Farm & Otter Sanctuary
Shiphay
Compton
Compton Castle
Torquay
Torre Abbey
Kent's Cavern Prehistoric Caves
Staverton
Cockington
Wellswood
Hope's Nose
Dartington
Littlehempston
Marldon
Living Coasts
Cider Press Centre Dartington
Dartington Hall Gardens
Berry Pomeroy Castle
Oldway Mansion
Hollicombe
Shinner's Bridge
Cott
South Devon Railway
Berry Pomeroy
Blagdon
Torbay
Kirkham
Paignton
Totnes
Castle
A385
Paignton & Dartmouth Steam Railway
Tigley
Motor Museum
Collaton St Mary
TORBAY
Belsford
Zoo & Environmental Park
Tor Bay
Harberton
Dart
Goodrington
Ashprington
Stoke Gabriel
Brixham
Berry Head
Harbertonford
Tuckenhay
Galmpton
Aquarium
Churston Ferrers
Cornworthy
St Mary's Bay
Crabadon
Washbourne
Dittisham
River Dart
Sharkham Pt.
Halwell
Allaleigh
Capton
Hillhead
Moreleigh
Woodland Leisure Park
Dartmouth
Newcomen Engine House
Woodford
Blackawton
Kingswear
Scabbacombe Hd.
Millcombe
Bayards Cove Fort
Warfleet
Coleton Fishacre
Bowden
Dartmouth Castle
Mew Stone
East Allington
Stoke Fleming
Blackpool
Goveton
Strete
South West Coast Path
Harleston
Slapton
Start Bay
Sherford
Frittiscombe
Slapton Sands
Slapton Ley
Frogmore
Stokenham
Charleton
Chillington
Torcross
Kernborough
Beeson
South Pool
Beesands
Kellaton
Hallsands
South Allington
Start Point
Devon
East Prawle
Lannacombe Bay
Prawle Pt.
A
B
C
D
E
F
5
6
7
8
9
30
31

1
2
3
4
5
A
B
C
D
E
F
NORTH
BIDEFORD
HARTLAND POINT
Titchberry
Windbury Pt.
CLOVELLY VILLAGE
Clovelly
Higher Clovelly
Stoke
Hartland Quay
Hartland
Philham
SOUTH WEST COAST PATH
Milford
ELMSCOTT
Eddistone
Elmscott
Tosberry
Buck's Cross
THE MILKY WAY ADVENTURE PARK
Woolfardisworthy
Hartland Forest
Alminstone Cross
South Hole
Knaps Longpeak
Welcombe
235
Meddon
Ashmansworthy
Gooseham
156
Woolley
Eastcott
Youlstone
Morwenstow
Dinworthy
Higher Sharpnose Pt.
Shop
A39
KILLARNEY SPRINGS FAMILY LEISURE PARK
Woodford
BROCKLANDS ADVENTURE PARK
Bradworthy
Bradworthy Cross
Lower Sharpnose Pt.
14
Waldon
Alfardisworthy
Coombe
Kilkhampton
Sutcombe
Stibb
Soldon Cross
CORNWALL
Strat
BUDE
DUNSDON
Poughill
Hersham
Flexbury
Bude Haven
1643
Stratton
Grimscott
Chilsworthy
Bude
A3072
Launcells
Tamar
9
Pancrasweek
Holsworthy
SS
BAY
Upton
B3254
Derril
Derriton
Marhamchurch
Bridgerule
Pyworthy
162
Chasty
Widemouth Bay
Widemouth Sand
Budd's Titson
Leworthy
Coppathorne
Millook
Dizzard Pt.
Poundstock
Deer
SOUTH WEST COAST PATH
Tregole
9
Treskinnick Cross
Whitstone
Claw
St Genny's
Trewint
Week St Mary
North Tamerton
PENHALLAM
Cambeak
Crackington Haven
Rosecare
Tetcott
Lana
Jacobstow
SX
Wainhouse Corner
Luffincott
Tresparrett Posts
B3263
West Curry
Fire Beacon Pt.
260
South Wheatley
Beeny
Maxworthy
A39
Northcott
BOSCASTLE HARBOUR
Tresparrett
Marshgate
Bennacott
Canworthy Water
Boyton
Brazacott
Boscastle
Lesnewth
Otterham
256
Trevalga
Warbstow
Trelash
Langdon
CASTLE
Tintagel Hd.
Tremaine
Ottery
Bridgetown
OLD POST OFFICE
TINTAGEL
Bossiney
North Petherwin
Tintagel
B3266
B3262
Hallworthy
Treneglos
Werrington
308
Yeolmbridge
Treknow
Davidstow
Trewarmett
8
Tremail
13
Tresmeer
Egloskerry
Langore
B3254
Start Pt.
Trewassa
Tregeare
THE ARTHURIAN CENTRE
St Stephen's
Dutson
Trebarwith
B3263
BRITISH CYCLING MUS.
Davidstow Moor
Cold Northcott
HIDDEN VALLEY DISCOVERY PARK
B3314
A395
Piper's Pool
Launceston
Treligga
CASTLE
SOUTH WEST COAST PATH
Tregadillett
Delabole
Camelford
St Clether
Laneast
A30
Trewen
TRETHORNE LEISURE FARM
Daw's House
A388
Valley Truckle
Crowdy Res.
B3254
Port Isaac Bay
B3314
Polyphant
70
Inny
Helstone
South Petherwin
B3267
Port Isaac
Port Quin Bay
Port Quin
High Moor
400 ROUGH TOR
Altarnun
Lewannick
Port Gaverne
B3267
St Teath
Trewint
LONG CROSS
B3257
Pendoggett
Trelights
5
veighan
420 BROWN WILLY
369
A30
5
Lezant
Polzeath
Michaelstow
Codda
Congdon's Shop
Trekenner
0 1 2 3 4 5 6 miles
0 1 2 3 4 5 6 7 8 9 10 km
331 GARROW TOR
BODMIN
Trebullett
St Mi
St Breward
MUSEUM OF SMUGGLING
Trebartha
Treburley
Pityme
3
Bolventor
18
4
Coad's Green
5
B3254
North Hill
Chapel Amble
St Kew
MOOR
B3257

LUNDY 2:15
Braunton Burrows
Chivenor
Barnstaple
Goodleigh
Brayford
High Bray
North Heasley
South Radworthy
Heasley Mill
Pilton
MUSEUM OF NORTH DEVON
Westacott
Gunn
Charles
Fremington
Yelland
Bickington
Bickleton
Newport
Landkey
Swimbridge
Newland
West Buckland
East Buckland
NORTH DEVON MARITIME MUSEUM
Instow
Bishops Tawton
NORTH DEVON FARM PARK
NORTHAM BURROWS
Appledore
BAY
DEVON
Westward Ho!
Northam
TAPELEY PARK GDNS
Westleigh
Tawstock
North Molton
Filleigh
Orchard Hill
Eastleigh
Horwood
Newton Tracey
Herner
Cobbaton
THE BIG SHEEP
Bideford
Ensis
East Stowford
QUINCE HONEY FARM
Abbotsham
BURTON GALL & MUS
East-the-Water
Hiscott
Chapelton
COBBATON COMBAT COLL
Chittlehampton
South Molton
Bish Mill
Handy Cross
Woodtown
Fishleigh Barton
Alverdiscott
ATLANTIC VILLAGE
Buck's Mills
Horns Cross
Pairy Cross
Ford
Landcross
Woodtown
Umberleigh
Clapworthy
Bishops Nympton
Yarnscombe
Atherington
Alswear
Littleham
Goldsworthy
Warkleigh
George Nympton
Satterleigh
Langridge Ford
Weare Giffard
Parkham
Monkleigh
Sherwood Green
High Bickington
Chittlehamholt
Buckland Brewer
High Bullen
Romansleigh
Parkham Ash
DARTINGTON CRYSTAL
St Giles in the Wood
King's Nympton
Frithelstock
Great Torrington
Frithelstock Stone
Taddiport
Tythecott
Kingscott
Roborough
Cadbury Barton
Week
R.H.S. GARDEN ROSEMOOR
West Putford
East Putford
Little Torrington
Burrington
Elstone
THE PIXIE KILN & GALLERY
Langtree
Beaford
Chulmleigh
West Worlington
Bulkworthy
Stibb Cross
Riddlecombe
Cheldon
Ashreigney
Abbots Bickington
Newton St Petrock
Peters Marland
Woolston
Winswell
Chawleigh
Venn Green
Milton Damerel
Merton
Huish
Dolton
Ashley
Torridge
Hollocombe
Filleigh
Buckland Filleigh
Dowland
Holsworthy Beacon
Shebbear
Petrockstow
Wembworthy
Eastington
Thornbury
Meeth
Iddesleigh
Winkleigh
Lapford
Morchard Bishop
Brushford
Coldridge
Nymet Rowland
Bradford
Woodacott
D
e
v
o
n
Sheepwash
Broadwood Kelly
Black Torrington
Cookbury
Monkokehampton
West Leigh
Holemoor
Bondleigh
East Leigh
Zeal Monachorum
Down St Mary
Highampton
Hatherleigh
Brandis Corner
Whimble
Hollacombe
Graddon Moor
Honeychurch
Chilla
WINSFORD WALLED GARDEN
Exbourne
Jacobstowe
North Tawton
Bow
Colebrooke
Halwill Junction
Sampford Courtenay
Nymet Tracey
Halwill
Beaworthy
Northlew
Inwardleigh
Oak Cross
Clawton
Itton
Hillerton
Patchacott
Ashbury
DARTMOOR RAILWAY
Quoditch
BROADBURY
Folly Gate
Taw Green
Spreyton
Ashwater
Eworthy
Okehampton
Sticklepath
South Tawton
Ettisleigh
Henford
Germansweek
Boasley Cross
Thorndon Cross
FINCH FOUNDRY
Belstone
South Zeal
Whiddon Down
Cheriton Bishop
Chapmans Well
Virginstow
CASTLE
OKEHAMPTON (Dartmoor)
Okehampton Camp
East Panson
Roadford Res.
Meldon
Crockernwell
SOURTON CROSS SERVICES
Grinacombe Moor
Bratton Clovelly
St Giles on the Hth.
Okehampton Common
COSDON HILL
Throwleigh
Drewsteignton
Gridley Corner
YES TOR
CASTLE DROGO
Broadwoodwidger
Bridestowe
Sourton
BLACK-A-TOR COPSE
HIGH WILLHAYS
Wonson
Sandypark
Thrushel
Bridestowe and Sourton Common
Gidleigh
Easton
Cross Green
Thrushelton
Murchington
Stowford
DINGLE'S STEAM VILLAGE
Lewdown
Shortacombe
OKEMENT HILL
Teigncombe
Chagford
DARTMOOR
Liftondown
Lifton
Portgate
Lewtrenchard
Lydford
HANGINGSTONE HILL
Frenchbeer
Moretonhampstead
Tinhay
LYDFORD
Coryton
Lettaford
THE MINIATURE PONY CENTRE
North Bovey
LYDFORD GORGE
NATIONAL
Lawhitton
North Brentor
Black Down
Willsworthy
CUT HILL
SITTAFORD TOR
Kelly
Chillaton
DARTMOOR
GRIMSPOUND
Manaton
Bradstone
HAMELDOWN TOR
PARK
Milton Abbot
Dunterton
Mary Tavy
Horndon
ROUGH TOR
Postbridge
Cudliptown
HOUND TOR
Rezare
Lamerton
Peter Tavy
FOREST
Bellever
Widecombe in the Moor
Bonehill
Haytor Vale
Sydenham Damerel
Wilminstone
WISTMAN'S WOOD
BELLEVER (Dartmoor)
GT. MIS TOR
PREHISTORIC SETTLEMENT
Merrivale
SS
SX
A39
A386
A361
A377
A3124
A3072
A3079
A388
A30
A382
B3233
B3232
B3227
B3226
B3217
B3220
B3042
B3096
B3215
B3206
B3212
B3362
B3387
Taw
Torridge
Mole
Yeo
Lew
Carey
Teign
Tamar
Dart

Brayford
High Bray
Radworthy
North Heasley
Heasley Mill
South Radworthy
Charles
West Buckland
East Buckland
Liscombe
Tarr Steps
Winsford
Bridgetown
Exton
Hawkridge
Molland Common
Twitchen
Dane's Brook
Withiel Florey
Clatworthy Res.
Brompton Regis
Wimbleball Lake
Huish Champflower
Upton
Haddon Hill
Heydon Hill
Skilgate
Chipstable
Anstey Common
West Anstey
East Anstey
Dulverton
Battleton
Barle
Nightcott
Brushford
Bury
Morebath
Petton
Shillingford
Clayhanger
North Molton
Molland
Filleigh
Quince Honey Farm
East Stowford
Chittlehampton
South Molton
Mole
Yeo
Yeo Mill
Oldways End
Exebridge
Bampton
Bish Mill
Newtown
Bishops Nympton
Ash Mill
Knowstone
Roachill
Oakfordbridge
Oakford
Clapworthy
Satterleigh
George Nympton
Alswear
Mariansleigh
Rose Ash
Huntsham
Hockworthy
Chittlehamholt
Romansleigh
Meshaw
King's Nympton
Creacombe
Stoodleigh Beacon
Stoodleigh
Cove
Exe Valley
Rackenford
Cadbury
Burrington
Elstone
Week
Queen Dart
Little Dart
Loxbeare
Washfield
Chevithorne
East Mere
Whitnage
Lutworthy
Witheridge
Templeton Bridge
Knightshayes Court
Uplowman
Bolham
Chettiscombe
Sampford Peverell
Chulmleigh
Cheldon
West Worlington
East Worlington
Drayford
Nomansland
Templeton
Calverleigh
Tiverton Castle
Cowleymoor
Halberton
Ashreigney
Chawleigh
Thelbridge Barton
Washford Pyne
Cruwys Morchard
Withleigh
Cotteylands
Tiverton
Grand Western Canal
Ashley
Pennymoor
Ash Thomas
Willand
Filleigh
Dalch
Black Dog
Puddington
Way Village
Well Town
Diggerland
Cullompton Services
Wembworthy
Eastington
Poughill
Cadeleigh
Butterleigh
Cullompton
Brushford
Coldridge
Nymet Rowland
Lapford
Morchard Bishop
Woolfardisworthy
Upham
Devonshire's Centre
Bickleigh Mill
Bickleigh Castle
Bickleigh
Devon Railway Centre
Kennerleigh
Stockleigh English
Oldborough
Cheriton Fitzpaine
Colebrook
West Leigh
East Leigh
Ash Bullayne
East Village
Cadbury
Fursdon House
Bradninch
Mutterton
Westcott
Zeal Monachorum
Down St Mary
Newbuildings
Stockleigh Pomeroy
Silverton
Culm
Copplestone
Sandford
Upton Hellions
Thorverton
Up Exe
Hele
Langford
Clyst Hydon
Honeychurch
North Tawton
Knowle
Bow
Coleford
The Collegiate Church of the Holy Cross
Shobrooke
Efford
Shute
Ellerhayes
Nether Exe
Killerton House
Clyst St Lawrence
Nymet Tracey
Colebrooke
Crediton
Sweetham
Brampford Speke
Rewe
Budlake
Westwood
Dartmoor Railway
Itton
Hillerton
Yeoford
Uton
Hookway
Newton St Cyres
Stoke Canon
Broadclyst
Clyst
Taw Green
Venny Tedburn
Upton Pyne
Poltimore
Whimple
Spreyton
Cowley
Dog Village
Jack in the Green
Hittisleigh
Tedburn St Mary
Pinhoe
Rockbeare
South Tawton
South Zeal
Whiddon Down
Cheriton Bishop
Whitestone
Exwick
Exeter
Cathedral
Whipton
Clyst Honiton
Exeter International
Marsh Green
Crockernwell
Heavitree
Sowton
Exeter Services
Aylesbeare
Cosdon Hill
Throwleigh
Drewsteignton
Longdown
Powderham
Wheatley
St Thomas
Countess Wear
Clyst St Mary
Farringdon
Castle Drogo
Sandypark
Ide
Crealy Adventure Park
Wonson
Teign
Easton
Dunsford
Shillingford St George
Alphington
Clyst St George
Woodbury
Salterton
Gidleigh
Murchington
Steps Bridge (Dartmoor)
Topsham
Ebford
Exminster
Exton
Teigncombe
Chagford
Doccombe
Bridford
Bridfordmills
Doddiscombsleigh
Kennford
Kenn
Black Hill
Frenchbeer
Moretonhampstead
Christow
Higher Ashton
Lower Ashton
Powderham
Lympstone
A La Ronde
Lettaford
The Miniature Pony Centre
North Bovey
Canonteign Falls
Kenton
Powderham Castle
Withycombe Raleigh
Ord Tor
Devon & Exeter
Trusham
Starcross
Littleham
Grimspound
Manaton
Lustleigh
Hennock
Cockwood
Exmouth
Hameldown Tor
Water
Bovey
Ashcombe
Dawlish Warren
Exmouth Model Railway
Straight Pt.
Postbridge
East Dartmoor Heaths
Bovey Tracey
Chudleigh
Chudleigh Knighton
Craft Centre
Brimley
Ideford
Luton
Little Haldon
Dawlish
Bell
Dart
Ilsington
Heathfield
Liverton
SS
SX
D
e
V
0 1 2 3 4 5 6 miles
0 1 2 3 4 5 6 7 8 9 10 km
A361
A396
A377
A3072
A3124
A30
A382
A38
A380
A379
A376
A373
M5
B3224
B3222
B3190
B3227
B3226
B3137
B3096
B3042
B3220
B3212
B3206
B3193
B3181
B3052
B3179
B3178
B3180
B3344
B3192
B3387

Taunton
Wellington
Wiveliscombe
Honiton
Axminster
Chard
Ilminster
Crewkerne
South Petherton
Merriott
Ottery St Mary
Sidmouth
Sidford
Seaton
Beer
Lyme Regis
Budleigh Salterton
Charmouth
Bridport
BLACKDOWN HILLS
B L A C K D O W N
H I L L S
E A S T D E V O N
VALE OF TAUNTON DEANE
Culm Valley
West Sedge Moor
L Y M E B A Y
Seaton Bay
Charlton Bay
Ladram Bay
Beer Hd.
Danger Pt.
ST
SY
Staplegrove
Bathpool
Bishop's Hull
Norton Fitzwarren
Cheddon Fitzpaine
Monkton Heathfield
Creech St Michael
Ruishton
Thornfalcon
Henlade
Stoke St Mary
Orchard Portman
Staple Fitzpaine
Pitminster
Corfe
Blagdon Hill
Trull
Staplehay
West Buckland
Rockwell Green
Thorne St Margaret
Holywell Lake
Sampford Arundel
Wrangway
Ford Street
Angersleigh
Holcombe Rogus
Westleigh
Burlescombe
Appledore
Uffculme
Culmstock
Hemyock
Churchstanton
Churchinford
Clayhidon
Rosemary Lane
Stapley
Bolham Water
Smeatharpe
Abbey
Craddock
Ashill
Smithincott
Blackborough
Kentisbeare
Sheldon
Dunkeswell
Upottery
Luppitt
Rawridge
Beacon
Wick
Monkton
Combe Raleigh
Awliscombe
Buckerell
Colestocks
Payhembury
Broadhembury
Kerswell
Dulford
Norman's Green
Plymtree
Tale
Talaton
Feniton
Fenny Bridges
Gittisham
Alfington
Fairmile
West Hill
Wiggaton
Tipton St John
Venn Ottery
Harpford
Bowd
Newton Poppleford
Hawkerland
Colaton Raleigh
Yettington
Otterton
East Budleigh
Knowle
Cotmaton
Salcombe Regis
Branscombe
Weston
Vicarage
Harcombe
Sidbury
Church Green
Farway
Broad Down
Northleigh
Southleigh
Colyton
Colyford
Axmouth
Musbury
Whitford
Shute
Kilmington
Offwell
Wilmington
Cotleigh
Dalwood
Stockland
Millhayes
Heathstock
Ham
Membury
Furley
Chardstock
Alston
Churchill
Smallridge
Yarcombe
Newcott
Marsh
Whitestaunton
Howley
Wambrook
Bishopswood
Buckland St Mary
Combe St Nicholas
Wadeford
Chaffcombe
Forton
Tatworth
South Chard
Tytherleigh
Thorncombe
Holditch
Hawkchurch
Birdsmoor Gate
Marshalsea
Marshwood
Bettiscombe
Pilsdon
Broad Oak
Whitchurch Canonicorum
Ryall
Morcombelake
Symondsbury
Chideock
Seatown
Eype
West Bay
Wootton Fitzpaine
Uplyme
Combpyne
Rousdon
Weycroft
Winsham
Wayford
Whatley
Cricket St Thomas
Hewish
Misterton
Clapton
Seaborough
Drimpton
Burstock
Broadwinds
Cudworth
Chillington
Cricket Malherbie
Dowlish Wake
Kingstone
Dinnington
Hinton St George
West Chinnock
Lopen
Seavington St Mary
Seavington St Michael
Over Stratton
Norton sub Hamdon
Chiselborough
Donyatt
Ashwell
Stocklinch
Shepton Beauchamp
Barrington
West Lambrook
East Lambrook
Westport
Puckington
Ilton
Hambridge
Kingsbury Episcopi
Martock
Bower Hinton
Isle Brewers
Isle Abbotts
Fivehead
Curry Mallet
Hatch Beauchamp
West Hatch
Wrantage
Beercrocombe
Hatch Green
Bickenhall
Curland
Ashill
Windmill Hill
Broadway
Horton
Crock Street
North Curry
Knapp
Meare Green
Stoke St Gregory
Curry Rivel
Drayton
Langport
Huish Episcopi
Muchelney
Pitney
Low Ham
High Ham
Henley
Othery
Pathe
Stathe
Burrowbridge
Athelney
Lyng
West Lyng
Durston
Creech Heathfield
North End
Hedging
North Newton
Northmoor Green or Moorland
Huntworth
North Petherton
Middlezoy
Aller
Thurloxton
West Monkton
Kingston St Mary
Nailsbourne
Pickney
Fulford
Bishops Lydeard
Cushuish
Cothelstone
Broomfield
Courtway
Goathurst
West Bagborough
Lydeard St Lawrence
Willett
Combe Florey
East Combe
Ash Priors
Tolland
Tarr
Brompton Ralph
Clatworthy
Langley Marsh
Maundown
Fitzhead
Halse
Preston Bowyer
Heathfield
Milverton
Hillcommon
Oake
Hillfarance
East Nynehead
Bradford on Tone
Nynehead
Runnington
Waterrow
Bathealton
Langford Budville
Kittisford
Appley
Ashbrittle
Nicholashayne
Langport
Sutton
GAULDEN MANOR GARDEN
FYNE COURT
TEMPLE OF HARMONY
HESTERCOMBE GARDENS
BRIDGWATER & TAUNTON CANAL MAUNSEL LOCKS
WILLOWS & WETLANDS VISITOR CENTRE
LANGPORT & R. PARRETT VISITOR CENTRE
STEMBRIDGE TOWER
ABBEY
SOMERSET CRICKET MUS.
SHEPPY'S FARMHOUSE CIDER
TAUNTON DEANE SERVICES
TAUNTON
BARRINGTON HILL
STAPLE HILL
BARRINGTON COURT
E. LAMBROOK MANOR
DILLINGTON HOUSE
HORNSBURY MILL
WILDLIFE PARK
FORDE ABBEY AND GARDENS
THE CRAFT AND DESIGN CENTRE
COLDHARBOUR MILL WORKING WOOL MUSEUM
HACKPEN HILL
BLACK DOWN
ESCOT PARK
FARWAY
BLACKBURY CAMP
SHUTE BARTON
BEER QUARRY CAVES
PECORAMA
MARINE HOUSE
SEATON ELECTRIC TRAMWAY COMPANY
SOUTH WEST COAST PATH
AXMOUTH TO LYME REGIS UNDERCLIFFS
CHARMOUTH HERITAGE COAST CENTRE
AQUARIUM
DINOSAURLAND
BICTON PARK
OTTERTON MILL
FAIRLYNCH ARTS CENTRE AND MUSEUM
WORLD OF COUNTRY LIFE
P&R
M5
A38
A358
A30
A303
A35
A373
A375
A3052
A361
A378
A372
A356
A3259
B3187
B3188
B3227
B3224
B3391
B3440
B3170
B3168
B3162
B3167
B3165
B3164
B3174
B3177
B3176
B3178
B3180
B3172
B3161
B3163
Tone
Parrett
Isle
Yarty
Axe
Otter
Char
Tale
5
6
7
8
9
A
B
C
D
E
F
G

King's Sedge Moor
Somerset Levels
Middlezoy
Othery
Pathe
High Ham
Henley
Dundon
Compton Dundon
Littleton
Butleigh
Baltonsborough
Southwood
Barton St David
West Lydford
East Lydford
Hornblotton Green
Sutton
Ansford
Castle Cary
Cole
Pitcombe
Hardway
Redlynch
Stoney Stoke
Alfred's Tower
Shepton Montague
Charlton Musgrove
Leigh Common
Hadspen Garden
Wincanton
Bratton Seymour
Bayford
Stoke Trister
Burrowbridge
Stathe
Athelney
Lyng
Stoke St Gregory
West Sedge Moor
Curry Rivel
Langport
Huish Episcopi
Low Ham
Pitney
Somerton
Stemple Tower Mill
Kingweston
Keinton Mandeville
Lydford-on-Fosse
Charlton Adam
Charlton Mackerell
Lytes Cary Manor
Babcary
North Barrow
South Barrow
Galhampton
Haynes Motor Mus
Yarlington
North Cadbury
Holton
Cary Fitzpaine
Kingsdon
Sparkford
Maperton
Lattiford
North Cheriton
South Cheriton
Langport & R. Parrett Visitor Centre
Willows & Wetlands Visitor Centre
Drayton
Muchelney
Abbey
Long Sutton
Podimore
West Camel
Queen Camel
South Cadbury
Compton Pauncefoot
Blackford
Horsington
Fivehead
Isle
Yeo
Northover
Bridgehampton
Fleet Air Arm Mus
Ilchester
Yeovilton
Limington
Chilton Cantelo
Marston Magna
Sutton Montis
Corton Denham
Charlton Horethorne
Abbas Combe
Curry Mallet
Isle Brewers
Isle Abbotts
Hambridge
Long Load
Kingsbury Episcopi
Stapleton
Ash
Coat
Tintinhull
Tintinhull Garden
Ashington
Rimpton
Sandford Orcas Manor House
Adber
Sandford Orcas
Stowell
Temple Combe
Yenston
Henstridge Marsh
Henstridge Ash
Henstridge
Milborne Wick
Westport
East Lambrook
West Lambrook
Martock
Treasurer's Ho
Hurst
Chilthorne Domer
Yeovil Marsh
Mudford
Trent
Poyntington
Oborne
Milborne Port
Stalbridge
Puckington
Ilton
Barrington
Barrington Court
E. Lambrook Manor
South Petherton
Bower Hinton
Stoke sub Hamdon
Montacute House
Montacute
Preston Plucknett
Yeovil
Nether Compton
Over Compton
Sherborne
Sherborne Old Castle
Goathill
Purse Caundle
Stocklinch
Shepton Beauchamp
Stoke-sub-Hamdon Priory
Norton sub Hamdon
Odcombe
Brympton
Sherborne Castle
Stalbridge Weston
Ashwell
Seavington St Michael
Over Stratton
Ham Hill
Chiselborough
West Coker
North Wootton
Haydon
Stourton Caundle
Ilminster
Dillington House
Donyatt
Seavington St Mary
Lopen
West Chinnock
North Coker
East Coker
Barwick
Stoford
Bradford Abbas
Alweston
Bishop's Caundle
Lydlinch
Dowlish Wake
Kingstone
Dinnington
Hinton St George
Merriott
East Chinnock
Hardington Moor
Hardington Mandeville
Thornford
Folke
Lillington
Longburton
Woodbridge
King's Stag
Cricket Malherbie
Hornsbury Mill
Chillington
Cudworth
Haselbury Plucknett
Closworth
Ryme Intrinseca
Beer Hackett
Yetminster
Holwell
Crouch Hill
Blackmore Vale
Chaffcombe
Crewkerne
Cricket St Thomas
Wildlife Park
Hewish
Misterton
North Perrott
Hardington Marsh
Pendomer
Holnest
Leigh
Glanvilles Wootton
Pulham
Hazelbury Bryan
Whatley
Winsham
Wayford
Clapton
Seaborough
South Perrott
Halstock
Melbury Osmond
Chetnole
Hermitage
Middlemarsh
Westfields
Forton
Drimpton
Mosterton
Chedington
Corscombe
West Chelborough
Melbury Sampford
Evershot
Melbury Bubb
Hilfield
Lyon's Gate
Duntish
Mappowder
Forde Abbey and Gardens
Thorncombe
The Craft and Design Centre
Broadwindsor
Burstock
Holyfield
Batcombe
Minterne Magna
Minterne Gardens
Buckland Newton
Holditch
Birdsmoor Gate
Rampisham
Frome St Quintin
Up Cerne
Alton Pancras
Plush
Hawkchurch
Marshalsea
Bettiscombe
Stoke Abbott
Beaminster
Wraxall
Up Sydling
Cerne Abbas Giant
Cerne Abbas
Piddletrenthide
Marshwood
Pilsdon
Netherbury
Mapperton
Hooke
Cattistock
Sydling St Nicholas
Chilfrome
Toller Porcorum
Nether Cerne
White Lackington
Piddlehinton
Melplash
North Poorton
Maiden Newton
Godmanstone
Wootton Fitzpaine
Broad Oak
Salwayash
West Milton
Powerstock
Toller Fratrum
Hog Cliff
Whitchurch Canonicorum
Ryall
Dottery
Nettlecombe
Wynford Eagle
Forston
Charlton Down
Morcombelake
Bradpole
Loders
Eggardon
Down
Uploders
West Compton
Frampton
Grimstone
Muckleford
Stratton
Charmouth
Charmouth Heritage Coast Centre
Lyme Regis
Aquarium
Dinosaurland
Symondsbury
Chideock
Seatown
Bridport
Walditch
Bothenhampton
Askerswell
Kingston Russell
Compton Valence
Bradford Peverell
Charminster
Hardy's Cottage Garden
Eype
West Bay
South West Coast Path
Shipton Gorge
Chilcombe
Litton Cheney
Long Bredy
Winterbourne Abbas
Nine Stones
The Tutankhamun Exhibition
Dorchester
Stinsford
Kingston Maurward
Military Museum
The Dinosaur Museum
Burton Bradstock
Poor Lot Barrows
Littlebredy
Winterbourne Steepleton
Martinstown
Maiden Castle
West Stafford
Whitcombe
Swyre
Puncknowle
Valley of Stones
Black Down
Hardy Monument
Winterborne Monkton
Winterborne Herringston
West Knighton
West Bexington
Kingston Russell Stone Circle
Portesham
South West Coast Path
Broadmayne
Abbotsbury
Tithe Barn Children's Farm
Sub Tropical Gardens
St. Catherine's Chapel
Swannery
Rodden
Upwey
Broadwey
Bincombe
White Horse
Poxwell
Littlemoor
Preston
Upton
Osmington
Langton Herring
Nottington
Overcombe
Jordan Hill Roman Temple
Osmington Mills
Radipole
Weymouth Sea Life Park
Chesil Beach
Chickerell
Water Gardens
Melcombe Regis
Westham
Weymouth
Charlestown
Nothe Fort
Brewer's Quay and Timewalk
Wyke Regis
Rodwell
Portland Harbour
Weymouth Bay
SY
ST
Dorset
Blackmore
Weymouth
Brewer's Quay and Timewalk
Rodwell
Wyke Regis
Portland Harbour
Guernsey 2:00
Jersey 3:15
St. Malo 5:00
Portland Castle
Portland
Fortuneswell
West Bay
Grove
Easton
Portland
Weston
Museum
Southwell
Bill of Portland
0 1 2 3 4 5 6 miles
0 1 2 3 4 5 6 7 8 9 10 km

Stourhead
Stourton
White Sheet Hill
Zeals
Mere
Penselwood
Bourton
Queen Oak
Bush Farm Bison Centre
The Green
West Knoyle
East Knoyle
Hindon
Berwick St Leonard
Fonthill Bishop
Fonthill Gifford
Vale of Wardour
Chilmark
Ridge
Farmer Giles Farmstead
Teffont Magna
Teffont Evias
Dinton
Chicksgrove
Grovely Wood
Baverstock
Barford St Martin
Wilton
Ditchampton
Stratford sub Castle
Old Sarum
Salisbury
Quidhampton
Burcombe
Wilton House
Netherhampton
West Harnham
East Harnham
Bemerton
Huntingford
Milton on Stour
Cucklington
Gillingham
Elm Hill
Ham Common
Wyke
Sedgehill
Newtown
Tisbury
Hatch
Sutton Mandeville
Fovant
Compton Chamberlayne
Swallowcliffe
Ansty
Semley
Old Wardour Castle
Cranborne
Prescombe Down
Broad Chalke
Bishopstone
Stratford Tony
Coombe Bissett
Odstock
Nunton
Homington
Buckhorn Weston
Kington Magna
Motcombe
Knap Corner
Donhead St Andrew
Donhead St Mary
White Sheet Hill
West End
Fifield Bavant
Stoke Farthing
Croucheston
Ebbesbourne Wake
Mount Sorrel
Alvediston
Berwick St John
Milkwell
West Stour
East Stour
Shaftesbury
Ivy Cross
Ludwell
Woodminton
Bowerchalke
Charlton
Cann
Cann Common
Win Green
Chase and
Rockbourne Down
Wick Down
Fifehead Magdalen
Stour Provost
Stour Row
Guy's Marsh
Todber
Melbury Abbas
Melbury Down
Martin Drove End
Martin
Martin Down
Tidpit
Whitsbury
Upper Street
Breamore House & Museum
Pillwell
Marnhull
Margaret Marsh
Bedchester
Tollard Royal
Chase
Woodyates
Deanland
Sixpenny Handley
Woodcutts
Compton Abbas
Ashmore
East Orchard
West Orchard
Hinton St Mary
Fontmell Magna
Larmer Tree Victorian Pleasure Garden
West
Pentridge
Pentridge Hill
Rockbourne
Outwick
Roman Villa
Burgate
Damerham
Sturminster Newton
Mill
Manston
Sutton Waldron
Cranborne
Dean
Farnham
Su
Sandleheath
Ashford
Fordingbridge
Fiddleford
Fiddleford Manor
Hammoon
Iwerne Courtney or Shroton
Iwerne Minster
Stubhampton
Chettle
Chettle House
Monkton Up Wimborne
Alderholt Mill
Alderholt
Newton
Broad Oak
Child Okeford
Hambledon Hill
Tarrant Gunville
Wiltshire
Cashmoor
Cranborne
Manor Gardens
Cripplestyle
Edmondsham Ho.
Edmondsham
Charing Cross
Bickton
Fifehead Neville
Shillingstone
Tarrant Hinton
Gussage St Michael
Wimborne St Giles
Knowlton Church
Okeford Fitzpaine
Stourpaine
Long Crichel
Gussage All Saints
Heavy Horse Centre
Knowlton
Verwood
Ibsley
Kingston
Pimperne
Tarrant Launceston
Moor Crichel
Woodlands
Ringwood Forest
Durweston
Tarrant Monkton
Royal Signals Museum
Downs
Manswood
Ibberton
Turnworth
Woolland
Blandford Forum
Bryanston
Tarrant Rawston
Witchampton
Chalbury
Horton
Chalbury Common
Blashford
Ringwood
Stoke Wake
Higher Ansty
Blandford St Mary
Tarrant Rushton
Hinton Martell
Mannington
Three Legged Cross
Moors Valley
Ashley
Winterborne Houghton
Winterborne Stickland
Tarrant Keyneston
Gaunt's Common
Ashley Heath
St Ives
Hilton
Charlton Marshall
Winterborne Clenston
Thorncombe
Tarrant Crawford
Honeybrook Victorian Farm
Stanbridge
Holt
Holt Heath
West Moors
St Leonards Services
Melcombe Bingham
Milton Abbey
Whatcombe
Milton Abbas
Spetisbury
Broom Hill
Avon Heath
St Leonards
Kingston
Charlton Down
Shapwick
Kingston Lacy
Hillbutts
Clapgate
Colehill
Canford Bottom
Trickett's Cross
The Matchams Experience
Cheselbourne
Winterborne Whitechurch
Sturminster Marshall
Pamphill
Walford Mill
Wimborne Minster
Stapehill
Ferndown
Knoll Gdns
Almer
Hampreston
Longham
West Parley
Bournemouth International
Dewlish
Winterborne Kingston
Winterborne Zelston
Corfe Mullen
East End
Oakley
Merley
Canford Magna
Parley Cross
Hurn
Avon
Sopley
Milborne St Andrew
Anderson
Bearwood
Adventure Wonderland
Ensbury
Martyrs Museum
Bere Regis
Hill View
Broadstone
Bear Cross
Kinson
Holdenhurst
Jumpers Green
Puddletown
Tolpuddle
Morden
East Morden
Lytchett Matravers
Canford Heath
Bournemouth
Moordown
Athelhampton
Burleston
Affpuddle
Turners Puddle
Bloxworth
Slepe
Lytchett Minster
Waterloo
Talbot Village
Winton
The Red House Mus.
Athelhampton
Tincleton
Briants Puddle
Lane End
Wareham Forest
Farmer Palmer's Farm Park
Upton
Newtown
Branksome
Pokesdown
Wick
Woodsford
Cloud's Hill
Morden Bog
Holton Heath
Hamworthy
Poole
R.N.L.I. Mus.
Parkstone
Lilliput
Westbourne
Branksome Park
Boscombe
Southbourne
Art Gall. and Mus.
Moreton
Bovington Camp
Trigon Hill
Sandford
Scaplen's Court Museum
Compton Acres
Canford Cliffs
Oceanarium
Crossways
Monkey World
Tank Museum
Northport
Purbeck Toy Mus.
Arne
Poole Harbour
Brownsea I.
Brownsea Island
Mill House Cider Museum
East Burton
Wool
Stokeford
Wareham
Stoborough
Ridge
Sandbanks
SZ
Poole Bay
Warmwell
Owermoigne
East Stoke
West Holme
Stoborough Green
Stoborough Heath
Hartland Moor
Ferry
Toll
Studland Beach and Nature Reserve
Studland
East Knighton
Winfrith Newburgh
Coombe Keynes
Middlebere Heath
Wytch Heath
Grange Heath
Newton Heath
Bay
Holworth
Chaldon Herring or East Chaldon
Lulworth Castle
The Blue Pool
Norden Heath
Isle of
Studland and Godlington Heath
Studland
Cherbourg 4:15
Chaldon Down
South West Coast Path
Dorset
East Lulworth
East Creech
Purbeck Hills
Castle
Church Knowle
Corfe Castle
Nine Barrow Down
The Foreland
South West Coast Path
Guernsey 2:30
Jersey 3:45
St. Malo 5:25
Cherbourg 2:15
(Apr-Oct)
(May-Sept)
Ringstead Bay
West Lulworth
Lulworth Cove
Steeple
Model Village & Gardens
Ulwell
New Swanage
Bay
Durdle Door
Tyneham
Purbeck
Kingston
Harman's Cross
Swanage Bay
Swanage
Swanage Railway
Lulworth Cove
Worbarrow Bay
Kimmeridge
Kimmeridge Bay
Langton Matravers Mus.
Langton Matravers
Peveril Pt.
Swanage
Durlston Head
Acton
Worth Matravers
Durlston
Tilly Whim Caves
Setbourne
A303
A350
A30
A354
A357
A338
A36
A31
A35
A348
A349
A351
A352
A3049
B3089
B3081
B3092
B3091
B3082
B3078
B3072
B3081
B3075
B3070
B3071
B3390
B3069
B3351
B3347
B3073
B3094
B3095
24
14

Salisbury
Wilton
Romsey
Southampton
SOUTHAMPTON
Totton
Lyndhurst
Ringwood
Fordingbridge
Brockenhurst
Lymington
LYMINGTON
New Milton
Barton on Sea
Milford on Sea
Highcliffe
CHRISTCHURCH
Bournemouth
Boscombe
Poole Bay
Christchurch Bay
Hengistbury Head
Sandbanks
Studland Bay
The Foreland
Swanage Bay
The Needles
Alum Bay
Totland
Totland Bay
Freshwater Bay
Yarmouth
Brighstone Forest
Brighstone Bay
Atherfield Pt.
Hampshire
New Forest National Park
Beaulieu
Beaulieu Heath
Blackfield
Hythe
Dibden Purlieu
Marchwood
Chandler's Ford
Verwood
Ferndown
West Moors
St Leonards
Burley
Sway
Setley
Burton
Mudeford
Cranborne
Alderholt
Downton
Redlynch
Whiteparish
West Tytherley
Broughton
Houghton
King's Somborne
Little Somborne
Up Somborne
Sparsholt
Stockbridge
Mottisfont
Michelmersh
Timsbury
Braishfield
Ampfield
Hursley
Standon
North Baddesley
Chilworth
Rownhams
Nursling
Bassett
Swaythling
Ower
Wigley
Cadnam
Ashurst
Minstead
Emery Down
Bank
Denny Lodge
Balmerlawn
Hatchet Gate
East Boldre
Bucklers Hard
Exbury
Lepe
Needs Ore Pt.
Newtown Bay
Hamstead
Cranmore
Shalfleet
Ningwood
Newbridge
Calbourne
Shalcombe
Mottistone
Brook
Hulverstone
Limerstone
Yafford
Thorncross
The Undercliff
Freshwater
Afton
Colwell Bay
Norton
Norton Green
Keyhaven
Hurst Castle
Pennington
Lower Pennington
Everton
Downton
Lymore
Ashley
Hordle
Golden Hill
Bashley
Wootton
Bransgore
Thorney Hill
Sopley
Avon
Ripley
Hurn
Holdenhurst
Jumpers Green
Purewell
Somerford
Southbourne
Wick
Pokesdown
Westbourne
Branksome
Branksome Park
Canford Cliffs
Lilliput
Parkstone
Talbot Village
Moordown
Kinson
Ensbury
Bear Cross
Parley Cross
West Parley
Longham
Stapehill
Trickett's Cross
Ashley Heath
St Ives
Three Legged Cross
Woodlands
Horton
Edmondsham
Cripplestyle
Harbridge
Ibsley
Mockbeggar
Rockford
Blashford
Linwood
Moyles Court
Picket Post
Linford
Burley Street
Bisterne Close
Kingston
Moortown
Hyde
Hungerford
North Gorley
South Gorley
Stuckton
Blissford
Godshill
Frogham
Fritham
Bramshaw
Brook
Newbridge
Stoney Cross
Bartley
Netley Marsh
Woodlands
Eling
Testwood
Copythorne
Winsor
Calmore
Canada
Nomansland
Landford
Plaitford
West Wellow
East Wellow
Sherfield English
Newtown
Upper Ratley
Awbridge
Abbotswood
Whitenap
Ridge
Lee
Upton
Toothill
Cupernham
Kent's Oak
Carter's Clay
Lockerley
East Dean
West Dean
East Tytherley
Butt's Green
Farley
East Grimstead
West Grimstead
Whaddon
Alderbury
Britford
Bodenham
Nunton
Odstock
Charlton-All-Saints
Morgan's Vale
Woodfalls
Lover
Hale
Woodgreen
Breamore
North Charford
Whitsbury
Rockbourne
Martin
Tidpit
Martin Drove End
Damerham
Sandleheath
Ashford
Bickton
Outwick
Burgate
Upper Street
Coombe Bissett
Homington
Stratford Tony
Bishopstone
Croucheston
Stoke Farthing
Netherhampton
Quidhampton
Bemerton
West Harnham
East Harnham
Stratford sub Castle
Old Sarum
Laverstock
Winterbourne Earls
Firsdown
Middle Winterslow
West Winterslow
East Winterslow
The Common
Pitton
Ditchampton
Burcombe
Barford St Martin
SU
SZ
The Solent
Isle of Wight
CHERBOURG 4:15
GUERNSEY 2:30
JERSEY 3:45
ST. MALO 5:25
CHERBOURG 2:15
(Apr-Oct)
(May-Sept)
0 1 2 3 4 5 6 miles
0 1 2 3 4 5 6 7 8 9 10 km

Winchester
Kings Worthy
Martyr Worthy
Itchen Abbas
Itchen Stoke
New Alresford
Alresford
Gundleton
Bishop's Sutton
North Street
Soldridge
Four Marks
Kitwood
Ropley
Ropley Dean
Monkwood
East Tisted
West Tisted
Newton Valence
Selborne
Blackmoor
Whitehill
Standford
Conford
Greatham
Liphook
Longmoor Camp
Colemore
Hawkley
Liss Forest
Langley
West Liss
East Liss
Liss
Rake
Milland
Hill Brow
Borden
Headbourne Worthy
Littleton
Easton
Avington
Ovington
Weeke
Winnall
Tichborne
Cheriton
Bramdean
New Cheriton
Hinton Ampner
Kilmeston
Brockwood
Privett
High Cross
Stoner Hill
Froxfield Green
Steep Marsh
Steep
Stroud
Sheet
Petersfield
Rogate
Chithurst
Dumpford
Trotton
Nyewood
Minsted
Stanmore
Chilcomb
Oliver's Battery
Compton
Longwood Warren
Morestead
Lane End
Beauworth
Twyford
Shawford
Otterbourne
Owslebury
Baybridge
Colden Common
Upham
Fisher's Pond
EASTLEIGH
Bishopstoke
Fair Oak
Lower Upham
Ashton
Dean
Newtown
Wintershill
Horton Heath
Durley
Bishop's Waltham
Hoe
Droxford
Swanmore
Long Common
West End
Hedge End
Botley
Curdridge
Shedfield
Waltham Chase
Shirrell Heath
Soberton Heath
Newtown
Hoe Gate
Anthill Common
Hambledon
Soberton
Chidden
Clanfield
Catherington
Horndean
Blendworth
Finchdean
Forestside
Rowlands Castle
Chalton
Lovedean
Denmead
Cowplain
Hundred Acres
North Boarhunt
FOREST OF BERE
Waterlooville
Purbrook
Southwick
Wickham
Curbridge
Burridge
Swanwick
Lower Swanwick
Park Gate
Locks Heath
Sholing
Thornhill
Old Netley
Bursledon
Lowford
Hound
Hamble-le-Rice
Warsash
Titchfield
Newtown
Fareham
Funtley
Boarhunt
Wallington
Portchester
Fleetlands
Peel Common
Stubbington
Bridgemary
Portsmouth
Brockhurst
Hardway
Hill Head
Lee-on-the-Solent
GOSPORT
Alverstoke
Gilkicker Pt.
Southsea
PORTSMOUTH
Portsea
Fratton
Milton
Eastney
Hilsea
Cosham
Drayton
Wymering
Bedhampton
HAVANT
Warblington
Emsworth
Southbourne
Hermitage
Langstone
Stoke
North Hayling
Northney
Fleet
West Town
HAYLING ISLAND
South Hayling
Eastoke
Thorney
West Thorney
CHICHESTER HARBOUR
Chichester
Fishbourne
Bosham
Apuldram
Donnington
Hunston
Chidham
Nutbourne
Broadbridge
Funtington
Woodmancote
West Ashling
East Ashling
Summersdale
Lavant
West Stoke
Woodend
Walderton
Stoughton
West Marden
North Marden
Compton
Up Marden
East Marden
West Dean
Bow Hill
Treyford
Didling
Elsted
Bepton
East Harting
South Harting
Nursted
Buriton
Weston
War Down
Butser Hill
Langrish
East Meon
Ramsdean
Coombe
West Meon
Warnford
Exton
Corhampton
Meonstoke
Brockbridge
East End
Leigh Park
Stockheath
Westbourne
West Itchenor
Shipton Green
Birdham
Street End
Sidlesham
Somerley
Highleigh
Earnley
Bracklesham
East Wittering
West Wittering
Acre Street
Selsey
SELSEY BILL
Norton
Fawley
Ashlett
Calshot
Stone Pt.
Cowes
East Cowes
Gurnard
Gurnard Bay
Rew Street
Northwood
Osborne Bay
Whippingham
Fishbourne
Wootton Bridge
RYDE
Binstead
Elmfield
Seaview
Nettlestone
Nettlestone Pt.
St Helens
Bembridge
Foreland
Lane End
Hillway
Whitecliff Bay
Culver Cliff
Yaverland
Sandown
Sandown Bay
Lake
Shanklin
Apse Heath
Luccombe Village
Luccombe Chine
Dunnose
Bonchurch
Ventnor
St Lawrence
The Undercliff
Isle of Wight
Parkhurst
Parkhurst Forest
Havenstreet
Wootton Common
Staplers
NEWPORT
Shide
Carisbrooke
Gunville
Hunny Hill
Clatterford
Bowcombe
Blackwater
Downend
Arreton
Alverstone
Newchurch
Brading
Steyne Cross
Merstone
Horringford
Rookley
Winford
Branstone
Sandford
Godshill
Whiteley Bank
Roud
Wroxall
Stenbury Down
Whitwell
Niton
Blackgang
Chale
Chale Bay
Chale Green
Bierley
Pyle
Little Atherfield
Kingston
Shorwell
Chillerton
Gatcombe
Medina
SOLENT
SPITHEAD
Stokes Bay
Southampton Water
Langstone Harbour
Portsmouth Harbour
CAEN 6:00
CHERBOURG 3:00 (March-Nov)
LE HAVRE 7:30
ST. MALO 8:45
BILBAO 35:00
GUERNSEY 6:30
JERSEY 10:00
SU
SZ
EAST HAMPSHIRE
M27
M3
M275
A3(M)
A27
A3
A32
A31
A272
26
16

Haslemere
Liphook
Petersfield
Midhurst
Petworth
Billingshurst
Pulborough
Storrington
Arundel
Chichester
Bognor Regis
LITTLEHAMPTON
Rustington
Angmering
Ferring
Worthing
Selsey
SELSEY BILL
East Wittering
West Wittering
Bosham
Southbourne
Middleton-on-Sea
West Sussex
SU
SZ
CHICHESTER HARBOUR
Guernsey
3½ miles to 1 inch
GUERNSEY
St Peter Port
Herm
Jethou
SHELL BEACH
CASTLE CORNET
POOLE 2:30 (Apr-Oct)
WEYMOUTH 2:00
PORTSMOUTH 6:30
SARK 0:45
ST. HELIER 2:00
ST. HELIER 0:50
ST. MALO 2:40
DIELETTE 1:15 (May-Sept)
Alderney
3½ miles to 1 inch
ALDERNEY
Braye
St Anne
Brehou
Clonque Bay
Longis Bay
Telegraph Bay
Quesnard Pt.
DIELETTE 1:00 (May-Sept)
0 1 2 3 4 5 6 miles
0 1 2 3 4 5 6 7 8 9 10km

Horsham
St Leonard's Forest
Roffey
Colgate
Pease Pottage
Tilgate Forest Row
Balcombe
Balcombe Lane
Selsfield Common
West Hoathly
Sharpthorne
Wakehurst Place
Priest House
Highbrook
Chelwood Gate
Wych Cross
Coleman's Hatch
Upper Hartfield
Lye Green
Friar's Gate
Boarshead
Crowborough
Ashdown Forest
Handcross
Nymans Garden
Staplefield
Ashfold Crossways
Mannings Heath
Monk's Gate
Southwater Street
Southwater
Nuthurst
Lower Beeding
Leonardslee Gardens
Warninglid
Slaugham
Slough Green
Brook Street
Borde Hill Garden
Whitemans Green
Ardingly
Horsted Keynes
Chelwood Common
Danehill
Nutley
Duddleswell
Jarvis Brook
Copsale
Crabtree
Maplehurst
Cuckfield
Lindfield
Haywards Heath
Heaven Farm
Sheffield Green
Sheffield Park
Fletching
The Bluebell Railway
Cackle Street
Splayne's Green
Fairwarp
Maresfield
High Hurstwood
Butcher's Cross
Hadlow Down
Pound Green
Buxted
Ringles Cross
Cross in Hand
Bolney
Ansty
Scayne's Hill
Cowfold
West Grinstead
Kent Street
Wineham
Hickstead
Wivelsfield
Wivelsfield Green
North Common
Newick
Grisling Common
Uckfield
Framfield
Blackboys
Partridge Green
Dial Post
Twineham
Jumping Course
Sayers Common
Burgess Hill
Ditchling Common
Chailey
South Street
Spithurst
Isfield
Ridgewood
Little Horsted
Waldron
Foxhunt Green
West End
Henfield
Ashurst
Blackstone
Albourne
Washbrooks Farm Centre
Hurstpierpoint
Hurst Wickham
Plumpton Green
Plumpton
Chiltington
Lavender Line Steam Railway
Halland
East Hoathly
Rose Hill
Woodmancote
Hassocks
Keymer
Ditchling
Ditchling Museum
Streat
East Chiltington
Barcombe Cross
Barcombe
Shortgate
Chiddingly
Whitesmith
Westmeston
Small Dole
Fulking
Poynings
Clayton
Pyecombe
Ditchling Beacon
Cooksbridge
Hamsey
Broyle Side
Laughton
Golden Cross
Ringmer
Offham
Mt. Harry
Steyning
Bramber
Upper Beeding
Edburton
Saddlescombe
Truleigh Hill
Devil's Dyke
Lewes
South Malling
Glyndebourne
Mark Cross
Lower Dicker
Wallands Park
Cliffe Hill
Ripe
Chalvington
St. Mary's House
Botolphs
Brighton and Hove
Patcham
Stanmer
Coldean
Falmer
Anne of Cleves Ho.
Lewes Downs (Mount Caburn)
Glynde
Glynde Place
Coombes
Mile Oak
Westdene
Withdean
Kingston near Lewes
Beddingham
Selmeston
Arlington
North Lancing
Portslade
Hove
West Blatchington
Moulsecoomb
Bevendean
Iford
Rodmell
Monks Ho.
West Firle
Firle Pl.
Charleston Farmhouse
Alciston
Firle Beacon
Sompting
Broadwater
Lancing
Kingston by Sea
Southwick
Preston Manor
Preston
Castle Hill
Woodingdean
Southease
South Downs Way
Berwick
Drusillas Park
Wilmington
Shoreham-by-Sea
Portslade-by-Sea
Brighton
Royal Pavilion
Kemp Town
Ovingdean
Tarring Neville
South Heighton
Alfriston
The Long Man of Wilmington
East Worthing
South Lancing
Marlipins Museum
Worthing
Brighton Sea Life
Volk's Electric Railway
Merchants Quay
Rottingdean
Telscombe
Saltdean
Piddinghoe
Newhaven
Denton
Norton
Paradise Park
Clergy House
Lullington Heath
Litlington
Charleston Manor
Telscombe Cliffs
Peacehaven
Bishopstone
Newhaven Fort
East Blatchington
Westdean
Seaford
Seven Sisters
Friston
Birling Gap
Dieppe 4:00
Le Havre 5:00 (May-Sept)
TQ
TV
South Downs
Jersey
3½ miles to 1 inch
Grosnez Pt.
Plémont Pt.
Sorel Pt.
Ronez Pt.
St John's Bay
Belle Hougue Pt.
North Coast Visitor Centre
St John's
Bouley Bay
Tour de Rozel
Rozel
St Mary's
Jersey Flower Centre
Trinity
La Coupe Pt.
JERSEY
St Ouens
Jersey Zoo & Wildlife Park
Carteret 0:45
Portbail 0:45 (Summer only)
Les Mielles Visitor Centre
Carrefour Selous
St Martin's
St Ouen's Bay
St Peter's
St Catherine's Bay
La Hougue Bie
Mont Orgueil Castle
Five Oaks
Red Houses
Gorey
Corbière Pt.
St Aubin
St Helier
Jersey Museum
Grouville
Royal Bay of Grouville
St Brelade
St Clements
St Brelades Bay
St Aubin's Bay
Sark 0:45 (Summer only)
Elizabeth Castle
Fort Regent Leisure Centre
La Rocque Pt.
St. Peter Port 0:50
Weymouth 3:15
Poole 3:45 (Apr-Oct)
Noirmont Pt.
Le Nez Pt.
St Clements Bay
St. Peter Port 2:00
Portsmouth 10:00
St. Malo 1:10
Granville 1:00 (Apr-Oct)
Dielette 1:30 (May-Sept)
Carteret 0:55 (Apr-Oct)
St. Malo 1:10

East Sussex
HIGH WEALD
WEALD
TQ
TV
ROYAL TUNBRIDGE WELLS
Uckfield
Newhaven
Eastbourne
Hastings
BEXHILL
Crowborough
Heathfield
Hailsham
Polegate
Seaford
Battle
Mayfield
Wadhurst
Hawkhurst
Cranbrook
Staplehurst
Headcorn
Southborough
Pembury
Paddock Wood
Penshurst
Bidborough
Speldhurst
Rusthall
Langton Green
Groombridge
Hartfield
Withyham
Frant
Lamberhurst
Goudhurst
Kilndown
Horsmonden
Brenchley
Matfield
Marden
Sissinghurst
Benenden
Rolvenden
Sandhurst
Newenden
Bodiam
Northiam
Robertsbridge
Salehurst
Etchingham
Burwash
Burwash Common
Burwash Weald
Ticehurst
Flimwell
Stonegate
Rotherfield
Jarvis Brook
Nutley
Duddleswell
Fairwarp
Maresfield
Buxted
Framfield
Blackboys
Cross in Hand
Broad Oak
Five Ashes
Hadlow Down
Waldron
Horam
Maynard's Green
Vine's Cross
Rushlake Green
Dallington
Brightling
Netherfield
Mountfield
Sedlescombe
Westfield
Three Oaks
Guestling Thorn
Brede
Broad Oak
Fairlight
Ore
St Leonards
Hollington
Crowhurst
Catsfield
Ninfield
Herstmonceux
Windmill Hill
Boreham Street
Wartling
Pevensey
Pevensey Bay
Westham
Stone Cross
Langney
Willingdon
Jevington
Friston
East Dean
Birling Gap
BEACHY HEAD
Alfriston
Berwick
Wilmington
Folkington
Litlington
West Firle
Glynde
Ripe
Chalvington
Arlington
Selmeston
Lower Dicker
Upper Dicker
Chiddingly
Golden Cross
Laughton
Ringmer
Halland
Shortgate
East Hoathly
Whitesmith
Ridgewood
Little Horsted
Isfield
Bishopstone
Norton
Denton
South Heighton
Tarring Neville
East Blatchington
Westdean
Cooden
Norman's Bay
Little Common
Sidley
Bulverhythe
West Marina
Silverhill
Baldslow
Hurst Green
Bedgebury Forest
ASHDOWN FOREST
Bewl Water
Pevensey Levels
DIEPPE 4:00
LE HAVRE 5:00 (May-Sept)
A21
A22
A26
A27
A259
A265
A267
A268
A271
A272
A229
A262
A264
A2100
17
29
0 1 2 3 4 5 6 miles
0 1 2 3 4 5 6 7 8 9 10km

Ashford
Willesborough
Sevington
Kingsnorth
Mersham
Smeeth
Hinxhill
Willesborough Lees
Brabourne
Brabourne Lees
Lymbridge Green
Stowting
Rhodes Minnis
Ottinge
Elham
Lyminge
Etchinghill
Postling
Paddlesworth
Hawkinge
Swingfield Minnis
Densole
Drellingore
West Hougham
Capel le-Ferne
CHANNEL TUNNEL
Folkestone
Sandgate
Saltwood
Hythe
Palmarsh
Cheriton
Newington
Beachborough
Stanford
Sellindge
Sellindge Lees
Newingreen
Pedlinge
Lympne
Court-at-Street
Aldington
Aldington Frith
Clap Hill
Bonnington
Bilsington
Cheeseman's Green
Bromley Green
Ruckinge
Hamstreet
Orlestone
Warehorne
Kenardington
Appledore
Appledore Heath
Snave
Newchurch
Burmarsh
West Hythe
Dymchurch
St Mary in the Marsh
St Mary's Bay
Ivychurch
Brenzett
Snargate
Brookland
Old Romney
New Romney
Littlestone on Sea
Romney Sands
Greatstone on Sea
Lydd
Lydd on Sea
Denge Marsh
Denge Beach
DUNGENESS
ROMNEY MARSH
Walland Marsh
Camber
Rye
Rye Harbour
Rye Bay
Winchelsea
Winchelsea Beach
Icklesham
Pett
Guestling Green
Cliff End
Fairlight
Fairlight Cove
Udimore
Playden
Rye Foreign
Peasmarsh
Iden
Houghton Green
East Guldeford
Beckley
Four Oaks
Wittersham
Ham Green
The Stocks
Stone
Peening Quarter
ISLE OF OXNEY
ROTHER LEVELS
Rolvenden Layne
Small Hythe
Reading Street
Leigh Green
Tenterden
Parkgate
St Michael's
Woodchurch
Brook Street
Shirkoak
Henghurst
High Halden
Biddenden
Tanden
Shadoxhurst
Stubbs Cross
Bethersden
Standen
Smarden
Smarden Bell
Haffenden Quarter
Wissenden
Maltman's Hill
Great Chart
HEADCORN
GODINTON HOUSE
McARTHUR GLEN ASHFORD
KENT AND EAST SUSSEX STEAM RAILWAY
SOUTH OF ENGLAND RARE BREEDS CEN.
HAM STREET WOODS
PORT LYMPNE WILD ANIMAL PARK AND GARDENS
ROMNEY, HYTHE AND DYMCHURCH LIGHT RAILWAY
MARTELLO TOWER
AERONAUTICAL MUSEUM
HORNE'S PLACE CHAPEL
SMALLHYTHE PLACE
FARM WORLD
RYE HERITAGE CENTRE
CAMBER CASTLE
WINCHELSEA COURT
HASTINGS
DUNGENESS POWER STATION & INFORMATION CENTRE
THE OLD LIGHTHOUSE
DUNGENESS
LYDD
BROCKHILL
ELHAM VALLEY RLY MUS.
KENT BATTLE OF BRITAIN MUSEUM
RUSSIAN SUB.
ROTUNDA
CLIFF LIFT
FOLKESTONE
Royal Military Canal
E. Stour
Rother
Tillingham
Brede
NORTH DOWNS WAY
TR
M20
A20
A28
A259
A2070
A262
A261
A268
B2067
B2080
B2082
B2075
B2089
B2068
30
31
ENGLISH CHANNEL
5
6
7
8
9
60
62
A
B
C
D
E
F
G

1
2
3
4
5
A
B
C
D
E
F
North West Point
North East Point
LUNDY MARINE NATURE RESERVE
LUNDY
142
ILFRACOMBE 2:15
BIDEFORD 2:15
South West Point
Surf Point
SS
NORTH DEVON
LUNDY 2:15
OLD CORN MILL
Rillage Pt.
Combe Martin Bay
Trentishoe
Ilfracombe
ILFRACOMBE MUSEUM
Hele
WATERMOUTH CASTLE
Girt Down
349
Heale
Bull Pt.
Lee
206
Rockham Bay
Whitestone
Slade
Berrynarbor
Sterridge
Combe Martin
WILDLIFE & DINOSAUR PARK
Morte Point
Mortehoe
ONCE UPON A TIME
269
A3123
Kentisbury
Woolacombe
MORTE BAY
Trimstone
Berry Down Cross
Berry Down
Cheglinch
Patchole
Kentisbury Ford
Woolacombe Sand
210
Dean
Bittadon
SOUTH WEST COAST PATH
Pickwell
West Down
East Down
North Buckland
Churchill
Baggy Pt.
Putsborough
Arlington
ARLINGTON COURT
Georgeham
Nethercott
Croyde Bay
Croyde
Darracott
Halsinger
Milltown
Loxhore
Muddiford
158
Lobb
Knowle
Marwood
Guineaford
Shirwell
Bratton Fleming
Saunton
Pippacott
198
Kingsheanton
Braunton
MARWOOD HILL GARDENS
Shirwell Cross
ELLIOT GALLERY
Heanton Punchardon
Prixford
Stoke Rivers
Saunton Sands
Wrafton
TOLL
Ashford
Burridge
Braunton Burrows
Chivenor
Barnstaple
Goodleigh
LUNDY 2:15
Taw
Pilton
MUSEUM OF NORTH DEVON
Gunn
Fremington
Westacott
Yelland
Bickington
P&R
Bickleton
Newport
Landkey
NORTH DEVON MARITIME MUSEUM
Bishops Tawton
Swimbridge Newland
NORTH DEVON FARM PARK
BIDEFORD BAY
NORTHAM BURROWS
Appledore
Instow
TAPELEY PARK GDNS
Swimbridge
Westward Ho!
Northam
Westleigh
Torridge
THE BIG SHEEP
Orchard Hill
Horwood
Newton Tracey
Eastleigh
Herner
Cobbaton
East Stowford
Titchberry
Bideford
Abbotsham
BURTON GALL & MUS
Ensis
Hiscott
Chapelton
COBBATON COMBAT COLL.
CLOVELLY VILLAGE
Handy Cross
East-the-Water
Woodtown
Chittlehampton
0 1 2 3 4 5 6 miles
0 1 2 3 4 5 6 7 8 9 10 km

Kenfig Hill
Cefn Cross
Aberkenfig
Tondu
Bryncethin
Sarn
Pyle (Y Pîl)
Cefn Cribbwr
Pen-y-fai
Pendre
Coity
Pencoed
Brynna
Llanharan
Brynsadler
Llanharry
Llanilid
Kenfig
Mawdlam
North Cornelly
Kenfig Burrows
South Cornelly
KENFIG POOL AND DUNES
SARN PARK SERVICES
McARTHUR GLEN BRIDGEND
COITY CASTLE
NEW CASTLE
Bridgend
(Pen-y-bont ar Ogwr)
Laleston
Oldcastle
Coychurch
Tythegston
Merthyr Mawr
Newton
Nottage
Clevis
Hutchwns
ROYAL PORTHCAWL
Porthcawl
OGMORE CASTLE
MERTHYR MAWR WARREN
Ogmore
Ewenny
Corntown
Treoes
St Mary Hill
Llangan
Llansannor
Craig Penllyn
Penllyn
Ystradowen
Maendy
Aberthin
Welsh St Donats
Colwinston
Pentre Meyrick
Ogmore-by-Sea
St Brides Major
Penuchadre
Llysworney
Cowbridge
(Y Bont-Faen)
Llanblethian
Llandow
Llandough
St Hilary
Tusker Rock
Southerndown
GLENMORGAN HERITAGE COAST CENTRE
Wick
Llanmihangel
St Mary Church
OLD BEAUPRE CASTLE
Broughton
Sigingstone
Monknash
Marcross
Llanmaes
Eglwys-Brewis
Flemingston
Llanbethery
St Donat's
Llantwit Major
(Llanilltud Fawr)
Boverton
St Athan
Rhoose
(Y Rhws)
East Aberthaw
CARDIFF INTERNATIONAL (MAES AWYR CAERDYDD CYMRU)
Nash Pt.
Trwyn yr As
Breaksea Pt.
Trwyn Breaksea
Vale of Glamorgan (Bro Morgannwg)
Walterston
Llantrithyd
Pendoylan
Talygarn
Miskin
Pont-y-clun
LLANERCH VINEYARD
MODEL CENTRE
Dolau
Brynycae
Ely
MÔR HAFREN
BRISTOL CHANNEL
SS
Highveer Pt.
Woody Bay
Lynmouth Bay
Foreland Pt.
Lynmouth
Lynton
CLIFF RAILWAY
Countisbury
WATERSMEET HOUSE
Martinhoe
LYNTON AND BARNSTAPLE RLY
Barbrook
Cheriton
Brendon
Malmsmead
Oare
CULBONE HILL
TOLL
Porlock Bay
Porlock Weir
Bossington
Porlock
Hurlstone Pt.
SOUTH WEST COAST PATH
SELWORTHY BEACON
EXMOOR FALCONRY
Allerford
Selworthy
Minehead
Woodcombe
WEST SOMERSET RAILWAY
SOMERWEST WORLD
Alcombe
Periton
Blue Anchor Bay
Marsh Street
Dunster
DOLL MUS.
MILL & MARKET
DUNSTER CASTLE (NT)
MINEHEAD
Carhampton
Blue Anchor
Old Cleeve
Withycombe
Bilbrook
CLEEVE ABBEY
Washford
Rodhuish
Roadwater
East Ilkerton
Martinhoe Cross
Furzehill
Shallowford
Parracombe
West Lyn
Brendon Common
EXMOOR
West Luccombe
Luccombe
HAWKCOMBE WOODS
Holnicote Estate
Wootton Courtenay
Cowbridge
VINEYARD
Timberscombe
Blackmoor Gate
EXMOOR FOREST
Challacombe Common
Pinkworthy Pond
DUNKERY BEACON
THE DUNKERY & HORNER WOOD
EXMOOR ZOO
Challacombe
Exe Plain
NATIONAL
Exe
BRENDON
CROYDON HILL
FOREST
Shoulsbarrow Common
Knightacott
Simonsbath
Edgcott
Luckwell Bridge
Cutcombe
Wheddon Cross
Exford
EXFORD
Leworthy
Bray
LYPE HILL
Luxborough
Kingsbridge
Monkslade
Yard
BRENDON HILLS
Benton
Lydcott
Barle
HORSEN HILL
Withypool
Treborough
Withypool Common
WINSFORD HILL
Winsford
North Radworthy
Exton
Brayford
High Bray
PARK
Withiel Florey
Clatworthy Res.
Charles
North Heasley
Liscombe
Bridgetown
Brompton Regis
West Buckland
Heasley Mill
South Radworthy
TARR STEPS
East Buckland
Molland Common
Dane's Brook
Hawkridge
Wimbleball Lake
Twitchen
Upton
Huish Champflower
Filleigh
North Molton
Mole
Anstey Common
HADDON HILL
HEYDON HILL
Molland
West Anstey
Dulverton
Battleton
Bury
Skilgate
Chipstable
South Molton
QUINCE HONEY FARM
East Anstey
Yeo Mill
Nightcott
Waterrow

Cardiff
(Caerdydd)
CARDIFF
(CAERDYDD)
PENARTH
BARRY
(Y BARRI)
Barry Island
Vale of Glamorgan
(Bro Morgannwg)
Cowbridge
(Y Bont-Faen)
Llantwit Major
(Llanilltud Fawr)
Pencoed
Llantrisant
Talbot Green
Rhoose
(Y Rhws)
Penarth
Sully Island
Ynys Sili
Flat Holm
Steep Holm
Lavernock Pt.
Breaksea Pt.
Trwyn Breaksea
ABER HAFREN
MOUTH OF THE SEVERN
MÔR HAFREN
BRISTOL CHANNEL
BRIDGWATER BAY
Weston-super-Mare
Weston Bay
Brean Down
Brean
BERROW FLATS
Burnham-on-Sea
Highbridge
STERT FLATS
Bridgwater
Minehead
Blue Anchor Bay
Watchet
Williton
Somerset
QUANTOCK HILLS
QUANTOCK FOREST
BRENDON HILLS
BRENDON FOREST
Wiveliscombe
Clatworthy Res.
Wimbleball Lake
VALE OF TAUNTON DEANE
Rumney
Newton
Peterstone Wentlooge
St Brides Wentlooge
Castleton
Marshfield
Nash
Pawlett
Puriton
Cannington
Nether Stowey
Stogursey
Holford
Dunster
Porlock
Wootton Courtenay
Cutcombe
Timberscombe
Carhampton
Washford
Kingsbridge
Brompton Regis
Upton
Bury
Milverton
Bishops Lydeard
Kingston St Mary
North Petherton
0 1 2 3 4 5 6 miles
0 1 2 3 4 5 6 7 8 9 10 km

BRISTOL
Bristol
North Somerset
Bath and N.E. Somerset
Somerset
MENDIP HILLS
Avonmouth
Portishead
Clevedon
Nailsea
Long Ashton
FILTON
Patchway
MANGOTSFIELD
Kingswood
Hanham
KEYNSHAM
Chipping Sodbury
Yate
Bath
Radstock
Midsomer Norton
Paulton
Peasedown St John
Shepton Mallet
Wells
Cheddar
Axbridge
Wedmore
Glastonbury
Street
Somerton
Castle Cary
Bruton
Wincanton
Evercreech
Frome
Wrington
Yatton
Congresbury
Banwell
Winscombe
Blagdon
Chew Magna
Pensford
Timsbury
Farrington Gurney
Chewton Mendip
Priddy
Wookey Hole
Westbury-sub-Mendip
Rodney Stoke
Draycott
Mark
Burtle
Meare
Shapwick
Butleigh
Keinton Mandeville
Charlton Mackerell
Langport
Sparkford
North Cadbury
Holton
Ditcheat
Pylle
Doulting
Cranmore
Oakhill
Holcombe
Coleford
Mells
Kilmersdon
Chilcompton
Emborough
Hinton Blewett
Compton Martin
West Harptree
East Harptree
Ubley
Burrington
Churchill
Sandford
Locking
Hewish
Puxton
Kingston Seymour
Claverham
Backwell
Flax Bourton
Barrow Gurney
Winford
Felton
Bristol International
Chew Valley Lake
Blagdon Lake
Cheddar Res.
Clifton Suspension Bridge
Wookey Hole Caves & Papermill
Bishop's Palace
Glastonbury Tor
Avon Valley Railway
East Somerset Railway
Haynes Motor Mus
Lytes Cary Manor
Somerset Levels
King's Sedge Moor
Polden Hills
M5
M4
M32
M49
A38
A37
A39
A361
A303
A371
A368
A370
A369
A4
A4174
A420
A46
A431
A36
A367
A362
A359
A372
A403
B3130
B3135
B3139
B3151
B3153
B3114
12
24
35
36

Yate
Chipping Sodbury
MANGOTSFIELD
Kingswood
Hanham
KEYNSHAM
Bath
Corsham
Chippenham
Calne
Melksham
Devizes
Bradford-on-Avon
Trowbridge
Westbury
Frome
Warminster
Radstock
Midsomer Norton
Paulton
Peasedown St John
Bruton
Castle Cary
Evercreech
Mere
Gillingham
Wiltshire
SALISBURY PLAIN
CRANBORNE CHASE
VALE OF WARDOUR
Great Ridge
Summer Down
Keysley Down
Littleton Down
West Lavington Down
Bruton Forest
COTSWOLDS
Avon
Kennet & Avon Canal
LEIGH DELAMERE SERVICES
WARMINSTER SERVICES
M4
A46
A4
A36
A350
A361
A303
A342
A3102
B4040
6 miles
10km
0 1 2 3 4 5 6 miles
0 1 2 3 4 5 6 7 8 9 10km

Swindon
Wootton Bassett
The Marsh
Coate
Hinton Parva
Idstone
Bishopstone
Wanborough
Liddington
Kingston Warren
Lambourn Downs
Bassett
The Ridgeway
Farnborough
Fawley
Upper Lambourn
South Fawley
Catmore
North Wroughton
Great Western (Maize) Maze
Elcombe
Wroughton
Chiseldon
Badbury
Lambourn
Brightwalton
Lilley
Broadtown Lane
Broad Town
Uffcott
Bushton
Clyffe Pypard
Barbury Castle
Upper Upham
Baydon
Eastbury
East Garston
Chaddleworth
Leckhampstead Thicket
Broad Hinton
Woodsend
Aldbourne
Membury Services
Woodlands St Mary
Leckhampstead
Clevancy
Marlborough Downs
Great Shefford
Winterborne Bassett
Hackpen Hill
Southend
Ogbourne St George
Shefford Woodlands
Berwick Bassett
Ogbourne St Andrew
Preston
Weston
Welford
Winterbourne
Windmill Hill
Winterborne Monkton
Rockley
Whittonditch
Westbrook
Yatesbury
The Ridgeway
Fyfield Down
Ogbourne Maizey
Ramsbury
Hungerford Newtown
Wickham
Boxford
Snelsmore Common
Avebury Manor
Avebury
Mildenhall
Axford
Chilton Foliat
Stone Circle
W. Kennett Avenue
Silbury Hill
Marlborough
Fyfield
Kennet
Hungerford
Halfway
Bagnor
Stockcross
Donnington
Beckhampton
West Kennett
Manton
Froxfield
Avington
Speen
Long Barrow
East Kennett
The Sanctuary
West Overton
Lockeridge
Savernake Forest
Cadley
Chisbury
Chisbury Chapel
Little Bedwyn
Kintbury
Laylands Green
Enborne
Newbury
Clench Common
Hamstead Marshall
Tan Hill
Milk Hill
Durley
Great Bedwyn
Bagshot
Inkpen
Upper Green
Horton
Allington
Pewsey Downs
Huish
Wootton Rivers
Oare
Shalbourne
Ham
West Woodhay
Ball Hill
Stanton St Bernard
West Stowell
Crofton
Crofton Beam Engines
North End
Woolton Hill
All Cannings
Alton Priors
New Mill
Stibb Green
Eastcourt
Walbury Hill
Broad Laying
Honey Street
Wilcot
Pewsey
Burbage
Wilton Windmill
Wilton
Rivar
Buttermere
East Woodhay
East End
Combe
Woodborough
Easton Royal
East Grafton
West Grafton
Marten
Highclere
Beechingstoke
Bottlesford
Milton Lilbourne
Patney
Manningford Bruce
Southcott
Wexcombe
Oxenwood
Wedhampton
Henge
Hilcott
Linkenholt
Faccombe
Highclere Castle
Chirton
Marden
North Newnton
Manningford Bohune
Tidcombe
Fosbury
Vernham Street
Netherton
Wilsford
Pewsey Down
Haydown Hill
Vernham Dean
Ashmansworth
Charlton
Brunton
Crux Easton
Rushall
Upavon
Aughton
Collingbourne Kingston
Upton
Woodcott
Lower Everleigh
Sunton
Cadley
Upper Chute
Chute Standen
Ibthorpe
Hurstbourne Tarrant
Dunley
Everleigh
Collingbourne Ducis
Lower Chute
Tangley
Binley
West Chisenbury
East Chisenbury
Collingbourne Forest
Doles Wood
Stoke
Compton
Black Heath
Compton Down
Enford
Fifield
Haxton Down
Ludgershall
Wildhern
St Mary Bourne
Coombe
Fittleton
Hatherden
Little London
West Down
Enford Down
Tidworth
North Tidworth
Clanville
Enham Alamein
Smannell
Netheravon
Orcheston Down
Dovecote
Appleshaw
Penton Mewsey
Picket Piece
Whitchurch
Figheldean
South Tidworth
Kimpton
Fyfield
Weyhill
Charlton
Finkley Down Farm Park
Hurstbourne Priors
Ablington
Knighton Down
Thruxton
Andover Down
Orcheston
Milston
Shipton Bellinger
Durrington
The Hawk Conservancy Trust
Weyhill Services
Andover
Middleton
Longparish
Elston
Shrewton
Larkhill
Bulford Camp
Beacon Hill
Quarley
Amport
Monxton
Anna Valley
Upper Clatford
Forton
Tidbury Ring
Woodhenge
Bulford
Abbotts Ann
Harewood Forest
Countess
Stonehenge
Cholderton Rare Breeds
Cholderton
Grateley
Goodworth Clatford
Wherwell
Bullington
Newton Stacey
Barton Stacey
West Amesbury
Amesbury
Winterbourne Stoke
Palestine
Wilsford
Newton Tony
Chilbolton
Sutton Scotney Services
Berwick St James
Lake
Allington
Fullerton
Boscombe
Great Durnford
Museum of Army Flying
Stapleford
Upper Woodford
Over Wallop
Middle Wallop
Longstock
Leckford
Little Wishford
Idmiston
Nether Wallop
Porton
Middle Woodford
Gomeldon
Great Wishford
Stoford
Winterbourne Dauntsey
Winterbourne Gunner
Lopcombe Corner
Stockbridge
Crawley
Worthy Down
Wood
South Newton
Lower Woodford
East Winterslow
Winterbourne Earls
Firsdown
Broughton
Little Somborne
Chilhampton
Middle Winterslow
The Common
Whiteshoot Hill
Houghton
Up Somborne
Littleton
Barford St Martin
Ditchampton
Stratford sub Castle
Old Sarum
New Sarum
All Saints Church
Flowerdown Barrows
Wilton
West Winterslow
King's Somborne
Ashley
Sparsholt
Burcombe
Quidhampton
Laverstock
Pitton
Horsebridge
Farley Mount
Weeke
Wilton House
Salisbury
Bemerton
Netherhampton
West Harnham
Milford
Farley
West Tytherley
East Tytherley
Stanmore
East Harnham
Mompesson House
Farley Mount
Salisbury Racecourse
Coombe Bissett
Britford
East Grimstead
West Dean
Mottisfont Abbey
Brook
Olivers Battery
Stratford Tony
Alderbury
Lockerley
Butt's Green
Standon
Odstock
Whaddon
West Grimstead
East Dean
Mottisfont
Michelmersh
Bishopstone
Homington
Nunton
Bodenham
Pepperbox Hill
Braishfield
Ebble
Avon
Bourne
Vale of Pewsey
North Wessex Downs
Salisbury
SU
M4
A4
A338
A346
A303
A36
A34
A30
A345
A342
A354
A360
A3026
A3057
A343
A419
A4361
B4192
B4000
B4001
B3087
B3086
B3083
B3084
B3048
B3400
B3420
B3049
B4005
B4494
B4009
B3093
37
38
26
14
S

West Berkshire
Berkshire
Hampshire
Reading
Newbury
Basingstoke
Andover
Winchester
Hungerford
Thatcham
Whitchurch
Overton
Tadley
Alton
Goring
Caversham
Tilehurst
Whitley
Sonning Common
Hook
Odiham
New Alresford
Kings Worthy
Stockbridge
Streatley
Moulsford
South Stoke
Compton
East Ilsley
West Ilsley
Farnborough
Catmore
Lilley
Stanmore
Beedon
Peasemore
World's End
Chieveley
Hermitage
Curridge
Boxford
Westbrook
Winterbourne
Wickham
Weston
Welford
Great Shefford
Shefford Woodlands
Leckhampstead
Leckhampstead Thicket
Chaddleworth
Brightwalton
South Fawley
Fawley
East Garston
Woodlands St Mary
Hungerford Newtown
Halfway
Stockcross
Bagnor
Donnington
Speen
Shaw
Cold Ash
Upper Bucklebury
Bucklebury
Chapel Row
Beenham
Midgham
Woolhampton
Aldermaston Wharf
Aldermaston
Padworth
Brimpton
Crookham
Wasing
Greenham
Enborne
Hamstead Marshall
Kintbury
Avington
Inkpen
Upper Green
West Woodhay
Ball Hill
Wash Common
Newtown
Headley
Plastow Green
Ashford Hill
Heath End
Baughurst
Pamber Green
Pamber Heath
Pamber End
Silchester
Mortimer
Mortimer West End
Stratfield Mortimer
Burghclere
Old Burghclere
Highclere
Whitway
Ecchinswell
Sydmonton
Kingsclere
Wolverton
Wolverton Common
Ramsdell
Monk Sherborne
Charter Alley
Sherborne St John
Chineham
Hannington
North Oakley
Ibworth
Upper Wootton
Wootton St Lawrence
Winklebury
Oakridge
Popley
Old Basing
Hatch
Up Nately
North Warnborough
Greywell
Mapledurwell
Worting
Buckskin
Kempshott
Oakley
East Oakley
Deane
Ashe
Newfound
Quidhampton
Cole Henley
Litchfield
Dunley
Binley
Woodcott
Crux Easton
Faccombe
Ashmansworth
Linkenholt
Netherton
Upton
Ibthorpe
Hurstbourne Tarrant
Doles Wood
Stoke
St Mary Bourne
Little London
Smannell
Enham Alamein
Picket Piece
Hurstbourne Priors
Charlton
Andover Down
Middleton
Longparish
Forton
Tufton
Laverstoke
Steventon
North Waltham
Dummer
Nutley
Axford
Popham
Woodmancott
Micheldever Forest
Micheldever
Micheldever Wood
Preston Candover
Brown Candover
Northington
East Stratton
West Stratton
Wonston
South Wonston
Sutton Scotney
Stoke Charity
Bullington
Barton Stacey
Newton Stacey
Chilbolton
Upper Clatford
Anna Valley
Goodworth Clatford
Harewood Forest
Wherwell
Fullerton
Longstock
Leckford
Crawley
Worthy Down
Little Somborne
Up Somborne
King's Somborne
Ashley
Sparsholt
Littleton
Headbourne Worthy
Weeke
Winnall
Easton
Avington
Ovington
Martyr Worthy
Itchen Abbas
Itchen Stoke
Old Alresford
Tichborne
Cheriton
West Tisted
Bramdean
Hinton Ampner
Kilmeston
Beauworth
New Cheriton
Chilcomb
Longwood Warren
Gundleton
Bighton
Bishop's Sutton
Ropley
Ropley Dean
North Street
Soldridge
Four Marks
Monkwood
Kitwood
Medstead
Wivelrod
Upper Wield
Lower Wield
Hattingley
South Town
Bradley
Holt End
Bentworth
Beech
Shalden
Lasham
Herriard
Ellisfield
Farleigh Wallop
Cliddesden
Winslade
Tunworth
Weston Patrick
Southrope
Upton Grey
South Warnborough
Long Sutton
Golden Pot
Holybourne
Anstey
Chawton
Upper Farringdon
Lower Farringdon
Newton Valence
Selborne
East Tisted
Colemore
Hawkley
Privett
High Cross
Stoner Hill
Brighton Hill
Broadmere
Bramley
Sherfield on Loddon
Church End
Rotherwick
Newnham
Little London
Stratfield Turgis
Turgis Green
Hazeley
Hound Green
Mattingley
Hartley Westpall
Lyde Green
West Green
Heckfield
Bramshill
Riseley
Fair Oak Green
West End Green
Stratfield Saye
Beech Hill
Swallowfield
Farley Hill
Spencers Wood
Arborfield
Threemile Cross
Shinfield
Grazeley
Wokefield Park
Burghfield Common
Burghfield Hill
Burghfield
Sulhamstead
Sheffield Bottom
Ufton Nervet
Theale
Englefield
Tutts Clump
Southend
Bradfield
Stanford Dingley
Clay Hill
Frilsham
Yattendon
Quicks Green
Upper Basildon
Pangbourne
Lower Basildon
Aldworth
Ashampstead
Hampstead Norreys
Purley
Tidmarsh
Sulham
Whitchurch Hill
Whitchurch
Mapledurham
Cray's Pond
Goring Heath
Woodcote
Checkendon
Stoke Row
Satwell
Highmoor Cross
Rotherfield Greys
Rotherfield Peppard
Shepherd's Green
Kidmore End
Cane End
Binfield Hth.
Tokers Green
Dunsden Green
Emmer Green
Play Hatch
Calcot Row
Lambourn
Little Hungerford
Oare
Longlane
Brook
Michelmersh
Braishfield
Laylands Green
Buttermere
Combe
East Woodhay
East End
North End
Woolton Hill
Broad Laying
Hurstbourne
Wellington
Alder...
THE RIDGEWAY
WELLPLACE ZOO
GREYS COURT
STREATLEY ON THAMES
ST BARTHOLOMEW'S
BEALE PARK
BASILDON PARK
THE LIVING RAINFOREST
MAPLEDURHAM
ENGLISH RURAL LIFE MUS
READING SERVICES
CHIEVELEY SERVICES
SNELSMORE COMMON
DONNINGTON CASTLE
NEWBURY
ASHFORD HILL
ROMAN TOWN
STRATFIELD SAYE HOUSE
WELLINGTON
SANDHAM MEMORIAL CHAPEL
TOT HILL SERVICES
HIGHCLERE CASTLE
THE VYNE
MILESTONES
PORTWAY
FINKLEY DOWN FARM PARK
TIDBURY RING
SUTTON SCOTNEY SERVICES
WINCHESTER SERVICES
NORTHINGTON GRANGE
CURTIS MUSEUM
JANE AUSTEN'S HO
MID-HANTS RAILWAY
GILBERT WHITE'S HOUSE
ALL SAINTS CHURCH
FLOWERDOWN BARROWS
FARLEY MOUNT
WINCHESTER
INTECH SCIENCE TECHNOLOGY CENTRE
ST. CATHERINE'S HILL
ASHFORD HANGERS
FLYING
P&R
M4
M3
A4
A34
A339
A303
A33
A30
A31
A32
A343
A338
A3057
A272
A4155
B4000
B4009
B4494
B4526
B4640
B3051
B3400
B3420
B3048
B3049
B3047
B3046
B3349
B3011
B3006
B3270
B4471
N O R T H   W E S S E X   D O W N S
N O R
SU
0 1 2 3 4 5 6 miles
0 1 2 3 4 5 6 7 8 9 10 km

Windsor
Slough
SLOUGH
Maidenhead
Henley-on-Thames
Burnham
Uxbridge
Hillingdon
Cowley
Yeading
Yiewsley
Hayes
Southall
West Drayton
Heathrow Airport
HOUNSLOW
Brentford
Isleworth
Heston
Harlington
Cranford
Longford
Sipson
Colnbrook
Datchet
Eton
WINDSOR
Old Windsor
Twyford
Woodley
Earley
Winnersh
Sindlesham
Wargrave
Binfield
WOKINGHAM
Bracknell
Ascot
Sunninghill
Sunningdale
South Ascot
Virginia Water
EGHAM
Englefield Green
Staines
Ashford
Feltham
Teddington
Sunbury-on-Thames
Walton-on-Thames
Hampton
CHERTSEY
Addlestone
WEYBRIDGE
Esher
Byfleet
Cobham
Oxshott
Woodham
Chobham
Bagshot
Windlesham
Lightwater
Crowthorne
Sandhurst
CAMBERLEY
Yateley
Frimley
Deepcut
WOKING
Knaphill
Horsell
Fleet
FARNBOROUGH
ALDERSHOT
Ash
Farnham
Guildford
Shalford
Godalming
Milford
Elstead
Haslemere
Hindhead
Grayshott
Bordon
Liphook
Cranleigh
Ewhurst
Dunsfold
Alfold
Chiddingfold
Fetcham
Great Bookham
East Horsley
West Horsley
Ripley
Send
Burpham
Merrow
Gomshall
Abinger Hammer
Westcott
Holmbury St Mary
Wotton
Forest Green
Ockley
Walliswood
Kingsfold
Warnham
Rowhook
Rudgwick
Slinfold
Billingshurst
Plaistow
Kirdford
Wisborough Green
Northchapel
Fernhurst
Henley
Milland
Liss
Steep Marsh
Rake
Greatham
Empshott
Blackmoor
Whitehill
Headley
Kingsley
Binsted
Frensham
Tilford
Churt
Wrecclesham
Rowledge
Puttenham
Compton
Seale
Tongham
Wood Street
Worplesdon
Pirbright
Mytchett
Brookwood
Crookham Village
Church Crookham
Dogmersfield
Hartley Wintney
Eversley
Finchampstead
Hurst
Twyford
Shamley Green
Bramley
Wonersh
Chilworth
Albury
Peaslake
Hascombe
Tuesley
Witley
Wormley
Thursley
Rushmoor
Hambledon
Loxhill
Heathrow
M4
M3
M25
A3
A31
A30
A322
A329
A331
A24
A272
A308
A316
A309
A312
A4
28
16
39
40
SU
TQ
Surrey
Forest
Hogs Back
North Downs Way
Hurt Wood

Uxbridge
Hillingdon
Yeading
Northolt
Perivale
Alperton
Willesden
Harlesden
Camden
Islington
Bethnal Green
Stratford
East Ham
Barking
West Ham
Beckton
Cowley
Hayes
Southall
Greenford
EALING
Acton
Paddington
Finsbury
Holborn
Shoreditch
City
Poplar
Yiewsley
West Drayton
Hanwell
Kensington
Hyde Park
Westminster
Southwark
Bermondsey
Blackwall Tunnel
Woolwich Ferry
North Woolwich
Woolwich
Harlington
Cranford
Heston
Brentford
Chiswick
Hammersmith
Chelsea
LAMBETH
Deptford
Greenwich
Charlton
Sipson
Longford
HEATHROW AIRPORT
HOUNSLOW
Isleworth
Kew Br.
Fulham
Battersea
Peckham
Camberwell
New Cross
Lewisham
Kidbrooke
Stanwell Moor
Stanwell
West Bedfont
East Bedfont
Richmond
Mortlake
Putney
Clapham
Brixton
Hither Green
Eltham
New Eltham
Roehampton
Wandsworth
Dulwich
Catford
Feltham
Twickenham
Ham
Wimbledon Common
Balham
Streatham
Grove Park
Mottingham
Staines
Ashford
Hanworth
Teddington
Bushy Park
Kingston Vale
Wimbledon
Merton
Upper Tooting
West Norwood
Sydenham
Penge
Chislehurst
BROMLEY
Laleham
Littleton
Sunbury-on-Thames
Hampton
Kingston upon Thames
Raynes Park
Morden
Mitcham
South Norwood
Thornton Heath
Beckenham
Elmers End
Bickley
Petts Wood
CHERTSEY
Shepperton
West Molesey
East Molesey
Thames Ditton
Surbiton
New Malden
Walton-on-Thames
Long Ditton
Tolworth
Worcester Park
St.Helier
Hackbridge
Selhurst
Addiscombe
Eden Park
West Wickham
Hayes
Bromley Common
WEYBRIDGE
Hersham
Esher
Hook
Chessington
Carshalton
Croydon
Shirley
Keston
Farnborough
Claygate
Cheam
Sutton
Wallington
Beddington
South Croydon
Addington
New Addington
Downe
New Haw
Byfleet
Whiteley Village
Ewell
Belmont
Purley
Selsdon
Leaves Green
West Byfleet
Cobham
Oxshott
EPSOM
Woodmansterne
Sanderstead
Hamsey Green
Farleigh
Biggin Hill
Cudham
Wisley
Pyrford
Ripley
Stoke D'Abernon
Downside
Wood Field
Ashtead
Great Burgh
Burgh Heath
BANSTEAD
Kenley
Coulsdon
Whyteleafe
Warlingham
South Street
Leatherhead Common
Martyr's Green
Ockham
Fetcham
Leatherhead
Tadworth
Chipstead
Hooley
Old Coulsdon
Tatsfield
Woldingham
Little Bookham
Kingswood
Walton on the Hill
Lower Kingswood
Chaldon
CATERHAM
Titsey
East Horsley
West Horsley
Effingham
Great Bookham
Headley
Mickleham
Merstham
Limpsfield
Westerham
Limpsfield Chart
Brewer Street
Godstone
Church Town
Oxted
Tandridge
Crockham Hill
East Clandon
Westhumble
Ranmore Common
Dorking
Pixham
Buckland
Redhill
Nutfield
Bletchingley
Newland's Corner
Betchworth
Reigate
Earlswood
South Nutfield
Crowhurst Lane End
Marlpit Hill
Gomshall
Albury
Abinger Hammer
Shere
Brockham
Westcott
Strood Green
Doversgreen
Ridge Green
South Godstone
Chilworth
Brook
Wotton
North Holmwood
Leigh
Sidlow
Salfords
Crowhurst
Crouch House Green
Edenbridge
Sutton
Abinger Common
Blindley Heath
Farley Green
Peaslake
Holmbury St Mary
South Holmwood
Nalderswood
Outwood
Horne
Marsh Green
Lingfield
Hurt Wood
Coldharbour
Parkgate
Norwood Hill
Meath Green
Weatherhill
Smallfield
Beare Green
Hookwood
Horley
Newchapel
Felcourt
Dormansland
Newdigate
Charlwood
GATWICK AIRPORT
Burstow
Rowly
Ewhurst
Forest Green
Ewhurst Green
Capel
Clark's Green
Copthorne
Lullenden
Hammerwood
Ockley
Cranleigh
Walliswood
County Oak
Felbridge
Blackwell
East Grinstead
Ifield
Three Bridges
Oakwoodhill
Kingsfold
Rusper
Lambs Green
Pound Hill
Worth
Crawley Down
Sunnyside
Ashurstwood
Ellen's Green
Crawley
Turners Hill
Saint Hill
Forest Row
Broadfield
Tilgate
Rowhook
Faygate
Warnham
Rudgwick
Alfold
Pease Pottage
Selsfield Common
West Hoathly
Tisman's Common
Bucks Green
Strood Green
Broadbridge Heath
Roffey
Colgate
Balcombe Lane
Sharpthorne
Wych Cross
Park Street
St Leonard's Forest
Tilgate Forest Row
Slinfold
Horsham
Balcombe
Highbrook
Chelwood Gate
The Haven
Handcross
Ardingly
Roundstreet Common
Ashfold Crossways
Staplefield
Horsted Keynes
Chelwood Common
Monk's Gate
Slaugham
Danehill
Nutley
Lower Beeding
Brook Street
Slough Green
Southwater
Warninglid
Whitemans Green
Billingshurst
M25
M3
M4
M23
0 1 2 3 4 5 6 miles
0 1 2 3 4 5 6 7 8 9 10 km

Dagenham
Thurrock
CANVEY ISLAND
Leigh Beck
Corringham
Stanford-le-Hope
Coryton
Thames Haven
THAMES ESTUARY
South Ockendon
Orsett
Rainham
Aveley
Wennington
Creekmouth
Thamesmead
Erith
Belvedere
Purfleet
Dartford Crossing
West Thurrock
Grays
Chadwell St Mary
West Tilbury
East Tilbury
Tilbury
Linford
Mucking
Halstow Marshes
St Mary's Marshes
St Mary Hoo
Allhallows
Lower Stoke
Isle of Grain
Cliffe
Cooling
High Halstow
Stoke
North Street
Welling
Bexleyheath
Crayford
DARTFORD
Greenhithe
Swanscombe
NORTHFLEET
GRAVESEND
Bexley
Sidcup
Wilmington
Darenth
Betsham
Southfleet
Perry Street
Singlewell
Chalk
Shorne
Higham
Church Street
Lower Higham
Cliffe Woods
Medway
Chattenden
Hoo St.Werburgh
Wainscott
Upnor
Frindsbury
Strood
ROCHESTER
CHATHAM
Gillingham
Brompton
Grange
Upchurch
Rainham
Ham Green
Foots Cray
North Cray
Hextable
Swanley Village
Swanley
St Paul's Cray
St Mary Cray
Crockenhill
Orpington
Sutton at Hone
South Darenth
Hawley
Horton Kirby
Farningham
Istead Rise
Longfield
New Barn
Hartley
Sole Street
Cobham
Meopham Station
Hook Green
Luddesdown
Meopham
Cuxton
North Halling
Halling
Upper Halling
Wouldham
Luton
Wayfield
Walderslade
Hempstead
Moor Street
Wigmore
Newington
Hartlip
Bredhurst
Stockbury
Eynsford
Fawkham Green
New Ash Green
Ash
West Kingsdown
Maplescombe
Chelsfield
Well Hill
Green Street Green
Pratt's Bottom
Badger's Mount
Halstead
Shoreham
Knockholt
Knockholt Pound
Otford
Kemsing
Chevening
Stansted
Fairseat
Culverstone Green
Vigo Village
Trottiscliffe
Snodland
Birling
Ryarsh
Burham
Blue Bell Hill
Eccles
Aylesford
New Hythe
Boxley
Detling
Thurnham
Bicknor
Hucking
Broad Street
South Green
Wrotham
Wrotham Heath
Heaverham
Borough Green
Addington
Leybourne
West Malling
Ditton
East Malling
Offham
Platt
Seal
Dunton Green
Chipstead
Riverhead
Sevenoaks
Sundridge
Brasted
Brasted Chart
The Chart
Ightham
Stone Street
Crouch
Claygate Cross
Plaxtol
Mereworth
Kent Street
King's Hill
Sandling
Maidstone
British Legion Village
East Barming
Roseacre
Bearsted
Tovil
Teston
Shepway
Otham
Leeds
Broomfield
Kingswood
Langley
Langley Heath
Warmlake
Chart Corner
Sutton Valence
Ulcombe
Cross Keys
Whitley Row
Ide Hill
Toy's Hill
Sevenoaks Weald
Underriver
Dunk's Green
Shipbourne
West Peckham
Wateringbury
Nettlestead
Nettlestead Green
West Farleigh
East Farleigh
Loose
Boughton Monchelsea
Coxheath
Pootings
Four Elms
Hildenborough
Hilden Park
Coldharbour
Oakhurst
Pittswood
Hadlow
Higham Wood
East Peckham
Hale Street
Yalding
Hunton
Linton
Benover
Laddingford
Chainhurst
Golden Green
Barnes Street
Beltring
Rabbit's Cross
How Green
Bough Beech
Chiddingstone Causeway
Leigh
Brook Street
TONBRIDGE
Five Oak Green
Whetsted
Queen Street
Collier Street
Cross-at-Hand
Milebush
Southernden
Headcorn
Hawkenbury
Hever
Chiddingstone
Penshurst
Bidborough
Tudeley
Paddock Wood
Claygate
Marden
Staplehurst
Sinkhurst Green
Markbeech
Chiddingstone Hoath
Southborough
High Brooms
Speldhurst
Castle Hill
Matfield
Brenchley
Marden Beech
Marden Thorn
Knox Bridge
Frittenden
Cowden
Fordcombe
Pembury
Petteridge
Horsmonden
Winchet Hill
Curtisden Green
Blackham
Ashurst
Langton Green
ROYAL TUNBRIDGE WELLS
Hawkenbury
Lamberhurst Quarter
Hazel Street
Goudhurst
Cranbrook Common
Three Chimneys
Groombridge
Bells Yew Green
Lamberhurst
Iden Green
Wilsley Pound
Sissinghurst
Hartfield
Withyham
Eridge Green
Frant
Hook Green
Kilndown
Cranbrook
East End
Parkgate
Upper Hartfield
Lye Green
Cousley Wood
Hartley
Coleman's Hatch
Friar's Gate
Boarshead
Wood's Green
Durgates
Wadhurst
Bedgebury Forest
Gill's Green
Benenden
Mark Cross
Three Leg Cross
Flimwell
High Street
Hawkhurst
Iden Green
Dingleden
Rolvenden
Crowborough
Poundfield
Riseden
Bestbeech Hill
Union Street
Four Throws
ASHDOWN FOREST
Town Row
Rotherfield
Tidebrook
Shover's Green
Wallcrouch
Ticehurst
Horns Corner
The Moor
Rolvenden Layne
Jarvis Brook
Stonegate
Swiftsden
Sandhurst
Duddleswell
Coggins Mill
Hurst Green
Sandhurst Cross
Cackle Street
Fairwarp
High Hurstwood
Butcher's Cross
Mayfield
Witherenden Hill
Etchingham
Bodiam
Newenden
Kent
North Downs Way
Bewl Water

Canvey Island
Coryton
Thames Haven
Leigh Beck
Shoeburyness
Cambridge Town
THAMES ESTUARY
42
43
(From Dartford) VLISSINGEN 9:30 ZEEBRUGGE 9:00
Halstow Marshes
St Mary's Marshes
Allhallows-on-Sea
Allhallows
St Mary Hoo
Cliffe
Cooling
High Halstow
Lower Stoke
Isle of Grain
Grain
Stoke
Cliffe Woods
North Street
Medway
Hoo St.Werburgh
Chattenden
Upnor
Frindsbury
Brompton
Grange
ROCHESTER
CHATHAM
Gillingham
Luton
Wayfield
Walderslade
Hempstead
Moor Street
Wigmore
Rainham
Upchurch
Ham Green
Lower Halstow
Iwade
Sheerness
West Minster
Halfway Houses
Minster
Queenborough
Rushenden
Chetney Marshes
Eastchurch
Warden Pt.
Warden
Leysdown-on-Sea
ISLE OF SHEPPEY
ELMLEY
The Swale
Isle of Harty
Shell Ness
WHITSTABLE
Tankerton
Swalecliffe
Seasalter
Chestfield
South Street
Yorkletts
Kemsley
Milton Regis
SITTINGBOURNE
Conyer
Uplees
Breach
Bobbing
Newington
Hartlip
Borden
Oad Street
Bapchild
Barrow Green
Teynham
Oare
Faversham
Graveney
Goodnestone
Dargate
Honey Hill
Tyler Hill
Bredhurst
Stockbury
South Green
Bredgar
Tunstall
Highsted
Rodmersham
Lynsted
Ospringe
Preston
Hernhill
Blean
Boughton Street
Dunkirk
Rough Common
Hales Place
Harbledown
Thanington
Sandling
Boxley
Detling
Thurnham
Bicknor
Hucking
Swanton Street
Milstead
Frinsted
Doddington
Newnham
Eastling
Sheldwich
North Street
Selling
South Street
Oversland
Chartham Hatch
Chartham
Old Wives Lees
Maidstone
Tovil
Bearsted
Roseacre
Broad Street
Wormshill
Hollingbourne
Eyhorne Street
West Street
Wichling
Throwley
Badlesmere
Shottenden
Chilham
Shalmsford Street
Street End
Garlinge Green
Petham
East Farleigh
Shepway
Otham
Leeds
Harrietsham
Warren Street
Stalisfield Green
Leaveland
Molash
Loose
Boughton Monchelsea
Langley
Langley Heath
Broomfield
Kingswood
Lenham
Sandway
Lenham Heath
Challock
Godmersham
Sole Street
Crundale
Waltham
Linton
Chart Corner
Chart Sutton
Warmlake
Sutton Valence
Ulcombe
Grafty Green
Boughton Malherbe
Charing
Charing Heath
Westwell Leacon
Boughton Aluph
Westwell
Bilting
Boughton Lees
Wye
Hassell Street
Bodsham
Stelling Minnis
Elmsted
Rabbit's Cross
Cross-at Hand
Milebush
Marden
Southernden
Egerton
Egerton Forstal
Little Chart
Ram Lane
Goat Lees
Pluckley
Pluckley Thorne
Hothfield
Kennington
Brook
Hastingleigh
Lymbridge Green
Staplehurst
Hawkenbury
Headcorn
Marden Beech
Marden Thorn
Sinkhurst Green
Smarden
Smarden Bell
Maltman's Hill
Great Chart
Ashford
Willesborough
Hinxhill
Willesborough Lees
Brabourne
Stowting
Brabourne Lees
Knox Bridge
Frittenden
Haffenden Quarter
Wissenden
Sevington
Winchet Hill
Curtisden Green
Lashenden
Standen
Bethersden
Collier's Green
Cranbrook Common
Three Chimneys
Biddenden
Tanden
Stubbs Cross
Kingsnorth
Mersham
Cheeseman's Green
Smeeth
Sellindge
Sellindge Lees
Postling
Beach Stanford
Wilsley Pound
Sissinghurst
High Halden
Shadoxhurst
Bromley Green
Aldington Frith
Clap Hill
Aldington
Newingreen
Cranbrook
East End
St Michael's
Henghurst
Shirkoak
Bonnington
Court-at-Street
Lympne
Pedlinge
Hartley
Parkgate
Woodchurch
Orlestone
Ruckinge
Bilsington
West Hythe
Tenterden
Benenden
Brook Street
Kenardington
Hamstreet
Warehorne
Royal Military Canal
Burmarsh
Palmarsh
Gill's Green
Iden Green
High Street
Hawkhurst
Dingleden
Rolvenden
Leigh Green
Small Hythe
Reading Street
Appledore Heath
Snave
Newchurch
Four Throws
Rolvenden Layne
ISLE OF OXNEY
Appledore
ROMNEY MARSH
St Mary in the Marsh
Dymchurch
St Mary's Bay
The Moor
Sandhurst
Peening Quarter
Stone
Snargate
Ivychurch
Brenzett
Brookland
Wittersham
Ham Green
The Stocks
Bodiam
GREAT DIXTER
0 1 2 3 4 5 6 miles
0 1 2 3 4 5 6 7 8 9 10km
M2
M20
A2
A20
A28
A229
A249
A251
A252
A299
A2070
A259
TQ
NORTH DOWNS WAY
NORTH DOWNS
KENT DOWNS
Medway
Kent

HERNE BAY
Reculver
RECULVER TOWERS AND ROMAN FORT
Minnis Bay
Hillborough
Beltinge
Greenhill
Herne
Broomfield
Birchington
Westgate on Sea
Margate
MARGATE
DREAMLAND
THE SHELL GROTTO
Cliftonville
Foreness Pt.
Kingsgate
NORTH FORELAND
LIGHTHOUSE
Northdown
St Peter's
BROADSTAIRS
BLEAK HOUSE
DICKENS HOUSE MUSEUM
Dumpton
RAMSGATE BOULEVARD
Ramsgate
MARITIME MUSEUM
OOSTENDE 4:00
QUEX HOUSE
Isle of Thanet
SPITFIRE AND HURRICANE MEM.
Northwood
Newington
Acol
Manston
KENT INTERNATIONAL
St Nicholas at Wade
WINDMILL
Sarre
Boyden Gate
Hoath
Chislet
Monkton
Minster
Way
Cliffsend
Pegwell
PEGWELL BAY
SANDWICH & PEGWELL BAY
ST. AUGUSTINE'S CROSS
Pegwell Bay
Calcott
Broadoak
Upstreet
Hersden
Stour
West Stourmouth
East Stourmouth
Westmarsh
Ware
Grove
STODMARSH
Preston
Westbere
Sturry
Stodmarsh
Elmstone
Hoaden
RICHBOROUGH CASTLE
AMPHITHEATRE
Great Stonar
Fordwich
Canterbury
Wickhambreux
Ickham
WINGHAM BIRD PARK
Sandwich Bay
Sandwich
ROYAL ST. GEORGE'S
TOLL
ST. AUGUSTINE'S ABBEY
CANTERBURY
Littlebourne
Wingham
Guilton
Ash
Marshborough
Woodnesborough
Stone Cross
HOWLETTS WILD ANIMAL PARK
Bekesbourne
Bramling
Staple
Worth
TR
Patrixbourne
Nackington
Goodnestone
GOODNESTONE PARK
Gore
Eastry
Ham
Finglesham
Adisham
Bridge
Lower Hardres
Chillenden
Knowlton
Betteshanger
Sholden
MARITIME AND LOCAL HISTORY MUSEUM
DEAL
THE DOWNS
DEAL CASTLE
Bishopsbourne
Aylesham
Easole Street
Northbourne
Kingston
Nonington
Upper Hardres Court
Snowdown
Tilmanstone
Elvington
Great Mongeham
Walmer
WALMER CASTLE AND GARDENS
Barham
Womenswold
Derringstone
Bossingham
Barfrestone
EAST KENT RLY.
Eythorne
East Studdal
Sutton
Ripple
Woolage Green
Ringwould
Kingsdown
West Langdon
Coxhill
Shepherdswell
Denton
Wingmore
LYDDEN
Wootton
Coldred
East Langdon
Martin
Martin Mill
Lyminge Forest
Elham
Selsted
Lydden
LYDDEN TEMPLE EWELL
Whitfield
Guston
St Margaret's at Cliffe
THE BAY MUSEUM
St Margaret's Bay
West Cliffe
THE PINES GARDEN
ST. JOHN'S COMMANDERY
Ewell Minnis
Temple Ewell
Rhodes Minnis
BUTTERFLY CENTRE
Swingfield Street
CRABBLE CORN MILL
SOUTH FORELAND
Swingfield Minnis
Buckland
Ottinge
Densole
Alkham
ROMAN PAINTED HOUSE
DOVER
WHITE CLIFFS (N.T.)
CASTLE & HELLFIRE CORNER
CALAIS 1:10
DUNKERQUE 1:50
KENT BATTLE OF BRITAIN MUSEUM
Drellingore
Maxton
Lyminge
West Hougham
Farthingloe
Paddlesworth
Hawkinge
Aycliff
DE BRADELEI WHARF
BOULOGNE 0:50
Etchinghill
CHANNEL TUNNEL
Capel le Ferne
SAMPHIRE HO.
EASTCLIFFS AND WARREN
East Wear Bay
Newington
ELHAM VALLEY RLY MUS.
Cheriton
Folkestone
Saltwood
ROTUNDA
CLIFF LIFT
Sandgate
Hythe
19
CHANNEL
TUNNEL

MYNYDD PRESELI
Pontfaen
Crymych
Tegryn
Cwmorgan
Tanglwst
Puncheston
Castlebythe
New Inn
Rosebush
Mynachlog-ddu
Pentre-galar
Hermon
Llanfyrnach
Hen-feddau fawr
Dinas
Trelech
Bryn-Iwan
Cwmduad
Tufton
Henry's Moat
Maenclochog
Llangolman
Glandy Cross
Glandwr
Hebron
Blaen-waun
Pen-y-bont
Blaen-y-coed
Cynwyl Elfed
Woodstock
Wallis
New Moat
Efailwen
Pant-y-Caws
Llanglydwen
Cefn-y-pant
CHOCOLATE FARM
Cwmbach
Llanwinio
Talog
LLYS-Y-FRAN RESERVOIR
Llys-y-frân
Walton East
Llanycefn
Maesgwynne
Cross-hands
Login
Cwmfelin Mynach
Llanboidy
Gellywen
Ty-hen
Abernant
Bwlchnewydd
Newchurch
Pen-ffordd
Llandissilio
SN
Dyffryn
Tre-vaughan
Clarbeston
Clarbeston Road
Bletherston
Hiraeth
Henllan Amgoed
Llanfallteg
Meidrim
Merthyr
Carmarthen (Caerfyrddin)
Clunderwen
Gelli
Cwmfelin Boeth
Llangynin
Sarnau
Bancyfelin
Llanllwch
CORS GOCH, LLANLLWCH
Wiston
LLAWHADEN CASTLE
Bethesda
GROVELANDS
Pwll-trap
Llawhaden
Robeston Wathen
Llanddewi Velfrey
Whitland
Trevaughan
Backe
St Clears (Sanclêr)
Llangynog
Llangain
The Rhos
Narberth (Arberth)
WILSON MUSEUM
Crinow
Lampeter Velfrey
Llwyn-y-brain
Afon Taf
Llanddowror
Blackpool
PICTON CASTLE GARDENS
HERONS BROOK
Morfa Bach
Afon Tywi
Minwear
OAKWOOD
Cross Hands
Templeton
Cold Blow
Princes Gate
Tavernspite
Halfpenny Furze
Llanybri
Landshipping
Red Roses
Llandawke
DYLAN THOMAS BOATHOUSE
Llansteffan
CASTLE
Landshipping Quay
Martletwy
Ludchurch
Llanteg
Llansadurnen
Brook
Laugharne
Broadway
Ferryside
Black Tar
Yerbeston
Longstone
FOLLY FARM
Reynalton
Marros
MUSEUM OF SPEED
Broadlay
Port Lion
Loveston
Thomas Chapel
Begelly
Stepaside
COLBY WOODLAND GARDEN
Pendine
East Marsh
Llansaint
LAWRENNY
Lawrenny
Cresswell Quay
Jeffreyston
Kilgetty
Amroth
Pendine Sands
Traeth Pentywyn
West Williamston
Cresselly
Broadmoor
Hill
Carew Newton
Cosheston
CAREW CASTLE
Milton
Carew
Redberth
East Williamston
Saundersfoot
PEMBROKESHIRE COAST
ARFORDIR PENFRO
Pembrey Forest
Pembroke (Penfro)
Sageston
Broadfield
New Hedges
Carew Cheriton
LAMPHEY BISHOP'S PALACE
MANOR HOUSE WILDLIFE PARK
TUDOR MERCHANT'S HOUSE
CARMARTHEN
St Florence
Gumfreston
Tenby (Dinbych-y-Pysgod)
PEMBREY
Lamphey
Hodgeston
Jameston
Penally
BAY
Freshwater East
Lydstep
Giltar Pt.
BAE CAERFYRDDIN
MANORBIER CASTLE
Manorbier
MANORBIER
Caldey Sound
Cheriton or Stackpole Elidor
Trewent Pt.
Trwyn Trewent
Old Castle Hd.
Caldey Island
Ynys Bŷr
Chapel Pt.
Trwyn Capel
Stackpole Hd.
Pen Stackpole
SS
Burry Holms
Rhossili Bay
Bae Rhossili
Worms Head
Penrhyn-Gŵyr
A40
A477
A478
A4075
A4066
A4139
B4329
B4313
B4314
B4315
B4316
B4318
B4328
B4298
B4299
B4312
B4333
B4584
B4586
A484
A4115
45
46
44
A
B
C
D
E
F
1
2
3
4
0 1 2 3 4 5 6 miles
0 1 2 3 4 5 6 7 8 9 10km

Carmarthenshire
(Sir Gaerfyrddin)
Swansea
(Abertawe)
Brechfa Forest
Dolgran
Gwernogle
Abergorlech
Afon Cothi
Talley
Cynwyl Elfed
Cwm-byr
Llandovery
Cwmdwr
Wauncluda
Llansadwrn
Llanwrda
Myrtle Hill
Alltwalis
Nant-y-ffin
Pen-y-garn
Cwmdu
Halfway
Felindre
Cilgwyn
Myddfai
Usk Reservoir
Llanpumsaint
Llanllawddog
Brechfa
Soar
Ashfield
Llangadog
Pontarsais
Horeb
Llanfynydd
Hermon
Manordeilo
Felindre
Pant-glas
Capel Isaac
Salem
Cwmifor
Talsarn
Llanddeusant
Rhydargaeau
Pant-teg
Felingwm uchaf
Pantgwyn
Rhosmaen
Bethlehem
Dyffryn Ceidrych
Twynllanan
Llanddeusant
Gwili Railway
Peniel
Felingwm isaf
Pen-y-banc
Pentrefelin
Vale of Tywi
Dyffryn Tywi
Pontbren Araeth
Pont-ar-llechau
Bronwydd Arms
Ffynnon Ddrain
Capel Gwyn
Llanfihangel-uwch-Gwili
Court Henry
Broad Oak
Dinefwr Park
Llangathen
Cilsan
Llandeilo
Trichrug
Capel Gwynfe
Pont Aber
White Mill
Pont-ar-gothi
Aberglasney
Neuadd
Lovespoon Gallery
Nantgaredig
Llanegwad
Felindre
Dryslwyn
Afon Tywi
Ffairfach
Abergwili
Carmarthen
Llanarthne
Gelli Aur
Golden Grove
Trapp
Carreg Cennen Farm Centre and Castle
Black Mountain
Mynydd Du
Foel Fraith
Llangunnor
Capel Dewi
Pensarn
Johnstown
Nantycaws
National Botanic Garden of Wales
Penrhiw-goch
Temple Bar
Milo
Llandyfan
Dre-fach
Cwmffrwd
Llanddarog
Maesybont
Carmel
Pentre-Gwenlais
Llandybie
Croesyceiliog
Cwmisfael
Porthyrhyd
Idole
Bancycapel
Gwendraeth Fach
Llyn Llech Owain
Foel-gastell
Bonsai Centre
Gorslas
Cefneithin
Caer-bryn
Twynmynydd
Brynamman
Rhosaman
Llangendeirne
Crwbin
Drefach
Pen-y-groes
Cwm-y-glo
Morfa
Saron
Tir-y-dail
Glanaman
Afon Aman
Garnant
Gwaun-Leision
Cwmllynfell
Ystradowen
Abercraf
Pontantwn
Bancffosfelen
Cwm-mawr
Cross Hands
Tumble
Penybanc
Ammanford
(Rhydaman)
Pontamman
Gwaun-Cae-Gurwen
Tairgwaith
Upper Cwm-twrch
Cwmgiedd
Llandyfaelog
Pontyberem
Pentre
Cwmgwili
Capel Hendre
Betws
Pantyffynnon
Tycroes
Cwmgors
Lower Cwm-twrch
Penrhos
Meinciau
Pont-Henri
Greynor
Garnswllt
Gurnos
Ystradgynlais
Ystalyfera
Four Roads
Kidwelly Industrial Museum
Mynyddygarreg
Pontyates
Llannon
Llwyn-teg
Mynydd y Gwair
Godre'r-graig
Kidwelly
(Cydweli)
Cynheidre
Sylen
Pont Abraham Services
Llanedi
Graig Fawr
Climaen-gwyn
Ynys-meudwy
Swansea Valley
Cwm Abertawe
Carway
Five Roads
Horeb
Lliedi Resrs.
Sardis
Pentrebach
SN
Rhyd-y-fro
Pontardawe
Glantawe Riverside
Cilybebyll
Crynant
Trimsaran
Pontarddulais
Gellinudd
Mynydd March-Hywel
Pembrey
Pinged
Waun-y-clyn
Hendy
Fforest
Cwm-Dulais
Rhyd-y-gwin
Craig-cefn-parc
Trebanos
Rhôs
Cefn Coed Colliery Mus.
Cwmbach
Allt
Felindre
Rhyd-y-pandy
Alltwen
Achddu
Pembrey
Furnace
Felinfoel
Llangennech
Waungron
Faerdre
Burry Port
(Porth Tywyn)
Pwll
Sandy
Dafen
Pontlliw
Clydach
Ynystawe
Glais
Cilfrew
Aberdulais
Falls
Clyne
Millennium Coastal Park
Llanelli
Llwyn-hendy
Bryn
Grovesend
Bynea
Yspitty
Swansea West Services
Pant-lasau
Heol-las
Bryn-coch
Rhydding
Tonna
Neath Abbey
Cadoxton-Juxta-Neath
Neath Museum
Neath
(Castell-Nedd)
Machynys
Morfa
Wildfowl and Wetlands Trust
Loughor
Penllergaer
Gorseinon
Llangyfelach
Morriston
Birchgrove
Skewen
Llansamlet
Swansea Vale Rly
Pentre-dwr
Whiteford Pt.
Trwyn Whiteford
Whiteford
Llanrhidian Sands
Traeth Llanrhidian
Pen-clawdd
Gowerton
Cadle
Landore
Fforest-fach
Bon-y-maen
Llandarcy
Cimla
Briton Ferry
The Gnoll
Pontrhydyfen
South Wales Miners Mu.
Crofty
Wernffrwd
Llanmorlais
Blue Anchor
Three Crosses
Waunarlwydd
Pentre-chwyth
Cwmdu
Foxhole
P&R
Swansea
(Abertawe)
Cwm
Crymlyn Bog and Pant-y-Sais
Pwll-y-glaw
Bryncoch
Llanmadoc
Cheriton
Landimore
Weobley Castle
Dunvant
Killay
Sketty
Plantasia
Port Tennant
Baglan
Mynydd Dinas
Bryn
Brynbryddan
Cwmafan
Llangennith
Burry Green
Gower
Llanrhidian
Llethrid
Upper Killay
Clyne Valley
Brynmill
Swansea Museum
Glynn Vivian
National Waterfront Museum
Aberavon
Port Talbot
Burry
Reynoldston
Swansea Airport
Ilston
Mayals
Black Pill
The Beacon
Lunnon
Kittle
Bishopston
West Cross
Swansea Bay
Goytre
Llanddewi
Knelston
Gower Heritage Centre
Parkmill
Pennard
Mansefield
Lovespoon Gallery
Oystermouth Castle
Taibach
Margam
Rhossili
Scurlage
Penrice
Nicholaston
Penmaen
Southgate
Oldway
Newton
The Mumbles
(Y Mwmbwls)
Bae Abertawe
Groes
Middleton
Pilton Green
Oxwich
Oxwich Bay
Bae Oxwich
Pwlldu Hd.
Pen Pwlldu
Mumbles Hd.
Trwyn yr Mwmbwls
Gower Coast
Horton
Oxwich Castle
Margam Mus.
Overton
Port-Eynon
Port Eynon Bay
Bae Port Eynon
Port Eynon Pt.
Trwyn Port Eynon
SS
Kenfig
Mawdlam
Kenfig Pool and Dunes
Kenfig Burrows
Royal Porthcawl
Hutchwns
Porthcawl
A
B
C
D
E
F
G
5
6
7
8

Llandovery
Halfway
Myrtle Hill
Llanwrda
Cilgwyn
Myddfai
Usk Reservoir
Llangadog
Trecastle
Cwmwysg
Pont ar Hydfer
Llywel
Sennybridge
(Pont Senni)
Defynnog
Pentre'r-felin
Trallong
Aberyscir
Penpont
Llanspyddid
Brecon
(Aberhonddu)
Llanfaes
Llanhamlach
Llanfrynach
Pencelli
Libanus
Tai'r-Bull
Mynydd Illtyd
MOUNTAIN CENTRE
Talsarn
Twynllanan
Llanddeusant
Glas Fynydd Forest
Crai
Felin-Crai
Heol Senni
LLWYN-Y-CELYN
CRAIG CERRIG GLEISIAD A FAN FRYNYCH
Glyn Tarell
Capel Gwynfe
Pont-ar-llechau
Pont Aber
Neuadd
SN
FAN BRYCHEINIOG
Cray Res.
PEN Y FAN
BRECON BEACONS
Neuadd Reservoirs
Talybont Res.
FAN GIHIRYCH
FAN FAWR
Beacons Res.
Ystradfellte Res.
FFOREST FAWR
BLACK MOUNTAIN
Y MYNYDD DU
DAN-YR-OGOF SHOWCAVES
DAN-YR-OGOF
CRAIG-Y-NOS
OGOF FFYNNON DDU
Glyntawe
Craig-y-nos
Penwyllt
Abercynafon
Cantref Res.
Nant-ddu
Pontsticill Reservoir
BRECON MOUNTAIN RAILWAY
GARWNANT
GARWNANT VISITOR CENTRE
Llwyn-on Res.
Pontsticill
Vaynor
Brynamman
Rhosaman
Pen-y-cae
Cwmllynfell
Ystradowen
Gwaun-Leision
Tairgwaith
Abercraf
Caehopkin
CEFN-YR-ERW
Coelbren
Cwmgiedd
Upper Cwm-twrch
Lower Cwm-twrch
Penrhos
Ystradfellte
Cwmgors
Gurnos
Ystradgynlais
Onllwyn
Dyffryn Cellwen
Ystalyfera
Seven Sisters
Nant-y-cafn
Pontneddfechan
Pontbren Llwyd
Penderyn
Cefn-coed-y-cymmer
Dowlais
Godre'r-graig
SWANSEA VALLEY
CWM ABERTAWE
Glyn-neath
(Glynedd)
Morfa Glas
Rhigos
Cwm-hwnt
Hirwaun
Gellideg
Pen-yr-Heolgerrig
Merthyr Tydfil
(Merthyr Tudful)
Climaen gwyn
Ynys-meudwy
Rheola Forest
VALE OF NEATH
CWM NEDD
Blaengwrach
Cwmgwrach
Tre-Gibbon
Penywaun
Trecynon
Llwydcoed
Cwmdare
ABERDARE
(ABERDAR)
Aber-nant
Cwmbach
Pentrebach
Abercanaid
Troedyrhiw
Rhyd-y-fro
Pontardawe
Cilybebyll
Gellinudd
Rhôs
Alltwen
Trebanos
Crynant
Mynydd March-Hywel
CEFN COED COLLIERY MUS.
RESOLVEN MTN.
Resolven
Neath
Rhondda
Aberaman
Faerdre
Clydach
Glais
Cilfrew
Aberdulais
Melincourt
Clyne
Port Talbot
(Castell-Nedd
Port Talbot)
Blaenrhondda
Tynewydd
Treherbert
Cynon
Cwmaman
MOUNTAIN ASH
(ABERPENNAR)
Penrhiwceiber
Aberfan
Bedlinog
Cwmfelin
Merthyr Vale
Treharris
Heol-las
Bryn-coch
Birchgrove
Rhydding
Neath Abbey
Cadoxton-Juxta-Neath
Tonna
NEATH MUSEUM
Skewen
Neath
(Castell-Nedd)
Glyncorrwg
Maerdy
Treorchy
(Treorci)
Pentre
Ferndale
St Gwynno Forest
Blaen-gwynfi
Aber-gwynfi
Cwm-parc
RHONDDA
Taff
Ynysboeth
Abercynon
Cimla
Briton Ferry
THE GNOLL
Duffryn
Cymer
Croeserw
Ton-Pentre
Ystrad
Gelli
Tylorstown
Pont-y-gwaith
Wattstown
Ynysybwl
SOUTH WALES MINERS MUSEUM
AFAN ARGOED
FOEL Y DYFFRYN
Caerau
Spelter
WERFA
Nant-y-moel
GRAIG Y GEIFRI
Clydach Vale
Llwynypia
CLYNDACH VALE
Tonypandy
Penygraig
Trealaw
Ynyshir
Porth
RHONDDA HERITAGE PARK
Glyncoch
Cilfynydd
Baglan
Pwll-y-glaw
Brynbryddan
MYNYDD DINAS
Cwmafan
Bryn
Dyffryn
Nantyffyllon
Blaengarw
Pontycymer
Wyndham
Price Town
MAESTEG
Cwmfelin
Garth
Trebanog
PONTYPRIDD
Trehafod
Glyntaff
Aberavon
Port Talbot
Goybre
Taibach
Margam
Groes
MYNYDD MARGAM
Llangynwyd
Pont Rhyd-y-cyff
Ogmore Vale
Ogmore Forest
Evanstown
Gilfach Goch
Hendreforgan
Lewistown
Pant-yr-awel
Glynogwr
Bryn
Golau
Tonyrefail
Rhondda Cynon Taf
Pen-y-coedcae
Treforest
Rhydyfelin
Hawthorn
SWANSEA BAY
BAE ABERTAWE
MOEL TON-MAWR
Bridgend
(Pen-y-bont ar Ogwr)
Bettws
Llangeinor
Blackmill
MYNYDD MAENDY
Castellau
Coedely
Upper Church Village
Llantwit Fardre
Church Village
Beddau
MARGAM
MARGAM ABBEY AND STONES MUSEUM
Coytrahen
BRYNGARW
Brynmenyn
Tondu
Aberkenfig
Bryncethin
Heol-y-Cyw
Brynna
MODEL CENTRE
Llantrisant
Efail Isaf
SS
Kenfig Hill
BEDFORD
Cefn Cross
Sarn
McARTHUR GLEN BRIDGEND
Talbot Green
Llanharan
Dolau
Bryncae
Pont-y-clun
Cross Inn
Creigiau
Kenfig
Mawdlam
KENFIG POOL AND DUNES
North Cornelly
Pyle
(Y Pîl)
Cefn Cribbwr
Pen-y-fai
Pendre
Coity
COITY CASTLE
Pencoed
Llanilid
Llanharry
Brynsadler
Miskin
Groes-faen
Capel Llanilltern
Kenfig Burrows
South Cornelly
NEW CASTLE
Bridgend
(Pen-y-bont ar Ogwr)
Laleston
Oldcastle
Coychurch
Talygarn
LLANERCH VINEYARD
ROYAL PORTHCAWL
Tythegston
St Mary Hill
Treoes
Craig Penllyn
Llansannor
Ystradowen
St Brides super Ely
Peterston super-Ely
Newton
Clevis
Merthyr Mawr
OGMORE CASTLE
Corntown
Llangan
Ogmore
Ewenny
Pendoylan
Porthcawl
MERTHYR MAWR WARREN
Pentre
Penllyn
Maendy
Aberthin
Welsh St Donats
George's
0 1 2 3 4 5 6 miles
0 1 2 3 4 5 6 7 8 9 10 km

BLACK MOUNTAINS
Mynydd Llangynidr
Mynydd Llangattock
Monmouthshire
Torfaen
Caerphilly
Newport
Cardiff
Abergavenny
Monmouth
Cwmbran
CARDIFF
EBBW VALE
Tredegar
New Tredegar
Rhymney
Blaina
Abertillery
Abersychan
Blaenavon
Brynmawr
Nantyglo
PONTYPOOL
Griffithstown
Pontnewydd
Usk
Raglan
Caerleon
Caldicot
Portishead
Avonmouth
Crickhowell
Gilwern
Govilon
Pandy
Grosmont
Skenfrith
Llanvihangel-Ystern-Llewern
Llangattock-Vibon-Avel
Blackwood
Oakdale
Crumlin
Newbridge
Abercarn
Crosskeys
Risca
Machen
Bedwas
Bargoed
Gelligaer
Hengoed
Ystrad-mynach
CAERPHILLY
Rhiwderin
Bassaleg
Malpas
Christchurch
Magor
Rogiet
Undy
Chepstow Pk. Wood
Whitchurch
Llanishen
Rumney
St Mellons
Llanrumney
St Fagans
Penarth
Devauden
Shirenewton
Llantrisant
Llangybi
Tredunnock
Langstone
Penhow
Llanmartin
Bishton
Nash
Goldcliff
Whitson
Redwick
Peterstone Wentlooge
St Brides Wentloog
Marshfield
Castleton
Coedkernew
Lisvane
Llanedeyrn
Tongwynlais
Taff's Well
Rhiwbina
Radyr
Heath
Cathays
Roath
Llandaff
Canton
Ely
Portskewett
Caldicot Level
Battery Pt.
Redcliff Bay
West Hill
SO
ST
M4
M48
A40
A465
A449
A4042
A470
A48(M)
48
49
36
22
23

Monmouthshire
(Sir Fynwy)
South Gloucestershire
Monmouth
(Trefynwy)
Chepstow
(Cas-gwent)
Ross-on-Wye
Cinderford
Lydney
Newent
Coleford
Caldicot
Thornbury
Yate
Chipping Sodbury
Dursley
Wotton-under-Edge
FILTON
MANGOTSFIELD
Patchway
FOREST OF DEAN
River Severn
The Noose
Frampton on Severn
Berkeley
Sharpness
Newnham
Blakeney
Awre
Tintern Parva
TINTERN ABBEY
St Briavels
ST. BRIAVELS CASTLE
Raglan
RAGLAN
Usk
Skenfrith
SKENFRITH CASTLE
GROSMONT CASTLE
Symonds Yat
Goodrich
Whitchurch
Mitcheldean
Ruardean
Drybrook
Littledean
Parkend
Yorkley
Bream
Aylburton
Woolaston
Tidenham
Tutshill
Sedbury
Portskewett
Sudbrook
Severn Beach
Pilning
Almondsbury
Olveston
Tockington
Alveston
Falfield
Tortworth
Charfield
Kingswood
Hawkesbury Upton
Horton
Old Sodbury
Westerleigh
Winterbourne
Frampton Cotterell
Iron Acton
Stoke Gifford
Hambrook
Frenchay
Henbury
Horfield
Westbury on Trym
Shirehampton
Hallen
Easter Compton
Redcliff Bay
Sheepway
Whitson
Redwick
Magor
Rogiet
Undy
Caerwent
Penhow
Mathern
Mounton
Shirenewton
Itton
St Arvans
Devauden
Trellech
Llandogo
Penallt
Mitchel Troy
Dingestow
Wonastow
Rockfield
Dixton
Wyesham
Staunton
Christchurch
Berry Hill
Newland
Redbrook
Clearwell
Milkwall
Ellwood
Whitecroft
Pillowell
Viney Hill
Bilson Green
Ruspidge
Upper Soudley
Flaxley
Westbury-on-Severn
Elton
Boxbush
Arlingham
Rodley
Longney
Hardwicke
Fretherne
Saul
Upper Framilode
Moreton Valence
Whitminster
Nupend
Eastington
Frocester
Coaley
Cambridge
Slimbridge
Moorend
Gossington
Breadstone
Wanswell
Halmore
Purton
Newtown
Stinchcombe
North Nibley
Nibley Green
Woodmancote
Uley
Alderley
Tresham
Hillesley
Wickwar
Cromhall
Tytherington
Itchington
Rangeworthy
Latteridge
Engine Common
Little Sodbury
Dodington
Wapley
Codrington
Tormarton
Pucklechurch
Hinton
Coalpit Heath
Stapleton
Fishponds
Ross-on-Wye
Walford
Weston under Penyard
Coughton
Pontshill
Lea
Aston Crews
Aston Ingham
Gorsley
Linton
Bromsash
Kilcot
Clifford's Mesne
Malswick
Kent's Green
Tibberton
Taynton
Highleadon
Hartpury
Rudford
Lassington
Highnam Green
Highnam
Churcham
Minsterworth
Bulley
Huntley
Birdwood
Longhope
Glasshouse Hill
Oakle Street
Elmore Back
Elmore
Farleys End
Northwood Green
Blaisdon
Nailbridge
Brierley
English Bicknor
Lydbrook
Welsh Bicknor
Kerne Bridge
Marstow
Llangarron
Llancloudy
Welsh Newton
St Maughans
Llanrothal
Newcastle
Llangattock-Vibon-Avel
Onen
Llanvihangel-Ystern-Llewern
Penrhôs
Tregare
Pen-y-clawdd
Cwmcarvan
Llangovan
Kingcoed
Twyn-y-Sheriff
Llandenny
Llansoy
Gwernesney
Llangwm
Wolvesnewton
Kilgwrrwg Common
Newchurch
Gaerllwyd
Earlswood
Pen-y-cae-mawr
Mynydd-bach
Parc-Seymour
Llanvaches
Llanbeder
Llanmartin
Wilcrick
Llandevenny
Caldicot Level
Summerleaze
Kilpeck
Wormbridge
Didley
St Devereux
Kivernoll
Much Dewchurch
Wormelow Tump
Orcop Hill
Orcop
Garway Hill
Garway
Broad Oak
Pencoyd
Llanwarne
Michaelchurch
St Owens Cross
St Weonards
Tretire
Three Ashes
Peterstow
Glewstone
Bridstow
Harewood End
Hoarwithy
Llandinabo
Red Rail
King's Caple
Sellack
Upper Grove Common
Brampton Abbotts
Foy
Hole-in-the-Wall
How Caple
Fawley Chapel
Penalt
Ballingham
Carey
Little Birch
Much Birch
Little Dewchurch
Aconbury
Callow
Dewshall Court
Thruxton
Winnal
Cockyard
Fownhope
Bolstone
Sollers Hope
Brockhampton
Falcon
Crossway
Lyne Down
Much Marcle
Donnington
Bromsberrow Hth.
Broom's Green
Ryton
Redmarley D'Abitot
Dymock
Kempley
Fishpool
Upton Bishop
Phocle Green
Crow Hill
Playley Green
Pendock
Staunton
Corse
Poolhill
Brand Green
Upleadon
Bronw's End
Monmouth Cap
Pontrilas
Kentchurch
Hoaldalbert
Bont
Cross Ash
Crossway
Wayne Green
Llanfaenor
Maypole
Buckholt
Ganarew
Howton
M50
M48
M4
M5
M49
M32
A40
A48
A449
A466
A4137
A417
A38
A46
A4135
A403
A4174
SEVERN ROAD BRIDGE
SECOND SEVERN CROSSING
TOLL
0 1 2 3 4 5 6 miles
0 1 2 3 4 5 6 7 8 9 10 km

Bushley
Long Green
Forthampton
Tewkesbury
Newtown
Eldersfield
Corse Lawn
Chaceley
Walton Cardiff
Ashchurch
Aston Cross
Teddington
Fiddington
Oxenton
Washbourne
Alderton
Toddington
Alstone
Dixton
Stanton
MANOR
SNOWSHILL LAVENDER
Snowshill
GLOUCESTERSHIRE WARWICKSHIRE STEAM RAILWAY
Stanway
STANWAY HOUSE
Didbrook
HAILES ABBEY
Hailes
Greet
Gretton
ODDA'S CHAPEL
Deerhurst
Tredington
Apperley
Tirley
Hasfield
Ashleworth
Leigh
Coombe Hill
Hardwicke
Stoke Orchard
Gotherington
Bishop's Cleeve
LANGLEY HILL
Winchcombe
WINCHCOMBE POTTERY
SUDELEY CASTLE AND GARDENS
RAILWAY MUS.
Farmcote
Ford
Temple Guiting
Condicote
Longborough
Donnington
Sezincote
ARBORETUM
Bourton on the Hill
SEZINCOTE
Stow-on-the-Wold
Maugersbury
STOW-ON-THE-WOLD
Woodmancote
Cleeve Hill
Elmstone Hardwicke
Swindon
Southam
CHELTENHAM
BELAS KNAP LONG BARROW
THE COTSWOLD WAY
Charlton Abbots
Guiting Power
Kineton
COTSWOLD FARM PARK
Upper Swell
Lower Swell
Barton
Naunton
Upper Slaughter
Lower Slaughter
THE OLD MILL
Wyck Rissington
MINIATURE WORLD
Bourton-on-the-Water
BIRDLAND PARK
Little Rissington
Clapton-on-the-Hill
Great Rissington
Severn
Norton
Boddington
Uckington
Staverton
Sandhurst
Down Hatherley
Staverton Bridge
Arle
Golden Valley
Sandfields
GALLERY & MUSEUM
Prestbury
Battledown
Cheltenham
Charlton Kings
NATURE IN ART
Twigworth
Maisemore
Longford
Parton
GLOUCESTERSHIRE AIRPORT
Lansdown
Up Hatherley
HOLST'S BIRTHPLACE
Longlevens
OVER BRIDGE
DOCKS NATIONAL WATERWAYS
Churchdown
Badgeworth
Leckhampton
Dowdeswell
Whittington
Syreford
Andoversford
Sevenhampton
Brockhampton
Hawling
NOTGROVE LONG BARROW
Notgrove
Salperton
Cold Aston
Turkdean
Hazelton
Shipton
Shipton Solers
Gloucester
Hucclecote
Barnwood
Shurdington
Ullenwood
CRICKLEY HILL
Bentham
Coberley
Cowley
Hempsted
Matson
Brockworth
Great Witcombe
Tuffley
ROBINSWOOD HILL
Quedgeley
Whaddon
Upton St Leonard's
VILLA
PRINKNASH ABBEY & BIRD PARK
Cranham
Birdlip
Brookthorpe
Brimpsfield
Elkstone
Colesbourne
Withington
Compton Abdale
Cassey Compton
COUNTRYSIDE COLLECTION
Hampnett
Farmington
Northleach
Yanworth
CHEDWORTH ROMAN VILLA
Chedworth
Eastington
LODGE PARK
Sherborne
Windrush
COTSWOLD COMMONS AND BEECHWOODS
Syde
Whiteway
Haresfield
ROCOCO GARDENS
Harescombe
Sheepscombe
Painswick
The Camp
Miserden
Winstone
Woodmancote
Rendcomb
Calmsden
Foss Cross
Fossebridge
Coln St Dennis
Coln Rogers
Winson
Aldsworth
Pitchcombe
Whiteshill
Randwick
MISERDEN PARK
Duntisbourne Abbots
Duntisbourne Leer
North Cerney
Ablington
ARLINGTON MILL
Arlington
Bibury
ARLINGTON ROW (N.T.)
Coln St Aldwyn's
AKEMAN
Eastleach Turville
Slad
Sudgrove
Bisley
Edgeworth
Duntisbourne Rouse
Bagendon
Daglingworth
Barnsley
Hatherop
Fyfield
Southrop
Quenington
Stonehouse
Ebley
Stroud
Rodborough
Eastcombe
Bournes Green
Chalford
Oakridge
Sapperton
Oakley Wood
Baunton
Stratton
King's Stanley
Leonard Stanley
Woodchester
Thrupp
Brimscombe
Brownshill
Frampton Mansell
Cirencester
Ampney Crucis
Ampney St Mary
Ampney St Peter
Poulton
Milton End
Fairford
Littleworth
NYMPSFIELD LONG BARROW
WOODCHESTER PARK
Amberley
Hyde
Coates
CIRENCESTER LOCK UP
Chesterton
ROMAN AMPHITHEATRE
Preston
Harnhill
Driffield
Meysey Hampton
Horcott
Lechlade-on-Thames
Windsoredge
Minchinhampton
Nailsworth
Box
Tarlton
Source of the Thames
Siddington
Whelford
Whiteway
Avening
Cherington
Rodmarton
Ewen
South Cerney
Marston Meysey
Dunfield
Inglesham
Horsley
TRULL HOUSE GDNS.
Kemble
Shorncote
Cerney Wick
Down Ampney
Kempsford
Kingscote
Tetbury Upton
Culkerton
Poole Keynes
KEYNES PARK
NEIGH BRIDGE
COTSWOLD WATER PARK
Latton
Castle Eaton
Hannington Wick
CHAVENAGE HOUSE
Ashley
Somerford Keynes
Ashton Keynes
NORTH MEADOW
THE THAMES PATH
Cricklade
Hannington
Beverston
Tetbury
Chedglow
Chelworth
Oaksey
Crudwell
Eastcourt
Swill Brook
Leigh
Chelworth Green
Highworth
Long Newton
Doughton
Leighterton
Hankerton
Upper Minety
Minety
Broad Blunsdon
SWINDON AND CRICKLADE RAILWAY
Blunsdon St Andrew
Stanton Fitzwarren
Sevenhampton
Shipton Moyne
Brokenborough
Perry Green
Purton Stoke
WESTONBIRT ARBORETUM
Westonbirt
Filands
Charlton
Garsdon
Purton
Widham
Haydon Wick
Penhill
Upper Stratton
Stratton St Margaret
South Marston
Oldbury on the Hill
Easton Grey
Malmesbury
Queen Street
Dogridge
Lydiard Millicent
Pinehurst
Gorse Hill
Didmarton
Sopworth
Foxley
Lea
Lydiard Green
Rodbourne
Cheney
Sherston
Cleverton
The Common
LYDIARD HOUSE
G.W.R. MUS.
Norton
Corston
Little Somerford
B4042
Hook
Rodbourne
Walcot
Swindon
Little Badminton
Badminton
Luckington
Brinkworth
Callow Hill
The Marsh
McARTHURGLEN SWINDON
Rodbourne
Dauntsey
Grittenham
Wootton Bassett
Coate
COATE WATER
Alderton
Hullavington
Startley
Great Somerford
Lower Stanton St Quintin
Lower Seagry
Tockenham Wick
North Wroughton
Wroughton
GREAT WESTERN (MAIZE) MAZE
Elcombe
Acton Turville
Littleton Drew
Grittleton
Leigh Delamere
Stanton St Quintin
Upper Seagry
Tockenham
Badbury
Chiseldon
Burton
LEIGH DELAMERE SERVICES
Sutton Benger
Christian Malford
Bradenstoke
Lyneham
Church End
Broad Town
West Kington
Nettleton
Castle Combe
CASTLE COMBE
Yatton Keynell
Kington St Michael
Kington Langley
Langley Burrell
Foxham
West End
Spirthill
Preston
Goatacre
Bushton
Clyffe Pypard
Broad Hinton
Uffcott
BARBURY CASTLE
North Wraxall
COTSWOLDS
Gloucester
SP
SU
Cotswold
Swindon

Moreton-in-Marsh
Bourton on the Hill
Batsford
Lemington
Great Wolford
Whichford
Hook Norton
Wigginton
South Newington
Barford St John
Barford St Michael
Deddington
Clifton
Hempton
Sezincote
Wellington Aviation Art Museum
Chastleton House
Barton on the Heath
Long Compton
Little Compton
Great Rollright
Swerford
Rollright Stones
Worton
Great Tew
Over Worton
Duns Tew
North Aston
Somerton
Middle Aston
Upper Heyford
Steeple Aston
Lower Heyford
Cutsdean
Ford
Temple Guiting
Cotswold Farm Park
Kineton
Condicote
Longborough
Donnington
Evenlode
Chastleton
Salford
Over Norton
Chipping Norton
Little Tew
Heythrop
Ledwell
Sandford St Martin
Westcott Barton
Middle Barton
Steeple Barton
Broadwell
Adlestrop
Cornwell
Upper Swell
Lower Swell
Stow-on-the-Wold
Oddington
Daylesford
Maugersbury
Lidstone
Church Enstone
Enstone
Gagingwell
Cleveley
Kiddington
Rousham House
Naunton
Upper Slaughter
Lower Slaughter
The Old Mill
Wyck Rissington
Kingham
Churchill
Bledington
Sarsden
Icomb
Chadlington
Spelsbury
Taston
Over Kiddington
Glympton
Tackley
Notgrove
Cold Aston
Bourton-on-the-Water
Birdland Park
Miniature World
Westcote
Bruern Abbey
Lyneham
Idbury
Fifield
Little Rissington
Upper Rissington
Clapton-on-the-Hill
Chilson
Ascott-under-Wychwood
Charlbury
Wootton
Milton under Wychwood
Shipton-under-Wychwood
Stonesfield
Fawler
Bunkers Hill
Shipton on Cherwell
Turkdean
Great Rissington
Farmington
Finstock
North Leigh Roman Villa
Woodstock
Combe
Blenheim Palace
Thrupp
Kidlington
Northleach
Sherborne
Great Barrington
Taynton
Leafield
Fordwells
Ramsden
Whiteoak Green
East End
North Leigh
Long Hanborough
Bladon
Begbroke
Eastington
Lodge Park
Windrush
Little Barrington
Burford
Fulbrook
Swinbrook
Asthall Leigh
Hailey
New Yatt
Freeland
Church Hanborough
Yarnton
Fossebridge
Coln St Dennis
Asthall
Minster Lovell
Minster Lovell Hall and Dovecote
Crawley
Witney
Barnard Gate
Cassington
Oxford Services
Coln Rogers
Winson
Aldsworth
Signet
Westwell
Holwell
Charterville Allotments
Cogges
South Leigh
Eynsham
Wolvercote
Ablington
Arlington Mill
Arlington
Arlington Row (N.T.)
Bibury
Coln St Aldwyn's
Bradwell Grove
Cotswold Wild Life Park
Shilton
Curbridge
Brize Norton
High Cogges
Cogges Manor Farm Mus.
Swinford
Wytham
Ashmolean Mus.
Farmoor
Farmoor Reservoir
Carterton
Ducklington
Hardwick
Sutton
Stanton Harcourt
Botley
North Hinksey
Conduit House
Hatherop
Quenington
Eastleach Turville
Eastleach Martin
Filkins
Alvescot
Kencot
Broadwell
Black Bourton
Lew
Yelford
West End
Cumnor
Chawley
Fyfield
Broughton Poggs
Southrop
Brighthampton
Standlake
Aston
Cote
Eaton
Boars Hill
Wootton
Little Faringdon
Langford
Bampton
Weald
Clanfield
Shifford
Northmoor
Bessels Leigh
Appleton
Lamborough Hill
Foxcombe Hill
Sunningwell
Poulton
Milton End
Fairford
Horcott
Meysey Hampton
Grafton
Radcot
Chimney
Chimney Meadows
Duxford
Thames or Isis
The Thames Path
Carswell Marsh
Hinton Waldrist
Longworth
Netherton
Fyfield
Tubney
Cothill
Lechlade-on-Thames
Kelmscot
Kelmscott Manor
Eaton Hastings
Whelford
Inglesham
Marston Meysey
Dunfield
Buckland
Southmoor
Kingston Bagpuize
Shippon
Kempsford
Down Ampney
Buscot
Buscot Park
Upper Inglesham
Littleworth
Pusey
Frilford
Garford
Marcham
Caldecott
Latton
Hannington Wick
Faringdon
Badbury Hill
Great Barn
Hatford
Charney Bassett
Castle Eaton
Hannington
Coleshill
Great Coxwell
Little Coxwell
Shellingford
Stanford in the Vale
Lyford
Drayton
Cricklade
Highworth
Fernham
Baulking
West Hanney
East Hanney
Milton
Steventon
Swindon and Cricklade Railway
Broad Blunsdon
Blunsdon St Andrew
Stanton Fitzwarren
Sevenhampton
Longcot
Goosey
Denchworth
Watchfield
Shrivenham
Uffington
Grove
Milton Hill
Rowstock
Harwell
Widham
Purton
Haydon Wick
Penhill
Upper Stratton
Stratton St Margaret
Pinehurst
Rodbourne Cheney
Lydiard Millicent
Gorse Hill
Rodbourne
Walcot
South Marston
Bourton
Woolstone
Compton Beauchamp
Kingston Lisle
Sparsholt
West Challow
East Challow
Childrey
West Hendred
East Hendred
Ardington
Ardington Ho.
Lockinge
Wantage
East Ginge
West Ginge
Uffington Castle
Whitehorse Hill
Wayland's Smithy
Letcombe Regis
Letcombe Bassett
The Ridgeway
Chilton
Swindon
McArthurGlen
Great Western (Maize) Maze
Ashbury
Idstone
Bishopstone
Hinton Parva
Wanborough
Coate
Coate Water
Liddington
Kingston Warren
Lambourn Downs
Upper Lambourn
Fawley
South Fawley
West Ilsley
Farnborough
East Ilsley
Catmore
Ashdown Park
North Wroughton
Wroughton
Badbury
Chiseldon
Broadtown Lane
Broad Town
Lambourn
Brightwalton
Lilley
Stanmore
Beedon
Baydon
Eastbury
East Garston
Chaddleworth
Leckhampstead Thicket
Peasemore
World's End
Aldbourne
Membury Services
Woodsend
Woodlands
Leckhampstead
Vale of White Horse
SP
SU
Oxford
0 1 2 3 4 5 6 miles
0 1 2 3 4 5 6 7 8 9 10 km

Buckingham
Bletchley
Croughton
Aynho
Souldern
Mixbury
Water Stratford
Finmere
Radclive
Tingewick
Gawcott
Thornborough
Nash
Whaddon
Tattenhoe
Far Bletchley
Singleborough
Newton Longville
Little Brickhill
Cottisford
Newton Purcell
Barton Hartshorn
Preston Bissett
Padbury
Adstock
Great Horwood
Fritwell
Baynard's Green
Hardwick
Hethe
Chetwode
Addington
Winslow
Winslow Hall
Drayton Parslow
Stoke Hammond
Fewcott
Ardley
Stoke Lyne
Cherwell Valley Services
Fringford
Hillesden
Steeple Claydon
Mursley
Swanbourne
North End
Soulbury
Stratton Audley
Twyford
Bucknell
Caversfield
Poundon
Middle Claydon
East Claydon
Claydon House
Granborough
Hoggeston
Stewkley
South End
Charndon
Calvert
Botolph Claydon
Dunton
Linslade
Burcott
Caulcott
Middleton Stoney
Highfield
Woodfield
Bicester
Launton
Marsh Gibbon
North Marston
Buckingham
Wing
Ascott
Chesterton
Bicester Village
Edgcott
Grendon Underwood
Quainton Windmill
Oving
Creslow
Whitchurch
Cublington
Kirtlington
Ambrosden
Quainton
Pitchcott
Aston Abbotts
Mentmore
Wendlebury
Blackthorn
Buckinghamshire Railway Centre
Hardwick
Wingrave
Weston-on-the-Green
Lower Arncott
Kingswood
Waddesdon
Weedon
Rowsham
Bletchingdon
Merton
Ludgershall
Westcott
Upper Arncott
Piddington
Wotton Underwood
Waddesdon Manor
Akeman Street
Bierton
Cheddington
Charlton on Otmoor
Murcott
Long Marston
Hampton Poyle
Oddington
Boarstall Tower
Boarstall
Brill Windmill
Brill
Dorton
Ashendon
Upper Winchendon
Aylesbury
Puttenham
Marsworth
Islip
Noke
Horton-cum-Studley
Upper Pollicott
Nether Winchendon House
Lower Winchendon
Wilstone
Woodeaton
Beckley
Little London
Oakley
Chilton
Cuddington
Stone
Southcourt
Buckland
Weston Turville
Aston Clinton
Elsfield
Easington
Chearsley
Dinton
Westlington
Stoke Mandeville
Halton
Summertown
Stanton St John
Marston
Forest Hill
Long Crendon
Townsend
Haddenham
Ford
Bishopstone
Kimble Wick
Nash Lee
Wendover
Headington
Barton
Worminghall
Aston Sandford
North Lee
Terrick
Butler's Cross
The Ridgeway Path
The Oxford Story
University
Botanic Garden
Oxford
Wheatley
Holton
Ickford
Waterperry
Waterperry Gardens
Waterstock
Shabbington
Thame
Kingsey
Owlswick
Little Kimble
Ellesborough
St Leonard's
Shotover
Horspath
Cowley
New Hinksey
Oxford Services
Tiddington
Rycote Chapel
Moreton
Towersey
Ilmer
Longwick
Meadle
Askett
Great Kimble
Dunsmore
South Hinksey
Iffley
Cuddesdon
Great Milton
Pitch Green
Monks Risborough
Little Hampden
The Lee
Kennington
Littlemore
Sandford on Thames
Denton
Garsington
Great Haseley
Tetsworth
Emmington
Henton
Manor House
Bledlow
Princes Risborough
Ballinger Common
Toot Baldon
Little Milton
Little Haseley
Sydenham
Saunderton
Great Hampden
Prestwood
Great Missenden
Radley
Nuneham Courtenay
Marsh Baldon
St Katherine's
Chislehampton
Stoke Talmage
Adwell
Postcombe
Oakley
Chinnor
Chinnor & Princes Risborough Railway
Loosley Row
Lacey Green
Speen
Kingshill
Stadhampton
South Weston
Crowell
Kingston Blount
Aston Rowant
Radnage
Bledlow Ridge
Walters Ash
Upper North Dean
Great Kingshill
Holmer Green
Abingdon
Easington
Lewknor
Bradenham
Naphill
Cryers Hill
Widmer End
Drayton St Leonard
Chalgrove
The City
Stokenchurch
Hughenden Valley
Hughenden Manor
Hazlemere
Clifton Hampden
Berinsfield
Newington
Brightwell Baldwin
Pyrton
Shirburn
Beacon's Bottom
West Wycombe
West Wycombe Caves
Downley
Culham
Burcot
Dorchester
Dorchester Abbey
Berrick Salome
Cuxham
Christmas Common
Ibstone
West Wycombe Park
Tylers Green
Pendon Mus
Long Wittenham
Watlington
The Ridgeway
Northend
Sutton Courtenay
Appleford
Little Wittenham
Shillingford
Warborough
Roke
Britwell Salome
Cadmore End
Bolter End
High Wycombe
Wycombe Marsh
Benson
Ewelme
Greenfield
Turville Heath
Turville
Fingest
Lane End
Booker
Loudwater
Didcot
Didcot Railway Centre
Brightwell-cum-Sotwell
Preston Crowmarsh
Cookley Green
Pishill
Wycombe Air Park
Flackwell Heath
Wallingford
Crowmarsh Gifford
Russell's Water
Skirmett
Frieth
Marlow Bottom
Little Marlow
Wooburn Green
East Hagbourne
North Moreton
Cholsey and Wallingford Railway
Park Corner
Stonor
Stonor
Rockwell End
Lower Woodend
Well End
West Hagbourne
South Moreton
Nuffield
Fawley
Hambleden
Bovingdon Green
Bourne End
Upton
Aston Upthorpe
Cholsey
Nettlebed
Middle Assendon
Greenlands
Marlow
Cookham Dean
Stanley Spencer
Blewbury
Aston Tirrold
North Stoke
Ipsden
Bix
Lower Assendon
Mill End
Cookham
Cookham Rise
Maharajahs Well
Highmoor Cross
Remenham
Aston
Medmenham
Bisham
Moulsford
South Stoke
Checkendon
Stoke Row
Greys Court
Satwell
Shepherd's Green
Remenham Hill
The Thames Path
Hurley
Windsor
Park Corner
Furze Platt
Woodcote
Rotherfield Greys
Henley-on-Thames
Pinkneys Grn.
Burchett's Green
Maidenhead
Streatley
Goring
Cray's Pond
Sonning Common
Rotherfield Peppard
Harpsden
River & Rowing Museum
Warren Row
Compton
Goring Heath
Cox Grn.
Bray Wick
Aldworth
Streatley on Thames
St Bartholomew's
Kidmore End
Lower Shiplake
Shiplake
Littlewick Green
Bray
Lower Basildon
Beale Park
Whitchurch Hill
Cane End
Binfield Hth.
Wargrave
White Waltham
Woodlands Park
Hampstead Norreys
The Living Rainforest
Ashampstead
Basildon Park
Whitchurch
Mapledurham
Tokers Green
Dunsden Green
Hare Hatch
Waltham St Lawrence
Holyport
Maidenhead
Quicks Green
Pangbourne
Upper Basildon
Purley
Maple-durham
Emmer Green
Sonning Eye
Sonning
Play Hatch
Charvil
Twyford
Ruscombe
Touchen End
Paley Street
Buckingham
Oxford
Windsor
Maidenhead
Chiltern Hills
SP
SU

Bletchley
Fenny Stratford
Far Bletchley
Woburn
WILD ANIMAL KINGDOM
Eversholt
Church End
WOBURN ABBEY
Tingrith
Pulloxhill
Westoning
Higham Gobion
Shillington
Apsley End
Pirton
Ickleford
Little Horwood
Newton Longville
Little Brickhill
Great Brickhill
Milton Bryan
Harlington
Sharpenhoe
Barton-le-Clay
Pegsdon
KNOCKING HOE
HITCHIN
Drayton Parslow
Stoke Hammond
KINGS WOOD
STOCKGROVE PARK
Potsgrove
Battlesden
Toddington
TODDINGTON SERVICES
SUNDON HILLS
Streatley
BARTON HILLS
Mursley
Swanbourne
North End
Soulbury
Heath and Reach
Hockliffe
Tebworth
Upper Sundon
Lower Sundon
GALLEY HILL
Lilley
Great Offley
Charlton
Gosmore
St Ippolitts
Stewkley
South End
Leighton Buzzard
Eggington
Wingfield
Chalton
Sundon Park
Limbury
Preston
Hoggeston
Dunton
SP
Burcott
Linslade
LEIGHTON BUZZARD RAILWAY
Tilsworth
Stanbridge
Houghton Regis
Luton
Stopsley
Cockernhoe Green
King's Walden
St Paul's Walden
Creslow
Wing
ASCOTT
Billington
MEAD OPEN FM.
Dunstable
Leagrave
Biscot
WARDOWN PARK MUS.
Hart Hill
Cublington
Ledburn
Lower End
Eaton Green
Totternhoe
PRIORY CHURCH OF ST PETER
Luton
LONDON LUTON
Breachwood Green
Whitwell
Whitchurch
Aston Abbotts
Slapton
Church End
Eaton Bray
Farley Hill
STOCKWOOD CRAFT MUS.
Hardwick
Mentmore
Wingrave
Horton
Edlesborough
DUNSTABLE DOWNS
Kensworth
Caddington
Peter's Green
Kimpton
Weedon
Rowsham
Ivinghoe Aston
Whipsnade
Slip End
East Hyde
Blackmore End
Ayot St Lawrence
WHIPSNADE WILD ANIMAL PARK
Kensworth Common
WOODSIDE FARM AND WILDFOWL PARK
Kinsbourne Green
Hulcott
Cheddington
Ivinghoe
IVINGHOE
Dagnall
Studham
Markyate
Batford
SHAW'S CORNER
Bierton
Long Marston
Marsworth
Pitstone Green
Pitstone
Ringshall
Jockey End
Flamstead
HARPENDEN
Marshall's Heath
Wheathampstead
Aylesbury
Puttenham
Wilstone
Tring Wharf
ASHRIDGE PARK
Little Gaddesden
Trowley Bottom
Hatching Green
Buckland
Drayton Beauchamp
New Mill
Aldbury
Great Gaddesden
Redbourn
Southcourt
Weston Turville
Aston Clinton
Tring
TOLL
Water End
Childwick Green
Sandridge
Stoke Mandeville
Halton
Wigginton
Nettleden
Piccotts End
Jersey Farm
Bishopstone
THE RIDGEWAY PATH
Hastoe
Northchurch
Potten End
BERKHAMSTED CASTLE
OLD GORHAMBURY HOUSE
Townsend
St Albans
Marshalswick
THE GALLERIA
Kimble Wick
North Lee
Nash Lee
Wendover
Berkhamsted
Gadebridge
ROMAN THEATRE OF VERULAMIUM
Fleetville
Little Kimble
Terrick
Butler's Cross
St Leonard's
Cholesbury
Bourne End
Boxmoor
St Stephens
ABBEY
The Camp
Meadle
Ellesborough
Great Kimble
Buckland Common
Ashley Green
Hemel Hempstead
Sopwell
Askett
Dunsmore
The Lee
Bellingdon
Whelpley Hill
Felden
GDNS. OF THE ROSE
Chiswell Green
London Colney
MANOR HOUSE
Monks Risborough
Lee Clump
Chartridge
Lye Green
Bovingdon
Bedmond
Princes Risborough
Little Hampden
Ballinger Common
Bovingdon Green
Primrosehill
Kings Langley
Colney Street
MOSQUITO AIRCRAFT MUS.
Great Hampden
South Heath
Botley
Leyhill
Chipperfield
Abbots Langley
Bricket Wood
Shenleybury
Shenley
Loosley Row
Great Missenden
Chesham
Flaunden
Prestwood
Hyde Heath
Radlett
Lacey Green
Little Kingshill
Chesham Bois
Latimer
Sarratt
Aldenham
Green Street
Speen
Walters Ash
Upper North Dean
Great Kingshill
Little Missenden
Chenies
CHENIES MANOR HO.
Letchmore Heath
BOREHAMWOOD
Bledlow Ridge
Bradenham
Naphill
Cryers Hill
Holmer Green
Widmer End
Amersham
Little Chalfont
Chorleywood
Watford
Croxley Green
ALDENHAM
Elstree
Hughenden Valley
HUGHENDEN MANOR
Penn Street
CHILTERN OPEN AIR MUS.
RICKMANSWORTH
Oxhey
Bushey
West Wycombe
WEST WYCOMBE CAVES
Downley
Hazlemere
Coleshill
Winchmore Hill
Chalfont St Giles
Bushey Heath
WEST WYCOMBE PARK
Tylers Green
Penn
South Oxhey
High Wycombe
Knotty Green
MILTON'S COTTAGE
RICKMANSWORTH AQUADROME
Maple Cross
Batchworth Heath
Eastbury
Stanmore
Edgware
Wycombe Marsh
Loudwater
Forty Green
BEKONSCOT MODEL VILLAGE
Seer Green
Jordans
JORDANS
Chalfont Common
Lane End
Booker
Beaconsfield
Chalfont St Peter
Northwood
Harrow Weald
WYCOMBE AIR PARK
Flackwell Heath
Harefield
Hatch End
Frieth
Marlow Bottom
Little Marlow
Wooburn Green
BAYHURST WOOD
RUISLIP WOODS
Pinner
Wealdstone
Ruislip Common
HARROW
Gerrards Cross
Denham Green
Eastcote
Greenhill
Lower Woodend
Bovingdon Green
Well End
Wooburn
ODDS FARM PARK
Hedgerley
DENHAM
Tatling End
Ruislip
Rayners Lane
Harrow on the Hill
HARROW SCH.
Hambleden
Marlow
Bourne End
Cores End
Hedsor
BURNHAM BEECHES
Fulmer
Denham
Ickenham
Wembley
Mill End
Medmenham
Bisham
Cookham Dean
Cookham
STANLEY SPENCER GALLERY
NORTHOLT
Cookham Rise
CLIVEDEN
Farnham Common
Stoke Poges
Uxbridge
Sudbury
Northolt
Alperton
Remenham Hill
Hurley
THE THAMES PATH
Windsor
Pinkneys Gm.
Burnham
Farnham Royal
Wexham Street
BLACK PARK
Iver Heath
Stoke Green
Hillingdon
Perivale
Burchett's Green
Maidenhead
Furze Platt
Taplow
George Green
LANGLEY PARK
Iver
Cowley
LONDON MOTORCYCLE MUSEUM
Yeading
Greenford
Warren Row
Slough
SLOUGH
Yiewsley
Hayes
Southall
EALING
Knowl Hill
Cox Grn.
West Drayton
Hanwell
Littlewick Green
Wargrave
Dorney
Eton Wick
Langley
Richings Park
THORNEY
OSTERLEY PARK HO.
HESTON SERVICES
Upton
Eton
WINDSOR
Harmondsworth
Harlington
Cranford
Heston
Brentford
Kew
Twyford
St Lawrence
Touchen End
Oakley Green
Datchet
WINDSOR CASTLE
Colnbrook
Poyle
Longford
Sipson
LONDON HEATHROW
HEATHROW
Isleworth
SYON HO.
KEW GDNS.
0 1 2 3 4 5 6 miles
0 1 2 3 4 5 6 7 8 9 10 km

Letchworth
Baldock
Stevenage
Knebworth
Welwyn
Welwyn Garden City
Hatfield
Hertford
Ware
Hoddesdon
Broxbourne
Cheshunt
Waltham Abbey
Potters Bar
Enfield
Barnet
Harlow
Bishop's Stortford
Stansted Mountfitchet
Stansted Airport
Sawbridgeworth
Epping
Chipping Ongar
Loughton
Chigwell
Brentwood
Romford
Hornchurch
Upminster
Dagenham
Barking
Ilford
Woodford
Walthamstow
Tottenham
Edmonton
Chingford
Southgate
Finchley
Hendon
Hornsey
Hampstead
Willesden
Camden
Islington
Hackney
Stoke Newington
Leytonstone
Leyton
Wanstead
Stratford
East Ham
West Ham
Poplar
Bethnal Green
Shoreditch
Finsbury
Holborn
City
Paddington
Kensington
Westminster
Chelsea
Hammersmith
Fulham
Battersea
Lambeth
Southwark
Bermondsey
Deptford
Greenwich
Woolwich
Erith
Purfleet
Aveley
Rainham
South Ockendon
Dartford Crossing
Blackwall Tunnel
Woolwich Ferry
Greater London
Hertford
TL
TQ
M25
M11
M1
A1(M)
A10
A414
A120
A12
A13
54
55
42
28
29

Stansted Mountfitchet
Bishop's Stortford
Stansted Airport
Thaxted
Great Dunmow
Braintree
Halstead
Coggeshall
Kelvedon
Witham
Tiptree
Maldon
Chelmsford
Great Baddow
Danbury
Chipping Ongar
Ingatestone
Brentwood
Billericay
Wickford
Hockley
Rayleigh
Rochford
Southend-on-Sea
Basildon
Laindon
Pitsea
Thundersley
Hadleigh
Leigh on Sea
Westcliff-on-Sea
South Benfleet
Canvey Island
Stanford-le-Hope
Corringham
Thurrock
Grays
Chadwell St Mary
Tilbury
Romford
Hornchurch
Upminster
Dagenham
Rainham
Aveley
South Ockendon
South Woodham Ferrers
Hullbridge
Harold Hill
Thames Estuary
Blackwater Navigation
Chelmer and Blackwater Navigation
M11
M25
A12
A120
A127
A130
A13
A414
0 1 2 3 4 5 6 miles
0 1 2 3 4 5 6 7 8 9 10 km

Bures
Nayland
Boxted
Stratford St Mary
Dedham
Brantham
Cattawade
Upper Street
Harkstead
Holbrook Bay
Shop Corner
Shotley Gate
HARWICH
NATURE RESERVE
Stour
Little Horkesley
Boxted Heath
Boxted Cross
Langham
Dedham Heath
BRIDGE COTTAGE
SIR ALFRED MUNNINGS ART MUSEUM
Lawford
MISTLEY TOWERS
Mistley
Manningtree
Bradfield
Wrabness
Parkeston
HARWICH REDOUBT
Upper Dovercourt
Dovercourt
Mount Bures
Wormingford
Great Horkesley
EAST ANGLIAN RAILWAY MUSEUM
Fordham
Horkesley Heath
West Bergholt
Mile End
Ardleigh
Bradfield Heath
Horsleycross Street
Horsley Cross
Little Bromley
Great Bromley
Wix
Little Oakley
Great Oakley
ESBJERG 20:00
HOEK VAN HOLLAND 6:00
GOTHENBURG 38:30
ROTTERDAM 8:00
Colne
Fordstreet
Aldham
Eight Ash Green
HIGHWOODS
Parson's Heath
Fox Street
Crockleford Heath
ST. BOTOLPH'S PRIORY
Colchester
Elmstead Market
Little Bentley
Tendring Green
Stone's Green
Beaumont
Horsey Island
The Naze
Marks Tey
Stanway
Lexden
Beacon End
EARTH WORKS
Abbey Field
Hare Green
Balls Green
Frating Green
Tendring
Thorpe Green
Thorpe-le-Soken
HAMFORD WATER
Kirby-le-Soken
MARITIME MUSEUM
Copford Green
Shrub End
Maypole Green
Old Heath
BOURNE MILL
Blackheath
Wivenhoe Cross
Wivenhoe
BETH CHATTO GDNS
Great Bentley
Weeley
Weeley Heath
Aingers Green
Walton-on-the-Naze
Kirby Cross
Frinton-on-Sea
Easthorpe
Hardy's Green
COLCHESTER ZOO
Heckfordbridge
Layer de la Haye
Rowhedge
Alresford
Fingringhoe
Thorrington
Row Heath
Little Clacton
CLACTON VILLAGE
Great Holland
HOLLAND HAVEN
Smythe's Green
Birch
Birch Green
Malting Green
Abberton
Abberton Reservoir
Langenhoe
Brightlingsea
St Osyth Heath
Layer Marney
Layer Breton
LAYER MARNEY TOWER
Peldon
River Colne
ST. OSYTH'S PRIORY
St Osyth
Great Clacton
Holland-on-Sea
Clacton-on-Sea
Paternoster Heath
Oxley Green
Great Wigborough
Mersea Island
East Mersea
CUDMORE GROVE
Point Clear
Salcott
COPT HALL MARSHES
Blue Row
COLNE ESTUARY
Jaywick
Tolleshunt D'Arcy
BLACKWATER ESTUARY
West Mersea
MERSEA ISLAND MUSEUM
Colne Pt.
Tolleshunt Major
The Nass
Virley Channel
Tollesbury
Goldhanger
Sales Pt.
ST. PETERS ON THE WALL
Bradwell Waterside
Blackwater
Osea I.
Bradwell on Sea
Ramsey Island
St Lawrence
TM
Tillingham
DENGIE
Steeple
Lower Mayland
Asheldham
Dengie
Mayland
Southminster
Ray Sand
Althorne
Stoneyhills
MANGAPPS RAILWAY MUS.
Montsale
Deal Hall
Ostend
Creeksea
Burnham-on-Crouch
MUS.
Foulness Sand
Foulness Pt.
TR
Crouch
Paglesham Churchend
WALLASEA WETLANDS
Courtsend
Paglesham Eastend
Churchend
Ballards Gore
Potton Island
FOULNESS ISLAND
MAPLIN SANDS
Barling
Little Wakering
Havengore Island
Great Wakering
Bournes Green
North Shoebury
Thorpe Bay
Shoeburyness
Cambridge Town
(From Dartford)
VLISINGEN 9:30
ZEEBRUGGE 9:00
A B C D E F G
5 60 6 7 62 8

PEMBROKESHIRE COAST
ARFORDIR PENFRO
Strumble Head
Pen Caer
ROSSLARE 3:30
ROSSLARE 1:50
(Apr-Sept)
Dinas Head
Tresinwen
PWLL DERI
Llanwnda
Goodwick
(Wdig)
Fishguard Bay
Bae Abergwaun
Brynhenllan
Dinas Cross
A487
Lower Town
Fishguard
(Abergwaun)
45
Trefasser
Penbwchdy
PEMBROKESHIRE COAST PATH
LLWYBR ARFORDIR PENFRO
TREGWYNT WOOLLEN MILL
Dyffryn
Manorowen
St Nicholas
A40
Llanychaer
Scleddau
Pontfaen
B4313
Ynysduellyn
Abercastle
Granston
Trecwn
Penclegyr
Porthgain
Trefin
TREFIN
Mathry
CHEESE CENTRE
Newbridge
CORSYDD LLANGLOFFAN
Abereiddy
Llanrhian
Penparc
Castlemorris
Croes-goch
B4331
Little Newcastle
Puncheston
ST. DAVID'S HEAD
PENMAEN DEWI
Treleddyd-fawr
Tretio
Carnhedryn
Treffynnon
Treglemais
Treddiog
Letterston
Castlebythe
Tufton
Whitesand Bay
Porth-mawr
ST. DAVID'S
Rhodiad
Llanreithan
Welsh Hook
St Dogwells
BISHOP'S PALACE
Caerfarchell
Llandeloy
Pont-yr-hafod
Wolf's Castle
Ambleston
Woodstock
B4329
Rhosson
CATHEDRAL
Whitchurch
Middle Mill
Trefgarn Owen
Hayscastle
Brimaston
Rinaston
Wallis
Ramsey Island
Ynys Dewi
RAMSEY ISLAND
Ramsey Sound
St David's
(Tyddewi)
Nine Wells
Solva
PENYCWM
Hayscastle Cross
Mountain Water
Treffgarne
Triffleton
LLYS-Y-FRAN RESERVOIR
Penycwm
DUDWELL MT.
Leweston
Spittal
Walton East
SCOLTON MANOR & COUNTRY PARK
Newgale
Pembrokeshire
Wolfsdale
Roch Gate
Roch
Camrose
Rudbaxton
Clarbeston Road
Keeston
(Sir Benfro)
Nolton Haven
Simpson Cross
PEMBROKE MOTOR MUSEUM
Tangiers
Leechpool
SM
Nolton
Pelcomb Cross
Crundale
Wiston
ST. BRIDES
BAY
BAE SAIN FFRAID
Druidston
Lambston
Slade
Haverfordwest
(Hwlffordd)
PEMBROKESHIRE COAST PATH
LLWYBR ARFORDIR PENFRO
Pelcomb Bridge
Portfield Gate
CASTLE MUSEUM AND ART GALLERY
The Rhos
BROAD HAVEN
Haroldston West
B4341
Dreenhill
Uzmaston
Broad Haven
B4327
Merlin's Bridge
Millin Cross
PICTON CASTLE GARDENS
Little Haven
Broadway
Pope Hill
Boulston
Minwear
Talbenny
Walton West
Landshipping
Tower Point
Trwyn Twr
Walwyn's Castle
North Johnston
Freystrop
Hook
Martletwy
St Bride's
Landshipping Quay
NATIONAL NATURE RESERVE
Wooltack Point
Trwyn Wooltack
Tiers Cross
Johnston
Skomer Island
Ynys Skomer
SKOMER ISLAND
Marloes
Hasguard
Robeston Cross
A4076
Llangwm
Black Tar
MARLOES SANDS
Rosemarket
Broad Sound
Thornton
Hill Mountain
Port Lion
LAWRENNY
Gateholm Island
Ynys Gateholm
St Ishmael's
Sandy Haven
Herbrandston
Steynton
A477
Houghton
Lawrenny
Milford Haven
(Aberdaugleddau)
Honeyborough
West Williamston
Dale
B4325
Burton
Hakin
Neyland
Skokholm Island
Ynys Skokholm
MILFORD HAVEN
ABERDAUGLEDDYF
Waterston
Llanstadwell
UPTON CASTLE GROUNDS
Cosheston
Pembroke Dock
(Doc Penfro)
TOLL
CAREW CASTLE
Milton
Angle
Angle Bay
Bae Angle
Pwllcrochan
Pennar
32
B4322
St Ann's Hd.
Pentir St. Ann
Rhoscrowther
Pembroke
(Penfro)
Sheep Island
Ynys y Defaid
Monkton
LAMPHEY BISHOP'S PALACE
ROSSLARE 3:45
B4320
Hundleton
Lamphey
Freshwater West
Maiden Wells
B4584
Hodgeston
B4319
St Twynnells
Freshwater East
Castlemartin
Warren
St Petrox
Stackpole Elidor
Chenton or East
Trewent Pt.
Trwyn Trewent
Merrion
Stackpole
Linney Hd.
Pentir Linney
ELEGUG STACKS
STACKPOLE
Bosherston
Stackpole Hd.
Pen Stackpole
The Wash
PEMBROKESHIRE COAST PATH
LLWYBR ARFORDIR PENFRO
St Govan's Hd.
Pen St Gofan
SR
0 1 2 3 4 5 6 miles
0 1 2 3 4 5 6 7 8 9 10 km

CARDIGAN
BAY
BAE
CEREDIGION
SN
Cwmtudu
Cwmtydu
Ynys-Lochtyn
Llangrannog
Blaencelyn
Pontgarreg
Penbryn
Penmorfa
Brynhoffnant
Parcllyn
Tresaith
Aberporth
Sarnau
Cardigan I.
Ynys Aberteifi
MWNT
Felinwynt
Cemaes Head
Pen Cemaes
Gwbert
Ferwig
Blaenannerch
Tan-y-groes
A487
Glynarthen
Tremain
Blaenporth
POPPIT SANDS
Cippyn
B4546
B4548
Cardigan
(Aberteifi)
CASTLE
Penparc
Bettws Ifan
Rhydlewis
Hawen
Beulah
PEMBROKESHIRE COAST
ARFORDIR PENFRO
St Dogmaels
ABBEY
Bridgend
Llangoedmor
B4570
Pantgwyn
Ponthirwaun
Bryngwyn
Brongest
Troedyraur
Maesllyn
Moylgrove
PEMBROKESHIRE COAST PATH
LLWYBR ARFORDIR PENFRO
Monington
COEDMOR
Llechryd
Llandygwydd
Capel Tygwydd
46
Croft
Pen-y-bryn
CILGERRAN CASTLE
Cilgerran
A484
Afon Teifi
Newport Bay
Dinas Head
Glanrhyd
Bridell
Carreg-wen
Cwm-cou
Llandyfriog
Aber-banc
Bae Trefdraeth
Berry Hill
Nevern
B4582
Pont-gareg
Llantood
CORACLE CENTRE & FLOUR MILL
Abercych
Cenarth
Newcastle Emlyn
(Castell Newydd Emlyn)
Pentrecagal
Fishguard Bay
Bae Abergwaun
Brynhenllan
TREFDRAETH
Parrog
Newport
(Trefdraeth)
Felindre Farchog
PENGELLI FOREST
A487
Rhos-hill
Newchapel
CLYNFYW
Aber-Arad
NATIONAL WOOLLEN MUS.
Lower Town
Dinas Cross
CASTELL HENLLYS FORT
Eglwyswrw
B4332
Cilwendeg
Penrherber
Felindre
Fishguard
(Abergwaun)
347
CARNINGLI
TY CANOL
DYFED SHIRES & LEISURE FARM
BROMEIGAN GARDENS
Llanfair-Nant-Gwyn
Boncath
CHEESE FARM
B4333
Cwmhiraeth
Llanychaer
Cilgwyn
Crosswell
Afon Nevern
Blaenffos
Bwlchygroes
Cwmcych
Capel Iwan
Pontyglasier
Eglwyswen
335
MOELFRE
44
Brynberian
Penygroes
Star
Clydey
Cwmorgan
Tanglwst
Pontfaen
395
Crymych
Tegryn
Trecwn
B4313
MYNYDD PRESELI
B4329
468
536
FOEL-CWMCERWYN
Pentre-galar
Hermon
Llanfyrnach
Hen-feddau fawr
247
B4299
Bryn-Iwan
Little Newcastle
Puncheston
New Inn
Rosebush
Mynachlog-ddu
32
Dinas
Trelech
Castlebythe
Glandwr
Afon Taf
289
0 1 2 3 4 5 6 miles
0 1 2 3 4 5 6 7 8 9 10 km
Hebron
Blaen-waun
Pen-y-bont
Blaen-y-coed
Glandy Cross
Pant-y-Caws
Llanglydwen
CHOCOLATE FARM
Cwmbach
Llanwinio
Ambleston
Woodstock
New Moat

Aberystwyth
Aberaeron
Aberarth
New Quay (Ceinewydd)
Lampeter (Llanbedr Pont Steffan)
Newcastle Emlyn (Castell Newydd Emlyn)
Ceredigion
Carmarthenshire (Sir Gaerfyrddin)
Llanrhystud
Llansantffraed
Llanon
Cross Inn
Synod Inn
Llandysul
Llanarth
Llangrannog
Aberporth
Tresaith
Penbryn
Cardigan Bay
Ynys-Lochtyn
Cwmtudu
SN
45
58
32
33
A487
A486
A485
A475
A484
B4337
B4342
B4338
B4459
B4336
B4334
B4321
B4333
B4576
B4577
B4578
B4343
B4310
B4301
B4299
Brechfa
Llanybydder
Pencader
Horeb
Henllan
Talgarreg
Mydroilyn
Llannon
0 1 2 3 4 5 6 miles
0 1 2 3 4 5 6 7 8 9 10 km

Hafren Forest
Llanidloes
Salem
Pen-bont Rhydybeddau
Dyffryn Castell
Pant Mawr
Glynbrochan
Cwmbelan
New Chapel
Capel Bangor
Dollwen
Goginan
LLYWERNOG SILVER LEAD MINE
Llanifyny
Cwmbrwyno
A44
Llangurig
Tylwch
GLYNDWR'S WAY
Llaithd
VALE OF RHEIDOL RAILWAY
Afon Rheidol
RHEIDOL HYDRO ELECTRIC STATION
Ystumtuen
Aberffrwd
COED RHEIDOL
Ysbyty-Cynfyn
David's Well
A4120
Pisgah
Llanfihangel-y-Creuddyn
Mynydd Bach
Devil's Bridge
610 PEN Y GARN
B4343
Blaenycwm
Nantgwyn
B4518
Trisant
Pant-y-dwr
493 RED LION H
Cnwch-coch
A470
Bwlch-y-sarnau
B4340
Abermagwr
New Row
B4574
Cwmystwyth
HAFOD ESTATE
Pont-rhyd-y-groes
571 GEIFAS
498
St Harmon
Wenallt
Llanafan
Ysbyty Ystwyth
Mynydd Bach
371
Wye (Gwy)
505 MOEL HYWEL
Ab
Tynygraig
Tanyrhydiau
572 TRAWSALLT
Craig-goch Res.
Ystradmeurig
CLAERWEN
WELSH ROYAL CRYSTAL
Rhayader (Rhaeadr Gwy)
Gaufron
Swydd-ffynnon
Ffair-Rhos
Pontrhydfendigaid
Penygarreg Res.
Llansantffraed Cwmdeuddwr
A44
Nantmel
STRATA FLORIDA ABBEY
Glan Teifi
Garreg-ddu Res.
Elan Village
B4518
THE GIGRIN RED KITE FEEDING CENTRE
Gwystr
530 DIBYN DU
Claerwen Reservoir
Nant-glas
CORS CARON
Llanwrthwl
digion
eredigion)
Caban-coch Res.
Argoed Mill
Llandrindod Wells (Llandrindod)
249
Ty'n-yr-eithin
Afon Claerwen
Llanyre
A470
A4081
B4343
BLAENCARON
Tywi
Powys
537 DRUM-DDU
WELSH GOLD CENTRE
Tregaron
Newbridge on Wye
Ithon
NATIONAL CYCLE COLLECT
508 Y DRUM
645 DRYGARN FAWR
Disserth
Howe
532 BRYN CRWN
Cross
Llanafan-fawr
Forest
DOLGOCH
A483
SN
Llanddewi-Brefi
Pentre-rhew
484 ESGAIR CERRIG
CORS Y LLYN
B4358
Cwmbach
TYNCORNEL
500
NANT IRFON
Pentre-llwyn-llwyd
Builth Road
463
Soar-y-Mynydd
Llyn Brianne Res.
Abergwesyn
Troed-rhiwdalar
Llanelw
484 BRYN BRAWD
Cilmery
Oakland
Beulah
456
Llanfechan
A483
Builth Wells (Llanfair-ym-Muallt)
487
Mynydd Trawsnant
Cwm Irfon
Garth
Tyn-y-graig
ALLT RHYD Y GROES
CAMBRIAN WOOLLEN MILL
Irfon
441
Llanddewi'r Cwm
Llanwrtyd
Maesmynis
Ystradffin
Alltm
440
Llanwrtyd Wells (Llanwrtud)
Llangammarch Wells
B4519
Afon Cothi
459
474 DRUM-DDU
Ffarmers
Mynydd Mallaen
Nant-y-Bai
Cefn-gorwydd
B4520
Cwrt-y-cadno
Rhandirmwyn
EPYNT
Pentre Dolau-Honddu
Gwenddwr
Mynydd
Crychan Forest
463 BRYN DU
Llandre
434 ESGAIR FERCHON
Caeo Forest
Tirabad
Cynghordy
Upper Chapel
Pumsaint
DOLAUCOTHI GOLD MINES
Cilycwm
433
341
Llanfair-ar-y-bryn
Caio
Llaneglwys
Divlyn
Porthyrhyd
456
Crugybar
B4302
A482
Siloh
Blaendyryn
Merthyr Cynog
Honddu
423
Lower Chapel
Pentre-ty-gwyn
Babel
Llandovery (Llanymddyfri)
A483
442
Mynydd Bwlch-y-groes
Llandeilo'r Fan
Llanfihangel Nant Bran
Pont-faen
Pwllgloyw
Garthbre
Cwmdwr
B4520
Halfway
Pentre-bach
Nant Bran
Sarnau
Wauncluda
Llansadwrn
Myrtle Hill
A40
Llandefaelog Fach
Llanwrda
A4069
Llywel
Llanddew
A40
Pentre'r-felin
Battle
Felindre
Cilgwyn
Usk
Trallong
BRECON GAER ROMAN FORT
CATHE
Myddfai
Aberyscir
Brecon (Aberhonddu)
Ashfield
440
Usk Reservoir
Sennybridge (Pont Senni)
Penpont
Llanfaes
Hermon
Llangadog
Trecastle
Llanspyddid
Felindre
Cwmwysg
Pont ar Hydfer
Defynnog
400
BRECKNOCK MUSEUM
Manordeilo
Mynydd Illtyd
Tai'r-Bull
A4067
Cwmifor
MOUNTAIN CENTRE
Talsarn

Rhayader
Rhaeadr Gwy
Llansantffraed Cwmdeuddwr
Welsh Royal Crystal
The Gigrin Farm Red Kite Feeding Centre
Gaufron
Nantmel
Nant-glas
Llanwrthwl
Argoed Mill
Llanyre
Llandrindod Wells
(Llandrindod)
Radnorshire Museum
Ridgebourne
National Cycle Collection
Newbridge on Wye
Disserth
Howey
Crossway
Llanafan-fawr
Pentre-llwyn-llwyd
Troed-rhiwdalar
Cwmbach
Builth Road
Cors y Llyn
Cilmery
Llanelwedd
Oaklands
Llanfaredd
Builth Wells
(Llanfair-ym-Muallt)
Llanfechan
Garth
Tyn-y-graig
Maesmynis
Llanddewi'r Cwm
Aberedw
Alltmawr
Llandeilo Graban
Erwood
Crickadarn
Gwenddwr
Upper Chapel
Llaneglwys
Merthyr Cynog
Lower Chapel
Pentre Dolau-Honddu
Blaendyryn
Llanfihangel Nant Bran
Pont-faen
Pwllgloyw
Sarnau
Garthbrengy
Talachddu
Llandefaelog Fach
Llanddew
Battle
Aberyscir
Brecon
(Aberhonddu)
Brecon Gaer Roman Fort
Cathedral
Llechfaen
Llanywern
Llanfihangel Tal-y-llyn
Talyllyn
Llannamlach
Llangors
Llangorse Lake
Llangasty Talyllyn
Mountain Centre
Bull
Llanfilo
Felinfach
Tredomen
Llandefaelog-tre'r-graig
Trefeca
Howell House
Trefeinon Open Farm
Tredustan
Talgarth
Bronllys
Llandefalle
Llyswen
Boughrood
Glasbury
Pipton
Three Cocks
Velindre
Tregoyd
Llanigon
Cusop
Llanelieu
Pengenffordd
Mynydd Troed
Black Mountains
Y Mynydd Duon
Hay Bluff
The Tumpa
Capel-y-ffin
Craswall
Llanveynoe
Longtown
Llanthony
Priory
Clodock
Offa's Dyke Path
Llwybr Clawdd Offa
Hay-on-Wye
(Y Gelli Gandryll)
Clyro
Llowes
Llanstephan
Rhydness
Cwmbach
The Begwns
Painscastle
Llanbedr
Llanbadarn-y-Garreg
Rhos-goch
Rhos Goch
Bryngwyn
Red Hill
Rhulen
Cregrina
Hundred House
Glascwm
Gwaunceste Hill
Llansantffraed-in-Elvel
Frank's Bridge
Llanfihangel-nant-Melan
Colva
Newchurch
Michaelchurch on Arrow
Dol-y-cannau
Rhydspence
Bronydd
Whitney-on-Wye
Clifford
Priory Wood
Winforton
Willersley
Merbach
Bredwardine
Letton
Gardens & Gallery
Brobury
Hardwicke
The Bage
Arthur's Stone
Dorstone
Snodhill
Peterchurch
Hinton
Llanrosser
Urishay Common
Upper Maes-coed
Michaelchurch Escley
Middle Maes-coed
Newton
Lower Maes-coed
Brilley
Millhalf
Eardisley
Kinnersley
Upcott
Ailey
Almeley
Lower Welson
Wootton
Hopley's Green
Holme Marsh
Lyonshall
Headbrook
Kington
Hergest Croft Gdns
Lower Hergest
Upper Hergest
Hergest Ridge
Oaklands Small Breeds Farm
Kingswood
Huntington
Hengoed
Gladestry
Dolyhir
Burlingjobb
Old Radnor
Walton
Stanner Rocks
Flintsham
Titley
Knill
Nash
Stansbatch
Combe
Rodd
Presteigne
(Llanandras)
Judges Lodging
Lugg
Stapleton
Discoed
Evenjobb
Beggar's Bush
Kinnerton
Maes-Treylow
Dolley Green
Norton
Whitton
Pilleth
Cascob
Radnor Forest
Llanfihangel Rhydithon
Dolau
Bleddfa
Monaughty
Rhos-y-meirch
Knighton
(Tref-y-Clawdd)
Milebrook
Stowe
Knucklas
Skyborry Green
New Invention
Purlogue
Llanfair Waterdine
Upper Treverward
Chapel Lawn
Hobarris
Churchbank
Clun
Clun Mill
Clunton
Castle
Llwyn
Bicton
Whitcott Keysett
Newcastle
Hall of the Forest
Lower Down
Anchor
Black Mt
Bettws-y-crwyn
Quabbs
Felindre
Beguildy
Dutlas
Black Mountain
Glyndwr's Way
Beacon Hill
Crug
Llangunllo
Llanbister
Llanbadarn Fynydd
Rhyd-moel-ddu
Red Lion Hill
David's Well
Cilfaesty Hill
New Chapel
Tylwch
Nantgwyn
Pant-y-dwr
Bwlch-y-sarnau
St Harmon
Moel Hywel
Abbey-cwm-hir
Llandewi Ystradenny
Fron
Crossgates
Gwystre
Penybont
Llandegley
New Radnor
Yardro
Drum-ddu
Powys
Herefordshire
SO
Wye
Irfon
Ithon
Honddu
Usk
Teme
Redlake
Arrow
Lower Maes-coed
0 1 2 3 4 5 6 miles
0 1 2 3 4 5 6 7 8 9 10 km

Herefordshire
SO
Craven Arms
Ludlow
Leominster
Hereford
Tenbury Wells
Bromyard
Ledbury
Stokesay
Stokesay Castle
Clunbury
Clungunford
Bromfield
Ludlow
Middleton
Henley
Bitterley
Cleobury Mortimer
Wyre Forest
Far Forest
Callow Hill
Bliss Gate
Leintwardine
Downton on the Rock
Burrington
Wigmore
Ashford Carbonell
Ashford Bowdler
Richards Castle
Woofferton
Little Hereford
Burford
Burford House & Meadow Gallery
Brimfield
Orleton
Croft Castle
Yarpole
Lucton
Water Mill and Battle Centre
Mortimer's Cross
Kingsland
Eye
Berrington Hall
Kimbolton
Pudleston
Hatfield
Collington
Shobdon
Pembridge
Eardisland
Burton Court
Monkland
Dunkertons Cider
Luntley
Dilwyn
Weobley
Marlbrook
Hope under Dinmore
Bodenham
Hampton Court
Queenswood
Working Dairy Farm
Sutton St Nicholas
Marden
Withington
Shucknall
Kenchester
Kenchester Water Gardens
Credenhill
Swainshill
The Weir
Cider Museum
Rotherwas
Hampton Bishop
Mordiford
Holme Lacy
Fownhope
Bolstone
Brockhampton
Court Gardens
Ballingham
Much Marcle
Hellens Mansion
Dymock
St Mary's Church
Kempley
Madley
Kingstone
Much Dewchurch
Kilpeck
Kilpeck Castle (Rems) & Church
Abbey Dore
Abbey Dore Court
Wormbridge
Pontrilas
Ewyas Harold
Rowlestone
Golden Valley
Vowchurch
Bredwardine
The Flits
Moccas
Bridge Sollers
Byford
Mansell Lacy
Tillington
Wellington
Canon Pyon
King's Pyon
Burghill
Stretton Sugwas
Lugwardine
Bartestree
Dormington
Stoke Lacy
Much Cowarne
Bishops Frome
Fromes Hill
Castle Frome
Canon Frome
Stretton Grandison
Yarkhill
Tarrington
Newtown
Ashperton
Trumpet
Pixley
Aylton
Putley
Little Marcle
Woolhope
Sollers Hope
Ledbury
Eastnor
Eastnor Castle
Hollybush
Bosbury
Colwall
Wellington Heath
Bradlow
Cradley
Stifford's Bridge
West Malvern
Mathon
Suckley
Acton Beauchamp
Stanford Bishop
Whitbourne
Brockhampton Estate
Heritage Centre
Tedstone Wafre
Tedstone Delamere
Edvin Loach
Clifton upon Teme
Shelsley Beauchamp
Stanford on Teme
Stockton on Teme
Eardiston
Lindridge
Newnham Bridge
Kyre Magna
Stoke Bliss
Rays Farm Country Matters
Kinlet
Buttonoak
Howle Hill
Ross Spur Services
Hole-in-the-Wall
Upton Bishop
Gorsley
A49
A44
A456
A4112
A4110
A417
A438
A4103
A465
A466
A449
A4172
A4117
A443
A4113
M50
B4368
B4367
B4365
B4364
B4361
B4362
B4360
B4529
B4214
B4204
B4203
B4220
B4216
B4215
B4224
B4399
B4348
B4349
B4352
B4230
B4457
B4385
B4202
B4197
B4221
B4024
60
61
50
35
36
Teme
Lugg
Arrow
Wye
Frome
Rea
Leadon
Corve

Worcestershire
Stourbridge
HALESOWEN
Kidderminster
Bewdley
Stourport on Severn
Bromsgrove
Redditch
Droitwich Spa
Worcester
Great Malvern
Malvern Link
West Malvern
Ledbury
Upton upon Severn
Tewkesbury
Pershore
Evesham
Bromyard
Bishop's Cleeve
Kinver
Wyre Forest
Abberley Hill
Teme
Severn
Avon
MALVERN HILLS
VALE
SO
M5
M50
A449
A456
A44
A38
A4103
A417
A46
A422
A441
A448
A4440
Catshill
Longbridge
Northfield
Hagley
Blakedown
Wolverley
Stone
Chaddesley Corbett
Hartlebury
Ombersley
Fernhill Heath
Claines
Warndon
St John's
Powick
Kempsey
Callow End
Madresfield
Colwall
Welland
Broadwas
Leigh
Alfrick
Knightwick
Martley
Tenbury
Eckington
Bredon
Twyning
Ripple
Longdon
Inkberrow
Feckenham
Hanbury
Fladbury
Cropthorne
Ashton under Hill
Beckford
Winchcombe
Gotherington
Stoke Orchard
Deerhurst
Tredington
Ashchurch
Northway
Bredon's Norton
Much Marcle
Dymock
Kempley
Redmarley D'Abitot
Staunton
Corse
Hasfield
Ashleworth
0 1 2 3 4 5 6 miles
0 1 2 3 4 5 6 7 8 9 10km
61
62
49
36
37

Warwick
Coventry
Solihull
Royal Leamington Spa
Warwick
Stratford-upon-Avon
Banbury
Kenilworth
Shirley
Olton
Dorridge
Henley-in-Arden
Studley
Alcester
Southam
Shipston-on-Stour
Moreton-in-Marsh
Chipping Norton
Stow-on-the-Wold
Broadway
Chipping Campden
Cubbington
Ryton-on-Dunsmore
Hampton in Arden
Meriden
Balsall Common
Knowle
Hockley Heath
Lapworth
Wootton Wawen
Snitterfield
Wellesbourne
Kineton
Gaydon
Harbury
Bishop's Itchington
Ettington
Halford
Tredington
Long Compton
Mickleton
Bidford-on-Avon
Welford-on-Avon
Ilmington
Blockley
Bourton on the Hill
Evenlode
Chastleton
Great Rollright
Hook Norton
Bloxham
Adderbury
Fenny Compton
Farnborough
Cropredy
Wroxton
Drayton
Long Itchington
Napton on the Hill
Stretton-on-Dunsmore
Wolston
Binley
Tile Hill
Earlsdon
Stivichall
Willenhall
Baginton
Stoneleigh
Ashow
Leek Wootton
Hatton
Budbrooke
Claverdon
Wolverton
Sherbourne
Barford
Bishop's Tachbrook
Radford Semele
Whitnash
Ufton
Chesterton
Moreton Morrell
Lighthorne
Ashorne
Newbold Pacey
Hampton Lucy
Charlecote
Loxley
Walton
Combrook
Butlers Marston
Pillerton Hersey
Pillerton Priors
Oxhill
Lower Tysoe
Middle Tysoe
Upper Tysoe
Whatcote
Idlicote
Honington
Barcheston
Willington
Burmington
Cherington
Stourton
Whichford
Ascott
Sibford Gower
Sibford Ferris
Swalcliffe
Tadmarton
Broughton
Shutford
Epwell
Winderton
Upper Brailes
Lower Brailes
Sutton under Brailes
Todenham
Little Wolford
Great Wolford
Barton on the Heath
Little Compton
Salford
Over Norton
Little Tew
Great Tew
Swerford
Wigginton
South Newington
Milcombe
Nether Worton
Over Worton
Duns Tew
Heythrop
Sandford St Martin
Westcott Barton
Middle Barton
Cornwell
Adlestrop
Daylesford
Oddington
Broadwell
Donnington
Longborough
Condicote
Temple Guiting
Kineton
Lower Swell
Upper Swell
Farmcote
Ford
Cutsdean
Didbrook
Stanway
Stanton
Snowshill
Laverton
Buckland
Childswickham
Willersey
Saintbury
Weston-Sub-Edge
Aston Subedge
Hidcote Boyce
Ebrington
Charingworth
Paxford
Broad Campden
Aston Magna
Draycott
Batsford
Sezincote
Stretton-on-Fosse
Tidmington
Darlingscott
Blackwell
Armscote
Newbold on Stour
Admington
Upper Quinton
Lower Quinton
Preston on Stour
Alderminster
Atherstone on Stour
Clifford Chambers
Ailstone
Wimpstone
Long Marston
Dorsington
Pebworth
Broad Marston
Honeybourne
Bretforton
Badsey
Wickhamford
Aldington
South Littleton
Middle Littleton
North Littleton
Offenham
Cleeve Prior
Harvington
Marlcliff
Barton
Salford Priors
Abbots Salford
Broom
Iron Cross
Dunnington
Weethley Gate
Arrow
Exhall
Wixford
Ardens Grafton
Temple Grafton
Binton
Shottery
Luddington
Billesley
Haselor
Walcote
Wilmcote
Bishopton
Ingon
Alveston
Tiddington
Wasperton
Aston Cantlow
Great Alne
Little Alne
Shelfield
Bearley
Langley
Edstone
Norton Lindsey
Preston Bagot
Ullenhall
Oldberrow
Mappleborough Green
Morton Bagot
Sambourne
Coughton
King's Coughton
New End
Cookhill
Ipsley
Gorcott Hill
Holt End
Beoley
Tanworth-in-Arden
Wood End
Branson's Cross
Portway
Earlswood
Wythall
Monkspath
Whitlock's End
Drakes Cross
Hollywood
King's Norton
Cotteridge
Sparkhill
Moseley
Springfield
King's Heath
Hall Green
Elmdon
Bickenhill
Elmdon Heath
Eastcote
Copt Heath
Barston
Temple Balsall
Balsall
Fen End
Catchems Corner
Burton Green
Crackley
Meer End
Honiley
Beausale
Wroxall
Chadwick End
Baddesley Clinton
Kingswood
Rowington
Lowsonford
Shrewley Common
Haseley
Kemps Green
Bentley Heath
Berkswell
Four Oaks
Eastern Green
Allesley
Coundon
Keresley
Hawkes End
Whoberley
Pinley
Brinklow
King's Newnham
Church Lawford
Bretford
Brandon
Binley Woods
Stretton under Fosse
Ansty
Shilton
Barnacle
Longford
Little Heath
Foleshill
Walsgrave on Sowe
Wyken
Tollbar End
Bubbenhall
Stareton
Weston under Wetherley
Wappenbury
Eathorpe
Princethorpe
Frankton
Marton
Draycote
Bourton on Dunsmore
Birdingbury
Leamington Hastings
Hunningham
Lillington
Old Milverton
Milverton
Offchurch
Bascote
Stockton
Ladbroke
Chapel Green
Marston Doles
Priors Hardwick
Knightcote
Northend
Temple Herdewyke
Burton Dassett
Avon Dassett
Claydon
Mollington
Warmington
Ratley
Radway
Little Kineton
Shotteswell
Hornton
Horley
Hanwell
Alkerton
Shenington
Balscott
Neithrop
Grimsbury
North Newington
Easington
Bodicote
West Adderbury
Milton
Barford St John
Barford St Michael
Hempton
Whitnash
Longbridge
Hampton on the Hill
Heath End
Norton Lindsey
Hatton
Edge Hill
E V E S H A M
O F
Avon
Stour
Grand Union Canal
Oxford Canal
SP
M42
M40
M6
M45
A45
A46
A429
A422
A3400
A44
A435
A34
A41
A423
A4177
A452
A425
A426
A428
A361
A424
A436
B4035
B4086
B4100
B4455
B4632

Coventry
Rugby
Daventry
Southam
Banbury
Brackley
Towcester
Buckingham
Middleton Cheney
Northa
SP
Barnacle
Shilton
Withybrook
Cross in Hand
Misterton
Husbands Bosworth
Ansty
Monks Kirby
Walcote
North Kilworth
Sibbertoft
Clipston
Pailton
South Kilworth
Sulby Reservoir
Binley
Brinklow
Churchover
Gibbet Hill
Welford
Naseby Field
Kelmarsh
Binley Woods
Easenhall
Harborough Magna
Swinford
Stanford on Avon
Naseby Reservoir
Bretford
King's Newnham
Newbold on Avon
Newton
Catthorpe
Naseby
Haselbech
Brandon
Church Lawford
Long Lawford
Lilbourne
Clay Coton
Cold Ashby
Thornby
Maidwell
Wolston
Clifton upon Dunsmore
Yelvertoft
Ryton-on-Dunsmore
Bilton
Hillmorton
Winwick
Cottesbrooke
Bubbenhall
Stretton-on-Dunsmore
Guilsborough
Creaton
Princethorpe
Bourton on Dunsmore
Dunchurch
Kilsby
Crick
West Haddon
Coton
Hollowell
Thurlaston
Barby
Ravensthorpe
Teeton
Brixworth
Weston under Wetherley
Wappenbury
Frankton
Draycote
Draycote Water
Ashby St Ledgers
Watford
Spratton
Cubbington
Eathorpe
Marton
Birdingbury
Kites Hardwick
East Haddon
Hunningham
Woolscott
Holdenby
Leamington Hastings
Willoughby
Long Buckby
Chapel Brampton
Grandborough
Braunston
Welton
Church Brampton
Offchurch
Broadwell
Sawbridge
Great Brington
Harlestone
Long Itchington
Nethercote
Whilton
Little Brington
Stockton
Norton
Bascote
Flecknoe
Brockhall
Queen's Park
Lower Shuckburgh
Nobottle
New Duston
Ufton
Napton on the Hill
Staverton
Harpole
Dallington
Dodford
Flore
Duston
Harbury
Chapel Green
Upper Catesby
Newnham
Upper Weedon
Upper Heyford
Upton
Chesterton
Ladbroke
Badby
Weedon Bec
Kislingbury
Nether Heyford
Marston Doles
Hellidon
Church Stowe
Bugbrooke
Cross Green
Bishop's Itchington
Priors Marston
Everdon
Upper Stowe
Rothersthorpe
Priors Hardwick
Charwelton
Farthingstone
Gayton
Lighthorne
Gaydon
Knightcote
Preston Capes
Litchborough
Grimscote
Pattishall
Eastcote
Milton Malsor
Wormleighton
Upper Boddington
Byfield
Cold Higham
Astcote
Blisworth
Northend
Temple Herdewyke
Fenny Compton
Lower Boddington
Hinton
Woodford Halse
Maidford
Tiffield
Caldecote
Kineton
Burton Dassett
Adstone
Duncote
Little Kineton
Claydon
Aston le Walls
Eydon
Canons Ashby
Blakesley
Shutlanger
Stoke Bruerne
Radway
Avon Dassett
Farnborough
Moreton Pinkney
Woodend
Greens Norton
Chipping Warden
Woodend Green
Bradden
Warmington
Mollington
Weston
Ratley
Edge Hill
Culworth
Slapton
Alderton
Cropredy
Wardington
Weedon Lois
Abthorpe
Shotteswell
Upper Wardington
Sulgrave
Wappenham
Pury End
Hornton
Great Bourton
Williamscott
Paulerspury
Middle Tysoe
Horley
Thorpe Mandeville
Helmdon
Silverstone
Whittlebury
Alkerton
Hanwell
Chacombe
Marston St Lawrence
Shenington
Wroxton
Drayton
Grimsbury
Greatworth
Syresham
Whittlewood Forest
Balscott
Neithrop
Thenford
Crowfield
Epwell
Overthorpe
Halse
Radstone
Lillingstone Dayrell
Lillingstone Lovell
Shutford
Warkworth
Biddlesden
North Newington
Easington
Farthinghoe
Whitfield
Wicken
Sibford Gower
Tadmarton
Broughton
Turweston
Dadford
Akeley
Leckhampstead
Swalcliffe
Bodicote
Upper Astrop
Newbottle
Shalstone
Sibford Ferris
Sor Brook
Astrop
Hinton-in-the-Hedges
Buffler's Holt
Chackmore
Bloxham
West Adderbury
King's Sutton
Charlton
Westbury
Maids Moreton
Milcombe
Milton
East Adderbury
Evenley
Great Ouse
Water Stratford
Radclive
Thornborough
Barford St John
Croughton
Mixbury
Finmere
Hook Norton
Wigginton
South Newington
Barford St Michael
Aynho
Tingewick
Gawcott
Clifton
Swerford
Hempton
Deddington
Souldern
Cottisford
Barton Hartshorn
Padbury
Adstock
Nether Worton
Newton Purcell
Preston Bissett
Great Tew
Over Worton
Duns Tew
North Aston
Fritwell
Baynard's Green
Hardwick
Hethe
Addington
Middle Aston
Somerton
Fewcott
Stoke Lyne
Fringford
Hillesden
Upper Heyford
Ardley
Twyford
Steeple Claydon
Westcott Barton
Middle Barton
Steeple Aston
Bucknell
Stratton Audley
East Claydon
Middle Claydon
Grand Union Canal
Oxford Canal
Boddington Reservoir
Daventry Reservoir
Stanford Reservoir
Cherwell
Nene
Itchen
Leam
Avon
Swift
M1
M6
M40
M45
A5
A14
A43
A45
A46
A361
A413
A421
A422
A423
A425
A426
A428
A4071
A4303
A4500
A5123
A5199
B4027
B4031
B4100
B4525
COOMBE ABBEY
STANFORD HALL
RYTON ORGANIC GARDENS
RYTON POOLS
DRAYCOTE WATER
COTON MANOR
HOLDENBY HOUSE AND FALCONRY CENTRE
ALTHORP
COTTESBROOKE HALL AND GDNS
WATFORD GAP SERVICES
DAVENTRY
CHESTERTON WINDMILL
WARWICK SERVICES
OLD DAIRY FARM CRAFT CENTRE
NORTHAMPTON SERVICES
HUNSBURY HILL
BURTON DASSETT HILLS
GRANARY MUSEUM OF BYGONES
CANONS ASHBY HOUSE
FARNBOROUGH HALL
CATANGER LLAMA TREKKING
SULGRAVE MANOR
TOWCESTER
STOKE PARK PAVILIONS
THE CANAL MUSEUM
SILVERSTONE
SWALCLIFFE BARN
BROUGHTON CASTLE
STOWE SCHOOL AND GARDENS
CHERWELL VALLEY SERVICES
51
63
64
38
39
0 1 2 3 4 5 6 miles
0 1 2 3 4 5 6 7 8 9 10 km

Braybrooke
Desborough
Rushton
Rothwell
Arthingworth
Harrington
Weekley
Newton
Geddington
Kettering
Orton
Loddington
Thorpe Malsor
Barton Seagrave
Cranford St Andrew
Cranford St John
Warkton
Grafton Underwood
Sudborough
Lowick
Slipton
Twywell
Aldwincle
Wadenhoe
Achurch
Islip
Thrapston
Titchmarsh
Thorpe Waterville
Barnwell All Saints
Wigsthorpe
Luddington in the Brook
Thurning
Clopton
Winwick
Great Gidding
Little Gidding
Steeple Gidding
Hamerton
Coppingford
Old Weston
Buckworth
Brington
Molesworth
Bythorn
Keyston
Leighton Bromswold
Barham
Catworth
Spaldwick
Easton
Stow Longa
Covington
Hargrave
Tilbrook
Kimbolton
Grafham Water
West Perry
Draughton
Great Cransley
Mawsley
Broughton
Pytchley
Isham
Burton Latimer
Great Addington
Little Addington
Woodford
Denford
Ringstead
Raunds
Lamport
Old
Scaldwell
Walgrave
Orlingbury
Finedon
Hannington
Little Harrowden
Great Harrowden
Irthlingborough
Stanwick
Chelveston
Caldecott
Holcot
Hardwick
Higham Ferrers
Pitsford Reservoir
Pitsford
Sywell
Wellingborough
Mears Ashby
Wilby
Little Irchester
Rushden
Knuston
Newton Bromswold
Shelton
Lower Dean
Upper Dean
Yelden
Swineshead
Melchbourne
Pertenhall
Moulton
Overstone
Sywell Reservoir
Irchester
Little Wymington
Wymington
Farndish
Boughton
Boothville
Kingsthorpe
Kingsley Park
Weston Favell
Ecton
Earls Barton
New Barton
Great Doddington
Podington
Knotting
Knotting Green
Riseley
Brook End
Keysoe
Little Staughton
Great Staughton
Hail Weston
Great Billing
Little Billing
Wollaston
Souldrop
Santa Pod
Hinwick
Strixton
Northampton
Cogenhoe
Little Houghton
Whiston
Grendon
Brafield-on-the-Green
Castle Ashby
Easton Maudit
Bozeat
Sharnbrook
Bletsoe
Keysoe Row
Bolnhurst
Staploe
Great Houghton
Hardingstone
Denton
Yardley Hastings
Odell
Harrold
Felmersham
Radwell
Thurleigh
Rootham's Green
Colmworth
Wootton
Collingtree
Hackleton
Yardley Chase
Chellington
Carlton
Pavenham
Milton Ernest
Duck's Cross
Colesden
Chawston
Quinton
Piddington
Horton
Warrington
Lavendon
West End
Stevington
Oakley
Clapham
Wilden
Ravensden
Roxton
Courteenhall
Salcey Forest
Cold Brayfield
Turvey
Bromham
Renhold
Salph End
Great Barford
Blunham
Roade
Eakley Lanes
Weston Underwood
Olney
Clifton Reynes
Newton Blossomville
Bedford
Goldington
Willington
Hartwell
Ravenstone
Emberton
Box End
Biddenham
Great Denham
Queen's Park
Kempston
Fenlake
Cople
Moggerhanger
Hatch
Ashton
Stoke Goldington
Filgrave
Tyringham
Stagsden
Cardington
Shortstown
Thorncote Green
Northill
Long Street
Milton Keynes
Hardmead
Astwood
Elstow
Grafton Regis
Hanslope
Tathall End
Gayhurst
Sherington
Chicheley
North Crawley
Keeley Green
Cotton End
Ickwell Green
Castlethorpe
Lathbury
Bourne End
Wootton
Kempston Hardwick
Littleworth
Yardley Gobion
Potterspury
Haversham
Newport Pagnell
Upper Shelton
Lower Shelton
Stewartby
Wilstead
Haynes
Old Warden
Southill
Cosgrove
Great Linford
Broad Green
Cranfield
Houghton Conquest
Haynes Church End
Old Stratford
Stony Stratford
Wolverton
New Bradwell
Willen
Moulsoe
Marston Moretaine
How End
Shefford
Passenham
Bradwell
Broughton
Salford
Ampthill
Maulden
Clophill
Beadlow
Calverton
Woolstone
Milton Keynes Village
Lidlington
Millbrook
Upper Weald
Loughton
Woughton on the Green
Brogborough
Campton
Beachampton
Shenley Church End
Simpson
Walton
Wavendon
Aspley Guise
Ridgmont
Denel End
Flitton
Upper Gravenhurst
Meppershall
Thornton
Shenley Brook End
Woburn Sands
Bow Brickhill
Aspley Heath
Husborne Crawley
Steppingley
Flitwick
Silsoe
Upper Stondon
Whaddon
Bletchley
Fenny Stratford
Woburn
Eversholt
Pulloxhill
Greenfield
Shillington
Nash
Tattenhoe
Far Bletchley
Church End
Westoning
Higham Gobion
Holwell
Singleborough
Little Brickhill
Tingrith
Apsley End
Great Horwood
Little Horwood
Newton Longville
Great Brickhill
Milton Bryan
Harlington
Barton-le-Clay
Pirton
Sharpenhoe
Hexton
Pegsdon
Drayton Parslow
Stoke Hammond
Potsgrove
Battlesden
Toddington
Streatley
Mursley
Winslow
Swanbourne
Heath and Reach
Tebworth
Upper Sundon
Lower Sundon
Lilley
Great Offley
Leighton Buzzard
Hockliffe
Wingfield
Chalton
Stewkley
Soulbury
Eggington
Sundon
Ouse
Great Ouse
Tove
Whaddon Chase
Til
SP
TL
A
B
C
D
E
F
G
A6003
A43
A6116
A605
A6
A14
A509
A510
A45
A43
A4500
A428
A508
A5
A421
A422
A4146
A507
A6
A603
A600
A5120
A4012
M1
B576
B662
B660
B663
B645
B574
B571
B5388
B565
B526
B4034
B4033
B530
B579
B4032
B655
A505
64
65
54
39
40
RUSHTON TRIANGULAR LODGE
ELEANOR CROSS
BOUGHTON HOUSE
FERMYN WOODS
HAMERTON ZOO PARK
WICKSTEED PARK
LAMPORT HALL
BRIXWORTH
CHICHELE COLLEGE
HERITAGE CENTRE
IRCHESTER
NARROW GAUGE RAILWAY MUS
SYWELL
BILLING AQUADROME
CASTLE ASHBY GARDENS
HARROLD-ODELL
GLENN MILLER MUSEUM
BODYFLIGHT
STEVINGTON WINDMILL
BROMHAM MILL
CECIL HIGGINS ART GALLERY AND MUS
PRIORY
BUSHMEAD PRIORY
MOGGERHANGER PARK
ELSTOW MOOT HALL
CHICHELEY HALL
GULLIVERS LAND
NEWPORT PAGNELL SERVICES
STEWARTBY LAKE
ENGLISH SCHOOL OF FALCONRY
MARSTON VALE MILLENNIUM
HOUGHTON HOUSE
ST LAWRENCE'S
BRADWELL VILLAGE
NATIONAL HOCKEY
DE GREY MAUSOLEUM
WREST PARK HOUSE
BLETCHLEY PARK
WOBURN
WILD ANIMAL KINGDOM
WOBURN ABBEY
KINGS WOOD
STOCKGROVE PARK
TODDINGTON SERVICES
SUNDON HILLS
BARTON HILLS
KNOCKING HOE
WINSLOW HALL
GALLEY HILL
P&R

Cambridge
Huntingdon
St Ives
St Neots
Eynesbury
Godmanchester
Brampton
Cambourne
Bedford
Kempston
Sandy
Biggleswade
Shefford
Stotfold
Baldock
LETCHWORTH
HITCHIN
Royston
Buntingford
Sawtry
Grafham Water
Great Ouse
Cottenham
Histon
Ampthill
Flitwick
Clophill
Barton-le-Clay
WIMPOLE HALL AND HOME FARM
SHUTTLEWORTH COLLECTION
THE SWISS GARDEN
HINCHINGBROOKE
CROMWELL MUS
HOUGHTON MILL
ROYSTON & DISTRICT MUS
WOOD GREEN ANIMAL SHELTER
SHEPRETH WILDLIFE PARK
BUSHMEAD PRIORY
HAMERTON ZOO PARK
CAMBRIDGE SERVICES
BALDOCK SERVICES
TL
0 1 2 3 4 5 6 miles
0 1 2 3 4 5 6 7 8 9 10km

Little Downham
Chettisham
West Fen
Shippea Hill Sta.
Prickwillow
Lakenheath
Wangford Warren
Thetford Warren
Brandon Park
Coveney
Witcham
Ely
Oliver Cromwell's House
Queen Adelaide
Kenny Hill
Lakenheath Warren
Elveden
East of England Tank Museum
Thetford Heath
Wentworth
Witchford
Middle Fen
Stuntney
Great Fen
Mildenhall Fen
Eriswell
Little Thetford
Broad Hill
Holywell Row
Beck Row
North Hill
Haddenham
Barway
Isleham Fen
Thistley Green
West Row
The King's Forest
Wilburton
Stretham
Soham Cotes
Windmill
Isleham
Priory Church
Mildenhall
Worlington
Soham
Soham Mere
Barton Mills
Icklingham
Freckenham
Cavenham Heath
Down Field Windmill
Tuddenham
West Stow
Ingham
Fordham
Wicken
Wicken Corn Mill
Wicken Fen
Chittering
Upware
New River
Chippenham
Red Lodge
Herringswell
Lackford
Culford
Cavenham
Flempton
Chippenham Fen
Hengrave
Hengrave Hall
Fornham All Saints
River Bank
Adventures Fen
Landwade
Kennett
Farmland Mus. & Denny Abbey
Snailwell
Reach
Burwell
Kentford
Higham
Risby
Waterbeach
Exning
Landbeach
Moulton
Packhorse Bridge
Westley
Little Saxham
Bury St Edmunds
Cathedral and Abbey Ruins
Swaffham Prior
Commercial End
Newmarket
Newmarket Heath
National Horseracing Museum
Gazeley
Barrow
Great Saxham
Milton
Lode Mill
Lode
Horningsea
National Stud
Dalham
Denham
Horringer
Ickworth House
Anglesey Abbey
Swaffham Bulbeck
Stow cum Quy
Cheveley
Ashley
Kings Hedges
Bottisham
Dunstall Green
Hargrave
Fen Ditton
Mus. of Technology
Chevington
Hawstead
Cambridge
Romsey Town
Teversham
Little Wilbraham
Saxon Street
Ousden
Whepstead
Fitzwilliam Mus.
Great Wilbraham
Stetchworth
Woodditton
Lidgate
Depden Green
Rede Hall
Ditton Green
Upend
Dullingham
Depden
Chedburgh
Cherry Hinton
Six Mile Bottom
Fulbourn
Westley Waterless
Kirtling
Kirtling Green
Rede
Burrough Green
Thorns
Trumpington
Wickhambrook
Clopton Green
Brockley Green
Brinkley
Cowlinge
Great Shelford
Wandlebury
Weston Colville
Great Bradley
Wickham Street
Hawkedon
Carlton
Denston
Stapleford
Weston Green
Stansfield
Hartest
Little Bradley
Stradishall
TL
Little Shelford
Granta
West Wratting
Little Thurlow
Boxted
Shimpling
Babraham
Balsham
Great Thurlow
Stanstead
Fourwentways Services
Little Abington
Sawston
West Wickham
Barnardiston
Great Abington
Great Wratting
Hundon
Poslingford
Glemsford
Whittlesford
Hildersham
Streetly End
Duxford Chapel
Pampisford
Horseheath
Withersfield
Cavendish
High Street
Sue Ryder Foundation Mus.
Linton
Little Wratting
Kedington
Chilton Street
Pentlow
Long Melford
Linton Zoo
Duxford
Bartlow
Haverhill
Boyton End
Clare
Duxford Airfield (Imperial War Museum) American Air Mus.
Hinxton
Shudy Camps
Clare Castle
Foxearth
Clare Ancient House
Stoke by Clare
Ickleton
Stump Cross
Hadstock
Castle Camps
Sturmer
Wixoe
Belchamp St Paul
Borley
Great Chesterford
Baythorn End
Little Chesterford
Ashdon
Ashen
Ovington
Helions Bumpstead
Birdbrook
Belchamp Otten
Ballingdon
Steeple Bumpstead
Church End
Ridgewell
Tilbury Juxta Clare
Belchamp Walter
Bulmer
Little Walden
Strethall
Littlebury
Little Yeldham
Elmdon
Saffron Walden
Stambourne
Bulmer Tye
Sewards End
Gestingthorpe
Saffron Walden
Audley End
Great Yeldham
Henny
Littlebury Green
Radwinter
Stambourne Green
Toppesfield
Bridge Green
Hempstead
Audley End
Great Henny
Wendens Ambo
Colne Valley Railway
Hedingham Castle
Duddenhoe End
Wimbish
Cornish Hall End
Wickham St Paul
Tye Green
Great Sampford
Gainsford End
Castle Hedingham
Twinstead Green
Highstreet Green
Arkesden
Wimbish Green
Great Maplestead
Alphamstone
Little Sampford
Sible Hedingham
Newport
Howlett End
Howe Street
Little Maplestead
Morris Green
Debden
Finchingfield
Clavering
Wicken Bonhunt
Priors Hall Barn
Debden Cross
Pant
Pebmarsh
Rickling
Widdington
Mole Hall Wildlife Park
Wethersfield
Starlings Green
Little Bardfield
Thaxted
Halstead
Quendon
Hamperden End
Cutlers Green
Blackmore End
Berden
Great Bardfield
Gosfield
Colne
Stort
St. Mary's Church
Shalford
Stocking Pelham
Ugley
Henham
Monk Street
Church End
Beazley End
Earls Colne
Glendale Forge
East End
Lindsell
Shalford Green
Greenstead Green
Ugley Green
House on the Hill Toy Mus.
Duton Hill
Jasper's Green
Bocking Churchstreet
Manuden
Broxted
Bardfield Saling
High Garrett
Farnham
Elsenham
Molehill Green
Brick End
Great Easton
Sible Hedingham

Thetford
Thetford Warren
Wangford Warren
Lakenheath Warren
Brandon Park
Warren Lodge
Ancient House Mus.
Brettenham
Shadwell
Rushford
Gasthorpe
Kenninghall Heath
North Lopham
South Lopham
Fersfield
Shelfanger
Mill Green
Walcot Green
Roydon
Diss
Bressingham
Bressingham Steam Museum and Gardens
Garboldisham
Blo' Norton
Thelnetham Windmill
Thelnetham
Redgrave
Wortham
Magpie Green
Palgrave
Stuston
Knettishall
Knettishall Heath
Coney Weston
Hopton
Market Weston
Hinderclay
Thrandeston
Brome
Euston
Euston Hall
Barnham
Elveden
Thetford Heath
East of England Tank Museum
Fakenham Magna
Barningham
Sapiston
Honington
Hepworth
Botesdale
Rickinghall
Burgate
Mellis
Langton Green
Yaxley
Eye
The King's Forest
Icklingham
Cavenham Heath
Tuddenham
West Stow
Ingham
Bardwell
Ixworth Thorpe
Troston
Stanton
Upthorpe
Wattisfield
Allwood Green
Walsham le Willows
Cranmer Green
Gislingham
Thornham Parva
Thornham Magna
Braiseworth
Ampton
Great Livermere
Ixworth
Abbey (Rem.)
Langham
Four Ashes
Wickham Street
Stoke Ash
Lackford
Culford
Flempton
Cavenham
Timworth Green
Conyers Green
Badwell Ash
Crownland
Long Thurlow
Westhorpe
Finningham
Wickham Skeith
Thorndon
Hengrave
Hengrave Hall
Fornham All Saints
Fornham St Martin
Stowlangtoft
Hunston
Great Ashfield
Wyverstone
Wyverstone Street
Bacton
Cotton
Thwaite
Brockford Street
Wetheringsett
Great Barton
Pakenham
Stanton Street
Earl's Green
Ford's Green
Risby
Higham
Little Saxham
Westley
Bury St Edmunds
Thurston
Norton
Bacton Green
Canham's Green
Mendlesham
Blacksmith's Green
Cathedral and Abbey Ruins
Barrow
Great Saxham
Tostock
Elmswell
Haughley Green
Ward Green
Mendlesham Green
Wetherup Street
Blackthorpe
Beyton
Rougham
Woolpit
Wetherden
Gipping
Haughley Park
Haughley
Woolpit Bygones Museum
Rushbrooke
Hessett
Drinkstone
Drinkstone Green
Saxham Street
Middlewood Green
Mickfield
Denham
Horringer
Ickworth House
Sicklesmere
Rougham Green
Bradfield St George
Harleston
Thorney Green
Stowupland
Little Stonham
Hargrave
Chevington
Little Welnetham
Rattlesden
Buxhall Fen Street
Forward Green
Stonham Aspal
Hawstead
Great Welnetham
Whepstead
Rede Hall
Bradfield St Clare
Bradfield Combust
Bradfield Woods
Gedding
Poystreet Green
Buxhall
Museum of East Anglian Life
Stowmarket
Earl Stonham
Creeting Bottoms
Crowfield
Depden Green
Chedburgh
Depden
Felsham
Hightown Green
Great Finborough
Combs Ford
Combs
Creeting St Mary
Beacon Hill Services
Thorns
Rede
Hoggard's Green
Cross Green
Great Green
High Street Green
Moats Tye
Needham Market
Coddenham
Wickhambrook
Clopton Green
Wickham Street
Brockley Green
Lawshall
Cockfield
Thorpe Green
Little Finborough
Battisford
Battisford Tye
Barking
Denston
Hawkedon
Stansfield
Brettenham
Charles Tye
Ringshall
Barking Tye
Baylham
Stradishall
Hartest
Shimpling Street
Thorpe Morieux
Cross Green
Wattisham Airfield Museum
Wattisham
Hitcham
Ringshall Stocks
Great Blakenham
Barham
Claydon
Boxted
Shimpling
Alpheton
Preston St Mary
Kettlebaston
Great Bricett
Nedging Tye
Willisham Tye
Offton
Little Blakenham
Stanstead
Lavenham
Guildhall
Bildeston
Naughton
Somersham
Akenham
Hundon
Poslingford
Glemsford
Kentwell Hall
Bridge Street
Monks Eleigh
Chelsworth
Flowton
Whitton
Chilton Street
Clare
Cavendish
Sue Ryder Foundation Mus.
Pentlow
High Street
Melford Hall
Long Melford
Brent Eleigh
Milden
Semer
Ash Street
Elmsett
Whatfield
Bramford
Westbourne
Clare Castle
Clare Ancient House
Foxearth
Little Waldingfield
Great Waldingfield
Acton
Lindsey
Chapel
Aldham
Sproughton
Ipswich
Borley
Kersey
Wolves Wood RSPB Reserve
Burstall
Chantry
Ashen
Ovington
Belchamp Otten
Sudbury
Mill Green
Edwardstone
Hadleigh
Hintlesham
Chattisham
Copdock
Ridgewell
Tilbury Juxta Clare
Belchamp Walter
Bulmer
Ballingdon
Great Cornard
Gainsborough's Ho.
Groton
Newton
Boxford
Layham
Coles Green
Mace Green
Belstead
Little Yeldham
Middleton
Little Cornard
Stone Street
Calais Street
Whitestreet Green
Raydon
Great Wenham
Capel St Mary
Great Yeldham
Bulmer Tye
Gestingthorpe
Henny Street
Assington
Polstead
Shelley
Holton St Mary
Tattingstone
Colne Valley Railway
Hedingham Castle
Audley End
Great Henny
Twinstead
Harrow Street
Stoke-by-Nayland
Bentley
Castle Hedingham
Wickham St Paul
Twinstead Green
Lamarsh
Honey Tye
Dedham Vale
Thorington Street
Higham
East Bergholt
The Heath
Alton Water Res.
Highstreet Green
Sible Hedingham
Great Maplestead
Little Maplestead
Alphamstone
Bures Green
Bures
Nayland
Stratford St Mary
Dedham
Bridge Cottage
East Bergholt Place
Brantham
Cattawade
Upper Street
Pebmarsh
Stour
Little Horkesley
Boxted
Boxted Cross
Boxted Heath
Langham
Sir Alfred Munnings Art Museum
Dedham Heath
Lawford
Mistley Towers
Mistley
Bradfield
Manningtree
Mount Bures
Wormingford
Great Horkesley
Halstead
Colne Engaine
Blackmore End
Gosfield
Wakes Colne
East Anglian Railway Museum
Horkesley Heath
Ardleigh
Bradfield Heath
Beazley End
Chappel
Fordham
West Bergholt
Mile End
Little Bromley
Horsley Cross
Horsleycross Street
Bocking Churchstreet
Fordstreet
Colne
Eight Ash Green
Highwoods
St Botolph's
Parson's Heath
Fox Street
Crockleford Heath
Great Bromley
Tendring Green
Little Bentley
Colchester
TL
Suffolk
0 1 2 3 4 5 6 miles
0 1 2 3 4 5 6 7 8 9 10km

Harleston
Garlic Street
Rushall
Shimpling
Dickleburgh
Thelveton
100TH BOMB GROUP MEMORIAL MUS.
Needham
Thorpe Abbotts
Scole
Brockdish
BILLINGFORD WINDMILL
Oakley
Hoxne
Syleham
Fressingfield
WINGFIELD OLD COLLEGE
Wingfield
Brome Street
Cross Street
Heckfield Green
Denham
Stradbroke
Battlesea Green
Pixey Green
Chippenhall Green
Cranley
Denham Street
Horham
Wilby
Wootten Green
Redlingfield
Athelington
Occold
Fingal Street
Southolt
Stanway Green
Rishangles
Bedingfield
Bedfield
Kenton
Monk Soham
SAXTEAD GREEN POST MILL
Saxtead
Saxtead Green
Debenham
Ashfield
Earl Soham
Winston
Winston Green
Peats Corner
Framsden
Pettaugh
HELMINGHAM HALL GARDENS
Helmingham
Gosbeck
Ashbocking
Hemingstone
Swilland
Otley
Clopton Corner
Clopton
Witnesham
Henley
Grundisburgh
Burgh
Tuddenham St Martin
Culpho
Boot Street
Great Bealings
Little Bealings
Playford
Westerfield
Rushmere St Andrew
CHRISTCHURCH MANSION
Ipswich
Kesgrave
Martlesham
Martlesham Heath
MARTLESHAM HEATH CONTROL TOWER
Rose Hill
Stoke
Maidenhall
Gainsborough
Warren Heath
Wherstead
ORWELL
Nacton
Freston
Woolverstone
Levington
Pin Mill
Chelmondiston
Holbrook
Lower Holbrook
Stutton
Harkstead
Erwarton
Shotley
Shotley Gate
Shop Corner
Holbrook Bay
Stour
HARWICH
Parkeston
HARWICH REDOUBT
Dovercourt
Upper Dovercourt
Wrabness
Ramsey
Little Oakley
Great Oakley
Wix
Stone's Green
Redenhall
Wortwell
Mendham
St Cross South Elmham
St Margaret South Elmham
SOUTH ELMHAM HALL
St Michael South Elmham
All Saints South Elmham
St James South Elmham
Withersdale Street
Metfield
Rumburgh
Spexhall
Wissett
Linstead Parva
Chediston
Halesworth
Little Whittingham Green
Silverley's Green
Cratfield
Swan Green
Ashfield Green
Banyard's Green
Huntingfield
Cookley
Walpole
Laxfield
Russel's Green
Foals Green
Brundish Street
Crown Corner
Brundish
Owl's Green
Heveningham
Ubbeston Green
Sibton Green
Peasenhall
Sibton
Worlingworth
Tannington
Badingham
Maypole Green
Dennington
Bruisyard
Brabling Green
Cransford
Rendham
Framlingham
Cole's Green
Lampardbrook
Brandeston
Cretingham
Kettleburgh
Parham
Great Glemham
Sweffling
Easton
EASTON FARM PARK
Hacheston
Marlesford
Monewden
AKENFIELD
Letheringham
Charsfield
Little Glemham
Lower Hacheston
Wickham Market
Dallinghoo
Debach
Pettistree
Campsey Ash
Bredfield
Rendlesham
Ufford
Hasketon
Melton
Bromeswell
Eyke
Woodbridge
SUTTON HOO ARCHAEOLOGICAL SITE
Maidensgrave
Waldringfield Heath
Waldringfield
Brightwell
Newbourne
Bucklesham
Hemley
Kirton
Falkenham
Thorpe Common
Trimley St Martin
Trimley Lower Street
Trimley St Mary
TRIMLEY MARSHES NATURE RESERVE
Walton
FELIXSTOWE
CHARLES MANNING'S AMUSEMENT PARK
Old Felixstowe
Felixstowe Ferry
Deben
Orwell
Ilketshall St Lawrence
Redisham
Stone Street
Cox Common
Mill Common
Brampton
Westhall
Broadway
Holton
Blyford
Wenhaston
Blackheath
Blyth
Thorington
Bramfield
High Street
Hemp Green
Darsham
Yoxford
Rotten End
Middleton Moor
Middleton
North Green
Theberton
Kelsale
Curlew Green
Carlton
Saxmundham
Benhall Street
Benhall Green
Stratford St Andrew
Sternfield
Friston
Farnham
Gromford
Knodishall
Coldfair Green
Snape
SNAPE MALTINGS RIVERSIDE CENTRE
BLAXHALL
Blaxhall
Iken
Tunstall
Tunstall Forest
Sudbourne
Chillesford
Butley
Rendlesham Forest
Butley High Corner
Capel St Andrew
ORFORD CASTLE
Orford
Orford Ness
ORFORDNESS-HAVERGATE
Boyton
Sutton
Shottisham
Duck Corner
Stores Corner
Hollesley
Hollesley Bay
Shingle Street
Alderton
Bawdsey
TM
Sotterley
Shadingfield
West End
Wrentham
Benacre
BENACRE
Covehithe
Stoven
Clay Common
Frostenden
South Cove
Cove Bottom
Wangford
Reydon Smear
Reydon
HEN REEDBED NATURE RESERVE
SOUTHWOLD MUSEUM
Southwold
Blythburgh
Walberswick
SUFFOLK COAST
Dunwich
Dunwich Forest
DUNWICH UNDERWATER EXPLORATION EXHIBITION
WESTLETON HEATH
Westleton
MINSMERE RSPB NATURE RESERVE
Eastbridge
LEISTON ABBEY
Leiston
Sizewell
Aldringham
Thorpeness
NORTH WARREN RSPB NATURE RESERVE
Aldeburgh
Aldeburgh Bay
High Street
Alde
ESBJERG 20:00
HOEK VAN HOLLAND 6:00
OOSTENDE (From Ipswich) 9:00
GOTHENBURG 38:30
ROTTERDAM 8:00
A140
A143
A144
A145
A12
A1120
A1094
A1152
A1214
A1156
A14
A154
A120
A1095
B1116
B1117
B1118
B1123
B1124
B1125
B1126
B1127
B1387
B1122
B1121
B1119
B1120
B1069
B1078
B1079
B1077
B1084
B1083
B1438
B1353
B1080
B1456
B1352
B1414
B1107
68
69
43
A
B
C
D
E
F
G
5
6
7
8
9

Gwynedd
SNOWDONIA NATIONAL PARK
PARC CENEDLAETHOL ERYRI
SH
SN
TREMADOG BAY
BAE TREMADOG
Morfa Harlech
Harlech
Glyn-cywarch
Eisingrug
623 MOEL YSGYFARNOGOD
Bronaber
Mynydd Bach
A470
Afon Eden
Llanfair
LLANFAIR SLATE CAVERNS
Llandanwg
Pen-sarn
Pen-y-bont
Pentre Gwynfryn
Llanbedr
LLANBEDR
720 RHINOG FAWR
RHINOG
COED Y BRENIN VISITOR CENTRE
RHAEADR MAWDDACH
Coed y Brenin Forest
SARN HELEN
Bed-y-coedwr
Pont Aber-Geirw
Cwm-hesgen
Capel Hermon
734 RHOBELL FAWR
Pont Fronwydd
Afon Wnion
A494
ALLT Y BENGLOG
Morfa Dyffryn
MORFA DYFFRYN
Coed Ystumgwern
Dyffryn Ardudwy
Llanenddwyn
Llanddwywe
Cors-y-Gedol
Tal-y-bont
754 Y LLETHR
DIFFWYS 750
COED GANLLWYD
Ganllwyd
Llanfachreth
Rhydymain
Blaen-y-cwm
71
Llanelltyd
CYMER ABBEY
Bont Newydd
Brithdir
B4416
Plas-canol
Pen-y-bryn
Bontddu
Caerdeon
Llanaber
Cutiau
TOLL
PENMAENPOOL CENTRE
Penmaenpool
Abergwynant
Dolgellau
A470
Y Gribin
A496
Barmouth (Abermaw)
RNLI LIFEBOAT MUSEUM
Afon Mawddach
Rhyd-wen
KINGS
Afon Cerist
670 WAUN-OER
BARMOUTH BAY
The Bar
FAIRBOURNE & BARMOUTH STEAM RAILWAY
BAE BERMO
Fairbourne
Arthog
Ynysgyffylog
A493
893 CADAIR IDRIS
CADER IDRIS
Mynydd Ceiswyn
Mynydd Dolgoed
Dyfi Forest
MEIRION MILL
Friog
Minffordd
Tal-y-llyn
A487
Corris Uchaf
Aberllefenni
Aberangell
Llwyngwril
Afon Dysynni
Llanfihangel-y-pennant
CASTELL Y BERE
KING ARTHUR'S LABYRINTH & CRAFT CENTRE
Corris
CORRIS RAILWAY AND MUSEUM
Cwm-Llinau
Dol-fôr
Cemmaes
Llangelynin
Abergynolwyn
B4405
Esgairgeiliog
Rhoslefain
Llanfendigaid
Llanegryn
Peniarth
309
Plas Llwyngwern
CENTRE FOR ALTERNATIVE TECHNOLOGY
Pantperthog
B4404
Llanwrin
Cemmaes Road
Tonfanau
633 TARRENHENDRE
Bryncrug
Pandy
VALLEY DYFI
Pen-y-bont
A489
Commins Coch
Abercegir
Darowen
Rhyd-yr-onen
TALYLLYN RAILWAY
SENEDD-DY-OWAIN GLYNDWR
Machynlleth
Penegoes
FELIN CREWI WATER MILL
Tal-y-wern
Tywyn
Cwrt
Pennal
DOVEY DYFI
Forge
Caethle
Derwenlas
Melinbyrhedyn
468 MOELFRE
Glaspwll
Pant-glâs
279
Aberhosan
Aberdovey
Glandyfi
Dovey Dyfi
YNYS HIR RESERVE
Eglwys Fach
DYFI FURNACE
Aberdovey Bar
Bae Aberdyfi
DYFI
Fochno
Glaslyn
Ynyslas
B4353
582
Llancynfelyn
Tre'r-ddôl
Tre-Taliesin
521 MOEL-Y-LLYN
BORTH
Borth
Source of R. Severn
Blaen Hafren
Nant-y-Moch Reservoir
Upper Borth
Tal-y-bont
Dôl-y-Bont
741
752
PLYNLIMON PUMLUMON FAWR
Source of R. Wye
Blaen Gwy
Llandre
Pen-y-garn
Bont-goch
B4572
ARTS CENTRE
NATIONAL LIBRARY
CLIFF RAILWAY
Bow Street
Salem
506
Clarach
Penrhyn-coch
Pen-bont Rhydybeddau
148
Plas Gogerddan
A4159
Capel Dewi
Aberystwyth
LLYWERNOG SILVER LEAD MINE
Dyffryn Castell
P&R
Comins Coch
Llanbadarn Fawr
Capel Bangor
Dollwen
Goginan
Trefechan
CASTLE
A44
Cwmbrwyno
Ponterwyd
564
Penparcau
Southgate
Glanrafon
VALE OF RHEIDOL RAILWAY
Afon Rheidol
RHEIDOL HYDRO ELECTRIC STATION
46
47
Rhydyfelin
Moriah
Capel Seion
Ystumtuen
Ysbyty-Cynfyn
A487
Aberffrwd
COED RHEIDOL
Llanfarian
Gors
Pisgah
A4120
Llanfihangel-y-Creuddyn
New Cross
Mynydd Bach
Devil's Bridge
610 PEN Y GARN
A485
Blaenplwyf
Trisant
Blaenycwm
0 1 2 3 4 5 6 miles
0 1 2 3 4 5 6 7 8 9 10 km

Parc
Rhos-y-gwaliau
Aber-Hirnant
Pennant
Blaen-y-Cwm
Tregeiriog
Llechrydau
Llangower
Llyn Tegid or Bala Lake
Dolhendre
Bala Lake Rly.
Llanuwchllyn
Pont Cwm Pydew
827
Moel Sych
Tyn-y-fedwen
Llanarmon Dyffryn Ceiriog
Tyn-y-ffridd
Rhiwlas
Cefn Canol
Llangadwaladr
Rhydycroes
72
Aberhirnant Forest
Pistyll Rhaeadr
Tan-y-pistyll
Pont-Rhyd-sarn
Tai-bach
534
Llansilin
Offa's Dyke Path
Llwybr Clawdd Offa
Tyn-y-coed
Moelfre
Talardd
Ty-nant
626
Foel y Geifr
666
Cwm Cynllwyd
Pencraig
607
Cefn Coch
Llangynog
Llanrhaeadr-ym-Mochnant
Trefonen
Treflach
Pennant Melangell
884
Y Berwyn
Alltforgan
Penybontfawr
Penygarnedd
Afon Tanat
Llangedwyn
Pen-y-bont
Nantmawr
907
Aran Fawddwy
Hirnant
Rhos-y-brithdir
389
Llanyblodwel
Porth-y-waen
Lake Vyrnwy
Ty-uchaf
Bwlchyddar
Aber-Rhiwlech
Pont y Pennant
540
Blaen-y-cwm
Abernaint
Llanfechain
Llansantffraid-ym-Mechain
Llanymynech
Cywarch
513
Llanymawddwy
Hen Gerrig
Llanwddyn
Abertridwr
Llanfyllin
Bryn Sion
Aber Cowarch
Ddôl-Cownwy
Dyfnant Forest
Tycrwyn
Bwlch-y-cibau
Waen Fach
Deuddwr
Tir Rhiwiog
545
Moel y Llyn
Mynydd y Gadfa
Pont-Llogel
Llanfihangel-yn-Ngwynfa
SJ
Main
Sarnau
Ardleen
Dinas-Mawddwy
Minllyn
Cwm-Cewydd
Afon Vyrnwy (Afon Efyrnwy)
60
Trefnanney
Geuffordd
Wern
Meifod
Pentrebeirdd
A458
Wern
16
Dolanog
Pontrobert
Maesgwyn-Isaf
Mallwyd
330
Glascoed
Pool Quay
Foel
Llangadfan
Groes-lwyd
Guilsfield
Ffridd Goch
Glyndŵr's Way
Llanerfyl
Heniarth
Cloddiau
Welshpool (Y Trallwng)
Buttington
523
Pen Coed
Four Crosses
Cyfronydd
Mynydd y Cemaes
Clegyrnant
Dolwen
Sychtyn
Melin-y-grug
Melin-y-ddôl
Welshpool & Llanfair Light Railway
Powysland
Neinthirion
Llanfair Caereinion
Powis Castle
Hope
Pentre-Celyn
Castle Caereinion
Pandy
Cwmderwen
Mynydd Waun Fawr
Bryn-penarth
364
Leighton
Waun
Llanbrynmair
Powys
Llwynderw
Fron
Tafolwern
Dolfach
440
Pant-y-ffridd
Kingswood
Llan
A470
Rhyd
Llanllugan
Manafon
Berriew
Stockton
Bont-Dolgadfan
Talerddig
Llanwyddelan
Adfa
New Mills
Forden
13
Brooks
Garthmyl
Pennant
Tregynon
Fron
Montgomery (Trefaldwyn)
Carno
458
Bettws Cedewain
Green Lane
Llandyssil
Dolforwyn Castle
Abermule
Dylife
Clatter
Llanwnog
398
265
Llanllwchaiarn
Pentreheyling
Staylittle
Caersws
Llawryglyn
Gleiniant
Milford
Llanmerewig
Hodley
Trefeglwys
Newtown (Y Drenewydd)
Glanmule
Sarn
Llyn Clywedog
Little London
Mochdre
Kerry
City
482
Fan Hill
Van
Oakley Park
307
Llandinam
Dolfor
497
Mainstone
Severn (Hafren)
Hafren Forest
Tan Hinon
Old Hall
Glan-y-nant
Pentre
SO
Clun Forest
Llanidloes
Anchor
Hall of the Forest
528
Cilfaesty Hill
Glynbrochan
Newchapel
Pant Mawr
Cwmbelan
448
Black Mt
Newcastle
Llanifyny
A44
Llangurig
Glyndŵr's Way
584
Felindre
Bettws-y-crwyn
Quabbs
Tylwch
Llaithddu
47
48
Beguildy
David's Well
Llanbadarn Fynydd
Black Mountain
Dutlas
Upper Treverward
Nantgwyn
493
Red Lion Hill
Rhyd-moel-ddu
547
Beacon
Llanfair Waterdine
Pant-y-dwr
A483
A489
A490
A495
B4393
B4396
B4391
B4580
B4580
B4392
B4395
B4382
B4389
B4390
B4385
B4388
B4386
B4368
B4355
B4568
B4569
B4518
B4403

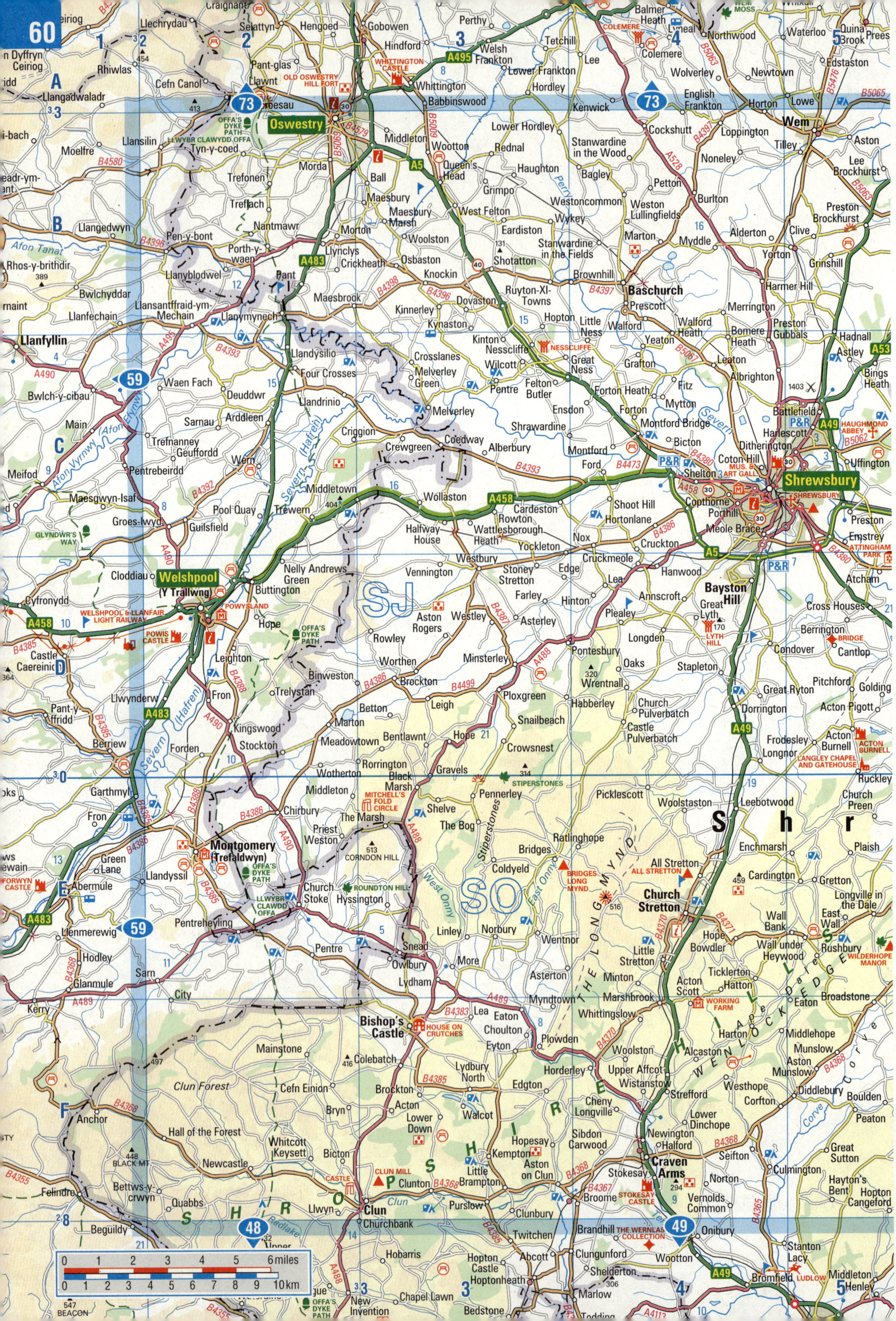
Llechrydau
Selattyn
Hengoed
Gobowen
Perthy
Welsh Frankton
Lower Frankton
Tetchill
Lee
Colemere
Northwood
Waterloo
Quina Brook
Prees
Edstaston
Wolverley
Newtown
English Frankton
Horton
Lowe
Wem
Aston
Tilley
Loppington
Cockshutt
Noneley
Lee Brockhurst
Rhiwlas
Cefn Canol
Pant-glas
Llawnt
Oswestry
Whittington
Babbinswood
Hordley
Kenwick
Llangadwaladr
Llansilin
Tyn-y-coed
Middleton
Wootton
Lower Hordley
Rednal
Stanwardine in the Wood
Moelfre
Trefonen
Morda
Queen's Head
Haughton
Bagley
Petton
Burlton
Ball
Maesbury
Maesbury Marsh
Grimpo
West Felton
Westoncommon
Weston Lullingfields
Preston Brockhurst
Llangedwyn
Treflach
Nantmawr
Morton
Woolston
Eardiston
Wykey
Marton
Myddle
Alderton
Clive
Pen-y-bont
Porth-y-waen
Llynclys
Crickheath
Osbaston
Shotatton
Stanwardine in the Fields
Yorton
Grinshill
Rhos-y-brithdir
Llanyblodwel
Pant
Knockin
Brownhill
Baschurch
Harmer Hill
Bwlchyddar
Llansantffraid-ym-Mechain
Llanymynech
Maesbrook
Kinnerley
Dovaston
Ruyton-XI-Towns
Prescott
Merrington
Llanfechain
Kynaston
Hopton
Little Ness
Walford
Walford Heath
Preston Gubbals
Bomere Heath
Llanfyllin
Llandysilio
Kinton
Nesscliffe
Yeaton
Hadnall
Astley
Four Crosses
Crosslanes
Melverley Green
Wilcott
Great Ness
Grafton
Leaton
Albrighton
Bings Heath
Waen Fach
Bwlch-y-cibau
Deuddwr
Pentre
Felton Butler
Forton Heath
Fitz
Llandrinio
Melverley
Ensdon
Forton
Mytton
Battlefield
Harlescott
Sarnau
Arddleen
Shrawardine
Montford Bridge
Bicton
Haughmond Abbey
Uffington
Main
Trefnanney
Geuffordd
Criggion
Crewgreen
Coedway
Alberbury
Montford
Ford
Ditherington
Coton Hill
Meifod
Pentrebeirdd
Wern
Middletown
Shelton
Shrewsbury
Maesgwyn-Isaf
Pool Quay
Trewern
Wollaston
Cardeston
Rowton
Shoot Hill
Hortonlane
Copthorne
Porthill
Preston
Groes-lwyd
Guilsfield
Halfway House
Wattlesborough Heath
Yockleton
Nox
Cruckton
Meole Brace
Emstrey
Attingham Park
Glyndŵr's Way
Westbury
Cruckmeole
Hanwood
Cloddiau
Welshpool (Y Trallwng)
Nelly Andrews Green
Buttington
Vennington
Stoney Stretton
Edge
Lea
Bayston Hill
Atcham
Cyfronydd
Powysland
Farley
Hinton
Annscroft
Great Lyth
Cross Houses
Welshpool & Llanfair Light Railway
Powis Castle
Hope
Offa's Dyke Path
Aston Rogers
Westley
Asterley
Plealey
Lyth Hill
Berrington
Bridge
Castle Caereinion
Rowley
Longden
Condover
Cantlop
Leighton
Worthen
Minsterley
Pontesbury
Oaks
Stapleton
Binweston
Brockton
Wrentnall
Great Ryton
Pitchford
Golding
Llwynderw
Fron
Trelystan
Ploxgreen
Habberley
Church Pulverbatch
Dorrington
Acton Pigott
Pant-y-ffridd
Betton
Leigh
Snailbeach
Castle Pulverbatch
Kingswood
Marton
Bentlawnt
Hope
Frodesley
Acton Burnell
Berriew
Forden
Stockton
Meadowtown
Crowsnest
Longnor
Langley Chapel and Gatehouse
Rorrington
Black Marsh
Gravels
Wotherton
Stiperstones
Ruckley
Garthmyl
Middleton
Mitchell's Fold Circle
Pennerley
Picklescott
Woolstaston
Leebotwood
Church Preen
Chirbury
Shelve
Fron
The Marsh
The Bog
Priest Weston
Ratlinghope
Corndon Hill
Bridges
Enchmarsh
Plaish
Montgomery (Trefaldwyn)
Green Lane
Llandyssil
Coldyeld
All Stretton
Cardington
Gretton
Longville in the Dale
Abermule
Church Stoke
Hyssington
Roundton Hill
Bridges Long Mynd
Church Stretton
Wall Bank
East Wall
Llanmerewig
Pentrehelyng
Llwybr Clawdd Offa
Linley
Norbury
Wentnor
Hope Bowdler
Wall under Heywood
Rushbury
Wilderhope Manor
Hodley
Pentre
Snead
Owlbury
More
Little Stretton
Asterton
Minton
Tickleton
Hatton
Sarn
Lydham
Acton Scott
Marshbrook
Broadstone
Kerry
City
Bishop's Castle
House on Crutches
Lea
Eaton
Myndtown
The Long Mynd
Working Farm
Eaton
Choulton
Whittingslow
Plowden
Harton
Middlehope
Mainstone
Colebatch
Eyton
Woolston
Alcaston
Munslow
Upper Affcot
Wistanstow
Aston Munslow
Lydbury North
Horderley
Strefford
Westhope
Corfton
Diddlebury
Boulden
Clun Forest
Cefn Einion
Brockton
Edgton
Wenlock Edge
Acton
Cheny Longville
Lower Dinchope
Peaton
Anchor
Bryn
Lower Down
Walcot
Sibdon Carwood
Newington
Halford
Seifton
Great Sutton
Hall of the Forest
Whitcott Keysett
Hopesay
Kempton
Craven Arms
Black Mt
Newcastle
Bicton
Clun Mill
Clunton
Aston on Clun
Stokesay
Culmington
Hayton's Bent
Hopton Cangeford
Little Brampton
Stokesay Castle
Norton
Vernolds Common
Felindre
Bettws-y-crwyn
Quabbs
Llwyn
Clun
Purslow
Broome
Churchbank
Clunbury
Brandhill
The Wernlas Collection
Onibury
Beguildy
Twitchen
Stanton Lacy
Hobarris
Hopton Castle
Abcott
Clungunford
Wootton
Hoptonheath
Shelderton
Bromfield
Ludlow
Middleton
Henley
Chapel Lawn
Bedstone
Marlow
New Invention
Beacon
SJ
SO
Shropshire
0 1 2 3 4 5 6 miles
0 1 2 3 4 5 6 7 8 9 10 km

Market Drayton
Stone
Stafford
Eccleshall
Newport
Telford
and
Wrekin
Wellington
Hadley
Oakengates
Donnington
Dawley
Madeley
Shifnal
Albrighton
Codsall
Tettenhall
Wolverhampton
Willenhall
Bilston
Sedgley
Tipton
Dudley
Wombourne
Kingswinford
Brierley Hill
Wordsley
Stourbridge
HALESOWEN
Kinver
Kidderminster
Bridgnorth
Much Wenlock
Broseley
Ironbridge
Coalport
Penkridge
Gnosall
Brewood
Shawbury
Hodnet
Sandford
Darliston
Bletchley
Longford
Hales
Chatcull
Wetwood
Croxton
Fairoak
Cotes
Millmeece
Slindon
Yarnfield
Walton
Little Stoke
Aston-By-Stone
Burston
Yarlet
Marston
Salt
Hopton
Holmcroft
Doxey
Forebridge
Moss Pit
Acton Trussell
Bednall
Dunston
Levedale
Longridge
Mitton
Whiston
Congreve
Lapley
Stretton
Gailey
Hatherton
Sutton
Woodseaves
Cheswardine
Chipnall
Bishop's Offley
Sugnall
Pershall
Chebsey
Norton Bridge
Great Bridgeford
Wootton
Ellenhall
Seighford
Ranton
Coton Clanford
Derrington
Whitecross
Haughton
Coppenhall
Bradley
Adbaston
Knighton
High Offley
Shebdon
Weston Jones
Norbury
Lawnhead
Knightley Dale
Long Compton
Soudley
Lockleywood
Hinstock
Ellerton
Sambrook
Pickstock
Puleston
Forton
Aqualate Mere
Coton
Gnosall Heath
Allimore Green
Apeton
Church Eaton
Outwoods
Moreton
High Onn
Orslow
Great Chatwell
Brineton
Marston
Blymhill
Wheaton Aston
Weston under Lizard
Bishop's Wood
Kiddemore Green
Tong Norton
Tong
Boscobel House & the Royal Oak
White Ladies Priory
Chillington Hall
Coven
Standeford
Shareshill
Featherstone
Codsall Wood
Oaken
Fordhouses
Oxley
Bushbury
Essington
Wergs
Pattingham
Perton
Trescott
Lower Penn
Penn
Bradmore
Trysull
Seisdon
Blakeley
Himley
Gornalwood
Swindon
Wall Heath
Bobbington
Halfpenny Green
Enville
Stourton
Amblecote
Netherton
Cradley Heath
Lye
Quarry Bank
Wollescote
Pedmore
Hasbury
Hagley
Clent
Blakedown
Churchill
Holy Cross
Belbroughton
Broom
Wolverley
Franche
Blakebrook
Trimpley
Cookley
Caunsall
Whittington
Blakeshall
Kingsford
Bodenham Arboretum & Earth Centre
Shatterford
Upper Arley
Pound Green
Low Habberley
Buttonoak
Wyre Forest
Romsley
Alveley
Birdsgreen
Hampton Loade
Sutton
Quatt
Chelmarsh
Tuckhill
Six Ashes
Four Ashes
Potter's Cross
Highley
Woodhill
Billingsley
Kinlet
Stottesdon
Chorley
Middleton Scriven
Sidbury
Glazeley
Eardington
Oldbury
Danesford
Quatford
Dudmaston Hall
Farmcote
Claverley
Heathton
Hopstone
Roughton
Hilton
Worfield
Rudge
Chesterton
Shipley
Badger
Ackleton
Stableford
Stockton
Norton
Beckbury
Burnhill Green
Ryton
Boningale
Grindle
Sutton Maddock
Kemberton
Brockton
Halesfield
Stirchley
Little Dawley
Coalbrookdale
Horsehay
Lawley
The Rock
Ketley
Ketley Bank
Priorslee
Crackleybank
Haughton
The Wyke
Lilleshall
Muxton
Heath Hill
Weston Heath
Lilyhurst
Sheriffhales
Trench
Donnington Wood
Church Aston
Longford
Chetwynd Aston
Brockton
Preston upon the Weald Moors
Eyton upon the Weald Moors
Kynnersley
Adeney
Edgmond
Edgmond Marsh
Tibberton
Cherrington
Waters Upton
Crudgington
Rowton
Great Bolas
Eaton on Tern
Howle
Ollerton
Child's Ercall
High Hatton
Radmoor
Ellerdine Heath
Cold Hatton
Edgebolton
Moreton Corbet
Muckleton
Great Wytheford
Walton
Poynton Green
High Ercall
Roden
Haughton
Rodington
Longdon on Tern
Sleapford
Bratton
Admaston
Withington
Upton Magna
Walcot
Wrockwardine
Charlton
Arleston
Aston
Uppington
Rushton
Norton
Wroxeter
Donnington
Eaton Constantine
Longwood
Little Wenlock
Dryton
Leighton
Buildwas
Cound
Cressage
Sheinton
Homer
Wyke
Benthall
Harley
Kenley
Stretton Westwood
Hughley
Presthope
Bourton
Easthope
Brockton
Weston
Shipton
Stanton Long
Holdgate
Tugford
Upper Heath
Abdon
Brown Clee Hill
Clee St Margaret
Burwarton
Aston Botterell
Loughton
Stoke St Milborough
Wheathill
Cleedownton
Farlow
Oreton
Silvington
Catherton
Cleeton St Mary
Bitterley
Foxwood
Doddington
Hopton Wafers
Cleobury North
Neenton
Ditton Priors
Middleton Priors
Chetton
Upton Cressett
Lower Netchwood
Monkhopton
Morville
Morville Heath
Aston Eyre
Tasley
Cross Lane Head
Haughton
Nordley
Astley Abbotts
Acton Round
Callaughton
Willey
Wolverhampton Business Airport
Wollerton
Stoke Heath
Wistanswick
Stoke on Tern
Ternhill
Marchamley
Lostford
Prees Green
Prees Lower Heath
Fauls
Wixhill
Weston
Moston
Hopton
Stanton upon Hine Heath
Hawkstone Park
Millgreen
Goldstone Hall
The Four Alls
Telford Services
Stafford Services
Hilton Park Services
Moseley Old Hall
Wightwick Manor
Weston Park
RAF Museum
David Austin Roses
Lilleshall Abbey
Hoo Farm Animal Kingdom
Granville
Wroxeter Roman City
The Wrekin
Telford Wonderland
Horsehay Steam Trust
Rosehill House
Mus. of Iron
Ironbridge Gorge
Blists Hill
Jackfield Tile Mus.
Buildwas Abbey
Benthall Hall
Morville Hall
Upton Cressett Hall
Stanmore
Cliff Railway
Watermill
Severn Valley Railway
Rays Farm Country Matters
Mottey Meadows
Izaak Walton Cottage Museum
Ancient High House
Himley Hall
Red House Glass Cone
Broadfield House Glass Mus.
Kingsford
Shropshire Union Canal
Belvide Res.
Severn
Worfe
Rea Brook
Borle Brook
Meese
Roden
Tern
Stour
Sow
M6
M54
A5
A41
A442
A458
A454
A449
A518
A5223
A49
A53
A34
A51
A456
A491
74
62
50
49
SJ
SO
o p s h i r e

Stone
Uttoxeter
Stafford
Eccleshall
Newport
Gnosall
Penkridge
Rugeley
Cannock Chase
Hednesford
Cannock
Lichfield
Brownhills
Shifnal
Albrighton
Codsall
Brewood
Wolverhampton
Wednesfield
Willenhall
Walsall
Bilston
Darlaston
Wednesbury
Aldridge
Sutton Coldfield
Sedgley
Coseley
Tipton
Wombourne
West Bromwich
Dudley
Oldbury
Rowley Regis
Smethwick
Birmingham
Erdington
Kingswinford
Brierley Hill
Stourbridge
Halesowen
Kinver
Solihull
Shirley
Longbridge
Abbots Bromley
Staffordshire
West Midlands
0 1 2 3 4 5 6 miles
0 1 2 3 4 5 6 7 8 9 10 km

Oaks Green
Sudbury
Foston
Church Broughton
Dalbury
Sutton on the Hill
Mickleover
Littleover
Burnaston
Osmaston
Normanton
Alvaston
Elvaston Castle
Borrowash
Breaston
Draycott
LONG EATON
Toton
Sawley
Thrumpton
Etwall
Findern
Allenton
Chellaston
Shardlow
Cavendish Bridge
Scropton
Hatton
Marston on Dove
Tutbury
Draycott in the Clay
Hanbury
Egginton
Rolleston on Dove
Willington
Stenson
Twyford
Barrow upon Trent
Swarkestone
Aston-on-Trent
Weston-on-Trent
Hemington
Lockington
Ratcliffe on Soar
Kingston on Soar
West Leake
East Leake
Gotham
New Kingston
Hanbury Woodend
Anslow Gate
Anslow
Stretton
Repton
Milton
Ingleby
Stanton by Bridge
King's Newton
Castle Donington
Kegworth
Melbourne
Isley Walton
Diseworth
Long Whatton
Sutton Bonington
Normanton on Soar
NEEDWOOD FOREST
Needwood
Horninglow
Newton Solney
Bretby
Foremark Res.
Ticknall
Calke
Breedon on the Hill
Tonge
Hathern
Stanford on Soar
Newchurch
Rangemore
Shobnall
Winshill
Burton upon Trent
Stapenhill
Upper Midway
Lower Midway
Hartshorne
Tatenhill
Branston
Newhall
Swadlincote
Church Gresley
Woodville
Smisby
Worthington
Belton
Thorpe Acre
Loughborough
Dunstall
Lount
Osgathorpe
Shepshed
Woodhouses
Barton-under-Needwood
Walton-on-Trent
Castle Gresley
Caldwell
Linton
Mount Pleasant
Blackfordby
Norris Hill
Ashby-de-la-Zouch
Coleorton
Newbold
Thringstone
Shelthorpe
Woodthorpe
Rosliston
Orgreave
Alrewas
Coton in the Elms
Overseal
Moira
Donisthorpe
Swannington
Whitwick
Charnwood Forest
Quorndon
Woodhouse
Woodhouse Eaves
Swithland
Fradley
Croxall
Oakthorpe
Packington
COALVILLE
Ravenstone
Greenhill
Copt Oak
Edingale
Lullington
Netherseal
Measham
Normanton le Heath
Hugglescote
Bardon
Elford
Harlaston
Haunton
Chilcote
Clifton Campville
Appleby Magna
Swepstone
Heather
Ellistown
Ibstock
Stanton under Bardon
Markfield
Cropston
Newtown Linford
Anstey
Whittington
Thorpe Constantine
No Man's Heath
Appleby Parva
Snarestone
Newton Burgoland
Battram
Bagworth
Field Head
Groby
Hademore
Norton-Juxta-Twycross
Shackerstone
Odstone
Nailstone
Thornton
Wigginton
Seckington
Newton Regis
Hopwas
Shuttington
Austrey
Congerstone
Barton in the Beans
Barlestone
Ratby
Glenfield
Botcheston
Leyfields
Tamworth
Alvecote
Amington
Twycross
Bilstone
Carlton
Market Bosworth
Newtown Unthank
Kirby Muxloe
Hints
Bonehill
Glascote
Warton
Orton-on-the-Hill
Wellsborough
Newbold Verdon
Desford
Leicester Forest East
Braunstone Town
Drayton Manor
Fazeley
Polesworth
St Helena
Birchmoor
Sheepy Magna
Sheepy Parva
Cadeby
Peckleton
Drayton Bassett
Wilnecote
Dordon
Grendon
Sibson
Shenton
Sutton Cheney
Kirkby Mallory
Dosthill
Grendon Common
Baddesley Ensor
Ratcliffe Culey
Upton
Stapleton
Thurlaston
Enderby
Middleton
Wood End
Atherstone
Dadlington
Earl Shilton
Narborough
Bodymoor Heath
Kingsbury
Baxterley
Witherley
Stoke Golding
Barwell
Elmesthorpe
Huncote
Littlethorpe
Bentley
Mancetter
Fenny Drayton
Higham on the Hill
Hinckley
Croft
Stoney Stanton
Wishaw
Over Green
Curdworth
Lea Marston
Hurley
Ridge Lane
Oldbury
Hartshill
Sutton in the Elms
Nether Whitacre
Church End
Camp Hill
Weddington
Sketchley
Burbage
Sapcote
Aston Flamville
Primethorpe
Broughton Astley
Minworth
Water Orton
Whitacre Heath
Furnace End
Over Whitacre
Galley Common
Chapel End
Stockingford
Nuneaton
Attleborough
Burton Hastings
Sharnford
Frolesworth
Dunton Bassett
Leire
Shustoke
Church End
Old Arley
Ansley
Chilvers Coton
Whitestone
Smockington
Claybrooke Magna
Claybrooke Parva
Ashby Parva
Coleshill
New Arley
Astley
Arbury Hall
Griff
Collycroft
Bedworth
Bramcote
Copston Magna
Wolvey
Wibtoft
Ullesthorpe
Kitt's Green
Tile Cross
Marston Green
Maxstoke
Fillongley
Corley Ash
Bedworth Heath
Bulkington
Sheldon
Chapel Green
Corley
Corley Moor
Ash Green
Neal's Green
Hawkesbury
Barnacle
Withybrook
Willey
Bitteswell
Lutterworth
Birmingham International
Butler's End
Keresley
Longford
Shilton
Ansty
Monks Kirby
Cross in Hand
Misterton
Elmdon
Bickenhill
Meriden
Hawkes End
Little Heath
Foleshill
Cotesbach
Elmdon Heath
Coundon
Allesley
Walsgrave on Sowe
Wyken
Pailton
Stretton under Fosse
Churchover
Gibbet Hill
Hampton in Arden
Eastern Green
Spon End
Great Heath
Coventry
Four Oaks
Eastcote
Whoberley
Coombe Abbey
Brinklow
Harborough Magna
Newbold on Avon
Copt Heath
Barston
Tile Hill
Earlsdon
Pinley
Binley
Binley Woods
Bretford
King's Newnham
Church Lawford
Long Lawford
Newton
Catthorpe
Knowle
Balsall Common
Stivichall
Willenhall
Brandon
Bentley Heath
Temple Balsall
Catchems Corner
Tollbar End
Wolston
Clifton upon Dunsmore
SK
SP
THE NATIONAL FOREST

Long Eaton
Clifton
Ruddington
Keyworth
Tollerton
Normanton-on-the-Wolds
Plumtree
Owthorpe
Colston Bassett
Langar
Barkestone-le-Vale
Woolsthorpe
Plungar
Belvoir
Harston
Stathern
Knipton
Bradmore
Bunny
Stanton-on-the-Wolds
Kinoulton
Hickling
Hose
Eaton
Branston
Croxton Kerrial
Eastwell
Castle Donington
Kegworth
Kingston on Soar
West Leake
East Leake
Costock
Wysall
Widmerpool
Willoughby-on-the-Wolds
Upper Broughton
Long Clawson
Goadby Marwood
Waltham on the Wolds
Sutton Bonington
Rempstone
Nether Broughton
Wycomb
Chadwell
Stonesby
Diseworth
Long Whatton
Normanton on Soar
Wymeswold
Old Dalby
Holwell
Scalford
Hathern
Stanford on Soar
Hoton
Grimston
Wartnaby
Ab Kettleby
Saxelbye
Melton Mowbray
Thorpe Arnold
Coston
Garthorpe
Freeby
Belton
Shepshed
Thorpe Acre
Loughborough
Cotes
Burton on the Wolds
Walton on the Wolds
Six Hills
Ragdale
Shoby
Asfordby
Asfordby Hill
Frisby on the Wreake
Brentingby
Wyfordby
Saxby
Stapleford
Burton Lazars
Shelthorpe
Woodthorpe
Barrow upon Soar
Seagrave
Hoby
Kirby Bellars
Nanpantan
Whitwick
Quorndon
Sileby
Thrussington
Rotherby
Charnwood Forest
Woodhouse
Mountsorrel
Ratcliffe on the Wreake
Rearsby
Great Dalby
Little Dalby
Whissendine
Woodhouse Eaves
Cossington
East Goscote
Gaddesby
Ashby Folville
Thorpe Satchville
Greenhill
Bardon
Copt Oak
Swithland
Rothley
Queniborough
Pickwell
Cold Overton
Leicestershire
Syston
Barsby
Twyford
Burrough on the Hill
Somerby
Langham
Markfield
Cropston
Thurcaston
Stanton under Bardon
Birstall
Barkby
South Croxton
Barleythorpe
Newtown Linford
Field Head
Anstey
Thurmaston
Marefield
Owston
Knossington
Thornton
Groby
Beeby
Lowesby
Hungarton
Cold Newton
Braunston-in-Rutland
Brooke
Ratby
Glenfield
Leicester
Keyham
Scraptoft
New Humberstone
Tilton on the Hill
Halstead
Botcheston
Newtown Unthank
Kirby Muxloe
Bushby
Thurnby
Braunstone Town
Leicester City
Evington
Stoughton
Houghton on the Hill
Billesdon
Skeffington
Loddington
Ridlington
Belton in Rutland
Newbold Verdon
Desford
Leicester Forest East
Stoneygate
Gaulby
Tugby
East Norton
Peckleton
Knighton
Oadby
King's Norton
Rolleston
Allexton
Wardley
Kirkby Mallory
Aylestone
Little Stretton
Stapleton
Thurlaston
Enderby
Glen Parva
Wigston
Great Glen
Illston on the Hill
Noseley
Goadby
Earl Shilton
Narborough
Blaby
South Wigston
Newton Harcourt
Carlton Curlieu
Burton Overy
Horninghold
Hallaton
Stockerston
Barwell
Elmesthorpe
Huncote
Littlethorpe
Whetstone
Shangton
Stonton Wyville
Glooston
Cranoe
Blaston
Eyebrook Reservoir
Croft
Countesthorpe
Kibworth Harcourt
Stoney Stanton
Cosby
Kilby
Tur Langton
Church Langton
Slawston
Great Easton
Sutton in the Elms
Kibworth Beauchamp
Medbourne
Burbage
Sapcote
Primethorpe
Peatling Magna
Fleckney
Smeeton Westerby
East Langton
Thorpe Langton
Welham
Drayton
Bringhurst
Aston Flamville
Broughton Astley
Arnesby
Saddington
Weston by Welland
Ashley
Cottingham
Willoughby Waterleys
Dunton Bassett
Ashby Magna
Shearsby
Bruntingthorpe
Foxton
Gumley
Sutton Bassett
Middleton
East Carlton
Frolesworth
Leire
Mowsley
Great Bowden
Claybrooke Magna
Claybrooke Parva
Ashby Parva
Peatling Parva
Laughton
Market Harborough
Dingley
Stoke Albany
Wilbarston
Copston Magna
Wibtoft
Ullesthorpe
Gilmorton
Walton
Lubenham
Little Bowden
Brampton Ash
Wolvey
Kimcote
Theddingworth
Marston Trussell
East Farndon
Pipewell
Bitteswell
Lutterworth
Willey
Withybrook
Misterton
Husbands Bosworth
Braybrooke
Cross in Hand
Walcote
North Kilworth
Sibbertoft
Great Oxendon
Desborough
Monks Kirby
Cotesbach
Pailton
South Kilworth
Sulby Reservoir
Clipston
Arthingworth
Rothwell
Churchover
Gibbet Hill
Welford
Harrington
Stretton under Fosse
Shawell
Stanford on Avon
Stanford Res.
Naseby Field
Kelmarsh
Orton
Loddington
Swinford
Naseby
Easenhall
Harborough Magna
Thorpe Malsor
King's Newnham
Coton
Haselbech
Great Cransley
Cold Ashby
Maidwell
Draughton
Clifton upon Dunsmore
Yelvertoft
Thornby
Mawsley
Broughton
SK
SP
Soar
Wreake
Swift
Sence
Eye
Res.
M1
M6
M69
A6
A46
A42
A50
A47
A14
A5
A4303
A563
A606
A607
A427
A508
A43
A453
A60
A6006
A512
B676
B6047
B5414
B581
B4114
B4669
B669
B664
B582
B4455
B4027
B5324
B6404
B4304
A5199
B591
B585
B587
B676
B5350
B4616
77
63
52
53
1645
NATURESCAPE WILD FLOWER FARM
GREAT CENTRAL RLY. (MAIN LINE)
RUSHCLIFFE
FIREWORK & 1930S MUS.
MANOR FARM
EAST MIDLANDS
DONINGTON PARK SERVICES
THE OLD RECTORY MUSEUM
CHARNWOOD MUSEUM
THE BELL FOUNDRY MUSEUM
CHARNWOOD LODGE
BEACON HILL
BROOMBRIGGS
TWINLAKES PARK
MELTON CARNEGIE MUS
BURROUGH HILL
LEICESTER SERVICES
BRADGATE PARK & SWITHLAND WOOD
BRADGATE HOUSE RUINS
CASTLE HILL
WATERMEAD
NATIONAL SPACE SCIENCE CENTRE
BELGRAVE HALL
GORSE HILL CITY FARM
ECO HOUSE
CATH
WILLIAM CAREY
MUSE. ART GAL
JOHN DORAN MUS
AYLESTONE MEADOWS
NAT. GAS MUS
BOTANIC GARDENS
LEICESTER FOREST EAST SERVICES
TROPICAL BIRD GARDENS
MALLORY PARK
BROCK'S HILL
THE NOOKS
BURBAGE COMMON & WOODS
FOSSE MEADOWS
CANAL MUS
FOXTON LOCKS
RUSHTON TRIANGULAR LODGE
STANFORD HALL
P&R
0 1 2 3 4 5 6 miles
0 1 2 3 4 5 6 7 8 9 10 km

Denton
Harlaxton
HARLAXTON MANOR
Old Somerby
Ropsley
Sapperton
Pickworth
Folkingham
Billingborough
Donington South Ing
Birthorpe
Humby
Hanby
Boothby Pagnell
Little Ponton
Stroxton
Great Ponton
A607
Laughton
Pointon
Westhorpe
Gosberton
Lenton
Aslackby
Millthorpe
Dowsby
Gosberton Clough
Risegate
Surfleet
Hungerton
Wyville
Ingoldsby
Graby
Keisby
Bassingthorpe
Bitchfield
Kirkby Underwood
Hawthorpe
Rippingale
Irnham
Crossgate
Stoke Rochford
Easton
Saltby
Skillington
Bulby
Dunsby
Northgate
Pinchbeck
Pinchbeck Bars
WOOLSTHORPE MANOR
Burton-le-Coggles
Corby Glen
Stainfield
Haconby
Woolsthorpe
Sproxton
Colsterworth
Twyford
Elsthorpe
Hanthorpe
Morton
Pinchbeck West
Buckminster
GRANTHAM SOUTH SERVICES
Birkholme
Grimsthorpe
Swinstead
Dyke
Spalding
Stainby
Swayfield
GRIMSTHORPE CASTLE
Cawthorpe
Pode Hole
Sewstern
Gunby
North Witham
Edenham
Little London
Scottlethorpe
Clay Lake
Bourne
Twenty
Creeton
Wymondham
South Witham
CRIBBS MEADOW
Castle Bytham
Little Bytham
Lound
Tongue End
Witham on the Hill
Northorpe
Edmondthorpe
Thistleton
Thurlby
Toft
Deeping St Nicholas
Deeping Fen
Market Overton
Clipsham
Teigh
Careby
THURLBY
Barrow
Stretton
Manthorpe
Thetford
RUTLAND RAILWAY MUS.
Carlby
Obthorpe
Greetham
Pickworth
Wilsthorpe
Hop Pole
Baston
Ashwell
Essendine
Braceborough
Cottesmore
Langtoft
Rutland
Exton
Greatford
TOLETHORPE HALL RUTLAND OPEN AIR THEATRE
Ryhall
Barholm
Towngate
Market Deeping
Little Casterton
Frognall
Burley
BARNSDALE PLANTS
Belmesthorpe
Deeping St James
Crowland
CROWLAND
Oakham
OAKHAM
Tickencote
Great Casterton
Whitwell
Deeping Gate
Empingham
Uffington
Tallington
West Deeping
Upper Hambleton
Northfields
Maxey
Northborough
Egleton
A606
Stamford
A16
RUTLAND WATER
Tinwell
Etton
Newborough
Normanton
BURGHLEY
Peakirk
Brooke
Edith Weston
Bainton
Glinton
Manton
Pilsgate
Barnack
Helpston
Bedford Level (North)
Ketton
Easton on the Hill
Ufford
Lyndon
North Luffenham
BARNACK HILLS AND HOLES
Eye Green
Chater
Preston
Pilton
Southorpe
Werrington
Gunthorpe
Wing
South Luffenham
Collyweston
Wittering
Peterborough
Eye
COLLYWESTON GREAT WOOD
Marholm
Walton
Dogsthorpe
Ayston
Morcott
SACREWELL FARM & COUNTRY CENTRE
CASTOR HANGLANDS
Newark
Stone Bridge Corner
Glaston
Thornhaugh
Upton
Duddington
Barrowden
Tixover
LONGTHORPE TOWER
PETERBOROUGH CATH
Bisbrooke
BEDFORD PURLIEUS
Wansford
Ailsworth
Longthorpe
Fengate
Stibbington
Castor
FLAG FEN BRONZE AGE EXCAVATIONS
Seaton
Wakerley
Sutton
NENE VALLEY RAILWAY
FERRY MEADOWS
RAILWORLD
Old Fletton
Stoke Dry
Lyddington
Harringworth
King's Cliffe
Yarwell
Sibson
Water Newton
Orton Longueville
Stanground
BEDE HOUSE
Thorpe by Water
Laxton
Alwalton
Whittlesey
Blatherwycke
Nassington
Orton Waterville
King's Delph
Apethorpe
Chesterton
CROWN LAKES
Farcet
Gretton
Bulwick
Woodnewton
PETERBOROUGH SERVICES
Caldecott
KIRBY HALL
SOUTHWICK HALL
Fotheringhay
Elton
ELTON HALL
CASTLE SITE
Haddon
Rockingham
ROCKINGHAM CASTLE
Deene
DEENE PARK
Deenethorpe
Southwick
Rockingham Forest
ROCKINGHAM MOTOR SPEEDWAY
Eaglethorpe
Warmington
Morborne
Farcet Fen
Whittlesey Mere
Yaxley
Tansor
Little Weldon
Glapthorn
Cotterstock
Norman Cross
Folksworth
Corby
Great Weldon
Upper Benefield
Lower Benefield
Oundle
Ashton
Stilton
Caldecote
HOLME FEN
Stanion
BARNWELL
Polebrook
Lutton
Denton
Holme
Ramsey St Mary's
Little Oakley
Harper's Brook
Stoke Doyle
Conington
Great Oakley
Barnwell St Andrew
Glatton
Ramsey Heights
Brigstock
LYVEDEN NEW BIELD
HILL FARM HERBS
FERMYN WOODS
Pilton
Hemington
WOODWALTON FEN
Nene
Luddington in the Brook
Barnwell All Saints
Wadenhoe
Sawtry
Newton
Geddington
ELEANOR CROSS
Church End
UPWOOD MEADOWS
Achurch
Great Gidding
Thurning
Little Gidding
Sudborough
Wigsthorpe
Aldwincle
Steeple Gidding
Wood Walton
Great Raveley
BOUGHTON HOUSE
Warkton
Grafton Underwood
Thorpe Waterville
HAMERTON ZOO PARK
Weekley
Lowick
Clopton
Winwick
Coppingford
MONKS WOOD
Islip
Titchmarsh
Hamerton
Kettering
Twywell
Thrapston
Upton
Wennington
Barton Seagrave
Cranford St Andrew
Cranford St John
Woodford
Old Weston
Alconbury Weston
Abbots Ripton
WICKSTEED PARK
Denford
Bythorn
Brington
Buckworth
Little Stukeley
Molesworth
Alconbury
A1
A1(M)
A15
A16
A43
A47
A605
A606
A6003
A6116
A6121
A427
A1139
A14
A151
B1176
B6403
B1443
B1166
B1397
B1180
B1356
B1525
B660
B1043
B1090
B670
B672
B662
B1040
TF
TL

Donington South Ing
End
Quadring
Bicker Haven
Gosberton
Westhorpe
Gosberton Clough
Fosdyke
Holbeach St Matthew
Holbeach St Marks
HOLBEACH MARSH
Gedney Marsh
Gedney Drove End
Daws
Lynn Channel
THE WASH
Risegate
Surfleet
Surfleet Seas End
Moulton Seas End
Saracen's Head
Holbeach Hurn
Holbeach Bank
Holbeach Clough
Gedney Dyke
Lutton
Guy's Head
Terrington
Crossgate
Northgate
Pinchbeck
Pinchbeck Bars
Pinchbeck West
Halesgate
BAYTREE OWL CENTRE
Weston
Moulton
Whaplode
Holbeach
Fleet Hargate
Gedney
Fleet
Gedney Broadgate
Chapelgate
Little London
BUTTERFLY & WILDLIFE PARK
Long Sutton
Sutton Bridge
Orange Row
Walpole Cross Keys
Spalding
SPRINGFIELDS SHOW GARDENS
MOULTON MILL
Low Fulney
Austendike
Pode Hole
Little London
Clay Lake
AYSCOUGHFEE HALL
Weston Hills
Sutton Crosses
Twenty
Whaplode St Catherine
MUS. OF ENTERTAINMENT
Tydd St Mary
Tydd Gote
Four Gotes
Walpole St Andrew
Walpole Marsh
Walpole St Peter
Hay Green
Tongue End
Cowbit
Moulton Chapel
Holbeach St Johns
Sutton St James
Deeping Fen
Deeping St Nicholas
Moulton Eaugate
TF
Tydd St Giles
Newton
Ingleborough
St John's Highway
Brotherhouse Bar
Hop Pole
Whaplode Drove
Tydd St Giles Fen
Sutton St Edmund
Fitton End
West Walton
St John Walpole Terrington Highway
West Walton Highway
Marshland St John's Fen End
Shepeau Stow
Holbeach Drove
Gedney Hill
Gorefield
Leverington
FENLAND AVIATION MUS.
Walsoken
Market Deeping
Frognall
Deeping St James
Crowland
CROWLAND ABBEY
Dowsdale
Throckenholt
Church End
PECKOVER HOUSE
Wisbech
WISBECH & FENLAND MUS.
New Walsoken
Marshland St James
North Fen
Parson Drove
Wisbech St Mary
Emneth
Emneth Hungate
Northborough
Nene Terrace
Morris Fen
Murrow
Tholomas Drove
Elm
Holly End
Peakirk
Newborough
Rogue's Alley
Glinton
Bedford Level (North)
Thorney Toll
Guyhirn Gull
Waldersey
Friday Bridge
Outwell
Stow
Eye Green
Thorney
Guyhirn
Ring's End
Coldham
Laddus Fens
WELE MANOR HALL
Upwell
Werrington
Gunthorpe
Eye
Walton
Dogsthorpe
Newark
Stone Bridge Corner
Chainbridge
Three Holes
Nene (Old Course)
Euximoor Fen
Upwell
LONGTHORPE TOWER
PETERBOROUGH CATH.
Peterborough
North Side
Eldernell
West Fen
Westry
Norwoodside
Euximoor Drove
South District
FERRY MEADOWS
Longthorpe
Fengate
FLAG FEN BRONZE AGE EXCAVATIONS
RAILWORLD
Old Fletton
Coates
March
Binnimoor Fen
Christchurch
Orton Longueville
Stanground
Whittlesey
Inham's End
Eastrea
Turves
Town End
Lakesend
Orton Waterville
King's Delph
CROWN LAKES
Farcet
TL
Tipsend
Upwell Fen
Welney
PETERBOROUGH SERVICES
Twenty Foot River
Ranson Moor
BEDFORD LEVEL (MIDDLE)
Flood's Ferry
Wimblington
Farcet Fen
Yaxley
Pondersbridge
White Fen
Gold Hill
Whittlesey Mere
Nene
Doddington
Norman Cross
Cambridge
Benwick
ISLE OF ELY
Manea
Middle Moor
Ramsey Mereside
Wimblington Fen
Sixteen Foot Drain
Stilton
HOLME FEN
Ramsey St Mary's
Forty Foot Drain
Vermuden's Drain
Purls Bridge
Fodder Fen
Denton
Holme
Ramsey Forty Foot
Chatteris
Horseway
Welches Dam
Pymoor
New Bedford River
Conington
Ramsey Heights
Ramsey Hollow
WILDLIFE TRUST WELNEY
Glatton
Ramsey
RURAL MUSEUM
Langwood Fen
Little Downham
WOODWALTON FEN
Bury
Tick Fen
Ferry Hill
Sawtry
Church End
UPWOOD MEADOWS
Chapel Head
Horseley Fen
Wardy Hill
Chettisham
West Fen
Little Gidding
Upwood
Coveney
Wood Walton
Wistow
Great Raveley
Pidley Fen
Mepal
Witcham
OLIVER CROMWELL'S HOUSE
Ely
CATHEDRAL AND MUS.
Coppingford
MONKS WOOD
Little Raveley
Warboys
Fenton
Chatteris Fen
Sutton
Wentworth
Witchford
Wennington
Pidley
Somersham
Old Hurst
Hill Row
Doles
North Hill
Haddenham
Little Thetford
Barway
Colne
Woodhurst
Ripton
Alconbury
Little Stukeley
A17
A16
A151
A1101
A47
A141
A1139
A605
A15
A1122
A1073
A1(M)
A142
A10
A1123
A1421
B1397
B1357
B1359
B1356
B1180
B1168
B1165
B1390
B1166
B1167
B1169
B1187
B1040
B1443
B1101
B1093
B1099
B1098
B1096
B660
B1090
B1043
B1050
B1381
B1411
B1525
79
65
54
55
0 1 2 3 4 5 6 miles
0 1 2 3 4 5 6 7 8 9 10 km

Snettisham
SNETTISHAM PARK
Ingoldisthorpe
Shepherd's Port
SNETTISHAM NATURE RESERVE
Shernborne
PEDDARS WAY
Great Bircham
BIRCHAM MILL
Bircham Newton
Bircham Tofts
Barmer
Syderstone
Blenheim Park
Bagthorpe
Wicken Green Village
Sculthorpe
West Barsham
East Barsham
Snoring
Dersingham
DERSINGHAM BOG
Anmer
HOUGHTON HALL
West Rudham
East Rudham
Tattersett
Coxford
Dunton
Shereford
Tatterford
Hempton
Toftrees
Fakenham
FAKENHAM
Little Ryburgh
Great Ryburgh
SANDRINGHAM
Sandringham
Wolferton
West Newton
Flitcham
New Houghton
Harpley
Helhoughton
West Raynham
East Raynham
South Raynham
Colkirk
Oxwick
Hamrow
Horningtoft
Castle Rising
CASTLE RISING
North Wootton
South Wootton
Hillington
PEDDARS WAY & NORFOLK COAST PATH
Little Massingham
Great Massingham
Weasenham St Peter
Weasenham All Saints
Whissonsett
Wellingham
EXTREME ADVENTURE
Tittleshall
Brisley
Stanfield
East Bilney
Marsh
Ongar Hill
Congham
CONGHAM HALL HERB GARDEN
Roydon
Grimston
Pott Row
ROYDON COMMON
Massingham Heath
King's Lynn
MARITIME EXHIBITION
GUILDHALL
Gaywood
Clenchwarton
Terrington St Clement
West Lynn
KING'S LYNN
Fairstead
Gayton
Leziate
Ashwicken
Gayton Thorpe
Rougham
Mileham
Bittering
NORFOLK RURAL LIFE MUSEUM
Gressenhall
Tilney High End
Tilney All Saints
Hardwick
Fair Green
Tower End
Middleton
East Winch
West Winch
North Runcton
Saddle Bow
Setchey
East Walton
West Bilney
Pentney
West Acre
Castle Acre
CASTLE ACRE PRIORY
South Acre
West Lexham
East Lexham
Newton
Litcham
Great Dunham
Little Dunham
Drury Square
Beeston
Longham
Sparrow Green
Crane's Corner
Wendling
TF
Tilney St Lawrence
Wiggenhall St Germans
Wiggenhall St Mary the Virgin
Wiggenhall St Mary Magdalen
Tottenhill Row
Blackborough End
Narborough
Watlington
Tottenhill
Norfolk
Wormegay
Great Fransham
Great Palgrave
Sporle
Little Fransham
HALL GDNS. & ARBORETUM
Scarning
Daffy Green
Runcton Holme
South Runcton
Shouldham
Marham
Marshland Fen
Shouldham Thorpe
Beachamwell Warren
Swaffham
PEDDARS WAY & NORFOLK COAST PATH
Necton
West End
North Pickenham
Holme Hale
Bradenham
Stowbridge
Stow Bardolph
Fincham
Barton Bendish
Beachamwell
Shingham
Cockley Cley
ICENI VILLAGE AND MUSEUMS
South Pickenham
Ashill
Crowshill
Shipdham
West Head
Wimbotsham
Stradsett
Crimplesham
Downham Market
Broomhill
Bexwell
Eastmoor
GOODERSTONE WATER GARDENS
Gooderstone
Saham Hills
Saham Toney
Ovington
Carbrooke
Bardolph Fen
Barroway Drove
Nordelph
Denver
Wereham
West Dereham
Boughton
Oxborough
OXBURGH HALL
Hilborough
Great Cressingham
Caudlesprings
Watton
Griston
Fen
Fordham
Wretton
Stoke Ferry
Whittington
Foulden
Bodney
Little Cressingham
Merton
Northacre
Old Bedford River
Hilgay
Wissey
Northwold
The Arms
Caston
Ten Mile Bank
Brookville
Thompson
Stow Bedon
Hilgay Fen
Southery
Cranwich
Ickburgh
LYNFORD ARBORETUM AND LAKES
Methwold Hythe
Methwold
Mundford
Methwold Fens
Southery Fens
Queen's Ground
TL
THETFORD
West Tofts
Great Hockham
Apes Hall
Brandon Creek
BRECKLAND
Feltwell
Brandon Bank
Feltwell Fens
Mare Fen
GRIMES GRAVES
Wretham
Burnt Fen
Hockwold cum Wilton
Weeting
FOREST
PEDDARS WAY & NORFOLK COAST PATH
WEETING HEATH
Hockwold Fens
Littleport
Little Ouse
Brandon
Santon Downham
Croxton
Bridgham
BEDFORD LEVEL (SOUTH)
BRANDON PARK
THETFORD WARREN LODGE
PARK
Brettenham
Shadwell
Shippea Hill Sta.
Thetford
Thetford Warren
Great Ouse
Prickwillow
Lakenheath
Wangford Warren
ANCIENT HOUSE MUS.
Rushford
Queen Adelaide
Kenny Hill
Lakenheath Warren
Knettishall
KNETTISHALL HEATH
Middle Fen
Stuntney
Great Fen
Mildenhall Fen
Eriswell
Elveden
EAST OF ENGLAND TANK MUSEUM
Barnham
Euston
EUSTON HALL
Coney Weston
Broad Hill
Lark
Holywell Row
Beck Row
Fakenham Magna
Barningham
WINDMILL
Isleham Fen
Thistley Green
West Row
A10
A47
A148
A149
A1078
A134
A1065
A1122
A11
A1066
A1075
A1088
A1101
A142
A1101
B1440
B1439
B1153
B1145
B1155
B1454
B1355
B1146
B1108
B1112
B1160
B1106
B1107
B1104
B1382
80
68
55
56

West Barsham
East Barsham
Great Snoring
Little Snoring
Thursford
Gunthorpe
Briningham
Melton Constable
Briston
Edgefield Street
Plumstead
Little Barningham
Aldborough
Wickmere
Alby Hill
Erpingham
Calthorpe
Colby
Suffield
MANNINGTON GARDENS
WOLTERTON PARK
Itteringham
Blenheim Park
Wicken Green Village
Sculthorpe
Dunton
Fakenham
Barney
Kettlestone
Fulmodestone
Swanton Novers
Corpusty
Saxthorpe
Shereford
Coxford
Tatterford
Hempton
Little Ryburgh
Stibbard
Hindolveston
Thurning
Norton Corner
Oulton
BLICKLING HALL
Ingworth
Blickling
Banningham
Toftrees
Great Ryburgh
Wood Norton
Guestwick
Wood Dalling
Heydon
Silvergate
Oulton Street
Aylsham
Dunkirk
Tuttington
Burgh next Aylsham
Helhoughton
West Raynham
East Raynham
Colkirk
Oxwick
Guist
Guestwick Green
Foulsham
Themelthorpe
Salle
Southgate
Fengate
Brampton
Marsham
South Raynham
Hamrow
Horningtoft
Gateley
Twyford
Broom Green
Bintree
FOXLEY WOOD
Reepham
Cawston
Booton
Little London
Eastgate
Buxton
Lamas
Whissonsett
Wellingham
Tittleshall
Brisley
North Elmham
Foxley
Whitwell Street
Brandiston
The Heath
EXTREME ADVENTURE
Stanfield
Billingford
Bawdeswell
Sparham
Haveringland
Hevingham
Stratton Strawless
Mileham
East Bilney
Worthing
NORFOLK WILDLIFE CENTRE
Alderford
Swannington
Upgate
Waterloo
West Lexham
Litcham
Beetley
Bittering
Mill Street
Lenwade
New Hainford
Hainford
East Lexham
NORFOLK RURAL LIFE MUSEUM
Gressenhall
Swanton Morley
Lyng
Elsing
DINOSAUR ADVENTURE PARK
Morton
Attlebridge
Felthorpe
Newton St Faith
Frettenham
Horsford
Beeston
Hoe
Woodgate
Primrose Green
Weston Longville
Thorpe Marriot
Spixworth
Newton
Great Dunham
Drury Square
Longham
Sparrow Green
Crane's Corner
Dereham
Etling Green
North Tuddenham
Weston Green
Ringland
Taverham
Drayton
Horsham St Faith
NORWICH INTERNATIONAL
Little Dunham
Great Fransham
Wendling
Hockering
Hellesdon
Old Catton
Sporle
Little Fransham
Scarning
MID-NORFOLK RAILWAY
Toftwood
Mattishall Burgh
Honingham
Costessey
Mile Cross
Upper Hellesdon
New Catton
BRADENHAM HALL GDNS. & ARBORETUM
Daffy Green
Yaxham
Clint Green
Mattishall
East Tuddenham
Easton
New Costessey
Necton
Westfield
Whinburgh
Welborne
Colton
Marlingford
Bowthorpe
Earlham
THE FORUM
West End
Bradenham
Brandon Parva
Bawburgh
SAINSBURY CENTRE FOR VISUAL ARTS
PEDDARS WAY & NORFOLK COAST PATH
Runhall
Barford
Colney
Lakenham
North Pickenham
Holme Hale
Shipdham
Garvestone
Thuxton
Barnham Broom
Great Melton
Little Melton
Cringleford
Eaton
Crowshill
Letton Green
Reymerston
Wramplingham
High Green
Danemoor Green
Carleton Forehoe
Hethersett
Keswick
South Pickenham
Ashill
Cranworth
Southburgh
Hardingham
Kimberley
Crownthorpe
Ketteringham
Caistor St Edmund
Dunston
Saham Hills
Woodrising
Wicklewood
Saham Toney
Ovington
Carbrooke
Hackford
Wymondham
East Carleton
Swardeston
Stoke Holy Cross
Great Cressingham
Caudlesprings
Hingham
Swainsthorpe
Deopham
Morley St Botolph
Mulbarton
Watton
Scoulton
Sifield
Griston
Little Ellingham
Suton
Bracon Ash
Hawes' Green
Little Cressingham
Deopham Green
Wreningham
Newton Flotman
Saxlingham Thorpe
Northacre
Rockland St Peter
Spooner Row
Ashwellthorpe
Florden
Saxlingham Nethergate
The Arms
Merton
Caston
Great Ellingham
Fundenhall
Hapton
Saxlingham Green
Stow Bedon
Rockland All Saints
Fundenhall Street
Tasburgh
Thompson
Besthorpe
Attleborough
Tacolneston
Forncett St Mary
Tharston
Hempnall
INDUSTRIAL STEAM MUSEUM
NFORD ARBORETUM
TROPICAL BUTTERFLY WORLD
Lower Stow Bedon
Bunwell
Forncett End
Stratton St Michael
Hempnall Green
Shropham
Forncett St Peter
Fritton
West Tofts
Puddledock
Carleton Rode
Long Stratton
Morningthorpe
PEDDARS WAY
OLD BUCKENHAM MILL
Old Buckenham
Wacton
Shelton Green
Great Hockham
Church Green
Hargate
Aslacton
Shelton
BRECKLAND
Wretham
Eccles Road
Wilby
New Buckenham
Tibenham
Great Moulton
Hardwick
SNETTERTON
Larling
Hunt's Corner
Pristow Green
Sneath Common
North Green
Quidenham
Banham
Goose Green
Tivetshall St Margaret
Bush Green
Croxton
Bridgham
BANHAM ZOO
Winfarthing
Tivetshall St Mary
Pulham Market
East Harling
Kenninghall
Dam Green
Gissing
Pulham St Mary
THETFORD WARREN LODGE
Kenninghall Heath
Mill Green
Starston
Thetford
Brettenham
Shadwell
North Lopham
Shelfanger
Burston
Shimpling
Garlic Street
Harleston
ANCIENT HOUSE MUS.
Fersfield
Rushall
Dickleburgh
Rushford
Gasthorpe
South Lopham
Bressingham
Walcot Green
Needham
Knettishall
Garboldisham
REDGRAVE & LOPHAM FEN
BRESSINGHAM STEAM MUSEUM AND GARDENS
Roydon
Diss
Thelveton
100TH BOMB GROUP MEMORIAL MUS.
Weybread
THETFORD HEATH
Euston
Blo' Norton
Thorpe Abbotts
Brockdish
THELNETHAM WINDMILL
Magpie Green
Palgrave
Scole
BILLINGFORD WINDMILL
EAST OF ENGLAND TANK MUSEUM
Coney
Hopton
Market Weston
Thelnetham
Redgrave
Wortham
Stuston
Oakley
Hoxne
Syleham
WINGFIELD OLD COLLEGE
Hinderclay
Thrandeston
Brome
Brome Street
Cross Street
Wingfield
Fakenham Magna
Botesdale
Langton
Heckfield
Battlesea Green
TF
TG
TL
TM
Norfolk
0 1 2 3 4 5 6 miles
0 1 2 3 4 5 6 7 8 9 10 km

5
6
7
8
9
A
B
C
D
E
F
G
Knapton
Bacton
Bradfield
Broomholm
Keswick
Walcott
Antingham
Edingthorpe
Swafield
Edingthorpe Green
Witton Bridge
North Walsham
Ridlington
Happisburgh
Spa Common
Crostwight
Whimpwell Green
Felmingham
Happisburgh Common
Eccles on Sea
EAST RUSTON GARDEN
Lessingham
Hempstead
Honing
81
Westwick
Bengate
East Ruston
Ingham Corner
Sea Palling
WAXHAM BARN
Waxham
Skeyton
Worstead
Ingham
Swanton Abbott
Sloley
Dilham
Stalham
Stalham Green
Smallburgh
Hickling
MUSEUM OF THE BROADS
Scottow
Pennygate
Sutton
Hickling Green
Barton Turf
Little Hautbois
Tunstead
ANT BROADS AND MARSHES
Wood Street
Hickling Heath
Horsey
Sco Ruston
Neatishead
Catfield
Hickling Broad
HORSEY WINDMILL
WINTERTON DUNES
WROXHAM BARNS
Barton Broad
HICKLING BROAD
MARTHAM BROAD
Ashmanhaugh
RA BOAT TRIP
East Somerton
Coltishall
Irstead
Sharp Street
Potter Heigham
West Somerton
Winterton-on-Sea
Threehammer Common
Hoveton
Thurne
Belaugh
Martham
Wroxham
Lower Street
Ludham
Bastwick
HILLSIDE ANIMAL SANCTUARY
Upper Street
Horning
LUDHAM MARSHES
Hemsby
Newport
Upper Street
Repps
Wroxham Broad
BURE MARSHES
Thurne
Rollesby
Scratby
Crostwick
Woodbastwick
Ormesby St Michael
California
TG
Ranworth
Clippesby
Filby Broad
Ormesby St Margaret
Rackheath
Salhouse
FAIRHAVEN GARDEN TRUST
New Rackheath
Panxworth
South Walsham
Billockby
Burgh St Margaret
Filby
CAISTER ROMAN TOWN
Caister-on-Sea
P&R
Mautby
Little Plumstead
Upton
Thrigby
West Caister
Sprowston
THE CANDLEMAKER WORKSHOP
THRIGBY HALL WILDLIFE GARDENS
Thorpe End
Hemblington
Runham
Blofield Heath
North Burlingham
Stokesby
West End
NORTH DENES
YARMOUTH
NORWICH
Great Plumstead
Acle
Bure
Thorpe St Andrew
Blofield
Damgate
GREAT YARMOUTH
Brundall
Lingwood
Beighton
Tunstall
THE
Runham
Great Yarmouth
A47
Postwick
Moulton St Mary
Halvergate Marshes
SEA LIFE GREAT YARMOUTH
Strumpshaw
South Burlingham
Breydon Water
Trowse Newton
Surlingham
Halvergate
Cobholm Island
ELIZABETHAN HOUSE, MARITIME NELSON/TOLHOUSE MUSEUMS
Kirby Bedon
Buckenham
BROADS
Burgh Castle
Southtown
EXHIBITION GALLERIES
A146
Hassingham
Freethorpe
AMAZONIA-WORLD OF REPTILES
Bramerton
Wickhampton
Arminghall
MID YARE
Southwood
BERNEY ARMS AND MILL
Framingham Pigot
Rockland St Mary
Cantley
Limpenhoe
Bradwell
PLEASURE BEACH
Gorleston-on-Sea
Framingham Earl
Claxton
Poringland
Hellington
Yare
PETTITTS ANIMAL ADVENTURE PARK
Belton
Ashby St Mary
Reedham
Yelverton
Bergh Apton
Langley Street
Hardley Street
A143
REDWINGS HORSE SANCTUARY
Howe
Thurton
Ferry
ST OLAVES PRIORY
Fritton
A12
Hopton on Sea
Shotesham
Brooke
Chedgrave
Lower Thurlton
The Dell
Lound
Stubb's Green
Sisland
Loddon
Chet
Thurlton
Thorpe
SOMERLEYTON HALL
Seething
Hales
Blundeston
Kirstead Green
Mundham
Stubbs Green
B1136
Herringfleet
Corton
Raveningham
Somerleyton
PLEASUREWOOD HILLS LEISURE PARK
HALES HALL BARN & GARDENS
RAVENINGHAM GARDENS
Haddiscoe
Maypole Green
Thwaite St Mary
TM
Oulton
LOWESTOFT AND EAST SUFFOLK MARITIME MUSEUM
Kirby Cane
Toft Monks
Road Green
Woodton
Stockton
Normanston
Hedenham
Wheatacre
HERITAGE/VISITOR CENTRE
Burgh St Peter
Topcroft
Cobbler's Green
Ellingham
Kirby Row
Aldeby
Oulton Broad
Topcroft Street
LOWESTOFT MUSEUM
Lowestoft
Geldeston
Gillingham
CARLTON MARSHES NATURE RESERVE
Ditchingham
Broome
Waveney
Kirkley
Beccles
Shipmeadow
Barnby
Great Green
Earsham
Mettingham
Pakefield
Bungay
Barsham
Worlingham
Carlton Colville
Denton
North Cove
Mutford
Ringsfield
Gisleham
NORFOLK AND SUFFOLK AVIATION MUSEUM
Ilketshall St Andrew
Ringsfield Corner
Hulver Street
Rushmere
Alburgh
Flixton
Ellough
Kessingland
Ilketshall St Margaret
Henstead
Kessingland Beach
Homersfield
AFRICA ALIVE
St Cross South Elmham
St Michael South Elmham
Ilketshall St Lawrence
Redisham
Sotterley
Benacre
Wortwell
Redenhall
Shadingfield
Mendham
St Margaret South Elmham
Stone Street
West End
Wrentham
SOUTH ELMHAM HALL
All Saints South Elmham
Cox Common
BENACRE
Brampton
Stoven
Clay Common
Withersdale Street
Rumburgh
Frostenden
Covehithe
St James South Elmham
Spexhall
Mill Common
South Cove
Metfield
Uggeshall
57
Westhall
Cove Bottom
Broadway
Wangford
Reydon Smear
Linstead Parva
Chediston
Reydon
Fressingfield
Little Whittingham Green
Holton
Halesworth
Blyford
HEN REEDBED NATURE RESERVE
SOUTHWOLD MUSEUM
Southwold
Chippenhall Green
Silverley's Green
Cratfield
Cookley
Wenhaston
A47
A1062
A149
A1064
A143
A146
A144
A145
A140
A12
A1117
B1159
B1150
B1354
B1140
B1152
B1074
B1332
B1062
B1127
B1437
B1375
B1123
B1124
B1126
B1116
A1095

Malltraeth Bay
Bae Malltraeth
Newborough Forest
MODEL VILLAGE
SEIONT II MARITIME MUSEUM
CASTLE & REGIMENTAL MUS.
Llanddwyn I.
Ynys Llanddwyn
The Bar
Abermenai Pt.
Trwyn Abermenai
CAERNARFON AIR MUSEUM
Morfa Dinlle
Dinas Dinlle
Llandwrog
GLYNLLIFON
C A E R N A R F O N
B A Y
B A E
C A E R N A R F O N
Pontllyfni
Aberdesach
82
WELSH LIFE
Clynnog-fawr
Tainlon
Capel Uchaf
Gyrn-goch
A499
Bryn-yr-eryr
509 BWLCH MAWR
522 GYRN DDU
SH
Trefor
564 YR EIFL
Llanaelhaearn
Pen-sarn
L L E Ŷ N
B4417
Llithfaen
Carreg Ddu
Porth Dinllaen
Pistyll
Llwyndyrys
Pencaenewydd
Llangybi
Morfa Nefyn
Nefyn
LLEYN HISTORIAL MARITIME MUSEUM
Fron
Llanarmon
Edern
Tan-y-graig
B4354
Rhos-fawr
Y Ffôr
Chwilog
Porth Ysgadan
Glanrhyd
PENARTH FAWR MEDIEVAL HOUSE
Rhos-y-llan
CORS GEIRCH
Boduan
A497
Llannor
Abererch
Tudweiliog
BODVEL HALL ADVENTURE PARK
HAVEN
Efailnewydd
Dinas
Rhyd-y-clafdy
Denio
Pwllheli
Porth Golmon
Garnfadryn
B4415
Carreg yr Imbill
South Beach
Bryn-mawr
Llaniestyn
Penrhos
P E N R H Y N   L L Y N
Pen-y-graig
Llangwnnadl
Rhedyn
Penrhyn Mawr
Sarn Meyllteyrn
Pen-y-groeslon
B4413
Llanbedrog
Ty-hen
Botwnnog
Nanhoron
Bryncroes
Mynytho
Trwyn Llanbedrog
Methlem
Rhydlios
Llandegwning
304 MYNYDD RHIW
PLAS-YN-RHIW
Capel Carmel
Rhoshirwaun
Llawr Dref
Llangian
St Tudwal's Road
Angorfa St Tudwal
Abersoch
191
Rhiw
Porth Neigwl or Hell's Mouth
Llanengan
Uwchmynydd
Aberdaron
Llanfaelrhys
Sarn Bach
Bwlchtocyn
St Tudwal's Island East
Ynys St Tudwal Dwyrain
Marchroes
St Tudwal's Island West
Ynys St Tudwal Gorllewin
Bodermid
Bardsey Sound
Swnt Enlli
Pen-y-cil
Cilan Uchaf
Trwyn Cilan
167
YNYS ENLLI
Bardsey Island
Ynys Enlli
0 1 2 3 4 5 6 miles
0 1 2 3 4 5 6 7 8 9 10 km

Caernarfon
Waterloo Port
Llanrug
Deiniolen
Clwt-y-bont
Brynrefail
Pont-rug
Cwm-y-glo
Caeathro
Llyn Padarn
Dinorwic
Llanberis
Ceunant
Croesywaun
Groeslon
Waunfawr
Llanfaglan
Bontnewydd
Saron
Glan-rhyd
Rhostryfan
Rhosgadfan
Llanwnda
Ffrwd
Groeslon
Penyffridd
Fron
Carmel
Cilgwyn
Nantlle
Penygroes
Talysarn
Tan-yr-allt
Llanllyfni
Nebo
Nasareth
Betws-Garmon
Llyn Cwellyn
Rhyd-Ddu
Ffridd-Uchaf
Bethania
Nant Peris
Pass of Llanberis
Llyn Peris
1085 SNOWDON YR WYDDFA
Llyn Llydaw
Llyn Gwynant
Pen-y-Gwryd Hotel
Pont Pen-y-benglog
Llyn Ogwen
Pont Rhyd-goch
999 GLYDER FAWR
1064 CARNEDD LLYWELYN
1044 CARNEDD DAFYDD
Marchlyn Mawr Res.
Capel Curig
Pont Cyfyng
Llyn Cowlyd
Llyn Crafnant
Cornel
GWYDYR FOREST PARK
Trefriw
Tal-y-Cafn
Llanddoged
Tai
Gwydyr Uchaf
Llanrwst
Melin-y-coed
Pentre-tafarn-y-fedw
Betws-y-Coed
Capel Garmon
Fairy Glen
Nebo
Mynydd Cribau
872 CARNEDD MOEL SIABOD
Pont-y-pant
Dolwyddelan
Pentre-bont
Garnedd
Conwy Falls Rhaeadr Conwy
Gwydyr Forest
Penmachno
Glan-Conwy
Padog
Ysbyty Ifan
Beddgelert Forest
Beddgelert
Nantgwynant
Llyn Dinas
Pass of Aberglaslyn
782 MOEL HEBOG
Nantmor
Croesor
623 MOEL PENAMNEN
Cwm Penmachno
Carrog
Llyn Conwy
Rhiwbryfdir
Blaenau Ffestiniog
Bethania
Tanygrisiau
770 MOELWYN MAWR
Congl-y-wal
Llan Ffestiniog
Pont yr Afon-Gam
Migneint
689 ARENIG FACH
Llyn Celyn
Pant-glas
Dafarn Faig
Upper Clynnog
Cenin
Bryncir
Glan-Dwyfach
Llecheiddior
Garndolbenmaen
Dolbenmaen
Llanfihangel-y-pennant
Tyddyn-mawr
552 MOEL-DDU
Golan
Prenteg
Garreg
Tan-lan
Rhyd
Llanfrothen
Rhyd-y-sarn
Tan-y-bwlch
Maentwrog
Gellilydan
Bont Newydd
Rhoslan
Penmorfa
Tremadog
Pentrefelin
Llanystumdwy
Porthmadog
Criccieth
Morfa Bychan
Borth-y-Gest
Minffordd
Portmeirion
Penrhyndeudraeth
Cilfor
556 GRAIG WEN
Llyn Arenig fawr
854 ARENIG FAWR
Pont Dolydd Prysor
Cwm Prysor
Trawsfynydd
Llyn Trawsfynydd
Caerwych
Traeth Bach
Llanfihangel-y-traethau
Talsarnau
Glan-y-wern
Eisingrug
Glyn-cywarch
623 MOEL YSGYFARNOGOD
TREMADOG BAY
BAE TREMADOG
Morfa Harlech
Harlech
750 MOEL LLYFRANT
Buarthmeini
Mynydd Bryn-llech
Bronaber
Mynydd Bach
Dolhendre
Gwynedd
720 RHINOG FAWR
Llanfair
Llandanwg
Pen-sarn
Pen-y-bont
Pentre Gwynfryn
Llanbedr
Bed-y-coedwr
Pont Aber-Geirw
Cwm-hesgen
Pont-Rhyd-sarn
SARN HELEN
Coed y Brenin
Forest
Capel Hermon
734 RHOBELL FAWR
Pont Fronwydd
Morfa Dyffryn
754 Y LLETHR
Ganllwyd
Coed Ystumgwern
Llanenddwyn
Dyffryn Ardudwy
Cors-y-Gedol
750 DIFFWYS
Llanfachreth
Rhydymain
Llanddwywe
Blaen-y-cwm
Tal-y-bont
Nannau
Plas-canol
Llanaber
Caerdeon
Bontddu
Pen-y-bryn
Llanelltyd
Bont Newydd
Brithdir
Cywarch
Y Gribin
Cutiau
Penmaenpool
Abergwynant
Dolgellau
Rhyd-wen
Barmouth (Abermaw)
Afon Mawddach
Arthog
Ynysgyfflog
BARMOUTH BAY
The Bar
BAE BERMO
Fairbourne
Friog
893 CADAIR IDRIS
670 WAUN-OER
Dinas-Mawddwy
Mynydd Ceiswyn
Mynydd Dolgoed
Cwm-Cewydd
Dyfi Forest
Minffordd
Llwyngwril
Tal-y-llyn
Llanfihangel-y-pennant
Corris Uchaf
Aberllefenni
Aberangell
Corris
Abergynolwyn
Llangelynin
Rhoslefain
Llanegryn
Esgairgeiliog
Dol-fôr
Cwm-Llinau
Cemmaes
SH
PARC CENEDLAETHOL ERYRI
SNOWDONIA NATIONAL PARK
82
83
72
59
58

Tramway
Toll
Llandudno
Great Orme Copper Mines
Alice in Wonderland
Penrhynside
Penrhyn Bay
Craig-y-don
Conwy Sands
Traeth Conwy
Deganwy
Llanrhos
Tywyn
Llandrillo-yn-Rhos
Rhos-on-Sea
Colwyn Bay (Bae Colwyn)
Llandudno Junction (Cyffordd Llandudno)
Welsh Mountain Zoo
Mochdre
Old Colwyn
Conwy
Gyffin
Aberconwy House/Plas Mawr
Dolwyd
Glan Conwy
Bryn-y-maen
Llanelian-yn-Rhos
Llanddulas
Llysfaen
Abergele
Rhyd-y-foel
Abergele Roads
Angorfa Abergele
Pensarn
Kinmel Bay
Towyn
Rhyl (Y Rhyl)
Seaquarium
Y-Ffrith
Prestatyn
Gronant
Gwespyr
Ffynnongroyw
Picton
Gwaenysgor
Llanasa
Meliden
Offa's Dyke Path
Llwybr Clawdd Offa
Axton
Trelawnyd
Dyserth
Cwm
Whitford
Pant-y-Wacco
Rhuddlan
Bodelwyddan
Rhuallt
Pen-y-cefn
Tremeirchion
Caerwys
Afon-wen Craft and Antique Centre
St Asaph (Llanelwy)
St Asaph Cathedral
Waen
Groesffordd Marli
Glascoed
Bodelwyddan
St George
Dolwen
Henryd
Felin Isaf Water Mill
Pentrefelin
Dawn
Betws-yn-Rhos
Moelfre Isaf
Moelfre Uchaf
Hafod-lom
Rowen
Tal-y-cafn
Bodnant
Graig
Ty'n-y-groes
Pontwgan
Eglwysbach
Vale of Conwy
Dyffryn Conwy
Dr-y-cennin
Tal-y-Bont
Pentre'r Felin
Gell
Cefn-coch
Pentre-Isaf
Llangernyw
Llanfair Talhaiarn
Bryn-nantllech
Llannefydd
Bryn Rhyd-yr-Arian
Cefn Berain
Bont-newydd
Plas-yn-Cefn
Trefnant
Vale of Clwyd
Dyffryn Clwyd
Bodfari
Green
Henllan
Denbigh (Dinbych)
Fron
Castle & Town Walls
Castell
Offa's Dyke Path
Llwybr Clawdd Offa
Llangwyfan
Waen
Llandyrnog
Dolgarrog
Coed Dolgarrog
Bryn-glas
Hendre-ddu
Llansannan
Llanddoged
Pandy Tudur
Tŷ'n-y-felin-isaf
Tan-y-fron
Clwt-grugoer
Groes
Llanrhaeadr
Llangynhafal
Moel Famau
Woollen Mill
Trefriw
Tan-lan
Tai
Gwydyr Uchaf
Llanrwst
Pentre-tafarn-y-fedw
Melin-y-coed
Gwytherin
Bylchau
Waen
Nantglyn
Peniel
Prion
Pentre Llanrhaeadr
Llanynys
Gellifor
Hirwaen
Cornel
Gwydyr Forest
Gwydyr Uchaf Chapel
Conwy
Ty-draw
Bryn Trillyn
Gorsedd Bran
Saron
Meifod
Rhewl
Llanbedr-Dyffryn-Clwyd
Craft Centre
Ruthin (Rhuthun)
Llanfwrog
Bontuchel
Cyffylliog
Swallow Falls
Betws-y-Coed
Conwy Valley Railway Museum
Nebo
Moel Seisiog
Llyn Aled
Llyn Alwen
Mynydd Hiraethog
Brenig Res.
Hafod Elwy Moor
Llyn Brenig Visitor Centre
Alwen Reservoir
Tai-Ucha
Nant Uchaf
Nilig
Pennant
Denbighshire (Sir Ddinbych)
Efenechtyd
Pwll-glas
Llanfair-Dyffryn-Clwyd
Clocaenog
Clawdd-newydd
Clocaenog Forest
Pentre-celyn
Mynydd Cribau
Capel Garmon
Burial Chamber
Fairy Glen
Conwy Falls
Rhaeadr Conwy
Penmachno Woollen Mill
Ty Mawr Wybrnant
Gwydyr Forest
Penmachno
Glan-Conwy
Hafod-Dinbych
Mwdwl-eithin
Pentrefoelas
Padog
Rhydlydan
Glasfryn
Cefn-brith
Pentre-llyn cymmer
Afon Alwen
Llanfihangel Glyn Myfyr
Derwen
Rhyd-y-meudwy
Llanelidan
Snowdonia National Park
Cwm Penmachno
Carrog
Llyn Conwy
Ysbyty Ifan
Garn Prys
Cerrigydrudion
Afon Ceirw
Melin-y-Wig
Bryn Saith Marchog
Ty Mawr Cwm
Pen-y-gop
Betws Gwerfil Goch
Gwyddelwern
Bryneglwys
Ty-nant
Dinmael
Maerdy
Morfydd
Carnedd y Filiast
Migneint
Pont yr Afon-Gam
Llangwm
Tai-mawr
Wenallt
Foel Goch
Glan-yr-afon
Druid
Glassblobbery
Corwen
Cynwyd Forest
Llangollen Steam Railway
Carrog
Llidiart-y-parc
Glyndyfrdwy
Arenig Fach
Llyn Celyn
Ciltalgarth
Glan-yr-afon
Cynwyd
Sarnau
Bethel
Moel Fferna
Llyn Arenig fawr
Frongoch
Cefn-ddwysarn
Cwm Prysor
Arenig Fawr
Parc Cenedlaethol Eryri
Lidiardau
Rhyd-uchaf
Rhiwlas
Llandderfel
Llandrillo
Bala (Y Bala)
Llanfor
Pale
Cefn Coch
Moel Llyfnant
Llanycil
Parc
Rhos-y-gwaliau
Pennant
Buarthmeini
Mynydd Bryn-llech
Llyn Tegid or Bala Lake
Aber-Hirnant
Blaen-y-Cwm
Mynydd Bach
Bala Lake Rly
Llangower
Dolhendre
Pont Cwm Pydew
Aberhirnant Forest
Berwyn
Tyn-y-fedwen
Tyn-y-ffridd
Moel Sych
Pistyll Rhaeadr
Gwynedd
Llanuwchllyn
Cwm-hesgen
Pont-Rhyd-y-fen
Tyn-y-pistyll
Bed-y-coedwr
Rhaeadr Mawddach
Talardd
Ty-nant
Foel y Geifr
Pennant Melangell
Pencraig
Llangynog
Cefn Coch
Llanrhaeadr-ym-Mochnant
Capel Hermon
Cwm Cynllwyd
SH
0 1 2 3 4 5 6 miles
0 1 2 3 4 5 6 7 8 9 10 km
59 71 83 85

River Dee
Afon Dyfrdwy
Thurstaston
Irby
Thingwall
Storeton
Port Sunlight
Pensby
Barnston
Brimstage
Heswall
Bromborough
Eastham
Eastham Ferry
Mostyn Quay
Mostyn
Glan-y-don
Dawpool Bank
Gayton
Thornton Hough
Raby
Garston
Speke Hall
Speke
Liverpool John Lennon
Liverpool Airport
Hale
Halton
Runcorn
Weston
Preston Brook
Sutton Weaver
Mersey
Ellesmere Port
Boat Museum
Ince Banks
Parkgate
Neston
Willaston
Hinderton
Hooton
Childer Thornton
Little Sutton
Overpool
Whitby
Stanlow
Ince
Elton
Frodsham
Newtown
Overton
Fivecrosses
Greenfield
Greenfield Valley Heritage Park
Holywell Bank
Gayton Sands
Carmel
Walwen
Little Neston
Ness
Ness Gardens
Great Sutton
Whitbyheath
McArthur Glen Cheshire Oaks
Chester Services
Helsby
Gorsedd
Holywell (Treffynnon)
Bagillt
Brynford
Dolphin
Babell
Burton
Two Mills
Ledsham
Stanley Woods
Little Stanney
Thornton-le-Moors
Elton Green
Hapsford
Alvanley
Newton
Kingsley
Birch Hill
Delamere
Delamere Forest Park
Puddington
Capenhurst
Backford
Backford Cross
Blue Planet Aquarium
Stoak
Dunham-on-the-Hill
Manley
Mouldsworth
Pentre Halkyn
Flint (Y Fflint)
Mount Pleasant
Ysceifiog
Lixwm
Rhes-y-cae
Halkyn Mountain
Halkyn
Oakenholt
Flint Mountain
Connah's Quay
Shotwick
Saughall
Mollington
Wervin
Chester Zoo
Picton
Bridge Trafford
Mickle Trafford
Little Barrow
Great Barrow
Ashton
Nannerch
Rhosesmor
Hendre
Northop
Northop Hall
Garden City
Sealand
Upton
Guilden Sutton
Rhydymwyn
Shotton
Queensferry
Sandycroft
Mancot
Greenacres
Blacon
Chester
Hoole
Newton
Littleton
Christleton
Stamford Bridge
Tarvin
Kelsall
Kelsall Hill
Oscroft
Willington Corner
Utkinton
Cotebrook
Flintshire (Sir Y Fflint)
Soughton
New Brighton
Ewloe
Ewloe Grn
Hawarden (Penarlâg)
Hawarden
Dewa
Grosvenor
Handbridge
Saltney
Brown Heath
Rowton
Waverton
Duddon
Clotton
Cilcain
Gwernaffield
Mold (Yr Wyddgrug)
Loggerheads
Moel Famau
Buckley (Bwcle)
Drury
Mynydd Isa
Spon Green
Llong
Broughton
Bretton
Lower Kinnerton
Balderton
Eccleston
Saighton
Milner's Heath
Hargrave
Huxley
Burton
Birch Heath
Brassey Green
Tafarn-y-gelyn
Cadole
Gwernymynydd
Maeshafn
Nercwys
Pontblyddyn
Penyffordd
Dodleston
Higher Kinnerton
Hatton Heath
Bruera
Gatesheath
Shropshire Union Canal
Tiverton
Llanferres
Leeswood
Coed-Talon
Waun-y-Llyn
Hope (Yr Hôb)
Burton Green
Pulford
Lavister
Aldford
Milton Green
Tattenhall
Beeston
Beeston Castle
Bunbury Heath
Eryrys
Treuddyn
Caergwrle
Rossett
Trevalyn
Handley
Higher Burwardsley
Burwardsley
Llanarmon-yn-Ial
Llanfynydd
Cefn-y-bedd
Llay
Marford
Churton
Aldersey Green
Chowley
Peckforton
Cheshire Workshops
Graianrhyd
Rhydtalog
Ffrith
Coddington
Harthill
Craig-fechan
Farndon
Clutton
Broxton
Barnhill
Bulkeley
Gallantry Bank
Brymbo
Bwlchgwyn
Alyn Waters
Moss
Gwersyllt
Gresford
Holt
Crewe
Barton
Stretton
Fuller's Moor
Bickerton
Cholmondeley Castle Gdns
Llandegla
Four Crosses
Gwynfryn
Rhosrobin
Garden Village
Borras Head
Pen-y-stryt
Lead Mines
Minera
Acton
Llan-y-pwll
Ridleywood
Tilston
Duckington
Edge Green
Offa's Dyke Path
Coedpoeth
New Broughton
Rhosnesni
Isycoed
Castletown
Horton Green
Bersham
Bersham Heritage Centre
Wrexham (Wrecsam)
Wrexham Industrial Estate
Hampton Heath
Bickley Moss
Llwybr Clawdd Offa
Cyrn y Brain
Esclusham Mountain
King's Mills
Bowling Bank
Shocklach
Ebnal
Rhostyllen
Erddig
Talwrn
Chorlton Lane
No Man's Heath
Malpas
Maesyrychen Mtn.
Llantysilio Mountain
Pentredwr
Eglwyseg Mountain
Tainant
Johnstown
Farm World
Marchwiel
Sontley
Cross Lanes
Worthenbury
Cuddington Heath
Bell o' th' Hill
Marbury
Llandynan
Rhewl
Rhosllanerchrugog
Ruabon Mountain
Penycae
Stryt-issa
Gyfelia
Eyton
Wrexham (Wrecsam)
Cock Bank
Bangor
Bangor-is-y-coed
Threapwood
Higher Wych
Wirswall
Eliseg's Pillar
Valle Crucis Abbey
Llangollen Motor Mus.
Canal Exhibition Centre
Acrefair
Cefn-mawr
Ruabon (Rhiwabon)
Overton Bridge
Cloy
Tallarn Green
Brooklands
Chemistry
Whitchurch
Dyfrdwy
Llangollen
Llangollen Exhibition Centre
Plas Newydd
Garth
Pont
Cysyllte
Ty Mawr
New Bridge
Rhos-y-Madoc
Erbistock
Overton (Owrtyn)
Lightwood Green
Horseman's Green
Eglwys Cross
The Chequer
Redbrook
Waymills
Froncysyllte
Pentre
Halton
Sandy Lane
Knolton
Knolton Bryn
Penley
Street Lydan
Hanmer
Arowry
Bronington
Alkington
Chwarel Wynne Mine & Museum
Glyn-Ceiriog
Pontfadog
Chirk Castle
Chirk (Y Waun)
Dudleston
Street Dinas
Ifton Heath
Dudleston Heath
Breaden Heath
Fenn's, Whixall and Bettisfield Mosses
Tilstock
Plas Nantyr
Tyn-y-celyn
Bronygarth
Chirk Bank
Preesgweene
Weston Rhyn
Llwynmawr
St Martin's
Elson
Welshampton
Llangollen Canal
Bettisfield
Hollinwood
Welsh End
Pandy
New Marton
Ellesmere
Balmer Heath
Wem Moss
Whixall
Craignant
Tregeiriog
Llechrydau
Selattyn
Hengoed
Gobowen
Perthy
Colemere
Lyneal
Northwood
Waterloo
Quina Brook
Prees
Llanarmon Dyffryn Ceiriog
Rhiwlas
Pant-glas
Hindford
Welsh Frankton
Tetchill
Lee
Edstaston
Cefn Canol
Llawnt
Old Oswestry Hill Fort
Whittington Castle
Whittington
Lower Frankton
Hordley
Wolverley
Newtown
Llangadwaladr
Rhydycroesau
Babbinswood
Kenwick
English Frankton
Horton
Lowe
Oswestry
Lower Hordley
Wem
Loppington
Tai-bach
Moelfre
Llansilin
Tyn-y-coed
Middleton
Wootton
Rednal
Cockshutt
Stanwardine in the Wood
Tilley
Aston
Noneley
Morda
Queen's Head
Haughton
Bagley
Pett
Trefonen
Treflach
Ball
Maesbury
Grimpo
Perry
Westoncommon
Weston
Burlton
West Felton
Preston
Wales

Halton
Runcorn
Hale
Hale Bank
Widnes
Weston
Ince Banks
Frodsham
Helsby
Keckwick
Daresbury
Moore
Catalyst
Norton Priory Mus & Gardens
Preston on the Hill
Dutton
Sutton Weaver
Aston
Newtown
Overton
Fivecrosses
Hatton
Appleton Thorn
Stretton
Lower Stretton
Higher Whitley
Lower Whitley
Swarton Heath
High Legh
Arley Hall
Arley
Hoo Green
Mere
Bucklow Hill
Rostherne Mere
Rosthernе
Ashley
Tatton House
Tatton Park
Thorns Green
New Mills
Morley Green
Styal
Quarry Bank Mill
Wilmslow
Davenport Green
Knutsford
Over Knutsford
Mobberley
Knolls Green
Alderley Edge
Nether Alderley
Ollerton
Marthall
Chelford
Over Peover
Peover Heath
Monks Heath
Capesthorne Hall
Jodrell Bank Visitor Centre
Withington Green
Siddington
Lower Withington
Gleadsmoss
Swettenham
Holmes Chapel
Cranage
Twemlow Green
Goostrey
Blackden Heath
Peover Hall
Lower Peover
Swan Green
Smithy Green
Plumley
Tabley
Knutsford Services
Over Tabley
Bate Heath
Holehouses
Cheshire County Show
Pickmere
Higher Wincham
Great Budworth
Gib Hill
Comberbach
Dones Green
Little Leigh
Anderton Boat Lift
Marbury
Barnton
Anderton
Marston
Wincham
Northwich
Lostock Gralam
Lostock Green
Broken Cross
Rudheath
Salt Mus
Lach Dennis
Weaverham
Hartford
Cuddington
Farmer for a Day
Acton Bridge
Crowton
Kingsley
Commonside
Newton
Alvanley
Birch Hill
Delamere Forest
Norley
Hatchmere
Sandiway
Delamere
Oakmere
Manley
Mouldsworth
Dunham-on-the-Hill
Bridge Trafford
Picton
Elton
Ince
Chester Services
Hapsford
Elton Green
Little Barrow
Great Barrow
Ashton
Kelsall
Kelsall Hill
Guilden Sutton
Stamford Bridge
Oscroft
Littleton
Christleton
Cheshire
Davenham
Moulton
Whitegate
Bostock Green
Byley
Puddinglake
Foxwist Green
Wharton Green
Wharton
Salterswall
Winsford
Little Budworth
Over
Church Hill
School Green
Middlewich
Sproston Green
Occlestone Green
Moston Green
Bradwall Green
Elworth
Sandbach
Sandbach Crosses
Sandbach Services
Sandlow Green
Brereton Green
Brereton Heath
Newsbank
Hulme Walfield
West Heath
Arclid
Astbury
Brownlow
Brownlow Heath
Brookhouse Green
Fourlanes End
Little Moreton Hall
Hassall Green
Hassall
Wheelock
Wheelock Heath
Thurlwood
Rode Heath
Scholar Green
Church Lawton
Mount Pleasant
Alsager
Kidsgrove
Radway Green
Talke
Freeport Talke Outlet Mall
Red Street
Audley
Chesterton
Alsagers Bank
Bradwell
Knutton
Silverdale
Newcastle-under-Lyme
Keele
Keele Services
Clayton
Madeley Heath
Madeley
Halmer End
Betley
Barthomley
Englesea-brook
Balterley
Gorstyhill
Wrinehill
Blakenhall
Checkley
Onneley
Madeley Park
Whitmore
Hanchurch
Baldwin's Gate
Willoughbridge
The Dorothy Clive Garden
Pipe Gate
Aston
Woore
Ireland's Cross
Knighton
Bearstone
Blackbrook
Maer
Chapel Chorlton
Stableford
Beech
Mucklestone
Ashley Heath
Ashley
Podmore
Cranberry
Hookgate
Loggerheads
Almington
Standon
Cotes
Chatcull
Millmeece
Wetwood
Croxtonbank
Croxton
Slindon
Fairoak
Sugnall
Sturbridge
Bishop's Offley
Pershall
Eccleshall
Adbaston
Knighton
Wootton
Shebdon
High Offley
Woodseaves
Ellenhall
Sutton
The Four Alls
Woodseaves
Chipnall
Cheswardine
Soudley
Goldstone Hall
Lockleywood
Hinstock
Ellerton
Child's Ercall
Hales
Market Drayton
Longford
Tern Hill
Rosehill
Stoke Heath
Wistanswick
Millgreen
Stoke on Tern
Moreton Say
Sandford
Darliston
Fauls
Bletchley
Prees
Prees Heath
Prees Higher Heath
Prees Lower Heath
Prees Green
Lostford
Wollerton
Wollerton Old Hall
Hawkstone Park
Marchamley
Hodnet
Hodnet Hall
Hopton
Weston
Wem
Lowe
Horton
Loppington
Cockshutt
Petton
Burlton
Preston
English Frankton
Wolverley
Newtown
Edstaston
Quina Brook
Waterloo
Whixall
Welsh End
Hollinwood
Tilstock
Alkington
Fenn's, Whixall and Bettisfield Mosses
Wem Moss
Bettisfield
Lyneal
Northwood
Colemere
Llangollen Canal
Welshampton
Bronington
Arowry
Hanmer
The Chequer
Eglwys Cross
Redbrook
Whitchurch
Chemistry
Brooklands
Grindley Brook
Waymills
Broughall
Ash Magna
Ightfield
Calverhall
New Street Lane
Burleydam
Wilkesley
Lightwood Green
Coxbank
Adderley
Kinsey Heath
Norton in Hales
Betton
Audlem
Buerton
Hankelow
Hatherton
Hunsterson
Walgherton
Wybunbury
Stapeley
Stapeley Water Gardens
Butt Green
Hough
Shavington
Weston
Gresty Green
Willaston
Wells Green
Crewe
Wistaston
Wistaston Green
Worleston
Woolstanwood
Haslington
Winterley
Maw Green
Coppenhall Moss
Barrows Green
Bradfield Green
Warmingham
Wettenhall
Church Minshull
Cholmondeston
Aston juxta Mondrum
Wardle
Barbridge
Haughton Moss
Radmore Green
Burford
Burland
Acton
St Mary's
Nantwich
Faddiley
Larden Green
Ravensmoor
Sound
Sound Heath
Broomhall
Aston
Newhall
Marley Green
Wrenbury
Norbury
Marbury
Wirswall
Higher Wych
Bell o' th' Hill
Cuddington Heath
Threapwood
Malpas
No Man's Heath
Hampton Heath
Bickley Moss
Ebnal
Shocklach
Chorlton Lane
Horton Green
Castletown
Tilston
Edge Green
Duckington
Bickerton
Cholmondeley Castle Gdns
Chorley
Gallantry Bank
Bulkeley
Fuller's Moor
Broxton
Barnhill
Harthill
Cheshire Workshops
Peckforton
Higher Burwardsley
Burwardsley
Spurstow
Bunbury
Bunbury Heath
Water Mill
Beeston
Beeston Castle
Tattenhall
Gatesheath
Newton
Huxley
Hargrave
Milner's Heath
Hatton Heath
Handley
Chowley
Clutton
Barton
Tiverton
Alpraham
Calveley
Tilstone Fearnall
Four Lane Ends
Rhuddall Heath
Tarporley
Birch Heath
Brassey Green
Clotton
Eaton
Rushton
Oulton Park
Shire Horse Centre
Cotebrook
Utkinton
Willington Corner
Duddon
Burton
Waverton
Cotton Heath
Bruera
Milton Green
Golborne
Shropshire Union Canal
Weaver
SJ

0 1 2 3 4 5 6 miles
0 1 2 3 4 5 6 7 8 9 10km

Kitt's Moss
Handforth
Bodford
Poynton
Midway
Hope Green
Wood Lanes
Lyme Park
Newtown
Furness Vale
Black Hill
Bridgemont
Mills
Whaley Bridge
Buxworth
Chinley
Chinley Head
Chapel Milton
Malcoff
Chestnut Centre
Whitehough
Slackhall
Chapel-en-le-Frith
Sparrowpit
Perryfoot
Blue John Cavern
Barber Booth
Mam Tor
Treak Cliff Cavern
Peak Cavern
Speedwell Cavern
Castleton
Peveril
Hope
Aston
Thornhill
Bamford
Brough
Bradwell
Hathersage
Athersage
Dean Row
Adlington Hall
Whiteley Green
Pott Shrigley
Kettleshume
Horwich End
Taxal
Lower Crossings
Combs
Dove Holes
Peak Forest
Coplow Dale
Little Hucklow
Great Hucklow
Abney
Bretton
Grindleford
Upper Padley
Nether Padley
Hough
Mottram St Andrew
Prestbury
Bollington
Bollington Cross
Fernilee
Fernilee Res.
Peak Dale
Upper End
Wheston
Tideswell
Litton
Lane Head
Foolow
Grindlow
Eyam
Eyam Hall
Froggatt
Nether Alderley Mill
Tytherington
West Park
Hurdsfield
Rainow
Walker Barn
Shining Tor
Buxton
Fairfield
Tunstead
Hargatewall
Miller's Dale
Wormhill
Derbyshire Dales
Wardlow
Burnt Heath
Stoney Middleton
Calver
Curbar
Henbury
Broken Cross
Heritage Centre
Macclesfield
Paradise Mill
Lower Pexhill
Tegg's Nose
Gurnett
Langley
Macclesfield Forest
Burbage
Buxton Mus. & Art Gallery
Poole's Cavern
Ravenstor
Cressbrook
Little Longstone
Rowland
Hassop
Blackwell
Great Longstone
Warren
Gawsworth
Sutton Lane Ends
Shutlingsloe
Haddon
Wildboarclough
Canholes
Cowdale
King Sterndale
Harpur Hill
Chelmorton
Taddington
Ashford in the Water
Pilsley
Edensor
Marton
Highlane
Gawsworth Hall
Oakgrove
Axe Edge
Brand Side
Sterndale Moor
Flagg
Sheldon
Bakewell
Rodeheath
North Rode
Allgreave
Flash
Earl Sterndale
Monyash
Over Haddon
Haddon Hall
Peak Village
Rowsley
Bosley
Wincle
Danebridge
Gradbach Mill
Hollinsclough
Glutton Bridge
Crowdecote
Caudwell's Mill
Youlgreave
Alport
Stanton in Peak
Eaton
Lower Heath
Buglawton
Key Green
Dane
Longnor
Arbor Low Henge
Nine Ladies Stone Circle
Bradford
Congleton
Rushton Spencer
Fawfieldhead
Newtown
Pilsbury
Parsley Hay
Middleton
Churchtown
Timbersbrook
Heaton
Hightown
Ryecroft Gate
Meerbrook
Upper Hulme
Brund
Sheen
Birchover
Darley Bridge
Mossley
Whitemore
Newtown
Hartington
Hartington Hall
Heathcote
Newhaven
The Pennine Bridleway
Elton
Winster
Poolfold
Biddulph Grange
Rudyard
Rudyard Res.
Tittesworth Res.
Upper Elkstone
Lower Elkstone
Hulme End
Biggin
Pikehall
Brightgate
Marsh Green
Gillow Heath
Biddulph Moor
Rudyard
Poolend
Ball Haye Green
Brindley Mill and Mus.
Thorncliffe
Warslow
Biggin Dale
Grangemill
Ible
Mow Cop
Mow Cop Castle
Biddulph
Horton
Knypersley
Blackwood Hill
Leek
Lowe Hill
Butterton
Wetton
Alstonefield
Alsop en le Dale
Aldwark
Longcliffe
Greenway Bank
Dunwood
Longsdon
Bradnop
Onecote
Ford
Grindonmoor Gate
Grindon
Hope
Milldale
Parwich
Ballidon
Middleton Engine Ho.
Newchapel
Brindley Ford
Endon Bank
Horse Bridge
Brown Edge
Goldenhill
Chell Heath
Endon
Deep Hayes
Flint Mill
Leekbrook
Cheddleton Railway Centre
Bottom House
New Street
Manifold
Dove Dale
Tissington
Bradbourne
Brassington
Carsington
Carsington Res.
Sandyford
Tunstall
Norton-in-the-Moors
Stanley
Baddeley Green
Cheddleton
Basford Green
Churnet Valley Rly
Blackbrook
Winkhill
Waterfall
Waterhouses
Dovedale
Ilam Hall
Ilam
Thorpe
Fenny Bentley
Hognaston
Bradeley
Ford Green Hall
Burslem
Bagnall
Ipstones
Calton
Kniveton
Stoke-on-Trent
Milton
Wetley Rocks
Consall Hall Gdns.
Cauldon
Blore
Atlow
Wolstanton
Etruria
Abbey Hulton
Bucknall
Consall
Kingsley Bird & Falconry Cent.
Foxt
Swinscoe
Mapleton
Hulland Ward
Hanley
Potteries Mus. & Art Gal.
Werrington
Cellarhead
Froghall
Ashbourne
Hulland
Trent
Blakeley Lane
Kingsley
Whiston
Cotton
Weaver Hills
Stanton
Mayfield
Bradley
Stoke-on-Trent
Park Hall
Kingsley Holt
Oakamoor
Ramshorn
Wootton
Church Mayfield
Clifton
Fenton
Boothen
Trent Vale
Longton
Hulme Quarry
Weston Coyney
Dilhorne
Cheadle
Farley
Dimmingsdale
Alton Towers
Threapwood
Alton
Ellastone
Snelston
Osmaston
Dresden
Caverswall
Foxfield Steam Railway
Forsbrook
Freehay
Gallows Green
Quixhill
Norbury
Wyaston
Shirley
Brailsford
Hanford
Trentham
Gladstone Pottery
Lightwood
Meir
Blythe Bridge
Mobberley
Bradley in the Moors
Denstone
Roston
Darley Moor
Ednaston
Draycott in the Moors
Trentham
Rough Close
Wedgwood Visitor Centre
Meir Heath
Croxden Abbey
Greatgate
Croxden
Rocester
Yeaveley
Rodsley
Hollington
Kirk
Tittensor
Barlaston
Cresswell
Upper Tean
Lower Tean
Checkley
Hollington
Cubley Common
Great Cubley
Bentley Fields Open Farm
Alkmonton
Hollington Grove
Knenhall
Fulford
Fole
Combridge
Marston Montgomery
Thurvaston
Longlane
Moddershall
Waldley
Longford
Swynnerton
Meaford
Oulton
Upper Leigh
Beamhurst
Crakemarsh
Longfordlane
Middleton Green
Lower Leigh
Stramshall
Heritage Centre
Somersal Herbert
Boylestone
Cotwalton
Church Leigh
Trusley
Hilderstone
Withington
Dalbury
Stone
Garshall Green
Dods Leigh
Field
Uttoxeter
Doveridge
Oaks Green
Church Broughton
Walton
Dayhills
Bramshall
Sutton on the Hill
Yarnfield
Little Stoke
Milwich
Blount's Green
Uttoxeter
Sudbury
Foston
Coton
Coton Hill
Stafford Services
Fradswell
Gratwich
Marchington
Sudbury Hall
Scropton
Norton Bridge
Aston-By-Stone
Burston
Sandon
Hatton
Hilton
Egginton on Dove
Chebsey
Izaak Walton Cottage Museum
Yarlet
Whitgreave
Gayton
Grindley
Kingstone
Gorsty Hill
Marchington Woodlands
Draycott in the Clay
Tutbury
Great Bridgeford
Marston
Salt
Chartley Moss
Hanbury
Rolleston on Dove
Weston
Stowe-by-Chartley
Drointon
Shugborough Working Farm
Hopton
Hixon
Newton
Newborough
Hanbury Woodend
Anslow Gate
Anslow
Stretton
Peak District National Park
SK
Stafford
A523
A5102
A537
A54
A5004
A6
A623
A6187
A625
A6020
A619
A536
A515
A53
A520
A52
A50
A5012
A521
A522
A34
A518
A51
A511
B5470
B5087
B5055
B5053
B5054
B5056
B5057
B5035
B5032
B5033
B5030
B5027
B5029
B5066
B5013
B5017
B5026
B5405
B6049
B6465
B6001
B6521
B5012
B5056
M6
87
88
76
62
5
6
7
8
9
A
B
C
D
E
F
G
a
f
o
r
d
r
e
P E A K D I S T R I C T N A T I O N A L P A R K

Aston
Bamford
Ringinglow
Millhouses
Norton
Woodseats
Gleadless
Beighton
Swallownest
Todwick
Kiveton Park
South Anston
Castleton
Brough
Hathersage
Whirlow
Abbeydale
Dore
Totley
Beauchief
Bradway
Jordanthorpe
Hackenthorpe
Highlane
Mosborough
Holbrook
Norwood
Wales
Thorpe Salvin
Peveril
Bradwell
88
89
Coal Aston
ECKINGTON
Marsh Lane
Harthill
Netherthorpe
Woodall Services
Coplow Dale
Great Hucklow
Little Hucklow
Abney
Bretton
Upper Padley
Longshaw
Owler Bar
Dronfield
Dronfield Woodhouse
Apperknowle
Renishaw Hall Gardens
Spinkhill
Renishaw
Barlborough
Grindleford
Nether Padley
Holmesfield
Unstone
Unstone Green
Middle Handley
West Handley
Mastin Moor
Whitwell
Hodthorpe
Eyam
Eyam Hall
Grindlow
Foolow
Lane Head
Froggatt
Common Side
Revolution House
Clowne
Tideswell
Litton
Derbyshire Dales
Burnt Heath
Stoney Middleton
Calver
Moorhall
Wildaygreen
Barlow
New Whittington
Old Whittington
Staveley
Woodthorpe
Creswell
Wardlow
Curbar
Overgreen
Cutthorpe
Newbold
Poolsbrook
Stanfree
Elmton
Holbeck
Cressbrook
Little Longstone
Rowland
Baslow
Old Brampton
Chesterfield
Brimington
Tapton
Duckmanton
Long Duckmanton
Shuttlewood
Holbeck Woodhouse
Whaley
Ravenstor
Ashford in the Water
Great Longstone
Hassop
Eastmoor
Brampton
Hady
Calow
Bolsover
Whaley Thorns
Nether Langwith
Langwith
Taddington
Pilsley
Chatsworth House
Wadshelf
St Mary & All Saints
Arkwright Town
Sutton Hall
Scarcliffe
Langwith Junction
Edensor
Holymoorside
Walton
Birdholme
Hasland
Sutton Scarsdale
Palterton
Sheldon
Bakewell
Hob Hursts House
Slatepit Dale
Swathwick
Temple Normanton
Shirebrook
Flagg
Haddon Hall
Peak Village
Beeley
Wingerworth
Grassmoor
Grassmoor Heath
Glapwell
Derby
75
Monyash
Over Haddon
Rowsley
Tupton
Holmewood
Doe Lea
New Houghton
Caudwell's Mill
Uppertown
Old Tupton
Stainsby
Pleasley
Mansfield Woodhouse
Youlgreave
Arbor Low Henge
Alport
Stanton in Peak
Northwood
Brockhurst
North Wingfield
Parsley Hay
Nine Ladies Stone Circle
Bradford
Kelstedge
Alton
Clay Cross
Hardwick Hall
Radmanthwaite
Churchtown
Two Dales
Parkhouse Green
Hardstoft
Teversal
Mansfield
Middleton
Birchover
Darley Bridge
Peak Rail
Upper Hackney
Ashover
Fallgate
Pilsley
Skegby
The Pennine Bridleway
Elton
Wensley
Milltown
Tansley Knoll
Stretton
Tibshelf
Tibshelf Services
Stanton Hill
Heathcote
Newhaven
Winster
Matlock
Woolley
Morton
Stonebroom
Biggin
Pikehall
Brightgate
The Heights of Abraham
Tansley
Brackenfield
Higham
Newton
Huthwaite
Sutton in Ashfield
Bonsall
Starkholmes
Grangemill
Gulliver's Kingdom
Matlock Bath
Lea
Wessington
Shirland
Westhouses
Blackwell
Hilcote
Biggin Dale
Ible
Arkwright's Cromford Mill
Masson Mills
Wheatcroft
South Normanton
Kirkby in Ashfield
Aldwark
Cromford
Holloway
The National Tramway Mus.
Fourlane Ends
Alfreton
Cox Moor
Alsop en le Dale
Longcliffe
Middleton
National Stone Cen.
Leawood Pumphouse
South Wingfield
McArthur Glen Mansfield
Middleton Top Engine House
Bolehill
Oakerthorpe
Pinxton
Nuncargate
Newstead Abbey
Milldale
Ballidon
Wirksworth
Wirksworth Moor
Whatstandwell
Wingfield Manor
Alfreton Services
Somercotes
Dove Dale
Parwich
Brassington
Crich
Fritchley
Swanwick
Leabrooks
Selston
Annesley
Annesley Woodhouse
Bradbourne
Carsington
Miller's Green
Alderwasley
Bullbridge
Pentrich
Riddings
Tissington
Ecclesbourne Valley Rly
Shining Cliff
Carsington Res.
Ambergate
Ridgeway Cottage Industrial Centre
Midland Railway Centre
Ironville
Jacksdale
Newstead
Papplewick
Thorpe
Fenny Bentley
Hognaston
Toadmoor
Heage
Bagthorpe
Felley Priory
Linby
Beighton Hill
Ripley
New Brinsley
Underwood
Kniveton
Belper Lane End
Nether Heage
Codnor
Brinsley
Hucknall
Kirk Ireton
Shottle
Derwent Valley Visitor Cen.
Broadholme
Marehay
Atlow
Biggin
Idridgehay
Mount Pleasant
Far Laund
Cross Hill
Westville
Mapleton
Hulland Ward
Hillclifflane
Blackbrook
Openwoodgate
Loscoe
Aldercar
Moorgreen
D H Lawrence Birthplace Mus.
Ashbourne
Hulland
Cowers Lane
Shottlegate
De Bradelei Mill
Belper
Denby
Heanor
Eastwood
Bradley
Cross o' th' hands
Turnditch
Hazelwood
Kilburn
Horsley Woodhouse
Marlpool
Watnall
Mayfield
Church Mayfield
Clifton
Windley
Milford
Horsley
Shipley
Kimberley
Nuthall
Bulwell
Osmaston
Holbrook
Smalley
Awsworth
Old Basford
Snelston
Wyaston
Weston Underwood
Coxbench
Cotmanhay
Mapperley
Erewash Museum
Swingate
Cossall
Duffield
Shipley
Nottingham
Darley Moor
Shirley
Mugginton
Brailsford
Ednaston
Kedleston
Flaxholme
Little Eaton
Stanley Common
Morley
West Hallam
Ilkeston
Strelley
Castle Museum & Gallery
Yeaveley
Rodsley
Hollington
Quarndon
Breadsall
Kirk Hallam
Trowell
Trowell Services
Bentley Fields Open Farm
Cubley Common
Great Cubley
Alkmonton
Hollington Grove
Kirk Langley
Kedleston Hall
Allestree
Stanley
Dale Abbey
Stanton-by-Dale
Wollaton
Wollaton Hall
Marston Montgomery
Thurvaston
Longlane
Langley Common
Mackworth
Chaddesden
Bramcote
Beeston
Longford
Lees
Derby City
Sandiacre
Risley
Stapleford
Longfordlane
Radbourne
Spondon
Ockbrook
Chilwell
Boylestone
Trusley
Mickleover
City Mus. & Art Gall.
Borrowash
Breaston
Attenborough
Oaks Green
Dalbury
Littleover
Osmaston
Elvaston Castle & Mus.
Draycott
Long Eaton
Barton in Fabis
Church Broughton
Sutton on the Hill
Burnaston
Normanton
Alvaston
Elvaston
Thrumpton
Sudbury
Foston
Etwall
Allenton
Thulston
Sawley
Scropton
Sudbury Hall
Hatton
Hilton
Findern
Chellaston
Shardlow
Cavendish Bridge
Gotham
Tutbury
Marston on Dove
63
Stenson
Aston-on-Trent
Ratcliffe on Soar
Willington
Twyford
Swarkestone
Shardlow Services
Lockington
New Kingston
Barrow upon Trent
Weston-on-Trent
Hemington
Castle Donington
Kingston on Soar
Repton
Ingleby
Stanton by Bridge
King's Newton
Donington Park
Grand Prix Racing Cars
Nottingham East Midlands
Kegworth
West Leake
Hanbury Woodend
Anslow Gate
Anslow
Milton
Melbourne
Newton Solney
0 1 2 3 4 5 6 miles
0 1 2 3 4 5 6 7 8 9 10 km

Woodsetts
Wigthorpe
Gateford
Shireoaks
Rhodesia
Darfoulds
Worksop
Kilton
Manton
Scofton
Ranby
Babworth
West Retford
Ordsall
RETFORD
BASSETLAW MUSEUM
Clarborough
Hayton
North Leverton with Habblesthorpe
NORTH LEVERTON WINDMILL
Welham
Le Steeple
Littleborough
Sutton
South Leverton
Coates
Marton
Gate Burton
Stow
Normanby by Stow
Cammeringham
Thorpe in the Fallows
Aisthorpe
Scampton
Sturton by Stow
Brampton
Torksey
Bransby
Brattleby
Ingleby
Broxholme
North Carlton
South Carlton
Saxilby
Kettlethorpe
Fenton
Odder
Burton
MUSEUM OF LINCOLNSHIRE LIFE
Grove
Treswell
SUNDOWN ADVENTURELAND
Rampton
Cottam
Eaton
Headon
Woodbeck
Stokeham
Church Laneham
Laneham
Gamston
Upton
Laughterton
Dunham
Newton on Trent
Elkesley
Askham
East Drayton
West Drayton
Markham Moor
Darlton
Ragnall
MARKHAM MOOR SERVICES
Milton
West Markham
East Markham
WALKS OF LIFE
Tuxford
Fledborough
Thorney
Broadholme
Skellingthorpe
North Clifton
Harby
DODDINGTON HALL
Doddington
Birchwood
Boultham
Bracebridge
HARTSHOLME
High Marnham
Low Marnham
Normanton on Trent
South Clifton
Spalford
Wigsley
Eagle Moor
Eagle
LINCOLNSHIRE ROAD TRANSPORT MUSEUM
Whisby
WHISBY NATURE WORLD
Grassthorpe
Weston
Sutton on Trent
Girton
North Scarle
Eagle Barnsdale
Thorpe on the Hill
North Hykeham
South Hykeham
Besthorpe
Carlton on Trent
South Scarle
Swinderby
Morton
Haddington
Aubourn
Harmston
Cromwell
Collingham
Thurlby
Bassingham
Norwell
THE VINA COOKE MUSEUM OF DOLLS
Norwell Woodhouse
Ossington
Holme
Langford
Brough
Norton Disney
Stapleford
Carlton le Moorland
North Muskham
Bathley
Little Carlton
South Muskham
Winthorpe
NEWARK AIR MUSEUM
Kelham
Coddington
Beckingham
Brant Broughton
Welbourn
Averham
Staythorpe
Newark-on-Trent
Balderton
Barnby in the Willows
Stragglethorpe
Leadenham
Fulbeck
Hawton
Fenton
Claypole
MANOR STABLES CRAFT WORKSHOPS
Caythorpe
Stubton
Brandon
Dry Doddington
Frieston
Hough-on-the-Hill
Gelston
Carlton Scroop
West Willoughby
Normanton
Long Bennington
Hougham
Westborough
Marston
MARSTON
Honington
Foston
Barkston
Syston
Belton
BELTON HOUSE
Great Gonerby
Manthorpe
Londonthorpe
GRANTHAM NORTH SERVICES
BOUNDARY MILLS
Allington
Sedgebrook
Barrowby
Grantham
GRANTHAM MUS.
Earlsfield
Cold Harbour
Old Somerby
Little Ponton
Harlaxton
HARLAXTON MANOR
Stroxton
Great Ponton
Woolsthorpe
Denton
Wyville
Stoke Rochford
Easton
Skillington
Bassingthorpe
WOOLSTHORPE MANOR
Colsterworth
Hungerton
Croxton Kerrial
Saltby
Branston
Knipton
Harston
Eaton
Eastwell
Waltham on the Wolds
Goadby Marwood
Long Clawson
Hose
Harby
Stathern
Plungar
Belvoir
BELVOIR
Barkestone-le-Vale
Redmile
Stenwith
MUSTON MEADOWS
Muston
Bottesford
Easthorpe
Normanton
Alverton
Kilvington
Staunton in the Vale
Flawborough
Hawksworth
Thoroton
Orston
Scarrington
Car Colston
Screveton
Sibthorpe
Shelton
Cotham
Flintham
Syerston
Elston
East Stoke
Thorpe
Fiskerton
Farndon
Rolleston
Morton
Upton
THE WORKHOUSE
Southwell
SOUTHWELL MINSTER
Easthorpe
SOUTHWELL
Halam
Normanton
Hockerton
Edingley
Farnsfield
Kirklington
Winkburn
Caunton
Knapthorpe
Maplebeck
Eakring
Kersall
Kneesall
Ompton
Wellow
BETH SHALOM HOLOCAUST CENTRE
Laxton
Moorhouse
Egmanton
Boughton
New Ollerton
Ollerton
Kirton
Walesby
Bevercotes
Haughton
Bothamsall
Hardwick
CLUMBER PARK
Carburton
CRESWELL CRAGS MUSEUM
Great Lake
Norton
Cuckney
Perlethorpe
HAMLYN LODGE COTTAGE INDUSTRY
Church Warsop
Meden Vale
Budby
SHERWOOD FOREST
Market Warsop
SHERWOOD FOREST VISITORS CENTRE
Edwinstowe
Lidgett
SHERWOOD FOREST
SHERWOOD FOREST FARM PARK
Old Clipstone
RUFFORD
SHERWOOD PINES FOREST PARK
Clipstone
Forest Town
Bilsthorpe
Bilsthorpe Moor
Rainworth
WONDERLAND PLEASURE PARK
WHITE POST FARM CENTRE
White Post
Blidworth
Haywood Oaks
Ravenshead
LONGDALE RURAL CRAFT CENTRE
PAPPLEWICK PUMPING STATION
BURNTSTUMP
Oxton
Halloughton
Park Hill
Thurgarton
Bleasby
Hoveringham
Gonalston
Epperstone
Calverton
Woodborough
BESTWOOD
Bestwood Village
Lowdham
TUMBLE TOWN
ARNOLD
Bestwood
Lambley
Caythorpe
Kneeton
Gunthorpe
East Bridgford
Bulcote
Burton Joyce
Gedling
Porchester
Mapperley Park
Carlton
GREENS MILL & SCIENCE CENTRE
THE TALES OF ROBIN HOOD
Nottingham
Colwick
Radcliffe on Trent
Stoke Bardolph
Shelford
Newton
Saxondale
Bingham
Aslockton
Whatton
Elton
Harlequin
Holme Pierrepont
HOLME PIERREPONT
Lenton
TRENT BRIDGE CRICKET GRD.
Bassingfield
WEST BRIDGFORD
Wilford
Edwalton
Cotgrave
NOTTINGHAM
Cropwell Butler
Tithby
Sutton
Granby
Barnstone
Langar
NATURESCAPE WILD FLOWER FARM
VALE OF BELVOIR
Cropwell Bishop
Owthorpe
Colston Bassett
Tollerton
Normanton-on-the-Wolds
Plumtree
Clifton
FRAMEWORK KNITTERS MUS.
Ruddington
RUSHCLIFFE
GREAT CENTRAL RLY. (NOTT'M)
Bradmore
Keyworth
Kinoulton
Stanton-on-the-Wolds
Bunny
Hickling
Upper Broughton
Widmerpool
Wysall
Willoughby-on-the-Wolds
East Leake
Costock
MANOR FARM
Nether Broughton
Wycomb
Nottingham
SK

by Stow
Normanby by Stow
Ingham
Cold Hanworth
Friesthorpe
Lissington
East Torrington
South Willingham
Donington on Bain
Stow
Cammeringham
Hackthorn
Snarford
Wickenby
West Torrington
Benniworth
Thorpe in the Fallows
Brattleby
Welton Hill
Holton cum Beckering
REDHURST B&B
East Barkwith
Sturton by Stow
Aisthorpe
DAMBUSTERS INN & HERITAGE CENTRE
Welton
Snelland
West Barkwith
Market Stainton
Brampton
Scampton
Dunholme
Fulnetby
Rand
RAND FARM PARK
Sotby
Torksey
Bransby
Stainton by Langworth
Panton
Wragby
Ranby
Broxholme
North Carlton
Scothern
Bullington
Ingleby
Fenton
South Carlton
Sudbrooke
Langworth
WOODSIDE FALCONRY AND CONSERVATION CENTRE
Langton by Wragby
Hatton
Great Sturton
Kettlethorpe
Saxilby
Odder
Riseholme
Nettleham
Apley
Kingthorpe
Newton on Trent
Burton
Reepham
Hemingby
MUSEUM OF LINCOLNSHIRE LIFE
Bunker's Hill
North Greetwell
Cherry Willingham
Low Barlings
Minting
Baumber
Broadholme
Ermine
ELLIS MILL
Thorney
Skellingthorpe
St Giles
CATH
Fiskerton
Stainfield
Gautby
Wispington
Clifton
Harby
New Boultham
Lincoln
Washingborough
Young Wood
Edlington
DODDINGTON HALL
Wigsley
Doddington
Birchwood
Boultham
Canwick
Branston Booths
Bardney
Bucknall
Thimbleby
Spalford
HARTSHOLME
Heighington
Langton
Horsington
LINCOLNSHIRE ROAD TRANSPORT MUSEUM
Bracebridge
Eagle Moor
Whisby
Bracebridge Heath
Branston
Potterhanworth Booths
BARDNEY LIMEWOODS
Thornton
Eagle
WHISBY NATURAL WORLD
Southrey
Old Woodhall
North Scarle
North Hykeham
Bracebridge Low Fields
Potterhanworth
Stixwould
Reeds Beck
Martin
Dalderby
Eagle Barnsdale
Thorpe on the Hill
South Hykeham
Nocton
Wasps Nest
Sots Hole
Roughton Moor
Roughton
Morton
Waddington
Dunston
COTTAGE MUSEUM
Woodhall Spa
Haltham
South Scarle
Swinderby
Haddington
Metheringham
Kirkstead
Kirkby on Bain
Aubourn
Harmston
Martin Dales
Toft Hill
Collingham
Thurlby
Coleby
Blankney
Martin
Tattershall Thorpe
Bassingham
Boothby Graffoe
METHERINGHAM AIRFIELD VISITOR CENTRE
TIMBERLAND ART & DESIGN
TATTERSHALL COLLEGE
Norton Disney
Navenby
Scopwick
Timberland
Tattershall
Coningsby
Brough
BATTLE OF BRITAIN MEMORIAL FLIGHT
Stapleford
Carlton le Moorland
SK
TF
Kirkby Green
Thorpe Tilney
Walcott
Tattershall Bridge
COLLEGIATE CHURCH OF THE HOLY TRINITY
NEWARK AIR MUSEUM
Wellingore
Rowston
BILLINGHAY COTTAGE
Hawthorn Hill
Witham
Brant
Ashby de la Launde
Dogdyke
Scrub Hill
New York
Coddington
Digby
Billinghay
Chapel Hill
Welbourn
Bloxholm
Beckingham
Brant Broughton
Stragglethorpe
Leadenham
Dorrington
North Kyme
Haven Bank
Wildmore
Barnby in the Willows
ERMINE STREET
Fenton
Ruskington
Anwick
Fulbeck
Cranwell
MANOR STABLES CRAFT WORKSHOPS
South Kyme
Holland Fen
Claypole
BUBBLE CAR MUSEUM
Leasingham
Stubton
Caythorpe
South Kyme Fen
Brandon
Evedon
Amber Hill
Dry Doddington
Frieston
North Rauceby
CRANWELL AVIATION HERITAGE CENTRE
Ewerby
Ewerby Thorpe
Hough-on-the-Hill
Holdingham
COGGLESFORD WATERMILL
Kirkby la Thorpe
Long Bennington
Normanton
South Rauceby
Howell
HOLLAND FEN
Gelston
Carlton Scroop
Sleaford
Asgarby
East Heckington
Hougham
Sudbrook
Quarrington
Swineshead Bridge
Westborough
West Willoughby
Ancaster
Heckington
THE PEAROOM CENTRE
Marston
MARSTON HALL
Silk Willoughby
HECKINGTON WINDMILL
Great Hale
Foston
Honington
Wilsford
Burton Pedwardine
Little Hale
North End
Syston
Barkston
Kelby
Northbeck
Helpringham
BOUNDARY MILLS
GRANTHAM NORTH SERVICES
Culverthorpe
Swarby
Swineshead
Allington
Belton
Oasby
Heydour
Scredington
Drayton
Great Gonerby
BELTON HOUSE
Aswarby
Sedgebrook
Aisby
Aunsby
Osbournby
Spanby
Bicker
Manthorpe
Welby
Dembleby
Swaton
Londonthorpe
Grantham
Haceby
Newton
Northorpe
Donington
Barrowby
Earlsfield
GRANTHAM MUS
Cold Harbour
Braceby
Walcot
Threekingham
Bridge End
Horbling
Church End
Stow
Woolsthorpe
Ropsley
Sapperton
Pickworth
Billingborough
Donington South Ing
Birthorpe
Denton
Old Somerby
Folkingham
Quadring
HARLAXTON MANOR
Humby
Hanby
Harlaxton
Little Ponton
Boothby Pagnell
Laughton
Pointon
Gosberton
Stroxton
Lenton
Aslackby
Westhorpe
Millthorpe
Great Ponton
Dowsby
Gosberton Clough
Hungerton
Ingoldsby
Graby
Risegate
Croxton Kerrial
Keisby
Bitchfield
Kirkby Underwood
Hawthorpe
Rippingale
Irnham
Surfleet Seas End
Northgate
Bulby
Dunsby
Saltby
Skillington
WOOLSTHORPE MANOR
Burton-le-Coggles
Stainfield
Pinchbeck Bars
Pinchbeck
0 1 2 3 4 5 6 miles
0 1 2 3 4 5 6 7 8 9 10 km
A1500
A156
A57
A46
A15
A158
B1190
B1188
B1178
B1202
B1191
B1189
B1192
A153
A607
A17
B1429
B1209
B6403
B1395
A52
B1394
B1177
B1176
B1174
A607
A1
B1397
B1181
A152
B1356
90
91
77
65

Raithby
Withcall
Little Cawthorpe
South Reston
Gayton le Marsh
Trusthorpe
Tathwell
North Reston
Muckton
Strubby
Maltby le Marsh
Thorpe
Sutton on Sea
Haugham
Withern
Tothill
Stenigot
CADWELL PARK
Cawkwell
Authorpe
Sandilands
Burwell
Woodthorpe
Beesby
Maidenwell
WOODY'S TOP
Belleau
CLAYTHORPE WATER MILL AND WILDFOWL GARDENS
Saleby
Hannah
Goulceby
Markby
Scamblesby
Farforth
Ruckland
White Pit
Aby
Swaby
Oxcombe
South Thoresby
ALFORD WINDMILL
Asserby
Ketsby
Bilsby
ALFORD MANOR HOUSE
Alford
Huttoft
Belchford
South Ormsby
Calceby
Rigsby
Haugh
Anderby
ON YOUR MARQUES
Tetford
Farlesthorpe
Mumby
Authorpe Row
Driby
Brinkhill
Well
Fulletby
Cumberworth
Salmonby
Somersby
Ulceby
Chapel St Leonards
Helsey
West Ashby
Bag Enderby
Sutterby
Bonthorpe
Hogsthorpe
Claxby
Ashby Puerorum
Harrington
Willoughby
High Toynton
Langton
Greetham
Sloothby
Aswardby
HARDY'S ANIMAL FARM
Skendleby
Horncastle
Hagworthingham
Sausthorpe
Ingoldmells
Scrafield
SNIPE DALES
Partney
FANTASY ISLAND CHILDREN'S PLAYDROME & THE MILLENNIUM ROLLERCOASTER
Addlethorpe
Welton le Marsh
Mareham on the Hill
Lusby
Scremby
Hameringham
Mavis Enderby
Raithby
Candlesby
Orby
FUNCOAST WORLD
Orby Marsh
Scrivelsby
Asgarby
Spilsby
Ashby by Partney
GUNBY HALL
Hareby
Old Bolingbroke
Hundleby
Burgh le Marsh
Winthorpe
Seathorne
NORTHCOTE HEAVY HORSE CENTRE
Great Steeping
Bratoft
Wood Enderby
BOLINGBROKE
Toynton All Saints
Halton Holegate
NATURELAND SEAL SANCTUARY
Moorby
Miningsby
West Keal
Irby in the Marsh
BURGH LE MARSH WINDMILL
CHURCH FARM MUS
Skegness
OSLINC OSTRICH FARM
East Keal
Toynton St Peter
Firsby
THE LIFEBOAT STATION
East Kirkby
Little Steeping
Toynton Fen Side
Mareham le Fen
LINCOLNSHIRE AVIATION HERITAGE CENTRE
Keal Cotes
Thorpe Culvert
Thorpe St Peter
Croft
Revesby
Seacroft
Thorpe Fendykes
Croft Marsh
Revesby Bridge
Wainfleet All Saints
Stickford
GIBRALTAR POINT
Wainfleet Bank
New Bolingbroke
Fen Side
MAGDALEN MUSEUM
Wainfleet Tofts
Wainfleet St Mary
GIBRALTAR POINT
New Leake
Midville
Tumby Woodside
Stickney
Friskney Eaudike
Medlam
Eastville
Wainfleet Sand
Sandy Bank
East Fen
Friskney
Carrington
Bunker's Hill
Lade Bank
West Fen
Wrangle Bank
Friskney Tofts
Hundle Houses
Northlands
Leake Commonside
SIBSEY TRADER MILL
Friskney Flats
Wrangle Lowgate
Sibsey
Old Leake
Frithville
Gipsey Bridge
Wrangle
Fishtoft Drove
Hurn's End
Langrick
Anton's Gowt
Boston Long Hedges
Leverton Outgate
BOSTON DEEPS
Hilldyke
Leverton Highgate
Frith Bank
Leverton
Cowbridge
Leverton Lucasgate
LYNN DEEPS
Brothertoft
Benington
Boston West
Boston
Haltoft End
Butterwick
TF
GUILDHALL
Freiston
Chain Bridge
Skirbeck
Skirbeck Quarter
Kirton Holme
Wyberton
THE WASH
Frampton West End
Fishtoft
Scrane End
Hunstanton
SEA LIFE SANCTUARY
Fenhouses
Kirton End
Frampton
Kirton
Sandholme
Asperton
Heacham
Skeldyke
Wigtoft
Seadyke
Sutterton
Bucklegate
Algarkirk
Lynn Channel
Fosdyke
Risegate Haven
Holbeach St Matthew
SNETTISHAM NATURE RESERVE
Holbeach St Marks
Dawsmere
Surfleet Seas End
HOLBEACH MARSH
Gedney Marsh
Gedney Drove End
DERSINGHAM
Surfleet
Moulton Seas End
Saracen's Head
Holbeach Hurn
THE WASH
Wolferton
Holbeach Bank
Gedney Dyke
Halesgate
Holbeach Clough
Lutton
Guy's
BAYTREE

NATURELAND SEAL SANCTUARY
THE LIFEBOAT STATION
Skegness
Seacroft
GIBRALTAR POINT
Wainfleet Sand
TF
NORFOLK COAST
BRANCASTER ROADS
LYNN DEEPS
79
Holkham Bay
SCOLT HEAD ISLAND
Brancaster Bay
HOLME DUNES
BIRD OBSERVATORY RESERVE
Holme next the Sea
Titchwell
Brancaster Staithe
Burnham Deepdale
Brancaster
Burnham Norton
Westgate
Burnham Market
Burnham Overy Staithe
Burnham Overy Town
Burnham Thorpe
PEDDARS WAY & NORFOLK COAST PATH
HOLKHAM
Holkham
HOLKHAM HALL
WELLS-NEXT-THE-SEA
Wells-Next-The-Sea
Warham
WELLS AND WALSINGHAM RAILWAY
Old Hunstanton
Hunstanton
SEA LIFE SANCTUARY
HUNSTANTON
Ringstead
Thornham
Summerfield
Heacham
NORFOLK LAVENDER
Docking
Sedgeford
Stanhoe
CREAKE ABBEY
New Holkham
North Creake
South Creake
SOUTH CREAKE MAIZE MAZE
Waterden
Wighton
Copy's Green
Great Walsingham
Little Walsingham
SHIREHALL MUS.
North Barsham
Houghton St Giles
West Barsham
Great Snoring
East Barsham
Snettisham
SNETTISHAM PARK
Fring
Bircham Newton
Great Bircham
Barmer
Syderstone
Blenheim Park
Wicken Green Village
Sculthorpe
SNETTISHAM NATURE RESERVE
Shepherd's Port
Ingoldisthorpe
Shernborne
BIRCHAM MILL
Bircham Tofts
Bagthorpe
PEDDARS WAY
Dersingham
Anmer
HOUGHTON HALL
West Rudham
East Rudham
Tattersett
Coxford
Dunton
Shereford
Tatterford
Hempton
Fakenham
FAKENHAM
Toftrees
67
DERSINGHAM BOG
SANDRINGHAM
Sandringham
Wolferton
West Newton
Flitcham
New Houghton
Harpley
Helhoughton
West Raynham
East Raynham
Colkirk
Oxwick
Hamrow
Horningtoft
Castle Rising
CASTLE RISING
North Wootton
South Wootton
Hillington
Little Massingham
Great Massingham
South Raynham
Whissonsett
Terrington Marsh
Ongar Hill
King's Lynn
MARITIME EXHIBITION
ROYDON COMMON
Roydon
Congham
CONGHAM HALL HERB GARDEN
Grimston
Pott Row
Massingham Heath
Weasenham St Peter
Weasenham All Saints
EXTREEME ADVENTURE
Wellingham
Tittleshall
Stanfield
Clenchwarton
Terrington St Clement
GUILDHALL
Gaywood
West Lynn
KING'S LYNN
Fairstead
Hardwick
Gayton
Ashwicken
Leziate
Rougham
Mileham
Tilney All Saints
Tilney High End
Fair Green
Tower End
Gayton Thorpe
West Lexham
Litcham
Bittering
East Lexham
Middleton
West Winch
North Runcton
East Winch
East Walton
Castle Acre
CASTLE ACRE PRIORY
Newton
Beeston
Longham
Terrington St John
Tilney St Lawrence
Saddle Bow
Wiggenhall St Germans
Wiggenhall St Mary the Virgin
Setchey
Blackborough End
West Bilney
Pentney
West Acre
South Acre
Great Dunham
Drury Square
Sparrow Green
Crane's Corner
Little Dunham
Great Fransham
Wendling
Tottenhill Row
Narborough
Wormegay
Great Palgrave
Sporle
Little Fransham
BRADENHAM HALL GDNS. & ARBORETUM
Wiggenhall St Mary Magdalen
Watlington
Tottenhill
Runcton Holme
Shouldham
Marham
Necton
West End
Swaffham
Bradenham
Beachamwell Warren
Holme Hale
North Pickenham
West Head
Wimbotsham
Stow Bardolph
Fincham
Barton Bendish
Beachamwell
Crowshill
A149
A148
A1065
A47
A10
A134
A1122
A1078
B1153
B1155
B1355
B1105
B1454
B1440
B1439
B1145
B1146
0 1 2 3 4 5 6 miles
0 1 2 3 4 5 6 7 8 9 10km

TG
NORFOLK
COAST
Blakeney Point
BLAKENEY
GUILDHALL
CLEY MILL
Cley next the Sea
PEDDARS WAY AND NORFOLK COAST PATH
Salthouse
Morston
Blakeney
Wiveton
Newgate
Kelling
Stiffkey
Cockthorpe
Langham
Glandford
MUCKLEBURGH COLLECTION
Weybourne
SHERINGHAM PARK
NORTH NORFOLK RAILWAY
Sheringham
PRIORY MAZE & GARDENS
NORFOLK SHIRE HORSE CENTRE
CROMER MUSEUM
Cromer
West Runton
East Runton
Upper Sheringham
Beeston Regis
High Kelling
Bodham
East Beckham
West Beckham
Aylmerton
Felbrigg
FELBRIGG HALL
Overstrand
Northrepps
Sidestrand
Trimingham
Crossdale Street
Westgate
Binham
Saxlingham
Letheringsett
Holt
Field Dalling
WAYSIDE CROSS
THE TEXTILE CENTRE
Lower Green
LETHERINGSETT WATERMILL
PICTURECRAFT GALLERY
HOLT
BACONSTHORPE CASTLE
Gresham
Frogshall
Southrepps
Gimingham
Mundesley
STOW WINDMILL
Bale
Sharrington
Hempstead
Baconsthorpe
Sustead
Roughton
Hindringham
Brinton
Thornage
Hunworth
Bessingham
Hanworth
Thurgarton
Thorpe Market
Lower Street
Trunch
Paston
THURSFORD COLLECTION
Thursford
Gunthorpe
Stody
Briningham
Edgefield
Plumstead
Matlaske
Aldborough
Alby Hill
Knapton
Bacton
Keswick
Broomholm
Little Snoring
Barney
Swanton Novers
Melton Constable
Briston
Edgefield Street
Little Barningham
Wickmere
ALBY CRAFTS
ALBY GARDENS
Antingham
Bradfield
Edingthorpe
Swafield
Kettlestone
Fulmodestone
MANNINGTON GARDENS
WOLTERTON PARK
Calthorpe
Erpingham
Colby
Suffield
STRAW MUSEUM
North Walsham
Edingthorpe Green
Witton Bridge
Ridlington
Spa Common
Crostwight
Corpusty
Saxthorpe
Itteringham
PENSTHORPE NATURE RESERVE & GARDENS
Stibbard
Little Ryburgh
Great Ryburgh
Hindolveston
Thurning
BLICKLING HALL
Ingworth
Blickling
Banningham
Felmingham
EAST RUSTON GARDEN
Honing
East Ruston
Wood Norton
Norton Corner
Oulton
Silvergate
Dunkirk
Tuttington
Westwick
Guestwick
Guestwick Green
Wood Dalling
Heydon
Oulton Street
Aylsham
Burgh next Aylsham
Skeyton
Bengate
Worstead
Guist
Swanton Abbott
Sloley
Dilham
Smallburgh
Twyford
Foulsham
Themelthorpe
Salle
Southgate
Fengate
Gateley
Broom Green
Bintree
FOXLEY WOOD
Reepham
Cawston
Little London
Marsham
Brampton
BURE VALLEY RAILWAY
Scottow
Pennygate
Foxley
Booton
Eastgate
Buxton
Lamas
Little Hautbois
Tunstead
Brisley
North Elmham
Whitwell Street
Brandiston
The Heath
Sco Ruston
ANT BROADS AND MARSHES
Neatishead
Billingford
Bawdeswell
Haveringland
Hevingham
Stratton Strawless
WROXHAM BARNS
Ashmanhaugh
Coltishall
East Bilney
Worthing
Sparham
NORFOLK WILDLIFE CENTRE
Alderford
Swannington
Waterloo
Threehammer Common
Beetley
Mill Street
Lenwade
Upgate
New Hainford
Hainford
Belaugh
Hoveton
NORFOLK RURAL LIFE MUSEUM
Swanton Morley
Lyng
DINOSAUR ADVENTURE PARK
Frettenham
Wroxham
Lower Street
Upper Street
Gressenhall
Hoe
Elsing
Morton
Attlebridge
Felthorpe
Horsford
Newton St Faith
HILLSIDE ANIMAL SANCTUARY
Horning
Wroxham Broad
BURE MARSHES
Woodgate
Primrose Green
Weston Longville
Thorpe Marriott
Crostwick
Woodbastwick
Etling Green
North Tuddenham
Weston Green
Ringland
Taverham
Drayton
Horsham St Faith
Spixworth
Rackheath
Salhouse
Dereham
Hockering
NORWICH INTERNATIONAL
New Rackheath
Panxworth
MID-NORFOLK RAILWAY
Mattishall Burgh
Honingham
Costessey
Hellesdon
Old Catton
Sprowston
Thorpe End
Little Plumstead
Hemblington
Scarning
Toftwood
Clint Green
Mattishall
East Tuddenham
Easton
Mile Cross
Upper Hellesdon
Blofield Heath
Daffy Green
Yaxham
New Costessey
THE FORUM
New Catton
Thorpe St Andrew
Great Plumstead
Westfield
Whinburgh
Welborne
Colton
Marlingford
Bowthorpe
Earlham
CATHEDRAL
NORWICH
Brundall
Blofield
Brandon Parva
Bawburgh
SAINSBURY CENTRE FOR VISUAL ARTS
Runhall
Barford
Colney
Lakenham
Postwick
Shipdham
Garvestone
Thuxton
Barnham Broom
Great Melton
Little Melton
Cringleford
Letton Green
Reymerston
Danemoor
Wramplingham
High Green
Eaton
Trowse Newton
Kirby Bedon
Surlingham
A148
A149
A1082
B1156
B1110
B1354
B1149
B1436
A140
B1145
B1150
B1354
A1067
B1147
B1110
B1146
A47
A1074
A1151
B1140
B1108
B1135
A1075
68
69
P&R

Isle of Anglesey
(Sir Ynys Môn)
Holyhead
(Caergybi)
Holy Island
Ynys Gybi
The Skerries
Ynysoedd y Moelrhoniaid
Carmel Head
Pen Carmel
Wilfa Head
Pen Wilfa
Cemlyn Bay
Bae Cemlyn
Cemaes Bay
Bae Cemaes
WYLFA POWER STATION AND OBSERVATION TOWER
Bull Bay
Porth Llechog
Point Lynas
Trwyn Eilian
Dulas Bay
Bae Dulas
Church Bay
Porth Swtan
HOLYHEAD BAY
BAE CAERGYBI
DUBLIN 1:49
DUN LAOGHAIRE 1:40
DUBLIN 3:00
North Stack
BREAKWATER
HOLYHEAD MOUNTAIN
220
South Stack
ELLINS TOWER RSPB RESERVE
PENRHOS FEILW STANDING STONES
Penrhyn Mawr
Cymyran Bay
Bae Cymyran
SH
LLYNON WINDMILL
Alaw Res.
CORS ERDDREINIOG
CORS GOCH
THE STONE SCIENCE
CORS BODEILIO
ORIEL YNYS MON
HENBLAS COUNTRY PARK
JAMES PRINGLE WEAVERS
PILI PALAS
PLAS NEWYDD
PLAS COCH GARDEN ZOO
SEA ZOO
BIRD WORLD
FOEL FARM PARK
MODEL VILLAGE
NEWBOROUGH WARREN AND YNYS LLANDDWYN
Malltraeth Bay
Bae Malltraeth
Llanddwyn I.
Ynys Llanddwyn
Newborough Forest
SEIONT II MARITIME MUSEUM
CASTLE & REGIMENTAL MUS.
SEGONTIUM FORT
MENAI STRAIT AFON MENAI
Caernarfon
WELSH HIGHLAND RAILWAY
INIGO JONES TUDOR SLATEWORKS
CAERNARFON AIR MUSEUM
GLYNLLIFON
WELSH LIFE
The Bar
Abermenai Pt.
Trwyn Abermenai
CAERNARFON BAY
BAE CAERNARFON
ANGLESEY
YNYS MÔN
Amlwch
Amlwch Port
Llanbadrig
Porthllechog
Burwen
Cemaes
Tregele
Llanfechell
Rhosbeirio
Bodewryd
Llaneilian
Pengorffwysfa
Penysarn
Nebo
Dulas
City Dulas
Brynrefail
Moelfre
Ty-mawr
Llanallgo
Marianglas
Benllech
Red Wharf Bay
Tan-y-graig
Pentraeth
Llanfairynghornwy
Llanfflewyn
Rhosgoch
Carreglefn
Rhydwyn
Llanrhyddlad
Llanfaethlu
Llanbabo
Gwredog
Rhosybol
Tyn-y-pwll
Llandyfrydog
Mynydd Bodafon
Hebron
Llanddeusant
Elim
Llanerchymedd
Bachau
Maenaddwyn
Brynteg
Tynygongl
Llanfwrog
Llanfachraeth
Llantrisant
Carmel
Capel Coch
Pen-llyn
Llechcynfarwy
Llanynghenedl
Newlands Park
Llangoch
Goferydd
Kingsland
Penrhosfeilw
Trearddur
Glan-traeth
Four Mile Bridge
Valley
Caergeiliog
Bodedern
Trefor
Tregaian
Llanbedrgoch
Llangwyllog
Llynfaes
Glan Gors
Rhosmeirch
Llanddyfnan
Talwrn
Pen-y-garnedd
Bryngwran
Llanfihangel yn Nhowyn
Gwalchmai
Bodffordd
Heneglwys
Llangefni
Rhoscefnhir
Ceint
Penmynydd
Rhoscolyn
Llanfairyneubwll
Capel-gwyn
Ddrydwy
Cerrigceinwen
Llangristiolus
Porthaethwy
Llanfaelog
Rhosneigr
Bryn Du
Pencarnisiog
Soar
Capel Mawr
Pentre Berw
Gaerwen
Llanfairpwll-gwyngyll
Bethel
Trefdraeth
Afon Cefni
Llanddaniel Fab
Capel-y-graig
Llangwyfan-isaf
Llangadwaladr
Aberffraw
Hermon
Malltraeth
Llangaffo
Brynsiencyn
Bodorgan
Y Felinheli
Seion
Llanddeiniolen
Newborough
Dwyran
Pen-lon
Bethel
Saron
Waterloo Port
Llanrug
Pont-rug
Cwm-y-glo
Caeathro
Ceunant
Llanfaglan
Saron
Bontnewydd
Croesywaun
Groeslon
Waunfawr
Glan-rhyd
Morfa Dinlle
Llanwnda
Rhostryfan
Rhosgadfan
Dinas Dinlle
Ffrwd
Penyffridd
Betws-Garmon
Llandwrog
Groeslon
Fron
Carmel
Cilgwyn
Nantlle
Penygroes
Talysarn
Pontllyfni
Tan-yr-allt
Llanllyfni
Nebo
Aberdesach
Tainlon
Clynnog-fawr
Nasareth
Gyrn-goch
Capel Uchaf
Bryn-yr-eryr
Pant-glas
509 BWLCH MAWR
522 GYRN DDU
Uchaf Clynnog
Dafarn Faig
Trefor
734
Afon Dwyfor
A5
A55
A5025
A4080
A5114
A487
A499
A4085
A5108
A5111
B5109
B5110
B5111
B5112
B5420
B4419
B4421
B4422
B4545
B4366
B4418
70
71
0 1 2 3 4 5 6 miles
0 1 2 3 4 5 6 7 8 9 10 km

5
6
7
8
9
A
B
C
D
E
F
G
Great Ormes Head
Pen-y-Gogarth
TRAMWAY
TOLL
GREAT ORME
GREAT ORME COPPER MINES
Llandudno
ALICE IN WONDERLAND
Penrhynside
Penrhyn Bay
ORIEL MOSTYN
Craig-y-don
Rhos-on-Sea
Conwy Sands
Traeth Conwy
Llanrhos
Llandrillo-yn-Rhos
COLWYN BAY
(BAE COLWYN)
Abergele Roads
Angorfa Abergele
Puffin Island
Ynys Seiriol
CONWY BAY
BAE CONWY
Mariandyrys
Glan-yr-afon
Caim
Penmon
Llanddona
Llangoed
Llanfaes
Beaumaris
GAOL AND COURTHOUSE
B5109
Llansadwrn
Llandegfan
Lavan Sands
Traeth Lafan
Menai Bridge
Garth
TEGFRYN
Hirael
PENRHYN
BANGOR
Bangor
Glan Adda
Minffordd
Llandegai
Tal-y-bont
COCHWILLAN OLD HALL
Llanllechid
Rachub
BANGOR SERVICES
Glasinfryn
Tregarth
Pentir
Sling
A4244
B4409
Bethesda
Gerlan
Braichmelyn
Rhiwlas
Penisarwaun
Deiniolen
Ty'n-y-maes
Clwt-y-bont
Brynrefail
Marchlyn Mawr Res.
Llyn Padarn
Dinorwic
LLANBERIS LAKE RAILWAY
PADARN
POWER OF WALES
SLATE MUS
Llanberis
LLANBERIS
DOLBADARN
Llyn Peris
Nant Peris
Pass of Llanberis
A4086
726
SNOWDON RANGER
SNOWDON MOUNTAIN RAILWAY
1085
SNOWDON YR WYDDFA
YR WYDDFA
Rhyd-Ddu
Ffridd-Uchaf
747
Bethania
Beddgelert Forest
Nantgwynant
Llyn Gwynant
Llyn Dinas
SYGUN COPPER MINE
Beddgelert
Pass of Aberglaslyn
782
MOEL HEBOG
Nantmor
A498
Dwygyfylchi
Penmaenmawr
Penmaenan
Capelulo
Conwy
CONWY
Gyffin
ABERCONWY HOUSE/PLAS MAWR
Deganwy
Tywyn
BUTTERFLY JUNGLE
A470
Llandudno Junction
(Cyffordd Llandudno)
WELSH MOUNTAIN ZOO
Mochdre
Old Colwyn
Llanddulas
Llysfaen
Abergele
A55
Pensarn
St Ge
B5383
Llanelian-yn-Rhos
Rhŷd-y-foel
Dolwen
Bryn-y-maen
Dolwyd
Glan Conwy
Llanfairfechan
Nant-y-pandy
SH
Henryd
FELIN ISAF WATER MILL
Pentrefelin
B5381
Dawn
Betws-yn-Rhos
MOELFRE ISAF
317
Abergwyngregyn
Crymlyn
COEDYDD ABER
Aber Falls
Rhaeadr Aber
610
TAL-Y-FAN
ROWEN
Rowen
Tal-y-cafn
BODNANT
Graig
Hafod-lom
396
MOELFRE UCHAF
Ty'n-y-groes
Pontwgan
COED GORSWEN
Llanbedr-y-cennin
Tal-y-Bont
B5106
Eglwysbach
Llanfair Talhaiarn
Pentre'r Felin
B5113
389
Gell
Cefn-coch
Pentre-Isaf
Bryn-nantllech
A544
SNOWDONIA NATIONAL PARK
942
FOEL FRAS
Afon Dulyn
Llyn Eigiau
Dolgarrog
COED DOLGARROG
VALE OF CONWY
DYFFRYN CONWY
Llangernyw
Bryn-glas
Hendre-ddu
B5382
Llansannan
A548
Afon Ddu
WOOLLEN MILL
A470
Tan-lan
Llanddoged
Pandy Tudur
Tŷ'r-felin-isaf
Clwt-g
1064
CARNEDD LLYWELYN
1044
CARNEDD DAFYDD
Llyn Cowlyd
Trefriw
Pentre-tafarn-y-fedw
B5384
Byl
A5
Llyn Ogwen
Pont Rhyd-goch
Tai
Llyn Crafnant
Gwydyr Uchaf
Llanrwst
Gwytherin
Pont Pen-y-benglog
IDWAL COTTAGE
CWM GLAS CRAFNANT
Cornel
GWYDYR FOREST
GWYDYR UCHAF CHAPEL
Melin-y-coed
B5113
BRYN TRILLYN
496
Ty-draw
CWM IDWAL
999
GLYDER FAWR
PARC
Capel Curig
CAPEL CURIG
Conwy
PARK
SWALLOW FALLS
Pont Cyfyng
CONWY VALLEY RAILWAY MUSEUM
Nebo
468
MOEL SEISIOG
Llyn Aled
Llyn Alwen
A543
Mynydd Hiraethog
PEN-Y-PASS
Pen-y-Gwryd Hotel
BETWS-Y-COED
Betws-y-Coed
Capel Garmon
BURIAL CHAMBER
Fairy Glen
Mynydd Cribau
B5113
Alwen Reservoir
HAFOD ELWY MOOR
B4501
CENEDLAETHOL
Llyn Llydaw
872
CARNEDD MOEL SIABOD
Pont-y-pant
532
Hafod-Dinbych
Mwdwl-eithin
Conwy Falls
Rhaeadr Conwy
PENMACHNO WOOLLEN MILL
Glan-Conwy
Dolwyddelan
DOLWYDDELAN
TY MAWR WYBRNANT
Pentre-bont
Gwydyr Forest
Penmachno
B4406
ERYRI
Garnedd
Pentrefoelas
BRYN GWYNANT
A498
A470
Padog
Rhydlydan
Glasfryn
Cefn-brith
A5
71
72
623
MOEL PENAMNEN
Afon Machno
Ysbyty Ifan
539
GARN PRYS
Cerrigydrudion
LLECHWEDD SLATE CAVERNS
Blaenau Ffestiniog
Cwm Penmachno
Carrog
B4407
Conwy
Llyn Conwy
Ty Mawr Cwm
Rhiwbryfdir
Tanygrisiau
Bethania
ANGLESEY
YNYS MÔN

NX
SC
POINT OF AYRE
The Ayres
Rue Pt.
Glentruan
Cranstal
The Lhen
Dhowin
Bride
Andreas
MANX CROSSES
Jurby Head
Jurby East
Jurby West
JURBY SOUTH
Ballasalla
Sandygate
St Judes
Regaby
The Cronk
Dhoor
RAMSEY BAY
CURRAGHS WILDLIFE PARK
Sulby
GROVE MUSEUM
Ramsey
MANX ELECTRIC RAILWAY
Churchtown
Orrisdale
Ballaugh
T.T.Course
Port e Vullen
Glen Auldyn
Maughold
Maughold Head
Rhencullen
Ravensdale
Dreemskerry
MANX CROSSES
Kirk Michael
565 NORTH BARRULE
Ballajora
Isle of Man
CELTIC CRAFT CENTRE
Corrany
Cornaa
Ballaleigh
SNAEFELL 621
Glen Mona
Barregarrow
Druidale
Dhoon
MURRAYS MOTORCYCLE MUSEUM
Agneash
LAXEY WHEEL AND MINES
Knocksharry
SNAEFELL MOUNTAIN RAILWAY
Bulgham Bay
MANX TRANSPORT MUSEUM
544
Ballaquine
Laxey
Cronk-y-Voddy
St Patrick's I.
487 COLDEN
LAXEY WOOLLEN MILLS
Old Laxey
PEEL
Peel
Res.
BALLALHEANNAGH GARDENS
Laxey Head
HOUSE OF MANANNAN
Fairy Cottage
Contrary Head
TYNWALD CRAFT CENTRE
Laxey Bay
KIPPER MUSEUM
TYNWALD HILL
Creg-ny-Baa
Ballacannel
Patrick
St John's
Greeba
Baldwin
Baldrine
Glenmaye
333
Clay Head
Lower Foxdale
Crosby
MANX CROSSES
Dalby Pt.
Glen Vine
Strang
HEYSHAM 3:30
Dalby
Onchan
GROUDLE GLEN RAILWAY
Niarbyl
Foxdale
Union Mills
Tromode
Eairy
HEYSHAM 2:00 (Summer Only)
ONCHAN PLEASURE PARK
Niarbyl Bay
Braaid
Spring Valley
Douglas
483 SOUTH BARRULE
222
Cooil
Douglas Bay
Close Clark
Ellenbrook
Douglas Head
CAMERA OBSCURA
Ballamodha
St Mark's
Ballaveare
Newtown
LIVERPOOL 2:30
Ronague
Little Ness
Lingague
Fleshwick Bay
Grenaby
ISLE OF MAN STEAM RAILWAY
LIVERPOOL 4:00 (Winter Only)
Surby
Ballabeg
RUSHEN ABBEY
Santon Head
Bradda Head
Bradda
Colby
Ballasalla
Port Erin
Port Greenaugh
RAILWAY MUS.
Four Roads
BILLOWN
ISLE OF MAN
The Howe
Castletown
Derbyhaven
Cregneash
CASTLE RUSHEN
NAUTICAL MUS.
St Michael's I.
Port St Mary
SCARLETT VISITOR CENTRE
OLD HOUSE OF KEYS
CREGNEASH VILLAGE FOLK MUSEUM
128
Calf of Man
Spanish Head
Scarlett Point
Dreswick Pt.
Chicken Rock
BELFAST 2:45
DUBLIN 2:45
(April-Sept)
0 1 2 3 4 5 6 miles
0 1 2 3 4 5 6 7 8 9 10 km

IRISH SEA
LIVERPOOL BAY
SD
SJ
Merseyside
LIVERPOOL
Blackpool
South Shore
BLACKPOOL PLEASURE BEACH
CYBERDOME CRYSTAL MAZE
Hawes Side
Mereside
Common Edge
Squires Gate
Little Plumpton
Great Plumpton
Westby
Moss Side
Wrea Green
Kirkham
Dowbridge
Newton
Scales
Freckleton
Warton
Lytham St Anne's
St Annes
Ansdell
Lytham
LYTHAM HALL
Fairhaven
Salters Bank
TOY AND TEDDY BEAR MUSEUM
ROYAL LYTHAM & ST ANNES
Ribble
Banks Sands
Great Bank
RIBBLE MARSHES
Hesketh Bank
Becconsall
Hundred End
Banks
Tarleton
Horse Bank
Crossens
Marshside
ECO VISITOR CENTRE
Southport
Churchtown
Mere Brow
Holmeswood
NEW MODEL VILLAGE
Blowick
Rufford
Birkdale
Brown Edge
MARTIN MERE WILDFOWL AND WETLAND CENTRE
Snape Green
Bescar
Scarisbrick
Hillside
ROYAL BIRKDALE
Ainsdale-on-Sea
Ainsdale
Shirdley Hill
New Lane
Pinfold
Burscough
Burscough Bridge
Woodvale
Halsall
Formby Hills
AINSDALE SAND DUNES
Barton
Haskayne
ORMSKIRK
Westhead
Freshfield
Formby
Formby Pt.
Downholland Cross
Little Altcar
Great Altcar
Aughton Park
Blaguegate
CABIN HILL
Aughton
Stanley Gate
Royal Oak
Bickerstaffe
Hightown
Ince Blundell
Lydiate
Maghull
Barrow Nook
Little Crosby
Lunt
Sefton
Melling Mount
Thornton
Netherton
Melling
Great Crosby
Kirkby
Aintree
LITHERLAND
Southdene
Waterloo
Seaforth
Orrell
Fazakerley
Knowsley
Crosby Channel
BELFAST 8:00
DOUGLAS 4:00 (Winter only)
DUBLIN 7:45
DOUGLAS 2:30
Bootle
New Brighton
Walton
Norris Green
CROXTETH
Kirkdale
Anfield
West Derby
Mockbeggar Wharf
NEW PALACE
Liscard
Egremont
Longview
Wallasey
HISTORIC WARSHIPS
Everton
WALKER GALL
Knotty Ash
Huyton
Leasowe
Seacombe
MARITIME MUS.
Roby
Meols
Moreton
Bidston
Poulton
HOYLAKE
Edge Hill
Wavertree
Childwall
Claughton
Netherley
West Hoyle Bank
Hilbre I.
Upton
TATE
Toxteth
Greasby
Birkenhead
Dingle
Mossley Hill
Gateacre
Grange
Woodchurch
Rock Ferry
West Kirby
Frankby
Tranmere
Allerton
Woolton
Welsh Channel
Prenton
SUNLIGHT VISION MUS.
Aigburth
ARROWE
Point of Ayr
Yr Parlwr Du
New Ferry
Grassendale
HALEWOOD
Talacre
Caldy
BEBINGTON
LADY LEVER ART GALLERY
Hunt's Cross
River Dee
Afon Dyfrdwy
Irby
Thingwall
Storeton
Port Sunlight
Garston
Gronant
Gwespyr
Thurstaston
Barnston
Brimstage
Pensby
SPEKE HALL
Speke
Prestatyn
Gwaenysgor
Picton
Ffynnongroyw
WIRRAL
Bromborough
LIVERPOOL JOHN LENNON
Liverpool Airport
OFFA'S DYKE PATH
LLWYBR CLAWDD OFFA
Llanasa
Mostyn Quay
Heswall
Eastham
Eastham Ferry
Dawpool Bank
Thornton Hough
Mersey
Axton
Mostyn
Trelogan
Gayton
Raby
Trelawnyd
Eastham
Parkgate
Hinderton
Willaston
Hooton
Ellesmere Port
Ince Banks
GREENFIELD VALLEY HERITAGE PARK
Holywell Bank
Gayton Sands
Neston
Childer Thornton
RIVACRE
BOAT MUSEUM
Walwen
Little Neston
Little Sutton
Overpool
Stanlow
Ince
Holywell
Ness
Great Sutton
Whitby
Elton
NESS
M55
M58
M57
M53
A583
A584
A565
A570
A59
A577
A580
A57
A5058
A562
A561
A552
A553
A540
A41
A550
A548
A55
A506
A5147
B5259
B5261
B5246
B5243
B5242
B5240
B5195
B5193
B5422
B5192
B5138
B5137
B5136
B5151
B5178
92
86
72
73
0 1 2 3 4 5 6 miles
0 1 2 3 4 5 6 7 8 9 10 km

Preston
Fulwood
Ribbleton
Freckleton
Lytham
Ansdell
Kirkham
Wesham
Warton
Banks Sands
Ribble Marshes
Hesketh Bank
Becconsall
Much Hoole
Longton
Walmer Bridge
LEYLAND
Bamber Bridge
Farington
Clayton-le-Woods
Whittle-le-Woods
Wheelton
Brinscall
Blackburn
Darwen
Lancashire
Tarleton
Bretherton
Croston
Eccleston
CHORLEY
Coppull
Adlington
Horwich
Standish
Blackrod
Bolton
Westhoughton
Hindley
Wigan
Orrell
Skelmersdale
Upholland
ORMSKIRK
Burscough
Burscough Bridge
Parbold
Rufford
Halsall
Banks
Crossens
Churchtown
Blowick
Scarisbrick
Shirdley Hill
Aughton
Maghull
Lydiate
Kirkby
Rainford
Billinge
ASHTON-IN-MAKERFIELD
Golborne
Haydock
Newton-le-Willows
Leigh
ATHERTON
Tyldesley
Worsley
Astley Green
Irlam
Partington
Cadishead
Glazebury
Chat Moss
St Helens
Knowsley
Prescot
Huyton
Roby
Merseyside
LIVERPOOL
Everton
Walton
Anfield
Wavertree
Childwall
Garston
Speke
Liverpool Airport
Widnes
Runcorn
Halton
Warrington
Lymm
Birchwood
Culcheth
Daresbury
Frodsham
Helsby
Hale
Rock Ferry
Port Sunlight
Bromborough
Eastham
Arley
Great Budworth
Comberbach
Anderton
Marston
Pickmere
Lower Whitley
Higher Whitley
Stretton
Appleton Thorn
Grappenhall
Thelwall
Dunham Town
Rostherne
Bucklow Hill
Mere
Over Tabley
Bate Heath
Holehouses
Plumley
Irlams o' th' Height
Aintree
Melling
Lunt
Sefton
Netherton
Crosby
Bootle
0 1 2 3 4 5 6 miles
0 1 2 3 4 5 6 7 8 9 10 km

Burnley
ACCRINGTON
Haslingden
RAWTENSTALL
Bacup
Todmorden
Hebden Bridge
Mytholmroyd
Queensbury
Halifax
Sowerby Bridge
BRIGHOUSE
Elland
Huddersfield
Ramsbottom
Whitworth
Littleborough
Rochdale
Milnrow
Bury
HEYWOOD
Middleton
ROYTON
Shaw
Oldham
Chadderton
Radcliffe
Whitefield
PRESTWICH
Marsden
Meltham
HOLMFIRTH
Mossley
Ashton-under-Lyne
STALYBRIDGE
MANCHESTER
SALFORD
Eccles
URMSTON
Trafford Park
Stretford
Droylsden
Dukinfield
Denton
Hyde
GLOSSOP
SALE
GATLEY
Cheadle
Stockport
Bredbury
Romiley
Marple
Altrincham
Hale
HAZEL GROVE
Bramhall
Manchester Airport
WILMSLOW
Knutsford
Poynton
Bollington
New Mills
Whaley Bridge
Chapel-en-le-Frith
Low Leighton
HOPE FOREST
Castleton
Tideswell
Heptonstall Moor
Forest of Rossendale
Hollingworth Lake
Moss Moor
Wessenden Moor
Saddleworth Moor
Dove Stone Res.
Greater Manchester
SE
SK
M60
M62
M66
M67
M56
A6
A34
A58
A62
A628
A646
93
94
88
74
75

West Yorkshire
South Yorkshire
PEAK DISTRICT NATIONAL PARK
HIGH PEAK
HOPE FOREST
SK
Bradford
LEEDS
GARFORTH
PUDSEY
Halifax
Queensbury
Illingworth
BRIGHOUSE
Elland
Sowerby Bridge
Cleckheaton
BATLEY
MORLEY
Birstall
Heckmondwike
Liversedge
Dewsbury
OSSETT
Mirfield
Horbury
Wakefield
Rothwell
Middleton
CASTLEFORD
Pontefract
Featherstone
Normanton
Huddersfield
Marsden
Meltham
Slaithwaite
HOLMFIRTH
Honley
Skelmanthorpe
Denby Dale
Clayton West
Darton
Royston
Barnsley
Cudworth
Hemsworth
South Kirkby
Darfield
Wombwell
Worsbrough
Hoyland
Wath upon Dearne
Swinton
Penistone
Dodworth
Stocksbridge
Chapeltown
Sheffield
Rawmarsh
Beighton
Handsworth
Dronfield
ECKINGTON
Hathersage
GLOSSOP
Charlestown
Chapel-en-le-Frith
Crowden
Midhope Moors
Howden Moors
Broomhead Moor
Bradfield Moors
Shelf Moor
Kippax
Ledston Luck
Crigglestone
Sandal Magna
Emley
Flockton
Kirkburton
Shelley
Thurstonland
Crow Edge
Oxspring
Thurgoland
Tankersley
Ecclesfield
Grenoside
Wadsley Bridge
Dore
Totley
Bamford
Castleton
Edale
Hope
Aston
Tideswell
Eyam
Grindleford
Froggatt
Ladybower Res.
Derwent Res.
Howden Res.
KINDER SCOUT 636
BLEAKLOW HILL 633
FEATHERBED TOP 544
BLACK HILL 582
PENNINE WAY
M1
M62
M606
M621
A616
A628
A629
A635
A638
A642
A57
A61
A6102
94
95
87
75
76
0 1 2 3 4 5 6 miles
0 1 2 3 4 5 6 7 8 9 10 km

Sherburn in Elmet
Fenton
Selby
Selby Abbey
Osgodby
Menthorpe
Aeroplane Museum
Breighton
Spaldington
Newthorpe
Steeton Hall Gateway
Thorpe Willoughby
Lund
South Duffield
Cliffe
Hambleton
South Milford
Brayton
East Common
Hemingbrough
Wressle
Brind
North Howden
Portington
Hive
Ledsham
Lumby
Monk Fryston
Newsholme
Howden Minster
Cavil
Eastrington
Sandholme
Gilberdyke
Staddlethorpe
Hillam
Barlow
Barmby on the Marsh
Long Drax
Howden
Asselby
Knedlington
Kilpin Pike
Kilpin
Balkholme
Fairburn
Burton Salmon
Gateforth
Burn
Yorkshire Garden World
West Haddlesey
Chapel Haddlesey
Brotherton
Birkin
Drax
Boothferry
New Fryston
Temple Hirst
Camblesforth
Newland
Airmyn
Hook
Skelton
Laxton
Ferrybridge
Beal
Kellington
Hirst Courtney
Sutton
Kellingley
Eggborough
Hensall
Carlton
Saltmarshe
Yokefleet
Blacktoft
Goole
Knottingley
Rawcliffe
Waterways Museum & Adventure Centre
Reedness
Swinefleet
Ousefleet
Blacktoft RSPB
Whitgift
Little Reedness
Ferrybridge Services
High Eggborough
Gowdall
Snaith
East Cowick
West Cowick
Rawcliffe Bridge
Old Goole
Chequerfield
Cridling Stubbs
Whitley
Great Heck
Pollington
Southfield Reservoir
Dutch River
Adlingfleet
Darrington
East Hardwick
Womersley
Balne
Aire and Calder Navigation
Goole Fields
Fockerby
Garthorpe
Burton Stather
Wentbridge
Little Smeaton
Walden Stubbs
Went
Sykehouse
Pincheon Green
Goole Moors
Luddington
Low Ackworth
Kirk Smeaton
Fenwick
SE
Moorends
Humberhead Peatlands
Thorne Waste or Moors
Amcotts
Thorpe Audlin
Barnsdale Bar Services
Norton
Badsworth
Campsall
Fosterhouses
Moss
Far Bank
Fishlake
Thorne
Crowle
Wrangbrook
Upton
Instoneville
Askern
Doncaster North Services
Stainforth & Keadby Canal
Windsor
North Elmshall
Sutton
Haywood
Braithwaite
Canal Side
Wike Well End
Ealand
Keadby
Gunness
Moorthorpe
South Elmsall
Skelbrooke
Burghwallis
Owston
Thorpe in Balne
Kirk Bramwith
Stainforth
Hatfield
Hatfield Chase
Hampole
Skellow
Carcroft
Adwick le Street
Barnby Dun
Burringham
Althorpe
Hooton Pagnell
Almholme
Dunscroft
Derrythorpe
Clayton
Brodsworth
Woodlands
Toll Bar
Kirk Sandall
Hatfield Woodhouse
Sandtoft
The Trolleybus Museum at Sandtoft
Woodhouse
Grey Green
Westgate
Highfields
Dunsville
West End
Belton
Beltoft
Thurnscoe
Brodsworth Hall
Arksey
Bentley
Edenthorpe
Church Town
East Butterwick
West Butterwick
Thurnscoe East
Hickleton
Scawsby
Museum & Art Gallery
Armthorpe
Hatfield Moors
Isle of Epworth
Goldthorpe
Marr
Cusworth
Wheatley
Intake
Nutwell
Doncaster
Melton Wood
Epworth
Old Rectory
Bolton upon Dearne
Barnburgh
Newton
Cusworth Hall Museum
Wroot
Epworth Turbary
Axholme
Harlington
Sprotbrough
Hyde Park
Cantley
Branton
Low Burnham
Kelfield
Susworth
Scotterthorpe
Adwick upon Dearne
High Melton
Balby
Bessacarr
Auckley
Mexborough
Cadeby
Lakeside Village
Aeroventure
Lidget
Blaxton
Upperthorpe
Owston Ferry
Warmsworth
Haxey
Laughton Forest
Denaby Main
Old Denaby
New Edlington
Finningley
Westwoodside
East Lound
East Ferry
Conisbrough
Conisbrough Ivanhoe
Loversall
Rossington
Robin Hood Airport Doncaster Sheffield
Craiselound
Wildsworth
Kilnhurst
Old Edlington
New Rossington
Idle
Laughton
Hooton Roberts
Clifton
Wadworth
Thrybergh
Ravenfield
Micklebring
Misson
Misterton
West Stockwith
Blyton
Dalton
Braithwell
Stainton
Austerfield
Newington
East Stockwith
SK
Spital Hill
Bawtry
Walkerith
Bramley
Hellaby
Maltby
Tickhill
Harworth
Walkeringham
Gringley on the Hill
Gainsborough Old Hall
Morton
Gainsborough
Wickersley
Hooton Levitt
Bircotes
Scaftworth
Everton
Scrooby
Styrrup
Stone
Carr
Cuckoo Hill
Wiseton
Beckingham
Thurcroft
Roche Abbey
Serlby
Mattersey Thorpe
Mattersey
Firbeck
Oldcotes
Blyth Services
Ranskill
Clayworth
Saundby
Ulley
Brampton en le Morthen
Laughton en le Morthen
Letwell
Langold
Torworth
North Wheatley
Bole
Lea
Aughton
Laughton Common
Dinnington
Blyth
Lound
Knaith Park
Aston
Gildingwells
Wetlands Waterfowl Reserve
South Wheatley
Sturton le Steeple
Knaith
North Anston
Carlton in Lindrick
Barnby Moor
Sutton
Hayton
Swallownest
Todwick
Woodsetts
Clarborough
Kiveton Park
South Anston
Wigthorpe
North Leverton with Habblesthorpe
Littleborough
Gate Burton
Rother Valley
Wales
Bassetlaw Museum
Welham
North Leverton Windmill
Marton
Norwood
Thorpe Salvin
Gateford
West Retford
Killamarsh
Scofton
Ranby
Babworth
Retford
Coates
Harthill
Shireoaks
Netherthorpe
South Leverton
Sturton
Woodall Services
Rhodesia
Kilton
Ordsall
Grove
Cottam
Brampton
Spinkhill
Darfoulds
Treswell
Sundown Adventureland
Rampton
Torksey
Manton
Eaton
Barlborough
Worksop
Woodbeck
Whitwell
Hodthorpe
Headon
Stokeham
Church Laneham
Fenton
Mastin Moor
Clowne
Clumber Park
Gamston
Upton
Laneham
Laughterton
Kettlethorpe
M62
M18
M180
M181
A1(M)
M1
A1
A19
A63
A614
A645
A638
A630
A635
A6182
A631
A57
A60
A620
A619
A18
A161
A156
A159
A628
A639
A616
A1041
A1146
B1222
B1228
B1230
B1392
B1216
B1396
B1403
B6045
B6079
B6420
B6463
B6422
B6474
B6376
B6094
B6093
B6060
B6410
B6059
B1241
95
96
90
76
77
Ouse
Aire
Derwent
Selby Canal
Foulness
Trent
Thorne

North
Lincolnshire
SE
SK
HUMBER
Humber Bridge
KINGSTON UPON HULL
Kingston-upon-Hull
Scunthorpe
Gainsborough
Goole
Howden
Gilberdyke
North Cave
South Cave
North Ferriby
Hessle
Anlaby
Kirk Ella
Cottingham
Barton-upon-Humber
Barrow upon Humber
Winterton
Brigg
Broughton
Messingham
Scotter
Kirton in Lindsey
Hibaldstow
Caistor
Market Rasen
Faldingworth
Wragby
Epworth
Crowle
ISLE OF AXHOLME
Beckingham
Walkeringham
Laughton Forest
Redcliff Channel
Read's Island
Goole Fields
Goole Moors
HUMBERSIDE INTERNATIONAL
THE DEEP
FERENS ART GALLERY
WILBERFORCE HOUSE
STREETLIFE
HUMBER BRIDGE
SKIDBY WINDMILL
YORKSHIRE WOLDS WAY
WATERS EDGE
ST PETER'S CHURCH
BAYSGARTH HO. MUS.
THORNTON ABBEY
JULIAN'S BOWER (TURF MAZE)
BLACKTOFT SANDS RSPB
NORMANBY HALL
ELSHAM HALL
THE TROLLEYBUS MUSEUM AT SANDTOFT
OLD RECTORY
GAINSTHORPE DESERTED MEDIEVAL VILLAGE
GAINSBOROUGH OLD HALL
NORTH LEVERTON WINDMILL
DAMBUSTERS INN & HERITAGE CENTRE
REDHURST B&B
RAND FARM PARK
WOODSIDE FALCONRY AND CONSERVATION CENTRE
MARKET RASEN
M62
M180
M181
A63
A15
A18
A159
A631
A46
A1103
A180
A156
A158
A614
A164
A165
A1033
A1077
89
96
97
77
78
0 1 2 3 4 5 6 miles
0 1 2 3 4 5 6 7 8 9 10km

Hedon
Withernsea
Keyingham
Patrington
Immingham
Grimsby
CLEETHORPES
Humberston
North East Lincolnshire
Waltham
New Waltham
Holton le Clay
Laceby
Healing
Keelby
Binbrook
North Thoresby
Louth
North Somercotes
Saltfleet
Mablethorpe
Alford
SPURN HEAD
MOUTH OF THE HUMBER
Donna Nook
ROTTERDAM 12:30
ZEEBRUGGE 12:45
ROTTERDAM
ZEEBRUGGE
HOEK VAN HOLLAND 13:00
OOSTENDE 15:00
BREVIK 33:00
CUXHAVEN 22:00
ESBJERG 22:00
GOTHENBURG 26:00
KRISTIANSAND 30:00
ROTTERDAM 11:45
ZEEBRUGGE 14:00
LINCOLNSHIRE WOLDS
CLEETHORPES COAST LIGHT RAILWAY
PLEASURE ISLAND THEME PARK
NATIONAL FISHING HERITAGE CENTRE
LINCOLNSHIRE WOLDS RLY
ALVINGHAM MILL
RUSHMOOR
CADWELL PARK
WOODY'S TOP
CLAYTHORPE WATER AND WILDFOWL GARDENS
ALFORD WINDMILL
ALFORD MANOR HOUSE
SEAL SANCTUARY & NATURE CENTRE
SALTFLEETBY THEDDLETHORPE
DONNA NOOK
SPURN
FORT PAULL
WALTHAM WINDMILL
TA
TF
97
78
79

Whicham
Millom
MILLOM FOLK MUSEUM
DUDDON ESTUARY
Haverigg
The Hill
Kirkby-in-Furness
Beck Side
Soutergate
Broughton Beck
Penny Bridge
Greenodd
Arrad Foot
Mansriggs
ROUDSEA WOOD AND MOSSES
LAUREL & HARDY MUS
Ulverston
Pennington
Askam in Furness
Ireleth
DUDDON SANDS
Lindal in Furness
Swarthmoor
SOUTH LAKES WILD ANIMAL PARK
SANDSCALE HAWS
Dalton-in-Furness
DALTON CASTLE
Stainton with Adgarley
Great Urswick
Little Urswick
Scales
Bardsea
Baycliff
Aldingham
NORTH WALNEY
BARROW (WALNEY ISLAND)
Hawcoat
BOW BRIDGE
Ormsgill
Newbarns
Newton
FURNESS ABBEY
GLEASTON WATERMILL
Gleaston
Dendron
Yarlside
Barrow-in-Furness
North Scale
CUSTOM HO
THE DOCK MUSEUM
Vickerstown
Barrow Island
Newbiggin
Leece
Roosebeck
Biggar
Rampside
Roa Island
Foulney Island
Piel Island
South End
Isle of Walney
South End Point
South Channel
Haverthwaite
ARTCRYSTAL
Backbarrow
Ayside
High Newton
Witherslack
Low Newton
Town End
Field Broughton
CARTMEL
CARTMEL PRIORY
Cartmel
HOLKER HALL
Holker
Allithwaite
Lindale
Grange-over-Sands
CONISHEAD PRIORY & BUDDHIST TEMPLE
Cartmel Sands
Cark
Flookburgh
Kents Bank
Ravenstown
LAKELAND RIDING CENTRE
Humphrey Head Pt.
Meathop
Leasgill
Heversham
Milnthorpe
Crooklands
Farleton
Storth
Beetham
HERON CORN MILL
Holme
CLAW FELL
ARNSIDE
Arnside
GAIT BARROWS
LAKELAND WILDLIFE OASIS
Clawthorpe
Burton-in-Kendal
Yealand Redmayne
Yealand Conyers
ARNSIDE AND SILVERDALE
Silverdale
BURTON-IN-KENDAL (Northbound On
Priest Hutton
LEIGHTON HALL
Warton
Borwick
Capernwray
Warton Sands
OLD RECTORY
Millhead
Carnforth
Over Kellet
Nether Kellet
Bolton le Sands
MORECAMBE
BAY
Hest Bank
Bolton Town End
Aughton
Caton Green
Halton
Slyne
Bare
Morecambe
Torrisholme
Skerton
Caton Brook
Sandylands
White Lund
MARITIME MUS.
Heysham
Lancaster
ASHTON MEMORIAL
PRIORY CHURCH
Aldcliffe
CITY MUS.
LEISURE PARK
Heaton
Scotforth
Quernmore
Middleton
Overton
DOUGLAS 3:30
DOUGLAS 2:00 (Summer Only)
BELFAST 9:00 DUBLIN 9:00
Glasson
Conder Green
Sunderland Pt.
Shoulder of Lune
Thurnham
Galgate
Smith Green
Ortner
LARNE 8:00
Dolphinholme
Cockerham Sands
Cockerham
LANCASTER (FORTON) SERV
Braides
Forton
Street
Hollins Lane
Knott End-on-Sea
Dam Side
Pilling Lane
Pilling
Stake Pool
Winmarleigh
Scorton
Fleetwood
Rossall Point
Preesall
FREEPORT FLEETWOOD
Cabus
Oakenclough
SD
Eagland Hill
Garstang
GARSTANG DISCOVERY CENTRE
Calder Vale
Stalmine
Staynall
Nateby
Bowgreave
Wyre
MARSH MILL-IN-WYRE
WYRE ESTUARY
Cleveleys
Trunnah
Hambleton
Out Rawcliffe
Moss Edge
Churchtown
Catterall
Claughton
Anchorsholme
Norbreck
Thornton
Ratten Row
Little Eccleston
TOLL
St Michael's on Wyre
Bispham
Carleton
Skippool
Little Singleton
Great Eccleston
Bilsborrow
Inglewhite
Blackpool
Warbreck
North Shore
Poulton-le-Fylde
Singleton
Elswick
Crossmoor
Myerscough
Queenstown
Normoss
Thistleton
Inskip
Cuddy Hill
Roseacre
Barton
Layton
Esprick
Blackpool
BLACKPOOL TOWER
SEA LIFE CENTRE
LOUIS TUSSAUD'S WAXWORKS
ZOO PARK
Great Marton
Staining
Corner Row
Catforth
Wharles
Lanca
Weeton
Woodplumpton
Broughton
CYBERDOME CRYSTAL MAZE
BLACKPOOL PLEASURE BEACH
South Shore
Hawes Side
Mereside
Great Plumpton
Little Plumpton
Wesham
Treales
Lower Bartle
Higher Bartle
Sharoe Green
Common Edge
Kirkham
Dowbridge
Lancaster Canal
Cottam
Ingol
Cadley
Fulwood
Westby
Squires Gate
BLACKPOOL
Moss Side
Wrea Green
Lea Town
Newton
Scales
Clifton
Higher Ballam
Preston
TOY AND TEDDY BEAR MUSEUM
ROYAL LYTHAM & ST ANNES
LYTHAM HALL
Freckleton
P&R
St Annes
Ansdell
Lytham
Warton
Higher Penwortham
Lytham St Anne's
Fairhaven
Bottom of Hutton
Middleforth Green
Salters Bank
Ribble
Hutton
Longton
Lostock Hall
New
0 1 2 3 4 5 6 miles
0 1 2 3 4 5 6 7 8 9 10km

YORKSHIRE DALES NATIONAL PARK
FOREST OF BOWLAND
SD
Kirkby Lonsdale
Old Town
Barbon
Mansergh
Lupton
Kearstwick
Casterton
Hutton Roof
Whittington
Cowan Bridge
Leck
Ireby
Masongill
Nether Burrow
Westhouse
Newton
Tunstall
Cantsfield
Ingleton
Arkholme
Melling
Wrayton
Burton in Lonsdale
Low Bentham
Bentham Pottery
Gressingham
Tatham
Wennington
Hornby
High Bentham
Newby
Clapham
Austwick
Feizor
Farleton
Wray
Claughton
Mewith Head
Keasden
Lawkland
Caton Moor
Salter
Goodber Common
Lowgill
Tatham Fells
Burn Moor
Eldroth
Crossgill
Haylot Fell
Catlow Fell
Docker Park Farm
Deepdale
Crag Hill
Whernside
Blea Moor
Gayle Moor
Scales Moor
Chapel-le-Dale
Ingleborough
Simon Fell
White Scar Caves
Ingleborough Common
Gaping Gill
Ingleborough Show Cave
Leck Fell
Ribblehead
Cam Fell
Langstrothdale Chase
Oughtershaw
Cragdale Moor
Middle Tongue
Yockenthwaite
Hubberholme
Cray
Buckden
High Birkwith
Foxup
Halton Gill
Horton Moor
New Houses
Pen-y-ghent
Horton in Ribblesdale
Litton
Scoska Wood
Littondale
Arncliffe
Kettlewell
Hawkswick
Darnbrook Fell
Fountains Fell
Pennine Way
Helwith Bridge
Wharfe
Little Stainforth
Stainforth
Malham Tarn
The Settle Loop
Stackhouse
Watershed Mill Visitor Centre
Langcliffe
Giggleswick
Giggleswick School Chapel
Settle
Yorkshire Dales Falconry and Conservation Centre
Malham Cove
Kirkby Fell
Malham
Bordley
New House Farm, Malham
Kilnsey Park
Wham
Hanlith
Mearbeck
Rathmell
Horses Health Farm
Kirkby Malham
Long Preston
Airton
Calton
Winterburn
Hetton
Ribblesdale
Otterburn
Hellifield
Bell Busk
Flasby
Eshton
Wigglesworth
Tosside
Gisburn Forest
Stocks Reservoir
Grunsagill
Knotts
Halton West
Coniston Cold
Bank Newton
Gargrave
Nappa
Broughton
East Marton
Paythorne
Newsholme
Horton
West Marton
Elslack
Carleton
Ward's Stone
Mallowdale Fell
White Hill
Lee Fell
Tarnbrook Fell
Croasdale Fell
Tarnbrook
Lee
Abbeystead
Marshaw
Trough of Bowland
Whins Brow
Hawthornthwaite Fell
Fell Top
Sykes
Slaidburn
Newton
Hareden
Dunsop Bridge
Sykes Fell
Forest Becks
Lane Ends
Easington Fell
Holden
Bolton-by-Bowland
Bracewell
Gisburn
Lane End
Thornton in Craven
Earby
Coates
Barnoldswick
Salterforth
Kelbrook
Lothersdale
Bleasdale Moors
Fair Snape Fell
Whitewell
Bleasdale
Cow Ark
Leagram Gardens
Grindleton
Sawley
Abbey
West Bradford
Newby
Rimington
Twiston
Downham
Chatburn
Waddington
Beacon Fell
Chipping
Bashall Eaves
Walker Fold
Clitheroe
Clitheroe Castle Museum
Worston
Low Moor
Whitechapel
Hesketh Lane
Pendle Hill
Barley
Blacko
Roughlee
Colne Edge
Foulridge
Pendle Heritage Centre
Newchurch
Barrowford
Laneshaw Bridge
Colne
Winewall
Wycoller
Trawden
Hollin Hall Sewing Centre
British in India Mus.
Nelson
Little Marsden
The Forest of Trawden
Pendleton
Longridge Fell
Knowle Green
New Row
Great Mitton
Barrow
Wiswell
Sabden
The Forest of Pendle
Fence
Longridge
Goosnargh
Hurst Green
Whalley
Whalley Abbey
Higham
Brierfield
Haggate
Boulsworth Hill
St Saviour's Church
Little Town
Old Langho
Billington
Simonstone
Trapp Forge
Gawthorpe Hall
Padiham
Harle Syke
Burnley Lane
Ribchester
Mus. of Childhood
Roman Museum
Read
Rose Grove
Burnley
Worsthorne
Walshaw Dean Res.
Haighton Green
Grimsargh
Copster Green
Langho
Great Harwood
Altham
Habergham
Hapton
Brunshaw
Widdop Res.
Weavers Triangle
Walk Mill
Hurstwood
Mereclough
Heptonstall Moor
Ribbleton
Balderstone
Salesbury
Osbaldeston
Wilpshire
Clayton-le-Moors
Rishton
Huncoat
Lane Ends
Rose Hill
Samlesbury Hall
Samlesbury
Mellor Brook
Mellor
Brownhill
Pleckgate
Towneley Hall Art Gallery & Mus.
Holme Chapel
Colden
County and Regimental Mus.
Walton-le-Dale
Higher Walton
Samlesbury Bottoms
Lewis Textile Museum
Church
Milnshaw
Accrington
Clow Bridge
Dunnockshaw
Love Clough
Blackshaw Head
Blackburn
Hoghton Tower
Coup Green
Gregson Lane
Bamber Bridge
Pleasington
Riley Green
Hoghton
Feniscowles
Shadsworth
Oswaldtwistle
Scaitcliffe
West End
Baxenden
Thieveley Pike
Cornholme
Charlestown
Lydgate
Portsmouth
Forest of Rossendale
Goodshaw Chapel
Goodshaw
Water
Ewood
Lower Darwen
Guide
A65
A683
A687
A682
A59
A56
A6068
A671
A666
A680
A678
A679
A646
M6
M65
B6254
B6480
B6479
B6255
B6478
B6243
B6245
B5269
B6246
B6251
B6383
B6252
B6230
B6231
B6238
B6160
99
100
94
86
87

YORKSHIRE
DALES
NATIONAL
PARK
North
NIDDERDALE
SD
SE
Cragdale Moor
Oughtershaw
MIDDLE TONGUE
Kidstones
Walden Head
Carlton Moor
Walden
Gammersgill
West Scrafton
Horsehouse
Coverdale
Braidley
Woodale
Hindlethwaite Moor
Colsterdale Moor
Colsterdale
Masham Moor
GREAT HAW
Ellingstring
High Ellington
Low Ellington
Low Burton
Masham
Fearby
Healey
UREDALE GLASS
THEAKSTON BREWERY
VISITOR CENTRE
Swinton
Binsoe
Leighton
Warthermarske
Ilton
Leighton Res.
Roundhill Res.
Yockenthwaite
Hubberholme
Cray
BUCKDEN PIKE
Buckden
Foxup
Halton Gill
Starbotton
LITTLE WHERNSIDE
Scar House Res.
Angram Res.
Nidd
Grewelthorpe
Kirkby Malzeard
Litton
SCOSKA WOOD
Skirfare
Wharfe
Littondale
KETTLEWELL
GREAT WHERNSIDE
Middlesmoor
Stean
Lofthouse
NIDDERDALE
HAMBLETON HILL
Carlesmoor
Swetton
Laverton
Greygarth
Riggs Moor
Darnbrook Fell
FOUNTAINS FELL
PENNINE WAY
Kettlewell
Arncliffe
Hawkswick
Bouthwaite
Dallowgill Moor
Dallow
Low Grantley
Stean Moor
Ramsgill
Gouthwaite Res.
Grantley
Conistone Moor
Heathfield Moor
Wath
Pateley Moor
Eavestone
Risplith
Sawley
Kilnsey
KILNSEY PARK
Conistone
Malham Tarn
MALHAM TARN
THE SETTLE LOOP
MALHAM COVE
KIRKBY FELL
MALHAM
Malham
Bordley
NEW HOUSE FARM, MALHAM
Threshfield
Grassington
UPPER WHARFEDALE MUSEUM
Linton
Hebden Moor
Grimwith Res.
Greenhow Hill
Hebden
NIDDERDALE MUSEUM
Pateley Bridge
Bewerley
Glasshouses
Wilsill
BRIMHAM ROCKS
STUMP CROSS CAVERNS
Low Laithe
New York
Dacre Banks
Summer Bridge
Hanlith
Thorpe
Burnsall
PARCEVALL HALL GARDENS
Pockstones Moor
Skyreholme
Dacre
Kirkby Malham
Threapland
Cracoe
Appletreewick
Padside
Darley Head
Darley
Birstwith
Airton
Calton
Winterburn
Hetton
Rylstone
Upper Barden Res.
Drebley
Barden Fell
Thruscross Res.
Thornthwaite
Long Preston
Otterburn
West End
Kettlesing Bottom
Hellifield
Bell Busk
Flasby
Barden Scale
Lower Barden Res.
Forest Moor
Ribble
Eshton
BOLTON ABBEY ESTATE
Bolton Abbey
Hill End
Blubberhouses
Kettlesing Head
Coniston Cold
Halton West
Gargrave
Eastby
Halton East
Embsay
EMBSAY STEAM RAILWAY
BUFFERS
Pace Gate
Fewston Res.
Fewston
Hazlewood
Swinsty Res.
Bland Hill
Bank Newton
Nappa
PENNINE WAY
Thorlby
SKIPTON
Bolton Bridge
Beamsley
Timble
Jack Hill
Newsholme
Broughton
East Marton
Skipton
Draughton
Langbar
Horton
West Marton
Carleton
Addingham
Middleton
Denton
Lindley Wood Res.
Lindley Green
Braythorn
Elslack
Low Bradley
Cringles
Bracewell
Farnley
Stainburn
Lane End
Thornton in Craven
EARBY
Cononley
ILKLEY
Askwith
Clifton
Weston
Coates
Earby
Farnhill
Newall
Leathley
Barnoldswick
Kildwick
Silsden
Ilkley Moor
Burley in Wharfedale
Otley
Pool
Salterforth
Lothersdale
Glusburn
Eastburn
RUMBALDS MOOR
Kelbrook
Lane Ends
Steeton
Menston
CHEVIN FOREST
East Carlton
Old Bramhope
Cowling
Sutton-in-Craven
CLIFFE CASTLE
Riddlesden
EAST RIDDLESDEN HALL
Guiseley
New Road Side
Keighley
East Morton
Yeadon
LEEDS BRADFORD INTERNATIONAL
Blacko
Colne Edge
Foulridge
Braithwaite
Micklethwaite
Hawksworth
Cookridge
Roughlee
Laycock
Knowle Park
Thwaites
Crossflatts
Laneshaw Bridge
Goose Eye
Thwaites Brow
Eldwick
BRACKEN HALL COUNTRYSIDE CENTRE
Baildon
Esholt
Rawdon
Barrowford
COLNE
Winewall
Wycoller
Exley Head
VINTAGE RAILWAY CARRIAGE MUS.
Tinshill
KEIGHLEY MOOR
Oakworth
Ingrow
BINGLEY
Trawden
WYCOLLER
BRITISH IN INDIA MUS.
HOLLIN HALL SEWING CENTRE
1853 GALLERY
Saltaire
Apperley Bridge
Horsforth
NELSON
Little Marsden
THE FOREST OF TRAWDEN
Oldfield
Lees
BRONTE PARSONAGE MUS.
HAWORTH
Harden
Cottingley
SHIPLEY
Idle
Calverley
Rodley
Stanbury
Haworth
Cullingworth
Wilsden
Moorhead
Eccleshill
BRADFORD IND. MUS.
Brierfield
PENISTONE HILL
Marsh
Lingbob
Frizinghall
Farsley
Bramley
BOULSWORTH HILL
PENNINE WAY
Haworth Moor
KEIGHLEY AND WORTH VALLEY RAILWAY
Oxenhope
CARTWRIGHT HALL ART GALLERY
Heaton
Undercliffe
Stanningley
Harle Syke
Haggate
Burnley
Manningham
Thornbury
Walshaw Dean Res.
Wadsworth Moor
Denholme
Allerton
Bradford
Swinnow Moor
Denholme Gate
Well Heads
Thornton
Lidget Green
Little Horton
COLOUR MUS.
Laisterdyke
PUDSEY
Brunshaw
Worsthorne
Widdop Res.
Denholme Clough
Clayton
Great Horton
Bowling
Holme Wood
New Farnley
WEAVERS' TRIANGLE
Walk Mill
Hurstwood
Mereclough
Warley Moor Res.
Causeway Foot
Mountain
NAT. MUS. OF PHOTOGRAPHY
West Bowling
BOLLING HALL
Tong
Heptonstall Moor
Dean Head Res.
Queensbury
Wibsey
Bierley
TOWNELEY HALL ART GALL & MUS.
Holme Chapel
Colden
Pecket Well
Illingworth
Ambler Thorn
Buttershaw
Low Moor
Birkenshaw
Drighlington
Gildersome
Heptonstall
Chiserley
Wainstalls
Shelf
Stone Chair
Oakenshaw
Adwalton
Hebden Bridge
Mount Tabor
Booth
Ovenden
BANKFIELD MUSEUM
Northowram
Wyke
OAKWELL HALL RED HOUSE
Birstall
Midgley
Wheatley
SHIBDEN HALL
Scholes
Gomersal
BAGSHAW MUS.
WALKLEY CLOGS
Mytholmroyd
Luddenden
Halifax
Water
Portsmouth
Lydgate
0 1 2 3 4 5 6 miles
0 1 2 3 4 5 6 7 8 9 10 km

Thirsk
Sowerby
Helmsley
Rye Dale
Ampleforth
Coxwold
Byland Abbey
Kilburn
Oldstead
Ripon
Harrogate
Knaresborough
Boroughbridge
Aldborough
Easingwold
Wetherby
Boston Spa
Tadcaster
Bramham
Garforth
LEEDS
Rothwell
Middleton
Morley
Selby
Sherburn in Elmet
York
Bishopthorpe
Copmanthorpe
Haxby
Strensall
Stillingfleet
Cawood
Barlby
Hovingham
Dishforth
Topcliffe
Skipton-on-Swale
Baldersby
Melmerby
Wath
North Stainley
Studley Roger
Fountains Abbey
Pateley Bridge
Spofforth
Collingham
Harewood
Kippax
Swillington
Methley
Great Preston
Aberford
Barwick in Elmet
Hemingbrough
Escrick
Naburn
Acaster Malbis
Fulford
Heslington
Upper Poppleton
Nether Poppleton
Rufforth
Marston Moor
Long Marston
Hessay
Tockwith
Cattal
Green Hammerton
Kirk Hammerton
Whixley
Nun Monkton
Linton-on-Ouse
Tollerton
Alne
Huby
Stillington
Crayke
Brandsby
Yearsley
Sutton-on-the-Forest
Shipton
Skelton
Wigginton
Y o r k s h i r e
City of York
SE
Swale
Ure
Nidd
Ouse
Wharfe
Aire
A1(M)
A1
A19
A59
A64
A168
A61
A170
M1
M62
M621
A63
A162
A658
A661
A660
A6120
A659
101
102
96
88
89
Marton
Upper Dunsforth
Great Ouseburn
Little Ouseburn
Thorpe Underwood
Allerton Mauleverer
Hopperton
Goldsborough
Flaxby
Staveley
Arkendale
Ferrensby
Farnham
Scotton
Killinghall
Hampsthwaite
Bishop Monkton
Roecliffe
Minskip
Langthorpe
Kirby Hill
Norton-le-Clay
Cundall
Helperby
Brafferton
Raskell
Tholthorpe
Flawith
Myton-on-Swale
Lower Dunsforth
Aldwark
Youlton
Newton on Ouse
Beningbrough
Moor Monkton
Hutton Wandesley
Askham Bryan
Askham Richard
Bilbrough
Catterton
Healaugh
Wighill
Walton
Thorp Arch
Clifford
Newton Kyme
Stutton
Kirkby Wharfe
Ulleskelf
Church Fenton
Little Fenton
Biggin
Barkston
Saxton
Towton
Bolton Percy
Appleton Roebuck
Colton
Holme Green
Acaster Selby
Riccall
Kelfield
Wistow
Osgodby
Thorpe Willoughby
Hambleton
Brayton
Gateforth
Burn
West Haddlesey
Chapel Haddlesey
Birkin
Hillam
Monk Fryston
South Milford
Lumby
Ledsham
Ledston
Fairburn
Brotherton
Burton Salmon
New Fryston
Allerton Bywater
Mickletown
Castleford

Helmsley
Rye Dale
DUNCOMBE PARK
Nawton
Wombleton
Welburn
Great Edstone
Marton
Pickering
PICKERING CASTLE
Ellerburn
Thornton-le-Dale
Wilton
Allerston
Ebberston
Snainton
Brompton
Harome
Sproxton
Normanby
Muscoates
NUNNINGTON HALL
Nunnington
West Ness
East Ness
Salton
Little Barugh
FLAMINGO LAND
Kirby Misperton
Great Barugh
Brawby
Wass
BYLAND ABBEY
Ampleforth
Oswaldkirk
Coxwold
Stonegrave
South Holme
Butterwick
Little Habton
Great Habton
Ryton
High Marishes
Low Marishes
Derwent
Yedingham
East Heslerton
West Knapton
East Knapton
Scampston
SCAMPSTON HALL
Gilling East
Cawton
HOWARDIAN HILLS
Yearsley
Hovingham
Wath
HOVINGHAM HALL
Fryton
Slingsby
Barton-le-Street
Wykeham
Rillington
WOLDS WAY LAVENDER
West Heslerton
Coulton
Brandsby
Scackleton
Appleton-le-Street
Amotherby
EDEN CAMP MUSEUM
Swinton
Broughton
Thorpe Bassett
Wintringham
Place Newton
Stearsby
Dalby
Terrington
Malton
Old Malton
Norton-on-Derwent
Scagglethorpe
Settrington
Skewsby
Crayke
YORKSHIRE LAVENDER
Ganthorpe
Coneysthorpe
CASTLE HOWARD
Whenby
Whitewall Corner
East Lutton
West Lutton
High Hutton
North Grimston
Stillington
Farlington
Bulmer
Welburn
Low Hutton
Langton
Kirby Grindalythe
Duggleby
Sheriff Hutton
SHERIFF HUTTON
Whitwell-on-the-Hill
Firby
Kirkham
KIRKHAM PRIORY
Kennythorpe
Birdsall
Wharram le Street
Sledmere
SLEDMERE HOUSE
Huby
Sutton-on-the-Forest
SUTTON PARK
Thornton-le-Clay
Foston
Crambe
Westow
Burythorpe
WHARRAM PERCY MEDIEVAL VILLAGE
West Lilling
Barton-le-Willows
Howsham
Leavening
Flaxton
Harton
Leppington
Acklam
Thixendale
Strensall
Bossall
Fimber
Claxton
Scrayingham
Kirby Underdale
Towthorpe
Sand Hutton
Shipton
Wigginton
Haxby
City
of
York
Earswick
Moor End
Upper Helmsley
Buttercrambe
Skirpenbeck
Bugthorpe
Painsthorpe
Fridaythorpe
Wetwang
Skelton
Huntington
Stockton on the Forest
Gate Helmsley
Stamford Bridge
Youlthorpe
YORKSHIRE WOLDS WAY
Overton
West Huntington
New Earswick
Warthill
Holtby
Full Sutton
Bishop Wilton
Huggate
Upper Poppleton
Rawcliffe
Low Catton
Gowthorpe
Great Givendale
Clifton
YORK MINSTER
Murton
Dunnington
High Catton
Fangfoss
Knapton
York
Heworth
JORVIK CENTRE
Osbaldwick
YORKSHIRE MUSEUM OF FARMING
Bolton
Meltonby
Millington
North Dalton
Holgate
Acomb
NATIONAL RAILWAY MUSEUM
CASTLE MUS
Grimston
Kexby
Wilberfoss
Yapham
Warter
Nunthorpe
Heslington
Kilnwick Percy
Woodthorpe
Fulford
Barmby Moor
Middleton-on-the-Wolds
Askham Bryan
Newton upon Derwent
Pocklington
BURNBY HALL GARDENS & MUSEUM TRUST
YORKSHIRE AIR MUSEUM
Elvington
Nunburnholme
McARTHUR GLEN YORK
Bishopthorpe
Crockey Hill
Allerthorpe
Copmanthorpe
YORK WEST SERVICES
Sutton upon Derwent
Burnby
Acaster Malbis
Naburn
Wheldrake
Thornton
Hayton
Londesborough
Colton
Deighton
Storwood
Melbourne
Pocklington Canal
Bielby
Thorpe le Street
Goodmanham
Appleton Roebuck
Escrick
LOWER DERWENT VALLEY
Shiptonthorpe
Market Weighton
Acaster Selby
Thorganby
East Cottingwith
Seaton Ross
Everingham
Holme Green
Stillingfleet
Harswell
Ryther
Ellerton
Laytham
Sancton
Kelfield
Water End
Aughton
Skipwith
North Duffield
Hartlhorpe
Moor End
Holme-on-Spalding-Moor
Cawood
Riccall
Foggathorpe
Sand Hole
North Cliffe
North Newbald
Bubwith
Highfield
Rascal Moor
Wistow
Gunby
Gribthorpe
South Cliffe
South Newbald
Willitoft
Hotham
Barlby
Osgodby
Menthorpe
THE REAL AEROPLANE MUSEUM
Breighton
Spaldington
Bursea
SELBY ABBEY
Lund
South Duffield
Foulness
North Cave
Everthorpe
Selby
Cliffe
Thorpe Willoughby
Wressle
Brind
North Howden
Portington
Hive
South Cave
East Common
Sandholme
West End
Brayton
Hemingbrough
Newsholme
Cavil
Scalby
Newport
Selby Canal
HOWDEN MINSTER
Eastrington
Gilberdyke
Brantingham
Ellerker
Barmby on the Marsh
Howden
Staddlethorpe
Market Weighton Canal
Asselby
Knedlington
Kilpin
Balkholme
Elloughton
YORKSHIRE GARDEN WORLD
Kilpin Pike
Broomfleet
Brough
Haddlesey
Drax
Boothferry
Ouse
Aire
0 1 2 3 4 5 6 miles
0 1 2 3 4 5 6 7 8 9 10 km

Yons Nab
CLEVELAND WAY
Filey Brigg
Filey
Filey Bay
Primrose Valley
Hunmanby Moor
Reighton Sands
Reighton Gap
Hunmanby
Seamer
Irton
Eastfield
Cayton
Lebberston
Gristhorpe
Wykeham
Ruston
Flixton
Folkton
Muston
Staxton
Willerby
CARRS
Ganton
Sherburn
Potter Brompton
YORKSHIRE WOLDS WAY
Fordon
Wold Newton
Foxholes
Burton Fleming
Reighton
Speeton
Buckton
Bempton
Flamborough
FLAMBOROUGH HEAD
Grindale
Butterwick
Weaverthorpe
Helperthorpe
Octon
Thwing
Octon Cross Roads
SEWERBY HALL AND GARDENS
Sewerby
BONDVILLE MODEL VILLAGE
PRIORY
BAYLE MUSEUM
Bridlington
OLD PENNY MEMORIES
Boynton
Rudston
Langtoft
Bessingby
Carnaby
West Hill
Hilderthorpe
Cottam
Haisthorpe
Thornholme
BURTON AGNES HALL
Kilham
BURTON AGNES MANOR HOUSE
PARK ROSE POTTERY AND LEISURE PARK
Burton Agnes
BRIDLINGTON BAY
Ruston Parva
Harpham
Fraisthorpe
Lowthorpe
Garton-on-the-Wolds
Nafferton
Gransmoor
Barmston
Driffield
Little Driffield
Elmswell
Great Kelk
Lissett
Gembling
Ulrome
Kelleythorpe
Foston on the Wolds
Wansford
Tibthorpe
SKIPSEA CASTLE
Skipsea
Skipsea Brough
Kirkburn
Southburn
Skerne
CRUCKLEY ANIMAL FARM
Church End
Beeford
Brigham
Hutton
North Frodingham
Bainton
Hutton Cranswick
Rotsea
Dunnington
Hempholme
Bewholme
Atwick
Watton
North Cliff
Kilnwick
Burshill
Hornsea
Lund
Beswick
Brandesburton
FREEPORT HORNSEA
HORNSEA MUSEUM
Holme on the Wolds
Lockington
Baswick Steer
Seaton
Hornsea Bridge
Thorpe
Hornsea Mere
Rolston
South Dalton
Scorborough
Leven
Sigglesthorne
Goxhill
Aike
Leven Canal
Catwick
Arram
Mappleton
Etton
Leconfield
Eske
Little Hatfield
Gardham
Cherry Burton
Routh
Rise
Great Hatfield
Great Cowden
Tickton
Long Riston
Arnold
Withernwick
Molescroft
BEVERLEY
Beverley
Meaux
Skirlaugh
New Ellerby
Aldbrough
Bishop Burton
Weel
Marton
West Newton
East Newton
BEVERLEY FRIARY
MINSTER
Woodmansey
Walkington
Wawne
Old Ellerby
BURTON CONSTABLE HALL
Flinton
Thearne
Bentley
Swine
Coniston
Garton
High Hunsley
Dunswell
Grimston
Thirtleby
Sproatley
Humbleton
Fitling
Skidby
Bransholme
Hilston
Kingston-upon-Hull
Sutton on Hull
Ganstead
Little Weighton
SKIDBY WINDMILL
Rowley
Inglemire
Bilton
Lelley
Owstwick
Cottingham
Sutton Ings
Elstronwick
Tunstall
Eppleworth
Newland
Stoneferry
Riplingham
Burton Pidsea
Preston
Roos
North End
Summergangs
Willerby
Sculcoates
WILBERFORCE HOUSE
West End
Kirk Ella
Waxholme
Owthorne
Salt End
Hedon
Marfleet
West Ella
Anlaby
STREETLIFE
THE DEEP
Rimswell
Swanland
Haven Side
Burstwick
Halsham
Withernsea
Welton
HUMBER BRIDGE
Hessle
FERENS ART GALLERY
KINGSTON UPON HULL
Paull
Thorngumbald
Camerton
Easington
North Ferriby
Keyingham
TA
WOLDS
East Riding of Yorkshire

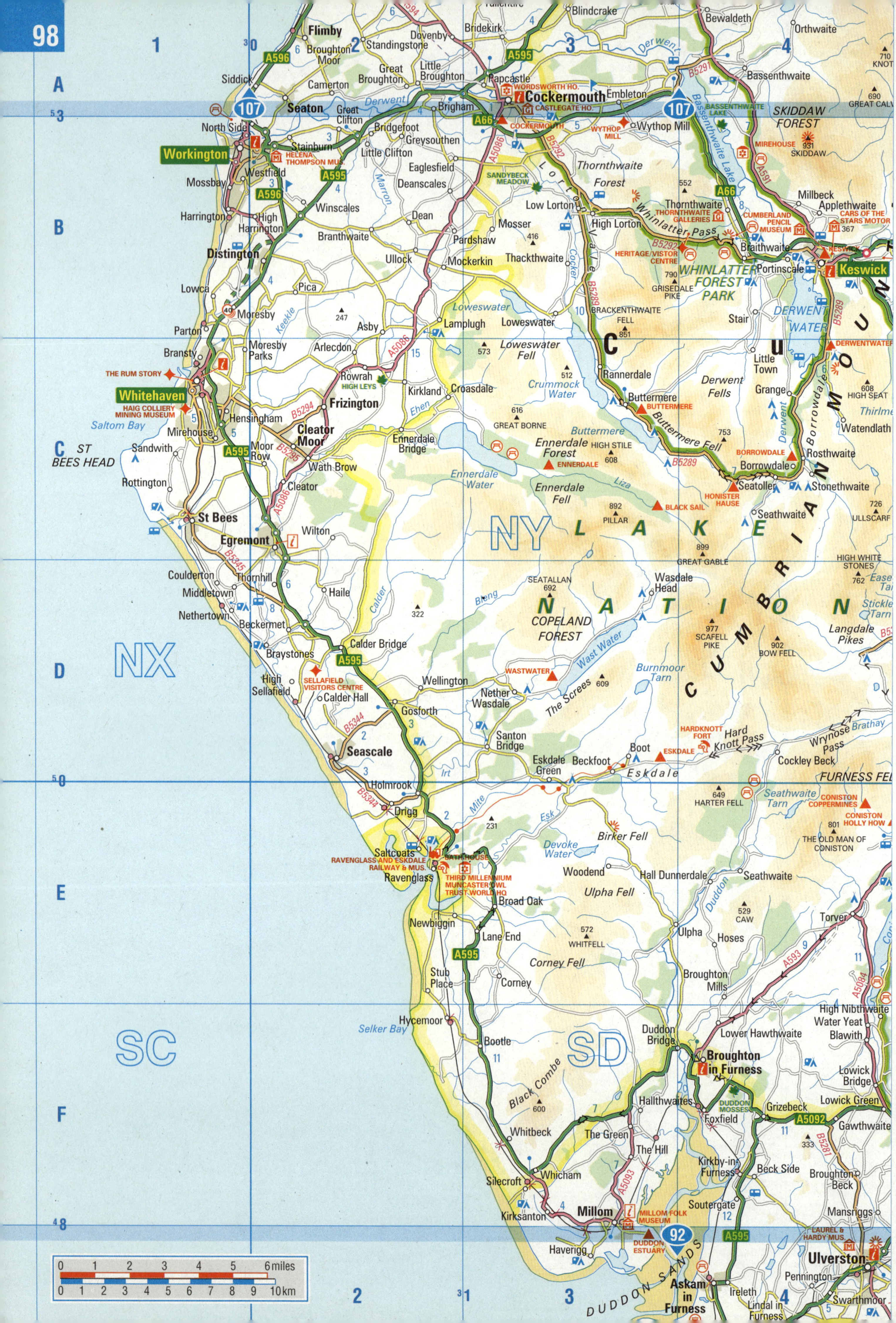

Flimby
Broughton Moor
Dovenby
Bridekirk
Blindcrake
Bewaldeth
Orthwaite
Standingstone
Siddick
Camerton
Great Broughton
Little Broughton
Papcastle
Cockermouth
WORDSWORTH HO.
CASTLEGATE HO.
Embleton
Bassenthwaite
GREAT CALVA
Seaton
Great Clifton
Brigham
Derwent
COCKERMOUTH
WYTHOP MILL
Wythop Mill
BASSENTHWAITE LAKE
SKIDDAW FOREST
North Side
Bridgefoot
Greysouthen
Workington
Stainburn
HELENA THOMPSON MUS.
Little Clifton
Eaglesfield
Thornthwaite Forest
Bassenthwaite Lake
MIREHOUSE
SKIDDAW
Mossbay
Westfield
Deanscales
SANDYBECK MEADOW
Marron
Lorton Vale
Harrington
High Harrington
Winscales
Dean
Low Lorton
High Lorton
Thornthwaite
THORNTHWAITE GALLERIES
Whinlatter Pass
CUMBERLAND PENCIL MUSEUM
Millbeck
Applethwaite
CARS OF THE STARS MOTOR
Branthwaite
Mosser
Pardshaw
Distington
Ullock
Mockerkin
Thackthwaite
Cocker
HERITAGE/VISITOR CENTRE
Braithwaite
Portinscale
KESWICK
Keswick
Lowca
Pica
GRISEDALE PIKE
WHINLATTER FOREST PARK
DERWENT WATER
Moresby
Keekle
Loweswater
Lamplugh
BRACKENTHWAITE FELL
Stair
Parton
Asby
Arlecdon
Loweswater Fell
DERWENTWATER
Bransty
Moresby Parks
Rowrah
HIGH LEYS
Kirkland
Croasdale
Crummock Water
Rannerdale
Little Town
THE RUM STORY
Whitehaven
HAIG COLLIERY MINING MUSEUM
Frizington
Ehen
GREAT BORNE
Buttermere
BUTTERMERE
Derwent Fells
Grange
HIGH SEAT
Thirlmere
Saltom Bay
Hensingham
Cleator Moor
Ennerdale Bridge
Buttermere Fell
Watendlath
Mirehouse
Ennerdale Forest
HIGH STILE
ENNERDALE
Borrowdale
BORROWDALE
Rosthwaite
ST BEES HEAD
Sandwith
Moor Row
Wath Brow
Ennerdale Water
Liza
Seatoller
HONISTER HAUSE
Stonethwaite
Rottington
Cleator
Ennerdale Fell
PILLAR
BLACK SAIL
Seathwaite
ULLSCARF
St Bees
Egremont
Wilton
NY
LAKE
GREAT GABLE
HIGH WHITE STONES
Coulderton
Thornhill
SEATALLAN
Wasdale Head
Middletown
Haile
Nethertown
Calder
Bleng
NATIONAL
CUMBRIAN MOUNTAINS
COPELAND FOREST
SCAFELL PIKE
BOW FELL
Langdale Pikes
Beckermet
Calder Bridge
NX
Braystones
Wast Water
Burnmoor Tarn
High Sellafield
SELLAFIELD VISITORS CENTRE
Calder Hall
Wellington
WASTWATER
Nether Wasdale
The Screes
Gosforth
HARDKNOTT FORT
Hard Knott Pass
Wrynose Pass
Brathay
Seascale
Santon Bridge
Boot
ESKDALE
Cockley Beck
Eskdale Green
Beckfoot
Eskdale
FURNESS FELLS
Holmrook
Irt
HARTER FELL
Seathwaite Tarn
CONISTON COPPERMINES
Drigg
Mite
Esk
CONISTON HOLLY HOW
Birker Fell
THE OLD MAN OF CONISTON
Saltcoats
RAVENGLASS AND ESKDALE RAILWAY & MUS.
BATH HOUSE
Ravenglass
THIRD MILLENNIUM MUNCASTER OWL TRUST WORLD HQ
Devoke Water
Woodend
Hall Dunnerdale
Seathwaite
Ulpha Fell
Duddon
Broad Oak
CAW
Torver
Newbiggin
WHITFELL
Lane End
Ulpha
Hoses
Corney Fell
Broughton Mills
Stub Place
Corney
High Nibthwaite
Water Yeat
Blawith
Hycemoor
Selker Bay
Bootle
Duddon Bridge
Lower Hawthwaite
SC
SD
Broughton in Furness
Lowick Bridge
Black Combe
Hallthwaites
DUDDON MOSSES
Foxfield
Grizebeck
Lowick Green
Gawthwaite
Whitbeck
The Green
The Hill
Kirkby-in-Furness
Beck Side
Broughton Beck
Silecroft
Whicham
Millom
MILLOM FOLK MUSEUM
Soutergate
Kirksanton
Mansriggs
LAUREL & HARDY MUS.
Haverigg
DUDDON ESTUARY
Ulverston
DUDDON SANDS
Askam in Furness
Pennington
Ireleth
Lindal in Furness
Swarthmoor
0 1 2 3 4 5 6 miles
0 1 2 3 4 5 6 7 8 9 10km

HIGH PIKE
Hutton Roof
Moseдale
Johnby
Little Blencow
Catterlen
Laithes
Langwathby
Winskill
Ousby
Skirwith
Kirkland
Great Blencow
Newton Reigny
Fair Hill
Edenhall
Greystoke
Penrith
Carleton
MAYBURGH HENGE
Blencarn
Crowdundle Beck
Mungrisdale
Berrier
Motherby
Newbiggin
BECKSTONES ART GALLERY
BROUGHAM CASTLE
Culgaith
Milburn
ACORN BANK
Newbiggin
SADDLEBACK OR BLENCATHRA
Scales
Penruddock
Stainton
Eamont Bridge
Temple Sowerby
Knock
TARN MOSS
DALEMAIN
RHEGED
Sockbridge
LILLIPUT LANE
CLIFTON HALL
Clifton
Threlkeld
Troutbeck
Hutton
Dacre
Tirril
WETHERIGGS COUNTRY POTTERY
Lowmoor Row
CLIBURN MOSS
Kirkby Thore
Dufton
DUFTON
LAKELAND BIRD OF PREY CENTRE
Melkinthorpe
Cliburn
Long Marton
Brampton
Wreay
Pooley Bridge
Askham
Lowther
CASTLERIGG STONE CIRCLE
Matterdale End
Longthwaite
Watermillock
Hackthorpe
Helton
Great Strickland
Morland
Bolton
Crackenthorpe
AIRA FORCE
Dockray
Knotts
Whale
King's Meaburn
Colby
Dowthwaitehead
ULLSWATER
STREET
Little Strickland
Newby
Appleby-in-Westmorland
Stanah
Sandwick
Howtown
Sleagill
LOADPOT HILL
Bampton Grange
Burrells
Fisher Place
HELVELLYN
Glenridding
Bampton
Hoff
Martindale Common
Bampton Common
Reagill
Dale Head
Rosgill
Maulds Meaburn
Great Ormside
Patterdale
PATTERDALE
HELVELLYN
Grisedale Beck
Bridgend
Angle Tarn
Haweswater Reservoir
SHAP ABBEY
Shap
Drybeck
Wythburn
Keld
Crosby Ravensworth
Hartsop
Brothers Water
Oddendale
Great Asby
Wythburn Fells
Grisedale Tarn
Ralfland Forest
Res.
D I S T R I C T
HIGH STREET
Crosby Ravensworth Fell
GREAT ASBY SCAR
GRASMERE THORNEY HOW
HARTER FELL
Shap Fells
Little Asby
Orton
GRASMERE BUTTERLYP HOW
Kirkstone Pass
Raisbeck
DOVE COTTAGE AND WORDSWORTH MUSEUM
Inn
P A R K
Grasmere
Rydal
RYDAL MOUNT
TEBAY SERVICES
SMARDALE
Chapel Stile
HOMES OF FOOTBALL
NY
Sadgill
Greenholme
Gaisgill
Kelleth
Rydal Water
Long Sleddale
Bretherdale Head
Lune
ELTERWATER
LANGDALE
Elterwater
Ambleside
Kentmere
Tebay
Bowderdale
Little Langdale
Clappersgate
Waterhead
Borrowdale
Weasdale
ROMAN FORT
AMBLESIDE
Troutbeck
Skelwith Bridge
WINDERMERE SUBMARINE
TOWNEND
Kent
BROCKHOLE NAT. PK VISITOR CENTRE
WINDERMERE
Lowbridge House
Forest Hall
Ravenstonedale Common
Low Wray
HOLEHIRD GARDENS
Langdale Fell
Outgate
Troutbeck Bridge
Elfhowe
HAWKSHEAD COURTHOUSE
High Wray
Garnett Bridge
Hawkshead Hill
Colthouse
WINDERMERE STEAMBOATS & MUS.
Ings
Staveley
Watchgate
Howgill Fell
Coniston
BEATRIX POTTER GALLERY
Hawkshead
Windermere
Bowston
Patton Bridge
GONDOLA
Esthwaite Water
Bowness-on-Windermere
THE WORLD OF BEATRIX POTTER
Garth Row
Grayrigg
Lowgill
THE CALF
Bowmanstead
HAWKSHEAD
BRANTWOOD
Near Sawrey
Ferney Green
Burneside
Meal Bank
Beck Foot
Brant Fell
GRIZEDALE FOREST PARK VISITOR CENTRE
Grizedale
Far Sawrey
HILL TOP
Crook
LAKELAND CLIMBING CENTRE
Lambrigg Fell
Cautley
Forest
Storrs
Winster
SD
G R I Z E D A L E
Underbarrow
Kendal
KENDAL
Sedbergh
FARFIELD MILL ARTS & HERITAGE CENTRE
Satterthwaite
Crosthwaite
New Hutton
KILLINGTON SERVICES (Southbound Only)
Force Mills
K VILLAGE
K VILLAGE HERITAGE CEN.
Millholme
Millthrop
Gregg Hall
Oxenholme
FOREST SPINNERS
Brigsteer
Natland
Killington
F U R N E S S
LAKESIDE
Bowland Bridge
Row
Middleshaw
Rusland
STOTT PARK BOBBIN MILL
Finsthwaite
Cartmel Fell
The Howe
SIZERGH
Barrows Green
Old Hutton
RUSLAND MOSS
Oxen Park
Lakeside
Gawthrop
F E L L S
AQUARIUM OF THE LAKES
FELL FOOT
Cotes
Sedgwick
Dent
Colthouse
Booth
WHITBARROW
Levens
Stainton
Gatebeck
Middleton
Newby Bridge
Staveley
Sampool Bridge
Hincaster
Spark Bridge
LAKESIDE AND HAVERTHWAITE RAILWAY
Endmoor
CALF TOP
LEVENS HALL
Backbarrow
Witherslack
Mill Side
Crooklands
ARTCRYSTAL
Penny Bridge
Haverthwaite
Ayside
High Newton
Town End
Leasgill
Old Town
Barbon
CRAG HILL
Greenodd
Low Newton
Heversham
Mansergh
Field Broughton
Milnthorpe
Lupton
Arrad Foot
Meathop
Farleton
Kearstwick
ROUDSEA WOOD AND MOSSES
Lindale
Storth
Beetham
HERON CORN MILL
Casterton
CART PRIORY
CARTMEL
Cartmel
CLAWTHORPE FELL
Kirkby Lonsdale
Holme
LECK FELL
ARNSIDE
Arnside
LAKELAND WILDLIFE OASIS
Hutton Roof
HOLKER HALL
Grange-over-Sands
GAIT BARROWS
Clawthorpe
Holker
Allithwaite
Yealand Redmayne
Burton-in-Kendal
Leck
CONISHEAD PRIORY & BUDDHIST TEMPLE
Cartmel Sands
Cark
Kents Bank
BURTON-IN-KENDAL SERVICES
Whittington
Cowan Bridge
Ireby
Chapel
108
109
100
92
93

Ousby
Skirwith
Kirkland
893 CROSS FELL
Tees
MILBURN FOREST
MOOR HOUSE-UPPER TEESDALE
Trout Beck
639 VIEWING HILL
Harwood Beck
Harwood
Langdon Common
696 CHAPELFELL TOP
Westernhope Moor
675
Bollihope Common
Blencarn
Crowdundle Beck
Langdon Beck
LANGDON BECK
Newbiggin Common
Middleton Common
109
772
Widdybank Fell
Forest
110
Bulgaith
Milburn
Cow Green Reservoir
Ettersgill
ACORN BANK
Newbiggin
Dufton Fell
767
CAULDRON SNOUT
Tees
HIGH FORCE
BOWLEES VISITOR CENTRE
Newbiggin
565
Temple Sowerby
Knock
PENNINE WAY
Maize Beck
Cronkley Fell
TEESDALE
Lowmoor Row
Holwick
Middleton-in-Teesdale
Kirkby Thore
Dufton
DUFTON
Murton Fell
NORTH
Mickle Fell
Cliburn
Long Marton
Brampton
673
776
LUNE FOREST
Lune Moor
Bowbank
Mickleton
Eggleston
EGGLESTON HALL
Morland
Bolton
Thringarth
Romaldkirk
Crackenthorpe
Murton
Grassholme Reservoir
Grassholme
King's Meaburn
Newby
Colby
Hilton
Warcop Fell
Lune
Selset Reservoir
Hunderthwaite
Hury
Appleby-in-Westmorland
DOW CRAG 549
Hunderthwaite Moor
Burrells
Eden
PENNINES
Hury Reservoir
Hoff
Great Ormside
Stainmore Common
Balderhead Reservoir
Clove Lodge
BALDERSDALE
Reagill
99
Cotherstone Moor
Maulds Meaburn
Sandford
North Stainmore
Hillbeck
Warcop
Deep Dale
Drybeck
BROUGH CASTLE
A66
Deepdale Beck
Bowes
Crosby Ravensworth
Brough
South Stainmore
PENNINE WAY
Great Asby
Bleatarn
Great Musgrave
Little Musgrave
Brough Sowerby
Moudy Mea
Gilmonby
Oddendale
Kaber
Barras
Soulby
Winton
Heggerscales
Bowes Moor
STAINMORE FOREST
GREAT ASBY SCAR
Crosby Ravensworth Fell
Sleightholme
Hartley
Crosby Garrett
Scargill Moor
Little Asby
KIRKBY STEPHEN
Kirkby Stephen
Winton Fell
Orton
412
Sleightholme Moor
NY
Belah
Smardale
Waitby
Raisbeck
Nateby
SMARDALE GILL
510 CLEASBY HILL
M6
662
SERVICES
Lune
Gaisgill
Kelleth
Newbiggin-on-Lune
Ash Fell
Arkengarthdale Moor
Tebay
A685
Bowderdale
Coldbeck
385
A683
Stonesdale Moor
Whaw
Weasdale
Ravenstonedale
B6259
Ravenseat
ROGAN'S SEAT 671
Birkdale Common
West Stonesdale
583 GREAT PINSEAT
Outhgill
709
KELD
Keld
Melbecks Moor
Langdale Fell
Ravenstonedale Common
494
587
Angram
Kearton
Angram Common
Howgill Fell
708
Mallerstang
Common
Gunnerside
Feetham
Thwaite
Satron
Muker
Low Row
Lowgill
716
GREAT SHUNNER FELL
676 THE CALF
Crackpot
Beck Foot
Brant Fell
Abbotside Common
BUTTERTUBS PASS
YORKSHIRE
PENNINE WAY
Abbotside Common
SD
Cotterdale
Askrigg Common
Cautley
Baugh Fell
North Yo
99
Garsdale Head
High Shaw
Askrigg
Newbiggin
Sedbergh
FARFIELD MILL ARTS & HERITAGE CENTRE
676
A684
Mossdale Moor
Hardrow
Sedbusk
LOW MILL OUTDOOR CENTRE
KILLINGTON SERVICES (Southbound Only)
Millthrop
Garsdale
Appersett
DALES COUNTRYSIDE MUSEUM
Bainbridge
WENSLEYDALE POTTERY
Hawes
Worton
Woodhall
Killington
Dee
Garsdale
Widdale Fell
HAWES
Gayle
Burtersett
Cubeck
Thornton Rust
WENSLEYDALE
556 RISE HILL
Gawthrop
Cowgill
672
WENSLEYDALE CREAMERY
Countersett
Semer Water
Wether Fell
614
Carpley Green
BISHOPDALE VALLEY
Dent
Dentdale
Middleton
Stone House
Wold Fell
Dodd Fell
Marsett
Stalling Busk
609 CALF TOP
DENTDALE
Newbiggin
Deepdale
668
Bishopdale Beck
Old Town
PENNINE WAY
Barbon
682 CRAG HILL
Gayle Moor
Cragdale Moor
Mansergh
Whernside
736
NATIONAL
Blea Moor
Oughtershaw
643 MIDDLE TONGUE
Kidstones
Cam Fell
Walden Head
Casterton
93
LANGSTROTHDALE CHASE
94
Kirkby Lonsdale
627
Ribblehead
Yockenthwaite
Cray
702 BUCKDEN PIKE
Hubberholme
Buckden
INGLEBOROUGH
High Birkwith
Foxup
Halton Gill
610
Cowan Bridge
Ireby
PARK
0 1 2 3 4 5 6 miles
0 1 2 3 4 5 6 7 8 9 10km

Pikeston Fell
Fir Tree
Hunwick
Newfield
Byers Green
Spennymoor
Cornforth
Trimdon
Ferryhill
Fishburn
Middlestone Moor
Kirk Merrington
Ferryhill Station
Mainsforth
Bishop Middleham
Bedburn
Redford
Hamsterley
Witton Park
Toronto
Escomb
Binchester Blocks
Westerton
Coundon
Middlestone
Leasingthorne
Chilton
Sedgefield
Hamsterley Forest
Low Etherley
High Etherley
Bishop Auckland
Eldon
Rushyford
Bradbury
Butterwick
Morley
Toft Hill
Coundon Grange
Shildon
Old Eldon
Middridge
NEWTON AYCLIFFE
Mordon
Woodland
Howle
Butterknowle
West Auckland
St Helen Auckland
Woodland Fell
Copley
High Lands
Evenwood
Bildershaw
Royal Oak
Redworth
Aycliffe
Thorpe Larches
Foxton
Stillington
Cockfield
Evenwood Gate
Burnt Houses
Wackerfield
Bolam
Heighington
Elstob
Whitton
Redmarshall
Carlton
RABY CASTLE
Hilton
Great Stainton
Brafferton
Bishopton
Kinninvie
Ingleton
Houghton le-Side
Coatham Mundeville
Little Stainton
Staindrop
Langton
Killerby
Walworth Gate
Cotherstone
Stainton
Headlam
Summerhouse
Denton
Walworth
Beaumont Hill
Barmpton
Cleatlam
Little Newsham
Lartington
BARNARD CASTLE
THE BOWES MUSEUM
Gainford
Harrowgate Hill
Great Burdon
Sadberge
Elton
Startforth
Barnard Castle
Winston
Piercebridge
High Coniscliffe
Darlington
Haughton Le Skerne
Longnewton
Westwick
Whorlton
ROMAN BRIDGE
Low Coniscliffe
Urlay Nook
Boldron
EGGLESTONE ABBEY
ROKEBY PARK
Ovington
Caldwell
Manfield
Greta Bridge
Eppleby
Forcett
Cleasby
Middleton St George
Egglescliffe
Aislaby
Middleton One Row
Brignall
Hutton Magna
Lane Head
STANWICK IRON AGE FORTIFICATIONS
Carlton
Stanwick-St-John
Aldbrough St John
Stapleton
Blackwell
Low Dinsdale
Scargill
West Layton
Neasham
Low Worsall
Barningham
Newsham
East Layton
Newton Morrell
Croft-on-Tees
Hurworth Place
The Stang Forest
Barton
Eryholme
Girsby
Dalton
Ravensworth
Melsonby
Dalton-on-Tees
Gayles
BARTON PARK SERVICES
Sockburn
Kirby Hill
Hartforth
CROFT
Whashton
Middleton Tyas
SCOTCH CORNER SERVICES
Hornby
Appleton Wiske
NZ
Gilling West
Scotch Corner
Great Smeaton
Moulton
North Cowton
West Rounton
Langthwaite
Arkle Town
Washfold
Atley Hill
East Cowton
Birkby
Welbury
Hurst
Skeeby
Uckerby
Richmond
Deighton
Arkengarthdale
Skelton
EASBY ABBEY
Easby
Scorton
Marske
RICHMOND CASTLE
Healaugh
SWALEDALE FOLK MUSEUM
Hudswell
Colburn
Brompton-on-Swale
CATTERICK
Whitwell
Streetlam
Lovesome Hill
East Harlsey
Reeth
Fremington
Bolton-on-Swale
Catterick Bridge
Danby Wiske
Grinton
Marrick
Downholme
Hipswell
Walkerville
SWALE DALE
GRINTON LODGE
Catterick
Catterick Garrison
Brompton
Winton
Stainton
Great Langton
Kirby Sigston
Tunstall
Scotton
Hipswell Moor
Stainton Moor
East Appleton
Kirkby Fleetham
Yafforth
Bolton Moor
Redmire Moor
Barden
Hornby
Great Fencote
Bullamoor
East Hauxwell
Hackforth
Thrintoft
Northallerton
Garriston
Arrathorne
Little Fencote
Ainderby Steeple
Romanby
Castle Bolton
Bellerby
Hunton
Scruton
BOLTON CASTLE
Preston-under-Scar
SWINESIDE CERAMICS
Constable Burton
Patrick Brompton
Langthorne
Warlaby
Redmire
Leyburn
Little Crakehall
CRAKEHALL WATER MILL
Morton-on-Swale
Carperby
Wensley
Great Crakehall
Leeming
North Otterington
YORKSHIRE MUSEUM OF CARRIAGES
Swinithwaite
Harmby
WENSLEYDALE RLY
Finghall
Newton-le-Willows
Leeming Bar
Thornton-le-Moor
Spennithorne
Aiskew
Sowber Gate
Aysgarth
AYSGARTH FALLS
West Witton
WHITE ROSE CANDLES
Middleham
Cowling
Bedale
Gatenby
Newby Wiske
South Otterington
Thoralby
Agglethorpe
MIDDLEHAM CASTLE
Thornton Steward
JERVAULX ABBEY
Burrill
Londonderry
Maunby
Thornton-le-Street
West Burton
Coverham
East Witton
Exelby
Firby
Melmerby
Carlton
Caldbergh
Thirn
Thornton Watlass
Theakston
THORP PERROW ARBORETUM
Burneston
Snape
Carthorpe
Kirby Wiske
Newsham
SION HILL HALL & BIRDS OF PREY CENTRE
Ellingstring
Carlton Moor
Walden
Gammersgill
West Scrafton
High Ellington
Low Ellington
Pickhill
South Kilvington
AERIAL EXTREME
Holme
Sandhutton
Horsehouse
Colsterdale
URE DALE GLASS
Low Burton
Well
Sinderby
Kirklington
Ainderby Quernhow
Carlton Miniott
Braidley
Hindlethwaite Moor
Colsterdale Moor
Fearby
Healey
Nosterfield
Howe
Woodale
GREAT HAW
THEAKSTON BREWERY
VISITOR CENTRE
Masham
Binsoe
Thornborough
Sutton Howgrave
Skipton-on-Swale
Leighton
Warthermarske
Swinton
West Tanfield
MARMION TOWER
Middleton Quernhow
Baldersby
Catton
Masham Moor
Leighton Res.
Ilton
LITTLE WHERNSIDE
Scar House Res.
Roundhill Res.
Grewelthorpe
Mickley
North Stainley
NORTON CONYERS
Wath
Melmerby
Baldersby St James
Topcliffe
Swale
Tees
Ure
Skerne
Wiske
Greta
Yorkshire
A1(M)
A1
A66
A66(M)
A67
A68
A167
A6108
A684
A689
A688
A6072
A61
A168

Hartlepool
Stockton-on-Tees
Middlesbrough
Redcar and Cleveland
North York Moors
NZ
Trimdon
Fishburn
Ferryhill Station
Bishop Middleham
Sedgefield
Hardwick Hall
Bradbury
Mordon
Butterwick
High Throston
Elwick
West Park
Dalton Piercy
Rift House
Seaton Carew
Saint Hilda's Parish Church
Hartlepool's Maritime Experience
Hartlepool Bay
Tees Bay
Rotterdam 16:00
Zeebrugge 16:30
Greatham
Graythorp
Energy Information Centre
Teesmouth
Wynyard Village
Wynyard Woodland
Thorpe Larches
Foxton
Stillington
Elstob
Newton Bewley
Cowpen Bewley
Wolviston
Billingham
Billingham Art Gallery
Billingham Beck
Thorpe Thewles
Whitton
Carlton
Redmarshall
Norton
Roseworth
Haverton Hill
Port Clarence
South Bank
North Ormesby
Great Stainton
Bishopton
Little Stainton
Brafferton
Coatham Mundeville
Fairfield
Hartburn
Thornaby on Tees
Dorman Museum
Normanby
Eston
Grangetown
Lazenby
Wilton
Kirkleatham
Kirkleatham Old Hall Museum
Dormanstown
Coatham
Salt Scar
Redcar
Marske-by-the-Sea
Saltburn Smugglers Heritage Centre
Miniature Railway
Saltburn-by-the-Sea
Brotton
New Marske
Yearby
Upleatham
Dunsdale
Skelton
North Skelton
Tocketts Water Mill
Guisborough
Guisborough Priory
Boosbeck
Margrove Park
Lingdale
Stanghow
Kilton Thorpe
Charltons
Hutton Gate
Moorsholm
Beaumont Hill
Barmpton
Great Burdon
Sadberge
Elton
Longnewton
Preston Hall Museum
Acklam
Nature's World
Park End
Ormesby
Ormesby Hall
Marton
Captain Cook Birthplace
Coulby Newham
Hemlington
Nunthorpe
Hutton Village
Gisborough Moor
Newton under Roseberry
Commondale Moor
Commondale
Haughton Le Skerne
Darlington
Urlay Nook
Durham Tees Valley
Middleton St George
Middleton One Row
Egglescliffe
Eaglescliffe
Aislaby
Yarm
Ingleby Barwick
High Leven
Stainton
Thornton
Maltby
Newby
Tanton
Great Ayton
Little Ayton
New Row
Low Dinsdale
Neasham
Low Worsall
Kirklevington
Hilton
Seamer
Middleton-on-Leven
Stokesley
Easby
Kildale
Kildale Moor
Battersby
Castleton
Hurworth Place
Eryholme
Dalton-on-Tees
Girsby
Sockburn
Picton
Crathorne
Tame Bridge
Rudby
Hutton Rudby
Enterpen
Kirkby
Great Busby
Great Broughton
Ingleby Greenhow
Westerdale
Cleveland Way
Hornby
Appleton Wiske
Great Smeaton
West Rounton
East Rounton
Welbury
East Cowton
Birkby
Deighton
Potto
Carlton in Cleveland
Faceby
Whorlton
Swainby
Urra
Westerdale Moor
Farndale Moor
Ingleby Arncliffe
Seave Green
Cockayne Ridge
Cockayne
Wake Lady Green
Streetlam
Danby Wiske
Lovesome Hill
East Harlsey
Mount Grace Priory
Osmotherley
Whorlton Moor
Chop Gate
Church Houses
Blakey Ridge
Brompton
Winton
Ellerbeck
Kirby Sigston
Snilesworth Moor
Bilsdale West Moor
Bilsdale East Moor
Bransdale
Rudland Rigg
Low Mill
Yafforth
Great Fencote
Thrintoft
Northallerton
Romanby
Ainderby Steeple
Bullamoor
Thimbleby
Fangdale Beck
Over Silton
Arden Great Moor
Nether Silton
East Moors
Helmsley Moor
Skiplam Moor
Gillamoor
Fadmoor
Scruton
Morton-on-Swale
Warlaby
Leeming Bar
Leeming
Gatenby
Londonderry
Sowber Gate
North Otterington
Thornton-le-Beans
Thornton-le-Moor
Borrowby
Leake
Kepwick
Cowesby
Hawnby
Rievaulx Moor
Newby Wiske
South Otterington
Maunby
Knayton
Upsall
Kirby Knowle
Boltby
Old Byland
Carlton
Kirkbymoorside
Pockley
Beadlam
Thornton-le-Street
Kirby Wiske
Newsham
North Kilvington
Felixkirk
Thirlby
Rievaulx
Rievaulx Abbey
Helmsley
Nawton
Wombleton
Welburn
Burneston
Carthorpe
Sion Hill Hall & Birds of Prey Centre
Pickhill
South Kilvington
Thirsk
World of James Herriot
Old Thirsk
Bob Hunter - Home of the Wren
Sutton Bank Visitor Centre
Cold Kirby
Scawton
Rye Dale
Duncombe Park
Aerial Extreme
Holme
Sinderby
Sandhutton
Kirklington
Ainderby Quernhow
Sowerby
Carlton Miniott
Sutton-under-Whitestonecliffe
Monk Park Farm
Bagby
Balk
Oldstead
Harome
Sproxton
Muscoates
Nunnington
West Ness
East Ness
Howe
Skipton-on-Swale
Sutton Howgrave
Great Thirkleby
Little Thirkleby
Kilburn
High Kilburn
Mouseman Visitors Centre
Wass
Ampleforth
Byland Abbey
Coxwold
Oswaldkirk
Stonegrave
Cawton
South Holme
Hovingham
Gilling East
Carlton Husthwaite
Hutton Sessay
Dalton
Norton Conyers
St James
Hambleton Hills
Cleveland Hills
Cleveland
0 1 2 3 4 5 6 miles
0 1 2 3 4 5 6 7 8 9 10 km

5
6
7
8
A
B
C
D
E
F
G
NZ
OV
SE
TA
Skinningrove
Carlin How
Loftus
Boulby
Staithes
Easington
Port Mulgrave
Runswick Bay
Hinderwell
Runswick Bay
Roxby
Liverton
Newton Mulgrave
Kettleness
Goldsborough
Ellerby
Scaling
Lythe
Sandsend
Sandsend Wyke
THE DRACULA EXPERIENCE
SUTCLIFFE GALLERY
Whitby
Saltwick Bay
WHITBY ABBEY
WHITBY
CAPTAIN COOK MEMORIAL MUSEUM
Mickleby
East Barnby
West Barnby
East Row
Dunsley
Scaling Dam Res.
Ugthorpe
Newholm
Lealholm Moor
THE MOORS CENTRE
Danby
Stonegate
Ruswarp
Aislaby
Briggswath
Stainsacre
High Hawkser
Houlsyke
Lealholm
Sleights
Sneaton
Ugglebarnby
Ainthorpe
Esk
Egton
Grosmont
GROSMONT GALLERY
Sneatonthorpe
Raw
Ness Pt.
CLEVELAND WAY
Robin Hood's Bay
Low Garth
Street
Glaisdale
Egton Bridge
Esk Valley
Littlebeck
Fylingthorpe
BOGGLE HOLE
Robin Hood's Bay
Glaisdale
Glaisdale Moor
Egton High Moor
Beck Hole
Goathland
Old Peak
Ravenscar
Flask Inn
Fylingdales Moor
Rosedale Moor
WHEELDALE MOOR ROMAN ROAD
YORK MOORS
Staintondale
STAINTONDALE SHIRE HORSE FARM
CLEVELAND WAY
Harwood Dale Forest
Thorgill
Wheeldale Moor
Goathland Moor
Saltergate
Harwood Dale
Rosedale Abbey
PICKERING MOOR
Pickering Forest
Cloughton Newlands
Cloughton Wyke
Cloughton
ROSEDALE
NAL PARK
Langdale Forest
Broxa Forest
Derwent
Cropton
Hartoft End
Stape
Burniston
Cromer Pt.
Spaunton Moor
Seven
Forest
Newton Dale
MOORLAND EXPERIENCE
TOLL
Langdale End
Broxa
Silpho
Suffield
Scalby
SCARBOROUGH SEA LIFE AND MARINE SANCTUARY
Scalby Ness Rocks
KINDERLAND
North Bay
Lastingham
Levisham
Hackness
Spaunton
Newton-on-Rawcliffe
Lockton
LOCKTON
Staindale Forest
Wrench Green
Everley
Barrowcliff
Newby
SCARBOROUGH CASTLE
ROTUNDA MUSEUM
Scarborough
South Bay
Hutton-le-Hole
Appleton-le-Moors
Cropton
NORTH RIDING FOREST PARK
Wykeham Forest
Trouts Dale
NORTH YORKSHIRE MOORS RAILWAY
Low Dalby
Dalby Forest
FORGE VALLEY WOODLANDS
Falsgrave
Keldholme
Sinnington
Wrelton
Aislaby
ST PETER AND ST PAUL CHURCH
East Ayton
THE HONEY FARM
Cayton Bay
Kirkby Mills
Middleton
PICKERING CASTLE
West Ayton
Osgodby
Sawdon
Eastfield
Yons Nab
Great Edstone
Pickering
Ellerburn
Hutton Buscel
WORDSWORTH GALLERY
Irton
Seamer
Cayton
Marton
Thornton-le-Dale
Wilton
Allerston
Ebberston
Snainton
Ruston
Wykeham
Lebberston
Gristhorpe
Normanby
Brompton
Little Barugh
Costa Beck
FLAMINGO LAND
Salton
Kirby Misperton
Great Barugh
Yedingham
Flixton
Folkton
Muston
Staxton
THE CARRS WAY
Brawby
High Marishes
Derwent
East Heslerton
Sherburn
Ganton
YORKSHIRE WOLDS WAY
Butterwick
Low Marishes
Little Habton
Great Habton
Ryton
Scampston
West Knapton
East Knapton
Potter Brompton
Hunmanby
A174
A171
A169
A170
A165
A64
A1039
B1366
B1266
B1410
B1416
B1447
B1415
B1258
B1261
96
97

1
2
3
4
5
A
B
C
D
E
F
NW
Bennane Hd.
112
Colmonell
Knockdolian
265
B734
Ballantrae Bay
B7044
Heronsford
Glen Tig
Ballantrae
Balkissock
Downan Pt.
Auchencrosh
439
BENERAIRD
A77
LARNE 1:00
(April-Sept)
LARNE 1:45
BELFAST 3:15
BELFAST 1:45
Mark
Glen App
Milleur Pt.
Corsewall Pt.
17
257
Portencalzie
Barnhills
North Cairn
South Cairn
Corsewall
B738
Loch Connell
Kirkcolm
Cairnryan
Penwhirn Res.
Main Water of Luce
Dounan Bay
Mains of Airies
Ervie
Braid Fell
Low Salchrie
The Wig
B798
LOCH RYAN
Knocknain
Slouchnawen Bay
Leswalt
Craigencross
Innermessan
B7043
A718
A751
Black Loch
CASTLE KENNEDY GARDENS
Glenstockadale
Stranraer
Aird
White Loch
Castle Kennedy
Broadsea Bay
T H E R H I
CASTLE OF ST JOHN VISITOR CENTRE
Knockglass
WIGTOWN DISTRICT MUSEUM
Soulseat Loch
A75
Mark
Lochans
Black Hd.
182
B7077
Dunskey Ho.
A77
Torrs Wa
LITTLE WHEELS
B7084
Portpatrick
Awhirk
Stoneykirk
Luce Sa
A716
Port of Spittal Bay
B7042
Cairngarroch
Sandhead
KIRKMADRINE STONES
Sandhead Bay
Cairngarroch Bay
Money Hd.
Clachanmore
Hole Stone Bay
ARDWELL GDNS.
Ardwell
Ardwell Mains
Chapel Rossan Bay
Ardwell Pt.
Logan Mains
LOGAN BOTANIC GARDEN
Balgowan Pt.
Mull of Logan
LOGAN FISH POND MARINE LIFE CENTRE
Port Nessock or Port Logan Bay
Port Logan
Cairnywellan Hd.
B7065
A716
Clanyard Bay
Low Clanyard
Kirkmaiden
Laggantalluch Hd.
Drummore
164
Damnaglaur
B7041
Crammag Hd.
Ma
Cairngaan
Port Kemin
0 1 2 3 4 5 6 miles
0 1 2 3 4 5 6 7 8 9 10 km

Pinmore Mains
Poundland
Pinwherry
Bellamore
335 PINDONNAN
Ballochmorrie
Black Clauchrie
Water of Tig
Barrhill
Laggan
Eldrick
A714
112
Arecleoch Forest
Chirmorrie
B7027
Drumlamford Loch
Dornal
Loch Dornal
Loch Ochiltree
Loch Maberry
Miltonise
287
Craig Airie Fell
Loch Derry
Polbae
LAGGANGAIRN STANDING STONES
Knowe
Cross Water of Luce
Artfield Fell
244
Carseriggan
Black Loch
Loch Heron
Loch Ronald
New Luce
SOUTHERN UPLAND WAY
Auchmantle
Drumphail
205
Tarf Water
Water of Luce
Whitecairn
Carscreugh
GLENWHAN GARDENS
GLENLUCE ABBEY
Dunragit
CASTLE OF PARK
Glenluce
Knock Moss
Dernaglar Loch
A747
Whitefield Loch
Milton
Stairhaven
Castle Loch
Auchenmalg
Auchenmalg Bay
Culshabbin
Alticry
B7005
197
Loch Head
CHAPEL FINIAN
Elrig
Mochrum Loch
Barrachan
MOTE OF DRUCHTAG
Mochrum
Milton Pt.
Port William
LUCE BAY
Barsalloch Pt.
BARSALLOCH FORT
MONREITH ANIMAL WORLD, SHORE CENTRE AND MUSEUM
Monreith Bay
Monreith
Monreith Mains
Drumtroddan
DRUMTRODDAN STONES
Airyhassen
Drummoddie
Moor of Ravenstone
B7021
B7085
75
A747
Glasserton
146
FELL OF CARLETON
ST NINIAN'S CAVE
Port Castle Bay
Cailliness Pt.
ryport
MULL OF GALLOWAY
BURROW HEAD
Cutcloy
Isle of Whithorn
ST NINIAN'S CHAPEL
B7004
Cairn Hd.
Portyerrock Bay
WHITHORN TRUST DISCOVERY CENTRE
PRIORY AND MUSEUM
Whithorn
Bishopton
A746
Port Allen
Cults
CRUGGLETON CHURCH AND CASTLE
B7063
GALLOWAY HOUSE GARDENS
Garlieston
Eggerness Pt.
Sorbie
B7052
Whauphill
Kirkinner
Braehead
Baldoon Sands
Bladnoch
VISITOR CENTRE
Wigtown
SCOTLAND'S BOOK TOWN
Wigtown Sands
Culmazie
THE MACHARS
Fell Loch
Torhousemuir
TORHOUSE STONE CIRCLE
B733
Bladnoch
B7052
131
Spittal
High Mindork
Craighlaw Mains
Kirkcowan
B735
A75
Shennanton
213
NX
Benfield
123
Baltersan
Causeway End
Carsegowan
Newton Stewart
MINNIGAFF
Minnigaff
Creebridge
Challoch
Penninghame Forest
B7027
A714
Kirroughtree Forest
Clachaneasy
Dumfries and Galloway
Glentrool Village
GLENTROOL VISITOR CENTRE
Glentrool
Palgowan
Water of Minnoch
Loch Moan
Cree
GALLOWAY FOREST PARK
Glen Trool Lodge
Trool
Loch Trool
BRUCE'S STONE
1307
MERRICK 843
Loch Enoch
692 MULLWHARCHAR
Loch Neldricken
Loch Valley
SILVER FLOWE
Loch Dee
716 LAMACHAN HILL
Loch Middle
CORSERINE 814
RHINNS OF KELLS
Loch Harrow
Forrest Lodg
Loch Dungeon
746
Drumt
Clatteringshaws Forest
Clatteringshaws Loch
Loch Grannoch
WILD GOAT PARK
353
106
A712
Penkiln Burn
Palnure Burn
711 CAIRNSMORE OF FLEET
CAIRNSMORE OF FLEET
Clints of Dromore
Palnure
Cree
GEM ROCK MUSEUM
Creetown
Glen
456 CAIRNHARROW
Carsluith
CARSLUITH CASTLE
CAIRNHOLY CAIRNS
Ravenshall Pt.
Ringdoo Pt.
Fleet Bay
FELL

Loch Dungeon
Silver Flowe
Loch Valley
746
Drumbuie
Earlstoun Loch
St John's Town of Dalry
Millquarter
Bogue
A702
Corriedoo Forest
417
Loch Urr
Sundaywell
Milton
373
Clatteringshaws Forest
113
Garroch
Glenlee
Blackcraig
Knocklearn
Clatteringshaws Loch
Loch Dee
381
A762
B7075
A712
Balmaclellan
Gibbshill
New Galloway
Blowplain Open Farm
Glenkiln
AN HILL
Clatteringshaws Forest Wildlife Centre
Ironmacannie
317
Craig
Corsock
398
Glen
Raiders Road Forest Drive
Dumfries and Galloway
Merkland
Brooklands
353
Bennan
Dee
Cairn Edward Hill
Loch Ken
A713
Urr Water
Crocketford or Ninemile Bar
Wild Goat Park
Loch Grannoch
Forest
470
Fell of Fleet
Mossdale
Drumrash
Parton
Auchenreoch Loch
B794
Kirkpatrick Durham
Milton
Stroan Loch
Springholm
Cairnsmore of Fleet
711
Loch Skerrow
Woodhall Loch
Old Bridge of Urr
Crossmichael
Palnure Burn
105
Craig
Clarebrand
Haugh of Urr
Fleet Forest
Lochenbreck Loch
Townhead of Greenlaw
B795
Mote of Urr
Clints of Dromore
Laurieston
Palnure
Laurieston Forest
343
Loch Glentoo
Threave Castle
Castle Douglas
A745
Old Buittle Tower
182
Barhill
Big Water of Fleet
Cree
Loch Whinyeon
Loch Mannoch
Loch Bargatton
Kelton Mains Open Farm
Threave Gardens
Carlingwark Loch
Dalbeattie
Glengap
366
Bengray
Forest
Glengap
Bridge of Dee
Rhonehouse or Kelton Hill
B736
B721
Gem Rock Museum
Creetown
B796
A75
Gelston
Glen
Fleet
Ringford
A711
Palnackie
Wigtown Sands
Mill on the Fleet
Anworth
Gatehouse of Fleet
Valleyfield
Airieland
Barnbarroch
Wigtown
456
Cairnharrow
Cardoness Castle
B727
Orchardton Tower
Scotland's Book Town
Carsluith
Carsluith Castle
Valley
Girthon
Twynholm
Galloway Hydro Visitor Centre
391
Bengairn
Kippford or Scaur
Cairnholy Cairns
Tongland
Mote of Mark
Broughton House and Garden
East Stewartry Coast
Baldoon Sands
Ravenshall Pt.
Fleet Bay
Barharrow
Maclellan's Castle
Rough Island
Ringdoo Pt.
Sandgreen
A755
Whinnieliggate
Stewartry Museum
Kirkcudbright
Auchencairn
B7004
Islands of Fleet
Knockbrex
89
Kirkcarswell
Balcary Pt.
St Mary's Isle
Mutehill
135
Rascarrel
Sorbie
B7052
Kirkandrews
Borgue
Dundrennan
Rascarrel Bay
Garlieston
Wigtown Bay
Kirkcudbright Bay
Orroland
Eggerness Pt.
Townhead
Dundrennan Abbey
Borness
Galloway House Gardens
B7063
Netherlaw
Ross
Balmae
Port Mary
Borness Pt.
108
Abbey Hd.
Cults
Little Ross
Cruggleton Church and Castle
A746
Whithorn
Port Allen
Portyerrock Bay
Cairn Hd.
St Ninian's Chapel
Isle of Whithorn
Cutcloy
NX
0 1 2 3 4 5 6 miles
0 1 2 3 4 5 6 7 8 9 10 km

Ellisland Farm
Duncow
Applegarthtown
A74(M)
Galiaberry
Amisfield
Tinwald
Kirkton
A76
A701
Lochmaben
Marjoriebanks
Lochmaben Castle
Castle Loch
A709
Lockerbie
Bankshill
Newtonairds
Holywood
114
Locharbriggs
Dumfries and Galloway Aviation Mus.
Heck
Drumpark
Irongray
Heathhall
Newbridge
Lincluden College
The Grove
Torthorwald
Hightae
Birkshaw Forest
Castlemilk
Burnswark
Burnswark Fort
Waterbeck
Terregles Banks
Lincluden
Old Bridge House Mus.
Greystone
Rammerscales House
Kettleholm
Shawhead
Maxwelltown
Dumfries
Collin
Middleshaw
Middlebie
Burns House
Greenlea
A75
Cargenbridge
Robert Burns Centre
Dumfries Museum & Camera Obscura
Racks
Dalton
Ecclefechan
Thomas Carlyle's Birthplace
Eaglesfield
Brae
Lochfoot
Lochrutton Loch
Cleughbrae
Hoddomcross
Kingholm Quay
Mouswald
Kirtlebridge
Islesteps
Lochar Water
Carrutherstown
Hoddom Mains
Mabie Forest
Mabie
Kelton
Lochar Moss
Lochaber Loch
Kirkonnell Flow
Brydekirk
Creca
Beeswing
Loch Arthur
Drumcoltran Tower
Glencaple
Bankend
Clarencefield
Charlesfield
108
Kirkconnell
Ruthwell Cross
Shambellie House Costume Museum
River Nith
Ruthwell
Duncan Savings Bank Museum
Annan
Dornock
Kirkgunzeon
Shearington
Blackshaw
Cummertrees
Eastriggs
New Abbey
Caerlaverock Castle
Powfoot
Welldale
Shawhill
Sweetheart Abbey
Eastpark
New Abbey Pow
New Abbey Corn Mill
Nith
Bowhouse
Caerlaverock
Overton
Wildfowl and Wetland Centre
383 Long Fell
Loch Kindar
Blackshaw Bank
Estuary
Bowness-on-Solway
Port Carlisle
Drumburn
569 Criffell
Solway Coast
Glasson
Bowness Common
Drumburgh
Cardurnock
Carsethorn
Anthorn
Kirkbean
Arbigland Gardens
Drumburgh Moss
Drumstinchall
Whitrigg
Prestonmill
Caulkerbush
Kirkbride
Mainsriddle
John Paul Jones Birthplace Museum
Skinburness
Mersehead RSPB Nature Reserve
Newton Arlosh
Sandyhills
Colvend
Southerness
Wedholme Flow
Rockcliffe
Portling
Southerness Pt.
Calvo
Seaville
Mersehead Sands
Silloth
Greenrow
Causewayhead
South Solway Mosses
Castlehill Pt.
Kingside Hill
Blitterlees
Abbey Town
Waver
Kelsick
Oulton
Lessonhall
Highlaws
Dundraw
Waverbridge
Beckfoot
Pelutho
Wigton
Newtown
Blencogo
NX
Bromfield
Holme St Cuthbert
Waverton
Langrigg
Waterside
Mawbray
Dubmill Pt.
Edderside
New Cowper
Westnewton
Bolton Low Houses
Allonby
NY
Watchhill
Aspatria
A596
Mealsgate
Hayton
Allonby Bay
Ellen
Blennerhasset
Prospect
Boltongate
Oughterside
Sandale
Torpenhow
Allerby
Threapland
Crosscanonby
Crosby Villa
Parsonby
Plumbland
Whitrigg
Bothel
Ireby
Crosby
Bullgill
Gilcrux
Maryport Maritime Museum
Uldale
High Ireby
Maryport
447 Binsey
Over Water
Dearham
Tallentire
A595
Blindcrake
Sunderland
Bewaldeth
Flimby
Dovenby
Bridekirk
Broughton Moor
Standingstone
Derwent
Great Broughton
Little Broughton
Bassenthwaite
Siddick
Camerton
Papcastle
Wordsworth Ho.
Cockermouth
Embleton
Seaton
Great Clifton
Brigham
Castlegate Ho.
Bassenthwaite Lake
98
North Side
Bridgefoot
Cockermouth
Wythop Mill
Workington
Stainburn
Greysouthen
Helena Thompson Mus.
Little Clifton
Thornthwaite Forest
Mirehouse
931 Skiddaw
Westfield
Eaglesfield
Sandybeck Meadow
Mossbay
Deanscales
Marron
Low Lorton
Thornthwaite
Millbeck
Harrington
Winscales
Dean
Cumberland
Solway Firth

Lockerbie
Langholm
Kershopefoot
Kershope Forest
Tinnisburn Forest
Ecclefechan
Annan
Eastriggs
Gretna
Gretna Green
Longtown
Brampton
Carlisle
Wetheral
Wigton
Thursby
Aspatria
Kirkbride
Newton Arlosh
Dalston
Sebergham
Caldbeck
Lazonby
Penrith
SKIDDAW FOREST
NY
Cumbria
Inglewood Forest
A7
A74(M)
A75
A6071
A689
A69
A595
A596
M6
A66
A591
A6
115
107
98
99
Scale bar: 0 1 2 3 4 5 6 miles; 0 1 2 3 4 5 6 7 8 9 10 km

NORTHUMBERLAND
NATIONAL PARK
NORTH PENNINES
NY
Wark Forest
Bellingham
Redesmouth
Hesleyside
Bower
Ridsdale
Hopehouse
Sighty Crag
Whitelyne Common
The Flatt
Paddaburn Moor
Churnsike Lodge
White Preston
Kielder Mires
Blacka Burn
Warks Burn
Stonehaugh
Whygate
Wark
Birtley
Park End
Great Swinburne
Gunnerton
Colt Crag Reservoir
Bewcastle
Spadeadam Forest
Butterburn
Black Fell
Pennine Way
Haughton Common
Simonburn
Barrasford
Haughton Castle
Chollerton
Humshaugh
Chollerford
Spadeadam Farm
Wiley Sike
Thirlwall Common
Whiteside
Greenlee Lough
Broomlee Lough
Course of Hadrian's Wall
Hadrian's Wall Path
Old Repeater Station
Walwick
Low Brunton
Brunton Turret
Chesters Roman Fort
Wall
Hill Head
Housesteads Roman Fort
Visitor Centre
Vallum
West Hall
Gilsland Spa
Birdoswald Roman Fort
Birdoswald
Roman Army Museum
Hadrian's Wall
Once Brewed
Chesterholm Museum (Vindolanda)
Fourstones
Newbrough
Acomb
Gilsland
Greenhead
Upper Denton
Banks
Lanercost
Low Row
Haltwhistle
Henshaw
Bardon Mill
Chesterwood
Melkridge
Redburn
South Tyne
Haydon Bridge
Low Gate
Hexham
Moothall
Abbey
Border History Mus.
Plenmeller
Denton Fell
Plenmellar Common
Rowfoot
Langley
Milton
Talkin Tarn
Farlam
Talkin
Hallbankgate
Tindale
Tindale Tarn
Tindale Fells
Midgeholme
Halton Lea Gate
Lambley
Stonehouse
Forest Head
Whitfield
Bearsbridge
West Allen
Catton
Dye House
Dalton
Whitley Chapel
Slaley Forest
Maiden Way
Eals
Gelt
Cold Fell
Glendue Fell
King's Forest of Geltsdale
Geltsdale Middle
Knarsdale
Slaggyford
Whitfield Moor
Allendale Town
East Allen
Hexhamshire Common
Broadwell House
Devil's Water
Blanchland Moor
Ninebanks
Sinderhope
Allendale Common
Blanchland
Newbiggin
Croglin
Croglin Water
Ayle
Spartylea
Hunstanworth
Nookton Fell
South Tynedale Railway
Blagill
Gossipgate Gallery
Carrshield
Scale Houses
Watch Hill
Raise
Alston
Bayles
Nenthall
Coalcleugh
Dirt Pot
Allenheads
Bolt's Law
Gilderdale Forest
Middle Fell
Renwick
Haresceugh
Leadgate
Nenthead
Nenthead Mines Heritage Centre
Killhope Leadmining Centre
Rookhope
Rookhope Nurseries
High Bankhill
Garrigill
Lanehead
Middlehope Moor
Unthank
Cowshill
Wearhead
Weardale
Burnhope Reservoir
Gamblesby
Glassonby
Ireshopeburn
St John's Chapel
Westgate
Daddry Shield
Eastg
Great Salkeld
Melmerby
Melmerby Fell
Altston Moor
Little Salkeld
Burnhope Seat
Hunsonby
Round Hill
Ireshope Moor
Winskill
Langwathby
Ousby
Cross Fell
Tees
Harwood
Westernhope Moor
Briggle Beck
Skirwith
Edenhall
Kirkland
Milburn Forest
Trout Beck
Moor House-Upper Teesdale
Viewing Hill
Harwood Beck
Langdon Common
Chapelfell Top
Newbiggin Common
Eden
Blencarn
Crowdundle Beck
Langdon Beck
Forest
Ettersgill
Mayburgh Henge
Brougham Castle
Culgaith
Milburn
Widdybank Fell
Cow Green Reservoir
Bowlees Visitor Centre
Acorn Bank
Newbiggin
Dufton Fell
Cauldron Snout
High Force
Temple Sowerby
Knock
Cronkley Fell
Wetheriggs Country Pottery
Lowmoor Row
Maize Beck
Holwick
Middleton-in-Teesdale
Cliburn Moss
Kirkby Thore
Dufton
A69
A689
A686
A68
A6079
B6318
B6320
B6319
B6305
B6304
B6295
B6303
B6294
B6277
B6412
A66
116
110
99
100

Ridsdale
Wansbeck
Meldon
Molesden
Choppington
Clifton
Stepscott
Bedlington
Redemouth
Sweethope Loughs
Kirkharle
WALLINGTON
BOLAM LAKE
Bolam
Whalton
Tranwell
Nedderton
Great Bavington
Capheaton
Harnham
Shilvington
Saltwick
Thockrington
Little Bavington
Belsay
BELSAY HALL
Ogle
Stannington
PLESSEY WOODS
Birtley
Colt Crag Reservoir
Kirkheaton
KIRKLEY HALL
Wark
Great Swinburne
Hallington Reservoir
Hallington
Black Heddon
West Newham
Milbourne
Higham Dykes
Berwick Hill
NORTHUMBERLAND CHEESE FARM
Park End
Gunnerton
Colwell
Ryal
Ingoe
Brenkley
Simonburn
Barrasford
Fenwick
Heugh
Ponteland
Dinnington
Seaton Burn
Northumberland
Chollerton
Haughton Castle
Humshaugh
Bingfield
Matfen
Stamfordham
Dalton
Prestwick
Brunswick Village
Hazlerigg
COURSE OF HADRIAN'S WALL
HADRIAN'S WALL PATH
Chollerford
Walwick
Low Brunton
BRUNTON TURRET
Great Whittington
Ouston
Eachwick
Medburn
Darras Hall
High Callerton
NEWCASTLE INTERNATIONAL
Woolsington
Black Callerton
Kenton Bankfoot
CHESTERS ROMAN FORT
Wall
Hill Head
Harlow Hill
Gosforth
Kenton
Fourstones
Halton
HADRIAN'S WALL PATH
North Walbottle
Westerhope
Newbrough
Warden
AYDON CASTLE
Aydon
Sandhoe
ACOMB
Acomb
TYNE GREEN
Newton Hall
Horsley
Heddon-on-the-Wall
Throckley
Walbottle
NEWCASTLE UPON TYNE
GEORGE STEPHENSON'S BIRTHPLACE
WYLAM RAILWAY MUS.
Newburn
Low Gate
MOOTHALL
ABBEY
Corbridge
Newton
TYNE RIVERSIDE
Ovingham
Wylam
Clara Vale
Scotswood
Haydon Bridge
Hexham
BORDER HISTORY MUS.
DILSTON PHYSIC GDN
Dilston
Ovington
West Wylam
Crawcrook
Ryton
NEWCASTLE DISCOVERY
METROLAND
Dunston
CHERRYBURN
Branch End
Prudhoe
BLAYDON
HEXHAM
Riding Mill
Broomhaugh
Stocksfield
Mickley Square
High Mickley
Greenside
Coalburns
Winlaton
THORNS CENTRE
WHICKHAM
Whickham
Painshawfield
Barlow
Broomley
New Ridley
Leadgate
High Spen
Highfield
Sunniside
Street Gate
Chowdene
Dye House
Dalton
Slaley
Healey
HIGHLAND CATTLE CENTRE
Hedley on the Hill
Chopwell
Rowlands Gill
GIBSIDE
Byermoor
Marley Hill
Lamesley
Whitley Chapel
Whittonstall
Blackhall Mill
DERWENTCOTE STEEL FURNACE
Hamsterley
DERWENT WALK
Burnopfield
TANFIELD RAILWAY
Kibblesworth
ST. ANDREW'S CHURCH
Leazes
Hobson
Allendale Town
Slaley Forest
Kiln Pit Hill
Newlands
Ebchester
High Westwood
Tanfield
BEAMISH
Urpeth
Perkinsville
Medomsley
Tantobie
Beamish
Hexhamshire Common
Broadwell House
Devil's Water
DERWENT RES.
Shotleyfield
Dipton
Tanfield Lea
STANLEY
Sinderhope
Blanchland Moor
Shotley Bridge
Catchgate
West Pelton
Grange Villa
CHESTER-LE-STREET
Allendale Common
Carterway Heads
Leadgate
The Middles
POW HILL
Bridgehill
Consett
Annfield Plain
Craghead
Blanchland
Edmundbyers
EDMUNDBYERS
Templetown
Iveston
Waldridge
Spartylea
Muggleswick
Allensford
Knitsley
Delves
Maiden Law
Hunstanworth
Castleside
Burnhope
Edmondsley
NOOKTON FELL
Muggleswick Common
Lanchester
BROOM HO. FM MAIZE MAZE
Sacriston
Horsleyhope
Dirt Pot
Allenheads
NY
NZ
BOLT'S LAW
Waskerley
East Butsfield
DIGGERLAND
Witton Gilbert
Langley Park
NORTH
Rookhope
Res.
Cornsay
HALL HILL FARM
Cornsay Colliery
Quebec
Esh
Bearpark
Middlehope Moor
ROOKHOPE NURSERIES
Stanhope Common
Satley
Ushaw Moor
Broompark
Lanehead
Tunstall Res.
COLLIER LAW
Esh Winning
New Brancepeth
Cowshill
Crawleyside
Wolsingham Park Moor
High Stoop
Waterhouses
Wearhead
WEARDALE
DURHAM DALES CENTRE
Stanhope
Eastgate
Westgate
Tow Law
East Hedleyhope
Brandon
Ireshopeburn
St John's Chapel
Daddry Shield
WEARDALE RAILWAY
Sunniside
Brancepeth
Frosterley
Wolsingham
Thornley
Billy Row
Durham
Ireshope Moor
PENNINES
Hill End
Wear
Crook
Helmington Row
Oakenshaw
Willington
Page Bank
HARPERLEY P.O.W. CAMP
Fir Tree
Byers Green
Westernhope Moor
Bollihope Common
Howden-le-Wear
Hunwick
Newfield
Middlestone Moor
Langdon Common
CHAPELFELL TOP
Pikeston Fell
Bedburn
High Grange
Binchester
BINCHESTER FORT
Blocks
Westerton
Newbiggin Common
PAWLAW PIKE
Witton-le-Wear
Langdon Beck
LANGDON BECK
Middleton Common
Redford
Hamsterley
Witton Park
Toronto
AUCKLAND CASTLE
Coundon
Forest
Ettersgill
TOLL
ESCOMB CHURCH
Escomb
HIGH FORCE
BOWLEES VISITOR CENTRE
Hamsterley Forest
Low Etherley
High Etherley
Bishop Auckland
Tees
Morley
Toft Hill
ST HELEN'S
Coundon Grange
Eldon
Shildon
Cronkley Fell
Middleton-in-Teesdale
Woodland Fell
Woodland
Howle
Butterknowle
High
Evenwood
West Auckland
St Helen Auckland
0 1 2 3 4 5 6 miles
0 1 2 3 4 5 6 7 8 9 10 km

West Sleekburn
Cambois
Bedlington Station
East Sleekburn
Cowpen
BLYTH
117
Bebside
Newsham
East Hartford
New Delaval
Shankhouse
Nelson Village
New Hartley
Seaton
Seaton Sluice
SEATON DELAVAL HALL
Cramlington
Southfield
East Cramlington
Seaton Delaval
Hartley
ST MARY'S LIGHTHOUSE
St Mary's or Bait I.
Holywell
Seghill
Dudley
Annitsford
Burradon
Backworth
Earsdon
WHITLEY BAY
NEWCASTLE
Camperdown
Killingworth
Monkseaton
Shiremoor
Marden
Cullercoats
BLUE REEF AQUARIUM
STAVANGER 20:45
HAUGESUND 23:00
BERGEN 27:00
AMSTERDAM 15:00
TYNEMOUTH CASTLE & PRIORY
Longbenton
STEPHENSON RAILWAY MUSEUM
THE RISING SUN
North Shields
Tynemouth
ARBEIA ROMAN FORT AND MUSEUM
Jesmond
Willington
WALLSEND
ROYAL QUAYS
South Shields
SOUTH SHIELDS MUSEUM
Heaton
TOLL
Tyne Tunnel
THE LEAS AND MARSDEN ROCK
NEWCASTLE-U-TYNE
Jarrow
BEDE'S WORLD
ST PAUL'S MONASTERY
Westoe
Harton
Marsden Bay
Byker
SEGEDUNUM FORT
Walker
Marsden
CASTLE KEEP
Gateshead
Hebburn
SOUTER LIGHTHOUSE
INTERNATIONAL STADIUM
Hedworth
Whiteleas
Cleadon
Whitburn Colliery
Pelaw
Boldon Colliery
Whitburn
Felling
Boldon
Carr Hill
FULWELL WINDMILL
Low Fell
Downhill
Fulwell
Roker
Wear
Hylton Castle
Southwick
Wrekenton
BOWES RLY
Usworth
Castletown
Monkwearmouth
NATIONAL GLASS CENTRE
Springwell
STATION MUS.
SAINT PETER'S CHURCH
SUNDERLAND MINSTER
Blackfell
OLD HALL
WASHINGTON
South Hylton
Pallion
Birtley
WASHINGTON SERVICES
High Barnes
Sunderland
Lambton
Pennywell
Hendon
THE WILDFOWL & WETLANDS TRUST
PENSHAW MON.
NZ
Ouston
Barley Mow
Fatfield
Penshaw
East Herrington
New Silksworth
Rickleton
Tunstall
Ryhope
Shiney Row
New Herrington
Doxford Park
RYHOPE ENGINES MUS.
CHESTER-LE-STREET
Bournmoor
Newbottle
Burdon
THE ANKERS HOUSE
Fence Houses
Seaton
Northlea
SEAHAM
Chester Moor
Great Lumley
Colliery Row
HOUGHTON-LE-SPRING
West Lea
East Rainton
Dalton-le-Dale
Plawsworth
West Rainton
Hetton-le-Hole
Cold Hesledon
Kimblesworth
FINCHALE PRIORY
Murton
Pity Me
Leamside
Hawthorn
Low Moorsley
Easington Lane
Beacon Pt.
Framwellgate Moor
South Hetton
Pittington
Easington Colliery
DURHAM LIGHT INFANTRY MUS.
Carrville
Littletown
DALTON PARK
Haswell
Easington
Durham
Sherburn
Sherburn Hill
Haswell Plough
DURHAM CITY
DURHAM CATH.
Shotton Colliery
Horden
DURHAM UNIV. ORIENTAL MUS.
Ludworth
Shadforth
Shincliffe
Old Cassop
Thornley
PETERLEE
Shotton
CASTLE EDEN DENE
Blackhall Colliery
Cassop
Wheatley Hill
CASTLE EDEN WALKWAY
Blackhall Rocks
Old Quarrington
Castle Eden
High Hesleden
Sunderland Bridge
Bowburn
CASSOP VALE
Hesleden
DURHAM SERVICES
Quarrington Hill
Wingate
DURHAM COAST
Croxdale
Hett
Deaf Hill
Station Town
Hart Station
Tudhoe
Kelloe
Trimdon Grange
Trimdon Colliery
Hutton Henry
Sheraton
Hart
Coxhoe
JACKSONS LANDING
Spennymoor
Cornforth
Trimdon
SAINT HILDA'S PARISH CHURCH
Ferryhill
High Throston
THRISLINGTON
Ferryhill Station
Elwick
HARTLEPOOL'S MARITIME EXPERIENCE
Hartlepool Bay
West Park
Hartlepool
Kirk Merrington
Fishburn
Mainsforth
Bishop Middleham
Seaton Carew
Middlestone
Chilton Lane
Dalton Piercy
Rift House
Butterwick
Leasingthorne
Chilton
101
102
HARDWICK HALL
ROTTERDAM 16:00
ZEEBRUGGE 16:30
Rushyford
Sedgefield
Tees Bay
Greatham
Bradbury
SEDGEFIELD
ENERGY INFORMATION CENTRE
NEWTON AYCLIFFE
Graythorp
Middridge
Mordon
Wynyard Village
Newton Bewley
Salt Scar
Thorpe Larches
WYNYARD
Wolviston
COWPEN
TEESMOUTH

120
Troon
Barassie
Muirhead
North Bay
South Bay
ROYAL TROON
Lady Isle
LARNE 1:49 (March-Sept)
LARNE 4:30
DUNDONALD CASTLE
Loans
Symington
Bogend
Craigie
Crossroads
Hansel Village
Millburn
Auchmillan
Mossgiel
Cessnock Water
Monkton
GLASGOW PRESTWICK INTERNATIONAL
Tarbolton
BACHELOR'S CLUB
BURN'S HOUSE MUSEUM
Mauchline
Prestwick
AYR GORGE WOODLANDS
Failford
Haugh
St Quivox
Mossblown
Woodfield
Newton on Ayr
Wallacetown
Whitletts
Annbank
Stair
Crosshill
Lugar Water
Ayr
Trabboch
Ochiltree
Seafield
Belston
Masonhill
Coylton
Coalhall
Belmont
BURNS COTTAGE
MACLAURIN GALLERY & ROZELLE HOUSE
Joppa
Hillhead
Drongan
Heads of Ayr
HEADS OF AYR FARM PARK
Doonfoot
Alloway
Laigh Glengall
BURNS NATIONAL HERITAGE PARK
TAM O'SHANTER EXPERIENCE
Martnaham Loch
Barbieston
Fisherton
Sinclairston
Hayhill
Littlemill
Rankinston
Dunure
Culroy
Minishant
Dalrymple
Hollybush
ELECTRIC BRAE
Water of Coyle
Culzean Bay
Polnessan
KILMEIN HILL
NS
CULZEAN CASTLE
CULZEAN
Whitefaulds
Maybole
COLLEGIATE CHURCH
Patna
Burnfoot
Maidenhead Bay
Maidens
Kirkmichael
Aitkenhead
Loch Spallander Reservoir
Waterside
DOON VALLEY HERITAGE MUSEUM
BENBEOCH
SCOTTISH INDUSTRIAL RAILWAY CENTRE
Burnton
TURNBERRY
Turnberry Bay
Turnberry
Brest Rocks
Kirkoswald
SOUTER JOHNNIE'S COTTAGE
CROSSRAGUEL ABBEY
Crosshill
BLAIRQUHAN
Straiton
Bogton Loch
Dalmellington
CATHCARTSON VISITOR CENTRE
Bellsbank
Ruglen
Townhead
Wallacetown
Water of Girvan
South
Ayrshire
Dipple
Burnhead
Dailly
BIG HILL OF GLENMOUNT
BARGANY GARDENS
Old Dailly
Girvan
Penkill
Houdston
Glendoune
Linfern Loch
Tairlaw Forest
Loch Finlas
LOCH DOON
Lamloch
Penwhapple Res.
Loch Bradan
MULL OF MILJOAN
Dalwyne
LOCH DOON CASTLE
Craigmalloch
Woodland Bay
South Balloch
Tormitchell
Pinminnoch
CARRICK
Barr
Changue Forest
Auchensoul
Kennedy's Pass
GREY HILL
Pinmore
CARRICK FOREST
Loch Riecawr
Loch Macaterick
Stinchar
Merkland
Currarie
Straid
Lendalfoot
CRAIGENREOCH
MEAUL
Pinmore Mains
CARLETON CASTLE
CORSERINE
NX
Poundland
Pinwherry
PINDONNAN
GALLOWAY
Bellamore
MULLWHARCHAR
Loch Harrow
Colmonell
104
Knockfolian
Ballochmorrie
Black Clauchrie
Loch Moan
Cree
Water of Minnoch
MERRICK
Loch Enoch
RHINNS OF KELLS
Heronsford
Glen Tig
Water of Tig
Duisk
Palgowan
FOREST
Loch Neldricken
SILVER FLOWE
Loch Valley
Barrhill
Balkissock
Laggan
Eldrick
Glentrool
Glen Trool Lodge
BRUCE'S STONE
Trool
Clatt
Auchencrosh
Arecleoch Forest
105
Drumlamford Loch
Glentrool Village
GLENTROOL VISITOR CENTRE
Glen
Loch Trool
PARK
Loch Dee
Dornal
Loch Dornal
Bargrennan
LAMACHAN HILL
0 1 2 3 4 5 6 miles
0 1 2 3 4 5 6 7 8 9 10 km

East
Ayrshire
Dumfries
and
Galloway
NS
NX
Glengavel Reservoir
Avon
434 WEDDER HILL
466 MIDDLEFIELD LAW
522 NUTBERRY HILL
River Wethan
Coalburn
Braehead
CAIRN LODGE (HAPPENDON) SERVICES
Happendon
Uddington
Douglas West
Douglas Water
Glenbuck
465 HARESHAW HILL
Glespin
Roberton Law
Robert
392 AUCHENSAUGH HILL
Middle Muir
Netherwood
Smallburn
Muirkirk
Kames
SORN CASTLE
Catrine
Sorn
Airds Moss
Cronberry
Back Rogerton
Auchinleck
Lugar
Glenmuir
497 WARDLAW HILL
Glenmuirshaw
593 CAIRN TABLE
Glentaggart
Crawfordjohn
Duneaton Water
DRAKE LAW 483
Holmhead
Logan
KEIR HARDIE STATUE
BAIRD INSTITUTE MUS.
Cumnock
Netherthird
Craigens
Dalblair
Glenmuir Water
478 MOUNT STUART
Fingland
494 RAKE LAW
553 WELLGRAIN DOD
LOWTHER HILLS
DOON VALLEY RARE BREEDS CENTRE
509 KIRKLAND HILL
Kirkland
Crawick Water
Leadhills
Elvan Water
MUSEUM OF LEAD MINING
LEADHILLS & WANLOCKHEAD RLY.
WANLOCKHEAD BEAM ENGINE
Wanlockhead
Pathhead
Mansfield
Connel Park
Bankglen
Nith
New Cumnock
Kirkconnel
485 CONRIG HILL
732 GREEN LOWTHER
Kelloholm
Burnside
Dalleagles
THE KNIPE 575
Crawick
Sanquhar
Mennock Pass
725 LOWTHER HILL
TOLBOOTH MUSEUM
SANQUHAR POST OFFICE
SOUTHERN UPLAND WAY
Kello Water
Afton Water
Mennock
Potrail Water
569 ENOCH HILL
700 BLACKCRAIG HILL
Euchan Water
449 CAIRN HILL
Afton Reservoir
478
Durisdeermill
691 BALLENCLEUCH
DURISDEER PARISH CH.
Durisdeer
Enterkinfoot
Scar Water
554 CAIRNKINNA HILL
Enoch
Carsphairn Forest
Holestane
443
MORTON CASTLE
DRUMLANRIG CASTLE
797 CAIRNSMORE OF CARSPHAIRN
500
Carronbridge
Brochloch
Corlae
580 BENBRACK
Benbuie
Auchenbrack
Shinnel Water
Auchenbainzie
Gatelawbridge
Burnhead
Thornhill
Garryhorn
Water of Ken
Penpont
Carsphairn
SOUTHERN UPLAND WAY
Dalwhat Water
372
Tynron
CAIRN AVEL
Bardennoch
Dundeugh Forest
Keir Mill
Closeburn
THE GLENKENS
Knowehead
Craigdarroch
Moniaive
Kirkland
357
Park
Kendoon Loch
JAMES PATERSON MUSEUM
Castlemaddy
Glencrosh
MAXWELTON HOUSE
KENDOON
Black Water
Straith
Dundeugh
Kendoon
Glenhoul
385 WETHER HILL
Castlefairn
Dalmacallan Forest
Wallaceton
Glenmidge
Forrest Lodge
Carsfad Loch
Holmhead
Auldgirth
Lochinvar
432 BOGRIE HILL
Lochurr
Loch Dungeon
417
Dunscore
Loch Urr
Sundaywell
ELLISLAND FARM
Earlstoun Loch
Millquarter
Milton
Cairn Water
Drumbuie
St John's Town of Dalry
Bogue
Corriedoo Forest
240
373
Garroch
Glenlee
Blackcraig
Newtonairds
Holywood
Clatteringshaws Forest
Drumpark
Knocklearn
Clatteringshaws Loch
381
New Galloway
Balmaclellan
Gibbshill
Glenkiln Res.
Irongray
Newbridge
Glenkiln
BLOWPLAIN OPEN FARM
317
398
Terregles Banks
CLATTERINGSHAWS FOREST WILDLIFE CENTRE
Ironmacannie
Corsock
Glen
Shawhead
A76
A70
A702
A712
A762
A713
B729
B797
B740
B743
B7036
B705
B741
B7000
B7078
B7040
M74
121
114
106

Happendon
Uddington
Douglas
ST BRIDES
Roberton Law
M74
Wiston
Newton
DUNGAVEL HILL
Lamington
Symington
Coulter
A702
Clyde
Roberton
Cowgill Upper Reservoir
Culter Waterhead Reservoir
CULTER FELL 748
Rachan Mill
Drumelzier
BLAKEHOPE HEAD 543
Stanhope
PYKESTONE HILL 737
Langhaugh
Manor Water
Holms Water
817 DOLLAR LAW
696 BLACK LAW
Crookhaugh
Hearthstane
Tweedsmuir
688 GLENWHAPPEN RIG
392 AUCHENSAUGH HILL
Middle Muir
Glentaggart
B7078
ABINGTON SERVICES
Abington
569 TEWSGILL HILL
Camps Water
Camps Reservoir
Crawfordjohn
B740
DRAKE LAW 483
Kirkton
Crawford
Glenbreck
Tweed
A701
Talla Reservoir
840 BROAD LAW
Meggethead
Megget Reservoir
Talla Linnfoots
LOWTHER HILLS
WELLGRAIN DOD 553
494 RAKE LAW
B797
B7040
Elvanfoot
550
553 CRAIGMAID
546 CLYDE LAW
Fruid Reservoir
LOCHCRAIG HEAD 800
690
Loch Skeen
Birkhill
GREY MARE'S TAIL WATERFALLS
882 WHITE COOMB
Source of River Tweed
Elvan Water
Leadhills
MUSEUM OF LEAD MINING
LEADHILLS & WANLOCKHEAD RLY.
WANLOCKHEAD BEAM ENGINE
Wanlockhead
Watermeetings
March
A702
DEVIL'S BEEF TUB
808 HART FELL
753 SADDLE YOKE
Blackhope Burn
677
485
Mennock Pass
732 GREEN LOWTHER
725 LOWTHER HILL
Nether Howecleuch
Ericstane
Granton
Howslack
Roundstonefoot
Capplegill
B797
Mennock
SOUTHERN UPLAND WAY
Potrail Water
Daer Reservoir
SOUTHERN UPLAND WAY
B719
A74(M)
A708
Moffat Water
678 CAPEL FELL
692 ETTRICK PEN
449 CAIRN HILL
A76
NS
NT
Coatsgate
Moffat
MUSEUM
688 LOCH FELL
Durisdeermill
691 BALLENCLEUCH LAW
Durisdeer
DURISDEER PARISH CHURCH
Enterkinfoot
407
Easter Earshaig
Garpol Water
Dumcrieff
Beattock
Kinnelhead
Annan
Enoch
668 GANA HILL
A702
Holestane
443
MORTON CASTLE
DRUMLANRIG CASTLE
512 QUEENSBERRY
A701
484
Laverhay
Eskdal
Wamphray Water
Carronbridge
Locherben
399
Black Esk Reservoir
Auchenbainzie
Gatelawbridge
Lochwood
Scar Water
Burnhead
Penpont
Thornhill
NX
NY
Kinnel Water
Newton
Loch Ettrick
B7020
B7076
Waterhead
Sandyford
B723
Keir Mill
St Ann's
Closeburn
353
Forest of Ae
ANNANDALE WATER SERVICES
Johnstonebridge
Chapelhill
Dinwoodie Mains
Boreland
A702
357
Park
Blackacre
MAXWELTON HOUSE
Courance
A76
B729
Straith
Wallaceton
Ae Village
Water of Ae
Dryfe Water
Dumfries and
Dalmacallan Forest
Glenmidge
Parkgate
Nethermill
B7020
B7076
Sibbaldbie
Auldgirth
Nith
Templand
Corrie Common
Dalswinton
Auchencairn
Shieldhill
A701
Millhousebridge
Sundaywell
Dunscore
ELLISLAND FARM
Duncow
Applegarthtown
A74(M)
Milton
Cairn Water
Lochmaben
Marjoriebanks
B723
Gallaberry
Amisfield
Water of Milk
240
B729
Kirkton
Tinwald
LOCHMABEN CASTLE
Castle Loch
A709
Lockerbie
Bankshill
Newtonairds
Holywood
Locharbriggs
Heathhall
DUMFRIES AND GALLOWAY AVIATION MUS.
Heck
B7068
Drumpark
Glenkiln
Irongray
LINCLUDEN COLLEGE
The Grove
A709
Torthorwald
Hightae
287
Burnswark
BURNSWARK FORT
Birkshaw Forest
Castlemilk
Kettleholm
Middleshaw
OLD BRIDGE HOUSE MUS.
Greystone
RAMMERSCALES HOUSE
Collin
249
B7020
B7076
Middlebie
398
Glen
Shawhead
Maxwelltown
A75
0 1 2 3 4 5 6 miles
0 1 2 3 4 5 6 7 8 9 10 km

Traquair
Caddonfoot
Yair Hill Forest
Tweed
Abbotsford House
Boleside
Darnick
Melrose
Newstead
A6091
Priorwood Gdns.
Trimontium Exhibition
Abbey
Dryburgh
Eildon Hills
Newtown St. Boswells
St. Boswells
Mertoun Gdns.
Glen Ho
Kirkhouse
Minch Moor
Blake Muir
Broadmeadows
Ovenscloss
Lindean
Whitlaw Mosses
Bowden
Selkirk Glass
Selkirk
Sir Walter Scott's Courtroom
Halliwell's House Museum
Bowhill House & Country Park
Fastheugh Hill
Philiphaugh
Bowhill
Yarrow
Yarrow Water
Yarrow Feus
Douglas Burn
Southern Upland Way
Dryhope Tower
Mountbenger
Sundhope
Dryhope
Cappercleuch
St. Mary's Loch
Ettrickbridge
Kirkhope
Aikwood Tower James Hogg Exhibition
Scottish
Ettrick Forest
Black Knowe Head
Gilmanscleuch
The Wiss
Caver's Hill
Akermoor Loch
Loch of the Lowes
Crosslee
Newburgh
Ettrick Water
Tushielaw
Shaws Under Loch
Hellmoor Loch
Todrig
Ale Water
Smasha Hill
Borders
Ramsey Knowe
Wardlaw
Redfordgreen
Ettrick
Ettrickhill
Ramseycleuch
James Hogg Monument
Buccleuch
Borthwickshiels
Roberton
Borthwickbrae
Burnfoot
Deanburnhaugh
Glenkerry
Redcleuch Edge
Borthwick Water
Craik Forest
Nether Dalgliesh
Craik
Howpasley
Pike Hill
Davington
Kagyu Samye Ling Tibetan Centre
White Esk
Eskdalemuir Forest
Eskdalemuir
Jamestown
Meggat Water
Castle O'er Forest
Castle O'er
Georgefield
Bentpath
Eskdale
Galloway
Calkin Rig
Craigcleuch Castle Collection
Potholm
Langholm
Malcolm Monument
Paddockhole
Kirtleton
Kirtle Water
Waterbeck
Kirkconnel Churchyard
Evertown
Canonbie
Gilnockie Tower
Claygate
Rowanburn
Catlowdy
Crossings
Liddel Water
Liddesdale
Tinnisburn Forest
Caulside
Kershopefoot
Kershope Forest
Kershope Burn
Bewcastle Fells
Baileyhead
White Lyne
Whitelyne Common
Blackpool Gate
The Flatt
White Preston
Black Lyne
Glendhu Hill
Sighty Crag
Newcastleton Forest
Newcastleton or Copshaw Holm
Janet Armstrong House
Black Edge
Tarras Water
Ewes
Ewes Water
Pike Fell
Roan Fell
Tudhope Hill
Wisp Hill
Castleweary
Teviothead
Teviot
Riddell Monument
Northhouse
Broadhaugh
Newmill
Branxholme
Branxholm Park
Teviotdale
Allan Water
Dodburn
Priesthaugh
The Pike
Caldcleuch Head
Slitrig Water
Gorrenberry
Hermitage Castle
Hermitage
Newlands
Steele Road
Dinlabyre
Old Castleton
Larriston
Larriston Fells
Saughtree
Deadwater
Peel Fell
Kielder
Kielder Birds of Prey
Wauchope Forest
Langburnshiels
Fanna Hill
Singdean
Cragbank Wood
Southdean
Chesters
Cleuch Head
Hobkirk
Bonchester Bridge
Hallrule
Rubers Law
Kirkton
Cauldmill
Drumlanrig's Tower
Hawick
Museum and Scott Gallery
Wilton
Burnfoot
Appletreehall
Ashybank
Clarilaw
Horsleyhill
Denholm
Bedrule
Hassendean
Minto
Newton
Jedburgh Abbey
Mary Queen of Scots House
Lanton
Chesters
Ancrum
Bloomfield
Greenhouse
Belses
Longnewton
Ashkirk
Woll
Lilliesleaf
Clerklands
Midlem
Maxton
Rule Water
NT
NY
A7
A68
A708
A698
A699
A6088
B709
B711
B7009
B6399
B6357
B6400
B6359
B6453
B6405
B6358
B6318
B7068
B722
B725
B720
B7060
B6398
B6404
123
116
108

Kelso
Jedburgh
Hawick
Bellingham
THE CHEVIOT HILLS
NORTHUMBERLAND NATIONAL PARK
KIELDER FOREST PARK
KIELDER WATER
Wauchope Forest
Redesdale Forest
Kielder Forest
Wark Forest
Newcastleton Forest
Kidland Forest
Leithope Forest
REDESDALE
NT
NY
124
115
109
A68
A698
A699
A6088
A6091
A7
B6357
B6358
B6320
St. Boswells
Newtown St. Boswells
Maxton
Ancrum
Denholm
Bonchester Bridge
Camptown
Byrness
Catcleugh
Otterburn
Rochester
Kielder
Falstone
Town Yetholm
Kirk Yetholm
Morebattle
THE CHEVIOT
815
Craik Moor
Catcleugh Reservoir
Kielderhead Moor
PEEL FELL
602
Emblehope Moor
Wainhope Moor
Blackburn Common
Blakehope Fell
Troughend Common
Larriston Fells
Bewcastle Fells
Whitelyne Common
Langburnshiels
Saughtree
Deadwater
Steele Road
Newlands
Hermitage
Dinlabyre
Old Castleton
Baileyhead
Paddaburn
Hopehouse
Greenhaugh
Lanehead
Charlton
Hesleyside
Redesmouth
Ridsdale
West Woodburn
East Woodburn
Hareshaw Head
Elishaw
Horsley
Redesdale Camp
Sills
Featherwood
Alwinton
Linshiels
Shillmoor
Barrowburn
Blindburn
Hownam
Chatto
Oxnam
Swinside Hall
Falla
Mossburnford
Bairnkine
Mervinslaw
Hundalee
Bedrule
Hallrule
Hobkirk
Chesters
Southdean
Cleuch Head
Kirkton
Culdmill
Ashybank
Minto
Hassendean
Lanton
Newton
Bonjedward
Crailing
Crailinghall
Cessford
Eckford
Kalemouth
Nisbet
Heiton
Roxburgh
Linton
Crookhouse
Whitton
Mowhaugh
Sourhope
Hethpool
Kilham
Pawston
Mindrum
Westnewton
Kirknewton
Shipley Shiels
Gatehouse
The Eals
Bower
Stonehaugh
Whygate
Birtley
Wark
Scale: 0 1 2 3 4 5 6 miles; 0 1 2 3 4 5 6 7 8 9 10 km

NORTHUMBERLAND COAST
Steads
North Hazelrigg
Belford
Easington
Waren Mill
Glororum
Burton
Seahouses
Milfield
Fenton Town
Nesbit
Doddington
South Hazelrigg
Spindlestone
Mousen
Bradford
Elford
North Sunderland
Lanton
Coupland
Newtown
West Horton
East Horton
Bellshill
Warenton
Adderstone
Lucker
Newham Hall
Beadnell
Akeld
Weetwood Hall
Humbleton
Wooler
Chatton
Greendikes
Warenford
Swinhoe
Benthall
Beadnell Bay
Earle
Haugh Head
Newham
Fleetham
Newstead
Middleton Hall
Chillingham
CHILLINGHAM CASTLE
CHILLINGHAM WILD CATTLE
Rosebrough
Chathill
COLD LAW
North Middleton
Newtown
Lilburn Tower
Hepburn
Ellingham
Preston
PRESTON TOWER
Brunton
High Newton-by-the-Sea
Low Newton-by-the-Sea
Embleton Bay
Brockdam
Brownyside
North Charlton
Christon Bank
Embleton
South Middleton
East Lilburn
Doxford
Dunstan Steads
Castle Point
DUNSTANBURGH CASTLE
Ilderton
Langleeford
Roseden
Roddam
Old Bewick
West Ditchburn
South Charlton
Rock
Craster
Harthope Burn
Wooperton
New Bewick
Harehope
Eglingham
Dunstan
Rennington
Littlemill
Howick
DUNMOOR HILL
Brandon
NORTHUMBERLAND NATIONAL PARK VISITOR CENTRE
Beanley
Greensidehill
Powburn
Ingram
Branton
Shipley
HULNE ABBEY
Littlehoughton
Howick Haven
Shill Moor
Titlington
Glanton
Shawdon Hall
ALNWICK ABBEY
Denwick
Longhoughton
Boulmer
Glanton Pike
Bolton
Alnwick
Boulmer Haven
HAT LAW
Great Ryle
Abberwick
Broome Park
Hawkhill
Prendwick
Whittingham
Lemmington Hall
Lesbury
Alnham
Little Ryle
Thrunton
Bilton
Alnmouth
Yetlington
EDLINGHAM CASTLE
Alnmouth Bay
Scrainwood
Callaly
Thrunton Wood
Edlingham
Shilbottle
High Buston
Biddlestone
Lorbottle Hall
Low Buston
Netherton
Lorbottle
Birling
Burradon
High Trewhitt
Newton-on-the-Moor
Eastfield Hall
Warkworth
Harbottle
Sharperton
Cartington
Hazon
Gloster Hill
Amble
Coquet I.
Coquet
SHIRLAW PIKE
Swarland Estate
Brainshaugh
Guyzance
North Togston
Hauxley
LADY'S WELL
Warton
Snitter
CRAGSIDE
Holystone
Flotterton
Rothbury
CRAGSIDE HOUSE
Swarland
Acklington
Radcliffe
Caistron
Thropton
Togston
Hepple
Newtown
Whitton
NATIONAL PARK VISITOR CENTRE
Longframlington
Felton
Broomhill
South Broomhill
DRURIDGE BAY
Great Tosson
LONGFRAMLINGTON GARDENS
West Thirston
East Thirston
Red Row
BRINKBURN PRIORY
Weldon
Low Hesleyhurst
TOSSON HILL
ROTHBURY
Eshott
Druridge Bay
West Chevington
Forestburn Gate
Helm
Harwood Forest
Widdrington
Wingates
Longhorsley
Causey Park Bridge
Stobswood
Elsdon
Widdrington Station
The Scars
Cresswell
Fontburn Res.
Nunnykirk
Fallowlees Burn
Ellington
Ewesley
Fenrother
Tritlington
Ulgham
Linton
Lynemouth
Raylees
Northumberland
Rothley Shield East
Netherwitton
THE SANCTUARY WILDLIFE CENTRE
Stanton
Hebron
COLLIERY MUSEUM
Beacon Pt.
QUEEN ELIZABETH II
Woodhorn
HERTERTON HOUSE GARDEN
Longwitton
Font
Longhirst
Pegswood
Ashington
Rothley
Pigdon
Newbiggin-by-the-Sea
Hart Burn
NORTHUMBRIA CRAFT CENTRE
WANSBECK
Hirst
Hartburn
Mitford
Bothal
North Seaton
Knowesgate
Cambo
Scots' Gap
Throphill
Morpeth
Stakeford
Middleton
High Angerton
Kirkwhelpington
Guide Post
Scotland Gate
West Sleekburn
Wansbeck
Choppington
Cambois
WALLINGTON
Molesden
Hepscott
Meldon
Tranwell
Clifton
Bedlington Station
East Sleekburn
Bedlington
BLYTH
BOLAM LAKE
Bolam
Cowpen
Sweethope Loughs
Kirkharle
Whalton
Nedderton
Bebside
Great Bavington
Capheaton
Shilvington
Saltwick
Newsham
Thockrington
Harnham
Blyth
East Cramlington
New Delaval
PLESSEY WOODS
Stannington
Little Bavington
Belsay
BELSAY HALL
Ogle
Shankhouse
Colt Crag Reservoir
Kirkheaton
Nelson Village
New Hartley
Seaton
KIRKLEY HALL
NORTHUMBERLAND CHEESE FARM
Hallington Reservoir
Hallington
West Newham
Higham Dykes
Berwick Hill
Cramlington
Black Heddon
Southfield
Seaton Delaval
SEATON
DEVIL'S CAUSEWAY
FOREST
NT
NU
NY
NZ
A1
A697
A68
A189
A192
A193
A196
A197
A1068
A696
B6341
B6342
B6343
B6344
B6345
B6346
B6347
B6348
B6349
B1340
B1341
B1339
B1337
B6524
B1505
B1329
B1331
125
110

1
2
3
4
5
A
B
C
D
E
F
NR
Carraig Mhór
Ardtalla
Claggain Bay
Kintour
Ardmore Pt.
KILDALTON CHURCH AND CROSSES
Eilean Craobhach
Eilean a'Chuirn
Eilean Bhride
126
Eilean Garbh
West Tarbert Bay
East Tarbert Bay
Tarbert
Gigha Island
100
Druimyeon More
Ardminish
Ardminish Bay
ACHAMORE GARDENS
0:20
Gigalum Island
Cara Island
SOUND OF GIGHA
Ardpatrick Ho.
Ardpatrick Pt.
Eilean Tràighe
Ronachan Pt.
Achatachoillan
Gartnagrenach
A83
Clachan
Loch Ciaran
269 CRUACH NAM FIADH
B842
Balochroy
128
Crossaig Glen
Crossaig
Loch Garasdale
248 CRUACH MHIC GOUGAN
Rhunahaorine
Cour Bay
Cour
241 BEINN BHREAC
Tayinloan
322 CNOC NAN CRAOBH
Carradale Water
Grogport
Killean
Beacharr
CRUACH MHIC-AN T-SAOIR 364
354 CRUACH NAN GABHAR
Brackley
Clachaig Water
Muasdale
KINTYRE
KILBRANNAN SOUND
Carradale
Glenacardoch Pt.
Amod
Belloch
426 BEINN BHREAC
Port Righ
Bridgend
Glenbarr
Barr Water
Torrisdale-Square
CLAN MACALISTER CENTRE
Carradale Pt.
454 BEINN AN TUIRC
Carradale Bay
Cleongart
Saddell Glen
Bellochantuy Bay
Saddell
SADDELL ABBEY
Bellochantuy
341 A'CHRUACH
Saddell Bay
Killocraw
Lussa Loch
397 SGREADAN HILL
Ugadale
Tangy Loch
Skeroblingarry
Black Bay
Westport
Glenlussa Water
Kilchenzie
Peninver
Ardnacross Bay
Kilmichael
West Darlochan
Low Smerby
Machrihanish Bay
CAMPBELTOWN
CAMPBELTOWN HERITAGE CENTRE
Machrihanish
Trodigal
Campbeltown
Campbeltown Loch
Island Davaar
DAVAAR ISLAND CAVE PAINTING
Drumlemble
B843
Stewarton
Kilkerran
Kildalloig
Knocknaha
Earadale Pt.
Achinhoan Hd.
352 BEINN GHUILEAN
385 THE SLATE
Woodbank
446 CNOC MOY
Feochaig
Johnston's Pt.
Rubh'a'Mharaiche
Glen Breackerie
277 CNOC ODHAR
Conie Glen
NORTH CHANNEL
Keprigan
North Carrine
Strone Glen
Macharioch
Polliwilline Bay
428
Southend
Carskiey
Cove Pt.
Brunerican Bay
MULL OF KINTYRE
Port Mean
Rubha Chlachan
Sheep I.
123
Sanda Island
0 1 2 3 4 5 6 miles
0 1 2 3 4 5 6 7 8 9 10 km

Glenreasdell Mains
Skipness
SKIPNESS CASTLE
Skipness Pt.
Skipness Bay
Claonaig
B8001
Claonaig Bay
SOUND OF BUTE
Inchmarnock
Ardscalpsie Pt.
Scalpsie
Scalpsie Bay
Stravanan Bay
Kingarth
Kilchattan Bay
ST BLANE'S CHAPEL
HOUSE AND GARDEN
OLD KIRK
Largs
CHRISTIAN HERITAGE MUSEUM
Great Cumbrae Island
Downcraig Ferry
MUSEUM OF THE CUMBRAES
Millport
Fairlie Roads
Fairlie
KELBURN COUNTRY CENTRE
Muirhead Reservoir
KAIM HILL
Knocken Reservo
The Tan
Little Cumbrae Island
HUNTERSTON POWER STATION VISITOR CENTRE
A78
Garroch Hd.
Cock of Arran
128
129
Loch Ranza
LOCHRANZA CASTLE
Lochranza
LOCHRANZA
ISLE OF ARRAN DISTILLERY
Catacol Bay
Catacol
Millstone Pt.
Portencross
Thirdpart
Farland Hd.
Seamill
West Kilbride
BLACKSHAW FARM PARK
Giffordla
North Ayrshire
NORTH SANNOX FARM PARK
Sannox
Sannox Bay
A841
MEALL NAN DAMH
Thundergay
NORTH
Pirnmill
Loch Tanna
Glen Sannox
CIR MHÒR
BEINN BHARRAIN
BEINN TARSUINN
GOAT FELL
Whitefarland
Corrie
Imachar
ISLE OF ARRAN
Chapelhill
Dykes
Horse Isle
Ardrossan
NORTH AYRSHIRE MUSEUM
Saltcoats
A738
0:55
120
Glen Iorsa
Glen Rosa
BRODICK
BRODICK CASTLE
ARRAN AROMATICS VISITOR CENTRE
Brodick Bay
ISLE OF ARRAN HERITAGE MUSEUM
Brodick
Strathwhillan
Dougarie
Machrie Water
Auchagallon
Glenloig
A'CHRUACH
Glen Cloy
Machrie Bay
B880
Clauchlands Pt.
Tormore
MACHRIE MOOR STANDING STONES
Blairbeg
Margnaheglish
Lamlash
Lamlash Bay
Holy Island
Cordon
KING'S CAVE
BALMICHAEL VISITOR CENTRE
Balmichael
Drumadoon Pt.
Torbeg
Shiskine
FIRTH OF CLYDE
Blackwaterfoot
Drumadoon Bay
Kilpatrick
KILPATRICK DUN
TIGHVEIN
Auchencairn
Kingscross Pt.
Kingscross
Knockenkelly
Whiting Bay
North Kiscadale
South Kiscadale
Sliddery Water
Glenree
GLENASHDALE FALLS
WHITING BAY
Largymore
Brown Hd.
CARN BAN
Corriecravie
Kilmory Water
Largybeg
Sliddery
Dippen
Dippin Head
Lagg
Levencorroch
Kilmory
Bennan
SOUTH BANK FARM PARK
Kildonan
TORRYLINN CAIRN
Bennan Hd.
Sound of Pladda
Pladda
112
NR
NS
Dunure
Culzean Bay
CULZEAN CASTLE
CULZEAN
Maidenhead Bay
Maidens
A719
TURNBERRY
Turnberry Bay
Turnberry
Brest Rocks
Kirkoswal
SOUTER JOHNNIE'S COTTAGE
A77
Townhead
Wallace
Dipple
Burnhead
B741
A
B
C
D
E
F
5
6
7
8
9

Helensburgh
Rhu
Rosneath
Clynder
Kilcreggan
Gourock
Greenock
Port Glasgow
Dunoon
Kirn
Hunter's Quay
Sandbank
Innellan
Toward
Wemyss Bay
Skelmorlie
Inverkip
Largs
Fairlie
Millport
Great Cumbrae Island
West Kilbride
Seamill
Portencross
Farland Hd.
Ardrossan
Saltcoats
Stevenston
Kilwinning
Irvine
Troon
Prestwick
Monkton
Dreghorn
Kilmarnock
Riccarton
Kilmaurs
Stewarton
Dunlop
Beith
Kilbirnie
Dalry
Lochwinnoch
Kilmacolm
Bridge of Weir
Johnstone
Paisley
Renfrew
Clydebank
Bearsden
Barrhead
Neilston
Newton Mearns
Erskine Bridge
Dumbarton
Alexandria
Balloch
Bonhill
Renton
Galston
Newmilns
Mauchline
Catrine
Tarbolton
Symington
Fenwick
Waterside
Kingsford
Uplawmoor
Howwood
Kilbarchan
Houston
Langbank
Bishopton
Craigends
Linwood
Elderslie
Crosshouse
Hurlford
Crookedholm
Bogend
Loans
Muirhead
Barassie
Gatehead
Drybridge
Dundonald
Shortlees
Craigie
Mossgiel
Failford
Greenholm
Crossroads
Sornhill
Moscow
Laigh Fenwick
Onthank
Knockinlaw
Knockentiber
Springside
Perceton
Girdle Toll
Cunninghamhead
Torranyard
Bensile
Auchentiber
Dalgarven
Highfield
Blairlund
Drakemyre
Glengarnock
Longbar
Gateside
Barrmill
Greenhills
The Den
Lugton
Halket
Burnhouse
Fullwood
Gabroc Hill
Laighmuir
Chapelhill
Dykesmains
Fullarton
Glenburn
Foxbar
Millarston
Charleston
Nitshill
Thornliebank
Giffnock
Waterside
Auchenback
Gateside
Netherplace
Ranfurly
Crosslee
Brookfield
Quarrier's Homes
Mid Auchinlech
Devol
Bardrainney
Woodhall
Strone
Ravenscraig
Braeside
Larkfield
Levan
Ashton
Midton
Greenock West
Cardross
Castlehill
Brucehill
Milton
Bowling
Old Kilpatrick
Duntocher
Dalmuir
Inchinnan
Knightswood
Yoker
Scotstoun
Whiteinch
Hillington
Cardonald
Pollok
Craigendoran
Colgrain
Geilston
Jamestown
Auchincarroch
Stockiemuir
Craighat
Dumgoyne
Blairquhosh
Blairmore
Kilmun
Strone
Ardnadam
Cove
Portkil
Holy Loch
Cove Bay
Strone Pt.
Cloch Pt.
Lunderston Bay
Loch Thom
Gryfe Resrs.
Garvock
Shielhill
Upper Skelmorlie
Meigle
Routenburn
Downcraig Ferry
Tomont End
Kaim Hill
Knockendon Reservoir
Muirhead Reservoir
Camphill Reservoir
Kilbirnie Loch
Barr Loch
Castle Semple Loch
Rowbank Reservoir
Loch Libo
Long Loch
Hunterston Power Station Visitor Centre
Kelburn Country Centre
Vikingar!
Old Kirk
Christian Heritage Museum
Museum of the Cumbraes
Blackshaw Farm Park
Dalgarven Mill
Eglinton
Scottish Maritime Museum
The Big Idea
Glasgow Vennel Mus.
Dundonald Castle
Dean Castle
Loudon Castle Park
Dick Institute
Bachelor's Club
Burns's House Museum
Weaver's Cottage
Castle Semple
Nature Reserve Visitor Cen.
Muirshiel
Glenifer Braes
Finlaystone House & Gardens
Newark Castle
HM Customs & Excise Museum & Exhibition
McLean Mus. & Art Gall.
Highland Mary's Statue
John's Church
Geilston
Loch Lomond Shores
Balloch Castle
Linn Botanic Gardens
Kilmun Arboretum
Dumbarton Castle
Roman Bath House
Glasgow Prestwick International
Glasgow
Royal Troon
Horse Isle
Lady Isle
South Bay
Irvine Bay
The Tan
Fairlie Roads
Inverclyde
Renfrewshire
East Renfrewshire
West Dunbartonshire
North Ayrshire
Clyde-Muirshiel Regional Park
Cunninghame
Kilpatrick Hills
Duncolm 401
Dumbarton Muir
Flow Moss
Wallace Muir
Crins Hill 246
Hill of Stake 522
Queenside Muir
Waterhead Moor
Mistylaw Muir
Ladyland Moor
Irish Law 484
Creuch Hill 441
Duchal Moor
Kaim Hill 387
Firth of Clyde
Rothesay 0:35
Brodick 0:55
Larne 1:49 (March-Sept)
Larne 4:30
NS
A78
A8
A82
A737
A760
A71
A77
A76
A719
A736
A735
A761
A726
A809
A810
A811
A814
A815
A818
A880
A885
M8
M77
M898
B714
B780
B784
B706
B707
B778
B769
B751
B7081
B730
B739
B743
B744
B7037
B786
B788
B789
B790
B833
0 1 2 3 4 5 6 miles
0 1 2 3 4 5 6 7 8 9 10 km

Campsie Fells
Carron Valley Forest
Carron Valley Res.
Kilsyth Hills
East Dunbartonshire
Falkirk
North Lanarkshire
Lanarkshire
South Lanarkshire
Denny
Dunipace
Stenhousemuir
Larbert
Grangemouth
Bonnybridge
Falkirk
Kilsyth
Cumbernauld
Kirkintilloch
Milngavie
Bishopbriggs
Glasgow
Coatbridge
Airdrie
Rutherglen
Uddingston
Bothwell
Motherwell
Hamilton
Wishaw
East Kilbride
Carluke
Larkhall
Strathaven
Stonehouse
Lanark
Kirkmuirhill
Lesmahagow
Coalburn
Douglas
Muirkirk
Darvel
Eaglesham
Shotts
Harthill
Whitburn
Armadale
Fauldhouse
Caldercruix
Tinto Hills
Kype Muir
Rough Moss
Glengavel Reservoir
Clydesdale
NS

Torry Bay
Charlestown
Limekilns
Rosyth
Inverkeithing
Inverkeithing Bay
Dalgety Bay
Inchcolm
St Margaret's Hope
Forth Road Bridge
Inchmickery
Cramond I.
Grangemouth
Bo'ness
Grangepans
Carriden
Muirhouses
Blackness
Manderston
House of the Binns
Queensferry
Dalmeny
Dalmeny House
Cramond
Granton
Falkirk
Laurieston
Polmont
Brightons
Whitecross
Linlithgow
Linlithgow Bridge
Philipstoun
Old Philipstoun
Newton
Kirkliston
Davidson's Mains
Barnton
Cramond Bridge
Turnhouse
Edinburgh
Murrayfield
Corstorphine
Gorgie
Morningside
Ingliston
Gogar
Ratho Station
Ratho
Bridgend
Threemiletown
Winchburgh
Ecclesmachan
Broxburn
Uphall
Newbridge
Burnside
Dechmont
Wester Dechmont
Uphall Station
Pumpherston
Bonnington
Sighthill
Craiglockhart
Colinton
Hermiston
Juniper Green
Fairmilehead
Currie
Balerno
Malleny Mills
Kirknewton
Wilkieston
Burnwynd
West Lothian
Maddiston
California
Shieldhill
Standburn
Avonbridge
Westfield
Torphichen
Crossburn
Binniehill
Armadale
Windyknowe
Bathgate
Boghall
Deans
Livingston
Mid Calder
East Calder
Oakbank
Livingston Village
Seafield
Bellsquarry
Westrigg
Blackridge
Bathville
Mayfield
Whiteside
Blackburn
Harthill
Whitburn
East Whitburn
Croftmalloch
Eastfield
West Benhar
Longridge
Stoneyburn
Bents
Addiewell
Loganlea
West Calder
Polbeth
Fauldhouse
Greenburn
Breich
Shotts
Dykehead
Stane
Kirk of Shotts
Hirst
Allanton
Woodmuir Plantation
Cobbinshaw Reservoir
Crosswood Reservoir
Woolfords Cottages
Tarbrax
Harperrig Reservoir
Pentland Hills Regional Park
Threipmuir Reservoir
Harlaw Reservoir
Glencorse Res.
Easter Howgate
Milton Bridge
Penicuik
Silverburn
Scald Law
East Cairn Hill
West Cairn Hill
Nine Mile Burn
Baddinsgill Reservoir
Carlops
Leadburn
Howgate
Midlothian
Wilsontown
Rootpark
Climpy
Forth
Auchengray
Kingshill Plantation
Hare Hill
White Craig
Byrehope Mount
West Water Reservoir
West Linton
Cowdenburn
Whim Farm
Waterheads
Carluke
Yieldshields
Roadmeetings
Braehead
Bleak Law
Mendick Hill
Halmyre Mains
Wether Law
Damside
Romannobridge
Eddleston
Kilncadzow
Braidwood
Carstairs
West End
Carnwath
Kaimend
Carstairs Junction
Ravenstruther
Cartland
Newbigging
Dunsyre
Dolphinton
Walston
Black Mount
Melbourne
Mountain Cross
Blyth Bridge
Drochil
Kirkurd
Nemphlar
Kirkfieldbank
Lanark
New Lanark
Hyndford Bridge
Pettinain
Libberton
Elsrickle
Whitecastle
Shieldhill
Candy Mill
Broughton Heights
Black Meldon
White Meldon
Lyne Water
Hallyne
Neidpath Castle
Hawksland
Covington
Quothquan
Biggar
Skirling
Sandilands
Harleyhom
Thankerton
Broughton
Stobo
Kirkton Manor
Dreva
Upper Tweeddale
Broken Cross Muir
Douglas Water
Wolfclyde
Causewayend
Symington
Rachan Mill
Drumelzier
Bellspool
Castlehill
Tinto Hills
Tinto
Uddington
Happendon
Coulter
Wiston
Newton
Lamington
Dungavel Hill
Pykestone Hill
Langhaugh
Stob Law
Blakehope Head
Stanhope
Robertson Law
Douglas
Culter Fell
Cowgill Upper Reservoir
Culter Waterhead Reservoir
Crookhaugh
Hearthstane
Dollar Law
Black Law
Middle Muir
Auchensaugh Hill
NS
NT
M8
M9
A70
A702
A71
A72
0 1 2 3 4 5 6 miles
0 1 2 3 4 5 6 7 8 9 10 km

FIRTH OF FORTH
Inchkeith
ZEEBRUGGE 17:30
134
135
124
115
Black Rocks
HMY BRITANNIA
Newhaven
Leith
EDINBURGH
Portobello
Joppa
Duddingston
PALACE OF HOLYROOD HOUSE
ROYAL MUS. OF SCOTLAND
BRUNTSFIELD
Craigmillar
Newcraighall
CRAIGMILLAR CASTLE
ROYAL OBSERVATORY
Danderhall
Liberton
Gilmerton
Kaimes
Straiton
Loanhead
Bilston
Polton
Roslin
ROSSLYN CHAPEL
Auchendinny
EDINBURGH CRYSTAL VISITOR CENTRE
BUTTERFLY FARM
Eskbank
Dalkeith
DALKEITH PARK
Millerhill
Newbattle
Bonnyrigg and Lasswade
Rosewell
Carrington
ARNISTON HOUSE
Temple
Gorebridge
Arniston Engine
Newtongrange
Newlandrig
MINING MUSEUM
VOGRIE
Mayfield
Easthouses
North Middleton
Middleton
Musselburgh
MUSSELBURGH
INDUSTRIAL HERITAGE MUSEUM
NEWHAILES
INVERESK LODGE GDNS.
Inveresk
Wallyford
Whitecraig
EDINBURGH SERVICES
Prestonpans
Cockenzie and Port Seton
SETON COLLEGIATE CHURCH
Tranent
Elphinstone
Crossgatehall
Ormiston
Cousland
New Winton
Macmerry
Penston
Gladsmuir
New Town
Longniddry
Huntington
Elvingston
Samuelston
Pencaitland
GLENKINCHIE DISTILLERY
East Saltoun
West Saltoun
Peastonbank
Gilchriston
Peaston
Pathhead
Crichton
CRICHTON CASTLE
Humbie
Fala Dam
Fala
Tynehead
Fala Moor
Gilston
Gullane Bay
Gullane
MUIRFIELD
Dirleton
West Fenton
Fenton Barns
Aberlady Bay
Aberlady
MYRETON MOTOR MUSEUM
Craigielaw
Gosford Bay
GOSFORD HOUSE
Spittal
Ballencrieff
Drem
THE CHESTERS FORT
MUSEUM OF FLIGHT
Athelstaneford
HOPETOUN MON.
JANE WELSH CARLYLE MUSEUM
Haddington
ST MARY'S COLLEGIATE CH.
LENNOXLOVE
Bolton
Kingston
Whitekirk
East Fortune
Peffer Burn
East Linton
PRESTON MILL & PHANTASSIE DOOCOT
HAILES CASTLE
Traprain
Tyninghame
Preston
West Barns
Belhaven
JOHN MUIR
Tyne Mouth
Biel Water
Pitcox
Stenton
Luggate Burn
Papple
Garvald
Dunbar Common
East Lothian
Carfrae
Danskine
Gifford
Quarryford
Long Newton
Longyester
Stobshiel
Blegbie
Birns Water
LAMMER LAW
Hopes Reservoir
MEIKLE SAYS LAW
Whiteadder Reservoir
Spartleton Edge
Bothwell
LAMMERMUIR HILLS
HUNT LAW
Dye Water
Watch Water Reservoir
Midlothian
Rosebery Reservoir
Falahill
Heriot
Carcant
TORFICHEN HILL
MOORFOOT HILLS
Gladhouse Reservoir
Portmore Loch
Dewar
BLACKHOPE SCAR
Fountainhall
Gala Water
Kirktonhill
Hillhouse
Oxton
Addinston
Soonhope Burn
HOG'S LAW
COLLIE LAW
NT
Leader Water
THIRLSTANE CASTLE
Lauder
Thirlestane
Blythe
Thornydykes
Whiteburn
Houndslow
Westruther
Wedderlie
Torquhan
Killochyett
Stow
Lugate Water
Eden Water
Boon
Legerwood
GREEN KNOWE TOWER
LAUDERDALE
Scottish Borders
WHITEHOPE LAW
Glentress Forest
Leithen Water
WINDLESTRAW LAW
BLACK LAW
Peebles
TWEEDDALE MUS. & GALL.
Glentress
Colquhar
GREAT LAW
Bow
Caitha Bowland
Nether Blainslie
SOUTHERN UPLAND WAY
West Morriston
Fans
Kings Muir
KAILZIE GARDENS
Kirkburn
Cardrona
ST RONAN'S WELL INTERPRETATIVE CENTRE
ROBERT SMAIL'S PRINTING WORKS
Cardrona Forest
Walkerburn
Innerleithen
TRAQUAIR HOUSE
Traquair
Elibank and Traquair Forest
TWEEDDALE
Blackhaugh
Langshaw
Buckholm
Galashiels
Earlston
MELLERSTAIN HOUSE
PETER ANDERSON WOOLLEN MILL
Clovenfords
OLD GALA HOUSE
Caddonfoot
ABBOTSFORD HOUSE
Boleside
Gattonside
ABBEY
Darnick
Melrose
TRIMONTIUM EXHIBITION
PRIORWOOD GDNS
Eildon Hills
Newstead
Redpath
EILDON AND LEADERFOOT
Brotherstone
SMAILHOLM TOWER
Bemersyde
Clintmains
Dryburgh
ABBEY
MERTOUN GDNS.
Newtown St. Boswells
St. Boswells
Bowden
Rutherford
Maxton
Muirhouselaw
Kirkhouse
Glen Ho
Minch Moor
Yair Hill Forest
Glensax Burn
Tweed
Lindean
Ovenscloss
Blake Muir
Broadmeadows
BROADMEADOWS
SELKIRK GLASS
WHITLAW MOSSES
Selkirk
SIR WALTER SCOTT'S COURTROOM
Philiphaugh
HALLIWELL'S HOUSE MUSEUM
Bowhill
BOWHILL HOUSE & COUNTRY PARK
FASTHEUGH HILL
Yarrow Water
Yarrow
Yarrow Feus
Douglas Burn
SOUTHERN UPLAND WAY
DRYHOPE TOWER
Mountbenger
Midlem
Longnewton
Belses
SMAILHOLM TOWER
CUTHBERTS
Smailholm
Gordon
Manor

1
2
3
4
5
A
B
C
D
E
F
Scoughall
St. Baldred's Cradle
Tyne Mouth
135
JOHN MUIR BIRTHPLACE
Dunbar
Kingston
Whitekirk
East Fortune
Tyninghame
JOHN MUIR
Belhaven
West Barns
Preston
East Linton
Peffer Burn
PRESTON MILL & PHANTASSIE DOOCOT
HAILES CASTLE
Traprain
Biel Water
Pitcox
Spott
Broxburn
Barns Ness
East Barns
Skateraw
Meikle Pinkerton
Dry Burn
Thorntonloch
Luggate Burn
Stenton
Halls
Innerwick
COCKLAW HILL
319
DUNGLASS COLLEGIATE CHURCH
Cockburnspath
Reed Pt.
Cove
Siccar Pt.
Wheat Stack
FAST CASTLE
ST ABB'S HEAD
St. Abb's Head
KITTIWAKE GALLERY
Papple
Garvald
Oldhamstocks
Dunbar Common
397 BRANSLY HILL
398
Carfrae
Ecclaw
Lumsdaine
Coldingham Moor
Northfield
St Abbs
St. Abb's Haven
Coldingham
COLDINGHAM SANDS
COLDINGHAM PRIORY
Danskine
123
Quarryford
Longyester
LAMMERMUIR HILLS
Spartleton Edge
Bothwell Water
391 HEART LAW
Monynut Water
SOUTHERN UPLAND WAY
Grantshouse
Huxton
Ale Water
Eyemouth
Nether Monynut
Whiteadder Reservoir
535 MEIKLE SAYS LAW
Hopes Reservoir
Whiteadder Water
Cranshaws
379 CRANSHAWS HILL
Abbey St. Bathans
Houndwood
Eye Water
Cairncross
262
Auchencrow
Reston
AYTON CASTLE
Ayton
Ellemford
LAMMERMUIR
EDINSHALL BROCH
Prenderguest
495 HUNT LAW
Dye Water
Longformacus
Lintlaw
Preston
Chirnside
Watch Water Reservoir
HOG'S LAW
NT
JIM CLARK ROOM
398 DIRRINGTON GREAT LAW
Chirnsidebridge
Edrom
Buxley
Foulden
Clappers
FOULDEN TITHE BARN
Allanton
Scottish Borders
Wedderlie
Clockmill
Duns
Cheeklaw
CRUMSTANE FARM PARK
Blackadder West
Hutton
Paxton
PAXTON HOUSE
UNION SUSPENSION BRIDGE
Loanend
Choicelee
Gavinton
Sinclair's Hill
Whitsome
Fishwick
Westruther
Polwarth
285
389
Blythe
Thornydykes
Whiteburn
Halliburton
Sisterpath
Fogo
Bogend
Leet Water
Horndean
Horncliffe
Thorntonpark
Ladykirk
NORHAM CASTLE
Norham
Thirlestane
Houndslow
Eden Water
Greenlaw
Blackadder Water
Fogorig
Swinton
SWINTON KIRK
MERSE
Swintonmill
Simprim
Shoreswood
Boon
Grindon
Legerwood
Huntlywood
272
GREEN KNOWE TOWER
Gordon
Middlethird
Easter Howlaws
Lambden
Leitholm
Orange Lane
Felkington
Shellacres
Castle Heaton
Duddo
West Morriston
Fans
Fallsidehill
Hume
HUME CASTLE
Eccles
Lennel
Coldstream
TWEED BRIDGE
Cornhill-on-Tweed
THE HIRSEL
HEATHERSLAW LIGHT RAILWAY
Etal
Earlston
245
223
MELLERSTAIN HOUSE
Stichill
Birgham
Carham
Wark
West Learmouth
East Learmouth
Crookham
Ford
Branxton
1513
281
Nenthorn
Ednam
Tweed
Smailholm
Hadden
Pressen
Flodden
EILDON AND LEADERFOOT
Redpath
Brotherstone
Kerchesters
Holefield
246
Downham
Howtel
Newstead
SMAILHOLM TOWER
FLOORS CASTLE
KELSO ABBEY
Kelso
Sprouston
Windywalls
Maxwellheugh
Lempitlaw
Mindrum
Milfield
Melrose
PRIORWOOD GDNS.
TRIMONTIUM EXHIBITION
Bemersyde
Clintmains
Dryburgh
ABBEY
Manorhill
Trows
ROXBURGH CASTLE
Hoselaw
Pawston
Kilham
267
Glen
Eildon Hills
Newtown St. Boswells
St. Boswells
MERTOUN GDNS.
Rutherford
Roxburgh
Heiton
Blakelaw
Shotton
Westnewton
Lanton
Coupland
Bowden
Maxton
116
269
Kirknewton
0 1 2 3 4 5 6 miles
0 1 2 3 4 5 6 7 8 9 10 km
Kalemouth
TEVIOT WATER GARDENS
Kale Water
Frogden
282
Town Yetholm
KIRK YETHOLM
Kirk Yetholm
Hethpool
ST CUTHBERTS WAY
537
Nisbet
Belses
Eckford
Crookhouse
Linton
A1
A1107
A6112
A6105
A697
A698
A699
A68
A6091
A6089
A199
A198
B6355
B6370
B6365
B6456
B6460
B6437
B6438
B6461
B6470
B6397
B6404
B6398
B6350
B6396
B6352
B6351
B6353
B6354
B6436
B6401
B6400
B6359
B6360
B6356
B6364

5
40
6
7
8
43
9
A
68
B
C
D
E
F
63
G
Bay
EYEMOUTH MUSEUM
Burnmouth
Lamberton Beach
Lamberton
NU
1333
Highfields
Berwick-upon-Tweed
BARRACKS MUSEUM & RAMPARTS
TOWER HOUSE POTTERY
B6461
East Ord
Tweedmouth
Spittal
Tweed
A698
Prior Park
A1167
Redshin Cove
108
Murton
Thornton
Scremerston
DEVIL'S CAUSEWAY
West Allerdean
Shoresdean
Cheswick
Goswick
Ancroft
North Low
Haggerston
B6354
B6525
Berrington
South Low
Beal
A1
LINDISFARNE
Emmanuel Hd.
Holy Island (Lindisfarne)
Causeway
Holy Island
Holy Island Sands
LINDISFARNE CASTLE
Castle Pt.
HERITAGE CENTRE
LINDISFARNE PRIORY
Bowsden
82
12
Fenham
Guile Pt.
NORTHUMBERLAND COAST
HUT SMITHY WOOD WORKSHOP
Barmoor Castle
Barmoor Lane End
West Kyloe
Fenwick
B6353
Lowick
East Kyloe
Kyloe Hills
LADY WATERFORD HALL
Buckton
Farne Islands
ST CUTHBERT'S WAY
Elwick
Ross
Budle Bay
Staple Sound
FARNE ISLANDS
157
Holburn
Detchant
BAMBURGH CASTLE
Inner Sound
Middleton
Budle
Kimmerston
Hetton Steads
211
Bamburgh
Easington
Fenton Town
Nesbit
North Hazelrigg
Belford
B1342
Waren Mill
B1340
Spindlestone
Glororum
Burton
Doddington
South Hazelrigg
B6349
Seahouses
200
West Horton
Mousen
Bradford
B1341
Newtown
East Horton
Bellshill
Elford
North Sunderland
10
Warenton
Adderstone
Akeld
1402
Weetwood Hall
Lucker
Newham Hall
A697
117
Chatton
B6348
Warenford
Swinhoe
Benthall
Humbleton
B6348
Greendikes
Newham
Fleetham
Wooler
166
WOOLER
Newstead
Beadnell Bay
Earle
Haugh Head
CHILLINGHAM CASTLE
Chillingham
CHILLINGHAM WILD CATTLE
Rosebrough
Chathill
Ellingham
Preston
High Newton-by-the-Sea
Middleton Hall
Newtown

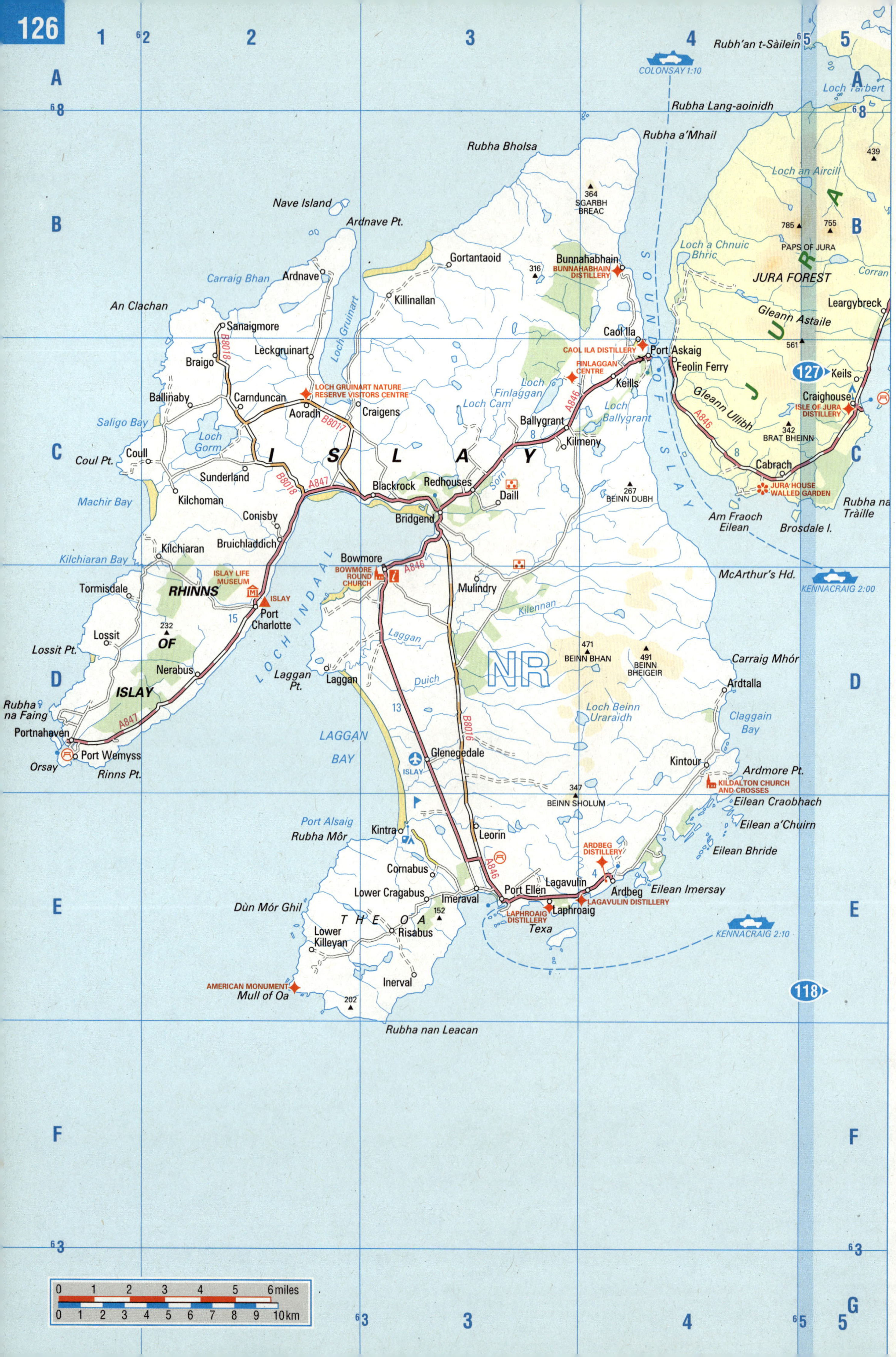

COLONSAY 1:10
Rubh'an t-Sàilein
Loch Tarbert
Rubha Lang-aoinidh
Rubha a'Mhail
Rubha Bholsa
364 SGARBH BREAC
Nave Island
Ardnave Pt.
Loch an Aircill
785
755
PAPS OF JURA
Loch a Chnuic Bhric
JURA FOREST
Corran
Leargybreck
Gleann Astaile
561
JURA
Gortantaoid
Bunnahabhain
BUNNAHABHAIN DISTILLERY
316
Carraig Bhan
Ardnave
An Clachan
Killinallan
Loch Gruinart
Sanaigmore
Leckgruinart
Braigo
Caol Ila
CAOL ILA DISTILLERY
Port Askaig
Feolin Ferry
FINLAGGAN CENTRE
Keills
127
Keils
Craighouse
ISLE OF JURA DISTILLERY
Gleann Ullibh
SOUND OF ISLAY
LOCH GRUINART NATURE RESERVE VISITORS CENTRE
Ballinaby
Carnduncan
Aoradh
Craigens
Loch Finlaggan
Loch Cam
Loch Ballygrant
Ballygrant
Kilmeny
Saligo Bay
Loch Gorm
Coull
Coul Pt.
ISLAY
342 BRAT BHEINN
Cabrach
JURA HOUSE WALLED GARDEN
Sunderland
Kilchoman
Machir Bay
Blackrock
Redhouses
Sorn
Daill
267 BEINN DUBH
Rubha na Tràille
Am Fraoch Eilean
Brosdale I.
Conisby
Bridgend
Bruichladdich
Kilchiaran
Kilchiaran Bay
Bowmore
BOWMORE ROUND CHURCH
ISLAY LIFE MUSEUM
McArthur's Hd.
KENNACRAIG 2:00
Tormisdale
RHINNS
ISLAY
Port Charlotte
Mulindry
Kilennan
LOCH INDAAL
232
OF
Lossit
Lossit Pt.
Laggan
471 BEINN BHAN
491 BEINN BHEIGEIR
Carraig Mhór
NR
Nerabus
Laggan Pt.
Duich
Ardtalla
ISLAY
Rubha na Faing
Loch Beinn Uraraidh
Claggain Bay
Portnahaven
LAGGAN BAY
Port Wemyss
Orsay
Rinns Pt.
Glenegedale
ISLAY
Kintour
Ardmore Pt.
KILDALTON CHURCH AND CROSSES
347 BEINN SHOLUM
Eilean Craobhach
Port Alsaig
Rubha Môr
Kintra
Leorin
Eilean a'Chuirn
Eilean Bhride
ARDBEG DISTILLERY
Cornabus
Lagavulin
Ardbeg
Eilean Imersay
Lower Cragabus
Imeraval
Port Ellen
LAGAVULIN DISTILLERY
Dùn Mór Ghil
LAPHROAIG DISTILLERY
Laphroaig
152
THE OA
Risabus
Texa
KENNACRAIG 2:10
Lower Killeyan
AMERICAN MONUMENT
Mull of Oa
Inerval
118
202
Rubha nan Leacan
A847
A846
B8018
B8017
B8016
0 1 2 3 4 5 6 miles
0 1 2 3 4 5 6 7 8 9 10 km

NM
NR
Garbh Eileach
Garvellachs
Eileach an Naoimh
SCARBA, LUNGA AND THE GARVELLACHS
Eilean Dubh Mòr
Lunga
Sound of Luing
CRUACH SCARBA 449
Scarba
Gulf of Corryvreckan
OBAN 2:20
Rubh'a'Geadha
Balnahard
Kiloran Bay
COLONSAY
KILORAN GARDENS
Kiloran
Kilchattan
B8086
B8087
136
Scalasaig
Loch Staosnaig
Garvard
B8085
Rubha Dubh
PRIORY
Dubh Eilean
Oronsay
Eilean nan Ron
Kinuachdrachd
Glengarrisdale Bay
296 CRUACH NA SEILCHEIG
130
Glendebadel Bay
365 BEN GARRISDALE
Lealt Burn
Corpach Bay
Lussa
467 BEINN BHREAC
Lealt
Gleann Aoistail
Ardlussa
Ardlussa Bay
Inverlussa
Lussagiven
Shian Bay
453 RAINBERG MOR
Shian
Loch Righ Mòr
318
A846
Barrahormid
B8025
Rubh'an t-Sàilein
1:10
Tarbert
KEILLS CHAPEL
Loch Tarbert
Rubha Lang-aoinidh
Keillmore
New Ulva
Loch na Cille
Island of Danna
Rubha a'Mhail
Rubha Bholsa
Lagg
439
Loch an Aircill
Loch Lesgamaill
364 SGARBH BREAC
JURA
Eilean Mòr
ST CORMAC'S CHAPEL
CHAPEL
Kilmory
Kilmory Bay
785
755
PAPS OF JURA
Loch a Chnuic Bhric
Gortantaoid
316
Bunnahabhain
BUNNAHABHAIN DISTILLERY
SOUND OF ISLAY
SOUND OF JURA
15
An Dùnan
128
JURA FOREST
Corran
Knockrome
Lowlandman's Bay
Leargybreck
Pt. of Knap
Gleann Astaile
Loch na Mile
126
Caol Ila
CAOL ILA DISTILLERY
561
Port Askaig
Feolin Ferry
FINLAGGAN CENTRE
Keills
Keils
Loch Finlaggan
Loch Cam
Loch Ballygrant
Gleann Ullibh
Craighouse
ISLE OF JURA DISTILLERY
Small Isles
Miller's Bay
Ballygrant
8
Kilmeny
342 BRAT BHEINN
Kilberry Hd.
SCULPTURED STONES
Redhouses
Sorn
Daill
267 BEINN DUBH
Cabrach
JURA HOUSE WALLED GARDEN
Rubha na Tràille
Bridgend
Am Fraoch Eilean
Brosdale I.
McArthur's Hd.
Mulindry
KENNACRAIG 2:00
0 1 2 3 4 5 6 miles
0 1 2 3 4 5 6 7 8 9 10 km
BEINN BHAN
491 BEINN
Carraig Mhór

Glengarrisdale Bay
Kinuachdrachd
296 CRUACH NA SEILCHEIG
Kinuachdrachd Harbour
Craignish
Island Macaskin
Kilmartin
GLEBE CAIRN
KILMARTIN HOUSE TRUST
KILMARTIN SCULPTURED STONES
RI CRUIN CAIRN
Slockavullin
Poltalloch
Crarae
CRARAE GLEN GARDENS
Minard
Glendebadel Bay
Glenn Airigh
Tullochgorm
Lachlan Bay
130
Loch Crinan
365 BEN GARRISDALE
Crinan
Killmahumaig
CUP AND RING MARKS
Kilmichael Glassary
Loch Glashan
MOINE MHOR
DUNADD FORT
Bridgend
Bellanoch
Mòine Mhòr
CAIRNBAAN CUP & RING MARKS
A83
Lephinmore
ROCK MARKINGS
Asknish
Lephinchapel
467 BEINN BHREAC
Lealt
Lussa
Lealt Burn
Lochgair
Cairnbaan
Gallachoille
KNAPDALE
Carsaig
Cam Loch
Crinan Canal
Lochgilphead
CRUACH CHUILCEACHAN
Ardlussa
Ardlussa Bay
Inverlussa
Lussagiven
Gleann Aoistail
JURA
Tayvallich
Achanamara
KILMORY CASTLE GARDENS
Carrick
Port Ann
Largiemore
KILMORY WOODLAND PARK
Kilmichael of Inverlussa
Ardrishaig
Achnaba
Otter Ferry
Glendaruel
Barrahormid
TAYNISH
Loch Gilp
Castleton
Clachan of Glendaruel
KILMODAN SCULPTURED STONES
Taynish
Loch Sween
Eilean Mòr
Ballimore
A846
Tarbert
127
KEILLS CHAPEL
Dunrostan
466 CRUACH LUSACH
Achabraid
Inverneill
Auchnaha
Keillmore
New Ulva
Loch na Cille
Island of Danna
CASTLE SWEEN
Lochead
458 CRUACH NAN CAORAC
Kilfinan Bay
Kilfinan
ST COLUMBA'S CAVE
Achahoish
B8024
477
454 BEINN BHREAC
KYLES
Drum
Eilean Mòr
ST CORMAC'S CHAPEL
CHAPEL
Kilmory
Kilmory Bay
Ellary
Clachbreck
NR
Erines
Melldalloch
Auchalick Bay
562 STOB ODHAR
Baile Boidheach
Port Driseach
Tighnabruaich
Ardmarnock Bay
Pt. of Knap
Loch Caolisport
Ormsary
Loch Chaorain
Barmore I.
Auchenlochan
Kames
Asgog Loch
SOUND OF JURA
Druimdrishaig
Millhouse
Kyles of Bute
Barfad
Glenan Bay
East Loch Tarbert
Portavadie
329
305
Loch nan Torran
Tarbert
Blair's Ferry
0:25
Miller's Bay
West Tarbert
Cretshengan
Asgog Bay
Kilbride Bay
CRUACH LAGAIN 264
A83
Corranbuie
Ardlamont Ho.
Coulaghailtro
Kilberry Hd.
SCULPTURED STONES
Kilberry
Torinturk
DUN
Rhu
Ardlamont Pt.
422 CNOC A'BHAILESHIOS
Kennacraig
Redhouse
Carse Ho.
Dunmore
WEST LOCH TARBERT
Rubha Leathan
Kilchamaig
Whitehouse
254
Loch Stornoway
Ardpatrick
B8001
Ardpatrick Ho.
Gartnagrenach
Glenreasdell Mains
Portachoillan
Skipness
SKIPNESS CASTLE
PORT ASKAIG 2:00
PORT ELLEN 2:10
Ardpatrick Pt.
Eilean Traighe
Skipness Pt.
Claonaig
Skipness Bay
269 CRUACH NAM FIADH
Ronachan Pt.
A83
Clachan
Claonaig Bay
SOUND OF
Loch Ciaran
Eilean Garbh
0:30
West Tarbert Bay
B842
East Tarbert Bay
Balochroy
Crossaig Glen
Cock of Arran
Tarbert
118
119
Crossaig
Loch Ranza
LOCHRANZA CASTLE
Gigha Island
100
Druimyeon More
Loch Garasdale
Lochranza
248 CRUACH MHIC GOUGAN
LOCHRANZA
Catacol Bay
Catacol
ISLE OF ARRAN DISTILLERY
444
Ardminish
Ardminish Bay
Rhunahaorine
Cour Bay
Cour
A841
0:20
ACHAMORE GARDENS
241 BEINN BHREAC
570 MEALL NAN DAMH
Thundergay
573
N
O
KINTYRE
KILBRANNAN SOUND
SOUND OF GIGHA
Gigalum Island
Tayinloan
322 CNOC NAN CRAOBH
Carradale Water
NORTH ARRAN
Cara Island
Killean
Grogport
Pirnmill
859
CRUACH MHIC-AN T-SAOIR 364
Glen Sa
798
Loch Tanna
CIR MHÒR
721 BEINN BHARRAIN
Whitefarland
354 CRUACH NAN GABHAR
Brackley
BEINN TARSUINN
874 GOAT FELL
825
Muasdale
Imachar
0 1 2 3 4 5 6 miles
0 1 2 3 4 5 6 7 8 9 10 km

A R G Y L L
F O R E S T
P A R K
Glen Sluain
Blairlomond
Loch Goil
Ardgoil Forest
Glen Douglas
Newton
Invernoaden
779 BEINN BHEULA
DOUNE HILL 734
Inverbeg
INVERBEG GALLERY
Rowardennan
ROWARDENNAN
Rowardennan Forest
Glenbranter
519 THE SADDLE
Glenmallan
Garbhallt
LACHLAN CASTLE
131
Glenbranter Forest
Carrick Castle
CARRICK CASTLE
Edentaggart
Loch Eck Forest
618 BEINN BHEAG
LOCH ECK
Whistlefield
Portincaple
Whistlefield
Glen Luss
THISTLE BAGPIPE WORKS
Inchlonaig
Luss
LOCH
Inchfad
Strathlachlan Forest
493
Caol Ghleann
713 BEINN CHAORACH
Garelochhead
593 BEINN RUISG
Aldochlay
Inchconnachan
LOMOND
Inchmurrin
Dunans
Bernice
741 BEINN MHOR
659 CREACHAN MOR
LONG
STRONE HOUSE GARDENS
Glen Fruin
BEINN RUADH 664
GLENFINART DEER FARM
Glen Finart
Faslane Port
Conchra
Glendaruel Forest
Glenmassan
Glenfinart
Ardentinny
Coulport
Rahane
GARE LOCH
Shandon
Duchlage
Blairglas
132
Glen Massan
YOUNGER BOTANIC GARDEN
Forest
Ardpeaton
681 SGORACH MOR
432 CRUACH NAN CUILEAN
Balliemore
Loch Tarsan
Benmore
Uig
Clynder
202
GLENARN GARDEN
THE HILL HOUSE
Arden
Craigendive
Ardbeg
KILMUN ARBORETUM
Rhu
A818
Bannachra Muir
BALLOCH CASTLE
Glen Lean
Invereck
Dalinlongart
Blairmore
Kilmun
LINN BOTANIC GARDENS
Cove Bay
Rosneath
Cove
Helensburgh
LOCH LOMOND
A82
Balloch
Craigendoran
LOMOND SHORES
Jamestown
Auchenbreck
405
Loch Riddon
Clachaig
Glen Kin
Holy Loch
Strone
Strone Pt.
Portkil
Rosneath Pt.
Colgrain
Sandbank
Ardnadam
Kilcreggan
0:30
578 CRUACH NAN CAPULL
Glenstriven
Hunter's Quay
0:10
GEILSTON
ALEXANDRIA
Bonhill
Geilston
Renton
ST JOHN'S CHURCH
Kirn
Gourock
Ashton
Greenock West
Greenock
Dunoon
0:20
HM CUSTOMS & EXCISE MUSEUM & EXHIBITION
Cardross
OF BUTE
506 BEINN BHREAC
LOCH STRIVEN
522 BLACK CRAIG
Inverchaolain
Midton
MCLEAN MUS. & ART GALL.
Levan
Larkfield
Braeside
NEWARK CASTLE
PORT GLASGOW
Castlehill
DUMBARTON
Ardentraive
Colintraive
Bullwood
HIGHLAND MARY'S STATUE
Cloch Pt.
Ravenscraig
Central
Brucehill
FINLAYSTONE HOUSE & GARDENS
Ferry
Algaltraig
Lunderston Bay
A78
A8
Strone
303
Woodhall
Devol
Mid Auchinlech
Bardrainney
Langbank
Kyles of Bute
418 CORLARACH HILL
Glen Fyne
Corlarach Forest
Loch Thom
Gryfe Resrs.
Inverkip
Shielhill
Inverclyde
Glen More
227
WINDY HILL 278
ISLAND OF BUTE
WAVE WHISPER GALLERY
Innellan
Garvock
Strathgryfe
Port Lamont
Newton Park
CLYDE
Wemyss Bay
Kilmacolm
Ardyne Pt.
441 CREUCH HILL
Upper Skelmorlie
Skelmorlie
Kames B.
Toward
St Colmac
Port Bannatyne
0:35
Toward Pt.
Duchal Moor
Quarrier's Homes
Houston
Ettrick Bay
ROTHESAY CASTLE
Rothesay Bay
Craigmore
NS
120
Bridge of Weir
Crosslee
Rothesay
ARDENCRAIG GARDENS
Montford
Meigle
MUIRSHIEL
Ranfurly
VICTORIAN FERNERY
Ascog
Noddsdale Water
Queenside Muir
522 HILL OF STAKE
Kilbarchan
WEAVER'S COTTAGE
Straad
Loch Fad
Kerrycroy
Routenburn
Waterhead Moor
REGIONAL
Mistylaw Muir
Calder
60
Scoulag
Largs Bay
VIKINGAR!
Largs
OLD KIRK
CASTLE SEMPLE
A737
Howwood
Inchmarnock
Scalpsie
Loch Quien
MOUNT STUART HOUSE AND GARDEN
Tomont End
CHRISTIAN HERITAGE MUSEUM
Ladyland Moor
Lochwinnoch
NATURE RESERVE VISITOR CEN.
484 IRISH LAW
Great Cumbrae Island
Downcraig Ferry
Ardscalpsie Pt.
Scalpsie Bay
Kingarth
Muirhead Reservoir
PARK
Barr Loch
Kilbirnie Loch
Rowbank Reservoir
KELBURN COUNTRY CENTRE
Stravanan Bay
Kilchattan Bay
MUSEUM OF THE CUMBRAES
Millport
Fairlie Roads
Fairlie
Camphill Reservoir
Kilbirnie
210
BUTE
157
Kilchattan Bay
Beith
ST BLANE'S CHAPEL
387 KAIM HILL
The Tan
Knockendon Reservoir
Rye Water
Glengarnock
Gateside
119
Garroch Hd.
HUNTERSTON POWER STATION VISITOR CENTRE
Longbar
Barrmill
Little Cumbrae Island
The Den
Greenhills
Girnhouse
stone Pt.
Thirdpart
Drakemyre
Garnock
Highfield
Blairland
Dunlop
Portencross
Giffordland
Dalry
BLACKSHAW FARM PARK
Farland Hd.
West Kilbride
A737
Auchentiber
Lugton Water
NORTH SANNOX FARM PARK
Seamill
rth Ayrshire
Sannox
Sannox Bay
Dalgarven
DALGARVEN MILL
ABBEY
Kilwinning
Torranyard
Annick Water
Corrie
Chapelhill
Horse Isle
Dykesmains
Bensli
Cunninghamhead
BRODICK 0:55
Ardrossan
NORTH AYRSHIRE MUSEUM
Stevenston
EGLINTON
Kilmaurs
Saltcoats
Girdle
FIRTH OF CLYDE

Sound of Mull
Island of Mull
Firth of Lorn
Lynn of Lorn
Lorn
Benderloch
Lismore
Kerrera
Oban
Seil
Luing
Shuna
Scarba
Lunga
Scarba, Lunga and the Garvellachs
Garvellachs
Eilean Dubh Mor
Eileach an Naoimh
Garbh Eileach
Gulf of Corryvreckan
Killundine
Larachbeg
Claggan
Kinlochaline Castle
Ardtornish Gardens
Achranich
Loch Aline
Lochaline
Loch Tearnait
Rannoch
437 Beinn a' Chaisil
Loch nan Clach
Glensanda
Shuna I.
Appin House
Portnacroish
Appin
Port Appin
Port Ramsay
Clachan
Eriska
North Shian
South Shian
Scottish Sea Life Sanctuary
Fiunary
Savary
Aros Mains
Rubha Mor
Salen
Pennygown
Fishnish Bay
Ardtornish Castle
Ardtornish Pt.
Glais Bheinn 479
An Sleaghach 513
Eignaig
Camas Gorm
Inninmore Bay
Garbh Shlios
Killbeg
Corrynachenchy
Garmony
412
Achnacroish
Rubha an Ridire
Bernera I.
Achinduin
Kilcheran
Eilean Dubh
Baravullin
Ferlochan
Kiel Crofts
Benderloch
Ledaig
Achnaba
Knock
Loch Bà
591 Beinn Ghraig
Glen Cannel
Scallastle Bay
Scallastle
Java
Craignure Bay
Craignure
Mull and West Highland Narrow Gauge Railway
766 Dun da Ghaoithe
761 Beinn Talaidh
Torosay Castle & Garden
Duart Bay
Duart Pt.
Duart Castle
Eilean Musdile
Ardmucknish Bay
North Connel
Connel
Black Crofts
Falls of Lora
Eilean Mor
Dunstaffnage Castle
Dunbeg
Lochdon
704 Corra-Bheinn
Glen More
Lussa
Castlebay 5:10
Coll 2:40
Tiree 3:40
Lochboisdale 5:15
Loch Don
Grass Pt.
Ganavan
Dunollie
Oban/Oban Lodge
McCaig's Tower
Oban Distillery
Oban Visitor Centre
Altnacraig
Oban Rare Breeds Farm Park
Black Lochs
Strathcoil
Coladoir
Loch Airdeglais
248
Balliemore
Glenamachrie
383
Ben Buie 717
698 Creach Beinn
Loch Spelve
Croggan
Rubha nan Sailthean
Bach I.
Ardmore
Sound of Kerrera
Gallanach
Loch Nell
Loch Fuaron
Kinlochspelve
Barrachandroman
Lochbuie
Loch Uisg
Rubha Seanach
Kilbride
Kilmore
Barran
503 Beinn na Croise
Am Buth
Loch Feochan
Glen Feochan
Glenfeochan House Gardens
Kilbride
Leidle
Carsaig
Loch Buie
405 Druim Fada
Laggan Deer Forest
Lord Lovat's Cave
Kilninver
Barochreal
Glen Euchar
368 A'Chruach
Musdale
Bragleenmore
Carsaig Bay
Rubha Dubh
Clachan Bridge
Insh I.
Sound of Insh
Clachan-Seil
Clachan
Loch Scamadale
438 Carn Dearg
515 Beinn Chapull
Frank Lockwood's Island
Easdale
An Cala Gardens
Easdale Island Folk Museum
Balvicar
Braes of Lorn
Blaran
267 Cruach Rarey
Loch Tralaig
Drissaig
Lochavich Ho
Kilmun
Dubh-fheith
Cuan
Cuan Ferry
Torsa
Seil Sound
Cullipool
94
Kilchoan
Ardanstur
Melfort
Kilmelford
Loch Avich
Loch Melfort
Glenmore
Lagalochan
Achafolla
Ardunaine Garden
Arduaine
Kames
365
491 Carn Ducharra
Inverliever Forest
Kilmaha
Sound of Luing
Garraron
Barbreck
Liever
Toberonochy
Shuna Sound
Craobh Haven
Barravullin
Lunga
Shuna Pt.
350 Cruach an Eachlaich
Arichamish
Torran
Crurach Scarba 449
Rubha Aird Luing
Kintraw
Ardfern
Ford
Finchairn
Finchairn Castle
Ederline
458 Cruach Fhionn
227 Creag Mhor
Eilean Righ
Carnassarie Castle
Aird
Loch Craignish
Rèisa an t-Sruith
Loch Gaineamhach
Kinuachdrachd
Craignish Pt.
Island Macaskin
Kilmartin
Glebe Cairn
Kilmartin House Trust
319
Glengarrisdale Bay
296 Cruach na Seilcheig
Kinuachdrachd Harbour
Kilmartin Sculptured Stones
Ri Cruin Cairn
Slockavullin
Poltalloch
Gleann Airigh
Glendebadel Bay
Loch Crinan
231 Dun Dubh
365 Ben Garrisdale
Crinan
Cup and Ring Marks
Kilmichael Glassary
Loch Glashan
Kilmahumaig
Bellanoch
Moine Mhor
Dunadd Fort
Bridgend
Cairnbaan Cup & Ring Marks
Rock Markings
Lochgair
Asknish
Lussa
Lealt
265
Colonsay 2:20
NM
NR
137
138
127
128
A828
A849
A848
A884
B8035
B8045
B844
B8003
B8002
A816
B8025
B841
B840
A83
0 1 2 3 4 5 6 miles
0 1 2 3 4 5 6 7 8 9 10km

Stockdale
Elleric
Glen Creran
Glen Ure
BEINN FHIONNLAIDH
Inverchannan
Glenceitlein
STOB DUBH
Allt Coire a'Chaorain
CLACH LEATHAD
BLACK MOUNT
Loch na h-Achlaise
An Iola
Invercreran
BEINN CHURALAIN
GLASDRUM WOOD
Glasdrum
Druimavuic
BEINN SGULAIRD
Gualachulain
STOB GHABHAR
WEST HIGHLAND WAY
Loch Tulla
Achallader
Creagan
South Creagan
BEINN TRILLEACHAN
STOB COIR'AN ALBANNAICH
Allt Dochard
Black Mount
Forest Lodge
Barcaldine
CREACH BHEINN
Abhainn
Allt Easach
BEN STARAV
Loch Dochard
Inveroran Hotel
Barcaldine Forest
Allt Hallater
BEINN NAN AIGHENAN
BIENN AN DOTHAIDH
Bridge of Orchy
Gleann Salach
B845
LOCH ETIVE
BEINN DORAIN
Allt Chonoghlais
ARDCHATTAN PRIORY GARDENS
ARDCHATTAN PRIORY
BEINN MHEADHONACH
Glen Kinglass
Glen Liver
Achnacloich
ACHNACLOICH GARDEN
Bonawe
BEINN MHIC-MHONAIDH
GLEN ORCHY
Arichastlich
Glen Noe
Glen Strae
BEINN EUNAICH
BEINN UDLAIDH
BEINN ODHAR
A85
BONAWE IRON FURNACE
INVERAWE FISHERIES AND SMOKERIES EXHIBITION
Brochroy
Fearnoch Forest
Taynuilt
Ichrachan
BEN CRUACHAN
Bridge of Awe
Allt Mhoille
B8074
Glen Lochy
Arrivain
Clifton
Tyndrum
BARGUILLEAN GARDENS
GLEN NANT
Glen Nant
Pass of Brander
Cruachan Reservoir
B8077
Awe
Stronmilchan
Strath of Orchy
Achnafalnich
Cononish
A82
Lonan
Falls of Cruachan
KILCHURN CASTLE
Lochawe
Dalmally
Inverlochy
BEN LUI
CRUACHAN DAM VISITOR CENTRE
Loch Nant
Loch Tromlee
ARDANAISEIG GARDENS
Ardanaiseig
Innis Chonain
MCINTYRE MONUMENT
Eas a'Ghaill
Inverherive
BEINN DUBHCHRAIG
INISHAIL CHAPEL
Inishail
Teatle Water
A819
NN
Allt Fionn Ghlinne
Sior Loch
Kilchrenan
MEALL NAN TIGHEARN
Annat
North Port
Cladich
Allt Fearna
Glen Falloch
Dubh Eas
Portsonachan
South Port
Cladich
Lochan Shira
Loch Sron Mor
Falls of Falloch
Argyll
TROISGEACH
Inverarnan
Ben Glas Burn
BEINN BHUIDHE
Fyne
Inverinan
B840
BEINN GHLAS
Shira
Allt na Lairige
Ballimeanoch
Brannie Burn
Glen Fyne
Ardlui
Allt Beochlich
Tullich
Glen Aray
Glen Shira
Glenfyne Lodge
MAOL BREAC
LOCH AWE
CRUACH MHOR
Dalavich
Blarghour
Kilblaan Burn
Clachan
ARDCHONNELL CASTLE
Portinnisherrich
Dubh Loch
Loch Sloy
BEN VORLICH
and
Drishaig
A83
Cairndow
INVERARAY CASTLE
BELL TOWER
ARDKINGLAS WOODLAND GARDEN
Eredine
COMBINED OPERATIONS MUSEUM
INVERARAY
Glen Kinglas
Inveruglas
ROB ROY'S CAVE
Ardno
A815
Inversnaid Hotel
INVERARAY JAIL
Inveraray
MARITIME MUSEUM
BEINN AN LOCHAIN
Rest and Be Thankful
BEINN IME
Durran
Newtown
St Catherine's
B828
WEST HIGHLAND WAY
AN SUIDHE
Douglas Water
B839
Hell's Glen
CRUACH NAN CAPULL
Monevechadan
Succoth
Dalchenna
Glen Croe
Tarbet
Eredine Forest
BEINN DEARG
BEN DONICH
Forest
Arrochar
Craig Rostan
Loch Leacann
Auchindrain
AUCHINDRAIN OPEN AIR MUSEUM
Ardgartan
Creggans
Stuckgowan
Bute
Strachur Bay
Clachan
Strachur
Drimsynie
Lochgoilhead
Ardmay
EUROPEAN SHEEP AND WOOL CENTRE
Ardgartan
Cur
Corrow
BEINN LOCHAIN
CNOC COINNICH
Furnace
Glen Sluain
Blairlomond
Glen Douglas
A886
A815
Crarae
Newton
Invernoaden
BEINN BHEULA
Ardgoil Forest
Loch Goil
LOCH LONG
A814
CRARAE GLEN GARDENS
DOUNE HILL
Inverbeg
INVERBEG GALLERY
Glenbranter
ARGYLL
Glenbranter Forest
Minard
Garbhallt
B8000
THE SADDLE
Glenmallan
Tullochgorm
LACHLAN CASTLE
Loch Eck
BEINN EICH
Lachlan Bay
Carrick Castle
CARRICK CASTLE
FOREST
Edentaggart
BEINN BHEAG
Strathlachlan Forest
Caol Ghleann
Portincaple
Whistlefield
Lephinmore
LOCH ECK
PARK
NS
Whistlefield
Glen Luss
THISTLE BAGPIPE WORKS
BEINN CHAORACH
Bernice
CREACHAN MOR
Garelochhead
A817
Aldochlay
Dunans
BEINN RUISG
Lephinchapel
138
139
132
129

LOCH LOMOND AND THE TROSSACHS NATIONAL PARK
Stirling
NN
NS
QUEEN ELIZABETH FOREST PARK
THE TROSSACHS
LOCH LOMOND
West Dunbartonshire
East Dunbartonshire
CAMPSIE FELLS
Glen Lochy
Arrivain
Clifton
Tyndrum
Cononish
Strath Fillan
Inverherive
Crianlarich
CRIANLARICH
BEN LUI
1130 BEN LUI
978 BEINN DUBHCHRAIG
901 BEINN ODHAR
BEINN UDLAIDH
1025 BEN CHALLUM
937 BEINN CHEATHAICH
Allt Ribhain
Auchlyne West Burn
GLEN DOCHART
Lochdochart House
Loch Iubhair
Loch Dochart
Benmore
Portnellan
1174 BEN MORE
1165 STOB BINNEIN
Auchlyne
Ledcharrie
Ardchyle
Dochart
Boreland
Finlarig
MOIRLANICH LONGHOUSE
KILLIN
Killin
BREADALBANE FOLKLORE CENTRE
Achmore
FALLS OF DOCHART
Glen Ogle
Beich Burn
Dalveich
Lochearnhead
EDINAMPLE FALLS
Edinample
Ardvorlich
852
WEST HIGHLAND WAY
Allt Fionn Ghlinne
Glen Falloch
Falloch
Falls of Falloch
Dubh Eas
739 MEALL NAN TIGHEARN
Fyne
733 TROISGEACH
Inverarnan
Ben Glas Burn
Allt na Lairige
Ardlui
645 MAOL BREAC
Loch Sloy
941 BEN VORLICH
916
Inveruglas
ROB ROY'S CAVE
1011 BEINN IME
849
881
Succoth
Glen Croe
Forest
A83
Arrochar
Tarbet
Ardgartan
Stuckgowan
Ardmay
Ardgartan
940 BEINN A'CHROIN
865 STOB A'CHOIN
770
Braes of Balquhidder
Monachylemore
Craigruie
Balquhidder
ROB ROY'S GRAVE
Auchtubh
Loch Doine
Loch Voil
Inverlochlarig
Ballimore
Calair Burn
Strathyre
Strathyre Forest
985 BEN VORLICH
771
687 BEINN BHREAC
820 BENVANE
811 BEINN EACH
Ardchullarie More
Loch Lubnaig
Keltie Water
Strath Gartney
Stronachlachar
LOCH KATRINE
Glen Finglas Res.
879 BEN LEDI
Anie
Pass of Leny
Leny Ho.
ROB ROY VISITOR CENTRE
FALLS OF LENY
Kilmahog
Bochastle
Callander
Inversnaid Hotel
Loch Arklet
Loch Ard Forest
TROSSACHS PIER COMPLEX
SS SIR WALTER SCOTT
The Trossachs
Trossachs Hotel
Brig o'Turk
Coilantogle
598
Frenich
B829
BEN VENUE
727
Loch Achray
Duncraggan
Lendrick Lodge
A821
Loch Chon
Craig Rostan
Loch Venachar
Achray Forest
Loch Drunkie
Menteith Hills
Torrie Forest
Loch Rusky
Kinlochard
Altskeith
FOREST PARK VISITOR CENTRE
Port of Menteith
974 BEN LOMOND
Milton
SCOTTISH WOOL CENTRE
TROSSACHS DISCOVERY CENTRE
DUNAVERIG FARMLIFE CENTRE
Ptarmigan Lodge
Loch Ard
Aberfoyle
Kirkton
Malling
INCHMAHOME PRIORY
Ruskie
Goodie Water
681
Glen Douglas
Rowardennan
ROWARDENNAN
596 BEINN UIRD
Duchray Water
Loch Ard Forest
Cobleland
Lake of Menteith
FLANDERS MOSS
Flanders Moss
DOUNE HILL 734
Inverbeg
INVERBEG GALLERY
Dykehead
Gartmore
Rowardennan Forest
577 BEINN BHREAC
Kelty Water
Dalmary
Flanders Moss
Forth
Glenmallan
BEINN EICH 702
Edentaggart
461
Arnprior
Cauldhame
Glen Luss
Inchlonaig
Milarrochy
B835
Buchlyvie
Portincaple
Whistlefield
713 BEINN CHAORACH
THISTLE BAGPIPE WORKS
Luss
Moor Park
A811
Garelochhead
Aldochlay
Inchfad
Balmaha
Milton of Buchanan
Garadhban Forest
Buchlyvie Muir
Kippen
Muir
593 BEINN RUISG
Inchcailloch
STRONE HOUSE GARDENS
Glen Fruin
ROWAN GALLERY
Balfron Station
Harvieston
Faslane Port
LOCH LOMOND
Drymen
Balfron
Fintry Hills
CULCREUCH CASTLE
Inchmurrin
Boquhan
Endrick Water
Ballikinrain
GARE LOCH
Shandon
Duchlage
Blairglas
Gartness
Gartocharn
Spittal
Killearn
Fintry
Croftamie
EARL'S SEAT 578
GLENARN GARDEN
THE HILL HOUSE
Arden
Craighat
Rhu
Bannachra Muir
BALLOCH CASTLE
Dumgoyne
GLENGOYNE DISTILLERY
202
Rosneath
LOCH LOMOND
Helensburgh
Stockiemuir
Blairquhosh
LOCH LOMOND SHORES
Auchincarroch
Balloch
Kilcreggan
Rosneath Pt.
Craigendoran
LOMOND SHORES
Blane Water
Strathblane Hills
Portkil
ALEXANDRIA
Jamestown
Netherton
Clachan of Campsie
Bonhill
Dumbarton Muir
Resrs
Blanefield
Strathblane
Gourock
Renton
Balgrochan
Greenock
Greenock West
401 DUNCOLM
MUGDOCK
Lennoxtown
Midton
MCLEAN MUS. & ART GALL.
HM CUSTOMS & EXCISE MUSEUM & EXHIBITION
Cardross
Castlehill
Townend
KILPATRICK HILLS
Mugdock
DUMBARTON
Blairskaith
Birdston
A85
A82
A84
A81
A821
A873
A811
A809
A818
A817
A814
A875
A891
A813
A812
B8074
B829
B837
B8034
B822
B834
B818
B821
B858
131
129
139
140
120
121
0 1 2 3 4 5 6 miles
0 1 2 3 4 5 6 7 8 9 10 km
0:10
0:30

Perth and Kinross
Clackmannanshire
Falkirk
NN
NS
140
141
134
121
122
Almond
CREAG UCHDAG
BEN CHONZIE
MEALL TARSUINN
MEALL NAN CAORAICH
Newton
Glen Almond
Little Glenshee
Logiealmond Lodge
Logiealmond
Harrietfield
Chapelhill
Buchanty
Loch Lednock Reservoir
Invergeldie
Loch Turret Reservoir
Glen Lednock
Funtullich
Glen Turret
Methven
Almondbank
Lochty
Keillour
Braegrum
Tibbermore
Monzie
Monzie Castle
Fowlis Wester
STANDING STONES
FALLS OF TURRET
Ochtertyre
Hosh
Gilmerton
St Fillans
Loch Earn
Ardtrostan
Dunira
MELVILLE MONUMENT
River Earn
Comrie
Lawers
Quoig
GLENTURRET DISTILLERY
Crieff
Keillour Forest
Pow Water
Madderty
Tullybannocher
EARTHQUAKE HOUSE
Ross
Dalginross
Lochlane
CRIEFF VISITORS' CENTRE
The Balloch
STUART CRYSTAL VISITOR CENTRE
Clathy
Findo Gask
St David's
Dupplin Castle
Forteviot
AUCHINGARRICH WILDLIFE & HIGHLAND CATTLE CENTRE
Forest of Glenartney
Water of Ruchill
Culloch
Torlum Wood
DRUMMOND CASTLE GARDENS
OLD CHURCH & TOWER
INNERPEFFRAY LIBRARY
Kirkton
Kinkell Bridge
Strathearn
Earn
Glen Artney
Dalchruin
Tigh-na-Blair
Ochtermuthill
Machany Water
Muthill
Aberuthven
Auchnashelloch
BEN CLACH
Tullibardine
TULLIBARDINE CHAPEL
Dunning
Langside
Auchterarder
Milton
Muirton
AUCHTERARDER HERITAGE
Glenlichorn
Knaik
Garrick
UAMH BHEAG
BLACKHALL ROMAN CAMPS
ARDOCH ROMAN CAMP
Gleneagles Hotel
GLENEAGLES
Braco
Strathallan
Blackford
Gleneagles House
Glen Eagles
Common of Dunning
Middle Rigg
Water of May
Bullie Burn
Muckle Burn
Braes of Ogilvie
STEEL'S KNOWE
INNERDOUNY HILL
Greenloaning
Allan Water
Ardoch Burn
Braes of Doune
Glendevon Resvrs.
GLENDEVON
Glendevon
Glen Devon
Burnfoot
Castle Hill Reservoir
South Queich
Carnbo
Drumvaich
Kinbuck
Balhaldie
Burn of Cambus
Ashfield
Sheriff Muir
Doune
Deanston
CATHEDRAL
Dunblane
Pisgah
LEIGHTON LIBRARY
BLAIRDENON HILL
BEN CLEUCH
Pool o' Muckhart
Yetts o' Muckhart
Drum
Crook of Devon
Thornhill
Blair Drummond
Easter Row
BLAIR DRUMMOND SAFARI PARK
KING'S SEAT HILL
CASTLE CAMPBELL
Rumbling Bridge
RUMBLING BRIDGE GORGE
Powmill
Blairdrummond Moss
Sunnylaw
Bridge of Allan
MILL TRAIL VISITOR CENTRE
Menstrie
Tillicoultry
Dollar
Blairlogie
Alva
Blairingone
Devon
Devonside
Drip Moss
Causewayhead
NATIONAL WALLACE MONUMENT
Tullibody
Fishcross
Coalsnaughton
GARTMORN DAM
Hill End
Kippen
Glentirranmuir
Gargunnock
STIRLING CASTLE
OLD TOWN JAIL
Raploch
Cambuskenneth
ABBEY
Branshill
Sauchie
Forest Mill
Stirling
Cambus
Kellarsbrae
SMITH ART GALL & MUSEUM
Balgonar
KNOCK HILL
CARLEATHERAN
Touch Hills
Cambusbarron
Torbrex
ALLOA
ALLOA TOWER
Fallin
Throsk
Clackmannan
South Alloa
Kennet
Kilbagie
Saline
Cowstrandburn
Gargunnock Hills
St Ninians
BANNOCKBURN HERITAGE CENTRE
Bannockburn
Earlsburn Reservoirs
Cowie
Dunmore
THE PINEAPPLE
Blairhall
Comrie
Gowkhall
Oakley
Carnock
Devilla Forest
Craigend
STIRLING SERVICES
Kincardine
CULROSS ABBEY
High Valleyfield
Loch Walton
Loch Coulter
Plean
Airth
CULROSS PALACE
Culross
Low Torry
Torryburn
Cairneyhill
Easter Cringate
PLEAN
Letham
Kincardine Bridge
Torry Bay
Carron
Torwood
Muirmill
Carron Bridge
Dunipace
Antonshill
Skinflats
CHARLESTOWN WORKSHOPS
Charlestown
Carron Valley Forest
Carron Valley Res.
DENNY
Stenhousemuir
SKINFLATS MUSEUM
GRANGEMOUTH
Fankerton
Stoneywood
Larbert
Carron
Bainsford
BO'NESS AND KINNEIL RAILWAY
Grangepans
Carriden
TOMTAIN
Head of Muir
FALKIRK MILLENNIUM WHEEL
Bo'ness
Muirhouses
BIRKHILL CLAY MINE
Blackness
Kilsyth Hills
Bonnybridge
Dennyloanhead
ROUGH CASTLE
FALKIRK
Laurieston
Grougfoot
Manners
COLZIUM HOUSE
Banton
Kilsyth
Banknock
Longcroft
High Bonnybridge
CALLENDAR HOUSE
Redding
Polmont
Brightons
Linlithgow
Milton of Campsie
Queenzieburn
Greenhill
Glen Village
Reddingmuirhead
Whitecross
Linlithgow Bridge
Philpstoun
Dullatur
Cumbernauld Village
Castlecary
Shieldhill
Maddiston
California
PALACE
Loan
Bridgend
Twechar
Croy
Abronhill
Jawcraig

Perth and Kinross
NO
NT
Stanley
Luncarty
Methven
Almondbank
Perth
Scone
Kinfauns
Glencarse
St Madoes
Errol
Carse of Gowrie
Braes of the Carse
Firth of Tay
Invergowrie
Longforgan
Kingoodie
Newburgh
Abernethy
Bridge of Earn
Forgandenny
Forteviot
Dunning
Auchterarder
Gleneagles House
Glenfarg
Auchtermuchty
Falkland
Lomond Hills
Fife Regional Park
Ladybank
Markinch
Leslie
Glenrothes
Milnathort
Kinross
Loch Leven
Dollar
Muckhart
Ballingry
Lochore
Lochgelly
Kelty
Cowdenbeath
Cardenden
Kirkcaldy
Kinghorn
Burntisland
Aberdour
Dalgety Bay
Inverkeithing
Rosyth
Dunfermline
Oakley
Kincardine
Culross
Grangemouth
Bo'ness
Forth Road Bridge
North Queensferry
Queensferry
Inchcolm
Inchmickery
Cramond
Granton
Newhaven
Leith
Edinburgh
Firth of Forth
M90
A9
A90
A91
A92
A977
A985
0 1 2 3 4 5 6 miles
0 1 2 3 4 5 6 7 8 9 10 km

Birkhill
Fintry
Downfield
Baldovie
Douglas & Angus
Dundee
Craigie
West Ferry
Lochee
Verdant Works
Mus. and Art Gall.
Mills Observatory
Stannergate
Broughty Ferry
Frigate Unicorn
Broughty Castle Museum
Barnhill
Monifieth
Souterrain Ardestie
Mains of Ardestie
Barry
Carnoustie
Barry Links
Buddon Ness
Dundee
Tay Bridge
Toll
Discovery Point
University Botanic Gardens
Newport-on-Tay
Tayport
Scotscraig
Tentsmuir Point
Tentsmuir Forest
Morton Lochs
Woodhaven
Tay Rail Bridge
Wormit
Kirkton
Bottomcraig
Balmerino
Gauldry
Pickletillem
Rhynd
Carrick
Kilmany
Lucklawhill
Leuchars
Leuchars Norman Church
Earlshall Castle and Gardens
Eden Mouth
Rathillet
Logie
Balmullo
Guardbridge
Eden Estivant Centre
St Andrews Bay
Dairsie or Osnaburgh
Kincaple
St Andrews
St Andrews Aquarium
British Golf Mus.
Cath. & St Rule's Tower
Kilmaron Castle
Cupar
Strathkinness
Newpark
Kemback
Blebocraigs
Balone
Brownhills
Buddo Ness
Craigtoun
St Andrews Botanic Garden
Boarhills
Babbet Ness
Cupar Muir
Pitscottie
Denhead
Prior Muir
Hill of Tarvit Mansionhouse
Bridgend
Ceres
Cameron Res.
Cameron Burn
Stravithie
Kingsbarns
Cambo Ness
Cambo Gardens
Carr Brigs
Tullybothy Craigs
Craigrothie
Baldinnie
Dunino
Balcomie
Craighead
Fife Ness
Scotstarvit Tower
Fife Folk Museum
Peat Inn
Radernie
Lathones
Lochty
Kingsmuir
Scotland's Secret Bunker
Crail Tolbooth
Woodside
New Gilston
Crail
Crail Museum and Heritage Centre
Montrave
Largoward
Carnbee
Pitcorthie
Pitkierie
West Ness
Wester Newburn
Praytis Farm Park
Scotland's Larder
Kellie Castle and Garden
Kilrenny
Fife Coastal Path
Kirkton of Largo
Arncroach
NO
Bonnybank
Lundin Links
Drumeldrie
Colinsburgh
Anstruther Easter
Scottish Fisheries Museum
Kennoway
Scoonie
Robinson Crusoe Statue
Lower Largo
Balchrystie
Abercrombie
Kilconquhar
Pittenweem
Anstruther Wester
St Fillan's Cave
St Monan's Windmill
Silverburn Estate
Ardross
St Monans
St Monan's Church
Letham Glen
Leven
Largo Bay
Ruddons Pt.
Innerleven
Methil
Earlsferry
Elie
Sauchar Pt.
Chapel Ness
Isle of May
Museum
Buckhaven
Fife Coastal Path
FORTH
Fidra
Craigleith
Bass Rock
Eyebroughy
North Berwick
Scottish Seabird Centre
Museum
Dirleton Castle & Gardens
Muirfield
Tantallon Castle
NT
Gullane Bay
Dirleton
Auldhame
Gullane
Scoughall
West Fenton
Kingston
Whitekirk
Fenton Barns
St. Baldred's Cradle
Aberlady Bay
Aberlady
Tyne Mouth
John Muir Birthplace
Myreton Motor Museum
Craigielaw
Drem
Tyninghame
John Muir
Dunbar
The Chesters Fort
Museum of Flight
East Fortune
Belhaven
Gosford Bay
Gosford House
Ballencrieff
West Barns
Preston
Broxburn
Barns Ness
Spittal
Athelstaneford
East Linton
Peffer Burn
Preston Mill & Phantassie Doocot
Cockenzie and Port Seton
Seton Collegiate Church
Hopetoun Mon.
Biel Water
Spott
Meikle
East Barns
Skateraw
Longniddry
Jane Welsh Carlyle Museum
Hailes
Traprain
Pitcox

1
2
3
4
A
B
C
D
E
F
G
144
Cairns of Coll
Eilean Mor
Rubha Mor
Sorisdale
Bousd
Cliad Bay
Arnabost
Gallanach
Grishipoll
B8072
B8071
COLL
OBAN 2:40
Ballyhaugh
Loch Cliad
Hogh Bay
Arinagour
Totronald
Feall Bay
Arileod
Acha
B8070
Loch Eatharna
Eilean Ornsay
Breachacha Castle
Friesland
Calgary Pt.
Gunna
Crossapol Bay
Soa
Loch Breachacha
TIREE
Vaul Bay
Salum
Caolas
Rubha Dubh
Balephetrish Bay
Vaul
B8069
Ruaig
B8068
Gott Bay
Kenovay
Scarinish
B8065
Heanish
Rubha Traigh an Duin
Crossapol
Hynish Bay
Balemartine
Mannal
0:55
NM
Ardnamurchan
ARDNAMURCHAN LIG
Quinish
Rubha an Aird
Caliach Pt.
Sunipol
Mornish
Calgary
Calgary Bay
Ensay
Treshnish Pt.
Haunn
B8073
Rubh a'Chaoil
Kilninian
Burg
Treshnish Isles
Fladda
LOCH
Eilean Dioghlum
Gometra
Lunga
Bearnus
Bac Mor
Little Colonsay
Staffa
STAFFA
FINGAL'S CAVE
Argyll
Erisgeir
(April-Oct) 0:45
0 1 2 3 4 5 6 miles
0 1 2 3 4 5 6 7 8 9 10 km
NL
Hough Skerries
R. Chraiginis
Balevullin
Kilkenneth
Moss
Middleton
Port Mor
Heylipol
Loch a'Phuill
Barrapol
B8067
Rinn Thorbhais
Balephuil
141
Balephuil Bay
Port Snoig
Hynish
TIREE
COLL 0:55
Eilean Annraidh
MACLEAN'S CROSS
IONA ABBEY AND CATHEDRAL
Rubha nan Cearc
Loch na Lathaich
IONA HERITAGE CENTRE
Kintra
Iona
Baile Mor
ST COLUMBA EXHIBITION & WELCOME CENTRE
Aridhglas
Eorabus
Stac an Aoineidh
Sound of Iona
Fionnphort
A849
Fidden
Tiraghoil
Bunessan
Loch Assapol
Erraid
ROSS OF
Soa I.
Ardalanish
Uisken
Ardchiavaig
Eilean a'Chalmain
125
Rubh Ardalanish

5
6
7
8
Rubha Aird Druimnich
Farquhar's Pt.
Eilean Shona
Invermoidart
Kinlochmoidart
MOIDART
Gaskan
A
Gorstan
Castle Tioram
Loch Moidart
Ardmolich
Brunery
Ockle Pt.
Sanna Point
144
Fascadale
Kilmory
Ockle
Ardtoe
Newton of Ardtoe
Shielfoot
145
A861
Dalnabreck
Dalelia
Polloch
Sanna
Sanna Bay
Branault
357 Beinn Bhreac
Kentra
Kentra Bay
Blain
Moss
Clash Moss
Portuairk
Achnaha
Achosnich
401
ARDNAMURCHAN
Acharacle
Ardshealach
Loch Mudle
SUNART
B8007
845 Beinn Resipol
B
Ariundle Centre
Ariundle
Scotstown
Anaheilt
Ardnastang
Kilchoan
Ormsaigmore
Ormsaigbeg
An Acairseid
Kilchoan Bay
Mingary Castle
528 Ben Hiant
Ardnamurchan Natural History Visitor Centre
490 Meall nan Each
Salen
Resipole
A861
19
Glenbeg
512 Ben Laga
Loch Sunart
Glencripesdale
11
Maclean's Nose
Ardslignish
Eilean Mor
Glenborrodale
Laga
Camuschoirk
0:35
Oronsay
Carna
Liddesdale
Ardmore Bay
Ardmore Pt.
Glencripesdale
516 Meall an Damhain
Bloody Bay
Auliston Pt.
169
138
Glengorm Castle
Mull and Iona Folklore Museum
Tobermory
Highland
582 Beinn nam Beathrach
571 Beinn Iadain
Lochuisge
B8043
Tobermory
Calve I.
Loch Teacuis
Quinish
Mishnish
'S Airde-Beinn
Tobermory Distillery
Upper Druimfin
Drimnin
Bonnavoulin
MORVERN
Gleann Dubh
A884
18
Loch Uisge
C
Beach
292
B8073
Mull Little Theatre
7
Penmore Mill
Dervaig
Achnadrish
451 Beinn Bhuidhe
Loch Arienas
A848
550 Stithean na Raplaich
Rhemore
Acharn
739 Beinn Mheadhoin
The Old Byre Heritage Centre
Speinne Mor 444
AROS
Ardnacross
Killundine
Gleann Geal
Lettermore
Loch Frisa
B849
Claggan
NM
Larachbeg
Kinlochaline Castle
Ardtornish Gardens
Achranich
Loch Tearnait
437 Beinn a' Chaisil
Bellart
Achnacraig
10
SOUND OF MULL
Fiunary
Savary
A884
Loch Aline
Rannoch
Loch nan Clach
Achleck
Aros
Fanmore 390
23
Crannich
Aros Mains
Lochaline
Glais Bheinn 479
D
An Sleaghach 513
Rubha Mor
Ballygown
A848
0:15
Ardtornish Castle
Eignaig
Eas Fors Waterfall
424 Beinn na Drise
Salen
Fishnish Bay
Ardtornish Pt.
Lagganulva
Pennygown
6
A884
Laggan Bay
Killiechronan
B8035
Killbeg
Corrynachenchy
A849
Inninmore Bay
Garbh Shlios
Camas Gorm
313
Oskamull
Kellan
B8073
Gruline
412
Forsa
Garmony
Scallastle Bay
Rubha an Ridire
Bernera I.
Achinduin
Ulva
Ulva House
Killiemor
Sound of Ulva
5
Kilcheran
Knock
ISLAND
Java
Craignure Bay
LOCH NA KEAL
Loch Bà
Scallastle
Lismore
Eorsa
Loch na Keal
B8035
591 Beinn a' Ghraig
Craignure
Mull and West Highland Narrow Gauge Railway
Inch Kenneth Chapel
Inch Kenneth
ISLE OF MULL
17
Derryguaig
OF
Glen Cannel
766 Dun da Ghaoithe
Duart Bay
Duart Pt.
Torosay Castle & Garden
Duart Castle
E
Eilean Musdile
Balnahard
761 Beinn Talaidh
130
and Bute
MULL
Lochdon
Oban 0:45
Mackinnon's Cave
561
966 Ben More
704 Corra-Bheinn
Glen More
17
Lussa
A849
Loch Don
Grass Pt.
519
Glen Seilisdeir
Beinn na Sreine
Strathcoil
ARDMEANACH
Killiemore House
B8035
Coladoir
A849
Loch Airdeglais
248
Ballimore
Aird of Kinloch
Ben Buie 717
698 Creach Beinn
Loch Spelve
Kerrera
The Burg
Kilfinichen Bay
Loch Fuaron
Ardmore
Croggan
Rubha nan Sailthean
Bach I.
Rubha Seanach
LOCH SCRIDAIN
Pennycross
Kinlochspelve
F
Torrans
Lochbuie
Barachandroman
Loch Uisg
503 Beinn na Croise
18
BROLASS
Leidle
Loch Buie
FIRTH OF LORN
Lee
Beach
Carsaig
405 Druim Fada
Laggan Deer Forest
Kilninver
376 Cruachan Min
376
Carsaig Bay
Rubha Dubh
Lord Lovat's Cave
Clachan Bridge
B844
MULL
Insh I.
Sound of Insh
Clachan-Seil
Clachan
Scoor
Carsaig Arches
Frank Lockwood's Island
Seil
An Cala Gardens
Malcolm's Pt.
Easdale
Easdale
Easdale Island Folk Museum
B844
G
Rubha nam Braithrean
5
6
7
17
8
Balvicar
B8003
Cruach

Loch Beoraid
Polnish
Lochailort
A830
Ranochan
796 SGURR AN UTHA
Glen Finnan
Glen Dubh Lighe
Glenn Suileag
Druim Fada
Ardnish
Inverailort
Loch Eilt
STATION MUSEUM
GLENFINNAN MONUMENT
Wauchan
Laggan
Loch Ailort
145
Glenfinnan
146
Alisary
869 DRUIM FIACLACH
Callop
Drumsallie
Kinlocheil
Fassfern
Roshven
882 ROIS-BHEINN
882 BEINN ODHAR BHEAG
LOCH EIL
A861
TREASURES OF THE EARTH
South Garvan
Duisky
Blaich
Corpach
Glen Garvan
Achaphubuil
Camusnagaul
Trislaig
666 BEINN GAIRE
755 MEALL NAN CREAG LEAC
Moidart
LOCH SHIEL
Kinlochmoidart
MOIDART
Gaskan
Scamodale
Stronchreggan
Ach'an Todhair
Ardmolich
Loch Moidart
Brunery
Gorstanvorran
SGOR AN TARMACHAIN 756
Cona Glen
770 STOB COIRE A'CHEARCAILL
Druimarbin
Glen Hurich
786 BEINN MHEADHOIN
Conaglen House
Blarmachfoldach
Dalnabreck
Dalelia
Polloch
Glenhurich
Loch Doilet
888 SGURR DHOMHNUILL
Scaddle
Aryhoulan
Inverscaddle Bay
Coruanan Lodge
CLAISH MOSS
Ardshealach
Kinlochan
Glen Scaddle
SUNART
Ardgour
SGURR NA H-EANCHAINNE 730
616 BEINN NA GUCAIG
Kiachnish
Resipole
845 BEINN RESIPOL
ARIUNDLE CENTRE
ARIUNDLE OAKWOOD
Glen Gour
Glenrigh Forest
LOCH SUNART
Ariundle
Scotstown
Strontian
701
Ardgour
Clovullin
Corran
Corran Narrows
Inchree
Anaheilt
Sallachan
Keppanach
Onich
GLENCRIPESDALE
Ardnastang
885 GARBH BHEINN
615
Camuschoirk
Glen Tarbert
Sallachan Pt.
A82
North Ballachulish
Liddesdale
Tarbert
Inversanda Bay
Inversanda
LOCH LINNHE
HIGHLAND MYSTERYWORLD
Glencoe
516 MEALL AN DAMHAIN
NM
South Ballachulish
Ballachulish
A828
583 CREACH BHEINN
Kentallen
582 BEINN NAM BEATHRACH
B8043
Glenduror Forest
Lochuisge
765 FUAR BHEINN
Kilmalieu
947
A884
Loch Uisge
Rubha Mor
Duror
571
D
Gleann Dubh
Cuil Bay
Beinn a'Bheithir
Glen an Fhiodh
Eilean Balnagowan
Keil
Glen Duror
Beach
Kingairloch
Salachan Glen
Camasnacroise
Loch a'Choire
Loch Arienas
879 FRAOCHAIDH
Acharn
739 BEINN MHEADHOIN
KINGAIRLOCH
Gleann Geal
Shuna I.
655
Appin House
959 BEINN FHIONNLAIDH
Claggan
137
Glen Stockdale
Elleric
Glen Creran
ARDTORNISH GARDENS
Loch Tearnait
A828
Fasnacloich
Achranich
437 BEINN A' CHAISIL
Portnacroish
An Iola
Invercreran
Glen Ure
Rannoch
KINLOCHLAICH HOUSE GARDENS
BEINN CHURALAIN 546
GLASDRUM WOOD
Loch Aline
Loch nan Clach
Glensanda
Appin
Glasdrum
937 BEINN SGULAIRD
E
Strath of Appin
Creagan
Port Ramsay
Port Appin
Druimavuic
GLAIS BHEINN 479
AN SLEAGHACH 513
LYNN OF
Clachan
Eriska
North Shian
839 BEINN TRILLEACHAN
ARDTORNISH CASTLE
Eignaig
South Creagan
Loch Creran
South Shian
Allt Easach
Lismore
B8045
LORN
Barcaldine
810 CREACH BHEINN
Abhainn Dalach
Inninmore Bay
Garbh Shlios
Camas Gorm
Achnacroish
SCOTTISH SEA LIFE SANCTUARY
Barcaldine Forest
LYNN OF LORN
LORN
Scallastle Bay
Rubha an Ridire
Bernera I.
130
Achinduin
Baravullin
Ferlochan
131
Kilcheran
Kiel Crofts
BENDERLOCH
Gleann Salach
Java
Craignure Bay
Eilean Dubh
Benderloch
B845
Ledaig
Craignure
MULL AND WEST HIGHLAND NARROW GAUGE RAILWAY
Achnaba
Ardmucknish Bay
ARDCHATTAN PRIORY GARDENS
ARDCHATTAN PRIORY
715 BEINN MHEADHONACH
LOCH ETIVE
Duart Bay
Duart Pt.
0:50
A828
TOROSAY CASTLE & GARDEN
DUART CASTLE
Eilean Musdile 0:45
Eilean Mor
DUNSTAFFNAGE CASTLE
North Connel
Connel
Black Crofts
FALLS OF LORA
Glen Liver
Lochdon
Dunbeg
Achnacloich
ACHNACLOICH GARDEN
Bonawe
Glen Noe
CASTLEBAY 5:10 COLL 2:40 TIREE 3:40 LOCHBOISDALE 5:15
Ganavan
A85
BONAWE IRON FURNACE
INVERAWE FISHERIES AND SMOKERIES EXHIBITION
A849
Loch Don
Dunollie
OBAN LODGE
MCCAIG'S TOWER
Black Lochs
Fearnoch Forest
Brochroy
Taynuilt
Ichrachan
BEN CRUACHAN 1126
Grass Pt.
OBAN VISITOR CENTRE
OBAN DISTILLERY
Altnacraig
OBAN RARE BREEDS FARM PARK
BARGUILLEAN GARDENS
Bridge of Awe
Pass of Brander
Cruachan Res.
COLONSAY 2:20
Kerrera
Oban
GLEN NANT
Awe
Glen Nant
897
Falls of Cruachan
Loch Spelve
0 1 2 3 4 5 6 miles
0 1 2 3 4 5 6 7 8 9 10km
Glenamachrie
383
Glen Lonan
Loch Nell
CRUACHAN DAM VISITOR CENTRE
Gallanach
Barran
515
Loch Nant
Loch Tromlee
Kilbride
Kilmore

Gairlochy
Glen Loy
Glen Loy Forest
Strone
Muirshearlich
Kilmonivaig
Brackletter
Highbridge
COMMANDO MEMORIAL
Spean Bridge
Inverroy
Roybridge
Bohuntine
Bohenie
Achluachrach
Murlaggan
Roughburn
A86
Killiechonate
Spean
MONESSIE FALLS
Braes o'Lochaber
GLEN SPEAN
1049 BEINN A' CHAORUINN
Moy Forest
Moy
Moy Lodge
1049 GEAL CHARN
146
147
TOR CASTLE
A82
B8004
Leanachan Forest
Banavie
NEPTUNE'S STAIRCASE LOCKS
Torlundy
NEVIS RANGE SKI CENTRE
Caol
Lochyside
INVERLOCHY CASTLE
Inverlochy
BEN NEVIS DISTILLERY VISITOR CENTRE
Claggan
Fort William
Achintee
WEST HIGHLAND MUSEUM
GLEN NEVIS VISITOR CENTRE
GLEN NEVIS
Glen Nevis House
Water of Nevis
The Cour
724 BEINN CHLIANAIG
Fersit
Allt Làire
1087 BEINN A'CHLACHAIR
Allt Cam
1177 STOB CHOIRE CLAURIGH
1106
Lairig Leacach
Allt na Lairige
1115 STOB COIRE EASAIN
LOCH TREIG
1046 CHNO DEARG
Loch Ghuilbinn
Ossian
1114 AONACH BEAG
1344 BEN NEVIS
1234 AONACH BEAG
1094
Uisge Labhair
1148 BEN ALDER
Amhainn Rath
Creaguaineach Lodge
937 BEINN NA LAP
Corrour Shooting Lodge
Prince Charlie's Cave
Achriabhach
Glen Nevis
LOCH OSSIAN
Loch Ossian
Corrour Forest
952 SGOR GAIBHRE
Blar a'Chaorainn
1099 SGURR A' MHAIM
1130 BINNEIN MOR
630
583
Allt na Cairn
140
Rannoch Forest
WEST HIGHLAND WAY
MAMORE FOREST
Loch Eilde Beag
789
Loch Eilde Mor
Ciaran Water
906 LEUM UILLEIM
796 MAM NA GUALAINN
Kinlochmore
Kinlochleven
THE ALUMINIUM STORY
B863
Leven
BLACKWATER RESERVOIR
Black Water
Loch Leven
867
GLENCOE AND NORTH LORN FOLK MUSEUM
AONACH 967
953
GLENCOE
NN
Rannoch Station
B846
GLENCOE VISITOR CENTRE
Glen Coe
Altnafeadh
857 BEINN A' CHRULAISTE
Black Corries Lodge
739 STOB NA CRUAICHE
Loch Eigheach
Gaur
Bridge of Gaur
BEN NEVIS AND GLEN COE
Kingshouse Hotel
Loch Gaineamhach
Loch Laidon
1150 BIDEAN NAM BIAN
925
Coupall
Royal Forest
GLENCOE SKI CENTRE
Etive
A82
RANNOCH MOOR
Allt Camghouran
994 SGOR NA H-ULAIDH
Dalness
MUSEUM OF SCOTTISH SKIING AND MOUNTAINEERING
Glen Etive
Alltchaorunn
1188
547
Loch Bà
931 MEALL BUIDHE
883 STOB DUBH
Allt Coire a Chaolain
1099 CLACH LEATHAD
Loch na h-Achlaise
Water of Tulla
Inverchanan
Glenceitlein
BLACK MOUNT
Loch an Daimh
879
Eas Daimh
Gualachulain
Allt Dochard
1090 STOB GHABHAR
WEST HIGHLAND WAY
Loch Tulla
Achallader
907 MEALL BUIDHE
960 STUCHD AN LOCHAIN
1044 STOB COIR'AN ALBANNAICH
Black Mount
1081 BEINN A' CHREACHAIN
Forest Lodge
Pubil
Cashlie
1078 BEN STARAV
Loch Dochard
Inveroran Hotel
Loch Lyon
Stronuich Reservoir
953 BEINN MHANACH
957 BEINN NAN AIGHENAN
Allt Hallater
1004 BIENN AN DOTHAIDH
Bridge of Orchy
BEINN HEASGARNICH 1076
639
1076 BEINN DÒRAIN
Allt Chonoghlais
Kenknock
Glen Lochay
701
Orchy
Glen Kinglass
A82
1047 CREAG MHOR
Breadalbane
796 BEINN MHIC-MHONAIDH
GLEN ORCHY
Arichastlich
901 BEINN ODHAR
989 BEINN EUNAICH
840 BEINN UDLAIDH
937 BEINN CHEATHAICH
Glen Strae
B8074
1025 BEN CHALLUM
Allt Mhoille
Glen Lochy
A85
Arrivain
Lochy
Clifton
Tyndrum
West Burn
Auchlyne
Allt Riobain
131
132
B8077
KILCHURN CASTLE
Lochawe
Stronmilchan
Strath of Orchy
Achnafalnich
880
Cononish
Strath Fillan
GLEN DOCHART
Inverlochy
Lochdochart House
A85
Dalmally
BEN LUI
A82
Loch Dochart
Loch Iubhair
MCINTYRE MONUMENT
Innis Chonain
1130 BEN LUI
Inverherive
Crianlarich
Benmore
Portnellan
Eas

Moy
Moy Lodge
Lochan na h-Earba
BEINN EILDE
Pattack
Gaick Forest
Loch Bhrodainn
Allt Gharbh Ghaig
A9
Ardverikie Forest
1049 GEAL CHARN
147
Loch Erich Forest
774 CREAGAN MOR
941 CARN NA CAIM
148
Loch an Duin
Allt Loraich
Loch Pattack
Ben Alder Lodge
Cama Choire
Sronphadruig Lodge
917
1087 BEINN A'CHLACHAIR
Allt Cam
936 A'BHUIDHEANACH BHEAG
Dail-na-Mine Forest
816 SRON A'CHLEIRICH
Loch Ghuilbinn
Allt a'Chaoil-reidhe
Ben Alder Forest
LOCH ERICHT
934 BEINN UDLAMAIN
803 THE SOW OF ATHOLL
Dalnacardoch Forest
FOREST
1114 AONACH BEAG
Dalnaspidal Lodge
Edendon Water
ATHOLL
Allt Glas Choire
Allt a'Mhuilinn
Ossian
Loch a' Bhealaich Bheithe
Corrievarkie Lodge
Dalnaspidal Forest
Allt a'Chireachain
Uisge Labhair
1148 BEN ALDER
Allt na Glaise
Loch Garry
775 MEALL NA LEITREACH
Dalnacardoch Lodge
GLEN GARRY
Loch Ossian
Corrour Shooting Lodge
Prince Charlie's Cave
855
Talla Bheith Forest
Loch Con
Garry
Corrour Forest
952 SGOR GAIBHRE
139
Allt Ghlas
Loch Errochty
Rannoch Forest
841 BEINN MHOLACH
612
NN
GRAMPIAN
Trinafour
Dalchalloch
B847
Errochty Water
GLEN ERROCHT
515 SRON BHEAG
Tummel Forest
891 BEINN A'CHUALLAICH
477
Killichonan Burn
Aulich Burn
Ericht
Craiganor Lodge
Kinloch Rannoch
B846
Dunalastair
Tummel Bridge
B8019
Dunalastair Water
Tummel
Bridge of Ericht
Killichonan
LOCH RANNOCH
Foss
Rannoch Station
Inverhadden
Carie
Loch Eigheach
Gaur
Finnart
Bridge of Gaur
Camghouran
Black Wood of Rannoch
Loch Kinardochy
Innerhadden Burn
Rannoch
Dall Burn
Allt na Bogair
1083 SCHIEHALLION
TAY FOREST
Allt Camghouran
Forest
Allt Mor
LOCH RANNOCH AND GLEN LYON
GLENGOULANDIE DEER PARK
B846
745 MEALL A'MHUIC
1042 CARN MAIRG
Keltney Burn
Appin of Dull
931 MEALL BUIDHE
1029 CARN GORM
Keltneyburn
Inververvar
ST FILLAN'S CHURCH & FORTINGALL YEW
Camusvrachan
Loch an Daimh
GLEN LYON GALLERY
Lyon
Fortingall
Taymouth Castle
Innerwick
Eas Daimh
Bridge of Balgie
Allt Conait
Gallin
Kenmore
A827
907 MEALL BUIDHE
960 STUCHD AN LOCHAIN
Allt Bail a'Mhuilinn
Allt Gleann Da-Eig
Fearnan
SCOTTISH CRANNOG CENTRE
Remony
780
1118
Acharn
Falls of Acharn
Pubil
Cashlie
Glen Lyon
Lawers Burn
LOCH TAY
Loch Lyon
Stronuich Reservoir
1214 BEN LAWERS
BEN LAWERS
Loch na Lairige
716 BEINN BHREAC
MEALL NAN TARMACHAN
Lawers
Quaich
1043
Ardtalnaig
BEIN HEASGARNICH
1076
BEN LAWERS VISITOR CENTRE (N.T.S.)
Carie
Gleann a'Chilleine
Kenknock
Glen Lochay
Breadalbane
Milton Morenish
888
Morenish
1047
F
FALLS OF LOCHAY AND FISH LIFT
Ardeonaig
Boreland
Finlarig
Finglen Burn
MOIRLANICH LONGHOUSE
KILLIN
Killin
BREADALBANE FOLKLORE CENTRE
937 BEINN CHEATHAICH
Achmore
637
879 CREAG UCHDAG
Allt Ribhainn
FALLS OF DOCHART
Auchlyne West Burn
Dochart
Loch Lednock Reservoir
Invergeldie Burn
931 BEN CHONZIE
A827
132
Auchlyne
133
Ardchyle
A85
Beich Burn
Glen Ogle
Invergeldie
Glen Lednock
Loch Iubhair
Dochart
Benmore
Portnellan
672 SRON MHOR
Comrie
0 1 2 3 4 5 6 miles
0 1 2 3 4 5 6 7 8 9 10km

CARN EALAR
AN SGARSOCH
Bynack Burn
CARN BHAC
Baddoch
UCHD A'CHLARSAIR
148
149
M O U N T A I N S
Tarf Water
BRAIGH SRON GHORM
BEINN DEARG
Glen Bruar
Bruar Lodge
BEINN IUTHARN MHOR
Loch nan Eun
Clunie Water
Loch Vrotachan
GLENSHEE SKI CENTRE
THE CAIRNWELL
Devil's Elbow
Caenlochan Forest
CARN AN TUIRC
GLAS MAOL
GLAS TULAICHEAN
Loch Loch
Tilt
O F A T H O L L
Forest Lodge
FINALTY HILL
Isla
BEINN A'GHLO
BEN GULABIN
Glen Diridh
Glen Tilt
Glenlochsie
MONAMEANACH
CARN LIATH
BEN VURICH
Gleann Fearnach
Spittal of Glenshee
BEN EARB
Loch Beanie
Auchavan
DUCHRAY HILL
BADENDU HILL
Falls of the Bruar
BLAIR CASTLE
CLAN DONNACHAIDH MUSEUM
Bruar Water
Pitagowan
Calvine
Struan
Blair Atholl
BLAIR ATHOLL MILL
Old Bridge of Tilt
Lude House
Ballentoul
BLAIR ATHOLL DISTILLERY
TULACH HILL
ATHOLL COUNTRY COLLECTION
Aldclune
Killiecrankie
KILLIECRANKIE VISITOR CENTRE
Bonskeid House
Glen Girnaig
MEALL UAINE
Glen Shee
Dalnaglar Castle
Meikle Forter
Folda
Cray
MOUNT BLAIR
Brewlands Bridge
Dalnavaid
Tarvie
Straloch
Enochdhu
Glen Brerachan
BEN VRACKIE
Ashintully Castle
Loch Bhac
LOCH TUMMEL
Tressait
Queen's View
QUEEN'S VIEW CENTRE
Falls of Tummel
LINN OF TUMMEL
Moulin
PITLOCHRY
Pitlochry
CREAG DHUBH
Kirkmichael
Blacklunans
STRATHARDLE
CAIRN GIBBS
Loch Faskally
HYDRO-ELECTRIC VISITOR CENTRE
Balmore
SCOTTISH PLANT COLLECTORS GARDEN
THEATRE FESTIVAL
EDRADOUR DISTILLERY
Milton of Edradour
BLAIR ATHOLL DISTILLERY VISITOR CENTRE
Loch Broom
MEALL REAMHAR
KNOCK OF BALMYLE
Black Water
Forest of Alyth
NN
NO
FARRAGON HILL
Loch Derculich
E S T P A R K
Tummel
Milton of Dalcapon
Ballintuim
Ardle
Strathtay
Ballechin
CHILDHOOD HERITAGE MUSEUM
CREAG NAM MIAL
Tulliemet
Grandtully
Tay
Ballinluig
Edradynate
CLUNY HOUSE GARDENS
Little Ballinluig
ST MARY'S CHURCH
Balnaguard
Logierait
Blackcraig Forest
Netherton
Forest of Clunie
Loch Ordie
Loch Benachally
Bridge of Cally
Tullymurdoch
CASTLE MENZIES
Camserney
Weem
Dull
WADE'S BRIDGE
Aberfeldy
ABERFELDY DISTILLERY & DEWAR'S WORLD OF WHISKY
Falls of Moness
BOLFRACKS GARDEN
Balnaguard Burn
Balmacneil
Kindallachan
Cochrage Muir
Tullyfergus
Riemore
Lornty Burn
Middleton
Bishopric
Kincraigie
Guay
Dowally
DEUCHARY HILL
Loch Skiach
Riechip
Westfields of Rattray
Lornty
Dalguise
Butterstone
Craigvinean Forest
Loch Kennard
Forneth
Achalader
Blairgowrie
Kinloch
Rattray
Urlar Burn
RIVER TAY
SCOTTISH HORSE REGIMENTAL MUS
Loch of Lowes
LOCH OF LOWES NATURE RESERVE
Concraigie
Loch of Clunie
Loch of Drumellie
Rosemount
Glen Cochill
Loch Hoil
Ballinloan Burn
Tombane Burn
CATH
Dunkeld
Little Dunkeld
Snaigow House
Clunie
Craigie
Kirkton of Lethendy
Scotston
THE HERMITAGE
Inver
Birnam
Lunan Burn
WATERFALL
Ballinlick
MEALL DEARG
Garrow
Trochry
Spittalfield
Delvine
Caputh
Perth
Glen Quaich
Cablea
Strathbraan
Obney Hills
Gellyburn
Meikleour
BEECH HEDGE
Kinclaven
Isla
Loch Freuchie
Braan
Upper Obney
Muir of Thorn
Murthly
Ardoch
Woodside
Burrelton
Amulree
Balquharn
Waterloo
Cargill
MEALL NAM FUARAN
Corrymuckloch
Ordie Burn
Bankfoot
Airntully
Whitefield
and
Little Glenshee
Tullybelton
Stanley
West Tofts
Saucher
Collace
Milton Burn
MEALL NAN CAORAICH
Wolfhill
Shochie Burn
Newton
Logiealmond Lodge
Guildtown
Kinrossie
Kirkton of Collace
Kinross
GLEN ALMOND
Logiealmond
Chapelhill
Downhill
Newmill
St Martins
Harrietfield
Moneydie
Balbeggie
133
134
MEALL TARSUINN
Luncarty
Loch Turret Reservoir
Shaggie Burn
Buchanty
Redgorton
PERTH
Almond
Pitcairngreen
CAITHNESS GLASS
PERTH MART VISITOR CENTRE
SCONE PALACE
Glen Turret
Methven
Almondbank
Huntingtower
Lochty
Muirton
Scone
Keillour
MUSEUM & ART GALLERY
POLE HILL
142

Baddoch
Glen Callater
Loch Callater
Dubh Loch
Glas-allt Shiel
Spittal of Glenmuick
Loch Muick
Glen Mark
Water of Mark
Burn of Branny
Water of Tarf
Glen Lee
Invermark Lodge
Auchronie
AWEE
Tarfside
Cairncross
Loch Lee
Inchgrundle
CAIRN BANNOCH
BROAD CAIRN
AN SOCACH
CARN AN TUIRC
TOLMOUNT
Clunie Water
Loch Vrotachan
GLENSHEE SKI CENTRE
THE CAIRNWELL
Devil's Elbow
GLAS MAOL
Caenlochan Forest
Glen Doll
Glendoll Lodge
Glendoll Forest
Braedownie
LAIR OF ALDARARIE
Water of Unich
MUCKLE CAIRN
Loch Brandy
Glen Effock
Water of Saughs
CRUYS
WEST KNOCK
CORRIE FEE
FINALTY HILL
DRIESH
BEN GULABIN
Clova
WHITE HILL
Hunthill Lodge
Wheen
Rottal
FINBRACKS
Angus
Glen Clova
MONAMEANACH
Spittal of Glenshee
Auchavan
Loch Beanie
Glen Prosen
Glenprosen Lodge
Kilburn
BADENDUN HILL
Balnaboth
Glenprosen Village
Glen Shee
MEALL UAINE
UCHRAY HILL
NO
Glenisla Forest
AULD DARKNEY
Clachnabrain
Glenmoy
Dalnaglar Castle
Meikle Forter
Folda
South Esk
Auchnacree
Cray
MOUNT BLAIR
Glenhead Farm
Easter Lednathie
Glenogil
Ogil
Fern
Ashintully Castle
Brewlands Bridge
Backwater Res.
Glenquiech
Freuchies
Hornieheugh
CAPTAIN SCOTT & DR. WILSON CAIRN
Dykehead
Newmill of Inshewan
Kirkmichael
Blacklunans
Kirkton of Glenisla
CAT LAW
Bellaty
CREIGH HILL
Balintore
Pearsie
Cortachy
Memus
Tannadice
CAIRN GIBBS
Black Water
Dykends
Balloch
Inverquharity
Murthill
Finavon
KNOCK OF BALMYLE
Forest of Alyth
MILE HILL
Shielhill
Oathlaw
Loch of Lintrathen
PEEL FARM TRAIL
Kirkton of Kingoldrum
Northmuir
Bridgend of Lintrathen
Kinnordy
LOCH OF KINNORDY NATURE RESERVE
Kirriemuir
BARRIE'S BIRTHPLACE
Carse Gray
Ardle
BALDUFF HILL
REEKIE LINN WATERFALL
Bridge of Craigisla
Auchrannie
Westmuir
Mosside
Lunanhead
RESTENNETH PRIORY
Blackcraig Forest
Netherton
Tullymurdoch
Kirkton of Airlie
Mains of Ballindarg
Padanaram
Forfar
FORFAR LOCH
THE MEFFAN GALLERY & MUSEUM
Bridge of Cally
Bamff
Craigton
Drumgley
Kingsmuir
Cochrage Muir
Shanzie
ST. ORLAND'S STONE
Lornty Burn
Tullyfergus
Ruthven
Leys of Cossans
Dean Water
Caldhame
Lownie Moor
Middleton
Alyth
Ruthven House
EASSIE SCULPTURED STONE
GLAMIS CASTLE
New Alyth
Westfields of Rattray
Glamis
Douglastown
Lornty
Balhary
Castleton
Charleston
Thornton
Kirkton
Achalader
Blairgowrie
Kinloch
Rattray
Leitfie
MEIGLE MUSEUM
Balkeerie
Eassie
ANGUS FOLK MUSEUM
Foffarty
Loch of Clunie
Loch of Drumellie
Rosemount
River Ericht
Kinloch
Meigle
Kirkinch
Milton
Inverarity
Gateside
Whigstreet
Clunie
Craigie
Muirton
Ardblair
Arthurstone
Wester Denoon
ARK HILL
Kirkton of Lethendy
Lunan Burn
Ardler
Newbigging
Newtyle
Nether Handwick
Gallowfauld
Spittalfield
Delvine
Coupar Angus
Keillor
Sidlaw Hills
Caputh
Meikleour
BEECH HEDGE
Kettins
Hallyburton House
Coldstream
Tay
Isla
Kinclaven
Marketmill
Long Loch
Bonnyton
Balkemback
Tealing
Monikie
Murthly
Campmuir
Kirkton of Auchterhouse
Newbigging
Ardoch
Woodside
Burrelton
Leys
Lundie
Auchterhouse
Leoch
Muir of Pert
Inveraldie
East March
Wellbank
Cargill
Pitcur
Buckler heads
Newbigging
Dronley
Bridgefoot
Burnside of Duntrune
Kellas
Drumsturdy
Whitefield
Littleton
Muirhead
Birkhill
CLATTO
SOUTERRAIN ARDESTIE
West Tofts
Stanley
Wolfhill
Saucher
KING'S SEAT
Fowlis
CAMPERDOWN AND TEMPLETON WOODS
Liff
Downfield
Fintry
Baldovie
Collace
Douglas & Angus
Guildtown
Kinrossie
Kirkton of Collace
Knapp
Denhead of Gray
Dundee
Craigie
West Ferry
Monifieth
St Martins
Abernyte
Benvie
Lochee
MILLS OBSERVATORY
VERDANT WORKS
MUS. AND ART GALL.
BROUGHTY CASTLE
Barnhill
Newmiln
Bandirran
Rossie Priory
Invergowrie
Stannergate
FRIGATE UNICORN
Broughty Ferry
BROUGHTY CASTLE MUSEUM
Dowhill
Braes of the Carse
Ballindean
Longforgan
Dundee
Tay Bridge
Balbeggie
Tayport
Luncarty
Kinnaird
Inchture
Castle Huntly
Kingoodie
UNIVERSITY BOTANIC GARDENS
DUNDEE
DISCOVERY POINT
Newport-on-Tay
Scotscraig
PERTH
PERTH MART VISITOR CENTRE
Scone
Kilspindie
POLE HILL
Grange
Woodhaven
Tay Rail Bridge
Wormit
Tentsmuir Forest
MORTON
MEGGINCH
Muirton
MUSEUM & ART GALLERY
0 1 2 3 4 5 6 miles
0 1 2 3 4 5 6 7 8 9 10 km

Burn of Tennet
778 MOUNT BATTOCK
Glen Dye
525 MELUNCART
Drumtochty Forest
464
Glenfarquhar Lodge
Tannachie
Carmont
Newbigging
Mains of Dellavaird
BURNS FAMILY MEMORIALS
Drumlithie
Glenbervie
Fiddes
Barras
Mill of Uras
Thornyhive Bay
Crawton
FOWLSHEUGH NATURE RESERVE
Crawton Bay
Catterline
Braidon Bay
Todhead Point
Roadside of Catterline
Pitforthie
Mondynes
Cairn o' Mount
Drumtochty Castle
THE RETREAT GLEN ESK FOLK MUS.
Millden Lodge
Clatterin Bridge
Strath Finella
Auchenblae
Glensaugh
Monboddo House
Brownmuir
East Cairnbeg
Fordoun
Parkneuk
Arbuthnott
Roadside of Kinneff
Kinneff
GRASSIC GIBBON CENTRE
ARBUTHNOTT CHURCH
ARBUTHNOTT HOUSE GARDENS
Mains of Allardice
Little John's Haven
Inverbervie
Bervie Bay
North Esk
Auchmull
Mains of Balnakettle
FASQUE HOUSE
Thainston
FETTERCAIRN DISTILLERY VISITOR CENTRE
Fettercairn
Howe of the Mearns
Scotston
678 HILL OF WIRREN
Bent
Mains of Thornton
Laurencekirk
Tulloch
Dalbog
Inch of Arnhall
Meikle Strath
Garvock
Garvock Hill
Redford
DAMSIDE GARDEN HERBS & ARBORETUM
Gourdon
Witton
Gannochy
Sauchieburn
Benholm
EDZELL CASTLE AND GARDENS
Edzell
Luthermuir
Luther Water
Dykelands
MILL OF BENHOLM
Bridgend
Balfield
West Water
Dunlappie
Johnshaven
440
Tillyarblet
BROWN CATERTHUN
North Water Bridge
North Esk
Marykirk
WHITE CATERTHUN
Inchbare
Pert
Ecclesgreig
Kirkton of Menmuir
Tigerton
Newtonmill
Craigo
Lochside
St Cyrus
Milton Ness
Logie Pert
Logie
Morphie
ST CYRUS
Mains of Balhall
Lochty
Belliehill
Little Brechin
Keithock
Muirton of Ballochy
Pathhead
West Muir
Trinity
Hillside
Kirkhill
BRECHIN CASTLE CENTRE
Brechin
HOUSE OF DUN
Dun
CALEDONIAN RAILWAY
Careston Castle
PICTAVIA
CATHEDRAL & ROUND TOWER
South Esk
Bridge of Dun
Montrose Basin
Montrose
MUSEUM AND ART GALLERY
Scurdie Ness
WILLIAM LAMB MEMORIAL STUDIO
Aldbar Castle
Kinnaird Castle
Barnhead
Inchbraoch
Netherton
Mains of Melgund
Middle Drums
MONTROSE BASIN NATURE RESERVE VISITOR CENTRE
Ferryden
Farnell
Bonnyton
Maryton
Kirkton of Craig
ABERLEMNO SCULPTURED STONES
Aberlemno
Montreathmont Forest
Carcary
Long Craig
Fishtown of Usan
Pitkennedy
Dunninald
Rossie Moor
Westerton
Boddin Pt.
252
Turin
Montreathmont Moor
Rescobie
Dubton
Bolshan
Braehead of Lunan
Reswallie
Balgavies
Glasterlaw
Lunan
NO
LUNAN BAY
Burnside
Milldens
Guthrie
Kinnell
Redcastle
Dunnichen
Letham
Pitmuies
HOUSE OF PITMUIES GARDEN
Friockheim
Boysack
Inverkeilor
Lang Craig
Lunan Water
Chapelton
Ethie Mains
Idvies
Red Head
Craichie
Leysmill
Cauldcots
Ethie Castle
Tulloes
Drunkendub
Letham Grange
Mosston
Colliston
Auchmithie
Greystone
Redford
Marywell
Meg's Craig
Kirkbuddo
St Vigeans
ST VIGEANS MUSEUM
Hayshead
Hayhillock
Carmyllie
Denhead of Arbilot
Cliffburn
The Deil's Heid
ARBROATH ABBEY
CROMBIE
Arbirlot
Arbroath
SIGNAL TOWER MUSEUM
Elliot
Res.
Kirkton of Monikie
Balmirmer
Craigton
Salmond's Muir
Monikie Burn
CARLUNGIE SOUTERRAIN
Muirdrum
East Haven
BARRY MILL
Panbride
Barry
Mains of Ardestie
Carnoustie
CARNOUSTIE
Barry Links
Buddon Ness
TENTSMUIR POINT
150
151
135
A90
A92
A935
A933
A934
A932
A930
B974
B966
B967
B9120
B9134
B9113
B965
B961
B978
B9128
B9127
A937
70
50
5
6
7
8
A
B
C
D
E
F
G

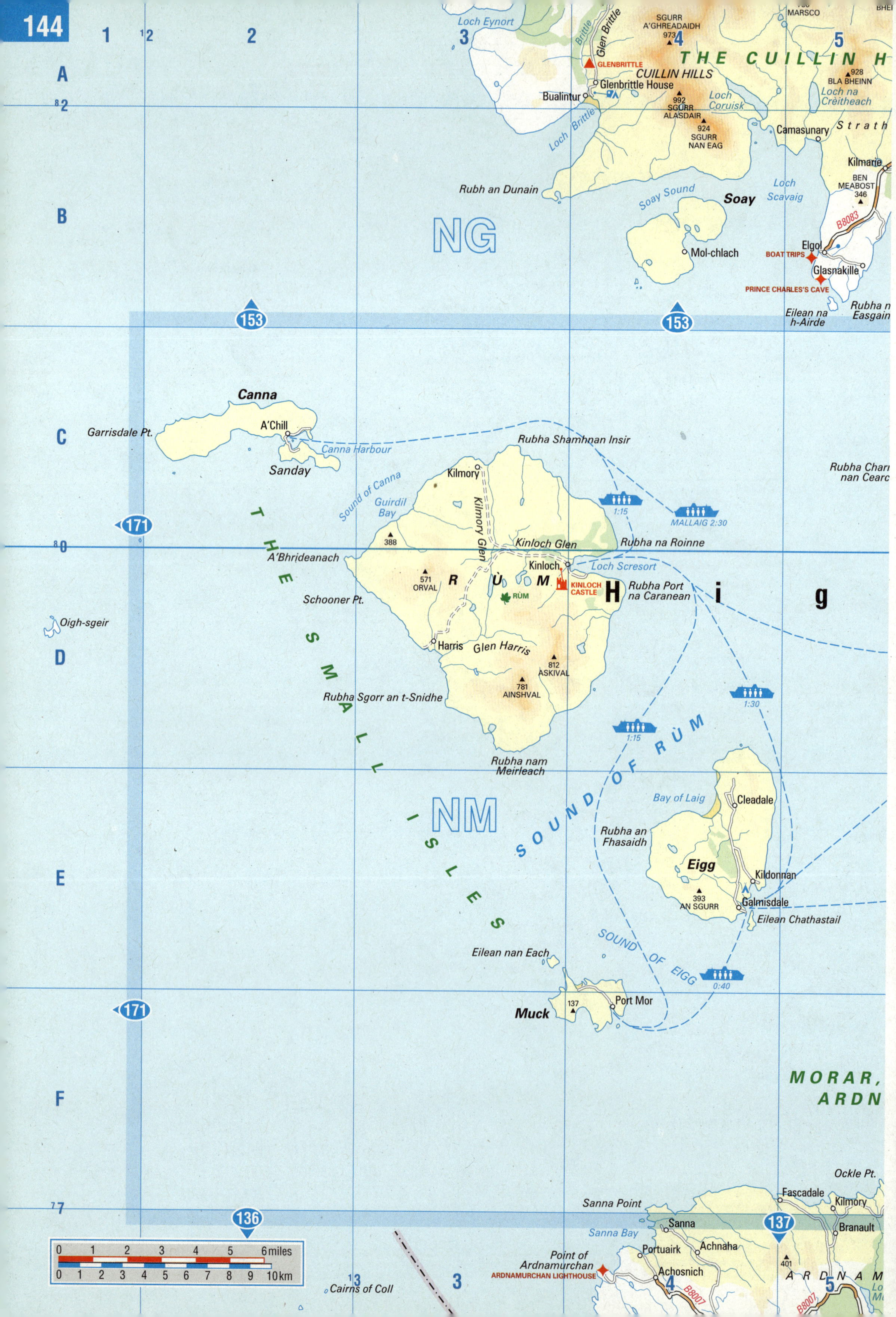

Loch Eynort
Glen Brittle
Brittle
SGURR A'GHREADAIDH 973
MARSCO
THE CUILLIN H
GLENBRITTLE
CUILLIN HILLS
Glenbrittle House
Bualintur
928 BLA BHEINN
Loch na Crèitheach
992 SGURR ALASDAIR
Loch Coruisk
924 SGURR NAN EAG
Loch Brittle
Camasunary
Strath
Kilmarie
BEN MEABOST 346
Rubh an Dunain
Soay Sound
Soay
Loch Scavaig
B8083
NG
Mol-chlach
Elgol
BOAT TRIPS
Glasnakille
PRINCE CHARLES'S CAVE
Eilean na h-Airde
Rubha n Easgain
153
153
Canna
A'Chill
Garrisdale Pt.
Canna Harbour
Sanday
Rubha Shamhnan Insir
Rubha Chari nan Cearc
Kilmory
Sound of Canna
Guirdil Bay
Kilmory Glen
1:15
MALLAIG 2:30
171
388
Kinloch Glen
Rubha na Roinne
THE SMALL ISLES
A'Bhrideanach
Kinloch
Loch Scresort
571 ORVAL
RÙM
KINLOCH CASTLE
Rubha Port na Caranean
Hig
Schooner Pt.
Oigh-sgeir
Harris
Glen Harris
812 ASKIVAL
781 AINSHVAL
Rubha Sgorr an t-Snidhe
1:30
1:15
SOUND OF RÙM
Rubha nam Meirleach
Bay of Laig
Cleadale
NM
Rubha an Fhasaidh
Eigg
Kildonnan
393 AN SGURR
Galmisdale
Eilean Chathastail
SOUND OF EIGG
Eilean nan Each
0:40
171
137
Port Mor
Muck
MORAR, ARDN
Ockle Pt.
Fascadale
Kilmory
Sanna Point
Sanna
Branault
136
137
Sanna Bay
Portuairk
Achnaha
401
Point of Ardnamurchan
ARDNAMURCHAN LIGHTHOUSE
Achosnich
ARDNAM
B8007
B8007
Cairns of Coll
0 1 2 3 4 5 6 miles
0 1 2 3 4 5 6 7 8 9 10 km

RED HILLS
732
BROADFORD
Corry
Broadford Bay
Waterloo
Broadford
Lower Breakish
Upper Breakish
Harrapool
Skulamus
WORLD OF WOOD
SKYE ENVIRONMENTAL CENTRE
A87
A851
155
Torrin
Kilbride
Suardal
B8083
Strath
Loch Slapin
Kirkibost
301
Heast
Kinloch
Drumfearn
Loch na Dal
Rubha Suisnish
Loch Eishort
Ord
Duisdalemore
Ornsay
Isleornsay
Camuscross
DUNSGIATH CASTLE
Tokavaig
Tarskavaig
Tarskavaig Pt.
Achnacloich
Teangue
KNOCK CASTLE
Knock Bay
Ferindonald
Kilbeg
Kilmore
Armadale Castle
ARMADALE GARDENS
Glen Meadhonach
CLAN DONALD CENTRE
ARMADALE
Armadale Bay
280
Calligarry
Ardvasar
Aird of Sleat
Ard Thurinish
0:25
Point of Sleat
SLEAT
SOUND OF SLEAT
Highland
SGURR NA COINNICH
739
KYLERHEA OTTER HAVEN
Kyle Rhea
Ferry
Glen Arroch
Allt Mòr
Kylerhea
610
BEN ASLAK
Bernera
Galltair
Glenelg
BERNERA BARRACKS
Glenelg Bay
Eilanreach
GLENELG BROCHS
Abhainn a' Ghlinne Bhig
Balvraid
Glen More
Upper Sandaig
742
BEINN A'CHAPAILL
Sandaig Is.
974
BEINN SGRITHEALL
BEINN NAN CAORACH
774
Arnisdale
Glen Arnisdale
Corran
LOCH HOURN
Ardintoul Pt.
Letterfearn
603
BEINN A'CHUIRN
Keppoch
Inverinate
Ruarach
Loch Duich
Ratagan
RATAGAN
Ault a'chruinn
Carn-gorm
Invershiel
Shiel Bridge
779
Glenshiel Forest
1010
THE SADDLE
146
Kinlochhourn Forest
713
DRUIM FADA
879
BUIDHE BHEINN
Kinloch
Rubha Ard Slisneach
Inverguseran
785
BEINN NA CAILLICH
Barrisdale Bay
Airor
NG
KNOYDART
1020
LADHAR BHEINN
894
Glen Barrisdale
Gleann na Guiserein
Sandaig
Sandaig Bay
Scottas
LUINNE BHEINN
939
Abhainn Chosaidh
Gleann an Dubh-Lochain
Inverie
Inverie Bay
Rubha Raonuill
MALLAIG HERITAGE CENTRE
MALLAIG MARINE WORLD
Mallaig
522
946
MEALL BUIDHE
BEINN BHUIDHE
855
Camusrory
Carnach
1040
SGURR NA CICHE
Glasnacardoch
A830
1:30
Beoraidbeg
LOCH NEVIS
Stoul
Kylesknoydart
Kylesmorar
Bracara
Bracorina
North Morar
Tarbet
859
Glen Dessarry
Morar
Brinacory
Swordland
Kinlochmorar
LOCH MORAR
B8008
829
CARN MOR
Glen Pean
Scamadale
Lettermorar
Oban
718
AN STAC
Portnaluchaig
Bunacaimb
Eilean Ighe
Back of Keppoch
South Morar
Meoble
965
SGURR NAN COIREACHAN
963
SGURR THUILM
Luinga Bheag
Kinloid
Arisaig
NM
710
MEITH BHEINN
Luinga Mhor
Loch nan Ceall
599
SIDHEAN MOR
LOCH NAN UAMH CAIRN
Kinlochbeoraid
Druimindarroch
Loch Beoraid
1:00
796
SGURR AN UTHA
Polnish
A830
Ranochan
Loch nan Uamh
Lochailort
STATION MUSEUM
GLENFINNAN MONUMENT
Glen Finnan
Glen Dubh Lighe
Ardnish
Inverailort
Loch Eilt
Glenfinnan
SOUND OF ARISAIG
Laggan
A861
138
Eilean nan Gobhar
Loch Ailort
Alisary
869
DRUIM FIACLACH
A830
Drumsallie
Callop
Samalaman I.
Glenuig Bay
Roshven
882
ROIS-BHEINN
882
BEINN ODHAR BHEAG
Smirisary
Glenuig
MOIDART AND ARDNAMURCHAN
666
BEINN GAIRE
755
MEALL NAN CREAG LEAC
Glen Garvan
Eilean Shona
Inversanda
Kinlochmoidart
MOIDART
Scamodale
Rubha Aird Druimnich
Farquhar's Pt.
Gaskan
LOCH SHIEL
Cona Glen
CASTLE TIORAM
Loch Moidart
Ardmolich
SGOR AN TARMACHAIN
756
Ardtoe
Newton of Ardtoe
Brunery
Gorstanvorran
Ockle
Shielfoot
B8044
A861
Hurich
Kentra
Blain
137
Dalnabreck
Dalelia
Glen Hurich
786
BEINN MHEADHOIN
357
BEINN BHREAC
Kentra Bay
Moss
Polloch
Glenhurich
Loch Doilet
CLAISH MOSS
Acharacle
Ardshealach
Kinlochan
888
SGURR DHOMHNUILL
Glen Scaddle
SUNART
Ardgour
A
B
C
D
E
F
G
5
6
7
8
9

1
2
3
4
5
A
B
C
D
E
F
155
156
145
138
139
Killilan Forest
899
AONACH BUIDHE
1069
1086
AN RIABHACHAN
1150
SGURR NA LAPAICH
Glencannich Forest
Liatrie
Mullardoch House
East Benula Forest
Loch Mullardoch
Glen Cannich
Gleann Udalain
Allt-nan-sùgh
Sallachy
SGUMAN COINNTICH
879
Loch Long
Camas-luinie
Carnach
Allt na Doire Gairbhe
Glen Elchaig
Elchaig
Loch nan Eun
Loch na Leitreach
FALLS OF GLOMACH
Gleann Sithidh
West Benula Forest
Gleann A'Choilich
1005
1053
TOLL CREAGACH
1111
TOM A CHOINICH
1183
CARN EIGE
Gleann nam Fiadh
Auchertyre
A87
Nostie
Ardelve
Bundalloch
Dornie
EILEAN DONAN CASTLE
Glas Eilean
Totaig
Keppoch
634
Letterfearn
SGURR AN AIRGID
841
Dorusduain
SGURR NAN CEATHREAMHNAN
1151
GLEN AFFRIC
Affric Lodge
Glen Affric
Loch Affric
Inverinate
603
BEINN A'CHUIRN
Loch Duich
Ruarach
Morvich
Carn-gorm
Ault a'chruinn
Ratagan
RATAGAN
Inverhiel
Shiel Bridge
Loch a'Bhealaich
GLEN AFFRIC
Affric
Glenaffric
Forest
BEINN FADA OR BEN ATTOW
1032
Glen Gniomhaidh
GLEN AFFRIC
Allt Garbh
539
Guisachan
Allt Riabhach
KINTAIL
Kintail Forest
GLENELG BROCHS
Glen More
779
Balvraid
1067
FIVE SISTERS
979
CISTE DHUBH
888
AONACH SHASUINN
706
CARN A CHAOCHAIN
NG
NH
Glen Shiel
1027
1719
1120
A'CHRALAIG
Glenshiel Forest
1010
THE SADDLE
BEINN NAN CAORACH
774
1109
SGURR NAN CONBHAIREAN
Ceannacroc Forest
Doe
Cluanie Inn
Ceannacroc Lodge
SGURR AN LOCHAIN
1004
918
Arnisdale
Glen Arnisdale
Kinlochhourn Forest
Cluanie Forest
Cluanie Lodge
LOCH CLUANIE
Lundie
A887
Bun Loyne
Corran
LOCH HOURN
879
BUIDHE BHEINN
906
SGURR THIONAIL
Glen Quoich
1021
AONACH AIR CHRITH
Bunloinn Forest
Beinneun Forest
788
713
DRUIM FADA
Kinloch Hourn
1027
SGURR A'MHAORAICH
Highland
1035
GLEOURAICH
Loyne
LOCH LOYNE
Barrisdale Bay
KNOYDART
894
Glen Barrisdale
Glenquoich Forest
540
13
Abhainn Chosaidh
LOCH QUOICH
Kingie
Aultnaslat
Inchlaggan
Ardochy House
LUINNE BHEINN
939
Garry
Tomdoun
Glen Garry
Greenfield
946
MEALL BUIDHE
919
GAIRICH
Glen Kingie
Kingie
1003
SGURR MOR
Allt Choire a'Bhalachain
556
GLAS BHEINN
901
BEN TEE
Carnach
1040
SGURR NA CICHE
Glengarry Forest
656
MEALL BLAIR
Loch Blair
804
GEAL CHARN
935
SRON A'CHOIRE GHAIRBH
858
880
SGURR MHURLAGAIN
859
Glen Dessarry
Dessarry
Murlaggan
Strathan
LOCH ARKAIG
829
CARN MOR
Glen Pean
Pean
Ardechvie
Achnasaul
B8005
Clunes Forest
Altrua
Oban
718
AN STAC
Gleann Camgharaidh
727
Locheil
Forest
Inver Mallie
Clunes
LOCH LOCHY
965
SGURR NAN COIREACHAN
963
SGURR THUILM
987
GAOR BHEINN
Glen Mallie
Mallie
Achnacarry
Bunarkaig
A82
Gloy
Kinlochbeoraid
NM
NN
796
BEINN BHAN
CLAN CAMERON MUSEUM
Gairlochy
Stronaba
796
SGURR AN UTHA
Glen Finnan
Glen Dubh Lighe
Gleann Suileag
Glen Loy
Loy
GREAT GLEN WAY
Kilmonivaig
COMMANDO MEMORIAL
Spean Bridge
STATION MUSEUM
GLENFINNAN MONUMENT
Wauchan
Druim Fada
Glen Loy Forest
Strone
Bracklette
Highbridge
Glenfinnan
Muirshearlich
Lochy
Killiechonate
Callop
Kinlocheil
Fassfern
B8004
TOR CASTLE
Leanachan Forest
A830
LOCH EIL
TREASURES OF THE EARTH
Corpach
Banavie
NEPTUNE'S STAIRCASE LOCKS
Torlundy
NEVIS RANGE SKI CENTRE
882
A861
South Garvan
Duisky
Blaich
Caol
INVERLOCHY
Lochyside
Achaphubuil
0 1 2 3 4 5 6 miles
0 1 2 3 4 5 6 7 8 9 10 km

Muchrachd
Balmore
Glass
457 CARN NAM BAD
MEALL NAN CAORACH
Balchraggan
A82
Dores
Cannich
CANNICH
A831
Glen Urquhart
Balbeg
465 MEALL NA H-EILRIG
A833
LOCH NESS MONSTER EXHIBITIONS
Loch Duntelchaig
Strathglass
Glen Affric
snakyle Forest
CAIRN
Corrimony
156
Buntait
Braefield
Balnain
Milton
Drumnadrochit
157
Achnabat
446
Shenval
A831
Loch Meiklie
Enrick
DRUM FARM
Urquhart Bay
464
STAC NA CATHAIG
DOG FALLS
Affric
Fasnakyle Ho
Glenurquhart Forest
Lewiston
Strone
URQUHART CASTLE
B852
B862
Tullich
Nairn
Tomich
Divach
Upper Lenie
Lower Lenie
COBB MEMORIAL
Torness
Loch Ruthven
East Croachy
Abhainn Deabhag
578
Enrick
Aberarder House
B851
Balcladaich
Balmacaan Forest
Coiltie
Bunloit
1:20 (May-Dec)
Fangaig
Balbeg
Inverfarigaig
ch Beinn Mheadhoin
PLODDA FALLS
MEALL A CHRATHAICH 679
Loch nam Breac Dearga
Easter Boleskine
FARIGAIG FOREST CENTRE
Aultnagoire
Erroogie
Loch ma Stac
Loch a' Chràthaich
Creagnaneun Forest
A82
Farigaig Forest
Dunmaglass Lodge
771
Loch nan Eun
Foyers
Lyne of Gorthleck
Forest
Loch na Beinne Baine
LOCH NESS
Alltsigh
Wester Aberchalder
Allt Bhlàraidh
Levishie Forest
Levishie
Achnaconeran
Lochgarthside
Loch Mhor
680
Dundreggan Forest
Invermoriston
Bailebeag
802 CARN ODHAR
Moriston
FALLS OF MORISTON
148
Allt na Muic
A887
Portclair Forest
Loch Knockie
Whitebridge
Aberchalder Burn
Allt Uisg an t-Sidhein
Dundreggan Lodge
Dundreggan
Portclair
588
811 CARN NA SAOBHAIDHE
Coignafearn Forest
Knockie Lodge
Dalchreichart
607 BURACH
River E.
Tomchrasky
Inverwick Forest
GREAT GLEN WAY
Glenbrein Lodge
Garrogie Lodge
MONADHLIATH
555
Feehlin
A82
Loch Tarff
B862
Inchnacardoch Hotel
CLANSMAN CENTRE
Glendoe Lodge
Loch Killin
809 CARN NA LARAICHE MAOILE
Eskin
Allt Phocaichain
Fort Augustus
Glendoebeg
Glen Brein
Killin Lodge
MOUNTAINS
Inchnacardoch Forest
NH
Glen Markie
826 CARN COIRE NA CREICHE
Auchteraw
Allt Breinag
Killin
828 BURRACH MOR
Abhainn Cro Chlach
UBH
Oich
Caledonian Canal
Allt Doe
Allt Cam Ban
Allt Lundie
l a n d
779 CARN EASGANN BANA
Bridge of Oich
Newtown
Allt Odhar
CARN A'CHUILINN 816
Glendoe Forest
Tarff
942 CARN BAN
Munerigie
Glen Tarff
ARRY
Calder Burn
Invergarry
Loch Oich
MEALL NA H-AISRE 862
Mandally
A82
Culachy Forest
Allt Choire Lain Oig
Feith Talagain
Glen Markie
Allt Madagain
LOCH LOCHY
LAGGAN LOCKS
WELLS OF THE SEVEN HEADS
896 GAIRBEINN
884 CARN LEAC
Corrieyairack Forest
925 GEAL CHARN
832 MARG NA CRAIGE
Laggan
Melgarve
Kilfinnan
815 CARN DEARG
Garvamore
Spey
Crathie
Balgowan
A86
Drummin
148
Laggan
Cluny Castle
Catlodge
LOCHY
NN
Loch Crunachdan
Glenshero Lodge
Strath Mashie
Strathmashie House
636
Turret
Brae Roy Lodge
622
Letterfinlay
Glen Roy
CARN LIATH 1006
Aberarder Lodge
Cromra
571
Glen Gloy
PARALLEL ROADS
Aberarder Forest
A86
Kinloch Laggan
Loch Caoldair
A889
Burn of Agie
Upper Glenfintaig
834 CARN DEARG
Aberarder
684
GLEN ROY
1128 CREAG MEAGAIDH
CREAG MEAGAIDH
LAGGAN
Mashie
915
Allt Glas Dhoire
LOCH
Lochan na h-Earba
674 BEINN EILDE
Dalwhinnie
DALWHINNIE DISTILLERY
1049 BEINN A' CHAORUINN
Moy Forest
911
Bohuntine
Bohenie
Moy
Moy Lodge
Ardverikie Forest
Pattack
Loch Ericht Forest
A9
Inverroy
Roybridge
Achluachrach
Murlaggan
Roughburn
A86
1049 GEAL CHARN
774 CREAGAN MOR
Spean
MONESSIE FALLS
Braes o'Lochaber
GLEN SPEAN
139
Loch Pattack
140
Ben Alder Lodge
ERICHT
Allt Luraich
917
724 BEINN CHLIANAIG
Fersit
1087 BEINN A'CHLACHAIR
Allt Cam
Allt a'Chaoil-reidhe
Ben Alder Forest
LOCH
A'BHUIDH BHEA
Allt Laire

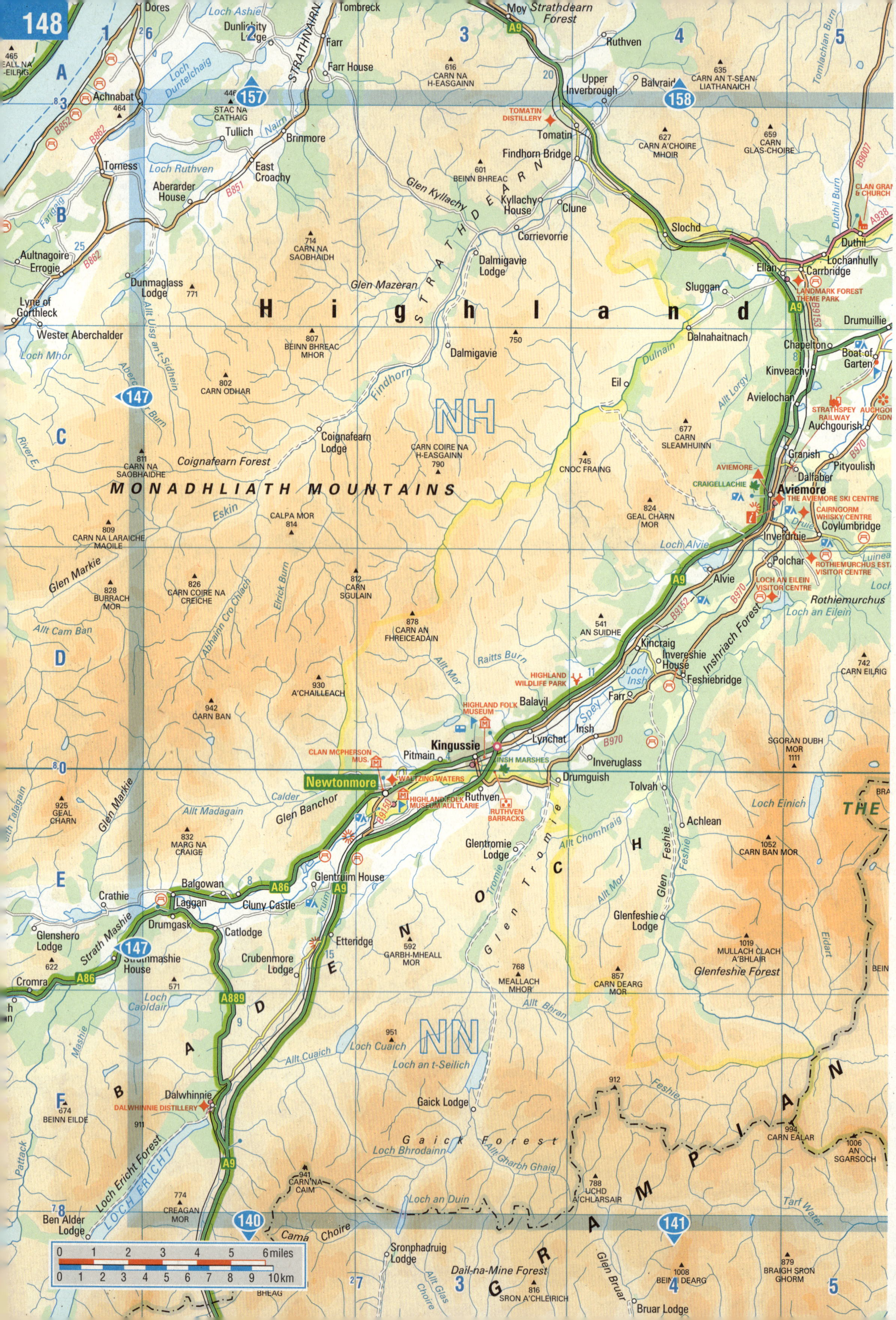

Dores
Loch Ashie
Dunlichity Lodge
STRATHNAIRN
Tombreck
Farr
Farr House
Moy
Strathdearn Forest
A9
Ruthven
616 CARN NA H-EASGAINN
Upper Inverbrough
Balvraid
635 CARN AN T-SEAN-LIATHANAICH
Tomlachlan Burn
465 EALL NA -EILRIG
Loch Duntelchaig
446 STAC NA CATHAIG
157
158
Achnabat
464
Tullich
Brinmore
Nairn
TOMATIN DISTILLERY
Tomatin
627 CARN A'CHOIRE MHOIR
659 CARN GLAS-CHOIRE
B9007
B852
B862
Torness
Loch Ruthven
East Croachy
Aberarder House
B851
601 BEINN BHREAC
Findhorn Bridge
Glen Kyllachy
STRATHDEARN
Kyllachy House
Clune
Corrievorrie
Slochd
CLAN GRANT & CHURCH
A938
Duthil Burn
Duthil
Farigaig
Aultnagoire
Errogie
714 CARN NA SAOBHAIDH
Dalmigavie Lodge
Ellan
Lochanhully
Carrbridge
LANDMARK FOREST THEME PARK
Dunmaglass Lodge
771
Glen Mazeran
Sluggan
Lyne of Gorthleck
Wester Aberchalder
Highland
807 BEINN BHREAC MHOR
750
Dalnahaitnach
B9153
Drumuillie
Chapelton
Boat of Garten
Loch Mhor
Allt Uisg an t-Sidhein
Dalmigavie
Dulnain
Findhorn
Kinveachy
Avielochan
Allt Lorgy
802 CARN ODHAR
Eil
147
NH
677 CARN SLEAMHUINN
STRATHSPEY RAILWAY
Auchgourish
River E.
Coignafearn Lodge
CARN COIRE NA H-EASGAINN 790
745 CNOC FRAING
Granish
B970
Pityoulish
811 CARN NA SAOBHAIDHE
Coignafearn Forest
MONADHLIATH MOUNTAINS
AVIEMORE
Dalfaber
CRAIGELLACHIE
Aviemore
THE AVIEMORE SKI CENTRE
824 GEAL CHARN MOR
CAIRNGORM WHISKY CENTRE
Coylumbridge
Eskin
CALPA MOR 814
809 CARN NA LARAICHE MAOILE
Inverdruie
Druie
Loch Alvie
Polchar
ROTHIEMURCHUS ESTATE VISITOR CENTRE
Glen Markie
826 CARN COIRE NA CREICHE
Elrick Burn
812 CARN SGULAIN
Alvie
A9
LOCH AN EILEIN VISITOR CENTRE
828 BURRACH MOR
Abhainn Cro Chlach
B970
B9152
Inshriach Forest
Rothiemurchus
Loch an Eilein
878 CARN AN FHREICEADAIN
Allt Cam Ban
541 AN SUIDHE
Kincraig
Invereshie House
Raitts Burn
HIGHLAND WILDLIFE PARK
Loch Insh
Feshiebridge
742 CARN EILRIG
930 A'CHAILLEACH
Allt Mor
942 CARN BAN
HIGHLAND FOLK MUSEUM
Balavil
Farr
Spey
Insh
Lynchat
Kingussie
B970
SGORAN DUBH MOR 1111
CLAN MCPHERSON MUS.
Pitmain
INSH MARSHES
Inveruglass
Drumguish
Newtonmore
WALTZING WATERS
Tolvah
925 GEAL CHARN
Calder
HIGHLAND FOLK MUSEUM AULTLARIE
Ruthven
RUTHVEN BARRACKS
Loch Einich
THE
Allt Madagain
Glen Banchor
B9150
Achlean
Glen Markie
832 MARG NA CRAIGE
Glentromie Lodge
Allt Chomhraig
Glen Feshie
Feshie
1052 CARN BAN MOR
Balgowan
A86
Glentruim House
A9
Crathie
Laggan
Cluny Castle
Truim
Glen Tromie
Tromie
Allt Mor
Glenfeshie Lodge
Glenshero Lodge
Strath Mashie
Drumgask
Catlodge
Etteridge
592 GARBH-MHEALL MOR
1019 MULLACH CLACH A'BHLAIR
Eidart
Glenfeshie Forest
622
Strathmashie House
Crubenmore Lodge
768 MEALLACH MHOR
857 CARN DEARG MOR
Cromra
A86
571
Loch Caoldair
A889
Allt Bhran
Mashie
951
NN
Loch Cuaich
Allt Cuaich
Loch an t-Seilich
Dalwhinnie
DALWHINNIE DISTILLERY
674 BEINN EILDE
911
Gaick Lodge
912
Feshie
994 CARN EALAR
1006 AN SGARSOCH
Gaick Forest
Loch Bhrodainn
Allt Gharbh Ghaig
Pattack
Loch Ericht Forest
LOCH ERICHT
A9
941 CARN NA CAIM
788 UCHD A'CHLARSAIR
GRAMPIAN
Tarf Water
774 CREAGAN MOR
Loch an Duin
Ben Alder Lodge
140
Cama
Choire
141
Glen Bruar
Sronphadruig Lodge
Dail-na-Mine Forest
1008 BEINN DEARG
879 BRAIGH SRON GHORM
Allt Glas Choire
816 SRON A'CHLEIRICH
Bruar Lodge
BHEAG
0 1 2 3 4 5 6 miles
0 1 2 3 4 5 6 7 8 9 10 km

Upper Derraid
Auchnagallin
Lettoch
Dalchirach
Favillar
Kirkhill
Fiddich
Glaschoil
Camerory
Delliefure
Mains of Dalvey
HILLS OF CROMDALE
Drumin
Glenfiddich Forest
Black Water
484 CARN-RUIGH CHARRACH
158
159
A95
B9102
B9008
B9009
Glenlivet
GLENLIVET DISTILLERY
Shenval
Auchbreck
742
Glenbeg
Grantown-on-Spey
Cromdale
Auchroisk
1690
Haughs of Cromdale
Achnahannet
471 BEINN MHOR
Anagach
Ballcorach
Tomnavoulin
Blackwater Forest
571 ROUND HILL
MAUSOLEUM
Craggan
Congash
732 CARN AN T-SUIDHE
Dulnain Bridge
Speybridge
REVACK ESTATE
569 CARN DAIMH
Skye of Curr
Lynemore
Strath Avon
Knockandhu
Livet
HEATHER HERITAGE CENTRE
722 CREGGAN A'CHAISE
Glenlivet Forest
632 HILL OF THREE STONES
Spey
Burn of Lochy
Clashnoir
Braes of Glenlivet
Chapeltown
A95
Cullachie
B970
Nethy Bridge
Dirdhu
Bridge of Brown
Fodderletter
LADDER HILLS
Badenyon
Birchfield
Dell Lodge
A939
GLENLIVET ESTATE
Glenbuchat Lodge
Lettoch
TOMINTOUL MUSEUM
Tomintoul
TOMINTOUL
588
East Croftmore
ABERNETHY FOREST NATURE RESERVE
568 BADDOCH
Delnabo
804 CARN MOR
Water of Buchat
Loch Garten
Abernethy Forest
Dorback Lodge
588 CARN MEADHONACH
150
Aundorach
Forest Lodge
ABERNETHY FOREST
Conglass Water
Water of Nochty
Braes of Abernethy
Blairnamarrow
CAIRNGORMS
Dorback Burn
688
Water of Ailnack
718 THE SOCACH
Bellabeg
Glen More Forest Park
NJ
LECHT SKI CENTRE
Glen Ernan
MEALL A'BHUACHAILLE 810
821 GEAL CHARN
Strathdon
The Queen's Forest
Avon
792 CARN EALASAID
Ernan Water
Inverernan Ho.
A944
CAIRNGORM LODGE
CAIRNGORM REINDEER CENTRE
Water of Caiplich
711
673
Candacraig Ho.
Glenmore Lodge
Nethy
Burn of Loin
Allt Tuileach
Colnabaichin
Don
Morlich
GLENMORE VISITOR CENTRE
742
742 BIG GARVOUN
Delnadamph
Cock Bridge
Corgarff
Tornahaish
NATIONAL
GLEN AVON
CORGARFF CASTLE
CAIRNGORM CHAIRLIFT, FUNICULAR RLY & SKI CENTRE
1090 BYNACK MORE
715 THE BRUACH
749
CAIRNGORM
Forest of Glenavon
823 BROWN COW HILL
744
Lairig Ghru
CAIRN GORM 1245
1245
Loch Builg
A939
Loch Avon
1107
10
Glen Fenzie
MOUNTAINS
1082
1171 BEN AVON
Gairnshiel Lodge
BEINN A'CHAORRUINN
Gairn
12
Lary
Loch Etchachan
BEN MACDUI 1309
B976
1089 CARN EAS
MOUNTAINS
900 CULARDOCH
743 GEALLAIG HILL
Glen Gairn
CAIRNGORM MOUNTAINS
1155 DERRY CAIRNGORM
Coilacriech
Culsh
PARK
931 BEINN BHREAC
Bush Crathie
CRATHIE CHURCH
Dee
A93
Littlemill
MCEWAN GALLERY
Glen Dee
Derry Burn
CARN NA DROCHAIDE 818
BALMORAL CASTLE AND GARDENS
Crathie
BRAEMAR
Inver
Invergelder
B976
150
BRAEMAR CASTLE
Easter Balmoral
ROYAL LOCHNAGAR DISTILLERY VISITOR CENTRE
Birkhall
Invercauld House
Mill of Sterin
1157
Glen Lui
Lui Water
Allanaquoich
Braemar
BRAEMAR HIGHLAND HERITAGE CENTRE
Glen Gelder
601
Mar Lodge
KINDROCHIT CASTLE
Forest of Mar
Claybokie
Tomintoul
Aucholzie
Ballochbuie Forest
LINN OF MUICK WATERFALL
LINN OF DEE
INVEREY
Muir
DEESIDE AND
Dee
Inverey
Auchallater
Glen Muick
BALMORAL FOREST
Geldie Burn
LOCHNAGAR
818 CARN LIATH
Glen Ey
NO
Callater Burn
850 CONACHCRAIG
674
Allt Connie
1150 LOCHNAGAR
GLENMUICK VISITOR CENTRE
721 FASHEILACH
Glen Callater
Loch Callater
Spittal of Glenmuick
Glen Mark
Bynack Burn
Baddoch
834
Dubh Loch
Glas-allt Shiel
A93
1012 CAIRN BANNOCH
Loch Muick
Glen Lee
920 CARN BHAC
998 BROAD CAIRN
939 AN SOCACH
1019 CARN AN TUIRC
Clunie Water
1048 BEINN IUTHARN MHOR
141
Loch Vrotachan
958 TOLMOUNT
142
Glen Doll
GLENSHEE SKI CENTRE
832 LAIR OF ALDARARIE
Water of Unich
Tilt
Loch nan Eun
933 THE CAIRNWELL
Glendoll Lodge
Devil's Elbow
1068 GLAS MAOL
Braedownie
Loch Brandy
Loch Loch
1051
Glendoll Forest

Ballochford
Tomnaven
Coynachie
Blackburn
Glens of Foudland
A96
Glen Fiddich
Clashindarroch Forest
Clashindarroch
Kirkney
Culdrain
Gartly
Cults
HILL OF FOUDLAND
Colpy
Largie
Wrangham
Bridgend
Inverharroch
Glenfiddich Forest
159
160
Kirkney Water
Milton of Lesmore
Milton of Noth
Kennethmont
Oldtown
Ardlair
The Shevock
Aulton
Insch
B992
B9002
Auchmair
Cabrach
Belhinnie
Rhynie
Cottown
742
571 ROUND HILL
Aldunie
Blackwater Forest
505
A941
Wheedlemont
Craig Castle
Clatt
Duncanston
Leslie
Kirkton
Auchleven
732 CARN AN T-SUIDHE
ST MARY'S CHURCH
Knockespock Ho.
Livet
721 THE BUCK
632 HILL OF THREE STONES
Clova
SCOTTISH SCULPTURE WORKSHOP
Lumsden
CORREEN HILLS
Coldwells Croft
Whitehaugh Forest
Muckletown
Chapeltown
A b e r d
Glenton
Tullynessle
Keig
Castle Forbes
Badenyon
Glenbuchat Lodge
LADDER HILLS
804 CARN MOR
NJ
Mossat
518 LORD ARTHUR'S CAIRN
Bridge of Alford
Montgarrie
Water of Buchat
149
658
Water of Nochty
Rinmore
Kildrummy
KILDRUMMY CASTLE & GARDEN
Don
Milltown of Kildrummy
A944
ALFORD VALLEY RAILWAY
HAUGHTON
GRAMPIAN TRANSPORT MUS
Gateside
Belnacraig
Kirkton of Glenbuchat
532
Auchintoul
Alford
HERITAGE CENTRE
Whitehouse
718 THE SOCACH
A939
Glenkindie
Towie
Sinnahard
Asloun
Hillockhead
A980
Bellabeg
Forbestown
Strathdon
Glen Ernan
Ernan Water
Milltown of Towie
Ley
Little Lynturk
Kirkton of Tough
Tillyfourie
Inverernan Ho.
A944
Candacraig Ho.
Heugh-head
Boultenstone
Muir of Fowlis
Bridgend
Tillyfour
673
Tornashean Forest
Milton of Cushnie
Leochel-Cushnie
Corrennie Moor
Corrennie Forest
Cock Bridge
Colnabaichin
531 CRAIG OF BUNZEACH
Hillockhead
A97
CRAIGIEVAR CASTLE
Kintocher
Corgarff
Tornahaish
619
494 BENAQUHALLIE
CORGARFF CASTLE
Deskry Water
Easter Davoch
B9119
Migvie
Douneside
Craskins
476
Tornaveen
Coynach
Findrack Ho.
Drumlasie
D
749
CULSH SOUTERRAIN
744
Logie Coldstone
Tarland
Lumphanan
871 MORVEN
C R O M A R
TOMNAVERIE STONE CIRCLE
PEEL RING OF LUMPHANAN
Milton of Auchinhove
B993
Glen Fenzie
Milton of Logie
Glendavan Ho.
Coull
Auchlossan
Torphins
Gairnshiel Lodge
Ordie
299 SCAR HILL
MUIR OF DINNET
SLUG OF DESS FALLS
Lary
604
Loch Davan
Mid Beltie
Milton of Campfield
Glen Gairn
BURN O VAT
Loch Kinord
Aboyne
Kincardine O'Neil
B976
743 GEALLAIG HILL
A93
Dinnet
Tillydrine
Milton of Tullich
Muir of Dinnet
Backhill of Trustach
Bush Crathie
Coilacriech
Culsh
Bridge of Gairn
Glascorrie
B976
Birsemore
Birse
B993
CRATHIE CHURCH
Dee
MCEWAN GALLERY
Ballater
BRAELOINE INTERPRETIVE CENTRE
Marywell
Burn of Cattie
Crathie
Littlemill
Glen Tanar House
CASTLE GARDENS
House of Glenmuick
310 TOM'S CAIRN
Easter Balmoral
ROYAL LOCHNAGAR DISTILLERY VISITOR CENTRE
Birkhall
529
Tillygarmond
Mill of Sterin
Glen Tanar
Water of Tanar
GLEN TANAR
525 CARNFERG
Finzean
Percie
Forest of Glen Tanar
601
Glen Gelder
Girnock Burn
CLACHAN YELL 526
Forest of Birse
Ballochan
Aucholzie
Water of Feugh
LINN OF MUICK WATERFALL
Glen Muick
617
Water of Aven
BALMORAL FOREST
727 COCK CAIRN
742 HILL OF CAT
MOUNT SHADE 507
Glendye Lodge
850 CONACHCRAIG
939 MOUNT KEEN
GLENMUICK VISITOR CENTRE
721 FASHEILACH
NO
Spittal of Glenmuick
Glen Mark
Water of Mark
Burn of Branny
Water of Tarf
Burn of Tennet
778 MOUNT BATTOCK
Glen Dye
Dubh Loch
Glas-allt Shiel
Loch Muick
Glen Lee
525 MELUNCART
696 MONAWEE
Invermark Lodge
Auchronie
Tarfside
Cairncross
THE RETREAT - GLEN ESK FOLK MUS.
Cairn o' Mount
142
143
Water of Unich
Loch Lee
Inchgrundle
North Esk
0 1 2 3 4 5 6 miles
0 1 2 3 4 5 6 7 8 9 10km
Glen Doll
Glen Effock
G L E N E S K
Glendoll Forest
Braedownie
Loch Brandy
CRUYS

Kirkton of Culsalmond
B922
Rothmaise
Newseat
Folla Rule
St Katherine's
Cross of Jackston
Chapel
Earlsford
HADDO HOUSE AND GARDENS
Wedderlairs
Ythanbank
Hilton
Mains of Birness
Nethermill
Leask
A920
Cairnhill
Tocher
Meikle Wartle
Jackstown
Balgove
Tulloch
Raxton
MEDIEVAL TOMB
West Kinharrachie
Inverebrie
Broomfield
A90
P&R
Artrochie
Auchmacoy
SLAINS CASTLE
Bonnyton
160
Craigdam
Tarves
Ythsie
Esslemont
Ellon
161
Kirkton of Rayne
Meldrum Ho.
Auquhorthies
Newton Ho.
Old Rayne
LOANHEAD STONE CIRCLE
Mounie Castle
F O R M A R T I N E
Kirkton of Logie Buchan
VISITOR CENTRE
Kirktown of Slains
Collieston
Pitmachie
Durno
Daviot
A920
TOLQUHON CASTLE
PITMEDDEN GARDENS
Pitmedden
Meikle Tarty
Waterside
Sands of Forvie
St Catherine's Dub
Hackley Hd. or Forvie Ness
Ardoyne
ARCHAEOLINK PREHISTORY PARK
Whiteford
Pitcaple
Fingask
Oldmeldrum
Cairnbrogie
B9000
Tipperty
FORVIE
Westhall
Barra Castle
Udny Green
Tarty Burn
Oyne
Kirkton of Oyne
Harlaw Ho.
NJ
Mill of Kingoodie
Hattoncrook
B9000
Foveran
Newburgh
A96
Chapel of Garioch
Kirkton of Bourtie
Pettymuick
Cultercullen
Foveran Burn
Pittodrie
Balhalgardy
Hillbrae
Whiterashes
Udny Station
Drums
Newburgh Bar
BENNACHIE 528
BATTLE OF HARLAW MEMORIAL
BRANDSBUTT STONE
Affleck
Tillygreig
Tillycorthie
Minnes
Rashiereive
518
Burgh Muir
INVERURIE MUSEUM
Nether Crimond
A R I O C H
Inverurie
Tillykerrie
Ardo Ho.
Delfrigs
Middlemuir
Manar Ho.
Straloch
Aberdeenshire
Upper Woodend
Bograxie
Port Elphinstone
Kinmuck
Middleton
Newmachar
Craigie
Burnhervie
Aquhythie
KINKELL CHURCH
Balbithan Ho.
Causeyend
Don
Whitecairns
Belhelvie
B977
BALMEDIE
Balmedie
Rorandle
Blairdaff
Dalmadilly
Clovenstone
Balbithan
Cairnpark
Kinmundy
Pitfichie
Wester Fintray
Pitfichie Forest
Grantlodge
Drumligair
Pitmunie
MONYMUSK ARTS CENTRE
Kemnay
Cottown
Kintore
Hatton of Fintray
OLD CHURCH
Cothall
A90
Monymusk
Craigearn
Potterton
Corby Loch
Todlachie
Leylodge
Overton
Dyce
Parkhill Ho.
Blackdog
B993
Lauchintilly
Mundurno
CASTLE FRASER
Blackburn
ABERDEEN
Haughs of Clinterty
A96
Aberdeen
Denmore
KIRKWALL 6:00
LERWICK 14:00
Ordhead
Sauchen
Achath
Lyne of Skene
Stoneywood
Bankhead
Bridge of Don
A944
East Auchronie
Bucksburn
Hayton
CRUICKSHANK BOTANIC GARDEN
BRIG O'BALGOWNIE
Milton of Corsindae
Old Kinnernie
Skene Ho.
266
City
Woodside
ST MACHAR'S CATHEDRAL
Old Aberdeen
Bankhead
Corsindae
Dunecht
Loch of Skene
Kirkton of Skene
Northfield
Mastrick
Kittybrewster
A90
KING'S COLLEGE VISITOR CENTRE
Midmar
STONE CIRCLE
Westhill
Kingswells
Aberdeen
Comers
Tillybirloch
274
Marionburgh
Elrick
A944
SATROSPHERE
MARISCHAL MUSEUM
B9119
Echt
B9119
Garlogie
Cairnie
B9119
ABERDEEN
P&R
GORDON HIGHLANDERS MUSEUM
Ferryhill
Torry
Girdle Ness
Midmar Forest
South Kirkton
Easter Ord
Blacktop
Mannofield
DUTHIE PARK WINTER GARDENS
Nigg Bay
Landerberry
Redhill
Leuchar Burn
Ruthrieston
Kincorth
Greg Ness
433
HILL OF FARE
B9125
West Cullery
Benthoul
Contlaw
Cults
Bieldside
Milton of Murtle
Garthdee
Burn of Corrichie
Hardgate
Craigton
Milltimber
A93
Nigg
Banchory-Devenick
Cove Bay
B977
DRUM CASTLE
Charlestown
Hirn
Peterculter
B9077
A956
A980
Myrebird
Drumoak
Mains of Drum
Kirkton of Maryculter
Auchlunies
A90
Hare Ness
Brathens
Maryculter
Marywell
Bridge of Canny
Upper Lochton
The Neuk
CRATHES CASTLE AND GARDENS
B9077
Hillside
Findon Ness
East Mains
Dee
Findon
BANCHORY MUSEUM
Woodside of Arbeadie
Crathes
Muirskie
Auchlee
Portlethen
Arbeadie
Banchory
ROYAL DEESIDE RLY.
Kirkton of Durris
Woodlands
Downies
Kirkhall Forest
Deebank
Bridge of Feugh
Denside
Upper Burnhaugh
Cammachmore Bay
Auchattie
A957
Crossroads
Cammachmore
Belts of Collonach
Borrowfield
Newtonhill
B974
Durris Forest
Netherley
Cookney
Strachan
CAIRN-MON-EARN
378
NO
B979
Muchalls
Lochton
RAEDYKES ROMAN CAMP
Bridge of Muchalls
Union Cottage
Garrol Hill
376
MONGOUR
Water of Dye
Burn of Sheeoch
Mergie
Rickarton
Garron Pt.
Cowie Water
534
KERLOCH
A957
Cowie
Bridge of Dye
Kirktown of Fetteresso
Fetteresso Forest
Tewel
TOLBOOTH MUSEUM
Stonehaven
Carmont
Tannachie
Castle Haven
DUNNOTTAR CASTLE
New Mill
A90
A92
Thornyhive Bay
Drumtochty
464 Forest
Mains of Dellavaird
Glenfarquhar Lodge
BURNS FAMILY MEMORIALS
Drumlithie
Glenbervie
Fiddes
Mill of Uras
Drumtochty Castle
Barras
Crawton
143
FOWLSHEUGH NATURE RESERVE
Strath Finella
Monboddo House
Mondynes
Pitforthie
Roadside of Catterline
Crawton Bay
Catterline
Glensaugh
Auchenblae
Clatterin Brig
Brownmuir
Braidon Bay
Todhead Point
East Cairnbeg
B974
Fordoun
Roadside of Kinneff
B966
B967
Parkneuk
Arbuthnott
A B C D E F G
5 6 7 8 9

Fladda-chùain
Eilean Trodday
Rubha Hunish
Rubha na h-Aiseig
TARBERT 1:45
LOCHMADDY 1:50
Duntulm Castle
Duntulm
Balmacqueen
Kilmaluag
Lub Score
Museum of Island Life
Hungladder
Borneskeitaig
Kilmuir
Flora MacDonald's Memorial
Eilean Flodigarry
Flodigarry
Meall na Suiramach 543
Digg
Staffin I.
Staffin Bay
Glashvin
The Quiraing
Brogaig
Kilvaxter
Balgown
Linicro
Totscore
Kilbride Point
Stenscholl
Staffin
Trotternish
Kilt Rock
Kilt Rock & Mealt Falls
466 Biod Buidhe
Elishader
Maligar
Loch Mealt
Valtos
Marishader
Garros
Rubha nam Brathairean
Idrigill
Uig
Uig Bay
Conon
Rha
Balnaknock
611 Beinn Edra
Breckrey
Culnaknock
Lealt
Lealt Falls
Lower Tote
Upper Tote
Waternish Point
Ascrib Islands
NG
Ru Chorachan
Loch Snizort
Earlish
A87
Peinlich
Hinnisdal
607 Creag A'Lain
Ard Beag
Ben Geary 284
Geary
Trumpan Church
Trumpan
Knockbreck
Gillen
Ardmore Pt.
Lower Halistra
Upper Halistra
Hallin
Waternish
Mingay
Isay
Dunvegan Head
Loch Dunvegan
Stein
Lusta
B886
Greshornish Pt.
Lyndale Pt.
Kingsburgh
Lyndale Ho.
Loch Greshornish
Loch Snizort Beag
Romesdal
719 The Storr
Old Man of Storr
Island of Rona
125
Eilean Garbh
Sound of Raasay
Galtrigill
The MacCrimmon Piping Heritage Centre
Borreraig
Borreraig Park Museum
Uig
Claigan
Loch Bay
327 Beinn Bhreac
Bay River
Greshornish
Flashader
Treaslane
Suladale
Eyre
Trotternish
Bearreraig Bay
Eilean Tigh
Caol Rona
Garbh Eilean
Loch a' Sguirr
An Caol
Husabost
Loch Pooltiel
An Ceannaich
Feriniquarrie
Lower Milovaig
Glasphein
Totaig
Dunvegan Castle
Edinbane
Blackhill
A850
The Aird
Kensaleyre
Bernisdale
Haultin
Holm I.
Loch Leathan
Eilean Fladday
254
Oisgill Bay
Upper Milovaig
Lephin
B884
Colbost Folk Museum
Colbost
Holmisdale
Glen Dale
Hamara
Toy Museum
Lighthouse
Neist Point
Moonen Bay
Skinidin
Dunvegan
Giant Angus MacAskill Museum
Kilmuir
Lonmore
Cruachan Beinn A'Chearcaill 266
B8036
Tote
Glen Bernisdale
Skeabost
Carbost
Borve
Loch Fada
A855
Prince Charles's Cave
Manish Pt.
Loch Arnish
Torran
Arnish
Healabhal Mhor
Roskhill
Uigshader
Drumuie
Achachork
392
Rubha na h Airde Glaise
Brochel Castle
Brochel
Highland
173
170
154
Loch Fionnsbhagh
Boirseam
Lingreabhagh

ISLAND OF RAASAY
Portree
Torvaig
AN TUIREANN ARTS CENTRE
THE AROS EXPERIENCE
Shulishadermor
Glengrasco
Heatherfield
Penifiler
BEN TIANAVAIG 413
Glenmore
Mugeary
Camastianavaig
Holoman Bay
Tianavaig Bay
Conordan
Lower Ollach
Upper Ollach
Gedintailor
The Braes
BATTLE OF THE BRAES MONUMENT
Peinchorran
BEN LEE 444
Raasay Ho.
Clachan
RAASAY OUTDOOR CENTRE
Narrows of Raasay
Inverarish
East Suisnish
Eyre
Eyre Point
Caol Mòr
North Fearns
Glame
Balmeanach
Balachuirn
Oskaig
DUN CAAN 443
385
Rubha na'Leac
Scalpay
Scalpay Ho.
Caolas Scalpay
Loch Sligachan
Sconser
GLAMAIG 775
Moll
Loch Ainort
Luib
Dunan
OLD SKYE CROFTER'S HOUSE
GLAS BHEINN MHOR 570
RED HILLS
Corry
BROADFORD
Harrapool
WORLD OF WOOD
732
Suardal
B8083
Torrin
Kilbride
Strath
301
Loch Slapin
BLA BHEINN 928
Loch na Creitheach
Strathaird
Kirkibost
Kilmarie
BEN MEABOST 346
Camasunary
Loch Scavaig
Soay
Soay Sound
Mol-chlach
Elgol
BOAT TRIPS
Glasnakille
PRINCE CHARLES'S CAVE
Eilean na h-Airde
Rubha na h-Easgainne
Rubha Suisnish
Loch Eishort
Ord
DUNSGIATH CASTLE
Tokavaig
Tarskavaig
Tarskavaig Pt.
Achnacloich
SLEAT
Glen Meadhonach
Rubha Charn nan Cearc
Sligachan Hotel
Glen Sligachan
MARSCO 736
SGURR NAN GILLEAN 964
SGURR A'GHREADAIDH 973
THE CUILLIN HILLS
CUILLIN HILLS
SGURR ALASDAIR 992
SGURR NAN EAG 924
Loch Coruisk
Glenbrittle House
GLENBRITTLE
Glen Brittle
Bualintur
Loch Brittle
Rubh an Dunain
MINGINISH
SKYE
DUIRINISH
Glen Varragill
A87
A863
B885
B883
B8009
Loch Connan
Tungadal
Loch Duagrich
Snizort
ROINEVAL 439
Crossal
Drynoch
Merkadale
Carbost
TALISKER DISTILLERY
Fernilea
ARNAVAL 369
Fiskavaig
Portnalong
Loch Harport
Gleann Oraid
Talisker
Talisker Bay
BEINN BHREAC 445
Eynort
Grula
Glen Brittle Forest
459
Loch Eynort
Rubha nan Clach
Oronsay
Coillore
Bracadale
Struan
Ullinish
Tarner I.
Wiay
Loch Bracadale
Harlosh I.
Idrigill Point
MACLEOD'S MAIDENS
Geodha Mor
Ose
Loch Caroy
Balmore
Harlosh
Vatten
Roag
Orbost
Loch Varkasaig
Macleod's Tables
HEALABHAL BHEAG 488
468
Ramasaig
Hoe Rape
Hoe Point
NG
Canna
A'Chill
Sanday
Canna Harbour
Garrisdale Pt.
MALLAIG 2:30
RUM 1:15
Kilmory
Rubha Shamhnan Insir
0 1 2 3 4 5 6 miles
0 1 2 3 4 5 6 7 8 9 10 km
171
155
144

Ullapool
Little Loch Broom
Gruinard Bay
Gruinard I.
Loch Ewe
Isle of Ewe
Loch Maree
Fionn Loch
Loch Gairloch
Gairloch
Gairloch Heritage Museum
Inverewe Garden
Poolewe
Aultbea
Laide
Kinlochewe
Torridon
Torridon Visitor Centre
Victoria Falls
Loch Maree Islands
Beinn Eighe National Nature Reserve
Wester Ross
Letterewe Forest
Fisherfield Forest
Strathnasheallag Forest
Flowerdale Forest
Kinlochewe Forest
Torridon Forest
Ledgowan Forest
Glen Torridon
Glen Docherty
Glen Grudie
Upper Loch Torridon
Loch Torridon
Loch Shieldaig
Island of Rona
Longa Island
Rubha Reidh
Redpoint
Melvaig
Cove
Carn Dearg
An Teallach 1062
Slioch 980
Beinn Eighe 1010
Liathach 1054
Beinn Alligin 985
Mullach Coire Mhic Fhearchair 1019
Beinn Dearg Mhor 908
Beinn Lair 860
A832
A896
B8021
B8056
B8057
NG
NH
162
163
173
152
156

Highland
Kyle of Lochalsh
Glen Carron
Glencarron and Glenuig Forest
Glen Fhiodhaig
Glencarron Lodge
Achnashellach Forest
West Monar Forest
Loch Monar
An Gead Loch
Loch an Tachdaidh
Achnashellach Forest
Craig
Lair
Loch Dughaill
Coulin
Coulin Forest
Balnacra
Coulags
New Kelso
Strathcarron
Achintee
Attadale Ho.
Attadale
Attadale Forest
Bendronaig Lodge
Loch Calavie
Loch Cruoshie
Killilan Forest
Killilan
East Benula Forest
West Benula Forest
Gleann a' Choilich
Gleann Sithidh
Falls of Glomach
Glen Affric
Glenaffric Forest
Glen Gniomhaidh
Carnach
Loch na Leitreach
Glen Elchaig
Camas-luinie
Loch nan Eun
Loch Long
Sallachy
Bundalloch
Dornie
Eilean Donan Castle
Keppoch
Loch Duich
Inverinate
Ruarach
Dorusduain
Morvich
Carn-gorm
Ault a' chruinn
Inverinate
Invershiel
Shiel Bridge
Ratagan
Kintail
Kintail Forest
Five Sisters
Glenshiel Forest
Glen More
Glenelg Brochs
Balvraid
Bernera Barracks
Glenelg
Glenelg Bay
Eilanreach
Upper Sandaig
Sandaig Is.
Kylerhea
Kylerhea Otter Haven
Bernera
Galltair
Letterfearn
Totaig
Ardelve
Nostie
Auchertyre
Allt-nan-sùgh
Gleann Udalain
Ardnarff
Stromeferry
Achmore
Craig Highland Farm
Strome Castle
Stromemore
Ardaneaskan
Lochcarron
Slumbay
Kirkton
Loch Carron
Achintraid
Sanachan
Ardarroch
Kishorn I.
Loch Kishorn
Plockton
Duirinish
Drumbuie
Erbusaig
Badicaul
Balmacara Square
Reraig
Balmacara
Lochalsh Woodland Garden
Loch Alsh
Ardintoul Pt.
Glas Eilean
Castle Moil
Brightwater Visitor Centre
Kyleakin
Glen Arroch
An Dubh-aird
Port Cam
Black Is.
Applecross
Applecross Forest
Applecross Bay
Applecross Ho.
Chapel of St Maelrubha
Camusterrach
Camusteel
Culduie
Ard-dhubh
Toscaig
Uags
Bealach na Ba
Meall Gorm
Beinn Bhan
Glenshieldaig Forest
Shieldaig
Loch Shieldaig
Balgy
Loch Damh
Ben-damph Forest
Annat
Rassal Ashwood
Loch Lundie
Croic-bheinn
Inner Sound
Crowlin Islands
Eilean Mór
Caolas Mór
Eilean na Bà
Longay
Pabay
Guillamon I.
Scalpay
Scalpay Ho.
Caolas Scalpay
Island of Raasay
Rubha na' Leac
Brochel Castle
Brochel
Arnish
Torran
An Caol
Caol Rona
Garbh Eilean
Eilean Tigh
Eilean Fladday
Manish Pt.
Callakille
Lonbain
North Fearns
Eyre Point
Eyre
East Suisnish
Raasay Outdoor Centre
Dun Caan
Red Hills
Broadford
Broadford Bay
Skye Serpentarium
Skye Environmental Centre
World of Wood
Harrapool
Waterloo
Skulamus
Lower Breakish
Upper Breakish
Corry
Strath Suardal
Kilbride
Torrin
Loch Slapin
Loch Eishort
Rubha Suisnish
Ord
Drumfearn
Kinloch
Loch na Dal
Old Skye Crofter's House
Luib
Dunan
Moll
Loch Ainort
A87
A890
A896
A851
B8083
NG
NH
6 miles
10 km

Inverbroom
Lael Forest
Strath More
Lael
928
735
Deanich Lodge
Gleann Beag
Diebidale
Sealga
Dundonnell
Forest
163
Auchindrean
Braemore
889
1084 BEINN DEARG
628
Tollomuick Forest
Crom Loch
714 BEINN THARSUINN
Glen Diebidale
Strath na Sealga
Fain
Dundonnell
A832
Abhainn Cuileig
CORRIESHALLOCH GORGE
MEALL LEACACHAIN 618
954
787 BEINN A'CHAISTEIL
Abhainn
Loch Vaich
914 BEINN A' CHLAIDHEIMH
Braemore Forest
Abhainn Droma
Dirrie More
Strathvaich Forest
772 MEALL A' GHRIANAIN
Inchbae Forest
807
Lochdrum
Loch Droma
742
Strathvaich Lodge
Strathrannoch
Loch a'Bhraoin
A835
Loch Glascarnoch
Strath Vaich
Strath Rannoch
1019 MULLACH COIRE MHIC FHEARCHAIR
934
1110 SGURR MOR
BEINN LIATH MHOR A 'GHIUBHAIS LI 766
748 GROBAN
999 A'CHAILLEACH
Lochan Fada
Aultguish Inn
H
i
g
h
Abhainn a'Chadh'Bhuidhe
949 MEALL GORM
Kinlochluichart Forest
Fannich
Forest
MEALL MHIC IOMHAIR 607
Garbat Forest
Garbat
154
BEINN NAN RAMH 711
Fannich Lodge
479
Kinlochewe Forest
LOCH FANNICH
Grudie
Aultdearg
Corriemoillie Forest
Black Water
LITTLE WYVIS 764
Heights of Kinlochewe
Leckie
Strath Chrombuill
Abhainn Bruachaig
Lochrosque Forest
558 AN CABAR
Corriemoillie
Strathgarve Forest
Incheril
933 FIONN BHEINN
Lochluichart
Achanalt
Grudie
Gorstan
A832
Loch Luichart
Garve
Strath Bran
Loch Achanalt
A835
Loch Garve
Glen Docherty
Badavanich
A832
Achnasheen
Bran
NH
Loch Bhad Ghaineamhaich
580 SGURR MARCASAIDH
Glenmarksie
Tarvie
Craigdarroch
Loch a'Chroisg
Abhainn Dubh
Ledgowan Forest
Little Scatwell
Loch Achilty
Loch Meig
Torrachilty Wood
550 CARN-BEAG
Loch Gowan
879 SGURR A'MHUILINN
Milton
Porin
Dalnacroich
Meig
STRATHCONON
D
538 CARN MHARTUIN
Gleann Meinich
Loch Achonachie
A890
STRATHCONON
591
678 CARN BREAC
Glen Carron
Loch Sgamhain
Scardroy
457
Loch Beannacharain
Carnoch
Inverchoran
673 CARN NA COINNICH
Cabaan Forest
Glencarron Lodge
928
FOREST
Orrin Reservoir
Orrin
Allt a' Chonais
Glencarron and Glenuig Forest
849 BAC AN EICH
Meig
Glen Fhiodhaig
Glen Orrin
Corriehallie Forest
Achnashellach Forest
Orrin
Loch na Caoidhe
Gleann Goibhre
862
E
1053
1007 MAOILE LUNNDAIDH
814
766
BEINN A'BHA'ACH ARD 862
155
West Monar Forest
East Monar Forest
1083 SGURR A'CHOIRE GHLAIS
Erchless Forest
Neaty Burn
Loch Laoigh
LURG MHOR 986
Loch Monar
Monar Lodge
GLEN
Culligran Falls
Inchmore
Erchless Castle
Aigas Forest
Craigdhu
Struy
Mid Main
Loch Calavie
An Gead Loch
Uisge Misgeach
Glen Strathfarrar
Farrar
Loch Beannacharan
Loch an Tachdaidh
Glenstrathfarrar Forest
STRATHFARRAR
Struy Forest
Mauld
Loch Cruoshie
Loch a'Mhuillidh
818 SGOR NA DIOLLAID
Carnoch
A831
706 AN CRUACHAN
F
1150 SGURR NA LAPAICH
676 CAIRN GORM
Glassburn
STRATHGLASS
Killilan Forest
1086 AN RIABHACHAN
Glencannich Forest
Muchrachd
Glass
457 CARN NAM BAD
AONACH BUIDHE 899
1069
Liatrie
Balmore
Cannich
Mullardoch House
East Benula Forest
Cannich
CANNICH
Fasnakyle Forest
Glen
Loch Mullardoch
Glen Cannich
CAIRN
Buntait
Braefield
Corrimony
Balnain
146
147
Shenval
A831
DOG FALLS
Loch Meiklie
Fasnakyle Ho
Affric
1053 TOLL CREAGACH
Glenurquhart
Tomich
Enrick
578
Deabhag
Balcladaich
Balmacaan Forest
1183 CARN EIGE
Gleann nam Fiadh
F GLOMACH
0 1 2 3 4 5 6 miles
0 1 2 3 4 5 6 7 8 9 10km

Forest
CARN CHUINNEAG
Loch a' Chairn
Easter Fearn Burn
Baileigh
Meikle Gluich
Aultnamain Inn
Tarlogie
Morangie
GLENMORANGIE DISTILLERY
ALDIE WATERMILL
ST DUTHUS'S CHAPEL
Tain
TAIN THROUGH TIME VISITOR CENTRE
TAIN TOLBOOTH
Quarryhill
Balnagall
Lochslin
Aldie
Hilton
Loch Eye
Morangie Forest
Rhynie
Fearn Station
Loch a' Chaorainn
BEINN THARSUINN
Kildermorie Forest
Kildermorie Lodge
Braeantra
Strath Rusdale
Black Water
Strath Rory
East Lamington
Lamington
Newfield
Logie Hill
Hill of Fearn
Fearn
FEARN ABBEY
Loans of Tulloch
Arabella
Loch Morie
Inchlumpie
CNOC CORR GUINIE
Torran
Scotsburn
Kildary
Ardross
Ardross Forest
Easter Ardross
Stittenham
Dalnavie
Wyvis Lodge
Boath
Ardross Castle
Tullich Muir
Milton
Tarbat Ho.
Ankerville
Chapelhill
QUEEN'S CAIRN
Loch Glass
NH
Wester Lealty
Alness
Stonyfield
Rhicullen
Kilmuir
Nigg Bay
Pitcalnie
Nigg
Culzie Lodge
Achandunie
Nonikiln
Barbaraville
Sands of Nigg
Highland
Mossfield
Tomich
Balintraid
Mount Canisp
King's Cave
Achnagarron
Rosskeen
Saltburn
Balnabruaich
Balnapaling
FYRISH MONUMENT
BEN WYVIS
Glen Glass
Eileanach Lodge
Dalmore
DALMORE DISTILLERY
Invergordon
Nigg Ferry
Castlecraig
Allt nan Caorach
Novar House
Assynt Ho.
Culcairn
Alness Bay
Balblair
Newhall Point
Cromarty
CROMARTY COURT HOUSE
Sutors of Cromarty
Redburn
Evanton
Cromarty Bay
HUGH MILLER'S COTTAGE
Swordale
Drummond
Resolis
Udale Bay
Newton
Foulis Castle
Cullicudden
Newhall House
Shore Mill
Jemimaville
Sgitheach
Strath Sgitheach
Clach Liath Forest
Ardullie
STOREHOUSE OF FOULIS
Cromarty Firth
Muirton
CIOCH MHOR
Woodlands
Shoreton
Millbuie Forest
Glenurquhart
Upper Eathie
Heights of Brae
Mountgerald
Findon Mains
Black Isle
Tulloch Castle
Culbo
Bottacks
Fodderty
Raddery
Balmungie
Auchterneed
Dingwall
Culbokie
HIGHLAND MUS. OF CHILDHOOD
Knockfarrel
MOUNT EAGLE
Killen
GROAM HOUSE MUSEUM AND PICTISH CENTRE
Rosemarkie
Whiteness Head
MACDONALD MONUMENT
Urquhart
Rosemarkie Bay
Strathpeffer
Loch Ussie
Alcaig
Millbuie
Fort George
Kirkton
Belmaduthy
FORTROSE CATHEDRAL
Fortrose
FORT GEORGE
QUEEN'S OWN HIGHLANDERS MUS.
Baddock
Tradespark
Jamestown
Maryburgh
Corntown
Duncanston
Rosehaugh Mains
Contin
Knockbain
Ardersier
Chanonry Pt.
TORR ACHILTY DAM FISH LIFT
Conon Bridge
Easter Kinkell
Suddie
HERITAGE EXHIBITION
Roskill House
Avoch
Moss-side
Conon House
Leanaig
Avoch Bay
Conon
Marybank
Gollanfield
Milton of Gollanfield
Muir of the Clans
Geddes
Muirton Mains
Urray
Muckernich
Munlochy
Munlochy Bay
Muir of Fairburn
Tore
Allangrange Mains
Lochside
GLEN ORD DISTILLERY
Balvaird
Kilcoy
Fettes
Drumderfit
BLACK ISLE WILDLIFE AND COUNTRY PARK
Moray Firth
Fisherton
INVERNESS
Clephanton
Cawdor
Bogallan
CASTLE STUART
Tornagrain
Muir of Ord
Arpafeelie
Ardnagrask
Redcastle
Kilmuir
Castle Stuart
Croy
KILRAVOCK CASTLE
CAWDOR CASTLE AND GARDENS
Loch nan Eun
Corry of Ardnagrask
Windhill
Milton
DOLPHINS & SEALS OF THE MORAY FIRTH
Alturlie Pt.
Clashandorran
Tomich House
Charlestown
Newton
Cantraywood
Easter Galcantray
North Kessock
Longman Pt.
Loch nam Bonnach
Beauly Firth
Ruilick
BEAULY PRIORY
Balloch
Culloden Forest
Kirkton of Barevan
Mains of
MADE IN SCOTLAND
Beauly
South Kessock
Culloden
Bunchrew
Smithton
Newlands
Cantraydoune
Kirkhill
Lentran
INVERNESS MUS. AND ART GALLERY
Cantraybruich
Assich Forest
CRAIG PHADRIG FORT
BALNAIN HOUSE
CULLODEN BATTLEFIELD
Kilmorack
Drumchardine
Leachkin
Culcabock
CLAVA CAIRNS
Allt Dearg
Breakachy
Balchraggan
HIGHLAND WINERIES
BUGHT FLORAL HALL VISITOR CENTRE
CASTLE GARRISON ENCOUNTER
Westhill
AIGAS DAM FISH LADDER
Easter Moniack
Newtonhill
Crask of Aigas
Beaufort Castle
Dunain Ho.
Castletown
Rireach Burn
Cabrich
Culburnie
Kiltarlity
The Aird
BEINN BHUIDHE MHOR
Caledonian Canal
Dochgarroch
House of Daviot
Camault Muir
AN LEACAINN
Leys Castle
Eskadale
Dochfour Ho.
DOCHFOUR GARDENS
Strath Dores
Ness
Essich
Daviot
Craggie
Lochend
Drummossie
BEINN BHREAC
CARN NAN TRI-TIGHEARNAN
Boblainy Forest
Lairgmore
Scatraig
Loch Bruicheach
Glen Convinth
Drumashie Moor
Moy Burn
GREAT GLEN WAY
MEALL MOR
MEALL A' BHREACRAIBH
Moy Hall
Loch Moy
Abriachan
ABRIACHAN GARDEN NURSERY
Balnafoich
Strathnairn
Moy
Strathdearn Forest
MEALL NAN CAORACH
Balchraggan
Dores
Tombreck
Loch Ashie
Dunlichity Lodge
Ruthven
Farr
Balbeg
Urquhart
LOCH NESS MONSTER EXHIBITIONS
MEALL NA H-EILRIG
Loch Ness
Farr House
Loch Duntelchaig
CARN NA H-EASGAINN
Upper Inverbrough
Balvraid
Milton
Achnabat
STAC NA CATHAIG
Drumnadrochit
Urquhart Bay
TOMATIN DISTILLERY
Enrick
Lewiston
DRUM FARM
Tullich
Brinmore
Tomatin
Strone
URQUHART CASTLE
Findhorn Bridge
CARN A' CHOIRE GHOIR
Divach
Upper Lenie
Lower Lenie
Loch Ruthven
East Croachy
BEINN BHREAC
COBB MEMORIAL
Torness
Aberarder House
Glen Kyllachy
Kyllachy House
Clune
Bunloit

MORAY FIRTH
NH
NJ
Highland
Tain
Portmahomack
Tarbat Discovery Centre
Glenmorangie Distillery
Tain Through Time Visitor Centre
Tain Tolbooth
Inver
Arboll
Balnagall
Lochslin
Tarrel
Rockfield
Loch Eye
Hilton
Aldie
Geanies House
Rhynie
Fearn Station
Fearn
Fearn Abbey
Hill of Fearn
Loans of Tullich
Hilton of Cadboll
Balintore
Shandwick
Shandwick Stone
East Lamington
Newfield
Logie Hill
Arabella
Kildary
Milton
Tarbat Ho.
Ankerville
Chapelhill
Pitcalnie
Kilmuir
Nigg Bay
Barbaraville
Sands of Nigg
Nigg
Mount Canisp
King's Cave
Port an Righ
Balnapaling
Balnabruaich
Castlecraig
Nigg Ferry
Cromarty
Cromarty Court House
Cromarty Bay
Sutors of Cromarty
Newton
Shore Mill
Upper Eathie
Balmungie
Groam House Museum and Pictish Centre
Rosemarkie Bay
Fort George
Queen's Own Highlanders Museum
Chanonry Pt.
Whiteness Head
The Bar
Nairn
Nairn Fishertown Museum
Nairn Literary Institute Museum
Kirkton
Baddock
Tradespark
Ardersier
Moss-side
Boath Dovecote
Auldearn
Earlsmill
Blackhills
Brodie Castle
Dyke
Culbin Forest
Kincorth Ho.
Kintessack
Moy Ho.
Forres
Sueno's Stone
Nelson Tower
Falconer Museum
Findhorn
Findhorn Bay
Kinloss
Kinloss Abbey
Springfield
Grange Hall
Burghead
Burghead Museum
Burghead Bay
Hopeman
Cummingston
Roseisle
Roseisle Forest
Lower Hempriggs
Miltonhill
Coltfield
Alves
Mains of Burgie
Monaughty Forest
Pluscarden Abbey
Barnhill
Blervie Castle
Califer
Dallas Dhu Distillery
Rafford
Altyre Ho.
Moor of Granary
Briach
Dallas Forest
Branchill
Dallas
Gollanfield
Milton of Gollanfield
Inverness
Muir of the Clans
Geddes House
Lochside
Rosefield
Regoul
Laiken Forest
Whitemire
Conicavel
Easter Milton
Wester Milton
Darnaway Forest
Altyre Woods
Newtyle Forest
Logie
Drumine Forest
Craigroy
Mill Buie
Clephanton
Cawdor
Piperhill
Culcharry
Littlemill
Kilravock Castle
Cawdor Castle and Gardens
Tornagrain
Croy
Mid Urchany
Newton
Cantraywood
Culloden Forest
Easter Galcantray
Achavraat
Relugas
Loch Dallas
Glenernie
Beachans
Kirkton of Barevan
Mains of Clunas
Redburn
Newlands of Fleenas Wood
Ardclach Tower
Mount
Ferness
Newlands
Cantraydoune
Cantraybruich
Assich Forest
Culloden Battlefield
Clava Cairns
Balmore
Castletown
Glenferness House
Carn Kitty
Dulsie
Carn Sgumain
Beinn Bhuidhe Mhor
Larig Hill
Dava
Aitnoch
Hill of Aitnoch
Daless
Beinn Bhreac
Carn nan Tri-Tighearnan
Moy Burn
Meall a'Bhreacraibh
Findhorn
Lochindorb
Lochindorb Castle
Lochindorb Lodge
Carn-Ruigh Charrach
Carn na Loine
Moy Hall
Loch Moy
Moy
Strathdearn Forest
Upper Derraid
Auchnagallin
Advie
Lettoch
Glaschoil
Ruthven
Upper Inverbrough
Balvraid
Carn an t-Sean-Liathanaich
Camerory
Cottartown
Dellefure
Mains of Dalvey
Tomatin Distillery
Carn Glas-Choire
Achnahannet
Beinn Mhor
Glenbeg
Grantown-on-Spey
Cromdale
Auchroisk
Haughs of Cromdale
Anagach
Craggan
Congash
Speybridge
Dulnain Bridge
Kyllachy House
Clune
0 1 2 3 4 5 6 miles
0 1 2 3 4 5 6 7 8 9 10 km

Halliman Skerries
Covesea Skerries
LOSSIEMOUTH FISHERIES & COMMUNITY MUSEUM
Covesea
Stotfield
Branderburgh
Lossiemouth
Duffus
Gordonstoun
Loch Spynie
Lossie Forest
DUFFUS CASTLE
PALACE OF SPYNIE
Spynie
SPEY BAY
Kingston
TUGNET ICE HOUSE
Spey Bay
Leuchars Ho.
Lochhill
Garmouth
Quarrywood
Newton
Bishopmill
Elgin
ELGIN MUSEUM
CATHEDRAL
CASHMERE VISITOR CENTRE
OLD MILLS
MORAY MOTOR MUSEUM
New Elgin
Urquhart
Lhanbryde
Lochs Crofts
Pittendreich
Miltonduff
Moss of Barmuckity
COXTON TOWER
Mosstodloch
Paddockhaugh
Auchtertyre
BIRNIE CHURCH
Longmorn
Blackhills
Foresterseat
Thomshill
MILLBUIES
Teindland Forest
Orbliston
Dipple
Kellas
Glenlatterach
Glen of Rothes
338
Auchinroath
Newlands
Incherry
Moray
365 CAIRN UISH
Rothes
GLEN GRANT DISTILLERY
Burn of Rothes
404 CARN NA CAILLICHE
Elchies Forest
369
Whiteacen
Dandaleith
LADYCROFT AGRICULTURAL MUSEUM
Archiestown
Ringorm
CARDHU DISTILLERY
Cardow
Upper Knockando
Knockando
Knockando Ho.
Carron
Daugh of Kinermony
Speyview
Craigellachie
SPEYSIDE COOPERAGE VISITOR CENTRE
Charlestown of Aberlour
Milltown of Edinvillie
SPEYSIDE WAY
Marypark
Bellehiglash
GLENFARCLAS DISTILLERY
Bridge of Avon
Dalchirach
Drumin
GLENLIVET DISTILLERY
Glenlivet
Shenval
Auchbreck
Ballcorach
Tomnavoulin
Glenlivet
Avon
840 BEN RINNES
Favillar
Kirkhill
MEIKLE CONVAL 569
Glen Rinnes
Dullan Water
Glenfiddich Forest
742
732 CARN AN
569
Blackwater Forest
Black Water
Fiddich
Glen Fiddich
Bridgend
Inverharroch
Ballochford
487 THE SCALP
AUCHINDOUN CASTLE
Kirktown of Mortlach
Dufftown
BALVENIE CASTLE
GLENFIDDICH DISTILLERY
Milltown of Auchindoun
417
Maggieknockater
Kininvie Ho.
Midtown of Buchromb
Drummuir Castle
Drummuir
Towiemore
339
KEITH AND DUFFTOWN RLY
Rosarie Forest
471 BEN AIGAN
SPEYSIDE WAY
Mulben
311
NJ
Wood of Ordiequish
Ordiequish
Speymouth Forest
Fochabers
FOCHABERS FOLK MUSEUM
BAXTERS HIGHLAND VILLAGE
Newlands of Tynet
Auchenhalrig
SPEYSIDE WAY
Bogmoor
Upper Dallachy
Nether Dallachy
Porttanachy
Slackhead
Braes of Enzie
Forgie
Aultmore
Newmill
Keith
STRATHISLA DISTILLERY
STRATH ISLA
Broadrashes
301 MILLSTONE HILL
Broadley
ST. GREGORY'S CHAPEL
Clochan
Cairnfield Ho.
Drybridge
Shiel Muir
Portgordon
Buckpool
Buckie
Gordonsburgh
THE BUCKIE DRIFTER
Findochty
Portknockie
Portessie
Rathven
Cullen
Cullen Bay
Logie Hd.
Sandend Bay
FINDLATER CASTLE
Sandend
Lintmill
320
Fordyce
Milton
Kirktown of Deskford
DESKFORD CHURCH
Ardiecow
Berryhillock
Craibstone
Little Toux
Deerhill
Grange Crossroads
Mains of Edingight
Edingight Ho.
Gordonstown
KNOCK HILL
Aultmore
Crannoch
Sillyearn
Bracobrae
Davoch of Grange
Knock
Glen Barry
Drumnagorrach
Farmtown
Knau
ISLA
366
Balloch Wood
Milltown of Rothiemay
Glen of Coachford
Ruthven
Edintore
Little Pitlurg
Coachford
Cairnie
THE BIN
The Bin Forest
Corse of Kinnoir
Daugh of Cairnborrow
Cairnborrow
NORDIC SKI CENTRE
HUNTLY CASTLE
Huntly
BRANDER MUS
Torry
Deveron
Haugh of Glass
Slioch
STRATHBOGIE
Bailieswarđ
Bridgend
Tillathrowie
Succoth
525
Tomnaven
Kirkhill
Shanquhar
Coynachie
Culdrain
Blackburn
Clashindarroch Forest
Clashindarroch
Kirkney
Gartly
Kirkney Water
Cults
434 KNOCKANDY HILL
LEITH HALL
Milton of Noth
Kennethmont
Ardlair
Cottown
Rhynie
Belhinnie
Wheedlemont
Clatt
Milton of Lesmore
Auchmair
505
Cabrach
571 ROUND HILL
Aldunie
149
150
160
A941
A96
A95
A98
A990
A942
A920
A97
B9040
B9135
B9103
B9012
B9015
B9014
B9016
B9018
B9022
B9117
B9118
B9002
B9010
B9102
B9138
B9008
B9009
B9136
B9115

Findochty
Portknockie
Cullen Bay
Logie Hd.
Sandend Bay
Redhythe Pt.
Boyne Bay
Knock Hd.
Boyndie Bay
Head of Garness
Gamrie Bay
Troup Hd.
Portessie
Rathven
Cullen
Lintmill
Findlater Castle
Sandend
Portsoy
Seatown
Joiner's Workshop
Fordyce
Whitehills
Easter Whyntie
Boyndie
Auds
Inverboyndie
Macduff
Macduff Marine Aquarium
Banff
Banff Museum
Colleonard Sculpture Garden & Gallery
Duff House
Doune Park
Easter Silverford
West Eserskares
Longmanhill
Crovie
Gardenstown
Pennan
Dubford
Drybridge
Milton
Kirktown of Deskford
Deskford Church
Ardiecow
Berryhillock
Shiel Muir
Wester Culbeuchly
Montcoffer Ho.
Cushnie
Minnonie
Netherbrae
Mid Cloch Forbie
Hill of Fishrie
Craibstone
Little Toux
Newmills of Boyne
Oldtown of Ord
Kirktown of Alvah
Keilhill
Gorrachie
Cornhill
Weachyburn
Fattahead
Greenlaw
The Pole of Itlaw
King Edward
Milltown of Craigston
Craigston Castle
Plaidy
Fintry
Deerhill
Mains of Edingight
Edingight Ho.
Grange Crossroads
Gordonstown
Knock Hill
Blacklaw
Finnygaud
Hill of Mountblairy
Muirden
New Byth
Crannoch
Sillyearn
Knock
Glen Barry
Knowes of Elrick
Bracobrae
Davoch of Grange
Drumnagorrach
Farmtown
Cranna
Aberchirder
Bogton
Forglen Ho.
Garmond
Whitestones
Muiryfold
Balthangie
Old Crombie
Knauchland
Strathisla Distillery
Marnoch
Clunie
Carnousie
Turriff
Delgatie Castle
Cuminestown
Middle Cairncake
Balloch Wood
Kirkton
Little Colp
Delgaty Forest
Milltown of Rothiemay
Mains of Mayen
Hillbrae
Inverkeithny
Mill of Muiresk
Hatton Castle
Darra
Howe of Teuchar
Rush-head
Glen of Coachford
Ruthven
Yonder Bognie
Bognie
Fourman Hill
Auchininna
Coachford
Cairnie
Aberdeen
Fortrie
Brownhill
Birkenhills
Crofts of Inverthernie
The Bin
The Bin Forest
Corse of Kinnoir
Glendronach Distillery
Drumblair
NJ
Dykeside
Cairnbanno Ho.
South Millbrex
Steinmanhill
Daugh of Cairnborrow
Nordic Ski Centre
Huntly Castle
Lessendrum
Denmoss
Balgaveny
Nether Lenshie
Inverythan
Gourdas
Tifty
Lethenty
Cottown
Monkshill
Cairnborrow
Huntly
Drumblade
Corse
Auchamie
Kirkton of Auchterless
Brander Museum
Brideswell
Slioch
Logie Newton
Backhill
Fyvie Castle
Fyvie
Gordonstown
Woodhead
Ardo
Crofts of Haddo
Strathbogie
Bailiesward
Thomastown
Denend
Ythanwells
Badenscoth
Redhill
Rothiebrisbane
Bridgend
Rothienorman
Petty
Collynie
Tillathrowie
Hillhead
Bainshole
Fisherford
Cromblet
Barthol Chapel
Kirkstile
Shanquhar
Glens of Foudland
Hill of Foudland
Kirkton of Culsalmond
Rothmaise
Newseat
Folla Rule
St Katherine's
Earlsford
Coynachie
Blackburn
Culdrain
Cross of Jackston
Balgove
Clashindarroch Forest
Kirkney
Gartly
Colpy
Cairnhill
Tocher
Jackstown
Tulloch
Clashindarroch
Largie
Meikle Wartle
Cults
Knockandy Hill
Wrangham
Bonnyton
Craigdam
Kirkney Water
Kirkton of Rayne
Meldrum Ho.
Auquhorthies
Milton of Lesmore
Milton of Noth
Kennethmont
Oldtown
Ardlair
Aulton
The Shevock
Insch
Newton Ho.
Old Rayne
Loanhead Stone Circle
Mounie Castle
Daviot
Formartine
Belhinnie
Rhynie
Cottown
Ardoyne
Pitmachie
Durno
Fingask
Oldmeldrum
Archaeolink Prehistory Park
Whiteford
Pitcaple
Barra Castle
Mill of Kingoodie
Wheedlemont
Craig Castle
Clatt
Duncanston
Leslie
Kirkton
Westhall
Oyne
Kirkton of Oyne
Chapel of Garioch
Harlaw Ho.
Kirkton of Bourtie
Hattoncrook
St Mary's Church
Knockespock Ho.
Auchleven
Gadie Burn
Pittodrie
Battle of Harlaw Memorial
Balhalgardy
Hillbrae
Nether Crimond
Coldwells Croft
Whitehaugh Forest
Bennachie
Brandsbutt Stone
Burgh Muir
Inverurie Museum
Inverurie
Tillykerrie
Clova
Scottish Sculpture Workshop
Lumsden
Corren Hills
Muckletown
Garioch
Glenton
Upper Woodend
Bograxie
Burnhervie
Manar Ho.
Port Elphinstone
Kinmuck
Middleton
Balbithan Ho.
Kinkell Church
Tullynessle
Mossat
Lord Arthur's
Keig
Castle Forbes
Aquhythie
Rorandle
Don
Pitfichie
Blairdaff
Dalmadilly
Clovenstone
Balbithan
Wester Fintray
Cairnpark
Kildrum
Montgarrie
Haughton
Pitfichie
Grantlodge
Drummy Garden
Auchintoul
Alford
Grampian Transport Mus.
Gateside
Pitfichie Forest
Monymusk Arts Centre
Kemnay
Cottown
Kintore
Hatton of Fintray
0 1 2 3 4 5 6 miles
0 1 2 3 4 5 6 7 8 9 10 km

Fraserburgh
Rosehearty
Sandhaven Meal Mill
Fraserburgh Heritage Museum
Pittulie
Broadsea
Kinnaird Head
Kinnaird Castle Lighthouse & Scotland's Lighthouse Museum
Pitsligo Castle
Sandhaven
Peathill
Quarry Hd.
Fraserburgh Bay
Cairnbulg Pt.
Inverallochy
Percyhorner
Pitblae
Coburty
Maggie's Hoosie
Towie
Upper Boyndlie
Mid Ardlaw
Cairnbulg Castle
St Combs
Inzie Head
New Aberdour
Tyrie
Memsie
Gowanhill
Memsie Burial Cairn
Strathellie
Ladysford
Whitewell
Rathen
Cairness
Loch of Strathbeg
Nether Glasslaw
Hillhead of Auchentumb
Crimonmogate
Craigmaud
Newburgh
Loch of Strathbeg Nature Reserve Visitor Centre
Lonmay
Rattray Head
Old Rattray
Crimond
Mormond Hill
New Pitsligo
Knowhead
Strichen
Nether Park
Blackhill
NJ
NK
New Leeds
Longhill
Balearn
Bonnykelly
Adziel
North Ugie Water
Leys
St Fergus Moss
Ironside
Little Skillymarno
Denhead
Backfolds
Kirktown
St Fergus
Scotstown Hd.
Oldwhat
Fetterangus
Hythie
Rora Moss
North Kirkton
Mains of Fedderate
Forest of Deer
Toux
Rora
Lunderton
Kirkton Hd.
Deer Abbey
Dunshillock
Woodside
Culsh
Maud
Aden
Mintlaw
Newseat
Inverugie
Water
Inverugie Castle
Ugie Salmon Fish House
Maud Railway Museum
Backhill of Clackriach
Old Deer
Longside
Torterston
Buchanhaven
New Deer
Flushing
Peterhead
Aberdeenshire Farming Museum
South Ugie
Stuartfield
Inverquhomery
Arbuthnot Museum & Art Gallery
Drymuir
Millbreck
Keith Inch
Bulwark
Hillhead of Cocklaw
Peterhead Maritime
Buchan
Aberdeenshire
Peterhead Bay
Nethermuir
Crichie
Mains of Crichie
Nether Kinmundy
Invernettie
Sandford Bay
Knaven
Kinnadie
Little Dens
Skelmuir
Clola
Boddam
Blackhill
Buchan Ness
Millbank
Crofts of Meikle Ardo
Barrack
Mains of Annochie
Kinknockie
Stirling
Sandfordhill
Cairnorrie
Auchnagatt
Backhill of Fortree
Smallburn
Brownhill
Mains of Inkhorn
Moss of Cruden
Coldwells
Backhill
Stoneygate
Longhaven
Skelmonae
Teuchan
Quilquox
Milton Coldwells
North Haven
Auchiries
Bullers of Buchan
Methlick
Drumwhindle
Muirtack
Arthrath
Eastertown of Auchleuchries
Hatton
Twa Havens
Ythan
Cruden Bay
Haddo
Toll of Birness
Port Erroll
Haddo House and Gardens
Bogbrae
Chapel Hill
Bay of Cruden
Ythanbank
Hilton
Mains of Birness
Wedderlairs
Inverebrie
Nether Leask
Whinnyfold
Raxton
Broomfield
Medieval Tomb
West Kinharrachie
P&R
Artrochie
Tarves
Auchmacoy
Ythsie
Esslemont
Ellon
Slains Castle
Formartine
Kirkton of Logie Buchan
Kirktown of Slains
Tolquhon Castle
Visitor Centre
Collieston
Pitmedden Gardens
Pitmedden
Waterside
St Catherine's Dub
Meikle Tarty
Tipperty
Forvie
Sands of Forvie
Cairnbrogie
Hackley Hd. or Forvie Ness
Udny Green
Tarty Burn
Newburgh
Pettymuick
Culterculen
Foveran
Affleck
Udny Station
Foveran Burn
Newburgh Bar
Whiterashes
Tillygreig
Tillycorthie
Minnes
Rashiereive
Drums
Ardo Ho.
Straloch
Delfrigs
Middlemuir
Newmachar
Craigie
Causeyend
Kinmundy
Whitecairns
Belhelvie
Balmedie
Drumligair
Cothall
A90
A950
A952
A981
A98
A948
A975
A947
A920
B9031
B9032
B9033
B9107
B9093
B9029
B9106
B9170
B9030
B9005
B999
B9000
B977
B979
151

1
2
3
4
A
B
C
D
E
F
166
154
Eilean Chrona
Culkein
Clashnessie Bay
Cluas Deas
Achnacarnin
Clashmore
Clashnessie
Balchladich
Rienachait
Stoer
Rubh'a' Mhill Dheirg
Bay of Stoer
Clachtoll
Loch Crocach
R. Leumair
Achmelvich Bay
B869
Rhicarn
Achmelvich
ACHMELVICH BEACH
ASSYNT VISITOR CENTRE
Rubha Rodha
Baddidarach
Lochinver
Soyea I.
Loch Inver
Kirkaig Pt.
Badnaban
A'Chleit
Inverkirkaig
Strathan
Loch Kirkaig
Rubha na Breige
Eilean Mór
Rubha Coigeach
ENARD BAY
Rubh'a' Choin
NB
Camas Eilean Ghlais
Rubha Mor
Inverpolly Lodge
Reiff
Brae of Achnahaird
Altandhu
SUMMER ISLES SMOKEHOUSE
Polly
Eilean Mullagrach
Loch Vatachan
Loch Osgaig
Aird of Coigach
Isle Ristol
Polbain
Glas-leac Mór
Loch Bad a'Ghaill
Achiltibuie
HYDROPONICUM GARDENS
Badentarbat Bay
Polglass
NC
Tanera Beg
Summer Isles
Tanera Mór
ACHENINVER
Horse Sound
Horse I.
Glas-leac Beag
Culnacraig
743 BEINN MO COIGAC
Achduart
Eilean Dubh
Priest I.
Bottle I.
Carn nan Sgeir
Camas M
Greenstone Point
Cailleach Hd.
Isle Martin
STORNOWAY 2:40
Rubha Beag
Annat Bay
Rhue
Opinan
Stattic Pt.
Scoraig
Carnach
Rubha Mor
LITTLE LOCH BROOM
NG
Mellon Udrigle
Rireavach
NH
635 BEINN GHOBHLACH
Gruinard I.
Badluarach
Eilean Furadh Mór
Mungasdale
Sròn a' Gheodha Dhuibh
Achgarve
Dundonnell
Rubha Reidh
Camas Mór
155
Gruinard Bay
Gruinard House
A832
Badcaul
Badrallach
Laide
Mellon Charles
First Coast
Loch an Draing
Sand
Cove
Ormiscaig
Second Coast
Inchina
Tighnafiline
Little Gruinard
302
Camusnagaul
296 AN CUAIDH
Isle of Ewe
Aultbea
Drumchork
Gruinard
Ardessie
767 SAIL MHOR
29
Loch Sguod
Loch a'Bhaid-luachraich
Dundonnell Hotel
Melvaig
LOCH EWE
Little Gruinard
Inverasdale
Aultgrishan
Midtown
Loch Fada
WESTER ROSS
Strathnasheallag Forest
Seana Chamas
Brae
B8057
Rubha 'Ard na Bà
14
AN TEALLACH 1062
Naast
Tournaig
Aird Dubh
Loch na Sealga
Peterburn
A832
INVEREWE GARDEN
Loch Bad a'Chreamh
680 BEINN A'CHAISGEIN BEAG
B8021
Port Erradale
9
Londubh
Fisherfield Forest
North Erradale
Poolewe
Loch Kernsary
FIONN LOCH
908 BEINN DEARG MHOR
Strath na Sealga
Rubha Bàn
Big Sand
Ewe
Loch Tolláidh
0 1 2 3 4 5 6 miles
0 1 2 3 4 5 6 7 8 9 10 km
MEALL AN DOIREAN 420
Dubh Loch
914 BEINN A' CHLAIDHEIMH
791
LOCH GAIRLOCH

Culkein
Drumbeg
Oldany
Drumbeg
Nedd
Loch Poll
B869
Kylesku
Unapool
Newton
Glendhu Forest
Loch Glendhu
Gleann Dubh
Loch Glencoul
Glen Coul
530
BEINN AIRD DA LOCH
Kinloch
A838
566
873
BEN HEE
Loch a'Ghorm-choire
Gleann Leireag
166
167
Loch Merkland
Merkland Lodge
792
BEINN LEOID
Loch an Eircill
Loch Dubh a'Chuail
Loch a'Ghriama
Loch Fiag
404
473
Loch an Leothaid
808
QUINAG
Loch Beannach
Lochassynt Lodge
A894
EAS COUL AULIN WATERFALL
776
BEINN UIDHE 740
Corrykinloch
312
CNOC AN ALASKIE
Glen Fiag
Fiag Plantation
LOCH ASSYNT
Skiag Bridge
ARDVRECK CASTLE
Gorm Loch Mor
Fionn Loch Mor
Overscaig Hotel
A837
Inver
Little Assynt
Brackloch
Glencanisp Lodge
Loch Feith an Leòthaid
540
Inchnadamph
Inchnadamph Forest
LOCH SHIN
512
MAOVALLY
Fiag Bridge
ASSYNT-
Glencanisp
Forest
SUILVEN
731
846
CANISP
Stronchrubie
INCHNADAMPH
998
BEN MORE ASSYNT
391
A838
Allt Car
Strath an Lòin
Kirkaig
Falls
Fionn Loch
Loch na Gainimh
718
BREABAG
MEALL AN AONAICH 715
Duchally
164
COIGACH
Loch Awe
Loanan
NC
Benmore Forest
Cam Loch
Loch Veyatie
Ledbeg
Loch Sionascaig
Ledmore
Glen Oykel
Glen Cassley
BEINN SGEIREACH 476
Allt a'Bhunn
HIGHLAND & RARE BREEDS FARM
Elphin
Altnacealgach Hotel
Loch Ailsh
Benmore Lodge
Inverpolly Forest
613
849
CUL MOR
Drumrunie Forest
Loch an Doire Dhuibh
Knockan
Loch Urigill
A837
364
AN STUC
BEINN AN EOIN 554
Loch Lurgainn
769
CUL BEAG
KNOCKAN CRAG
A835
CROMALT HILLS
517
Cromm Allt
Glencassley Castle
Loch na Fuaralaich
Drumrunie
Loch Craggie
Loch na Claise Moire
Glenrossal
402
CNOC A'CHOIRE
IGACH
Oykel Forest
Langwell Lodge
Rappach
Runie
Strathcanaird
Kanaird
Strath Kanaird
Strath nan Lon
578
MEALL AN FHUARAIN
Oykel
18
Lubcroy
Oykel Bridge
Strath Oykel
A837
Invercassley
Rosehall
Brae
Doune
Oape
Altass
Loch Kanaird
A835
415
Allt-Beinn Donuill
Rappach Water
340
Einig
Glen Einig
Ach
Ardmair
Highland
Rhidorroch Forest
493
BEINN ULBHAIDH
Morefield
Ullapool
Loch Achall
Rhidorroch Ho.
548
Loch an Daimh
Strath Mulzie
Corriemulzie Lodge
412
CREAG LOISGTE
Strath Cuileannach
507
MEALL DHEIRGIDH
ULLAPOOL MUSEUM
ULLAPOOL
Ullapool
LOCHBROOM MUSEUM
Glen Achall
Rhidorroch
East Rhidorroch Lodge
Corriemulzie
LOCH BROOM
Allt na h-Airbhe
A835
558
BEINN EILIDEACH
LECKMELM SHRUBBERY AND ARBORETUM
Leckmelm
Glasha Burn
701
CARN A' CHOIN DEIRG
CROICH CHURCH
Croich
The Craigs
Amat Forest
Amatnatua
Carron
Braelan
Wester Gruinards
Blarnalearoch
Rhiroy
Ardindrean
642
MEALL DUBH
677
MEALL NAM BRADHAN
Ardcharnich
Loch a'Choire Mhoir
Freevater
822
Forest
Alladale Lodge
Alladale
279
Glencalvie Lodge
Eilean Darach
Letters
Douchary
927
SEANA BHRAIGH
845
CARN BAN
Gleann Mòr
Glencalvie Forest
Inverlael Forest
EASTER ROSS
CARN SAL
Dundonnell House
Inverlael
LAEL FOREST GARDEN
Lael Forest
NH
928
735
Deanich Lodge
Diebidale
Forest
Inverbroom
Lael
Gleann Beag
Crom Loch
714
BEINN THARSUINN
Glen Diebidale
838
CARN CHUINNEAG
Strath More
Broom
628
Forest
Auchindrean
889
1084
BEINN DEARG
Tollomuick Forest
Abhainn na Glasa
156
Fain
more
954
787
BEINN A'CHAISTEIL
Loch a'Chaorainn
CORRIESHALLOCH GORGE
A832
Dundonnell
Abhainn Cuileig
MEALL LEACACHAIN
618
Loch Vaich
772
MEALL A' GHRIANAIN
Inchbae Forest
Kildermorie Forest
Kildermorie Lodge
Braemore Forest
Abhainn Droma
742
Loch Mor
A B C D E F G
5 6 7 8

873 BEN HEE
Loch a'Ghorm-choire
Clebrig
A836
Loch Truderscaig
Loch an Alltan Fhearna
Loch Badanloch
Badanloch Lodge
328
272
167
473
721 BEN KLIBRECK
Loch Choire Lodge
168
Loch Fiag
Merkland Lodge
404
Strath Vagastie
Kilbreck Burn
961 MEALL NAN CON
Loch Choire Forest
Loch Choire
Borrobol Forest
312 CNOC AN ALASKIE
542
18
704 BEN ARMINE
Gorm-loch Beag
Loch a'Bhealaich
581 MEALL A'BHATA
Glen Fiag
Fiag Plantation
Crask Inn
Overscaig Hotel
Loch Gaineamhach
713 CREAG MHOR
Gorm-loch Mór
365
486
Fiag Bridge
BEN ARMINE FOREST
Skinsdale
Strath Skinsdale
391
LOCH SHIN
A838
Strath Tirry
Tirry
Ben Armine Lodge
Glas-loch Mor
Strath na Seilge
Allt Car
Strath an Loin
163
461 MEALLAN LIATH MOR
Rhian
Shinness
Dalnessie
NC
Black Water
Glen Cassley
Achnairn
Loch Beannach
Allt a'Bhunn
BEINN SGEIREACH 476
Highland
Brora
Strath Brora
Dalchork
Dalchork Wood
Achnaluachrach
299
West Langwell
Allt na Luibe
Colaboll
BEINN AN EOIN 554
Sallachy
Saval
Lairg Lodge
Lairg Muir
Loch Craggie
Dalreavoch
Rhilochan
Glencassley Castle
Loch na Fuaralaich
Lairg
323
A839
FERRYCROFT COUNTRYSIDE CENTRE
East Langwell
Farlary
Strath Fleet
Glenrossal
Grudie Burn
Claonel
Gruids
Torroble
Muie
14
402 CNOC A'CHOIRE
Cassley
Oykel Forest
Rogart
Ardachu
Loch Cracail Mor
Pittentrail
Invercassley
Rosehall
B864
A836
Glen Achany
Achany
336
HECTOR MACDONALD MONUMENT
Rogart Station
466
BEINN LUNNDA
Oykel Bridge
Strath Oykel
A837
Brae
Doune
Oape
Altass
Shin Forest
Achinduich
Morvich
Fleet
Shin
FALLS OF SHIN VISITOR CENTRE
Linsidemore
11
Loch Laro
Loch Buidhe
Torboll Farm
Kirkton
A9
Achnahanat
Little Torboll
Inveran
Invershin
Cambusmore Lodge
Loch Fleet
493 BEINN ULBHAIDH
Craigton
349 BEINN DOMHNAILL
Cambusavie Farm
Kyle of Sutherland
CARBISDALE CASTLE
297
Skelbo
1650
Culrain
Balblair
Achvaich
Badninish
507 MEALL DHEIRGIDH
Strath Culleannach
Airdens
Clashcoig
Evelix
Rearquhar
Poles
Braelangwell Lodge
Proncy
Carron
Migdale
Strathcarron
B9168
701 CARN A'CHOIN DEIRG
Croich
Wester Gruinards
Soyal
Bonar Bridge
Gablon
Pitgrudy
CROICH CHURCH
The Craigs
Lower Gledfield
Loch Migdale
Evelix
HISTORYLINKS EXHIBITION
Amat Forest
Amatnatua
Dounie
Ardgay
Spinningdale
Ospisdale
Clashmore
Camore
Alladale Lodge
279
A949
10
Dornoch
Alladale
Glencalvie Lodge
Kincardine
DORNOCH FIRTH
Whiteface
Skibo Castle
DORNOCH CATHEDRAL
Lonemore
Upper Ardchronie
Fearn Lodge
Dornoch Sands
Glencalvie Forest
645 CARN SALACHAIDH
Meikle Ferry
Ardmore
Easter Fearn
Cambuscurrie Bay
Ferry Point
EASTER ROSS
B9176
Edderton
Balleigh
Wester Fearn Burn
GLENMORANGIE DISTILLERY
ALDIE WATERMILL
Crom Loch
Diebidale
Forest
Loch a'Chairn
NH
A836
Tarlogie
Meikle Gluich
Morangie
Tain
714 BEINN THARSUINN
Glen Diebidale
838 CARN CHUINNEAG
Easter Fearn Burn
546
TAIN THROUGH TIME VISITOR CENTRE
Aultnamain Inn
321
Quarryhill
Morangie Forest
602
Aldie
Hilton
Abhainn na Glasa
157
692 BEINN THARSUINN
157
0 1 2 3 4 5 6 miles
0 1 2 3 4 5 6 7 8 9 10 km
Braeantra
Strath Rusdale
East Lamington
Lamington
Newfield
Inchbae Forest
Black Water
Strath Rory
Ogie Hill
742
Loch Morie
CNOC CORR GUINIE
Torran
Scotsburn

Loch Arichlinie
Knockfin Heights
Achentoul
Strath Beg
Kinbrace
B871
A897
Helmsdale
168
318 CNOC LOCH MHADADH
Dunbeath Water
Berriedale Water
Braemore
169
Smerral
Latheronwheel Ho.
Latheronwheel
LAIDHAY CROFT MUSEUM
DUNBEATH HERITAGE CENTRE
Balnabruich
Dunbeath
Dunbeath Bay
DUNBEATH CASTLE
Knockally
283
Kinbrace Burn
438 CNOC COIRE NA PEARNA
Abhainn na Frithe
705 MORVEN
517 CNOC AN EIREANNAICH
Suisgill Burn
Ramscraigs
Altanduin
Borrobol Lodge
A897
Wag
626 SCARABEN
Langwell Forest
Borgue
Newport
Ceann Leathad nam Bò
STRATH OF KILDONAN
Kildonan Burn
387 CREAG NAM FIADH
555 CREAG SCALABSDALE
Aultibea
Langwell Water
Langwell Ho.
Berriedale
BADBEA CLEARANCE VILLAGE
Kildonan Lodge
BAILE AN ÒR GOLDRUSH SITE
BEINN DUBHAIN 414
422
Tuarie Burn
Craggie
Craggie Burn
Helmsdale
Torrish
Kilphedir
A897
A9
Ousdale
345
ELDRABLE HILL 417
Marrel
HELMSDALE
Navidale
Ord Point
West Helmsdale
TIMESPAN HERITAGE CENTRE
NC
628 BEINN DHORAIN
Glen Sletdale
Glen Loth
592
Gartymore
Helmsdale
ND
Portgower
Balnacoil
538 COL-BHEINN
Lothmore
Lothbeg
Gordonbush
Lothbeg Pt.
Loch Brora
A9
BEN HORN 521
Loch Horn
Achrimsdale
East Clyne
West Clyne
Clynelish
CLYNELISH DISTILLERY
Dalchalm
377 CAGAR FEOSAIG
Brora
Doll
Golspie Burn
Backies
DUNROBIN CASTLE MUSEUM & GARDENS
Golspie
Culmaily
LOCH FLEET
Littleferry
SKELBO CASTLE
Fourpenny
Embo
Embo Street
WITCHES STONE
OLD POST OFFICE VISITOR CENTRE
DORNOCH FIRTH
NH
NJ
Tarbat Ness
TARBAT NESS LIGHTHOUSE
Wilkhaven
Whiteness Sands
TARBAT DISCOVERY CENTRE
Bindal
Portmahomack
Rockfield
Inver
Arboll
Balnagall
Tarrel
Lochslin
Loch Eye
B9165
Rhynie
158
Geanies House
Fearn Station
B9165
Fearn
Hill of Fearn
FEARN ABBEY
Hilton of Cadboll
Loans of Tullich
Arabella
Balintore
5
6
7
8
A
B
C
D
E
F
G

1
2
3
4
5
A
B
C
D
E
F
CAPE WRATH
Kearvaig
371 SGRIBHIS-BHEINN
Geodha Ruadh na Fola
Bay of Keisgaig
Kearvaig
Inshore
Loch Keisgaig
Geodha Ruadh
457 FASHVEN
Am Balg
423 BEINN DEARG
Loch Airigh na Beinne
Sandwood Loch
485 CREAG RIABHACH
Rubh'an Fhir Léithe
Grudie
Loch na Gainimh
Strath Shinary
332 GHLAS BHEINN
Sheigra
Balchrick
Droman
Oldshore Beg
Oldshoremore
Eilean Roin Mor
521 FARRMHEALL
A838
NC
Loch Clash
Kinlochbervie
Gualin Ho.
19
Badcall
B801
Achriesgill
Strath Dionard
Bagh Loch an Roin
Loch Inchard
Achlyness
L. na Claise Carnaich
Loch Dughaill
Ceathramh Garbh
Rhiconich
Ardmore Pt.
Rubha Ruadh
Ardmore
GANU MOR 908
Foinaven
Fanagmore
Tarbet
Loch Laxford
NORTH-WEST SUTHERLAND
Handa Island
Foindle
Loch a' Garbh-bhaid Mór
Sound of Handa
Loch nam Brac
A894
Laxford Bridge
Loch an Easain Uaine
787 ARKLE
Scourie Bay
Laxford
Scourie More
Scourie
A838
Gorm Loch
Lochstack Lodge
Rubh'Aird an t-Sionnaich
Loch Stack
719 BEN STACK
Upper Badcall
Lower Badcall
Strath Stack
BEINN AUSKAIRD 386
Badcall Bay
18
Achfary
332
Eil. a'Bhreitheimh
LOCH A'MHUILINN
Loch Crocach
REAY FOREST
Lochmore Lodge
Rubha a'Mhucard
A894
Loch More
Meall Mór
Calbha Mór
Loch na Creige Duibhe
Duartmore Forest
Eddrachillis Bay
Calbha Beag
Loch a' Chairn Bhain
Loch an Leathaid Bhuain
Auitanrynie
Point of Stoer
Oldany Island
Kylestrome
547 Forest
Kinloch
Cirean Geardail
161
R. nan Còsan
Eilean Chrona
Culkein Drumbeg
Loch Nedd
Kylesku
Glendhu
Culkein
Clashnessie Bay
Oldany
Loch Glendhu
Gleann Dubh
Cluas Deas
Drumbeg
B869
Unapool
530 BEINN AIRD DA LOCH
566
Achnacarnin
Nedd
8
Newton
Loch Glencoul
Clashmore
Loch Poll
Gleann Leireag
Glen Coul
Balchladich
Clashnessie
13
Rienachait
162
163
Loch an Leothaid
808 QUINAG
792 BEINN LEOID
Loch an Eircill
Loch Crocach
Loch Beannach
EAS COUL AULIN WATERFALL
Lochassynt Lodge
A894
A837
R. Leumair
Achmelvich Bay
776
BEINN UIDHE
0 1 2 3 4 5 6 miles
0 1 2 3 4 5 6 7 8 9 10 km

5
6
7
8
9
A
B
C
D
E
F
G
168
163
164
Faraid Head
Balnakeil Bay
BALNAKEIL CHURCH
Balnakeil
DURNESS VISITOR CENTRE
SMOO CAVE
Durness
DURNESS
Achiemore
BALNAKEIL CRAFT VILLAGE
Sangomore
Leirinmore
Keoldale
Kyle of Durness
Sangobeg
Rispond
Sarsgrum
422 MEALL MEADHONACH
Eilean Hoan
Geodh'a' Bhrideoin
Eilean Clùimhrig
Whiten Head
Rubha Thormaid
Portnancon
LOCH ERIBOLL
Heilam
Hope
Lochside
230
Eilean Choraidh
Eriboll
772 BEINN SPIONNAIDH
800 STACKIE
Polla
A838
Strath Beag
30
521 AN LEAN-CHARN
Loch Hope
A'Mhoine
A838
408 BEN HUTIG
Strathan
Midfield
Port Vasgo
West Strathan
Talmine
Skinnet
Midtown
Tongue Bay
Rabbit Is.
Achuvoldrach
TONGUE
Kirkiboll
Tongue
CASTLE VARRICH
KYLE OF TONGUE
NC
Druim nan Cliar
A836
310
Ribigill
Kinloch Lodge
Loch na Seilg
Loch Dionard
Loch Crocach
927 BEN HOPE
Loch a' Ghobha-Dhuibh
764 BEN LOYAL
FEINNE-BHEINN MOR 465
Loch an Dherue
Loch Loyal Lodge
557 CNOC NAN CULLEAN
Alltnacaillich
DUN DORNAIGIL BROCH
Strathmore
Strath More
Loch Haluim
Loch Coulside
Glen Golly
416
Inchkinloch
Gobernuisgach Lodge
Loch Meadie
777
759
Highland
Meadie Burn
Allt a' Chraois
Loch Coire na Saidhe Duibhe
Mudale
Mudale
Altnaharra
Clebrig
A836
B873
Loch Naver
A838
873 BEN HEE
Loch a' Ghorm-choire
34
Loch Merkland
Merkland Lodge
473
Strath Vagastie
Klibreck Burn
Loch Dubh a' Chuail
404
Loch Fiag
Loch a' Ghriama
Corrykinloch
312 CNOC AN ALASKIE
A836
18
642
961 MEALL NAN CON
Loch Choire Forest
721 BEN KLIBRECK
Loch a' Bhealaich
Loch Choire
581 MEALL
Loch Choire Lodge
704 BEN ARMINE
Gorm-loch Beag
Eilean nan Ron
Caol Raineach
Neave I. or Coombe I.
Skerray
Achtoty
Airdtorrisdale
Torrisdale
Skullomie
Coldbackie
Torrisdale Bay
Borgie
Invernaver
A836
Borgie Forest
Borgie
Farr Pt.
Kirtomy Pt.
Kirtomy
Farr
Swordly
STRATHNAVER MUSEUM
Bettyhill
Achina
Clachan Burn
Leckfurin
ACHANLOCHY CLEARANCE VILLAGE
Skelpick
B871
Skelpick Burn
Achagary
Loch Craggie
STRATHNAVER
Carnachy
Rhifail
293 BEINN RIFA-GIL
527 BEINN STUMANADH
16
Loch Loyal
Skail
Langdale
Loch Syre
Syre
Dalvina Lo.
River Naver
B873
ROSAL CLEARANCE TRAIL
B871
Rimsdale Burn
294 POLE HILL
Loch Eileanach
11
Mallart
Naver Forest
Loch Rimsdale
Loch nan C
Loch Truderscaig
272
Loch an Alltan Fhearna
328
9

Brims Ness
ST. MARY'S CHAPEL
Crosskirk
Strathy Point
Totegan
Armadale Bay
Strathy Bay
Melvich Bay
Sandside Bay
Brawl
Altiphurst
Baligill
Portskerra
Red Pt.
Fresgoe
Dounreay
DOUNREAY EXHIBITION CENTRE
Buldoo
Bridge of Forss
Achreamie
Eilean nan Ron
Ardmore Pt.
Kirtomy Pt.
Farr Pt.
Neave I. or Coombe I.
Torrisdale Bay
Skerray
Achtoty
Airdtorrisdale
Torrisdale
Kirtomy
Farr
Swordly
Armadale
Lednagullin
Strathy
Melvich
Bighouse
Sandside Ho.
Isauld
Achvarasdal
Reay
CNOC FREKEDAIN CHAMBERED CAIRN
Shebster
STRATHNAVER MUSEUM
Bettyhill
Achina
Invernaver
Borgie
Leckfurin
Clachan Burn
Loch Meadie
Bowside Lodge
Golval
Loch Akran
Loch Thormaid
Loch Saorach
Forss Water
Broubster
Strathy Forest
Loch Buidhe Mor
Loch na Seilge
Shurrery
Borgie Forest
ACHANLOCHY CLEARANCE VILLAGE
Skelpick
Loch Meala
Achiemore
Upper Bighouse
Craigtown
Dalhalvaig
Shurrery Lodge
Loch Scye
Achagary
Loch Mor na Caorach
Skelpick Burn
NC
Trantlemore
Trantlebeg
BEINN NAM BAD MOR
Loch nan Clach
The Uair
Loch Tuim Ghlais
Loch Caluim
Torran Water
Highland
Carnachy
Rhifail
STRATHNAVER
STRATH HALLADALE
BEINN UMANADH
BEINN RIFA-GIL
Forsinain
Loch nam Breac
Loch Strathy
Skail
Loch na Saobhaidhe
SLETILL HILL
Loch Sletill
Altnabreac Station
Lochdhu
Loch Syre
Langdale
Syre
Dalvina Lo.
Naver
Forsinard
Loch Crocach
ROSAL CLEARANCE TRAIL
Forsinard Station
FORSINARD NATURE RESERVE
Loch Druim a'Chliabhain
BEN GRIAM BEG
Loch a' Mhuilinn
Rumsdale Water
Dalnawilla Lodge
POLE HILL
Rimsdale Burn
Garvault Hotel
BEN GRIAM MORE
Allt Airigh-dhamh
Achentoul Forest
BEN ALISKY
Glutt Lodge
Mallart
Naver Forest
Loch an Ruathair
Loch Rimsdale
Loch nan Clàr
Badanloch Forest
Lochside
Knockfin Heights
Glutt Water
Loch Arichlinie
Loch Badanloch
Loch Truderscaig
Loch an Alltan Fhearna
Badanloch Lodge
Strath Beg
Achentoul
Kinbrace
Helmsdale
CNOC LOCH MHADADH
Loch Choire Lodge
Kinbrace Burn
CNOC COIRE NA PEARNA
Loch Choire
MORVEN
Abhainn na Frithe
Suisgill Burn
NOC AN EIREANNAICH
BEN ARMINE
Altanduin
Borrobol Lodge
Wag
A836
A897
B871
B873
167
164
165
0 1 2 3 4 5 6 miles
0 1 2 3 4 5 6 7 8 9 10 km

5
6
7
8
9
A
B
C
D
E
F
G
Swona
ST MARGARETS HOPE 1:00
176
Langaton Point
Nethertown
Red Head
Island of Stroma
Mell Head
Uppertown
St John's Pt.
Men of Mey
BURWICK 0:45 (May-Sept)
Boars of Duncansby
Gills Bay
DUNCANSBY HEAD
DUNNET HEAD
Briga Hd.
Scarfskerry Pt.
Scarfskerry
East Mey
CASTLE OF MEY
Ham
Brough
Hunspow
Rattar
Mey
Gills
Kirkstyle
Huna
JOHN O'GROATS
John o' Groats
Canisbay
Stacks of Duncansby
STROMNESS 1:30
The Thirl
St John's Loch
MARY-ANN'S COTTAGE
NATURAL HISTORY DISPLAY
Corsback
Barrock
Dunnet
Spear Hd.
Holborn Hd.
Thurso Bay
Clardon Hd.
DUNNET BAY
Inkstack
Scrabster
THURSO CASTLE
THURSO FOLK MUSEUM
FLAGSTONE INTERPRETATIVE TRAIL
Castlehill
Loch Heilen
Brabster
Skirza
Skirza Head
Tofts
Clardon
Murkle
Thurso
Thurso East
Castletown
Greenland
Lochend
Gill Burn
Freswick
Freswick Bay
Millbank
Haimer
CASTLETOWN
Tain
Newlands of Geise
Olrig Ho.
Slickly
Ness Head
BUCHOLLY CASTLE
Reaster
Geise
Hilliclay
Durran
Alterwall
NORTHLANDS VIKING CENTRE
Westfield
Weydale
Bowermadden
Lyth
LYTH ARTS CENTRE
Nybster
Auckengill
Sortat
Lieurary
Buckies
Achingills
Barrock Ho.
Brough Head
Howe
Stemster
Sordale
Knockdee
Stemster Ho.
Bowertower
Keiss
KEISS CASTLE
Loch Calder
Mireland
Braal Castle
Halcro
Hastigrow
Calder Mains
Roadside
Gillock
Kirk
Loch of Wester
Halkirk
Clayock
Loch Scarmclate
North Watten
Myrelandhorn
SINCLAIR'S BAY
Brawlbin
Banniskirk Ho.
Killimster
Loch Olginey
Scotscalder Station
Harpsdale
Loch Watten
Mains of Watten
Loch Shurrery
Dorrery
Olgrinmore
CASTLE SINCLAIR
CASTLE GIRNIGOE
Noss Head
Reiss
Watten
Winless
Spittal
Backlass
Sealky Head
Ackergill
Bilbster
WICK
Staxigoe
Mybster
Loch of Toftingall
WICK HERITAGE CENTRE
Papigoe
Wick
Strath
Westerdale
Acharole
Stirkoke Ho.
Milton
Broadhaven
Burn of Acharole
Strath Burn
Achairn Burn
Wick Bay
Old Wick
Newton
South Hd.
Loch Meadie
Badlipster
CASTLE OF OLD WICK
Whiterow
Gote O'Tram
Tannach
Hempriggs House
Loch Eileanach
Strathmore Lodge
Little River
Loch Hempriggs
Loch Gaineimh
Camster Burn
Helman Hd.
Lochmore Cottage
ND
HILL OF OLICLETT
Thrumster
Rangag
Gansclet
GREY CAIRNS OF CAMSTER
Loch More
Sarclet
Loch of Yarrows
Sarclet Hd.
Loch Ruard
Achavanich
Loch Sand
Loch Thulachan
Loch Rangag
STEMSTER HILL
Camster
Ulbster
CAIRN OF GET
Whaligoe
Roster
Bruan
Loch Breac
Crofts of Benachielt
HILL O' MANY STANES
Rumster Forest
Upper Lybster
Mid Clyth
Braehungie
Loch Dubh
Reisgill Burn
LYBSTER ART GALLERY
West Clyth
CNOCAN CONACHREAG
Forse Ho.
Swiney
Lybster
Houstry
WAG OF FORSE
Burn of Houstry
Smerral
Forse
Latheron
CLAN GUNN HERITAGE CENTRE
Dunbeath Water
Latheronwheel Ho.
Latheronwheel
Braemore
LAIDHAY CROFT MUSEUM
165
Balnabruich
DUNBEATH HERITAGE CENTRE
Dunbeath
Knockally
Dunbeath Bay
DUNBEATH CASTLE
Ramscraigs
SCARABEN
Borgue
A9
A99
A836
A882
B855
B874
B876
B870

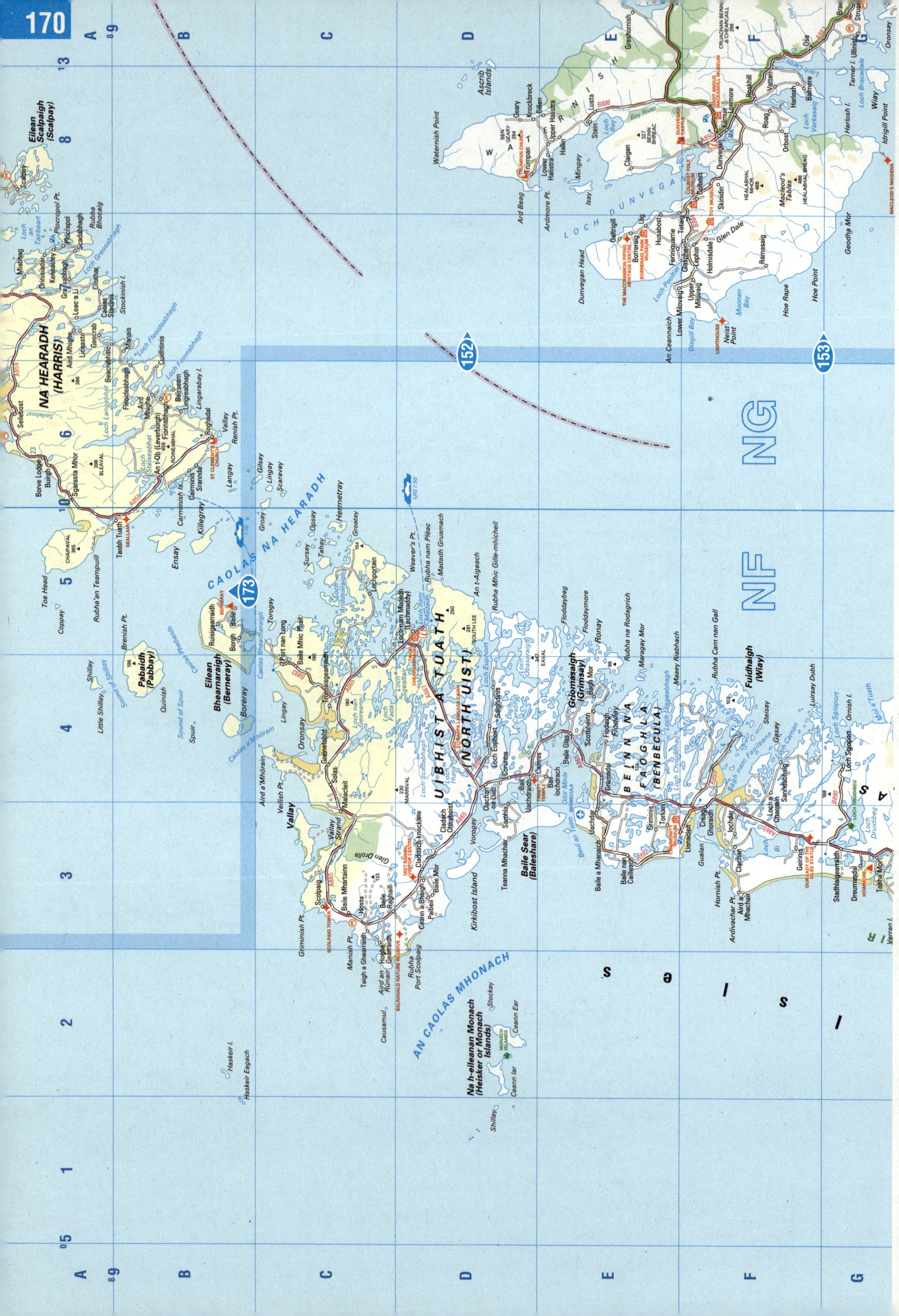

NA HEARADH (HARRIS)
Eilean Scalpaigh (Scalpay)
Scalpay
Tairbeart
Plocropol Pt.
Plocrapol
Scadabhagh
Rubha Bhocaig
Loch Greosabhagh
Stockinish I.
Manais
Loch Fleòideabhagh
Loch Fionnsbhagh
Lingarabay I.
Renish Pt.
Rodhadal
ST CLEMENT'S CHURCH
An t-Ob (Leverburgh)
Fionnsbhagh
Loch Steiseabhat
Sgarasta Mhor
BLEAVAL
Borve Lodge
Seilebost
Taobh Tuath
SEALLAM!
CHAIPAVAL
Toe Head
Rubha'an Teampuill
Coppay
Brenish Pt.
Shillay
Little Shillay
Sound of Shillay
Pabaidh (Pabbay)
Quinish
Sound of Spuir
Spuir
Ensay
Killegray
Carminish Is.
Langay
Gilsay
Lingay
Scaravay
Groay
Hermetray
CAOLAS NA HEARADH
Sursay
Opsay
Tahay
Grostay
Lochportain
Weaver's Pt.
Rubha nam Pleac
Madadh Gruamach
An t-Aigeach
Rubha Mhic Gille-mhicheil
Eilean Bhearnaraigh (Berneray)
Ruisigearraidh
Borgh
Baile
Boreray
Torogay
Caolas Bhearnaraigh
Caolas a'Mhòrain
Aird a'Mhòrain
Veilish Pt.
Vallay
Vallay Strand
Lingay
Oronsay
Port nan Long
Baile Mhic Phail
Grenetobht
Solas
Malacleit
Loch nam Madadh (Lochmaddy)
UIBHIST A TUATH (NORTH UIST)
Loch Euphort
Loch Obasaraigh
EAVAL
Floddaybeg
Floddaymore
Ronay
Rubha na Rodagrich
Maragay Mor
Griomasaigh (Grimsay)
Scolpaig
SCOLPAIG TOWER
Griminish Pt.
Baile Mhartainn
Manish Pt.
Hosta
Tigh a Ghearraidh
Baile Raghaill
Hogha Gearraidh
Aird an Runair
BALRANALD NATURE RESERVE
Rubha Port Scolpaig
Causamul
Paiblil
Baile Mor
Claddach-knockline
Cladach Chirceboist
Glen Drolla
UIST ANIMAL VISITOR CENTRE
MARRIVAL
Vorogay
Kirkibost Island
Teanna Mhachair
Baile Sear (Baleshare)
Cairinis
Uachdar
Baile a Mhanaich
Baile nan Cailleach
Griminis
Torlum
Liniclett
Gualan
BEINN NA FAOGHLA (BENBECULA)
Fuidhaigh (Wiay)
Rubha Cam nan Gall
Meavy Riabhach
Steisay
Gasay
Luirsay Dubh
Hornish Pt.
Ardivachar Pt.
Aird a Mhachair
Gerinish
OUR LADY OF THE ISLES STATUE
Loch Bi
Stadhlaigearraidh
Dreumasdal
HOWMORE
Tobha Mor
Loch Sgioport
Ornish I.
Loch Druidibeg
Yerran I.
AN CAOLAS MHONACH
Na h-eileanan Monach (Heisker or Monach Islands)
MONACH ISLANDS
Stockay
Ceann Ear
Ceann Iar
Shillay
Haskeir I.
Haskeir Eagach
Waternish Point
Ascrib Islands
W A T E R N I S H
Geary
Knockbreck
Gillen
Upper Halistra
Lower Halistra
Hallin
Trumpan
TRUMPAN CHURCH
Ard Beag
Ardmore Pt.
Mingay
Isay
Stein
Lusta
Bay River
Greshornish
Claigan
LOCH DUNVEGAN
DUNVEGAN CASTLE
Dunvegan
Kilmuir
Lonmore
Roskhill
Vatten
Roag
Harlosh
Orbost
Loch Vatten
Balmore
Ose
Loch Caroy
Ullinish
Tarner I.
Loch Bracadale
Harlosh I.
Wiay
Idrigill Point
MACLEOD'S MAIDENS
Oronsay
Macleod's Tables
HEALABHAL MHOR
HEALABHAL BHEAG
Geodha Mor
Hoe Point
Hoe Rape
Ramasaig
Glen Dale
Holmisdale
Skinidin
Colbost
Totaig
Husabost
Borreraig
Galtrigill
Dunvegan Head
THE MACCRIMMON PIPING HERITAGE CENTRE
BORRERAIG PARK MUSEUM
COLBOST FOLK MUSEUM
TOY MUSEUM
Uig
Feriniquarrie
Glasphein
Lephin
Upper Milovaig
Lower Milovaig
Loch Pooltiel
An Ceannaich
Oisgill Bay
Neist Point
LIGHTHOUSE
Moonen Bay
NG
NF
152
153
173

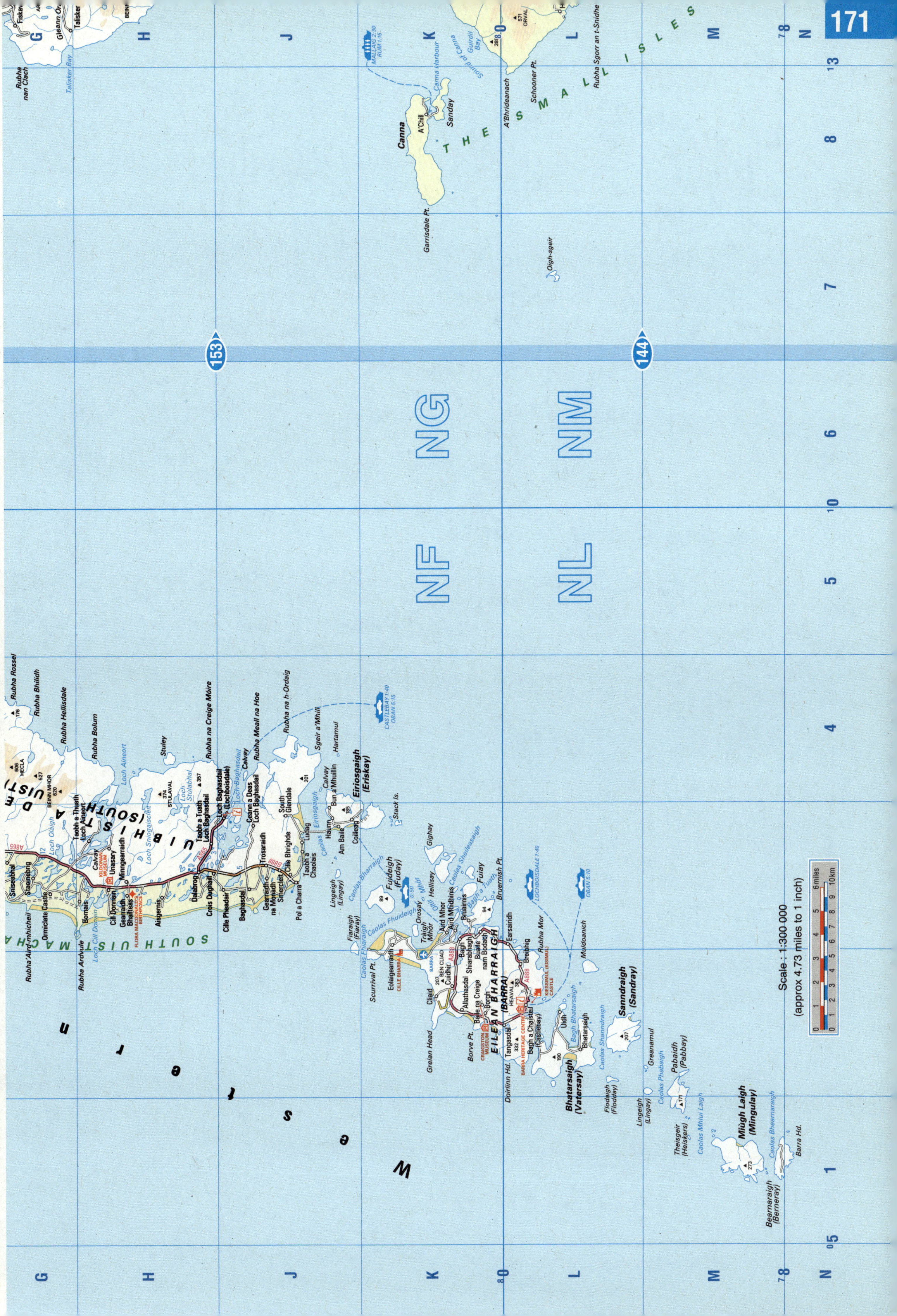
THE SMALL ISLES
Canna
Sanday
A'Chill
Canna Harbour
Sound of Canna
Garrisdale Pt.
Oigh-sgeir
Schooner Pt.
A'Bhrideanach
Rubha Sgorr an t-Snidhe
MALLAIG 2:30
RUM 1:15
153
144
NG
NM
NF
NL
UIBHIST A DEAS (SOUTH UIST)
SOUTH UIST MACHAIR
Loch Baghasdail (Lochboisdale)
Loch Aineort
Loch Sgioport
Stuley
Calvay
Rubha Rossel
Rubha Bhilidh
Rubha Hellisdale
Rubha Bolum
Rubha na Creige Mòire
Rubha Meall na Hoe
Rubha na h-Ordaig
HECLA
BEINN MHOR
STULAVAL
Taobh a Tuath Loch Aineort
Taobh a Tuath Loch Baghasdail
Ceann a Deas Loch Baghasdail
Cill Donnain
Gearraidh Bhailteas
Bornais
Dalabrog
Cille Pheadair
Baghasdal
Smercleit
Cille Bhrighde
South Glendale
Pol a Charra
Taobh a Chaolais
Ludag
Trosaraidh
Gearraidh na Monadh
Ormiclate Castle
Staoinebrig
Snaoiseabhal
Rubha Ardvule
Rubha 'Aird-mhichel
Loch Cill Donnain
Loch Olaigh
FLORA MACDONALD'S BIRTHPLACE
KILDONAN MUSEUM
A865
B888
Eiriosgaigh (Eriskay)
Am Baile
Haunn
Coilleag
Bun a' Mhuillin
Hartamul
Sgeir a' Mhill
Stack Is.
Caolas Eiriosgaigh
CASTLEBAY 1:40
OBAN 5:15
Fuideigh (Fuday)
Lingeigh (Lingay)
Fiaraigh (Fiaray)
Caolas Bharraigh
Caolas Fhiaraigh
Caolas Fhuideigh
Gighay
Hellisay
Fulay
Bruernish Pt.
Caolas Shelleasaigh
Bàgh a Tuath
Oitir Mhòr
Orosay
Tràigh Mhòr
Ard Mhòr
Ard Mhidhinis
Bruarnis
Bàgh Breibhig
Eolaigearraidh
CILLE BHARRA
BARRA
Scurrival Pt.
Greian Head
Cliaid
BEN CLIAD
Cuidhir
Allathasdal
Baile na Creige
Borgh
Borve Pt.
Buaile nam Bodach
Bàgh Shiarabhagh
Earsairidh
Breibhig
Rubha Mòr
HEAVAL
EILEAN BHARRAIGH (BARRA)
Bàgh a Chaisteil (Castlebay)
Tangasdal
Doirlinn Hd.
CRAIGSTON MUSEUM
BARRA HERITAGE CENTRE
KISIMUL CASTLE
A888
LOCHBOISDALE 1:40
OBAN 5:10
Muldoanich
Uidh
Bhatarsaigh (Vatersay)
Bàgh Bhatarsaigh
Sanndraigh (Sandray)
Caolas Shanndraigh
Flodaigh (Flodday)
Lingeigh (Lingay)
Greanamul
Pabaidh (Pabbay)
Caolas Phabaigh
Theisgeir (Heiskers)
Miùgh Laigh (Mingulay)
Caolas Mhiùl Laigh
Caolas Bhearnaraigh
Barra Hd.
Bearnaraigh (Berneray)
Sea of the Hebrides
Talisker
Talisker Bay
Gleann Òraid
Fiskavaig
Rubha nan Clach
ORVAL
Scale 1:300 000
(approx 4.73 miles to 1 inch)
0 1 2 3 4 5 6 miles
0 1 2 3 4 5 6 7 8 9 10km

St. Kilda
NA
NF
Boreray
Soay
ST KILDA
CONACHAIR
MULLACH BI
St Kilda or Hirta (Hiort)
Bagh a Bhaile
Dun
NB
NA
Western Isles
ISLE OF LEWIS (EILEAN LEODHAIS)
EILEAN LEODHAIS
RUBHA ROBHANAIS (BUTT OF LEWIS)
CHURCH OF ST MOLVAG
HARBOUR VIEW GALLERY
Coig Peighinnean
Eoropaidh
Port Nis
Lional
Tabost
Sgiogarstaigh
Cross Sands
Suainebost
Cros
Aird Dhail
Dail bho Dheas
Dail bho Thuath
Glen Cross
Cuiashader
Cellar Head
Gabhsann bho Thuath
Gabhsann bho Dheas
Mealabost Bhuirgh
Bail Ard Bhuirgh
Coig Peighinnean Bhuirgh
Siadar
Siadar Iarach
Siadar Uarach
Baile an Truiseil
Rubha Leathann
Aird Barvas
TRUSHAL STONE
Barabhas Iarach
Barabhas Uarach
Barabhas
BLACK HOUSE MUSEUM
Brù
Arnol
Labost
Bragar
Siabost bho Thuath
Siabost bho Dheas
SHAWBOST NORSE MILL
Pairc Shiaboist
Bàgh Dhail Beag
Dail Beag
Dail Mor
GEARRANNAN
Na Gearrannan
Borghastan
Carlabhagh
Campay
Floday
Harsgeir
Loch Charlabhaigh
Little Bernera
DUN CARLOWAY BROCH
Dun Charlabhaigh
Cirbhig
IRON AGE HOUSE
Crothair
AN CAOLAS
Pabay Mor
Tobson
Vacsay
Great Bernera
Breacleit
Circebost
Barraglom
Tolastadh a Chaolais
Keava
Eilean Kearstay
Calanais
CALLANISH STANDING STONES
CALLANISH VISITOR CENTRE
Linsiader
Breascleit
Gearraidh na h-Aibhne
Tobhtarol
Crulabhig
Taciet
Vuia Mor
Vuia Beag
Riof
Uigean
Bhaltos
Cliobh
Miabhig
Aird Uig
An Galan Uigeach
Bàgh Fhiabhaig
Timsgearraidh
Cradhlastadh
Càrnais
Ard More Mangersta
Mangurstadh
Eadar Dha Fhadhail
Cairisiadar
Geisiadar
SUAINAVAL
Loch Suaineabhal
Aird Fenish
Aird Brenish
Islibhig
Breanais
MEALISVAL
Einacleite
Gìosla
Loch Ròg
Loch Grunabhat
Loch Chaolartan
Loch Fuaroil
BEINN MHEADHONACH
Mealasta Island
Caolas an Eilein
Loch Morsgail
Loch Coirgerod
Loch Cro Criosdaig
Loch Beiniseabhal
Loch Bòdabhat
Morsgail Forest
Loch Tamnabhaigh
Loch Tealasabhaigh
Loch Crab
Kearstay
Scarp
Bràighe Mòr
LOCH LANGABHAT
Loch Tungabhat
Loch Smuaiseabhat
Loch Lacsabhat Ard
Loch nan Stearnag
Loch Urabhal
Loch a' Ghainmhich
Acha Mor
Glen Bragar
Gleann Bhruthadail
Gleann Mòr Barvas
Loch Urghag
Loch Breibhat
BEINN BRAGAR
Loch Scarabhat Mhor
Loch Mòr an Stàirr
BEINN MHOLACH
MUIRNEAG
Loch Langabhat
Loch Mòr Shanndabhat
Abhainn Ghearadha
Bail' Ur Tholastaidh
Tolastadh bho Thuath
Tolsta Head
Gleann Tholàstaidh
Port Bun a'Ghlinne
Creag Fhraoch
Loch Sgeireach Mor
Griais
Bac
Col
Col Uarach
Vatisker Pt.
Breibhig
Coll Sands
BROAD BAY OR LOCH A TUATH
Aird Thunga
Tunga
Sròn Ruadh
Rubha an t-Siumpain
Port Nan Giùran
Port Mholair
Cnoc
Amhlaigh
Aird
Sulaisiadar
Seisiadar
Garrabost
EYE PENINSULA
Pabail Uarach
Pabail Iarach
Aiginis
An Cnoc
Suardail
Bàgh Phabail
A'Chearc
Holm I.
Tolm
ST COLUMBA'S
Mealabost
STORNOWAY
Stornoway
MUSEUM NAN EILEAN
AN LANNTAIR GALLERY
LEWIS LOOM CENTRE
Sanndabhaig
Lacasdal
Newmarket
Grianan
An Gleann Ur
Arnish Moor
ULLAPOOL 2:40
Raerinish Pt.
Loch Orasaigh
Griomsidar
Ben Casgro
Liurbost
Ranais
Crosbost
Loch Tobhta Bridein
Loch nam Falcag
Loch Aiuigh na h-Airde
Soval Lodge
Loch Trealabhal
Barkin Is.
Tabhaidh Mhor
Eilean Chaluim Chille
Eilean Orasaidh
Eilean Thoraidh
Ceos
Lacasaidh
Loch Eireasort
Cromor
Gearraidh Bhaird
Cabharstadh
Baile Ailein
Sildinis
Cearsiadair
CEARSIADAIR
Tabost
Marbhig
Loch Strandabhat
Ceann Tarabhaigh
Airidh a Bhruaich
Aird an Troim
Ceann Shiphoirt
Loch Sgibacleit
Loch nan Eilean
Taobh a' Ghlinne
Grabhair
Calbost

SOUTH LEWIS
HARRIS AND
NORTH UIST
NA HEARADH (HARRIS)
UIBHIST A TUATH (NORTH UIST)
Eilean Bhearnaraigh (Berneray)
Pabaidh (Pabbay)
Tarasaigh (Taransay)
Eilean Scalpaigh (Scalpay)
Na h-Eileanan Mòra (Shiant Islands)
CAOLAS NAN EILEAN
LOCH A SIAR
CAOLAS NA HEARADH
SOUND OF RAASAY
LOCH SNIZORT
LOCH DUNVEGAN
TROTTERNISH
WATERNISH
Tairbeart (Tarbert)
An t-Ob (Leverburgh)
Loch nam Madadh (Lochmaddy)
Uig
Staffin
Duntulm
Kilmuir
Dunvegan Head
Waternish Point
Ascrib Islands
Rubha Hunish
Eilean Trodday
Kebock Head
Hushinish Pt.
Toe Head
Griomasaigh (Grimsay)
Baile Sear (Baleshare)
Vallay
Sound of Harris
Scale : 1:300 000
(approx 4.73 miles to 1 inch)
0 1 2 3 4 5 6 miles
0 1 2 3 4 5 6 7 8 9 10km
NF
NG
152
170

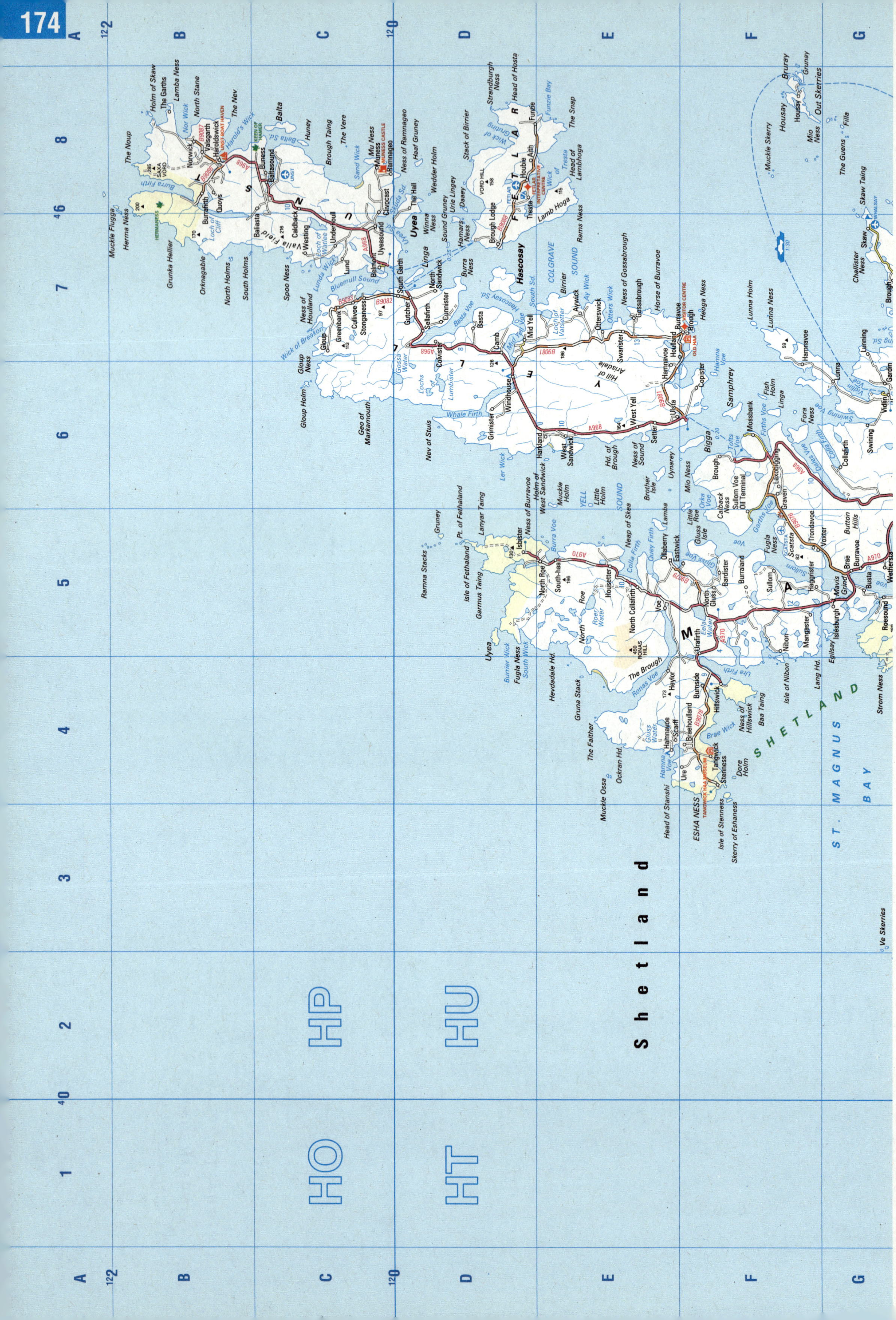
Shetland
HO
HP
HT
HU
UNST
YELL
MAINLAND
FETLAR
ST. MAGNUS BAY
SHETLAND
YELL SOUND
COLGRAVE SOUND
Muckle Flugga
Herma Ness
The Noup
Holm of Skaw
The Garths
Lamba Ness
North Stane
The Nev
Norwick
Valsgarth
Haroldswick
Baltasound
Balta
Huney
Brough Taing
The Vere
Burrafirth
Loch of Cliff
Quoys
Balliasta
Vallia Field
Caldback
Westing
Underhoull
Uyeasound
Belmont
Uyea
Muness
Mu Ness
Clivocast
Grunka Hellier
Orknagable
North Holms
South Holms
Spoo Ness
Lunda Wick
Bluemull Sound
Ness of Houlland
Gloup
Gloup Ness
Gloup Holm
Wick of Breakon
Greenbank
Cullivoe
Stonganess
Gutcher
Sellafirth
Colvister
Gossa Water
Geo of Markamouth
Basta
Basta Voe
Camb
Mid Yell
Mid Yell Voe
Hascosay
Hascosay Sd.
Linga
Burra Ness
Cunnister
North Sandwick
Windhouse
Grimister
Whale Firth
Nev of Stuis
Hill of Arisdale
Otterswick
Gossabrough
Swarister
Burravoe
Houlland
Hamnavoe
Brough
Copister
Ulsta
West Yell
Setter
Ness of Sound
West Sandwick
Harkland
Ness of Gossabrough
Horse of Burravoe
Heoga Ness
Samphrey
Bigga
Lunna Holm
Lunna Ness
Fish Holm
Mossbank
Firths Voe
Brough Lodge
Houbie
Tresta
Funzie
Funzie Bay
The Snap
Head of Hosta
Strandburgh Ness
Stack of Birrier
Lamb Hoga
Rams Ness
Head of Lambhoga
Muckle Skerry
Housay
Bruray
Grunay
Out Skerries
Mio Ness
Filla
The Guens
Skaw Taing
Skaw
Challister Ness
Brough
Lunning
Lunna
Vidlin
Gardin
Swining
Collafirth
Dales Voe
Laxobigging
Graven
Sullom Voe Oil Terminal
Calback Ness
Brough
Orka Voe
Little Roe
Gluss Isle
Lamba
Brother Isle
Uynarey
Mio Ness
Ollaberry
Eastwick
Quey Firth
Colla Firth
Bardister
Burraland
North Gluss
Sullom
Sullom Voe
Fugla Ness
Scatsta
Trondavoe
Voxter
Brae
Burravoe
Busta
Mavis Grind
Isbister
Ness of Burravoe
Burra Voe
Holm of West Sandwick
Muckle Holm
Little Holm
Neap of Skea
Isle of Fethaland
Pt. of Fethaland
Lanyar Taing
Gruney
Ramna Stacks
Garmus Taing
North Roe
South-haa
Roer Water
Housetter
North Collafirth
Voe
Urafirth
Eela Water
Ronas Hill
The Brough
Ronas Voe
Heylor
Uyea
Burrier Wick
Fugla Ness
South Wick
Hevdadale Hd.
Gruna Stack
The Faither
Ockran Hd.
Muckle Ossa
Head of Stanshi
Esha Ness
Isle of Stenness
Skerry of Eshaness
Stenness
Tangwick
Ure
Hamnavoe
Braehoulland
Burnside
Hillswick
Ness of Hillswick
Baa Taing
Dore Holm
Brae Wick
Nibon
Isle of Nibon
Mangaster
Islesburgh
Egilsay
Lang Hd.
Haggrister
Roesound
Wethersta
Strom Ness
Ve Skerries
A968
A970
B9081
B9082
B9083
B9084
B9086
B9087
B9076
B9078
B9079
B9088

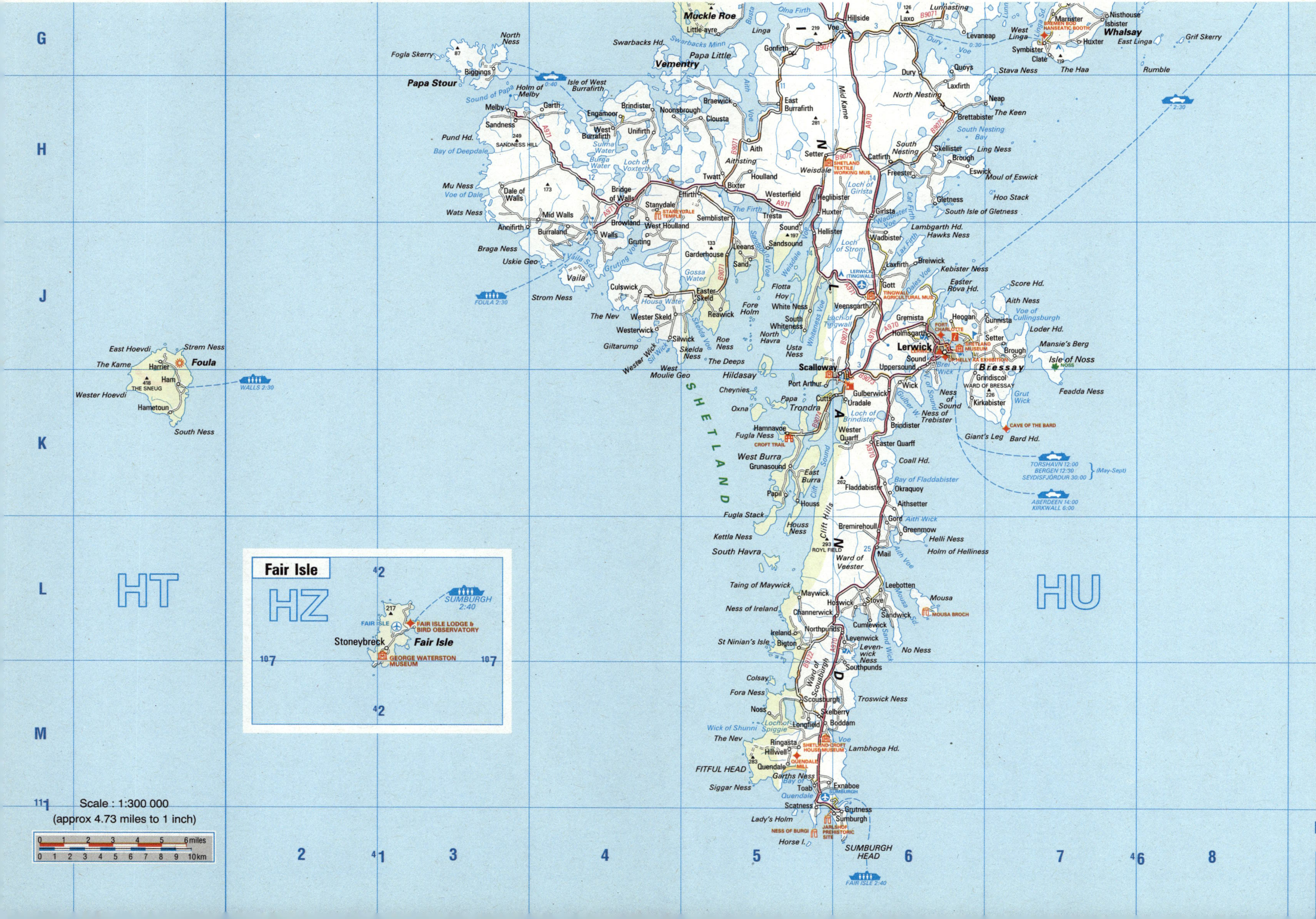
SHETLAND
Lerwick
Scalloway
Bressay
Isle of Noss
Whalsay
Muckle Roe
Vementry
Papa Little
Papa Stour
Vaila
Foula
Trondra
West Burra
East Burra
Mousa
Sumburgh
SUMBURGH HEAD
FITFUL HEAD
Fair Isle
Stoneybreck
FAIR ISLE LODGE & BIRD OBSERVATORY
GEORGE WATERSTON MUSEUM
SUMBURGH 2:40
FAIR ISLE 2:40
WALLS 2:30
FOULA 2:30
TORSHAVN 12:00
BERGEN 12:30
SEYDISFJORDUR 30:00
(May-Sept)
ABERDEEN 14:00
KIRKWALL 6:00
HT
HZ
HU
Scale : 1:300 000
(approx 4.73 miles to 1 inch)
0 1 2 3 4 5 6 miles
0 1 2 3 4 5 6 7 8 9 10km

Orkney
HY
ND
North Ronaldsay
Hollandstoun
Linklet Bay
Broch of Burrian
Strom Ness
North Ronaldsay Firth
Papa Westray
Holm of Papa
Bow Hd.
Aikerness
Holland
Backaskaill
Gayfield
Loch of St. Tredwell
Knap of Howar
Papa Westray
Bay of Skaill
Papa Sound
Noup Head
Rack Wick
Rackwick
Pierowall
Pierowall Church
Noltland Castle
Broughton
Braehead
Hd. of Moclett
Gentlemen's Cave
Westray
Fitty Hill
Midbea
Inga Ness
Langskaill
Cati Geo
Westside Church
Bay of Tuquoy
Skelwick
Spo Ness
Stanger Hd.
Rapness
Twiness
Berst Ness
Skea Skerries
Sulland
Weather Ness
The North Sound
Kirkwall 1:50
Holms of Ire
Scar
Burness
Otters Wick
Sellibister
Whitemill Pt.
Tafts Ness
North Loch
Lettan
Scuthvie Bay
Lop Ness
Ness of Brough
Bay of Brough
Newark
Bay of Lopness
Broughtown
Sanday
Lady
Overbister
Cata Sand
Kettletoft
Backaskaill Bay
Sty Wick
Quoyness Chambered Cairn
Els Ness
The Swarf
Bay of Newark
Tres Ness
Lashy Sound
Laminess
Braeswick
Stove
Quoy Ness
Bay of Stove
Hacks Ness
Sanday Sound
Pt. of Nevin
Wart Holm
Holm of Faray
Pt. of Huro
Faray
Rusk Holm
Fers Ness
Red Hd.
Grey Hd.
Calf of Eday
Carrick Ho.
Carrick House
Calfsound
Westray Firth
Sacquoy Hd.
Saviskaill Hd.
Saviskaill Bay
Faraclett Hd.
Kili Holm
Guith
Millbounds
Fersness Bay
Bay of London
Eday
Eday Sound
Spur Ness
Loth
Holm of Huip
Huip Ness
Huip Sound
Papa Stronsay
Grice Ness
Wasbister
Rousay
Sourin
Muckle Water
Mae Ness
Skaill
St Magnus Church
Egilsay
Seal Skerrie
Backaland
Veness
Links Ness
Odie
Stronsay
Whitehall Village
Linga Holm
Linga Sd.
Mill Bay
Odness
Costa Hd.
Eynhallow
Eynhallow Church
Midhowe Broch
Westness
Knowe of Yarso Cairn
Brinian
Frotoft
Rousay Sound
War Ness
Fall of Warness
Muckle Green Holm
St Catherine's Bay
Stronsay
Wardhill
Everbay
North Taing
Odin Bay
Brough Head
Brough of Birsay
The Barony
Abune-the-Hill
Loch of Swannay
Costa
Burgar
Aiker Ness
Eynhallow Sound
Broch of Gurness
Cubbie Roo's Castle and St Mary's Chapel
Wyre
Pt. of the Graand
Birsay Bay
Earl's Palace
Loch of Boardhouse
Loch of Hundland
Evie
Stenso
Redland
Marwick Head Nature Reserve
Marwick Hd.
Marwick
Stara
Kirbuster
Twatt
Burn of Hillside
Gairsay Sound
Wood Wick
Stronsay
Grobister
Bay of Holland
Dishes
Kirbister
Burgh Hd.
Rothiesholm
Mar Wick
Outshore Pt.
Loch of Isbister
Isbister
Beaquoy
Click Mill
Loch of Sabiston
Tingwall
Sweyn Holm
Gairsay
The Galt
Ness of Ork
Rothiesholm Hd.
Holland
Bay of Houseby
Lamb Hd.
Greenli Ness
Tor Ness
Scarwell
Northdyke
Pt. of Howana Geo
Quoyloo
Skeabrae
Dounby
Mirbister
Milldoe
Hackland
Gorseness
Veantrow Bay
Edmonstone
Bay of Skaill
Skaill
Row Hd.
Skara Brae
Skaill House
Kierfiold Ho.
Aith
Orkney Farm & Folklore Museum
Bay of Linton
Auskerry Sound
Shapinsay
Loch of Skaill
Hestwall
Tenston
Loch of Harray
Netherbrough
Brough
Bimbister
Settiscarth
Breck of Cruan
Isbister
Bay of Isbister
Broad Taing
Wide Firth
Balfour Castle
Balfour
Firth
Auskerry
Yesnaby
Voy
Arion
Pt. of Backaquoy
Helliar Holm
Newlot
Haco's Ness
Car Ness
Neban Pt.
Quholm
Loch of Stenness
Ring of Brogar
Stenness Standing Stones
Tormiston Mill
Maes Howe
Finstown
Bay of Firth
Damsay
Grimbister
Heddle
Nisthouse
Wideford Hill
Orkney Wireless Mus.
Ortak Visitor Centre
Tankerness House Museum
Work
Craigiefield
Hd. of Holland
Shapinsay Sound
Aberdeen 6:00
Lerwick 6:00
Rerwick Hd.
Bridge of Waith
Kirkwall
St Magnus Cathedral
Earl Patrick's Palace & Bishop's Palace
Berstane
Inganess Bay
Hall of Tankerness
Outertown
Breck Ness
Pier Arts Centre
Stromness
Stromness Museum
Clouston
Bay of Ireland
Ireland
Scapa
Highland Park Distillery
Tankerness
Den Wick
Mull Hd.
Hoy and West Mainland
Scrabster 1:30
Pt. of Oxan
Breckan
Clestrain Sound
Stenness
Ward Hill
Loch of Kirbister
Kirbister
Hobbister
Greenigoe
Tradespark
Whitecleat
Deer Sound
The Ness
North Halley
Sandside Bay
Kame of Hoy
Graemsay
Clestrain
Cairnton
Smoogro
Waulkmill
Lodge
Waulkmill Bay
Scapa Bay
Toab
Deerness
Skaill
Grindigar
Roana Bay
Gritley
Murra
North Hoy Nature Reserve
St John's Hd.
Hoy
Linksness
Quoyness
Peterstown
Orphir
Cryа
Gyre
Swanbister
St Nicholas Church
Swanbister Bay
Houton
Ve Ness
Foubister
North Dawn
Norwood Museum
Upper Sanday
Newark Bay
Pt. of Ayre
Old Man of Hoy
Ward Hill
Bring Deeps
Houton Head
Midland Ness
Scapa Flow
Bay of Sandoyne
St Mary's
Italian Chapel
Braehead
Corn Holm
Copinsay
Rackwick
South Burn
Dwarfie Stane
Scad Hd.
Cava
Howequoy Hd.
Lamb Holm
Cornquoy
Rora Head
Pegal Burn
Rack Wick
Knap of Trowieglen
Rysa Little
Glims Holm
Holm Sound
Rose Ness
Fossil and Vintage Centre
Echnaloch Bay
Northtown
Burray
Calf of Flotta
Roan Hd.
Hunda
Burray Village
Burray Ness
Hoy
Fara
Weddel Sd.
Scapa Flow Interpretation Centre
Pan Hope
Hillside
Southtown
Sneuk Hd.
Lyness
Rinnigill
Bow
Pan
Flotta
Water Sound
Uppertown
St. Margaret's Hope
Grimness
Rumley Pt.
Burn of Ore
Heldale Water
Little Rack Wick
Hoglinns Water
Little Ayre
Crockness
Longhope
Wyng
Hackness
Martello Tower
Swithe Sound
Hoxa
Herston
Quindry
Herston Hd.
Widewall
Papley
Grim Ness
Aikers
Newark Bay
Switha
Melsetter
Hurliness
Brims
Hoy (Longhope)
Kirk Hope
Cantick Hd.
South Walls
Garth Hd.
Brims Ness
Tor Ness
Sandwick
Sand Wick
Lythes
South Ronaldsay
Gills Bay 1:00
Suckquoy
Wind Wick
Linklater
North Hd.
Barth Hd.
Swona
Dundas Ho.
Burwick
Halcro Hd.
Cleat
Tomb of the Eagles and Bronze Age House
Old Hd.
Liddel
Brough Ness
Pentland Firth
Muckle Skerry
Pentland Skerries
Langaton Point
Nethertown
Red Head
Island of Stroma
Mell Head
Uppertown
John O'Groats (May-Sept) 0:45
Dunnet Head
169
Scale : 1:300 000
(approx 4.73 miles to 1 inch)
0 1 2 3 4 5 6miles
0 1 2 3 4 5 6 7 8 9 10km
A966
A967
A986
A965
A964
A960
A961
A963
A968
B9057
B9055
B9056
B9064
B9066
B9069
B9050
B9051
B9052
B9058
B9043
B9047
B9044
B9045
B9041
B9070
B9061
B9060
B9062
B9063
B9068
B9067
B9059
B9042

Aberdeen

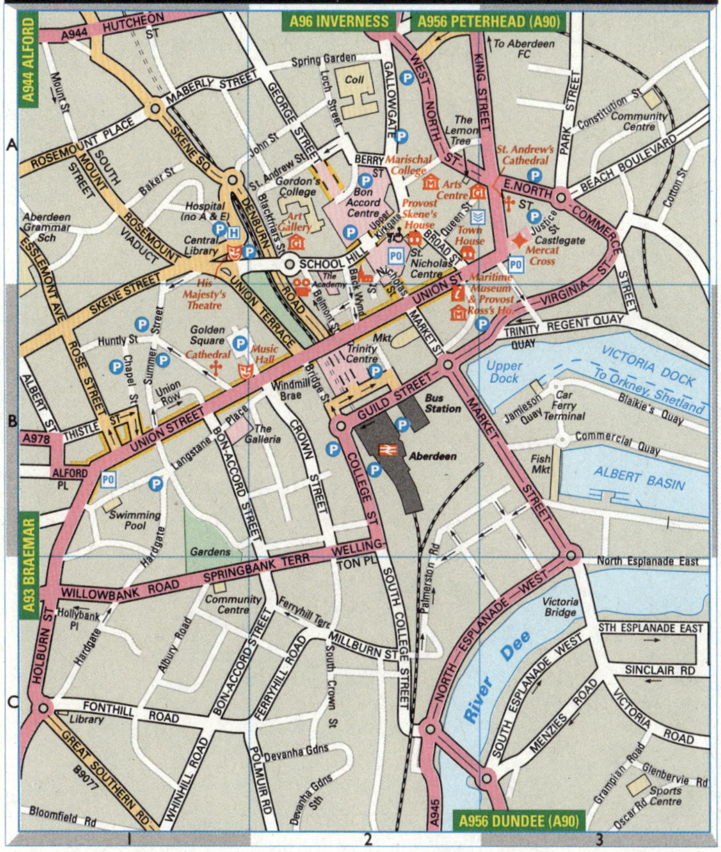

Bath

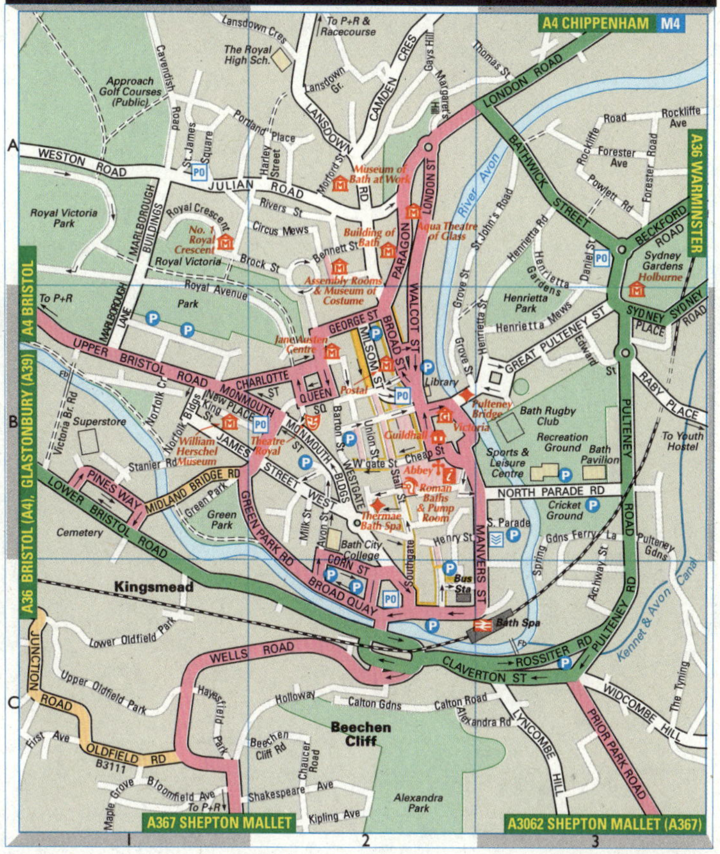

Birmingham

WEDNESFIELD
Perton
Coll
Molineux
West Park
Town Hall
WOLVERHAMPTON
Wightwick Manor
Bantock House Museum
Castlecroft
Bentley
Willenhall
Birchills Canal Museum
Arboretum
WALSALL
Bescot Stadium
BILSTON
DARLASTON
Penn
Staffordshire and Worcestershire Canal
Goldthorn Hill
COSELEY
WEDNESBURY
SEDGLEY
Tame Valley Canal
Tame Bridge Parkway
WOMBOURNE
Baggeridge Country Park
Nature Centre
Upper Gornal
TIPTON
Newton
Lyndon
Sandwell Valley Country Park
Himley Park
Himley Hall
Himley
Wildlife Centre
WEST BROMWICH
Black Country Museum
Dudley Zoological Gardens
Gornalwood
DUDLEY
Swindon
Wall Heath
Oakham
The Hawthorns
Sandwell
Pensnett
Kingswinford
Ashwood
Broadfield House Glass Museum
Ridgehill Wood
OLDBURY
Netherton
SMETHWICK
Langley Green
ROWLEY REGIS
Merry Hill Centre
BRIERLEY HILL
Old Hill
Blackheath
Red House Glass Cone
Wordsley
Stourbridge Canal
AMBLECOTE
Cradley Heath
Warley Woods
Hurst Green
Stourton
Lye
Cradley
Dudley Canal
World's End
Gibbet Wood
STOURBRIDGE
HALESOWEN
Woodgate Valley Country Park
Halesowen Abbey (rems)
Whittington Common
Bunker's Hill Wood
Pedmore
Wychbury Hill
Woodgate
Weoley Castle
Hagley Wood
Uffmoor Wood
Frankley Services
Bartley Resr
Shenley Fields
Hagley
Hagley Park
Twiland Wood
Frankley Resr
West Hagley
Clent
Clent Hills Country Park
Romsley
Ell Wood
Egg Hill
Frankley Hill
Frankley
Northfield
Blakedown
Holy Cross
Broome
Great Farley Wood
Hurcott Wood
Waseley Hills Country Park
Turves Green
Bissell Wood
Belbroughton
Rubery
Lickey Hills
Longbridge
Lickey Hills Country Park
Upper Bittell Reservoir
0 1 2 3 miles
0 1 2 3 4 5 km

ALDRIDGE
Little Aston
Hardwick
Roughley
Four Oaks
Streetly
Upper Nut Hurst
Bracebridge Pool
Blackroot Pool
Keeper's Pool
SUTTON PARK COUNTRY PARK
Town Hall
Westwood Coppice
Doe Bank Wood
Pheasey
Holly Hurst
Visitor Centre
Wyndley Pool
Powell's Pool
SUTTON COLDFIELD
Reddicap Heath
Trickley Coppice
New Park Wood
Middleton
ASH END HOUSE FARM
BROOMEY CROFT CHILDREN'S FARM
North Wood
Visitor Centre
KINGSBURY WATER PARK
Kingstanding
Over Green
Short Heath
Walmley
Curdworth
Perry Park
Witton Lakes
Erdington
Nature Centre
WATER ORTON
CASTLE BROMWICH
COLESHILL
Aston
Bromford
ASTON HALL
VILLA PARK
THE DRUM
CASTLE BROMWICH HALL
Winson Green
BIRMINGHAM
Kingshurst
Tile Cross
Chelmsley Wood
Lea Hall
Edgbaston Resr
NATIONAL INDOOR ARENA
Conv Centre
THINK TANK
ST ANDREW'S
BIRMINGHAM ECO PARK
BLAKESLEY HALL
Bordesley Green
Yardley
Marston Green
MARSTON GREEN
SHELDON COUNTRY PARK
Lyndon Green
Sheldon
BIRMINGHAM INTERNATIONAL AIRPORT
Bickenhill Plantations
NATIONAL EXHIBITION CENTRE
BIRMINGHAM BOTANICAL GARDENS
EDGBASTON
Cannon Hill Park
Nature Centre
Moseley
Acock's Green
RAILWAY MUSEUM
Terminal Building
BIRMINGHAM INTERNATIONAL
NATIONAL MOTOR CYCLE MUSEUM
Elmdon Park
Selly Park
Selly Oak
Moor Green
Univ
Ulverley Green
Olton Reservoir
Elmdon Heath
Hampton Coppice
CADBURY WORLD
Stirchley
Bournville
SAREHOLE MILL
Lode Heath
Barber's Coppice
Grand Union Canal
HAMPTON-IN-ARDEN
Catherine de Barnes Heath
YARDLEY WOOD
Yardley Wood
Stratford-Upon-Avon Canal
Shirley
SOLIHULL
Tudor Grange Park
Eastcote
King's Norton
Hillfield
Bill's Wood
Major's Green
Hawkesley
Hollywood
Trueman's Heath
WIDNEY MANOR
Monkspath
KNOWLE
Drakes Cross
Cheswick Green
Bentley Heath
Wythall
M6 Toll
M6
M42
A38(M)
River Tame
Birmingham & Fazeley Canal

Blackpool

Bournemouth

Bradford

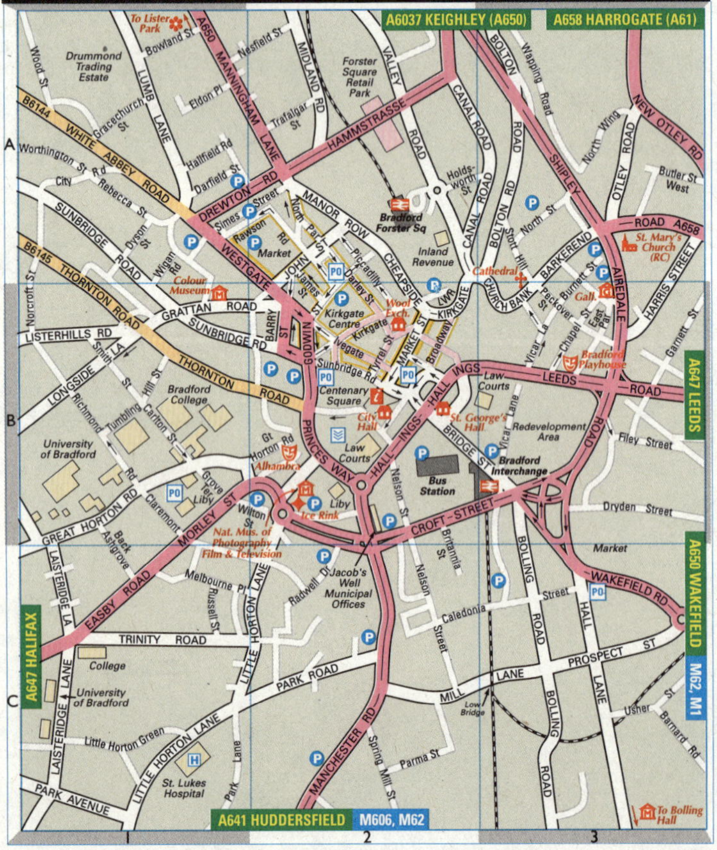

Brighton

Bristol

0 Miles ¼

Cambridge

0 Miles ¼

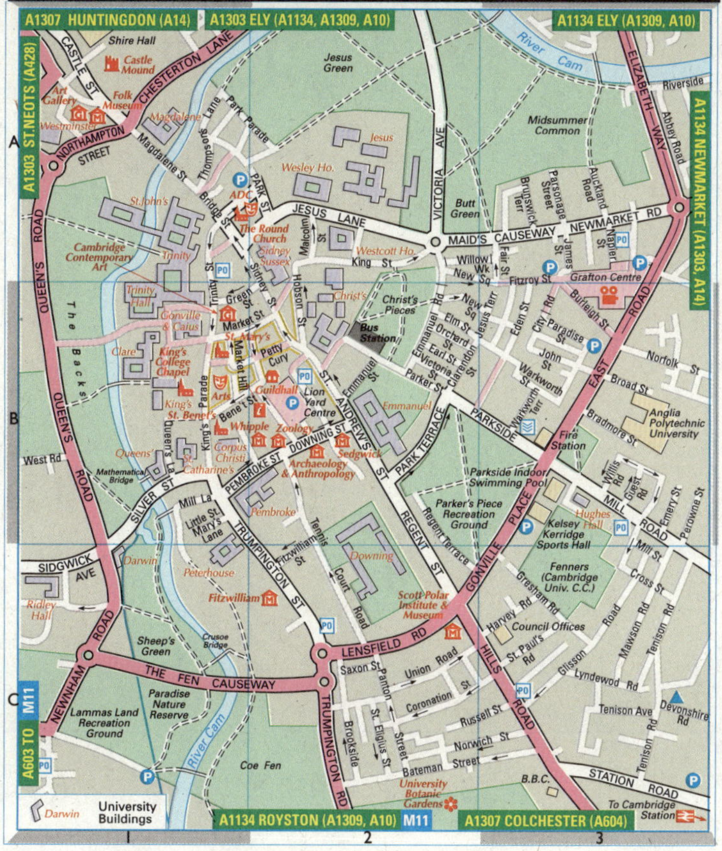

Canterbury

0 Miles ¼

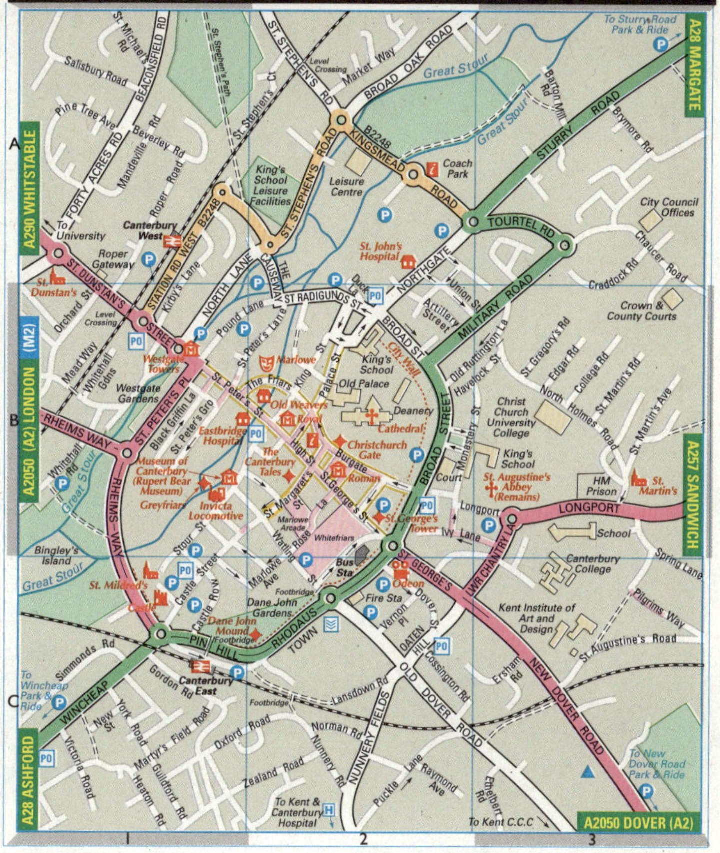

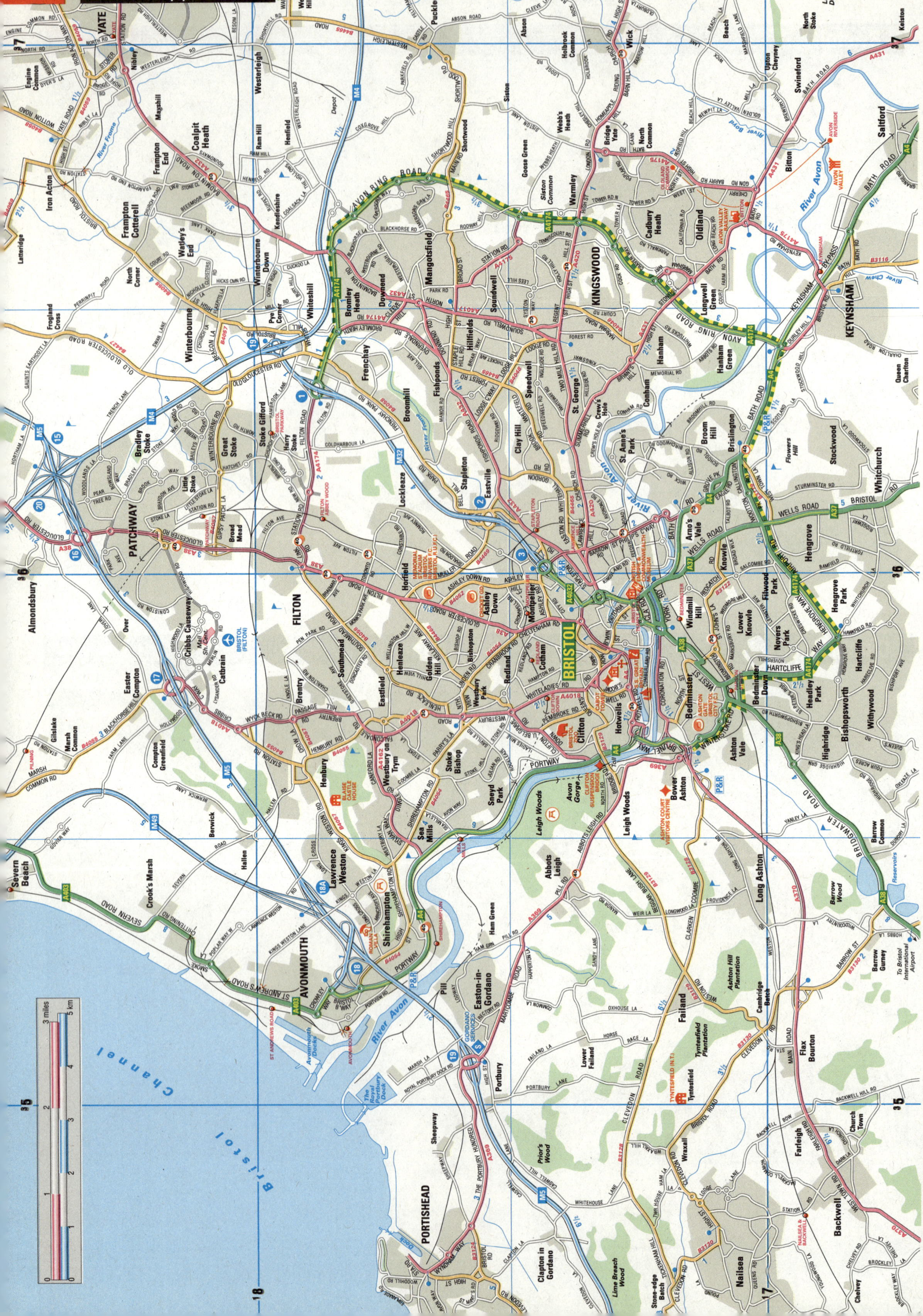

Yate
Pucklechurch
Wick
Westerleigh
Coalpit Heath
Frampton Cotterell
Iron Acton
Winterbourne
Winterbourne Down
Whiteshill
Mangotsfield
Kingswood
Downend
Bromley Heath
Frenchay
Fishponds
Hillfields
Soundwell
Warmley
Siston
Oldland
Cadbury Heath
Longwell Green
Hanham
Keynsham
Saltford
Bitton
Patchway
Bradley Stoke
Stoke Gifford
Filton
Almondsbury
Easter Compton
Cribbs Causeway
Henbury
Southmead
Horfield
Brentry
Lockleaze
Stapleton
Eastville
Speedwell
St. George
Conham
Brislington
Stockwood
Whitchurch
Hengrove
Knowle
Bedminster
Ashton Vale
Bishopsworth
Hartcliffe
Withywood
Headley Park
Bristol
Clifton
Hotwells
Redland
Cotham
Henleaze
Westbury on Trym
Stoke Bishop
Sneyd Park
Sea Mills
Shirehampton
Lawrence Weston
Avonmouth
Severn Beach
Pilning
Hallen
Leigh Woods
Abbots Leigh
Pill
Easton-in-Gordano
Portbury
Portishead
Clapton in Gordano
Failand
Long Ashton
Flax Bourton
Backwell
Nailsea
Wraxall
Tyntesfield
Chelvey
Barrow Gurney
River Avon
Avon Gorge
Bristol Channel
AVON RING ROAD

MOUTH OF THE SEVERN
ABER HAFREN
NEWPORT (CASNEWYDD)
CARDIFF (CAERDYDD)
CAERPHILLY (CAERFFILI)
Caerleon (Caerllion)
St Julian's
Maindee
Beechwood
Somerton
Pillgwenlly
Allt-yr-yn
Stelvio
Maes-glas
Duffryn
Ridgeway
Glasllwch
Gaer
High Cross
Pye Corner
Bassaleg
Rogerstone (Ty-du)
Rhiwderin
Garth
Fox Hill
Risca (Rhisga)
Pontymister
Ochrwyth
Danygraig
Park Wood
Michaelston-y-Fedw
Coedkernew (Coedcernyw)
Castleton
Marshfield
Blacktown
St Brides Wentlooge (Llansanffraid Gwynllŵg)
Peterstone Wentlooge (Llanbedr Gwynllŵg)
Wentlooge Level
Newton
St Mellons (Llaneirwg)
Trowbridge
Rumney (Rhymni)
Pwll-Mawr
Llanrumney
Began
Lower Machen
Chatham
Machen
Draethen
Coed Craig Ruperra
Coed Cefn-pwll-du
Cefn Mably Woods
Llanedeyrn
Pentwyn
Tremorfa
Splott
Roath
Roath Park
Cyncoed
Lisvane (Llys Faen)
Llwyncelyn
Coed Coesau-Whips
Bertlangollen
Rudry
Garth Place
Rhymney Valley
Waterloo
Graig-y-Rhacca
Trethomas
Bedwas
Lansbury Park
Coed Parc-y-Van
Van
The Warren
Thornhill
Llanishen
Heath
Cathays
Maindy
Gabalfa
Birchgrove
Rhiwbina
Whitchurch
Llandaff North
Llandaff (Llandaf)
Pontcanna
Canton
Riverside
Grangetown
Butetown
Cardiff Bay
Cardiff Bay Barrage
Llandough
Leckwith
Michaelston-le-Pit
Caerau
Ely (Trelái)
Fairwater
St Fagans (Sain Ffagan)
Michaelston-super-Ely
Culverhouse Cross
Wenvoe (Gwenfô)
Downs
Twyn-yr-odyn
Walston
St Lythans
St Nicholas (Sain Nicolas)
St Brides-super-Ely (Llansanffraid-ar-Elai)
St George's
Drope
Pentrebane
Radyr
Morganstown
Tongwynlais
Taff's Well (Ffynnon-Taf)
Coed-y-Wenallt
Pentwyn
Nantgarw
Groes-wen
Caerphilly Common
Watford
Trecenydd
Penyrheol
Energlyn
Pwllypant
Llanbradach
Abertridwr
Senghenydd
Mynydd Meio
Upper Boat
Glan-y-llyn
Garth Wood
Pentyrch
Gwaelod-y-garth
Grath Hill
Efail Isaf
Church Village
Rhydyfelin
Hawthorn
Glyntaff
Soar
River Taff
River Ely
River Usk
Ebbw River
Rhymney River
Llanishen Reservoir
Roath Basin
Bute E Dock
CARDIFF GATE SERVICES
CARDIFF WEST SERVICES
WELSH NATIONAL VELODROME
TREDEGAR HOUSE
FOURTEEN LOCKS
CAERPHILLY CASTLE
CASTELL COCH
FOREST FARM
LLANDAFF CATHEDRAL
MUSEUM OF WELSH LIFE
NATIONAL MUSEUM
MILLENNIUM STADIUM
CARDIFF CASTLE
TECHNIQUEST
CARDIFF BAY VISITOR CENTRE
WALES MILLENNIUM CENTRE
TINKINSWOOD BURIAL CHAMBER
PARC CEFN ONN
M4
A48(M)
A470
A4232
A48
A469
A467
A4042
A4050
3 miles
5 km

Cardiff road map page 22 • **Cheltenham** road map page 37 • **Chester** road map page 73

Cardiff / Caerdydd

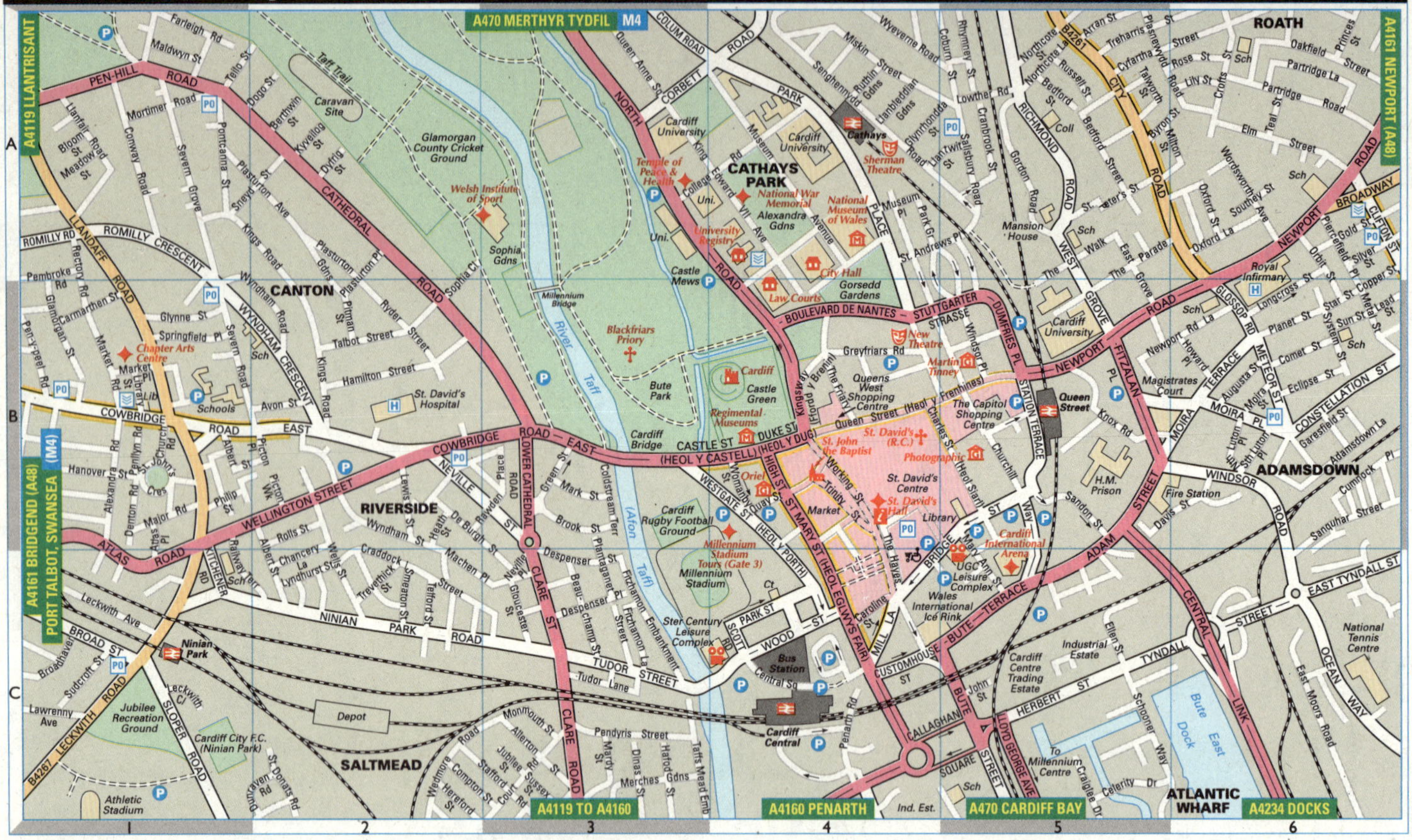

Cheltenham

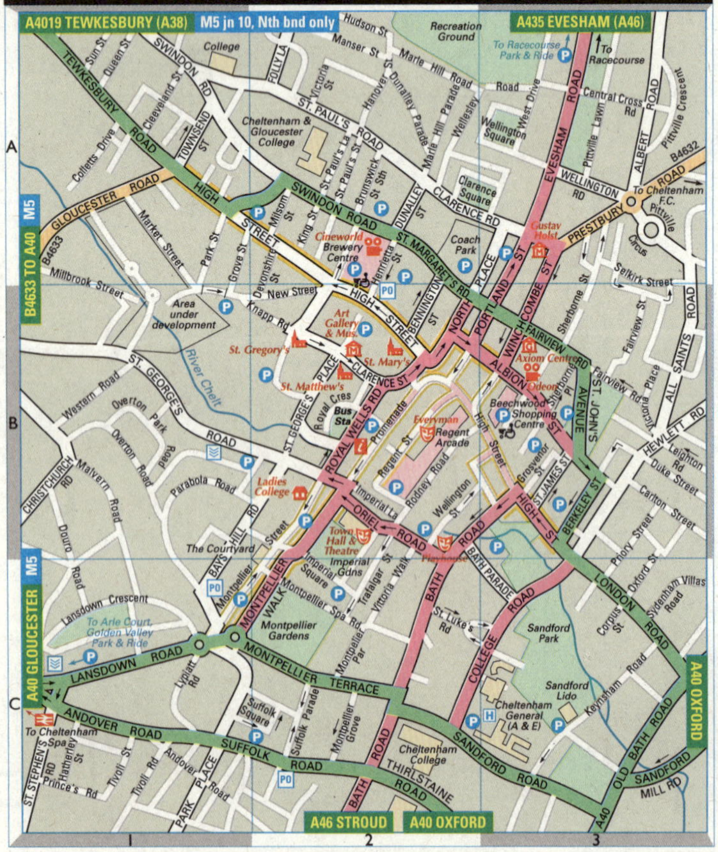

Chester

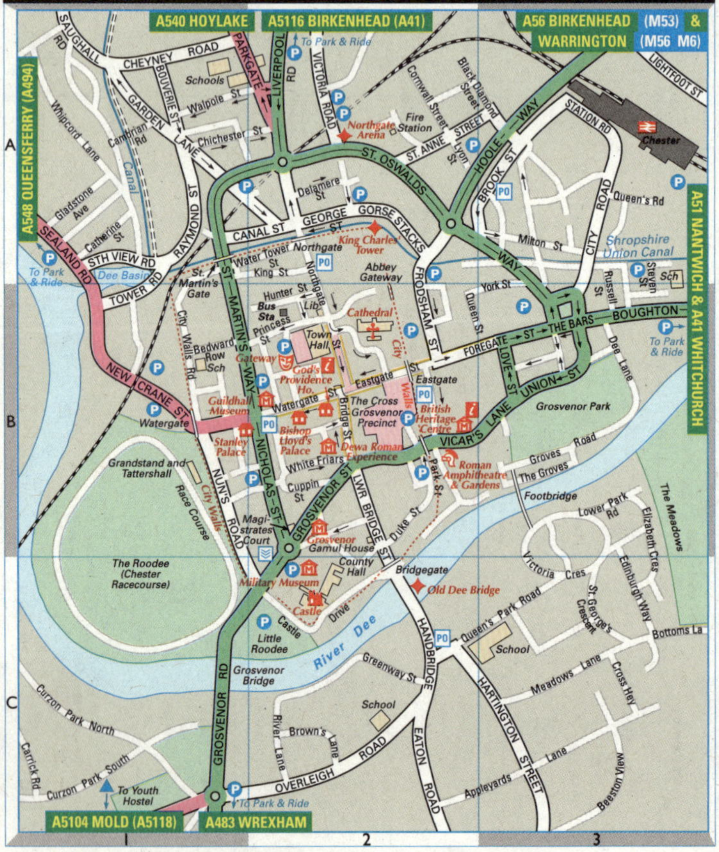

Colchester

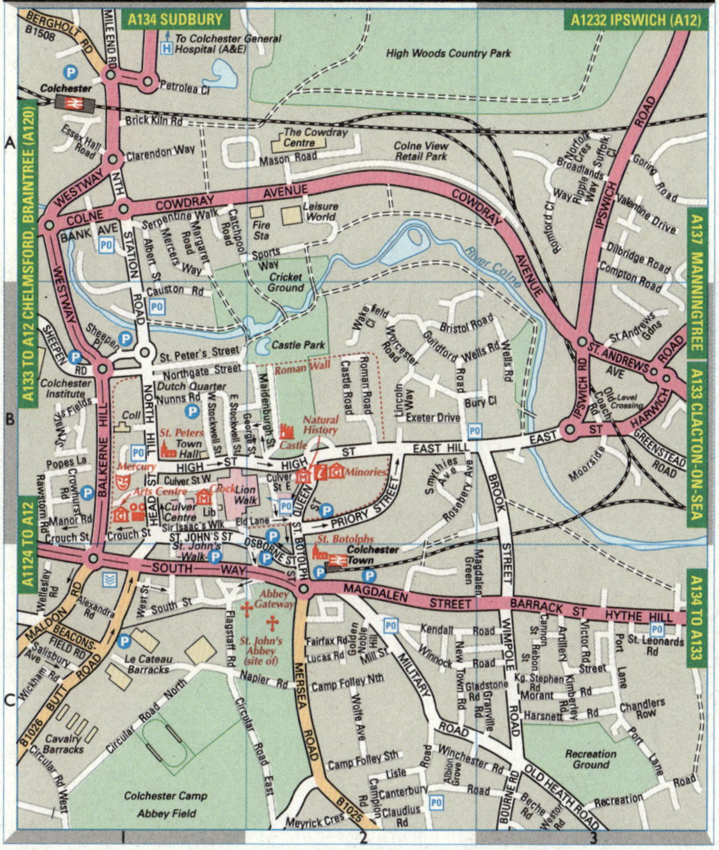

Coventry

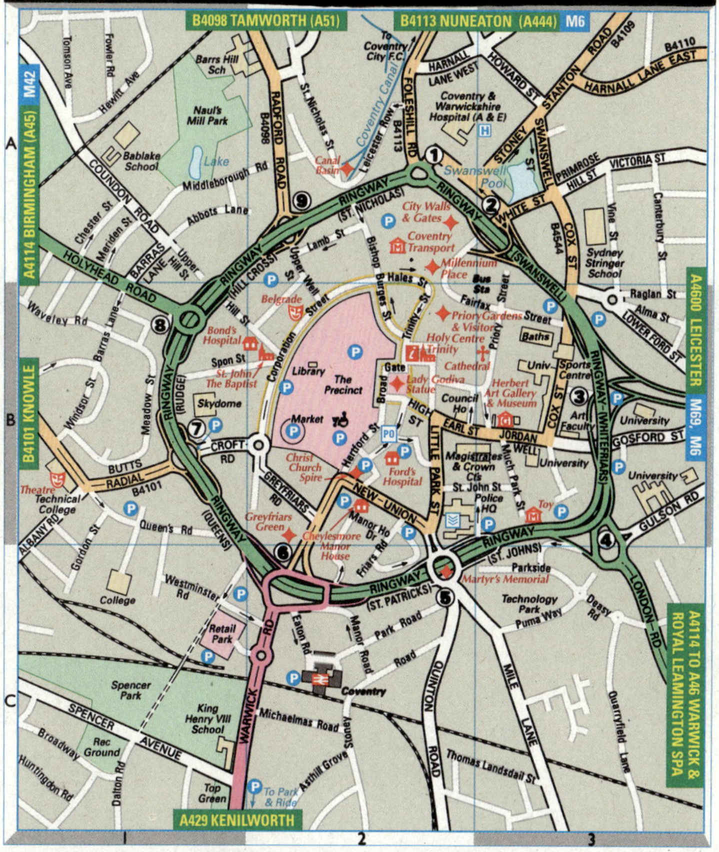

Derby

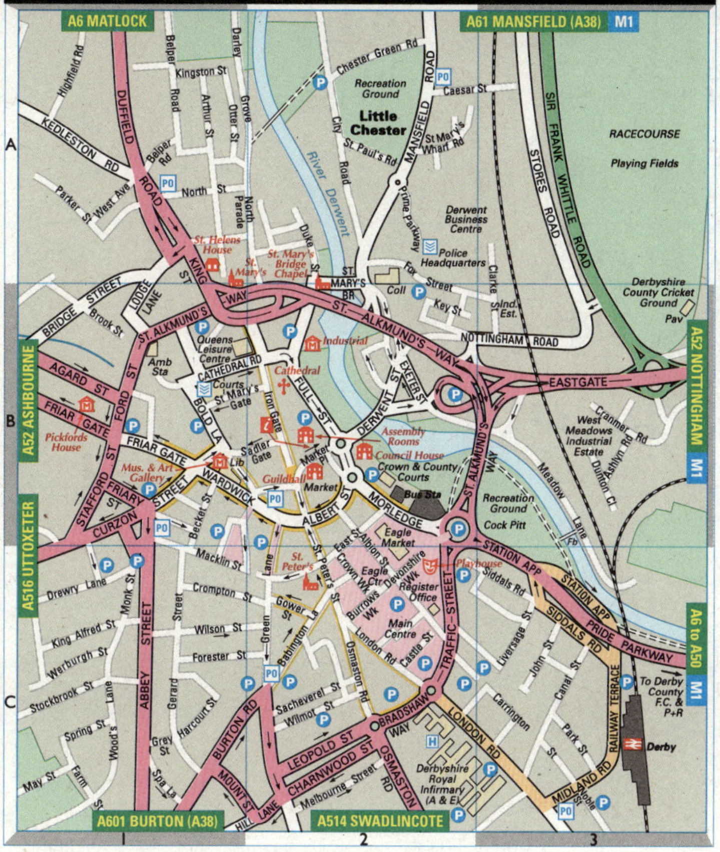

Durham

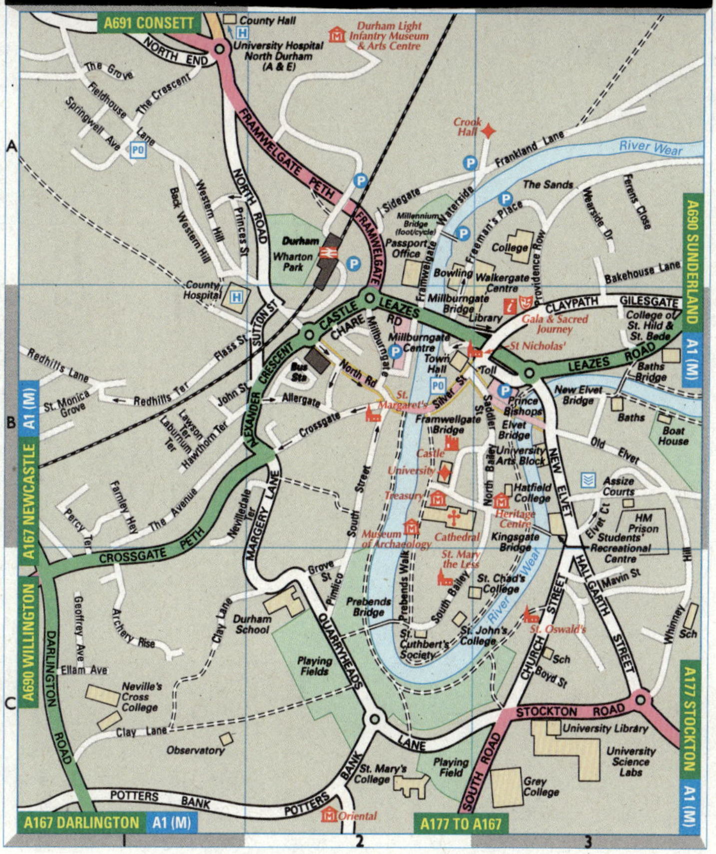

FIRTH OF FORTH
INCHKEITH
Inchcolm
Inchmickery
Cramond Island
Drum Sands
Middle Craigs
Eastern Craigs
Leith
Portobello
Musselburgh
Fisherrow Sands
Joppa
Newhaven
Granton
Granton Harbour
Wardie
Craigleith
Drylaw
Blackhall
Murrayfield
Corstorphine
Clermiston
Cramond
Cammo
Cramond Bridge
Turnhouse
Craigiehall
Dalmeny Park
Dalmeny House
Dalmeny
Inch Garvie
Forth Bridge
Forth Road Bridge
North Queensferry
Inverkeithing
Inverkeithing Bay
St Davids Harbour
Rosyth
St Margaret's Hope
Queensferry
Port Edgar
Dundas Castle
Kirkliston
Newbridge
Ratho Station
Ratho
Union Canal
River Almond
Edinburgh Airport
Royal Highland Showground
EDINBURGH
Calton Hill
Holyrood Park
Arthur's Seat
Dunsapie Loch
Duddingston Loch
Commonwealth Pool
Scottish Parliament
Royal Botanic Garden
Meadow Park
Merchiston
Churchill
Morningside
Craiglockhart
Colinton
Bonaly
Longstone
South Gyle
Baberton
Hermiston
Currie
Balerno
Kirknewton
Wilkieston
Juniper Green
Oxgangs
Comiston
Fairmilehead
Braid Hills
Liberton
Nether Liberton
Prestonfield
Craigmillar
The Inch
Moredun
Gilmerton
Danderhall
Niddrie
Bingham
Northfield
Craigentinny
Stoneybank
Old Craighall
Eastern Millerhill
Dalkeith
Eastthouses
Lasswade
Bonnyrigg
Loanhead
Muirhouse
Alnwickhill
Old Pentland
Eskgrove
Pentland Hills
Torphin
Clubbiedean Res
Harlaw Res
Dreghorn Services
Edinburgh Services
Hillend Ski Centre
Hillend Country Park
Bonaly Country Park
Malleny Garden
River Esk
Nature Trail
THE CITY OF EDINBURGH BY-PASS
GLASGOW ROAD
QUEENSFERRY ROAD
LANARK ROAD WEST
CALDER ROAD
A1
A7
A8
A70
A71
A90
A702
A720
A8000
M8
M9
P&R
32
33
57
68
0
1
2
3 miles
0
1
2
3
4
5 km

Edinburgh

0 Miles ¼

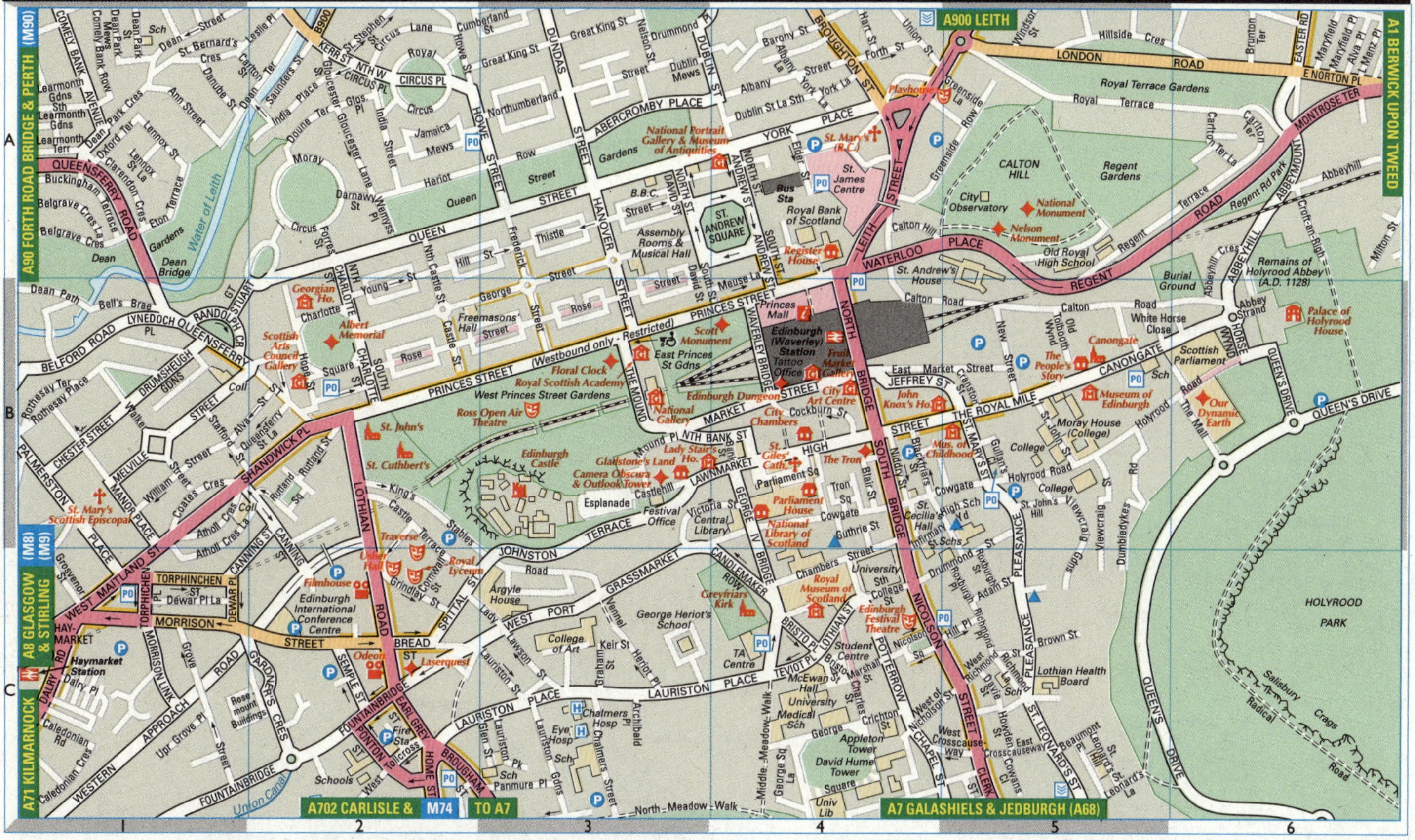

Glasgow

0 Miles ¼

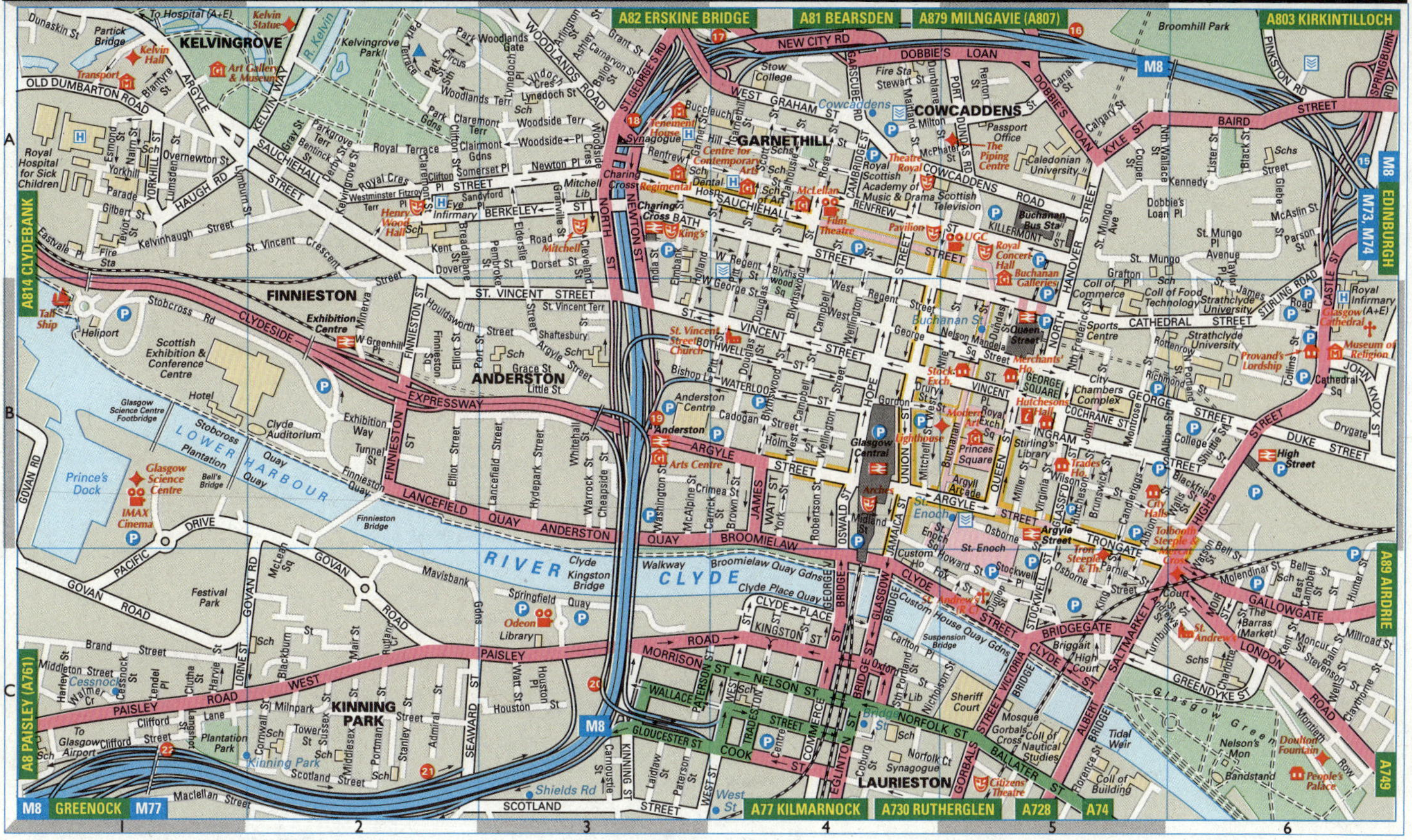

Kilpatrick Hills
Black Linn Reservoir
Fyn Loch
Lily Loch
Birny Hills
Cochno Loch
Black Loch
Loch Humphrey
Creigarestie
Greenside Reservoir
Jaw Reservoir
The Slacks
Carneddans Wood
Mugdock Wood
Mugdock
Mugdock Country Park
Loch Ardinning Nature Reserve
Craigend Muir
Craigmaddie Muir
Blairskaith Muir
Mugdock Reservoir
Craigmaddie Reservoir
MILNGAVIE
Dougalston Loch
Bardowie Loch
TORRANCE
Balmore
Kilpatrick Braes
DUNTOCHER
Faifley
BEARSDEN
OLD KILPATRICK
Erskine Bridge
Big Wood
Antonine Wall
Roman Bathhouse
Sports Complex
River Kelvin
Wilderness Plantation
Dalmuir
Drumchapel
Kessington
Bargarran
Drumry
ERSKINE
Newshot Island
CLYDEBANK
Clydebank Museum
Possil Loch
Nature Reserve
Forth and Clyde Canal
BISHOPBRIGGS
Inchinnan
Yoker
Knightswood
Dawsholm Park
Milton
Passenger Ferry
River Clyde
Blythswood
Jordanhill
Kelvinside
Springburn
Black Cart Water
Braehead Shopping Centre
Victoria Park
Firhill
White Cart Water
Glasgow International Airport
RENFREW
Partick
Kelvingrove Art Gallery
Transport Museum
GLASGOW
Clyde Tunnel
Govan
Exhibition Centre
Science Centre
LINWOOD
Gallowhill
PAISLEY
Hillington
Ibrox
Gallowgate
Ferguslie Park
Oldhall
Bellahouston Park
Pollokshields
ELDERSLIE
Crookston
Hagg's Castle
Pollok Country Park
Burrell Collection
Pollok House
Crossmyloof
Queen's Park
Govanhill
Richmond Park
Foxbar
Stanely Reservoir
Glenburn
Priesthill
Langside
RUTHERGLEN
Gleniffer Braes Country Park
Nitshill
Hillpark
Cathcart
King's Park
Croftfoot
Glenburn Reservoir
Brownside Braes
Crossmill
Muirend
Holmwood House
Harelaw Reservoir
Fereneze Hills
Orchard Park
Linn Park
Castlemilk
Giffnock
BARRHEAD
Waulkmill Glen Reservoir
Rouken Glen Country Park
Netherlee
Cathkin Braes Country Park
Lochliboside Hills
Williamwood
Balgray Reservoir
Ryatt Linn Reservoir
CLARKSTON
Carmunnock
NEILSTON
Crookfur
Broom
Busby
Museum of Scottish Country Life
Kirkton Dam
Greenbank Garden
Glanderston Dam
NEWTON MEARNS
Mearns
College Milton
Walton Dam
Snypes Dam
Thorntonhall
Craighall Dam
Knockenae Plantation
Waterfoot
Commore Dam
Hairmyres
Brother Loch
Moyne Moor
Long Loch
EAGLESHAM
Mossneuk
0 1 2 3 miles
0 1 2 3 4 5 km

LENNOXTOWN
Queenzieburn
KILSYTH
Milton of Campsie
Antermony Loch
Croy
Twechar
Bar Hill
Dullatur
Cumbernauld Village
Carrickstone
Abronhill
CUMBERNAULD
Balloch
Carbrain
Forth and Clyde Canal
KIRKINTILLOCH
River Kelvin
Westfield
Condorrat
Greenfaulds
Luggiebank
Palacerigg Country Park
Gartshore Moss
Broadwood Loch
Lenzie
Luggie Water
Auchinloch
Gadloch
Moodiesburn
Chryston
Greengairs
MUIRHEAD
Robroyston
STEPPS
Marnock
Glenboig
Balornock
Gartcosh
Johnston Loch
Frankfield Loch
Hogganfield Loch
Bishop Loch
Woodend Loch
Lochend Loch
Glenmavis
Plains
Craigend
Riddrie
Alexandra Park
Provan Hall
Easterhouse
Gartsherrie
Blairhill
AIRDRIE
Whinhall
Dunbeth
Drumgelloch
Dennistoun
Carntyne
Springboig
Swinton
COATBRIDGE
Whifflet
Gartlea
Bargeddie
Kirkwood
Dundyvan
Celtic Park
Tollcross Park
Mont Vernon
Braidfauld
Muirhead
Broomhouse
Cairnbroe
Shawhead
Calderbank
Chapelhall
River Clyde
North Calder Water
Tannochside
Hattonrig
CAMBUSLANG
Westburn
UDDINGSTON
Holytown
Mossend
New Stevenston
BELLSHILL
Orbiston
Newarthill
Flemington
Bothwell Castle
Bothwell Services (South only)
Carfin
Forgewood
Cleland
David Livingstone Centre
BOTHWELL
Strathclyde Country Park
Dechmont Hill
Strathclyde Loch
MOTHERWELL
Ravenscraig
Blantyre
Whitehill
Hamilton Services (North only)
Nerston
Udston
HAMILTON
Airbles
Craigneuk
WISHAW
Calderwood
East Mains
West Mains
EAST KILBRIDE
Earnock
Nature Reserve
River Clyde
Muirhouse
Netherton
St Leonards
Chatelherault Country Park
Eddlewood
Blantyre Muir
Calderglen Country Park
Whitehills
Hamilton High Parks
Carbarns Wood

Exeter

Miles ¼

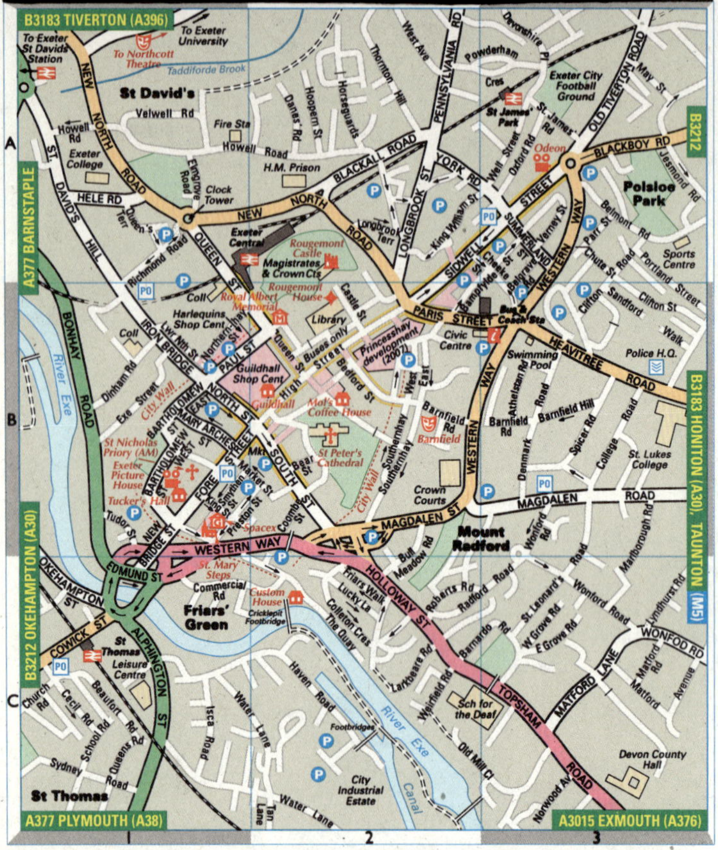

Gloucester

Miles

Hull

Miles ¼

Ipswich

0 Miles ¼

Leeds

0 Miles

Lancaster

0 Miles ¼

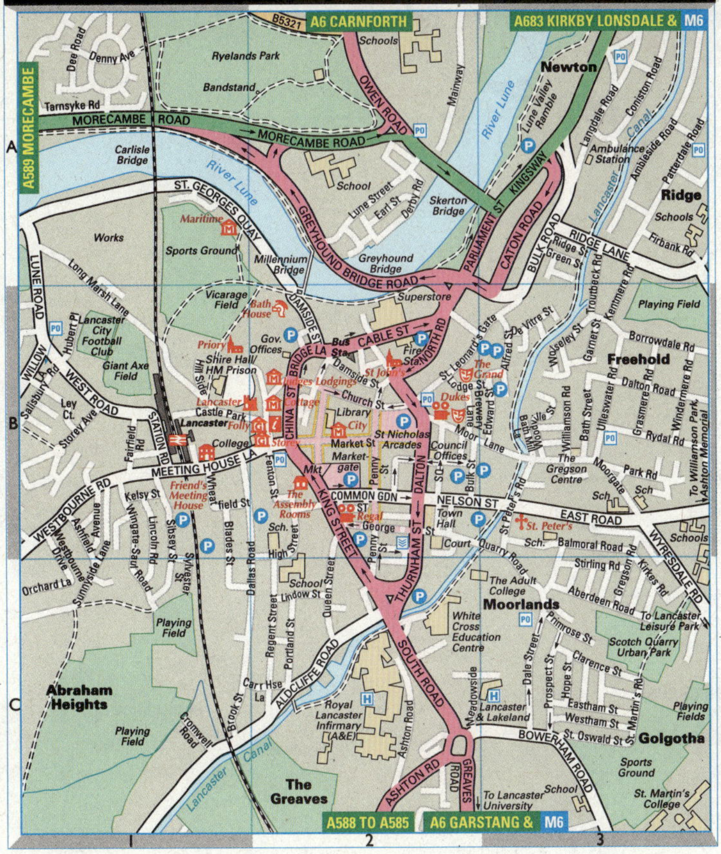

Leicester

0 Miles

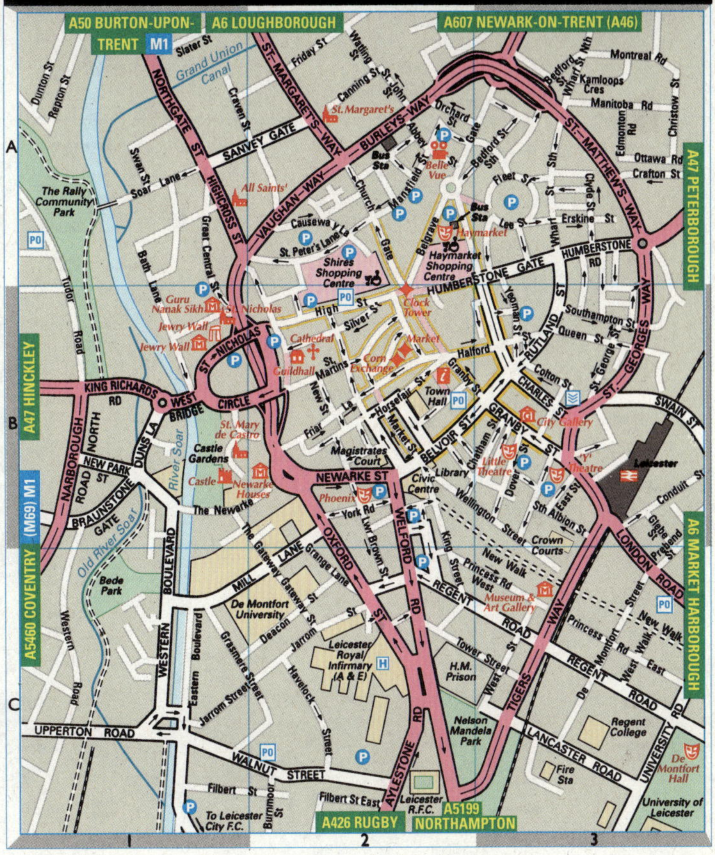

MENSTON
Guiseley Moor
Hawksworth Moor
RIDDLESDEN
Bingley Moor
East Morton
Kelcliff
GUISELEY
KEIGHLEY
Micklethwaite
Tranmere Park
Shaw Lane
YEADON
LEEDS BRADFORD INTERNATIONAL AIRPORT
Thwaites Brow
Eldwick
Baildon Moor
BAILDON
Esholt
Larkfield
RAWDON
BINGLEY
Ferncliffe
Harden
Buck Wood
Dawson Wood
Thackley End
Thackley
Simpson Green
West End
Cottingley
Nab Wood
SHIPLEY
West Royd
Thorpe
Greengates
CALVERLEY
Cullingworth
Wilsden
Moorhead
Frizinghall
Wrose
Eccleshill
Ravenscliffe
Farsley
DENHOLME
Heaton
Daisy Hill
Bolton
Fagley
Allerton
Fairweather Green
Barkerend
Thornbury
PUDSEY
THORNTON
BRADFORD
Stanningley
Clayton
Horton Bank
Tyersal
Fulneck
West Bowling
Holme Wood
QUEENSBURY
Bierley
Tong
Buttershaw
SHELF
East Bierley
Illingworth
Mixenden
Woodside
Wesley Place
Drighlington
BIRKENSHAW
Wyke
Ovenden
Wheatley
NORTHOWRAM
Hunsworth
GOMERSAL
Birstall
Woodlands
Pellon
HALIFAX
Hipperholme
Scholes
Moorend
Marsh
Bailiff Bridge
CLECKHEATON
Brown Hill
Nunroyd
Bank Top
Savile Park
Southowram
Hove Edge
LIVERSEDGE
SOWERBY BRIDGE
Siddal
BRIGHOUSE
Waring Green
HECKMONDWIKE
Norland Town
Clifton
Roberttown
Exley
Rastrick
Hartshead
Lindwell
GREETLAND
ELLAND
Dewsbury Moor
West Vale
Northope
MIRFIELD
Ravensthorpe
Fixby
Stainland
Holywell Green
Brackenhall
Cowcliffe

BRAMHOPE
Crag Wood
Bog Plantation
Harewood Park
Beech Bank
Eccup Reservoir
Lady Wood
West Woods
Bramham Park
Whittle Carr
Scarcroft
Thorner
Coakridge
York Gate Garden
Alwoodley
Slaid Hill
Blackwood
Shadwell
Adel
Govt Bldgs
Saw Wood
Horsforth
Ireland Wood
Park Villas
Tropical World
Roundhay Park
Lady Wood
Arthursdale
Barwick in Elmet
Barwick Bank
Cragg Hill
West Park
Meanwood
Monkswood
Scholes
Hawksworth
Met Univ
Beckett Park
Headingley
Oakwood
Brooklands
Swarcliffe
Kirkstall Abbey
Hyde Park
Parklands
Manston
Parlington Hollins
Bramley
Hill Top
Burley
University
Harehills
Leeds Industrial Museum
Austhorpe
Whitekirk
Garforth
Barrowby Park
Armley
Civic Hall
Town Hall
City Art Gall
Osmondthorpe
East End Park
Halton Moor
Colton
Swillington Common
Church Garforth
Pudsey
Park Spring
Upper Wortley
Bank
LEEDS
Royal Armouries
Farnley
Holbeck
Knowsthorpe
Home Farm
Temple Newsam House
Temple Newsam Country Park
Hunslet
Thwaitemills Industrial Museum
Dawson's Wood
Avenue Wood
Brecks Wood
New Farnley
Elland Road
River Aire
Aire & Calder Navigation
Beeston
Cross Flatts Park
South Leeds Stadium
Swillington
KIPPAX
Newsam Green
Little Preston
Country Park
Great Preston
Middleton Railway
Gildersome
Churwell
White Rose Centre
Middleton Park
Rothwell Haigh
Woodlesford
Cockpit Round
Morley
Troy Hill
Town Hall
ROTHWELL
Oulton
Bruntcliffe
Middleton
Robin Hood
Carlton
MORLEY
Topcliffe
Thorpe on the Hill
Ozelwell Green
Almshouses Wood
Mickletown
Copley Hill
Sports Centre
Moss Carr Wood
Methley
Bagshaw Museum
The Fall
Upper Batley
EAST ARDSLEY
Upper Green
Lee Moor
Lofthouse Gate
Fairies Hill
Ardsley Resr
River Calder
Lower Soothill
Haigh Moor
The Mill
Dum Wood
Stanley
Batley
Brandy Carr
Outwood
Nature Reserve
Altofts
Dogloitch Wood
Brag Lane End
Normanton
Batley Carr
Chidswell
Hanging Heaton
Newton Hill
Kirkhamgate
Wrenthorpe
Woodhouse
DEWSBURY
Gawthorpe
Ossett Street Side
Alverthorpe
Chickenley
Kirkthorpe
WAKEFIELD
Canal Museum
OSSETT
Flanshaw
Wakefield Westgate
Warmfield
Streethouse
Town Hall
Cath
Wakefield Kirkgate
Runtlings
Thornhill Lees
Calder & Hebble Navigation
Lupset
South Ossett
Belle Vue
Sharlston Common
Sharlston
3 miles
5 km

Liverpool road map page 85 • **Lincoln** road map page 78 • **Middlesbrough** road map page 102

Liverpool

0 Miles ¼

Lincoln

0 Miles ¼

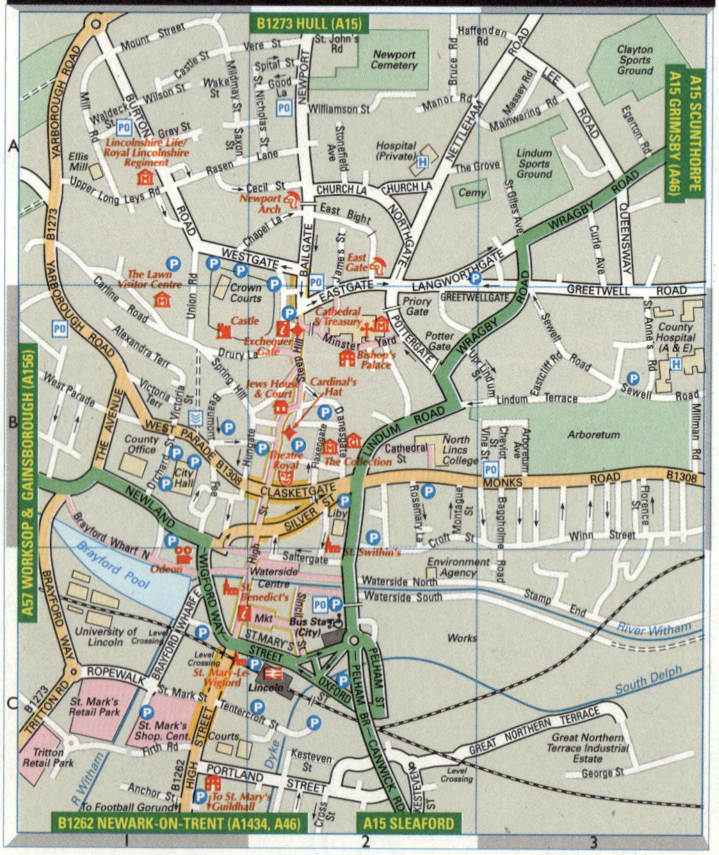

Middlesbrough

0 Miles ¼

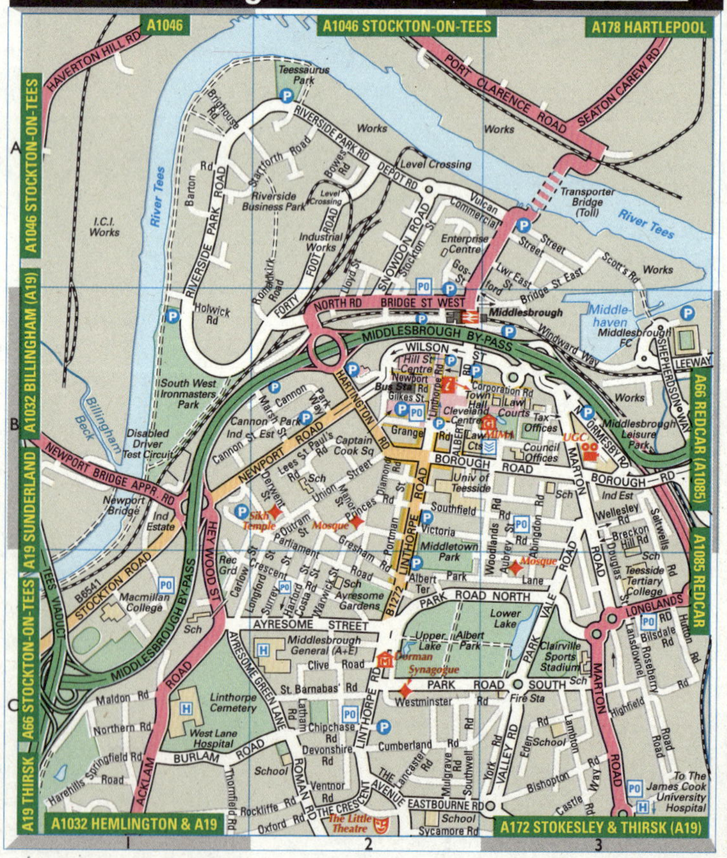

MAGHULL
Melling
CROSBY
Great Crosby
Waterloo
Seaforth
LITHERLAND
AINTREE
Kirkby Park
Westvale
KIRKBY
Fazakerley
Croxteth
Knowsley
Knowsley Park
BOOTLE
Walton
West Derby
Stockbridge Village
PRESCOT
New Brighton
WALLASEY
Anfield
Stanley Park
Newsham Park
HUYTON-WITH-ROBY
HUYTON
Roby
Broad Green
Edge Hill
Wavertree
Childwall
LIVERPOOL
BIRKENHEAD
Birkenhead Park
Oxton
Toxteth
Sefton Park
Dingle
Tranmere
Netherley
Woodlands
Woolton
Halewood
Aigburth
Otterspool
Allerton
Hunt's Cross
GARSTON
SPEKE
Hale
LIVERPOOL AIRPORT
LIVERPOOL JOHN LENNON AIRPORT
BEBINGTON
Port Sunlight
Spital
Brimstage
Bromborough
River Mersey
Eastham Ferry
Eastham
Thornton Hough
Raby
Manchester Ship Canal
Ince Banks
Hooton
WILLASTON
NESTON
Overpool
ELLESMERE PORT
Little Sutton
Whitby
0 1 2 3 miles
0 1 2 3 4 5 km

REGENT'S PARK
Institute of Archaeology (London Univ)
Open Air Theatre
Queen Mary's Gardens
The Holme
Regent's Park Lake
London Business School
Regents College
Royal Academy of Music
Madame Tussaud's
Lost Property Office (LT)
Baker Street
MARYLEBONE ROAD
REGENT'S PARK
Royal College of Physicians
Euston
Euston Square
National Temperance Hospital
SOMERS TOWN
St. Pancras
King's Cross
St. Pancras International Station under Construction (opens Nov 07)
British Library
PENTONVILLE ROAD
EUSTON ROAD
Wellcome Trust
Friends House
University College Hosp. (A&E)
University College
British Medical Association
Percival David Foundation
Coram's Fields (Children's Playground)
National Hospital
BLOOMSBURY
Royal Acad of Dramatic Art
University of London
Sch of Hygiene & Tropical Med
British Museum
FITZROVIA
British Telecom Tower
Pollock's Toy Mus
R.I.B.A.
Broadcasting Ho (BBC)
All Saints
Wallace Collection
Wigmore Hall
Royal Coll of Nursing
OXFORD STREET
SOHO
Marble Arch
Speakers Corner
Handel Hendrix Houses
Roosevelt Memorial
American Embassy
GROSVENOR SQUARE
MAYFAIR
Burlington House
Royal Acad of Arts
Piccadilly Circus
Trocadero Centre
Leicester Square
National Portrait Gall
National Gall
Nelson's Column
TRAFALGAR SQUARE
Charing Cross
St. Martin in the Fields
Covent Garden
Royal Opera House
London Transport Mus
Holborn
Victoria Embankment Gdns
Cleopatra's Needle
Savoy Pier
Embankment Pier
Hungerford Bridge (Footbridge)
ST. JAMES'S
PICCADILLY
Green Park
GREEN PARK
HYDE PARK
Diana, Princess of Wales Memorial Walk
Serpentine Rd
Achilles Statue
Apsley House Wellington Museum
Wellington Arch
Hyde Park Corner
Marlborough House
St. James's Palace
Clarence House
Lancaster House
ST. JAMES'S PARK
Duck Island
Horse Guards' Parade
Admiralty Arch
The Admiralty
Banqueting Ho.
Min of Defence
Cabinet War Rooms & Churchill Museum
Buckingham Palace
Buckingham Palace Gardens
Queen Victoria Memorial
Constitution Hill Closed to traffic on Sundays
The Mall Closed to traffic on Sundays
Guards Mus. & Chapel
Wellington Barracks
Queen's Gallery
Royal Mews
Home Office
New Scotland Yard
Westminster Abbey
Houses of Parliament
Westminster Pier
WESTMINSTER BRIDGE
London Aquarium
Dali Universe
F.A. Premier League Hall of Fame
County Hall
St. Thomas' Hospital
Florence Nightingale Museum
Westminster City Hall
Westminster Cathedral (R.C.)
Victoria
WESTMINSTER
Lambeth Pier
LAMBETH BRIDGE
Mus. of Garden History
Dept of Transport & Environment
Westminster School Playing Field
Burghers of Calais (Rodin)
Victoria Tower Gardens
Belgrave Square
KNIGHTSBRIDGE
BELGRAVIA
Sloane Street
Eccleston Bridge
Passport Office
Holy Trinity

FINSBURY
CLERKENWELL
HOLBORN
HOXTON
SHOREDITCH
THE CITY
SOUTHWARK
LAMBETH
RIVER THAMES
Pentonville Road
City Road
Old Street
Clerkenwell Road
London Wall
Holborn Viaduct
Newgate Street
Cheapside
Fleet Street
Strand
Victoria Embankment
Upper Thames Street
Lower Thames Street
Cannon Street
Queen Victoria Street
Fenchurch Street
Leadenhall Street
Cornhill
Bishopsgate
Moorgate
Farringdon Road
Blackfriars Road
Southwark Street
Borough High Street
Tooley Street
Tower Bridge Road
Blackfriars Bridge
Southwark Bridge
London Bridge
Tower Bridge
The Millennium Bridge (footbridge)
Jubilee Footbridge
Waterloo
Liverpool Street
Fenchurch Street
Cannon Street
London Bridge
Farringdon
Barbican
St. Paul's Cathedral
Museum of London
The Barbican Centre For Arts
Guildhall
Bank of England
Tate Modern
Shakespeare's Globe Theatre
The Tower of London
Royal National Theatre
BFI London IMAX Cinema
Imperial War Museum
Lincoln's Inn Fields
Royal Courts of Justice
Temple Church
Southwark Cathedral
Guy's Hospital
Bunhill Fields
Honourable Artillery Co HQ
River Bus Route
Congestion Charging Zone
Uncharged Roads
London Docklands
STEPNEY
POPLAR
CANNING TOWN
WAPPING
ROTHERHITHE
BERMONDSEY
MILLWALL
ISLE OF DOGS
DEPTFORD
GREENWICH
The Millennium Dome
World Trade Centre
Surrey Docks
Mudchute Park
Southwark Park
Miles 0 1

KINGS LANGLEY
ABBOTS LANGLEY
BRICKET WOOD
Bovingdon Green
Tower Hill
Chipperfield
Venus Hill
Hogpits Bottom
Flaunden
Belsize
Commonwood
Sarratt
Chenies
CHENIES MANOR HOUSE
Church End
Micklefield Green
Sarratt Bottom
Chandler's Cross
Whippendell Wood
Leavesden Green
Hunton Bridge
Garston
WATFORD
North Watford
Meriden
Waterdale
Woodside
Radlett
Aldenham
Colney Street
Letchmore Heath
Patchetts Green
ELSTREE AERODROME
Hilfield Park Reservoir
Loudwater
Chorleywood West
CHORLEYWOOD
Croxley Green
Cassiobury Park
BUSHEY
OXHEY
Bushey Heath
Holywell
Philipshill Wood
Heronsgate
CHILTERN OPEN AIR MUSEUM
Newland Park
Bottom Wood
RICKMANSWORTH
RICKMANSWORTH AQUADROME
Mill End
Stocker's Lake
MOOR PARK MANSION
Moor Park
Carpenders Park
South Oxhey
Oxhey Woods
Stanmore Common
STANMORE
Maple Cross
Chalfont Common
SHIRE HORSE CENTRE
NORTHWOOD
Eastbury
Hatch End
Harrow Weald
Headstone Lane
Headstone
Belmont
Grand Union Canal
West Hyde
Mount Pleasant
Harefield
CHALFONT ST. PETER
Copse Wood
Mad Bess Wood
Park Wood
RUISLIP LIDO
PINNER
HARROW MUSEUM
HARROW
Wealdstone
Greenhill
KENTON
South Harefield
DENHAM AERODROME
BAYHURST WOOD
Eastcote Village
North Harrow
West Harrow
Harrow on the Hill
Northwick Park
Denham Green
Higher Denham
Newyears Green
Eastcote
RUISLIP
Ruislip Manor
Rayners Lane
DENHAM
West Ruislip
ICKENHAM
Ickenham
Ruislip Gardens
South Ruislip
Roxeth
South Harrow
Sudbury
WEMBLEY
Fulmer
Rush Green
Tatling End
Swakeleys Rbdt
NORTHOLT AERODROME
Hillingdon Circus
New Denham
Polish War Memorial
NORTHOLT
UXBRIDGE
North Hillingdon
GREENFORD
Perivale
BLACK PARK
Blackpark Lake
Iver Heath
HILLINGDON
LONDON MOTORCYCLE MUSEUM
LANGLEY PARK
Langley Park
George Green
IVER
Shreding Green
Love Green
Cowley
Hayes End
Colham Green
Yeading
EALING
Wood End
HAYES
Hayes Town
SOUTHALL
Dormer's Wells
Drayton Green
West Ealing
HANWELL
YIEWSLEY
Middle Green
WEST DRAYTON
Norwood Green
Northfields
Osterley Park
Sutton
Colne Brook
River Colne
River Chess
Grand Union Canal
WESTERN AVENUE
NORTH ORBITAL ROAD
M25
M1
M40
M4
A40
A41
A312
A4020
0 1 2 3 miles
0 1 2 3 4 5 km

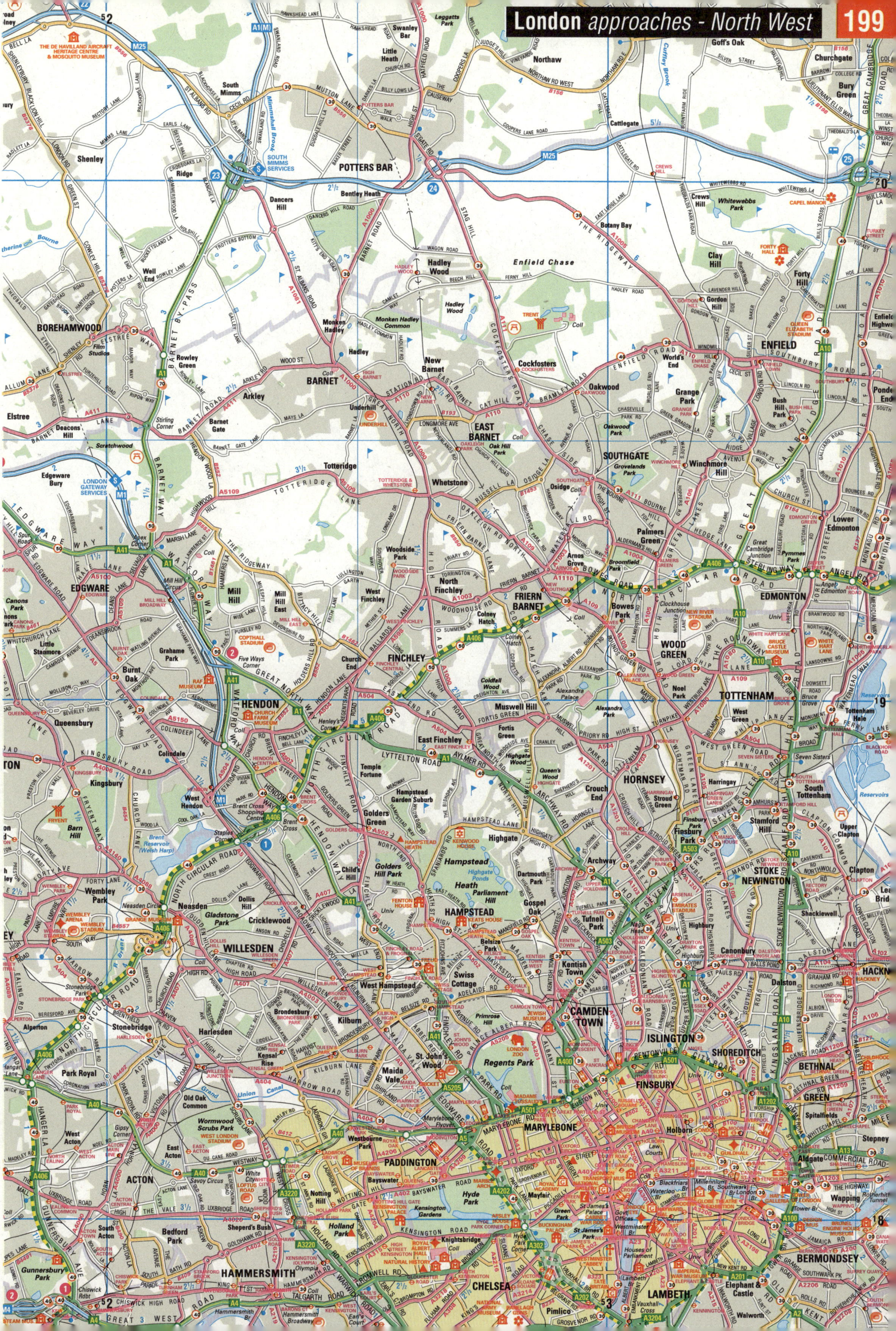
Potters Bar
South Mimms
Shenley
Borehamwood
Elstree
Barnet
Arkley
Hadley Wood
Enfield Chase
Cockfosters
New Barnet
East Barnet
Enfield
Southgate
Winchmore Hill
Totteridge
Whetstone
Edgware
Mill Hill
North Finchley
Friern Barnet
Palmers Green
Edmonton
Finchley
Hendon
Wood Green
Tottenham
Hornsey
Queensbury
Kingsbury
Muswell Hill
Highgate
Hampstead
Stoke Newington
Neasden
Willesden
Cricklewood
Kilburn
Camden Town
Islington
Shoreditch
Harlesden
Maida Vale
Regents Park
Finsbury
Bethnal Green
Park Royal
Acton
Paddington
Marylebone
Holborn
Notting Hill
Hyde Park
Hammersmith
Chelsea
Lambeth
Bermondsey
Kensington Gardens
Mayfair
Stepney
Wapping
Elephant & Castle

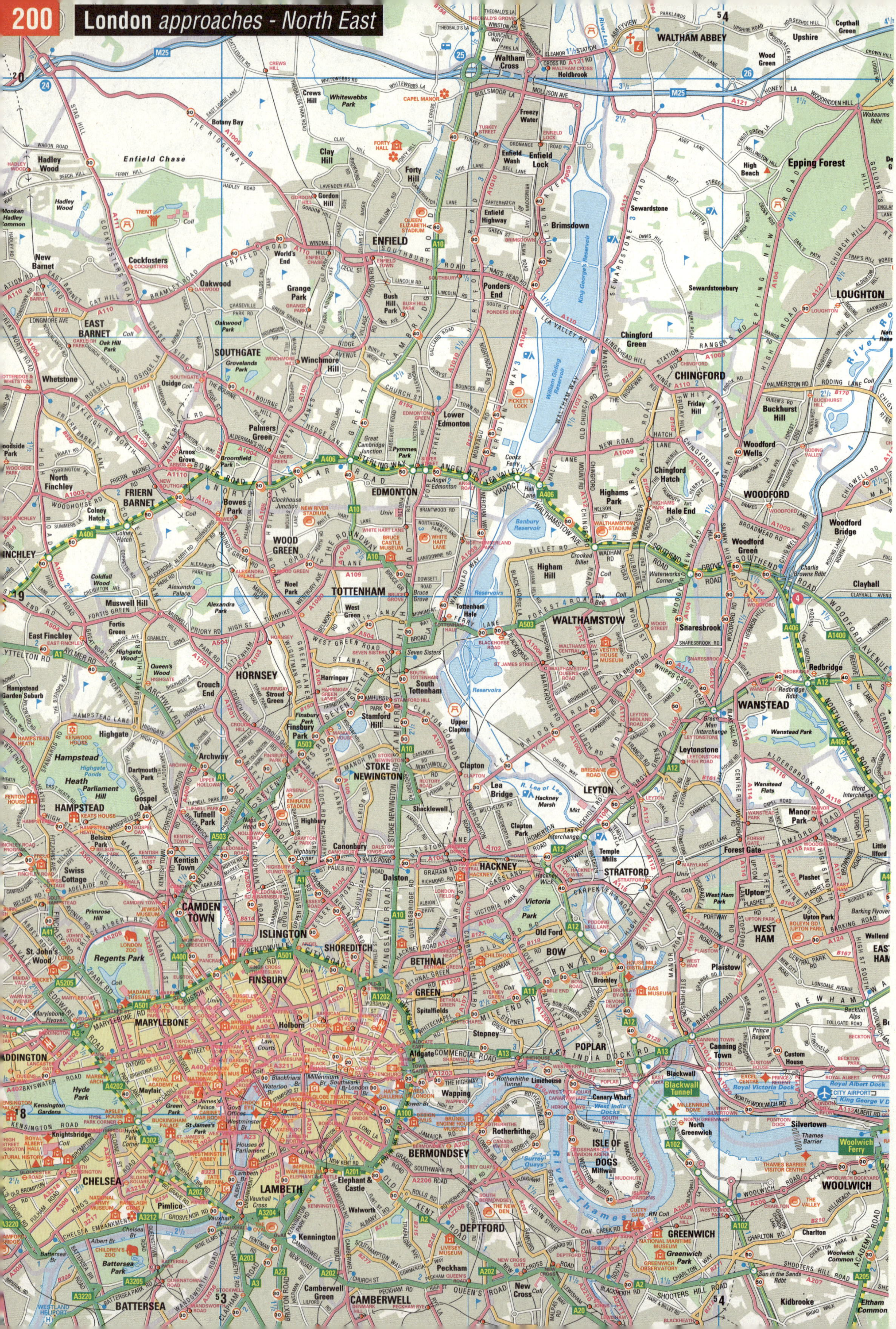
Waltham Abbey
Waltham Cross
Upshire
Copthall Green
Crews Hill
Whitewebbs Park
Capel Manor
Freezy Water
Enfield Wash
Enfield Lock
Botany Bay
Enfield Chase
Hadley Wood
Clay Hill
Forty Hill
Gordon Hill
Enfield Highway
Brimsdown
Epping Forest
High Beach
Sewardstone
Monken Hadley Common
New Barnet
Cockfosters
Enfield
World's End
Oakwood
Grange Park
Bush Hill Park
Ponders End
King George's Reservoir
Sewardstonebury
Loughton
East Barnet
Oak Hill Park
Southgate
Winchmore Hill
Grovelands Park
Chingford Green
Chingford
Whetstone
Osidge
William Girling Reservoir
Lower Edmonton
Friday Hill
Buckhurst Hill
Palmers Green
Arnos Grove
Broomfield Park
Great Cambridge Junction
Pymmes Park
Edmonton
Woodford Wells
North Finchley
Friern Barnet
Colney Hatch
Bowes Park
Clockhouse Junction
Chingford Hatch
Highams Park
Hale End
Woodford
Woodford Bridge
Woodford Green
Finchley
Coldfall Wood
Muswell Hill
Alexandra Palace
Alexandra Park
Wood Green
Banbury Reservoir
Higham Hill
Crooked Billet
Waterworks Corner
Charlie Browns Rdbt
Clayhall
Tottenham
Noel Park
West Green
Tottenham Hale
Walthamstow
Snaresbrook
Redbridge
East Finchley
Fortis Green
Highgate Wood
Queen's Wood
Crouch End
Hornsey
Harringay
Stroud Green
Seven Sisters
South Tottenham
Reservoirs
Wanstead
Hampstead Garden Suburb
Highgate
Hampstead
Heath
Parliament Hill
Dartmouth Park
Gospel Oak
Archway
Finsbury Park
Stamford Hill
Upper Clapton
Stoke Newington
Clapton
Lea Bridge
Hackney Marsh
Leyton
Leytonstone
Wanstead Park
Green Man Interchange
Wanstead Flats
Ilford Interchange
Manor Park
Little Ilford
Belsize Park
Swiss Cottage
Kentish Town
Tufnell Park
Highbury
Canonbury
Dalston
Shacklewell
Clapton Park
Hackney
Hackney Wick
Temple Mills
Stratford
Forest Gate
Upton
Plashet
Upton Park
Barking Flyover
Primrose Hill
Camden Town
Islington
Shoreditch
Victoria Park
Old Ford
Bow
West Ham
Plaistow
St. John's Wood
Regents Park
Finsbury
Bethnal Green
Spitalfields
Bromley
Marylebone
Holborn
Stepney
Poplar
Canning Town
Prince Regent
Beckton Alps
Custom House
Paddington
Hyde Park
Mayfair
Aldgate
Wapping
Limehouse
Rotherhithe Tunnel
Blackwall Tunnel
Canary Wharf
Royal Victoria Dock
Royal Albert Dock
City Airport
King George V Dock
Kensington Gardens
Green Park
St James's Park
Knightsbridge
Westminster
Houses of Parliament
Rotherhithe
Surrey Quays
Isle of Dogs
Millwall
North Greenwich
Silvertown
Thames Barrier
Woolwich Ferry
Bermondsey
Chelsea
Lambeth
Pimlico
Vauxhall Cross
Elephant & Castle
Walworth
Deptford
Greenwich
Woolwich
Charlton
Kennington
Battersea Park
Peckham
Camberwell
Camberwell Green
New Cross
Greenwich Park
Woolwich Common
Shooters Hill
Kidbrooke
Eltham Common
Battersea
River Thames
M25

0 1 2 3 miles
0 1 2 3 4 5 km
Theydon Bois
Theydon Garnon
Hobbs Cross
Theydon Mount
Stapleford Tawney
Mount End
Fiddlers Hamlet
Woodhatch
Stanford Rivers
Little End
Passingford Bridge
Stapleford Aerodrome
Abridge
Debden
Kelvedon Hatch
Secret Nuclear Bunker
Doddinghurst
Wyatt's Green
Swallows Cross
Navestock Heath
Navestock Side
Bentley
Crow Green
Coxtie Green
Pilgrims Hatch
Horseman Side
Watton's Green
South Weald Common
Navestock
Stapleford Abbots
Nuper's Hatch
Lambourne End
Chigwell Row
Hainault Forest
Chigwell
Grange Hill
Hainault
Fairlop
Fairlop Waters
Fulwell Cross
Barkingside
Gants Hill
Newbury Park
Seven Kings
Goodmayes
Chadwell Heath
Marks Gate
Little Heath
Havering-atte-Bower
Chase Cross
Collier Row
Rise Park
Noak Hill
Harold Hill
Harold Park
Harold Wood
Gallows Corner
Weald Park
St Vincents Hamlet
Old MacDonald's
South Weald
Brook Street
Shenfield
BRENTWOOD
Shenfield Common
Warley
Thorndon Park
Great Warley
Little Warley
ROMFORD
Ardleigh Green
Emerson Park
Heath Park
Rush Green
Hornchurch
Upminster
Cranham
Tithe Barn Agricultural & Folk Museum
Corbets Tey
Hacton
North Ockendon
South Ockendon
Elm Park
South Hornchurch
Rainham
Rainham Hall (NT)
Wennington
Wennington Marshes
Aveley
Aveley Marshes
Belhus Park
Belhus Woods
Purfleet
West Thurrock
Lakeside Shopping Centre
Chafford Hundred
South Stifford
North Stifford
GRAYS
Dartford Crossing
Dartford Tunnel
Queen Elizabeth II Bridge
West Thurrock Marshes
Dartford Marshes
Crayford Marshes
Slade Green
Barnehurst
Northumberland Heath
North End
Erith
Belvedere
Lessness Heath
West Heath
Abbey Wood
Bostall Woods
East Wickham
Welling
Shooters Hill
Plumstead
North Woolwich
Thamesmead
Crossness Pumping Station
River Thames
Creekmouth
Barking
DAGENHAM
Becontree
Heathway
Castle Green
Mayesbrook Park
Fair Cross
Loxford
ILFORD
Redbridge Museum
Cranbrook
Valentines Park
Eastbury Manor House
Movers Lane
Eastbrookend
Moby Dick
M25
M11
A12
A13
A127
A113
A118
A124
A125
A128
A1306
River Roding
River Ingrebourne
Channel Tunnel Rail Link (opens 2007)
Mar Dyke

HARLINGTON
Sipson
Harmondsworth
Colnbrook
Longford
Heathrow Airport
LONDON HEATHROW
Cranford
HESTON
BRENTFORD
HOUNSLOW
ISLEWORTH
Poyle
Horton
Sunnymeads
Stanwell Moor
Wraysbury
Wraysbury Reservoir
King George VI Reservoir
Staines Reservoirs
STANWELL
West Bedfont
East Bedfont
FELTHAM
Hounslow Heath
TWICKENHAM
Whitton
St Margarets
Ham
STAINES
ASHFORD
Ashford Common
Lower Feltham
HANWORTH
Hanworth Park
TEDDINGTON
EGHAM
Knowle Green
Queen Mary Reservoir
Laleham
Littleton
Charlton
SUNBURY
Sunbury Cross
Hampton
Bushy Park
Hampton Wick
Hampton Court Park
Thorpe
Virginia Water
Shepperton
Shepperton Green
Upper Halliford
Lower Halliford
East Molesey
Thames Ditton
Fieldcommon
WALTON-ON-THAMES
CHERTSEY
Lyne
Addlestonemoor
Woburn Park
WEYBRIDGE
ADDLESTONE
HERSHAM
ESHER
CLAYGATE
Hinchley Wood
Long Ditton
Ottershaw
Row Town
New Haw
St George's Hill
West End Common
Arbrook Common
Woodham
Anningsley Park
Brooklands
Byfleet
West Byfleet
Whiteley Village
Esher Common
Oxshott
Fairmile
Cobham
Malden Rushett
Prince's Coverts
Stoke Wood
Horsell Common
Sheerwater
Pyrford
Wisley
Painshill
Little Heath
Stoke D'Abernon
WOKING
Maybury
Pyrford Green
Wisley Common
Bolder Mere
Telegraph Hill
Cobham Park
Downside
Pachesham Park
Leatherhead Common
Ripley Green
Elm Corner
Bridge End
Martyr's Green
Ripley
Old Woking
Westfield
Ockham Park
Church End
Ockham
Banks Common
Great Bookham Common
Little Bookham Common
LEATHERHEAD
Effingham Common
Fetcham
Cartbridge
Send
Hungry Hill
Little Bookham
Sutton Green
East Horsley
Great Bookham
Fetcham Downs
Givons Grove
River Thames
River Wey
River Mole
River Colne
River Ember
0 1 2 3 miles
0 1 2 3 4 5 km

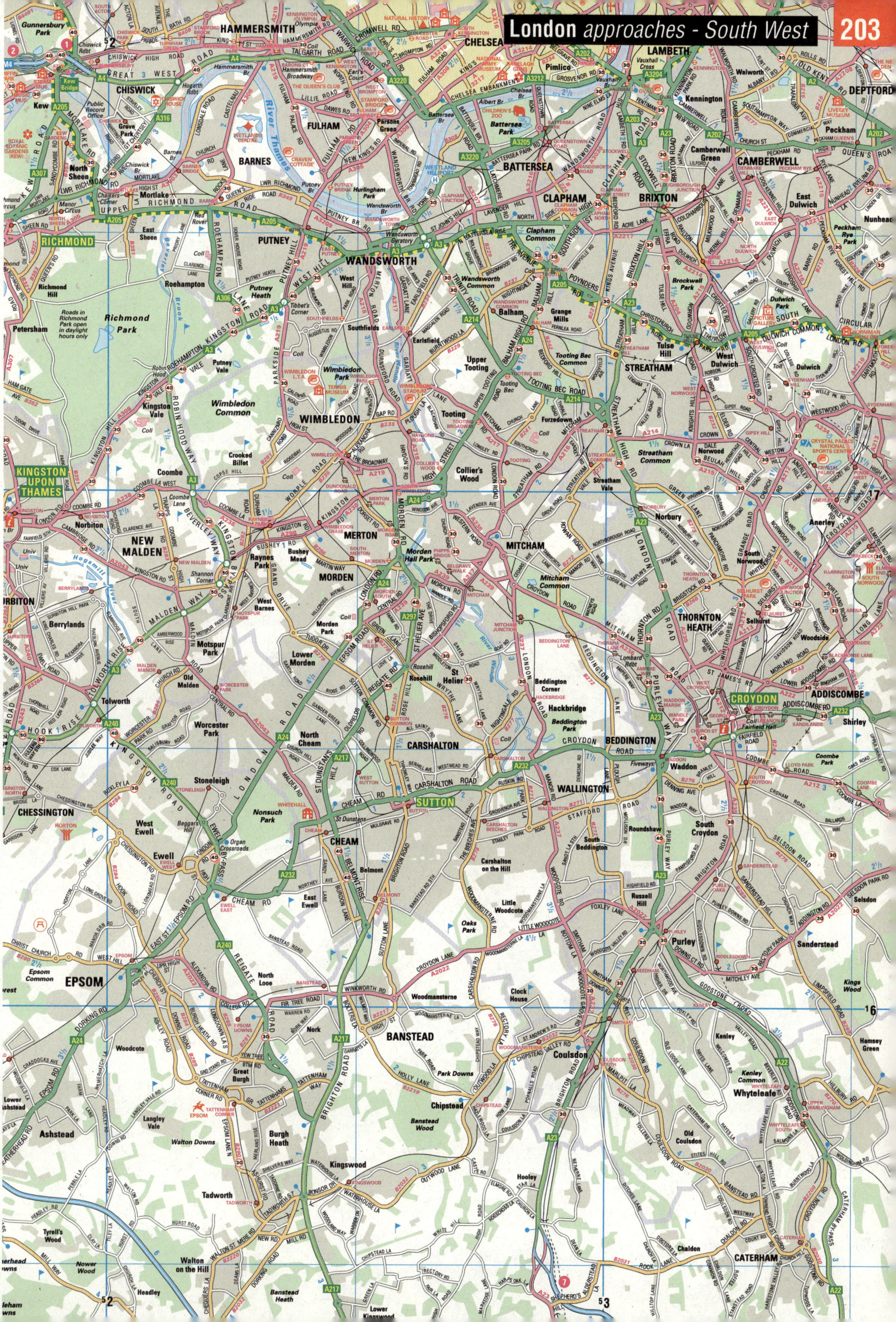
HAMMERSMITH
CHISWICK
Kew
FULHAM
CHELSEA
LAMBETH
Pimlico
Kennington
DEPTFORD
BARNES
BATTERSEA
CLAPHAM
BRIXTON
CAMBERWELL
Peckham
East Dulwich
RICHMOND
PUTNEY
WANDSWORTH
Roehampton
Richmond Park
Balham
Upper Tooting
STREATHAM
Dulwich
WIMBLEDON
Wimbledon Common
Tooting
KINGSTON UPON THAMES
Coombe
Norbiton
NEW MALDEN
MERTON
MORDEN
MITCHAM
Norbury
South Norwood
THORNTON HEATH
Anerley
Tolworth
Berrylands
Motspur Park
Worcester Park
CARSHALTON
BEDDINGTON
CROYDON
ADDISCOMBE
Shirley
WALLINGTON
SUTTON
CHEAM
Stoneleigh
CHESSINGTON
West Ewell
Ewell
EPSOM
Nonsuch Park
Belmont
South Croydon
Purley
Sanderstead
Selsdon
BANSTEAD
Woodmansterne
Coulsdon
Kenley
Whyteleafe
Ashtead
Burgh Heath
Kingswood
Tadworth
Walton on the Hill
Chipstead
CATERHAM
Headley

BARNES
BATTERSEA
CLAPHAM
BRIXTON
CAMBERWELL
Peckham
New Cross
Greenwich Park
BLACKHEATH
LEWISHAM
PUTNEY
WANDSWORTH
Brockley
Nunhead
East Dulwich
Catford
CATFORD
Forest Hill
Dulwich
West Dulwich
Tulse Hill
STREATHAM
Balham
Upper Tooting
Tooting
WIMBLEDON
Wimbledon Common
Streatham Common
PENGE
Beckenham Place Park
BECKENHAM
Norbury
Anerley
Elmers End
MERTON
MITCHAM
Mitcham Common
MORDEN
THORNTON HEATH
Shirley Oaks
West Wickham
CROYDON
ADDISCOMBE
Shirley
Upper Shirley
Addington
BEDDINGTON
Waddon
WALLINGTON
CARSHALTON
SUTTON
CHEAM
South Croydon
Selsdon
New Addington
Purley
Sanderstead
Kenley
Whyteleafe
BANSTEAD
Coulsdon
Chipstead
Warlingham
Woldingham
CATERHAM
Kingswood
Tadworth
Merstham
Walton Heath
Gravelly Hill
Winders Hill
M25

Dartford Crossing
Dartford Tunnel
Queen Elizabeth Bridge
Woolwich Common
East Wickham
Shooters Hill
Welling
Barnehurst
Slade Green
Kidbrooke
Eltham Common
Oxleas Wood
Blackheath Park
Falconwood
Bexleyheath
Crayford
Barnes Cray
Temple Hill
Danson Park
Danson Interchange
THE RED HOUSE
BEXLEY
ELTHAM
Avery Hill
Blackfen
Old Bexley
Black Prince Interchange
HALL PLACE
DARTFORD
Yorkshire Grey
Cliftons Rbdt
ELTHAM PALACE
Coldblow
New Eltham
Mottingham
SIDCUP
Grove Park
Longlands
Maypole
Wilmington
Fleet-Downs
North Cray
Joyden's Wood
Hook Green
Dareth
Lane End
Hawley
Elmstead Wood
Coll Elmstead
Sundridge Park
Chislehurst Common
CHISLEHURST
Frognal Corner
Scadbury Park Nature Reserve
Foots Cray
Critnall's Corner
Ruxley
Upper Ruxley
Hextable
Clement Street
Sutton-at-Hone
South Darenth
BROMLEY
Widmore
Bickley
St Paul's Cray
Hockenden
Swanley Village
Swanley
CHISLEHURST CAVES
Petts Wood
Poverest
St Mary Cray
Farningham Wood
Horton Kirby
JUBILEE
Southborough
Bromley Common
Kevingtown
Farningham
Hayes
Broom Hill
Crockenhill
Horton Wood
ORPINGTON
Crofton
Keston Mark
Goddington
Crown Wood
BIRD OF PREY CENTRE
Eynsford
EYNSFORD CASTLE
Locksbottom
Coney Hall
Keston
The Fantail
LULLINGSTONE ROMAN VILLA
LULLINGSTONE CASTLE
Farnborough
Chelsfield
Beechen Wood
Maplescombe
BRANDS HATCH
Nash
Green Street Green
Maypole
Well Hill
HIGH ELMS
Pratt's Bottom
Timberden Bottom
High Castle Wood
West Kingsdown
Cuckoo Wood
Leaves Green
Downe
Shoreham
Knatts Valley
DOWN HOUSE (CHARLES DARWIN MUSEUM)
Hazelwood
Halstead
Romney Street
BIGGIN HILL AERODROME
Luxted
Magpie Bottom
Woodlands
Newyears Wood
Single Street
Cudham
Knockholt Pound
Twitton
Otford
Berry's Green
Knockholt
Letts Green
Kemsing
Crowdleham
Heaverham
Biggin Hill
Horns Green
Chevening
Dunton Green
South Street
Tatsfield Green
Tatsfield
Longford
Greatness
Seal
Styants Bottom
Chipstead
Riverhead
Wildernesse
Hill Park
Force Green
Seal Chart
Godden Green
Titsey
Sundridge
Brasted
SEVENOAKS
Farley Common
QUEBEC HOUSE (N.T.)
CLACKET LANE SERVICES
Titsey Wood
Westerham
Kippington
KNOLE (N.T.)
Knole Park
Fawke Common
Lower Bitchet
Bitchet Green
SQUERRYES COURT
Brasted Chart
Mill Bank Wood
Limpsfield
Hosey Hill
French Street
Whitley Row
The High Chart
EMMETTS (N.T.)
Geathurst
River Hill
River Darent
M25
M20
M26
A20
A21
A25
A2
1 2 3 miles
1 2 3 4 5 km

Manchester

0 Miles ¼

Milton Keynes

0 Miles ¼

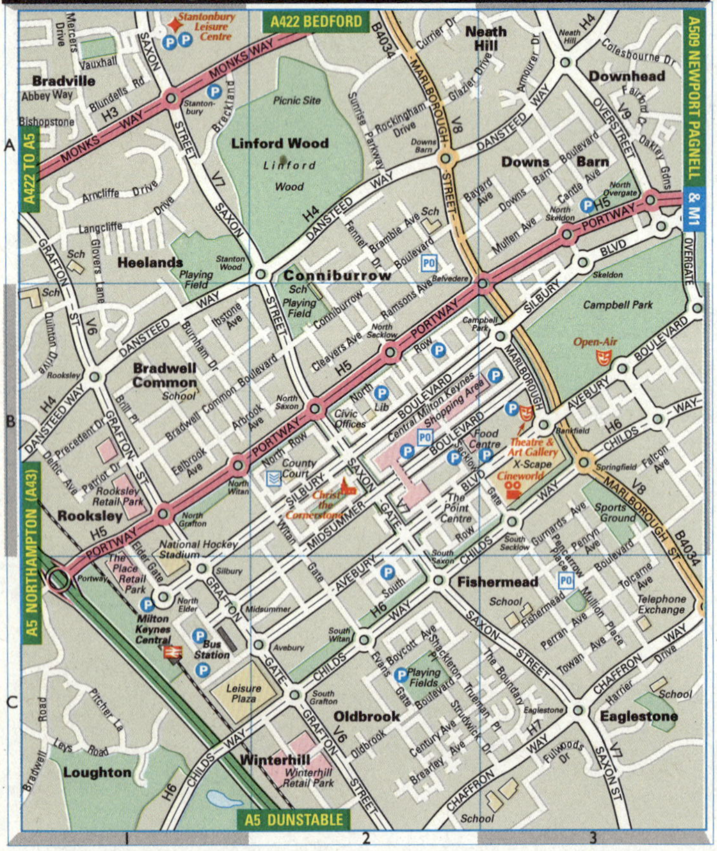

Northampton

0 Miles ¼

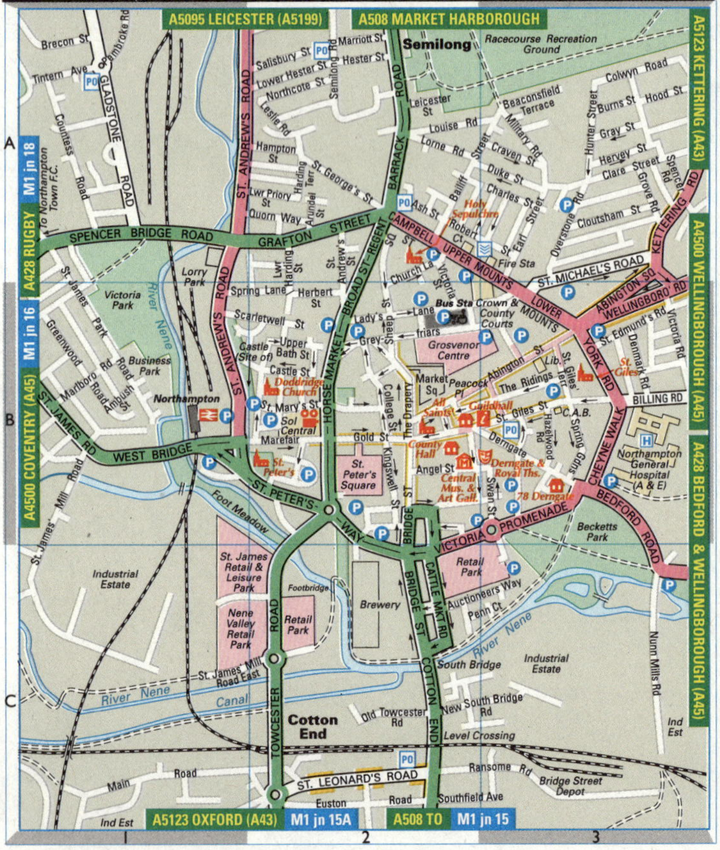

BOLTON
BURY
Redvales
Hollins
Unsworth
WHITEFIELD
Besses o' th' Barn
Simister
RADCLIFFE
LITTLE LEVER
Prestolee
Outwood
Ringley
KEARSLEY
Park Lane
Heaton Park
PRESTWICH
Linnyshaw
WALKDEN
Clifton Green
Newtown
SWINTON
PENDLEBURY
Kersal
Broughton Park
Crumpsall
Higher Blackley
Charlestown
Moston
Harpurhey
MIDDLETON
Langley
Rhodes
Birch
Hollins
Higher Boarshaw
Alkrington Garden Village
Moorclose
ROYTON
Heald Green
CHADDERTON
Busk
OLDHAM
Hollinwood
Lime Side
New Moston
FAILSWORTH
Woodhouses
Newton Heath
Miles Platting
Clayton
Greenside
DROYLSDEN
Openshaw
Gorton
Ardwick
MANCHESTER
SALFORD
Seedley
Little Bolton
Ellesmere Park
Westwood Park
Broadoak Park
Patricroft
ECCLES
Barton upon Irwell
TRAFFORD PARK
Salford Quays
Strangeways
Hulme
Old Trafford
Moss Side
Rusholme
Firswood
Longford Park
Whalley Range
STRETFORD
Davyhulme
URMSTON
Carrington
Ashton upon Mersey
SALE
Brooklands
Woodhouses
Chorlton-cum-Hardy
Barlow Moor
West Didsbury
Withington
Burnage
Levenshulme
REDDISH
North Reddish
South Reddish
Heaton Mersey
Heaton Norris
Dukinfield
Denton
Ryder Brow
Brinnington
STOCKPORT
Woodbank Park
Northern Moor
Broadheath
Timperley
ALTRINCHAM
Bowdon
HALE
Bowgreen
Roundthorn
WYTHENSHAWE
GATLEY
CHEADLE
Newall Green
Woodhouse Park
Well Green
Davenport Green
Halebarns
Heald Green
CHEADLE HULME
Bramhall Park
Ardswood
Gale Green
HAZEL GROVE
Norbury Moor
Kitt's Moss
BRAMHALL
Handforth
Ashley
Rostherne Mere
MANCHESTER AIRPORT
Terminal 2
Terminals 1 & 3
MANCHESTER INTERNATIONAL AIRPORT
River Irwell
River Mersey
Manchester Ship Canal
River Medlock
River Tame
Bridgewater Canal
Heaton Park Resr
Audenshaw Resrs
Gorton Resrs
Elton Resr
0 1 2 3 miles
0 1 2 3 4 5 km

Newcastle upon Tyne

Norwich

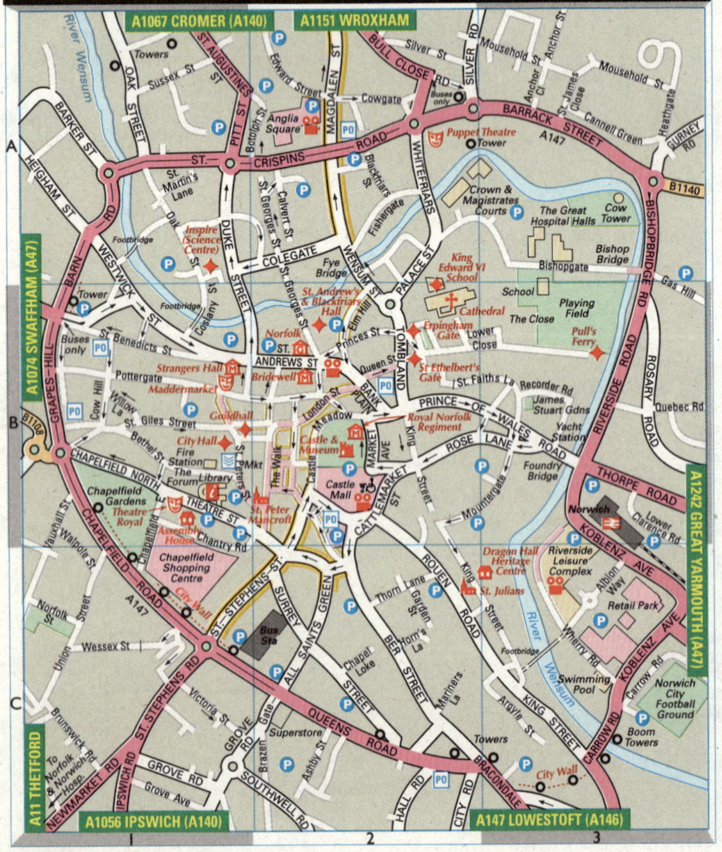

Oxford

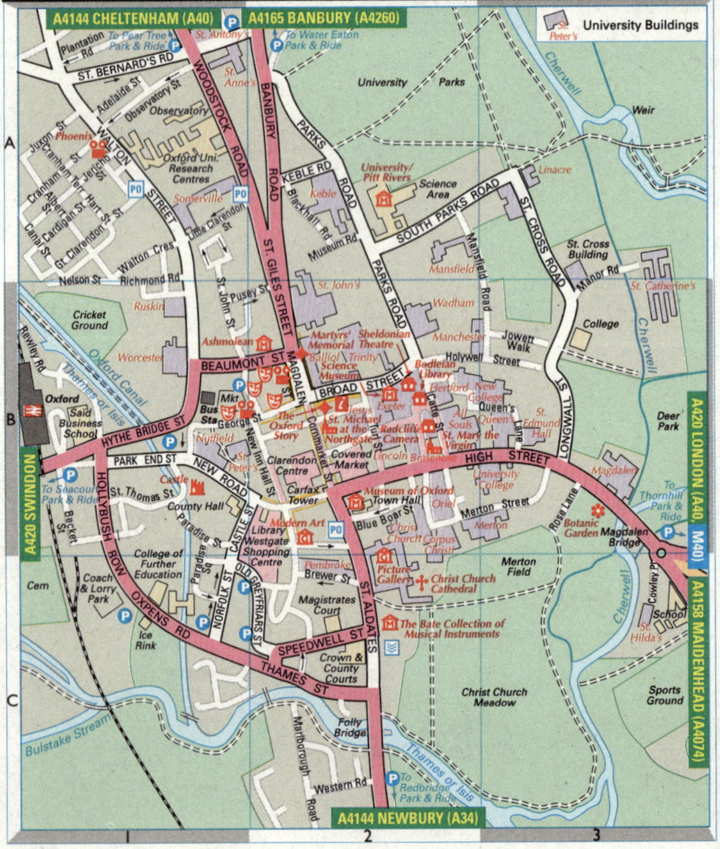

NEWCASTLE UPON TYNE
GATESHEAD
SEATON DELAVAL
Seghill
Dinnington
Brunswick Village
WIDE OPEN
DUDLEY
Prestwick
NEWCASTLE INTERNATIONAL AIRPORT
Hazlerigg
Camperdown
Killingworth
Backworth
Monkseaton
WHITLEY BAY
SHIREMOOR
Woolsington
Gosforth Lake
Gosforth Wood
LONGBENTON
Fawdon
Gosforth
Westerhope
Blakelaw
Jesmond
Heaton
WALLSEND
Willington
North Shields
Fenham
Benwell
Scotswood
Elswick
Byker
Walker
JARROW
HEBBURN
BLAYDON
Dunston
River Tyne
Tyne Tunnel
Bensham
Felling
Hedworth
Wardley
WHICKHAM
Lobley Hill
Sunniside
Wrekenton
Lyndhurst
Chowdene
Springwell
Usworth
WASHINGTON
Downhill
South Hylton
Kibblesworth
BIRTLEY
Biddock
Lampton
Tanfield
URPETH
OUSTON
Fatfield
PENSHAW
Harraton
Pelton
West Pelton
STANLEY
Grange Villa
Shiney Row
New Herrington
Lambton Park
Bournmoor
CHESTER-LE-STREET
Fence Houses
HOUGHTON LE-SPRING
River Wear
0 1 2 3 miles
0 1 2 3 4 5 km

Nottingham road map page 77 • **Plymouth** road map page 6 • **Portsmouth** road map page 15 • **Preston** road map page 86

Nottingham

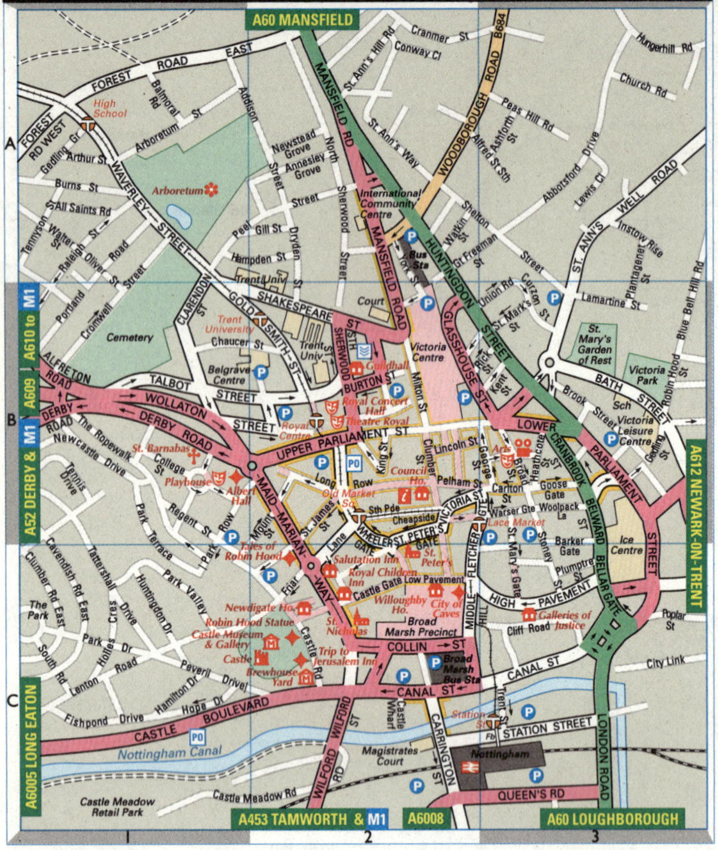

Plymouth

Portsmouth

Preston

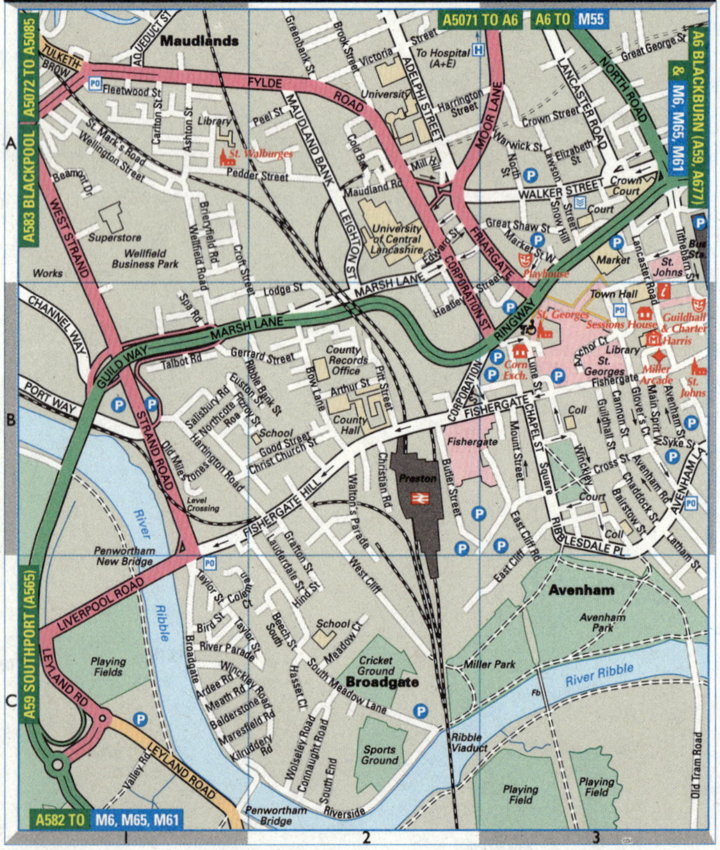

NOTTINGHAM
HUCKNALL
EASTWOOD
KIMBERLEY
BRINSLEY
ARNOLD
CARLTON
CALVERTON
ILKESTON
STAPLEFORD
BEESTON
WEST BRIDGFORD
ATTENBOROUGH
CLIFTON
LONG EATON
BREASTON
TOTON
RUDDINGTON
KEYWORTH
GOTHAM
KEGWORTH
BURTON JOYCE
Bulwell
Basford
Mapperley
Sherwood
Gedling
Netherfield
Colwick
Sneinton
Radford
Wollaton
Bramcote
Chilwell
Trowell
Strelley
Bilborough
Aspley
Cinderhill
Nuthall
Watnall
Awsworth
Cossall
Larklands
Sandiacre
Risley
Sawley
Trentlock
Tollerton
Edwalton
Gamston
Bassingfield
Plumtree
Lambley
Woodborough
Redhill
Bestwood
Papplewick
Lindy
Underwood
Bagthorpe
Moorgreen
Greasley
Giltbrook
Beauvale
Cotmanhay
Holme Pierrepont
NOTTINGHAM AIRPORT
Nottingham University
Meadows
Wilford
Ratcliffe on Soar
Kingston on Soar
Lockington
Bunny
Bradmore
Wysall
Thrumpton
Barton in Fabis
Stanton-by-Dale
Stanton on the Wolds
Normanton-on-the-Wolds
Clipston
Cropwell
Oxton
Thorndale Plantation
0 1 2 3 miles
0 1 2 3 4 5 km

Reading road map page 26 • **Salisbury** road map page 14 • **Sheffield** road map page 88

Reading

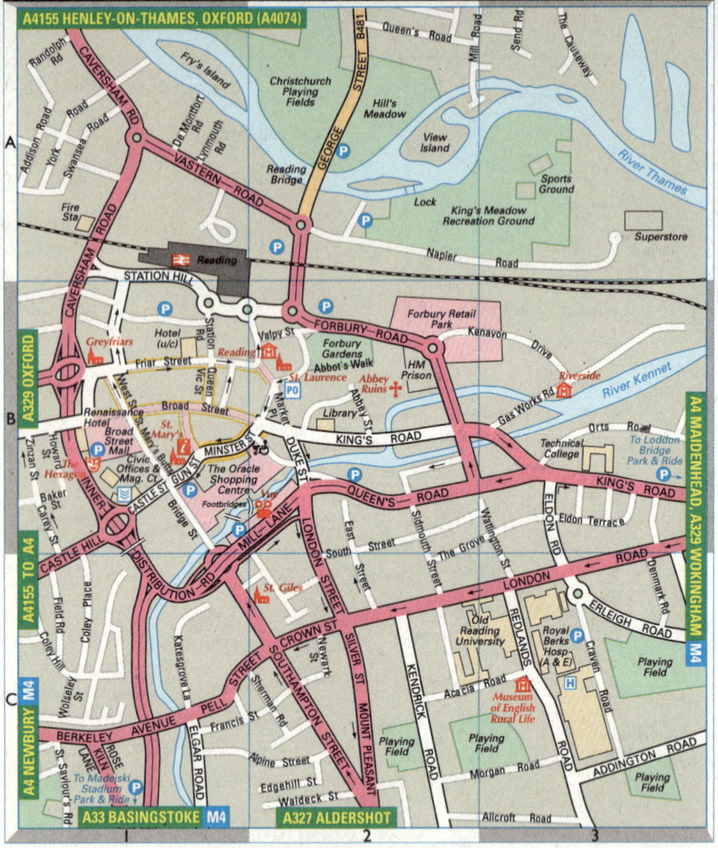

Salisbury

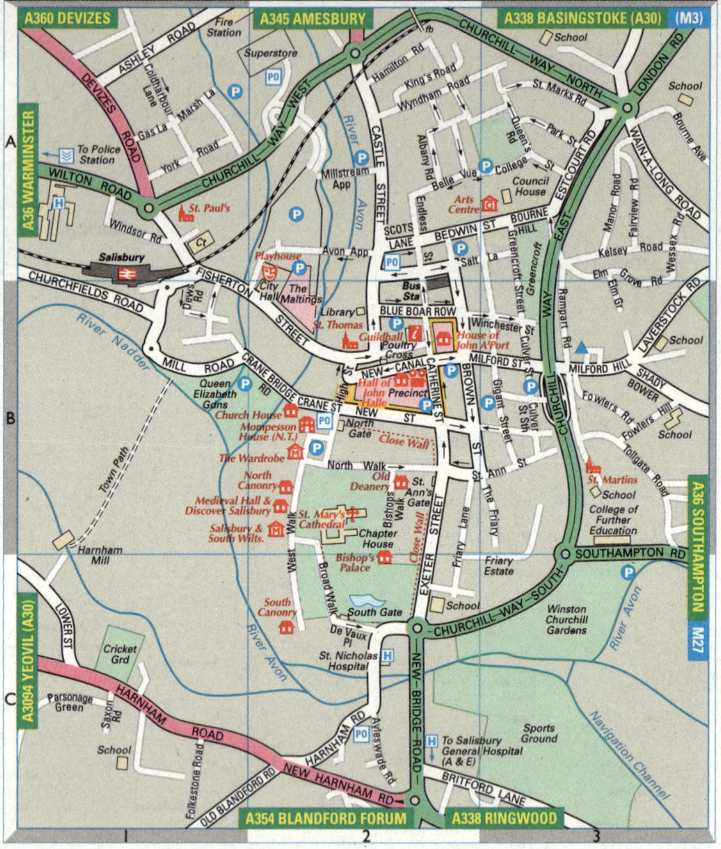

Sheffield

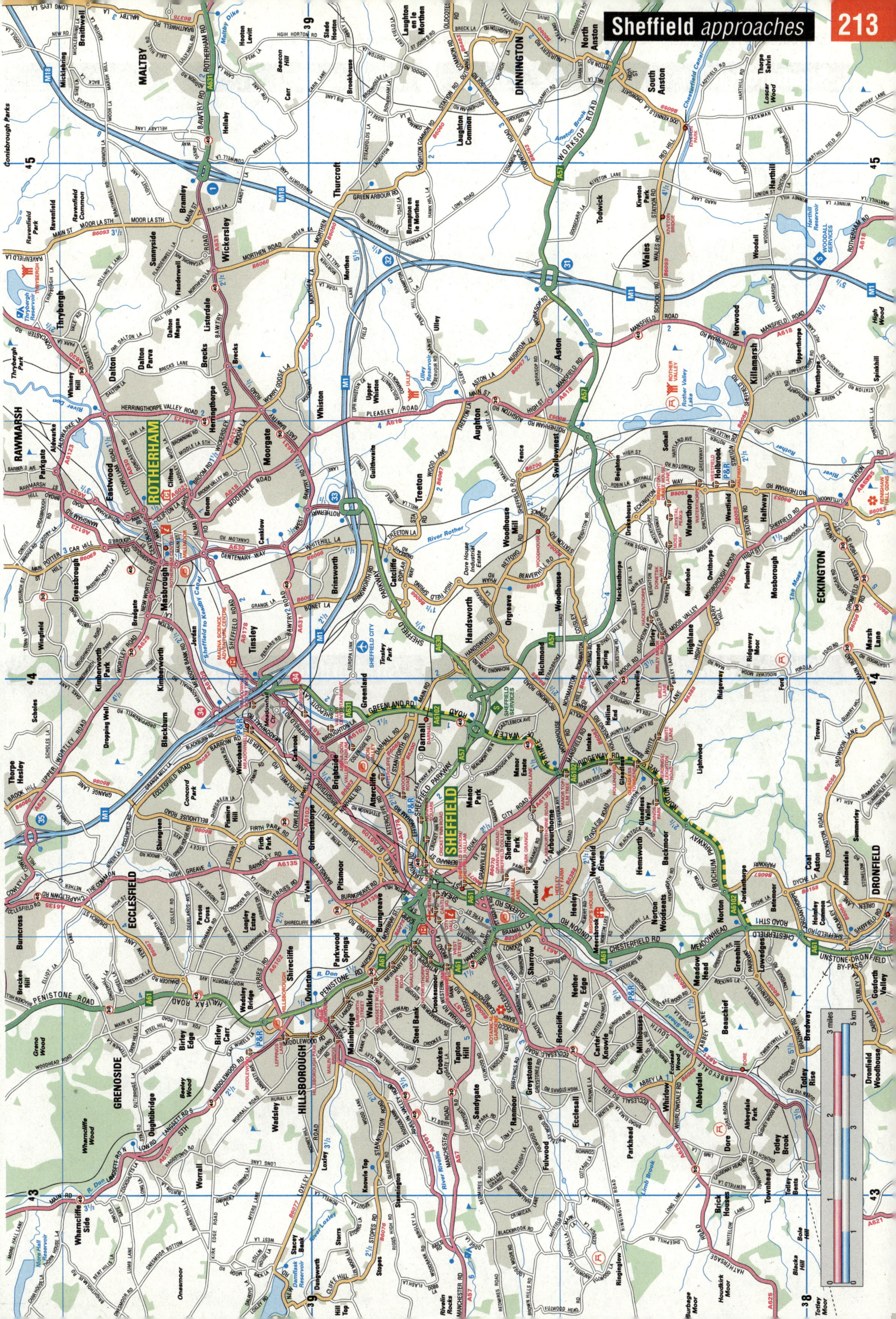
SHEFFIELD
ROTHERHAM
MALTBY
DINNINGTON
RAWMARSH
ECCLESFIELD
HILLSBOROUGH
GRENOSIDE
ECKINGTON
DRONFIELD
North Anston
South Anston
Thurcroft
Wickersley
Bramley
Whiston
Aughton
Swallownest
Woodhouse
Handsworth
Darnall
Attercliffe
Brinsworth
Catcliffe
Tinsley
Kimberworth
Masbrough
Greasbrough
Thrybergh
Dalton
Sunnyside
Killamarsh
Norwood
Kiveton Park
Wales
Todwick
Harthill
Aston
Ulley
Treeton
Orgreave
Mosborough
Halfway
Westfield
Waterthorpe
Beighton
Hackenthorpe
Frecheville
Intake
Gleadless
Norton
Heeley
Sharrow
Walkley
Crookes
Broomhill
Ecclesall
Millhouses
Beauchief
Abbeydale
Dore
Totley
Fulwood
Ranmoor
Sandygate
Stannington
Loxley
Wadsley
Worrall
Oughtibridge
Wharncliffe Side
Chapeltown
Burncross
Parson Cross
Shiregreen
Firth Park
Pitsmoor
Burngreave
Owlerton
Wincobank
Blackburn
Meadowhall
Coal Aston
Holmesfield
Gosforth Valley
Dronfield Woodhouse
M1
M18
A57
A61
A631
A630
A618
River Don
River Rother
Rother Valley Lake
Ulley Reservoir
Chesterfield Canal
Sheffield & Tinsley Canal
3 miles
5 km

Scarborough

0 Miles ¼

Southampton

0 Miles ¼

Stoke-on-Trent (Hanley)

0 Miles ¼

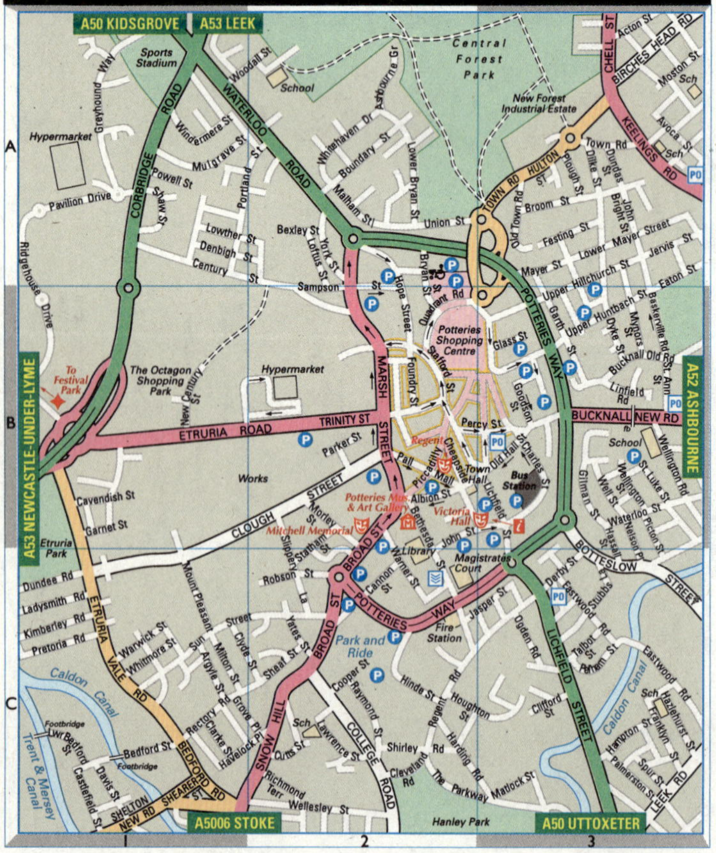

Stratford-upon-Avon

0 Miles ¼

Sunderland

0 Miles ¼

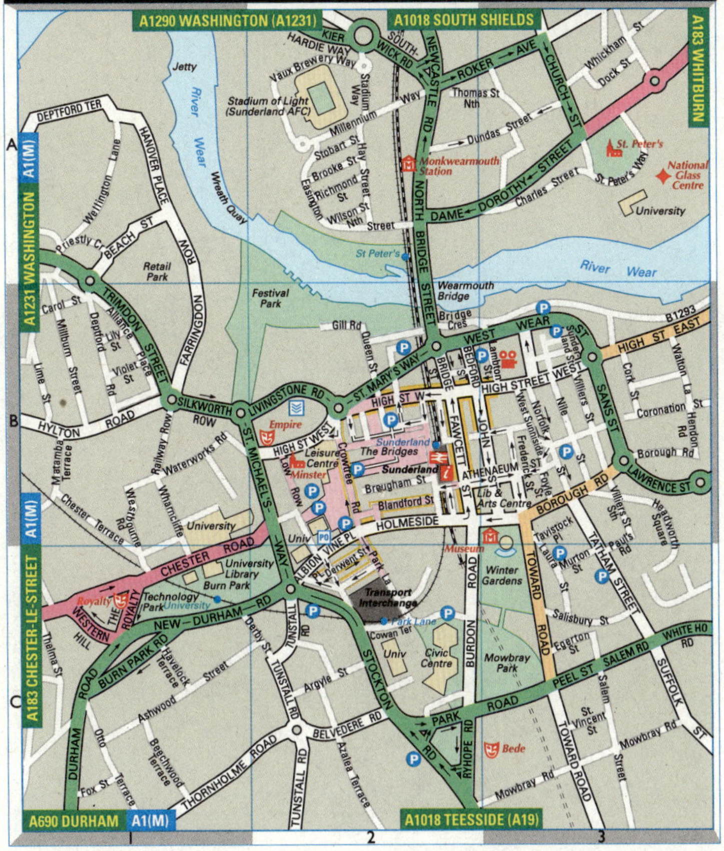

Swansea / Abertawe

0 Miles ¼

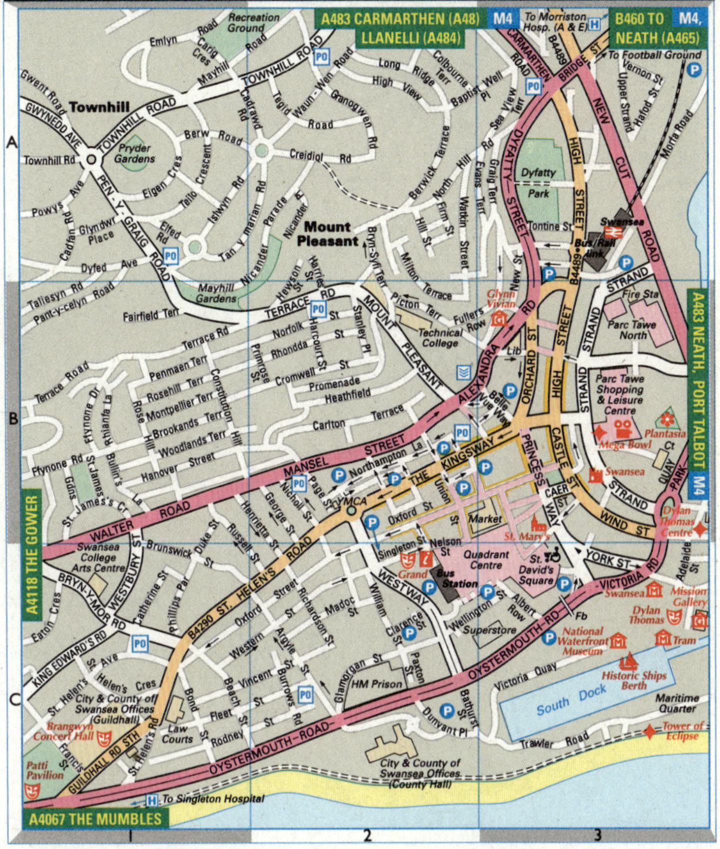

Telford

0 Miles ¼

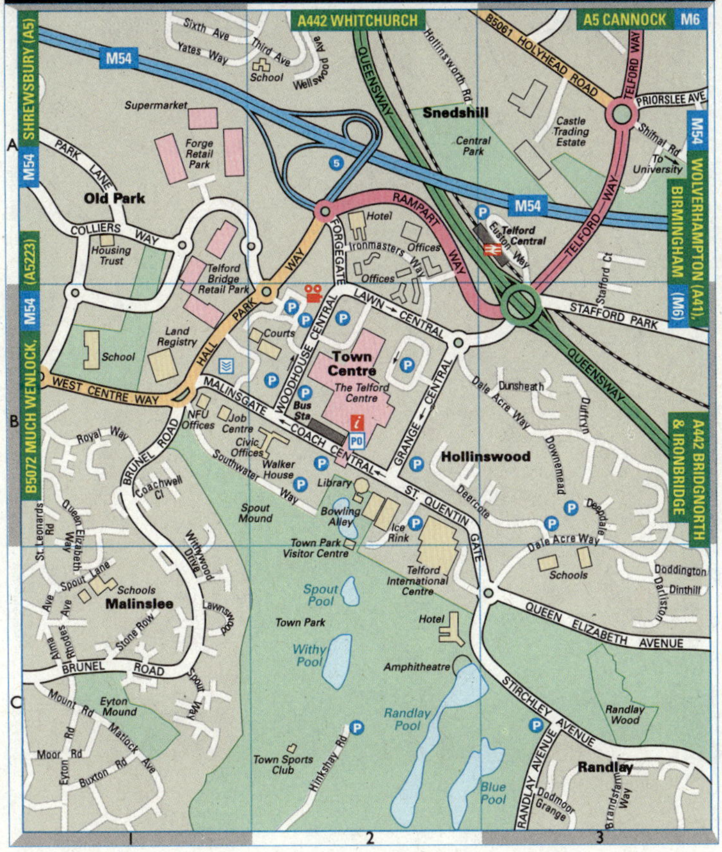

Torquay

0 Miles ¼

Winchester road map page 15 • **Windsor** road map page 27 • **Worcester** road map page 50 • **York** road map page 95

Winchester

0 Miles ¼

Windsor

0 Miles ¼

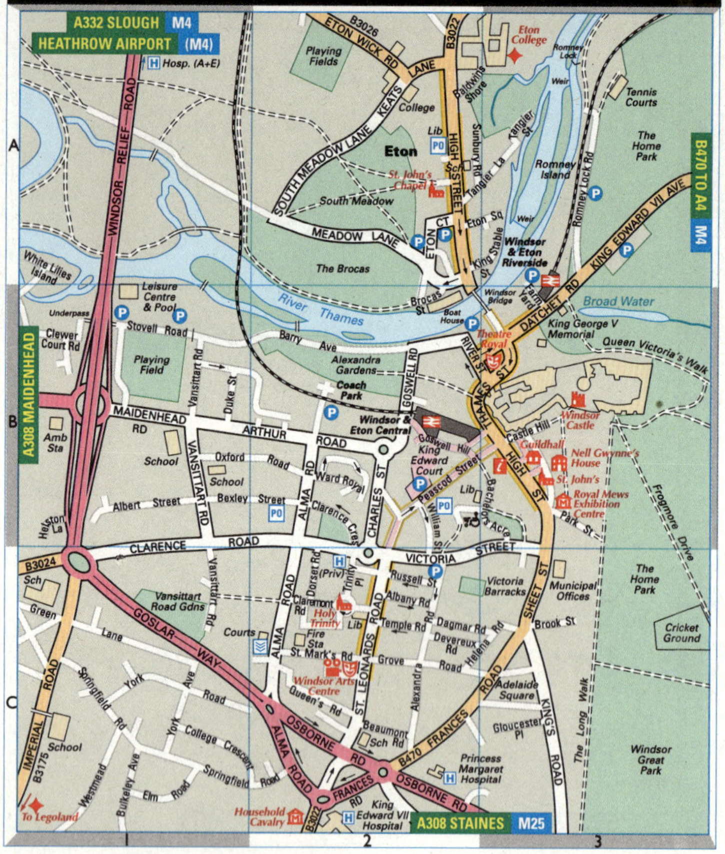

Worcester

0 Miles ¼

York

0 Miles ¼

M25 and routes into London

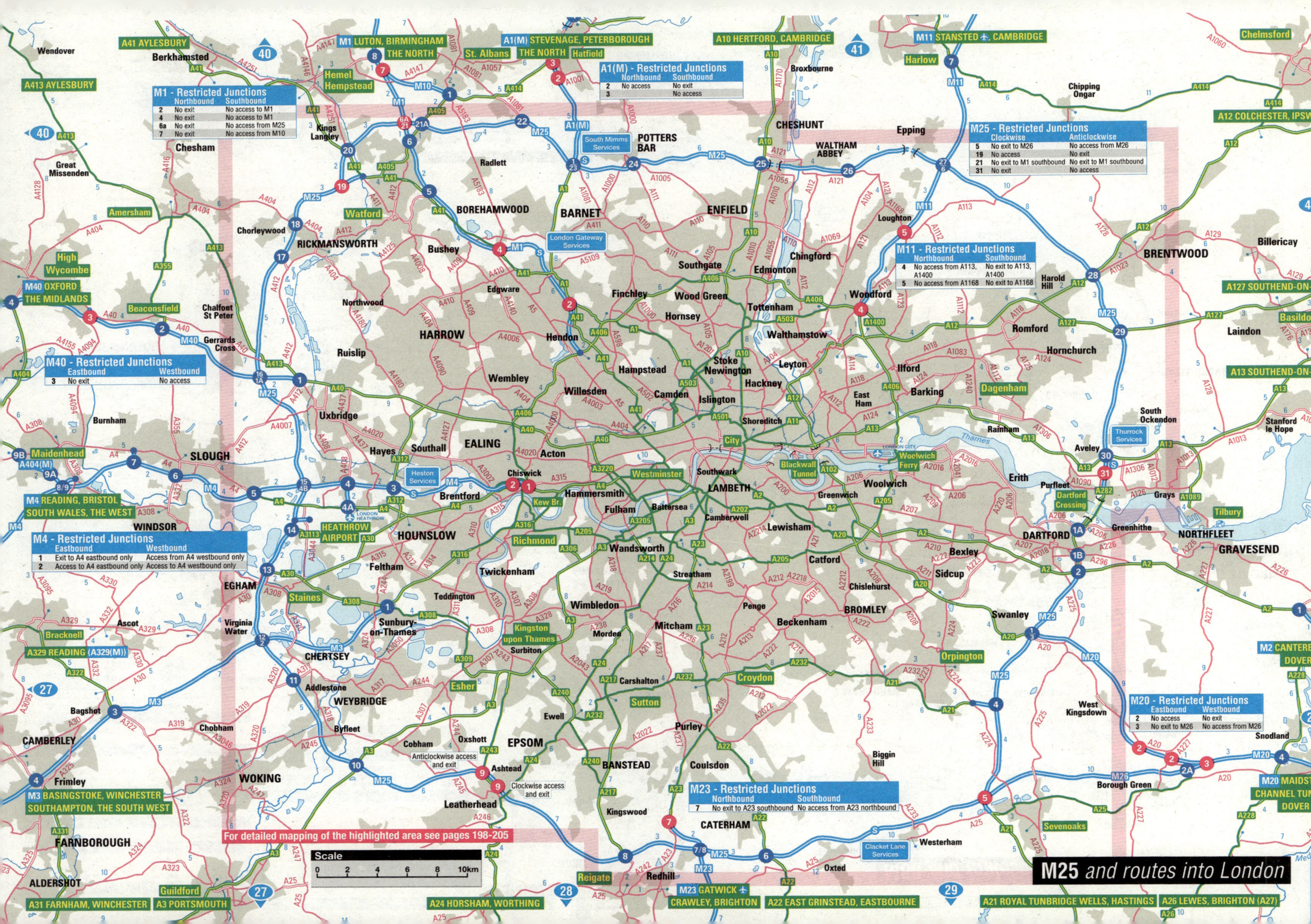

M60 and routes into Manchester and Liverpool

Restricted Junctions

M6	Northbound	Southbound
20	No exit to M56 eastbound	No access from M56 westbound
24	No exit	No access
25	No access from A49	No exit

M53	Northbound	Southbound
11	No exit to M56 westbound	No exit to M56 westbound

M56	Eastbound	Westbound
2	No exit	No access
3	No access	No exit
4	No exit	No access
7		No access
8	No exit or access	No exit
9	No access from M6 northbound	No access to M6 southbound
15	No exit to M53	No access from M53 northbound

M57	Northbound	Southbound
3	No exit	No access
5	No exit	No access

M58	Eastbound	Westbound
1	No exit	No access

M60	Clockwise	Anticlockwise
2	No exit	No access
3	No exit to A34 northbound	No exit to A34 northbound
4	No access to M56	No exit to M56
5	No exit to A5103 southbound	No exit to A5103 northbound
14	No exit to A580	No access from A580
16	No exit	No access
20	No access	No exit
22		No access
25	No access	
26		No exit or access
27	No exit	No access

M61	Northbound	Southbound
2	No access from A580 eastbound	No exit to A580 westbound
3	No access from A580 eastbound No access from A666 southbound	No exit to A580 westbound

M66	Northbound	Southbound
1	No access	No exit

M67	Eastbound	Westbound
1a	No access	No exit
2	No exit	No access

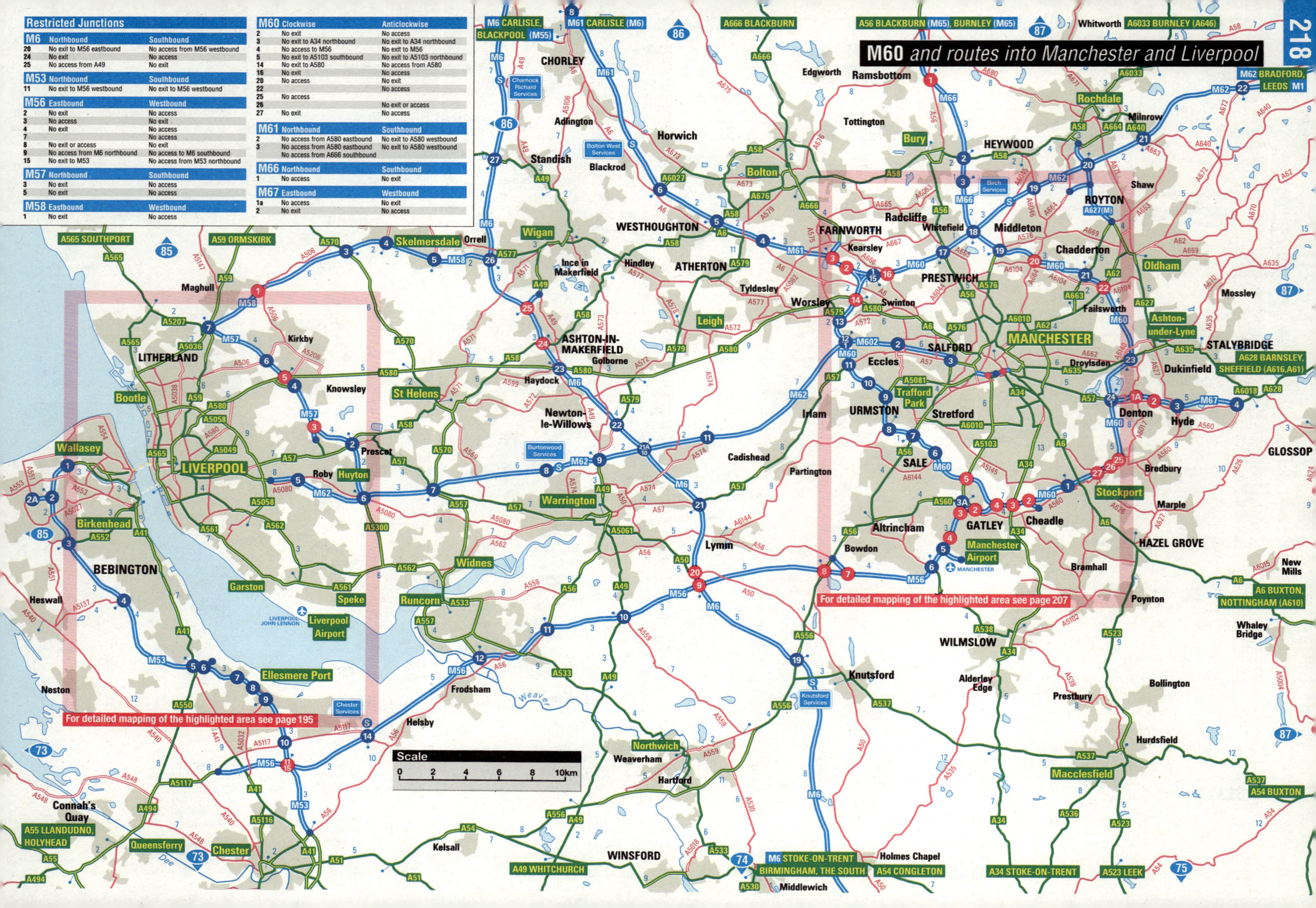

Heathrow Airport (London)

0 Miles ¼

Gatwick Airport (London)

0 Miles ¼

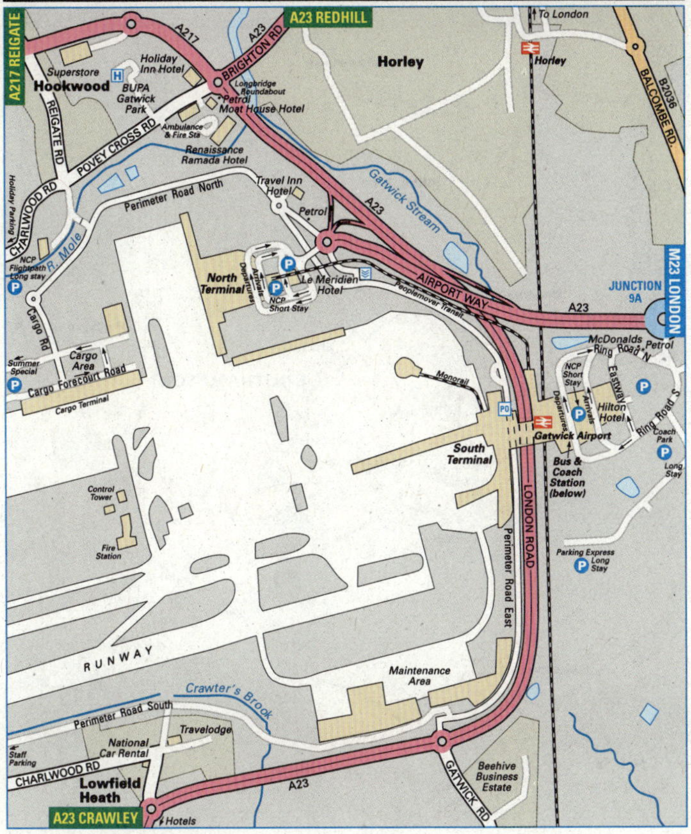

Manchester Airport

0 Miles ¼

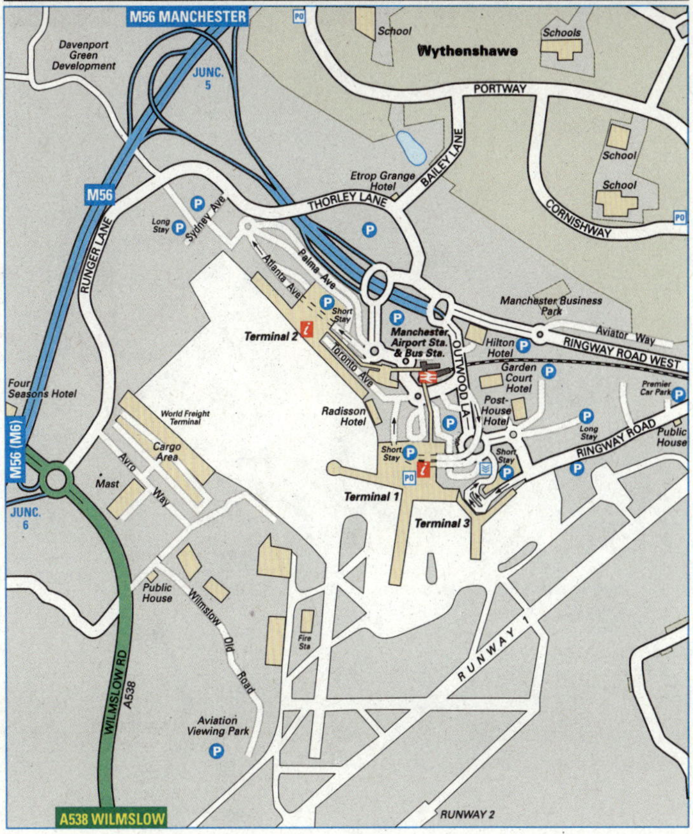

Dover road map page 31 • **Felixstowe** road map page 57 • **Portsmouth** road map page 15 • **Southampton** road map page 14

Port of Dover

0 Miles ¼

Port of Felixstowe

0 Miles ¼

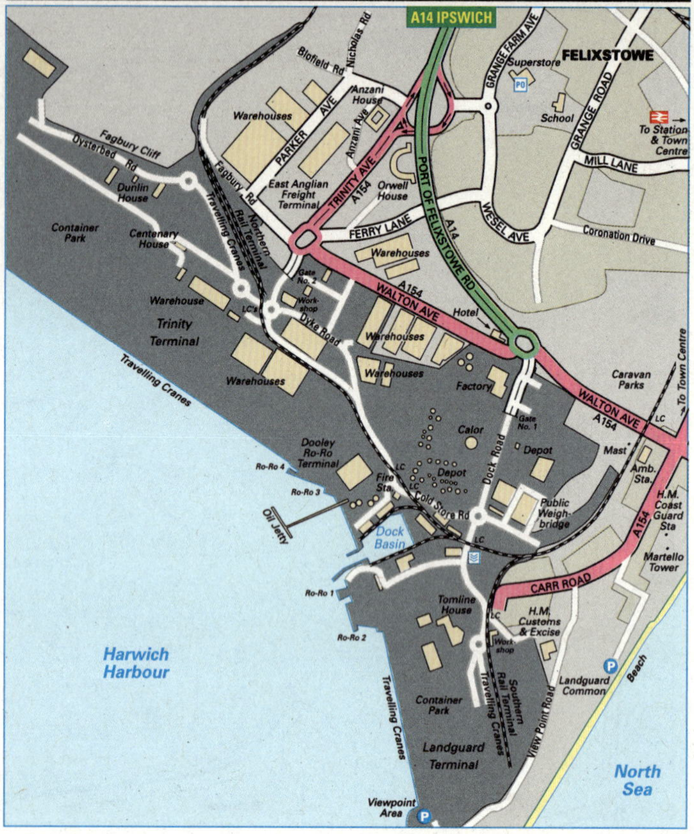

Portsmouth-Continental Ferry Port

0 Miles ¼

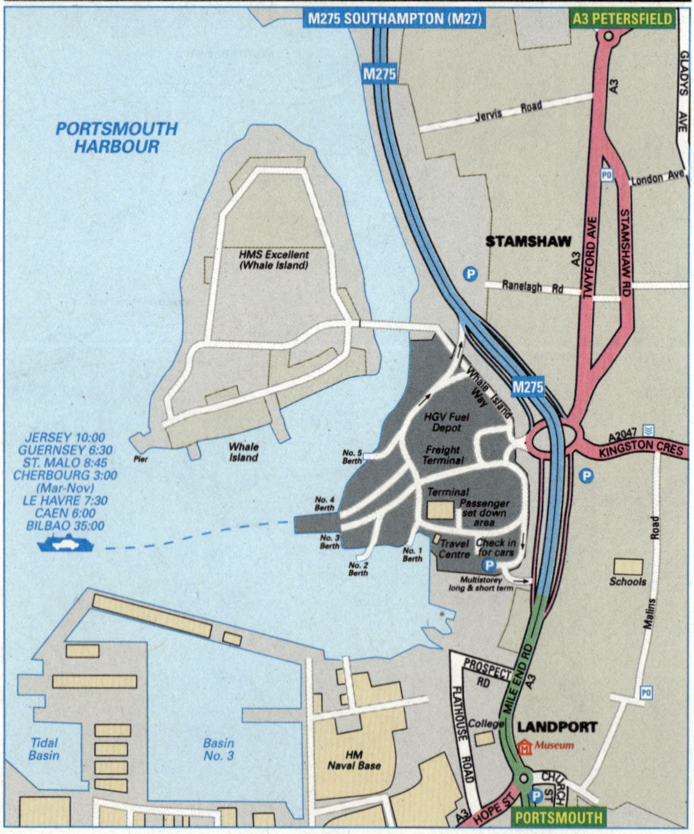

Port of Southampton

0 Miles 1

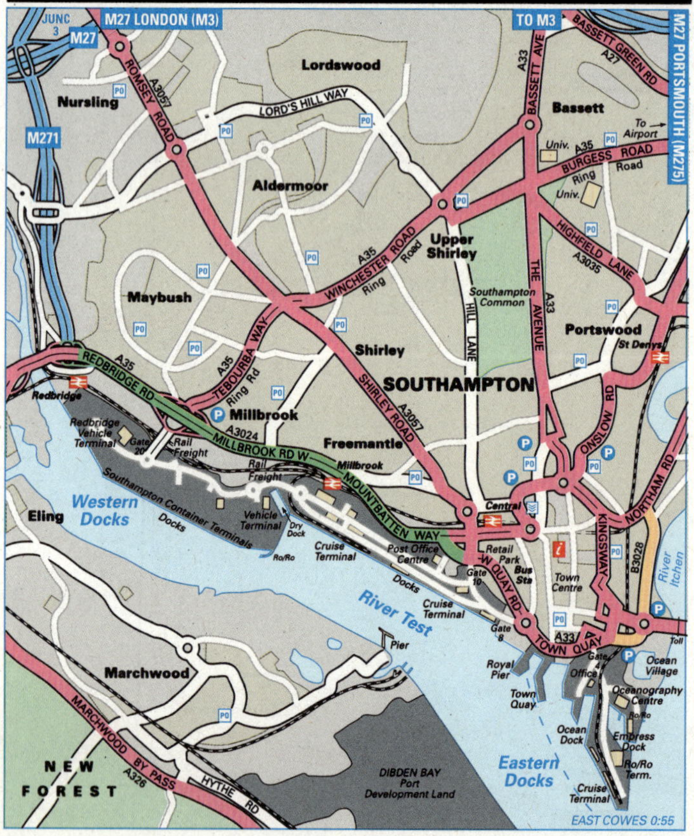

Boulogne

0 Miles ¼

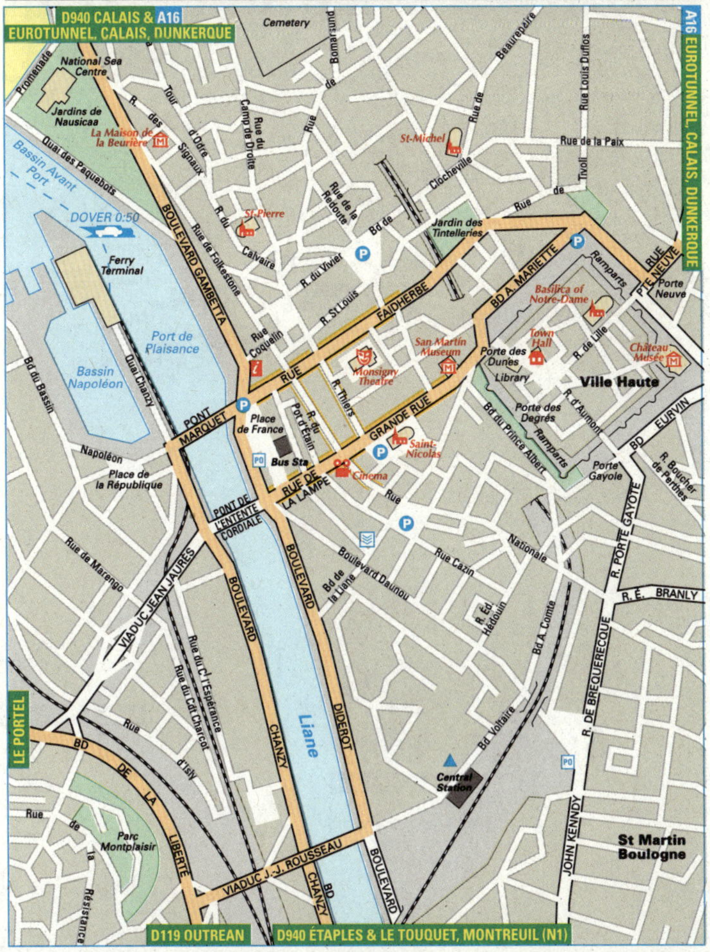

Calais

0 Miles ¼

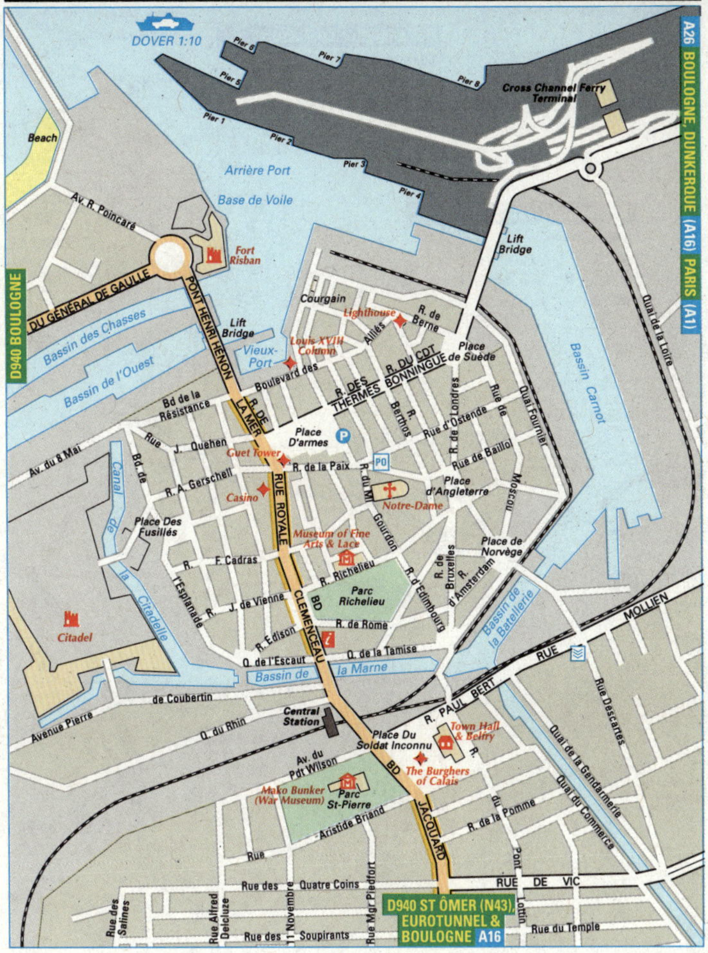

Boulogne and Calais *approaches*

Motorway full / restricted junction
Toll motorway
Principal trunk road single / dual carriageway
Other main road single / dual carriageway
Other important road
Other Road, scenic route
E25 European road number
A49 135 Motorway number, national road number
0 5 10 15 20 25 30miles
0 10 20 30 40km
Poole – St Malo via Guernsey and Jersey
Condor 5hrs:25mins May–Sept
Guernsey 2:30
Jersey 3:45 (Apr-Oct)
Bilbao 35:00
Poole – Cherbourg
Brittany Ferries
4hrs:15mins all year
5hrs:45mins all year
2hrs:15mins May–Sept
Guernsey 6:30
Jersey 10:00
Portsmouth – Cherbourg
Brittany Ferries
3hrs:00mins Mar-Nov
Condor
5hrs:30mins July-Sept (Sundays only)
Rosslare 17:30 (Mar-Dec)
Newhaven – Le Havre
LD Lines
5hrs May-Sept
Newhaven – Dieppe
Transmanche Ferries
4hrs all year
Portsmouth – Le Havre
LD Lines
5hrs:30mins all year
7hrs:30mins all year
Portsmouth – Caen
Brittany Ferries
6hrs:00mins all year
7hrs:00mins all year
3hrs:45mins Mar-Nov (Friday-Sunday)
Portsmouth – St Malo
Brittany Ferries
8hrs:45mins all year
10hrs:30mins all year
ENGLISH CHANNEL
Baie de la Seine
Côte de Nacre
Côte Fleurie
Baie du Mont-St. Michel
50°
49°
Portsmouth
Southampton
Bournemouth
Poole
Weymouth
Brighton
Newhaven
Eastbourne
Chichester
Worthing
Isle of Wight
Newport
Cherbourg
Le Havre
Caen
Bayeux
St. Lô
Fécamp
Honfleur
Lisieux
Alderney
Jersey
St. Helier
Guernsey
Granville
Avranches
St. Malo
Dinard
Vire
Flers
Argentan
Coutances

Brittany Ferries
www.brittany-ferries.com
08703 665 333

Condor Ferries
www.condorferries.co.uk
0870 243 5140

LD Lines
www.ldlines.com
0870 428 4335

Norfolk Line
www.norfolkline.com
0870 870 1020

P&O Ferries
www.poferries.com
08705 980 333

SeaFrance
www.seafrance.com
0870 443 1653

Speedferries
www.speedferries.com
0870 220 0570

Transeuropa Ferries
www.transeuropaferries.com
01843 595 522

Transmanche Ferries
www.transmancheferries.com
0800 917 1201

Index to road maps of Britain

How to use the index

Example

Trudoxhill Som **24** E2

- grid square
- page number
- county or unitary authority

Places of special interest are highlighted in magenta

Abbreviations used in the index

Aberdeen	Aberdeen City
Aberds	Aberdeenshire
Ald	Alderney
Anglesey	Isle of Anglesey
Angus	Angus
Argyll	Argyll and Bute
Bath	Bath and North East Somerset
Beds	Bedfordshire
Bl Gwent	Blaenau Gwent
Blkburn	Blackburn with Darwen
Blkpool	Blackpool
Bmouth	Bournemouth
Borders	Scottish Borders
Brack	Bracknell
Bridgend	Bridgend
Brighton	City of Brighton and Hove
Bristol	City and County of Bristol
Bucks	Buckinghamshire
Caerph	Caerphilly
Cambs	Cambridgeshire
Cardiff	Cardiff
Carms	Carmarthenshire
Ceredig	Ceredigion
Ches	Cheshire
Clack	Clackmannanshire
Conwy	Conwy
Corn	Cornwall
Cumb	Cumbria
Darl	Darlington
Denb	Denbighshire
Derby	City of Derby
Derbys	Derbyshire
Devon	Devon
Dorset	Dorset
Dumfries	Dumfries and Galloway
Dundee	Dundee City
Durham	Durham
E Ayrs	East Ayrshire
E Dunb	East Dunbartonshire
E Loth	East Lothian
E Renf	East Renfrewshire
E Sus	East Sussex
E Yorks	East Riding of Yorkshire
Edin	City of Edinburgh
Essex	Essex
Falk	Falkirk
Fife	Fife
Flint	Flintshire
Glasgow	City of Glasgow
Glos	Gloucesterhire
Gtr Man	Greater Manchester
Guern	Guernsey
Gwyn	Gwynedd
Halton	Halton
Hants	Hampshire
Hereford	Herefordshire
Herts	Hertfordshire
Highld	Highland
Hrtlpl	Hartlepool
Hull	Hull
I o M	Isle of Man
I o W	Isle of Wight
Invclyd	Inverclyde
Jersey	Jersey
Kent	Kent
Lancs	Lancashire
Leicester	City of Leicester
Leics	Leicestershire
Lincs	Lincolnshire
London	Greater London
Luton	Luton
M Keynes	Milton Keynes
M Tydf	Merthyr Tydfil
M'bro	Middlesbrough
Medway	Medway
Mers	Merseyside
Midloth	Midlothian
Mon	Monmouthshire
Moray	Moray
N Ayrs	North Ayrshire
N Lincs	North Lincolnshire
N Lnrk	North Lanarkshire
N Som	North Somerset
N Yorks	North Yorkshire
NE Lincs	North East Lincolnshire
Neath	Neath Port Talbot
Newport	City and County of Newport
Norf	Norfolk
Northants	Northamptonshire
Northumb	Northumberland
Nottingham	City of Nottingham
Notts	Nottinghamshire
Orkney	Orkney
Oxon	Oxfordshire
P'boro	Peterborough
Pembs	Pembrokeshire
Perth	Perth and Kinross
Plym	Plymouth
Poole	Poole
Powys	Powys
Ptsmth	Portsmouth
Reading	Reading
Redcar	Redcar and Cleveland
Renfs	Renfrewshire
Rhondda	Rhondda Cynon Taff
Rutland	Rutland
S Ayrs	South Ayrshire
S Glos	South Gloucestershire
S Lnrk	South Lanarkshire
S Yorks	South Yorkshire
Scilly	Scilly
Shetland	Shetland
Shrops	Shropshire
Slough	Slough
Som	Somerset
Soton	Southampton
Staffs	Staffordshire
Sthend	Southend-on-Sea
Stirl	Stirling
Stockton	Stockton-on-Tees
Stoke	Stoke-on-Trent
Suff	Suffolk
Sur	Surrey
Swansea	Swansea
Swindon	Swindon
T & W	Tyne and Wear
Telford	Telford and Wrekin
Thurrock	Thurrock
Torbay	Torbay
Torf	Torfaen
V Glam	The Vale of Glamorgan
W Berks	West Berkshire
W Dunb	West Dunbartonshire
W Isles	Western Isles
W Loth	West Lothian
W Mid	West Midlands
W Sus	West Sussex
W Yorks	West Yorkshire
Warks	Warwickshire
Warr	Warrington
Wilts	Wiltshire
Windsor	Windsor and Maidenhead
Wokingham	Wokingham
Worcs	Worcestershire
Wrex	Wrexham
York	City of York

A

Ab Kettleby Leics **64** B4
Ab Lench Worcs **50** D5
Abbas Combe Som **12** B5
Abberley Worcs **50** C2
Abberton Essex **43** C6
Abberton Worcs **50** D4
Abberwick Northumb **117** C7
Abbess Roding Essex **42** C1
Abbey Devon **11** C6
Abbey-cwm-hir Powys **48** B2
Abbey Dore Hereford **49** F5
Abbey Field Essex **43** B5
Abbey Hulton Stoke **75** E6
Abbey St Bathans Borders **124** C3
Abbey Town Cumb **107** D8
Abbey Village Lancs **86** B4
Abbey Wood London **29** B5
Abbeydale S Yorks **88** F4
Abbeystead Lancs **93** D5
Abbots Bickington Devon **9** C5
Abbots Bromley Staffs **62** B4
Abbots Langley Herts **40** D3
Abbots Leigh N Som **23** B7
Abbots Morton Worcs **50** D5
Abbots Ripton Cambs **54** B3
Abbots Salford Warks **51** D5
Abbotsbury Dorset **12** F3
Abbotsbury Sub Tropical Gardens Dorset **12** F3
Abbotsford House Borders **123** F8
Abbotsham Devon **9** B6
Abbotskerswell Devon **7** C6
Abbotsley Cambs **54** D3
Abbotswood Hants **14** B4
Abbotts Ann Hants **25** E8
Abcott Shrops **49** B5
Abdon Shrops **61** F5
Aber Ceredig **46** E3
Aber-Arad Carms **46** F2
Aber-banc Ceredig **46** E2
Aber Cowarch Gwyn **59** C5
Aber-Giâr Carms **46** E4
Aber-gwynfi Neath **34** E2
Aber-Hirnant Gwyn **72** F3
Aber-nant Rhondda **34** D4
Aber-Rhiwlech Gwyn **59** B6
Aber-Village Powys **35** B5
Aberaeron Ceredig **46** C3
Aberaman Rhondda **34** D4
Aberangell Gwyn **58** C5
Aberarder Highld **147** F7
Aberarder House Highld **148** B2
Aberarder Lodge Highld **147** F8
Aberargie Perth **134** C3
Aberarth Ceredig **46** C3
Aberavon Neath **33** E8
Aberbeeg Bl Gwent **35** D6
Abercanaid M Tydf **34** D4
Abercarn Caerph **35** E6
Abercastle Pembs **44** B3
Abercegir Powys **58** D5
Aberchirder Aberds **160** C3
Aberconwy House, Conwy Conwy **83** D7
Abercraf Powys **34** C2
Abercrombie Fife **135** D7
Abercych Pembs **45** E4
Abercynafon Powys **34** C4
Abercynon Rhondda **34** E4
Aberdalgie Perth **134** B2
Aberdâr = Aberdare Rhondda **34** D3
Aberdare = Aberdâr Rhondda **34** D3
Aberdaron Gwyn **70** E2
Aberdaugleddau = Milford Haven Pembs **44** E4
Aberdeen Aberdeen **151** D8
Aberdeen Airport Aberdeen **151** C7
Aberdesach Gwyn **82** F4
Aberdour Fife **134** F3
Aberdovey Gwyn **58** E3
Aberdulais Neath **34** D1
Aberedw Powys **48** E2
Abereiddy Pembs **44** B2
Abererch Gwyn **70** D4
Aberfan M Tydf **34** D4
Aberfeldy Perth **141** E5
Aberffraw Anglesey **82** E3
Aberffrwd Ceredig **47** B5
Aberford W Yorks **95** F7
Aberfoyle Stirl **132** D4
Abergavenny = Y Fenni Mon **35** C6
Abergele Conwy **72** B3
Abergorlech Carms **46** F4
Abergwaun = Fishguard Pembs **44** B4
Abergwesyn Powys **47** D7
Abergwili Carms **33** B5
Abergwynant Gwyn **58** C3
Abergwyngregyn Gwyn **83** D6
Abergynolwyn Gwyn **58** D3
Aberhonddu = Brecon Powys **34** B4
Aberhosan Powys **58** E5
Aberkenfig Bridgend **34** F2
Aberlady E Loth **135** F6
Aberlemno Angus **143** D5
Aberllefenni Gwyn **58** D4
Abermagwr Ceredig **47** B5
Abermaw = Barmouth Gwyn **58** C3
Abermeurig Ceredig **46** D4
Abermule Powys **59** E8
Abernaint Powys **59** B8
Abernant Carms **32** B4
Abernethy Perth **134** C3
Abernyte Perth **142** F2
Aberpennar = Mountain Ash Rhondda **34** E4
Aberporth Ceredig **45** D4
Abersoch Gwyn **70** E4
Abersychan Torf **35** D6
Abertawe = Swansea Swansea **33** E7
Aberteifi = Cardigan Ceredig **45** E3
Aberthin V Glam **22** B2
Abertillery = Abertyleri Bl Gwent **35** D6
Abertridwr Caerph **35** F5
Abertridwr Powys **59** C7
Abertyleri = Abertillery Bl Gwent **35** D6
Abertysswg Caerph **35** D5
Aberuthven Perth **133** C8
Aberyscir Powys **34** B3
Aberystwyth Ceredig **58** F2
Abhainn Suidhe W Isles **173** H3
Abingdon Oxon **38** E4
Abinger Common Sur **28** E2
Abinger Hammer Sur **27** E8
Abington S Lnrk **114** B2
Abington Pigotts Cambs **54** E4
Ablington Glos **37** D8
Ablington Wilts **25** E6
Abney Derbys **75** B8
Aboyne Aberds **150** E4
Abram Gtr Man **86** D4
Abriachan Highld **157** F6
Abridge Essex **41** E7
Abronhill N Lnrk **121** B7
Abson S Glos **24** B2
Abthorpe Northants **52** E4
Abune-the-Hill Orkney **176** D1
Aby Lincs **79** B7
Acaster Malbis York **95** E8
Acaster Selby N Yorks **95** E8
Accrington Lancs **87** B5
Acha Argyll **136** C2
Acha Mor W Isles **172** F6
Achabraid Argyll **128** B3
Achachork Highld **152** E5
Achafolla Argyll **130** D3
Achagary Highld **168** D2
Achahoish Argyll **128** C2
Achalader Perth **141** E8
Achallader Argyll **139** E7
Ach'an Todhair Highld **138** B4
Achanalt Highld **156** C3
Achanamara Argyll **128** B2
Achandunie Highld **157** B7
Achany Highld **164** D2
Achaphubuil Highld **138** B4
Acharacle Highld **137** B7
Acharn Highld **137** C8
Acharn Perth **140** E4
Acharole Highld **169** D7
Achath Aberds **151** C6
Achavanich Highld **169** E6
Achavraat Highld **158** E3
Achddu Carms **33** D5
Achduart Highld **162** D4
Achentoul Highld **168** F3
Achfary Highld **166** F4
Achgarve Highld **162** E2
Achiemore Highld **167** C5
Achiemore Highld **168** D3
A'Chill Highld **144** C2
Achiltibuie Highld **162** D4
Achina Highld **168** C2
Achinduich Highld **164** D2
Achinduin Argyll **130** B4
Achingills Highld **169** C6
Achintee Highld **139** B5
Achintee Highld **155** F5
Achintraid Highld **155** G4
Achlean Highld **148** E4
Achleck Argyll **137** D5
Achluachrach Highld **147** F5
Achlyness Highld **166** D4
Achmelvich Highld **162** B4
Achmore Highld **155** G4
Achmore Stirl **140** F2
Achnaba Argyll **130** B5
Achnaba Argyll **128** B4
Achnabat Highld **157** F6
Achnacarnin Highld **166** F2
Achnacarry Highld **146** F4
Achnacloich Argyll **131** B5
Achnacloich Highld **145** C5
Achnaconeran Highld **147** C7
Achnacraig Argyll **137** D5
Achnacroish Argyll **138** E2
Achnadrish Argyll **137** C5
Achnafalnich Argyll **131** C8
Achnagarron Highld **157** C7
Achnaha Highld **137** B5
Achnahanat Highld **164** E2
Achnahannet Highld **149** B5
Achnairn Highld **164** C2
Achnaluachrach Highld **164** D3
Achnasaul Highld **146** F4
Achnasheen Highld **156** D2
Achosnich Highld **137** B5
Achranich Highld **137** D8
Achreamie Highld **168** C5
Achriabhach Highld **139** C5
Achriesgill Highld **166** D4
Achrimsdale Highld **165** D6
Achtoty Highld **167** C8
Achurch Northants **65** F7
Achuvoldrach Highld **167** D7
Achvaich Highld **164** E4
Achvarasdal Highld **168** C4
Ackergill Highld **169** D8
Acklam M'bro **102** C2
Acklam N Yorks **96** C3
Ackleton Shrops **61** E7
Acklington Northumb **117** D8
Ackton W Yorks **88** B5
Ackworth Moor Top W Yorks **88** C5
Acle Norf **69** C7
Acock's Green W Mid **62** F5
Acol Kent **31** C7
Acomb Northumb **110** C2
Acomb York **95** D8
Aconbury Hereford **49** F7
Acre Lancs **87** B5
Acre Street W Sus **15** E8
Acrefair Wrex **73** E6
Acton Ches **74** D3
Acton Dorset **13** G7
Acton London **41** F5
Acton Shrops **60** F3
Acton Suff **56** E2
Acton Wrex **73** D7
Acton Beauchamp Hereford **49** D8
Acton Bridge Ches **74** B2
Acton Burnell Shrops **60** D5
Acton Green Hereford **49** D8
Acton Pigott Shrops **60** D5
Acton Round Shrops **61** E6
Acton Scott Shrops **60** F4
Acton Trussell Staffs **62** C3
Acton Turville S Glos **37** F5
Adbaston Staffs **61** B7
Adber Dorset **12** B3
Adderley Shrops **74** E3
Adderstone Northumb **125** F7
Addiewell W Loth **122** C2
Addingham W Yorks **94** E3
Addington Bucks **39** B7
Addington London **28** C4
Addington Kent **29** D7
Addinston Borders **123** D8
Addiscombe London **28** C4
Addlestone Sur **27** C8
Addlethorpe Lincs **79** C8
Adel W Yorks **95** F5
Adeney Telford **61** C7
Adfa Powys **59** D7
Adforton Hereford **49** B6
Adisham Kent **31** D6
Adlestrop Glos **38** B2
Adlingfleet E Yorks **90** B2
Adlington Lancs **86** C4
Admaston Staffs **62** B4
Admaston Telford **61** C6
Admington Warks **51** E7
Adstock Bucks **52** F5
Adstone Northants **52** D3
Adversane W Sus **16** B4
Advie Highld **158** F5
Adwalton W Yorks **88** B3
Adwell Oxon **39** E6
Adwick le Street S Yorks **89** D6
Adwick upon Dearne S Yorks **89** D5
Adziel Aberds **161** C6
Ae Village Dumfries **114** F2
Affleck Aberds **151** B7
Affpuddle Dorset **13** E6
Affric Lodge Highld **146** B4
Afon-wen Flint **72** B5
Afton I o W **14** F4
Agglethorpe N Yorks **101** F5
Agneash I o M **84** D4
Aigburth Mers **85** F4
Aiginis W Isles **172** E7
Aike E Yorks **97** E6
Aikerness Orkney **176** A3
Aikers Orkney **176** G3
Aiketgate Cumb **108** E4
Aikton Cumb **108** D2
Ailey Hereford **48** E5
Ailstone Warks **51** D7
Ailsworth P'boro **65** E8
Ainderby Quernhow N Yorks **102** F1
Ainderby Steeple N Yorks **101** E8
Aingers Green Essex **43** B7
Ainsdale Mers **85** C4
Ainsdale-on-Sea Mers **85** C4
Ainstable Cumb **108** E5
Ainsworth Gtr Man **87** C5
Ainthorpe N Yorks **103** D5
Aintree Mers **85** E4
Aintree Racecourse Mers **85** E4
Aird Argyll **130** E3
Aird Dumfries **104** C4
Aird Highld **154** C3
Aird W Isles **172** E8
Aird a Mhachair W Isles **170** F3
Aird a'Mhulaidh W Isles **173** G4
Aird Asaig W Isles **173** H4
Aird Dhail W Isles **172** B7
Aird Mhidhinis W Isles **171** K3
Aird Mhighe W Isles **173** J4
Aird Mhighe W Isles **173** K3
Aird Mhor W Isles **171** K3
Aird of Sleat Highld **145** C5
Aird Thunga W Isles **172** E7
Aird Uig W Isles **172** E3
Airdens Highld **164** E3
Airdrie N Lnrk **121** C7
Airdtorrisdale Highld **167** C8
Airidh a Bhruaich W Isles **172** G5
Airieland Dumfries **106** D4
Airmyn E Yorks **89** B8
Airntully Perth **141** F7
Airor Highld **145** C7
Airth Falk **133** F7
Airton N Yorks **94** D2
Airyhassen Dumfries **105** E7
Aisby Lincs **90** E2
Aisby Lincs **78** F3
Aisgernis W Isles **171** H3
Aiskew N Yorks **101** F7
Aislaby N Yorks **103** F5
Aislaby N Yorks **103** D6
Aislaby Stockton **102** C2
Aisthorpe Lincs **78** A2
Aith Orkney **176** E1
Aith Shetland **175** H5
Aith Shetland **174** D8
Aithsetter Shetland **175** K6
Aitkenhead S Ayrs **112** D3
Aitnoch Highld **158** F3
Akeld Northumb **117** B5
Akeley Bucks **52** F5
Akenham Suff **56** E5
Albaston Corn **6** B2
Alberbury Shrops **60** C3
Albert Dock, Liverpool Mers **85** F4
Albourne W Sus **17** C6
Albrighton Shrops **60** C4
Albrighton Shrops **62** D2
Alburgh Norf **69** F5
Albury Herts **41** B7
Albury Sur **27** E8
Albury End Herts **41** B7
Alby Hill Norf **81** D7
Alcaig Highld **157** D6
Alcaston Shrops **60** F4
Alcester Warks **51** D5
Alciston E Sus **18** E2
Alcombe Som **21** E8
Alcombe Wilts **24** C3
Alconbury Cambs **54** B2
Alconbury Weston Cambs **54** B2
Aldbar Castle Angus **143** D5
Aldborough Norf **81** D7
Aldborough N Yorks **95** C7
Aldbourne Wilts **25** B7
Aldbrough E Yorks **97** F8
Aldbrough St John N Yorks **101** C7
Aldbury Herts **40** C2
Aldcliffe Lancs **92** C4
Aldclune Perth **141** C6
Aldeburgh Suff **57** D8
Aldeby Norf **69** E7
Aldenham Herts **40** E4
Alderbury Wilts **14** B2
Aldercar Derbys **76** E4
Alderford Norf **68** C4
Alderholt Dorset **14** C2
Alderley Glos **36** E4
Alderley Edge Ches **74** B5
Aldermaston W Berks **26** C3
Aldermaston Wharf W Berks **26** C4
Alderminster Warks **51** E7
Alderney Airport Ald **16**
Alder's End Hereford **49** E8
Aldersey Green Ches **73** D8
Aldershot Hants **27** D6
Alderton Glos **50** F5
Alderton Northants **52** E5
Alderton Shrops **60** B4
Alderton Suff **57** E7
Alderton Wilts **37** F5
Alderwasley Derbys **76** D3
Aldfield N Yorks **95** C5
Aldford Ches **73** D8
Aldham Essex **43** B5
Aldham Suff **56** E4
Aldie Highld **164** F4
Aldingbourne W Sus **16** D3
Aldingham Cumb **92** B2
Aldington Kent **19** B7
Aldington Worcs **51** E5
Aldington Frith Kent **19** B7
Aldochlay Argyll **132** E2
Aldreth Cambs **54** B5
Aldridge W Mid **62** D4
Aldringham Suff **57** C8
Aldsworth Glos **38** C1
Aldunie Moray **150** B2
Aldwark Derbys **76** D2
Aldwark N Yorks **95** C7
Aldwick W Sus **16** E3
Aldwincle Northants **65** F7
Aldworth W Berks **26** B3
Alexandria W Dunb **120** B3
Alfardisworthy Devon **8** C4
Alfington Devon **11** E6
Alfold Sur **27** F8
Alfold Bars W Sus **27** F8
Alfold Crossways Sur **27** F8
Alford Aberds **150** C4
Alford Lincs **79** B7
Alford Som **23** F8
Alfreton Derbys **76** D4
Alfrick Worcs **50** D2
Alfrick Pound Worcs **50** D2
Alfriston E Sus **18** E2
Algaltraig Argyll **129** C5
Algarkirk Lincs **79** F5
Alhampton Som **23** F8
Aline Lodge W Isles **173** G4
Alisary Highld **145** F7
Alkborough N Lincs **90** B2
Alkerton Oxon **51** E8
Alkham Kent **31** E6
Alkington Shrops **74** F2
Alkmonton Derbys **75** F8
All Cannings Wilts **25** C5
All Saints Church, Godshill I o W **15** F6
All Saints South Elmham Suff **69** F6
All Stretton Shrops **60** E4
Alladale Lodge Highld **163** F8
Allaleigh Devon **7** D6
Allanaquoich Aberds **149** E7
Allangrange Mains Highld **157** D7
Allanton Borders **124** D4
Allanton N Lnrk **121** D8
Allathasdal W Isles **171** K2
Allendale Town Northumb **109** D8
Allenheads Northumb **109** E8
Allens Green Herts **41** C7
Allensford Durham **110** D3
Allensmore Hereford **49** F6
Allenton Derby **76** F3
Aller Som **12** B2
Allerby Cumb **107** F7
Allerford Som **21** E8
Allerston N Yorks **103** F6
Allerthorpe E Yorks **96** E3
Allerton Mers **86** F2
Allerton W Yorks **94** F4
Allerton Bywater W Yorks **88** B5
Allerton Mauleverer N Yorks **95** D7
Allesley W Mid **63** F7
Allestree Derby **76** F3
Allet Corn **3** B6
Allexton Leics **64** D5
Allgreave Ches **75** C6
Allhallows Medway **30** B2
Allhallows-on-Sea Medway **30** B2
Alligin Shuas Highld **154** E4
Allimore Green Staffs **62** C2
Allington Lincs **77** E8
Allington Wilts **25** F7
Allington Wilts **25** C5
Allithwaite Cumb **92** B3
Alloa Clack **133** E7
Allonby Cumb **107** E7
Alloway S Ayrs **112** C3
Allt Carms **33** D6
Allt na h-Airbhe Highld **163** E5
Allt-nan-sùgh Highld **146** B2
Alltchaorunn Highld **139** D5
Alltforgan Powys **59** B6
Alltmawr Powys **48** E2
Alltnacaillich Highld **167** E6
Alltsigh Highld **147** C7
Alltwalis Carms **46** F3
Alltwen Neath **33** D8
Alltyblaca Ceredig **46** E4
Allwood Green Suff **56** B4
Almeley Hereford **48** D5
Almer Dorset **13** E7
Almholme S Yorks **89** D6
Almington Staffs **74** F4
Alminstone Cross Devon **8** B5
Almondbank Perth **134** B2
Almondbury W Yorks **88** C2
Almondsbury S Glos **36** F3

Alne N Yorks 95 C7
Alness Highld 157 C7
Alnham Northumb 117 C5
Alnmouth Northumb 117 C8
Alnwick Northumb 117 C7
Alperton London 40 F4
Alphamstone Essex 56 F2
Alpheton Suff 56 D2
Alphington Devon 10 E4
Alport Derbys 76 C2
Alpraham Ches 74 D2
Alresford Essex 43 B6
Alrewas Staffs 63 C5
Alsager Ches 74 D4
Alsagers Bank Staffs 74 E5
Alsop en le Dale Derbys 75 D8
Alston Cumb 109 E7
Alston Devon 11 D8
Alstone Glos 50 F4
Alstonefield Staffs 75 D8
Alswear Devon 10 B2
Altandhu Highld 162 C3
Altanduin Highld 165 B5
Altarnun Corn 8 F4
Altass Highld 164 D1
Alterwall Highld 169 C7
Altham Lancs 93 F7
Althorne Essex 43 E5
Althorp House, Great Brington Northants 52 C4
Althorpe N Lincs 90 D2
Alticry Dumfries 105 D6
Altnabreac Station Highld 168 E5
Altnacealgach Hotel Highld 163 C6
Altnacraig Argyll 130 C4
Altnafeadh Highld 139 D6
Altnaharra Highld 167 F7
Altofts W Yorks 88 B4
Alton Derbys 76 C3
Alton Hants 26 F5
Alton Staffs 75 E7
Alton Pancras Dorset 12 D5
Alton Priors Wilts 25 C6
Alton Towers Staffs 75 E7
Altrincham Gtr Man 87 F5
Altrua Highld 146 F5
Altskeith Stirl 132 D3
Altyre Ho. Moray 158 D4
Alva Clack 133 E7
Alvanley Ches 73 B8
Alvaston Derby 76 F3
Alvechurch Worcs 50 B5
Alvecote Warks 63 D6
Alvediston Wilts 13 B7
Alveley Shrops 61 F7
Alverdiscott Devon 9 B7
Alverstoke Hants 15 E7
Alverstone I o W 15 F6
Alverton Notts 77 E7
Alves Moray 158 C5
Alvescot Oxon 38 D2
Alveston S Glos 36 F3
Alveston Warks 51 D7
Alvie Highld 148 D4
Alvingham Lincs 91 E7
Alvington Glos 36 D3
Alwalton Cambs 65 E8
Alweston Dorset 12 C4
Alwinton Northumb 116 D5
Alwoodley W Yorks 95 E5
Alyth Perth 142 E2
Am Baile W Isles 171 J3
Am Buth Argyll 130 C4
Amatnatua Highld 164 E1
Amber Hill Lincs 78 E5
Ambergate Derbys 76 D3
Amberley Glos 37 D5
Amberley W Sus 16 C4
Amble Northumb 117 D8
Amblecote W Mid 62 F2
Ambler Thorn W Yorks 87 B8
Ambleside Cumb 99 D5
Ambleston Pembs 44 C5
Ambrosden Oxon 39 C6
Amcotts N Lincs 90 C2
American Air Museum, Duxford Cambs 55 E5
Amersham Bucks 40 E2
Amerton Working Farm, Stowe-by-Chartley Staffs 62 B3
Amesbury Wilts 25 E6
Amington Staffs 63 D6
Amisfield Dumfries 114 F2
Amlwch Anglesey 82 B4
Amlwch Port Anglesey 82 B4
Ammanford = Rhydaman Carms 33 C7
Amod Argyll 118 C4
Amotherby N Yorks 96 B3
Ampfield Hants 14 B5
Ampleforth N Yorks 95 B8
Ampney Crucis Glos 37 D7
Ampney St Mary Glos 37 D7
Ampney St Peter Glos 37 D7
Amport Hants 25 E7
Ampthill Beds 53 F8
Ampton Suff 56 B2
Amroth Pembs 32 D2
Amulree Perth 141 F5
An Caol Highld 155 E2
An Cnoc W Isles 172 E7
An Gleann Ur W Isles 172 E7
An t-Ob = Leverburgh W Isles 173 K3
Anagach Highld 149 B6
Anaheilt Highld 138 C2
Anancaun Highld 154 D6
Ancaster Lincs 78 E2
Anchor Shrops 59 F8
Anchorsholme Blkpool 92 E3
Ancroft Northumb 125 E5
Ancrum Borders 116 B2
Anderby Lincs 79 B8
Anderson Dorset 13 E6
Anderton Ches 74 B3
Andover Hants 25 E8
Andover Down Hants 25 E8
Andoversford Glos 37 C7
Andreas I o M 84 C4
Anfield Mers 85 E4
Angersleigh Som 11 C6
Angle Pembs 44 E3
Angmering W Sus 16 D4
Angram N Yorks 95 E8
Angram N Yorks 100 E3
Anie Stirl 132 C4
Ankerville Highld 158 B2
Anlaby E Yorks 90 B4
Anmer Norf 80 E3
Anna Valley Hants 25 E8
Annan Dumfries 107 C8
Annat Argyll 131 C6
Annat Highld 155 E4
Annbank S Ayrs 112 B4
Anne Hathaway's Cottage, Stratford-upon-Avon Warks 51 D6
Annesley Notts 76 D5
Annesley Woodhouse Notts 76 D4
Annfield Plain Durham 110 D4
Annifirth Shetland 175 J3
Annitsford T & W 111 B5
Annscroft Shrops 60 D4
Ansdell Lancs 85 B4
Ansford Som 23 F8
Ansley Warks 63 E6
Anslow Staffs 63 B6
Anslow Gate Staffs 63 B5
Anstey Herts 54 F5
Anstey Leics 64 D2
Anstruther Easter Fife 135 D7
Anstruther Wester Fife 135 D7
Ansty Hants 26 E5
Ansty Warks 63 F7
Ansty Wilts 13 B7
Ansty W Sus 17 B6
Anthill Common Hants 15 C7
Anthorn Cumb 107 D8
Antingham Norf 81 D8
Anton's Gowt Lincs 79 E5
Antonshill Falk 133 F7
Antony Corn 5 D8
Anwick Lincs 78 D4
Anwoth Dumfries 106 D2
Aoradh Argyll 126 C2
Apes Hall Cambs 67 E5
Apethorpe Northants 65 E7
Apeton Staffs 62 C2
Apley Lincs 78 B4
Apperknowle Derbys 76 B3
Apperley Glos 37 B5
Apperley Bridge W Yorks 94 F4
Appersett N Yorks 100 E3
Appin Argyll 138 E3
Appin House Argyll 138 E3
Appleby N Lincs 90 C3
Appleby-in-Westmorland Cumb 100 B1
Appleby Magna Leics 63 D7
Appleby Parva Leics 63 D7
Applecross Highld 155 F3
Applecross Ho. Highld 155 F3
Appledore Devon 20 F3
Appledore Devon 11 C5
Appledore Kent 19 C6
Appledore Heath Kent 19 B6
Appleford Oxon 39 E5
Applegarthtown Dumfries 114 F4
Appleshaw Hants 25 E8
Applethwaite Cumb 98 B4
Appleton Halton 86 F3
Appleton Oxon 38 D4
Appleton-le-Moors N Yorks 103 F5
Appleton-le-Street N Yorks 96 B3
Appleton Roebuck N Yorks 95 E8
Appleton Thorn Warr 86 F4
Appleton Wiske N Yorks 102 D1
Appletreehall Borders 115 C8
Appletreewick N Yorks 94 C3
Appley Som 11 B5
Appley Bridge Lancs 86 D3
Apse Heath I o W 15 F6
Apsley End Beds 54 F2
Apuldram W Sus 16 D2
Aquhythie Aberds 151 C6
Arabella Highld 158 B2
Arbeadie Aberds 151 E5
Arbeia Roman Fort and Museum T & W 111 C6
Arberth = Narberth Pembs 32 C2
Arbirlot Angus 143 E6
Arboll Highld 165 F5
Arborfield Wokingham 27 C5
Arborfield Cross Wokingham 27 C5
Arborfield Garrison Wokingham 27 C5
Arbour-thorne S Yorks 88 F4
Arbroath Angus 143 E6
Arbuthnott Aberds 143 B7
Archiestown Moray 159 E6
Arclid Ches 74 C4
Ard-dhubh Highld 155 F3
Ardachu Highld 164 D3
Ardalanish Argyll 136 G4
Ardanaiseig Argyll 131 C6
Ardaneaskan Highld 155 G4
Ardanstur Argyll 130 D4
Ardargie House Hotel Perth 134 C2
Ardarroch Highld 155 G4
Ardbeg Argyll 126 E4
Ardbeg Argyll 129 B6
Ardbeg Distillery, Port Ellen Argyll 126 E4
Ardcharnich Highld 163 F5
Ardchiavaig Argyll 136 G4
Ardchullarie More Stirl 132 C4
Ardchyle Stirl 132 B4
Arddleen Powys 60 C2
Ardechvie Highld 146 E4
Ardeley Herts 41 B6
Ardelve Highld 155 H4
Arden Argyll 132 F2
Ardens Grafton Warks 51 D6
Ardentinny Argyll 129 B6
Ardentraive Argyll 129 C5
Ardeonaig Stirl 140 F3
Ardersier Highld 157 D8
Ardessie Highld 162 F4
Ardfern Argyll 130 E4
Ardgartan Argyll 131 E8
Ardgay Highld 164 E2
Ardgour Highld 138 C4
Ardheslaig Highld 154 E3
Ardiecow Moray 160 B2
Ardindrean Highld 163 F5
Ardingly W Sus 17 B7
Ardington Oxon 38 F4
Ardlair Aberds 150 B4
Ardlamont Ho. Argyll 128 D4
Ardleigh Essex 43 B6
Ardler Perth 142 E2
Ardley Oxon 39 B5
Ardlui Argyll 132 C2
Ardlussa Argyll 127 D4
Ardmair Highld 163 E5
Ardmay Argyll 131 E8
Ardminish Argyll 118 B3
Ardmolich Highld 145 F7
Ardmore Argyll 130 C3
Ardmore Highld 166 D4
Ardmore Highld 164 F4
Ardnacross Argyll 137 D6
Ardnadam Argyll 129 C6
Ardnagrask Highld 157 E6
Ardnarff Highld 155 G4
Ardnastang Highld 138 C2
Ardnave Argyll 126 B2
Ardno Argyll 131 E7
Ardo Aberds 160 E5
Ardo Ho. Aberds 151 B8
Ardoch Perth 141 F7
Ardochy House Highld 146 D5
Ardoyne Aberds 151 B5
Ardpatrick Argyll 128 D2
Ardpatrick Ho. Argyll 128 E2
Ardpeaton Argyll 129 B7
Ardrishaig Argyll 128 B3
Ardross Fife 135 D7
Ardross Highld 157 B7
Ardross Castle Highld 157 B7
Ardrossan N Ayrs 120 E2
Ardshealach Highld 137 B7
Ardsley S Yorks 88 D4
Ardslignish Highld 137 B6
Ardtalla Argyll 126 D4
Ardtalnaig Perth 140 F4
Ardtoe Highld 145 F6
Ardtrostan Perth 133 B5
Arduaine Argyll 130 D3
Ardullie Highld 157 C6
Ardvasar Highld 145 C6
Ardvorlich Perth 132 B5
Ardwell Dumfries 104 E5
Ardwell Mains Dumfries 104 E5
Ardwick Gtr Man 87 E6
Areley Kings Worcs 50 B3
Arford Hants 27 F6
Argoed Caerph 35 E5
Argoed Mill Powys 47 C8
Argyll & Sutherland Highlanders Museum (See Stirling Castle) Stirl 133 E6
Arichamish Argyll 130 E5
Arichastlich Argyll 131 B8
Aridhglas Argyll 136 F4
Arileod Argyll 136 C2
Arinacrinachd Highld 154 E3
Arinagour Argyll 136 C3
Arion Orkney 176 E1
Arisaig Highld 145 E6
Ariundle Highld 138 C2
Arkendale N Yorks 95 C6
Arkesden Essex 55 F5
Arkholme Lancs 93 B5
Arkle Town N Yorks 101 D5
Arkley London 41 E5
Arksey S Yorks 89 D6
Arkwright Town Derbys 76 B4
Arle Glos 37 B6
Arlecdon Cumb 98 C2
Arlesey Beds 54 F2
Arleston Telford 61 C6
Arley Ches 86 F4
Arlingham Glos 36 C4
Arlington Devon 20 E5
Arlington E Sus 18 E2
Arlington Glos 37 D8
Arlington Court Devon 20 E5
Armadale Highld 168 C2
Armadale W Loth 122 C2
Armadale Castle Highld 145 C6
Armathwaite Cumb 108 E5
Arminghall Norf 69 D5
Armitage Staffs 62 C4
Armley W Yorks 95 F5
Armscote Warks 51 E7
Armthorpe S Yorks 89 D7
Arnabost Argyll 136 C3
Arncliffe N Yorks 94 B2
Arncroach Fife 135 D7
Arne Dorset 13 F7
Arnesby Leics 64 E3
Arngask Perth 134 C3
Arnisdale Highld 145 B8
Arnish Highld 152 E6
Arniston Engine Midloth 123 C6
Arnol W Isles 172 D6
Arnold E Yorks 97 E7
Arnold Notts 77 E5
Arnolfini Gallery Bristol 23 B7
Arnprior Stirl 132 E5
Arnside Cumb 92 B4
Aros Mains Argyll 137 D6
Arowry Wrex 73 F8
Arpafeelie Highld 157 D7
Arrad Foot Cumb 99 F5
Arram E Yorks 97 E6
Arrathorne N Yorks 101 E7
Arreton I o W 15 F6
Arrington Cambs 54 D4
Arrivain Argyll 131 B8
Arrochar Argyll 131 E8
Arrow Warks 51 D5
Arthington W Yorks 95 E5
Arthingworth Northants 64 F4
Arthog Gwyn 58 C3
Arthrath Aberds 161 E6
Arthurstone Perth 142 E2
Artrochie Aberds 161 E7
Arundel W Sus 16 D4
Arundel Castle W Sus 16 D4
Aryhoulan Highld 138 C4
Asby Cumb 98 B2
Ascog Argyll 129 D6
Ascot Windsor 27 C7
Ascot Racecourse Windsor 27 C7
Ascott Warks 51 F8
Ascott-under-Wychwood Oxon 38 C3
Asenby N Yorks 95 B6
Asfordby Leics 64 C4
Asfordby Hill Leics 64 C4
Asgarby Lincs 78 E4
Asgarby Lincs 79 C6
Ash Kent 29 C6
Ash Kent 31 D6
Ash Som 12 B2
Ash Sur 27 D6
Ash Bullayne Devon 10 D2
Ash Green Warks 63 F7
Ash Magna Shrops 74 F2
Ash Mill Devon 10 B2
Ash Priors Som 11 B6
Ash Street Suff 56 E4
Ash Thomas Devon 10 C5
Ash Vale Sur 27 D6
Ashampstead W Berks 26 B3
Ashbocking Suff 57 D5
Ashbourne Derbys 75 E8
Ashbrittle Som 11 B5
Ashburton Devon 7 C5
Ashbury Devon 9 E7
Ashbury Oxon 38 F2
Ashby N Lincs 90 D3
Ashby by Partney Lincs 79 C7
Ashby cum Fenby NE Lincs 91 D6
Ashby de la Launde Lincs 78 D3
Ashby-de-la-Zouch Leics 63 C7
Ashby Folville Leics 64 C4
Ashby Magna Leics 64 E2
Ashby Parva Leics 64 F2
Ashby Puerorum Lincs 79 B6
Ashby St Ledgers Northants 52 C3
Ashby St Mary Norf 69 D6
Ashchurch Glos 50 F4
Ashcombe Devon 7 B7
Ashcott Som 23 F6
Ashdon Essex 55 E6
Ashe Hants 26 E3
Asheldham Essex 43 D5
Ashen Essex 55 E8
Ashendon Bucks 39 C7
Ashfield Carms 33 B7
Ashfield Stirl 133 D6
Ashfield Suff 57 C6
Ashfield Green Suff 57 B6
Ashfold Crossways W Sus 17 B6
Ashford Devon 20 F4
Ashford Hants 14 C2
Ashford Kent 30 E4
Ashford Sur 27 B8
Ashford Bowdler Shrops 49 B7
Ashford Carbonell Shrops 49 B7
Ashford Hill Hants 26 C3
Ashford in the Water Derbys 75 C8
Ashgill S Lnrk 121 E7
Ashill Devon 11 C5
Ashill Norf 67 D8
Ashill Som 11 C8
Ashingdon Essex 42 E4
Ashington Northumb 117 F8
Ashington Som 12 B3
Ashington W Sus 16 C5
Ashintully Castle Perth 141 C8
Ashkirk Borders 115 B7
Ashlett Hants 15 D5
Ashleworth Glos 37 B5
Ashley Cambs 55 C7
Ashley Ches 87 F5
Ashley Devon 9 C8
Ashley Dorset 14 D2
Ashley Glos 37 E6
Ashley Hants 14 E3
Ashley Hants 25 F8
Ashley Northants 64 E4
Ashley Staffs 74 F4
Ashley Green Bucks 40 D2
Ashley Heath Dorset 14 D2
Ashley Heath Staffs 74 F4
Ashmanhaugh Norf 69 B6
Ashmansworth Hants 26 D2
Ashmansworthy Devon 8 C5
Ashmore Dorset 13 C7
Ashorne Warks 51 D8
Ashover Derbys 76 C3
Ashow Warks 51 B8
Ashprington Devon 7 D6
Ashreigney Devon 9 C8
Ashtead Sur 28 D2
Ashton Ches 74 C2
Ashton Corn 2 D5
Ashton Hants 15 C6
Ashton Hereford 49 C7
Ashton Invclyd 129 C7
Ashton Northants 53 E5
Ashton Northants 65 F7
Ashton Common Wilts 24 D3
Ashton-In-Makerfield Gtr Man 86 E3
Ashton Keynes Wilts 37 E7
Ashton under Hill Worcs 50 F4
Ashton-under-Lyne Gtr Man 87 E7
Ashton upon Mersey Gtr Man 87 E5
Ashurst Hants 14 C4
Ashurst Kent 18 B2
Ashurst W Sus 17 C5
Ashurstwood W Sus 28 F5
Ashwater Devon 9 E5
Ashwell Herts 54 F3
Ashwell Rutland 65 C5
Ashwell Som 11 C8
Ashwellthorpe Norf 68 E4
Ashwick Som 23 E8
Ashwicken Norf 67 C7
Ashybank Borders 115 C8
Askam in Furness Cumb 92 B2
Askern S Yorks 89 C6
Askerswell Dorset 12 E3
Askett Bucks 39 D8
Askham Cumb 99 B7
Askham Notts 77 B7
Askham Bryan York 95 E8
Askham Richard York 95 E8
Asknish Argyll 128 A4
Askrigg N Yorks 100 E4
Askwith N Yorks 94 E4
Aslackby Lincs 78 F3
Aslacton Norf 68 E4
Aslockton Notts 77 F7
Asloun Aberds 150 C4
Aspatria Cumb 107 E8
Aspenden Herts 41 B6
Asperton Lincs 79 F5
Aspley Guise Beds 53 F7
Aspley Heath Beds 53 F7
Aspull Gtr Man 86 D4
Asselby E Yorks 89 B8
Asserby Lincs 79 B7
Assington Suff 56 F3
Assynt Ho. Highld 157 C6
Astbury Ches 74 C5
Astcote Northants 52 D4
Asterley Shrops 60 D3
Asterton Shrops 60 E3
Asthall Oxon 38 C2
Asthall Leigh Oxon 38 C3
Astley Shrops 60 C5
Astley Warks 63 F7
Astley Worcs 50 C2
Astley Abbotts Shrops 61 E7
Astley Bridge Gtr Man 86 C5
Astley Cross Worcs 50 C3
Astley Green Gtr Man 86 E5
Aston Ches 74 E3
Aston Ches 74 B2
Aston Derbys 88 F2
Aston Hereford 49 B6
Aston Herts 41 B5
Aston Oxon 38 D3
Aston Shrops 60 B5
Aston Staffs 74 E4
Aston S Yorks 89 F5
Aston Telford 61 D6
Aston W Mid 62 F4
Aston Wokingham 39 F7
Aston Abbotts Bucks 39 B8
Aston Botterell Shrops 61 F6
Aston-By-Stone Staffs 75 F6
Aston Cantlow Warks 51 D6
Aston Clinton Bucks 40 C1
Aston Crews Hereford 36 B3
Aston Cross Glos 50 F4
Aston End Herts 41 B5
Aston Eyre Shrops 61 E6
Aston Fields Worcs 50 C4
Aston Flamville Leics 63 E8
Aston Ingham Hereford 36 B3
Aston juxta Mondrum Ches 74 D3
Aston le Walls Northants 52 D2
Aston Magna Glos 51 F6
Aston Munslow Shrops 60 F5
Aston on Clun Shrops 60 F3
Aston-on-Trent Derbys 63 B8
Aston Rogers Shrops 60 D3
Aston Rowant Oxon 39 E7
Aston Sandford Bucks 39 D7
Aston Somerville Worcs 50 F5
Aston Subedge Glos 51 E6
Aston Tirrold Oxon 39 F5
Aston Upthorpe Oxon 39 F5
Astrop Northants 52 F3
Astwick Beds 54 F3
Astwood M Keynes 53 E7
Astwood Worcs 50 D3
Astwood Bank Worcs 50 C5
Aswarby Lincs 78 F3
Aswardby Lincs 79 B6
Atch Lench Worcs 50 D5
Atcham Shrops 60 D5
Athelhampton Dorset 13 E5
Athelington Suff 57 B6
Athelney Som 11 B8
Athelstaneford E Loth 123 B8
Atherington Devon 9 B7
Atherstone Warks 63 E7
Atherstone on Stour Warks 51 D7
Atherton Gtr Man 86 D4
Atley Hill N Yorks 101 D7
Atlow Derbys 76 E2
Attadale Highld 155 G5
Attadale Ho. Highld 155 G5
Attenborough Notts 76 F5
Atterby Lincs 90 E3
Attercliffe S Yorks 88 F4
Attleborough Norf 68 E3
Attleborough Warks 63 E7
Attlebridge Norf 68 C4
Atwick E Yorks 97 D7
Atworth Wilts 24 C3
Aubourn Lincs 78 C2
Auchagallon N Ayrs 119 C5
Auchallater Aberds 149 F7
Aucharnie Aberds 160 D3
Auchattie Aberds 151 E5
Auchavan Angus 142 C1
Auchbreck Moray 149 B8
Auchenback E Renf 120 D5
Auchenbainzie Dumfries 113 E8
Auchenblae Aberds 143 B7
Auchenbrack Dumfries 113 E7
Auchenbreck Argyll 129 B5
Auchencairn Dumfries 106 D4
Auchencairn Dumfries 114 F2
Auchencairn N Ayrs 119 D7
Auchencrosh S Ayrs 104 B5
Auchencrow Borders 124 C4
Auchendinny Midloth 123 C5
Auchengray S Lnrk 122 D2
Auchenhalrig Moray 159 C7
Auchenheath S Lnrk 121 E8
Auchenlochan Argyll 128 C4
Auchenmalg Dumfries 105 D6
Auchensoul S Ayrs 112 E2
Auchentiber N Ayrs 120 E3
Auchertyre Highld 155 H4
Auchgourish Highld 148 C5
Auchincarroch W Dunb 132 F3
Auchindrain Argyll 131 E6
Auchindrean Highld 163 F5
Auchininna Aberds 160 D3
Auchinleck E Ayrs 113 B5
Auchinloch N Lnrk 121 B6
Auchinroath Moray 159 D6
Auchintoul Aberds 150 C4
Auchiries Aberds 161 E7
Auchlee Aberds 151 E7
Auchleven Aberds 150 B5
Auchlochan S Lnrk 121 F8
Auchlossan Aberds 150 D4
Auchlunies Aberds 151 E7
Auchlyne Stirl 132 B4
Auchmacoy Aberds 161 E6
Auchmair Moray 150 B2
Auchmantle Dumfries 105 C5
Auchmillan E Ayrs 112 B5
Auchmithie Angus 143 E6
Auchmuirbridge Fife 134 D4
Auchmull Angus 143 B5
Auchnacree Angus 142 C4
Auchnagallin Highld 158 F4
Auchnagatt Aberds 161 D6
Auchnaha Argyll 128 B4
Auchnashelloch Perth 133 C6
Aucholzie Aberds 150 E2
Auchrannie Angus 142 D2
Auchroisk Highld 149 B6
Auchronie Angus 150 F3
Auchterarder Perth 133 C8
Auchteraw Highld 147 D6
Auchterderran Fife 134 E4
Auchterhouse Angus 142 F3
Auchtermuchty Fife 134 C4
Auchterneed Highld 157 D5
Auchtertool Fife 134 E4
Auchtertyre Moray 159 D5
Auchtubh Stirl 132 B4
Auckengill Highld 169 C8
Auckley S Yorks 89 D7
Audenshaw Gtr Man 87 E7
Audlem Ches 74 E3
Audley Staffs 74 D4
Audley End Essex 56 F2
Audley End House Essex 55 F6
Auds Aberds 160 B3
Aughton E Yorks 96 F3
Aughton Lancs 85 D4
Aughton Lancs 93 C5
Aughton S Yorks 89 F5
Aughton Wilts 25 D7
Aughton Park Lancs 86 D2
Auldearn Highld 158 D3
Aulden Hereford 49 D6
Auldgirth Dumfries 114 F2
Auldhame E Loth 135 F7
Auldhouse S Lnrk 121 D6
Ault a'chruinn Highld 146 B2
Aultanrynie Highld 166 F5
Aultbea Highld 162 F2
Aultdearg Highld 156 C3
Aultgrishan Highld 154 B3
Aultguish Inn Highld 156 B4
Aultibea Highld 165 B7
Aultiphurst Highld 168 C3
Aultmore Moray 159 D8
Aultnagoire Highld 147 B8
Aultnamain Inn Highld 164 F3
Aultnaslat Highld 146 D4
Aulton Aberds 150 B5
Aundorach Highld 149 C5
Aunsby Lincs 78 F3
Auquhorthies Aberds 151 B7
Aust S Glos 36 F2
Austendike Lincs 66 B2
Austerfield S Yorks 89 E7
Austrey Warks 63 D6
Austwick N Yorks 93 C7
Authorpe Lincs 91 F8
Authorpe Row Lincs 79 B8
Avebury Wilts 25 C6
Aveley Thurrock 42 F1
Avening Glos 37 E5
Averham Notts 77 D7
Aveton Gifford Devon 6 E4
Avielochan Highld 148 C5
Aviemore Highld 148 C4
Avington Hants 26 F3
Avington W Berks 25 C8
Avoch Highld 157 D8
Avon Hants 14 E2
Avon Dassett Warks 52 E2
Avonbridge Falk 122 B2
Avonmouth Bristol 23 B7
Avonwick Devon 6 D5
Awbridge Hants 14 B4
Awhirk Dumfries 104 D4
Awkley S Glos 36 F2
Awliscombe Devon 11 D6
Awre Glos 36 D4
Awsworth Notts 76 E4
Axbridge Som 23 D6
Axford Hants 26 E4
Axford Wilts 25 B7
Axminster Devon 11 E7
Axmouth Devon 11 E7
Axton Flint 85 F2
Aycliff Kent 31 E7
Aycliffe Durham 101 B7
Aydon Northumb 110 C3
Aylburton Glos 36 D3
Ayle Northumb 109 E7
Aylesbeare Devon 10 E5
Aylesbury Bucks 39 C8
Aylesby NE Lincs 91 D6
Aylesford Kent 29 D8
Aylesham Kent 31 D6
Aylestone Leicester 64 D2
Aylmerton Norf 81 D7
Aylsham Norf 81 E7
Aylton Hereford 49 F8
Aymestrey Hereford 49 C6
Aynho Northants 52 F3
Ayot St Lawrence Herts 40 C4
Ayot St Peter Herts 41 C5
Ayr S Ayrs 112 B3
Ayr Racecourse S Ayrs 112 B3
Aysgarth N Yorks 101 F5
Ayside Cumb 99 F5
Ayston Rutland 65 D5
Aythorpe Roding Essex 42 C1
Ayton Borders 124 C5
Aywick Shetland 174 E7
Azerley N Yorks 95 B5

B

Babbacombe Torbay 7 C7
Babbinswood Shrops 73 F7
Babcary Som 12 B3
Babel Carms 47 F7
Babell Flint 73 B5
Babraham Cambs 55 D6
Babworth Notts 89 F7
Bac W Isles 172 D7
Bachau Anglesey 82 C4
Back of Keppoch Highld 145 E6
Back Rogerton E Ayrs 113 B5
Backaland Orkney 176 C4
Backaskaill Orkney 176 A3
Backbarrow Cumb 99 F5
Backe Carms 32 C3
Backfolds Aberds 161 C7
Backford Ches 73 B8
Backford Cross Ches 73 B7
Backhill Aberds 160 E4
Backhill Aberds 161 E7
Backhill of Clackriach Aberds 161 D6
Backhill of Fortree Aberds 161 D6
Backhill of Trustach Aberds 150 E5
Backies Highld 165 D5
Backlass Highld 169 D7
Backwell N Som 23 C6
Backworth T & W 111 B6
Bacon End Essex 42 C2
Baconsthorpe Norf 81 D7
Bacton Hereford 49 F5
Bacton Norf 81 D9
Bacton Suff 56 C4
Bacton Green Suff 56 C4
Bacup Lancs 87 B6
Badachro Highld 154 C3
Badanloch Lodge Highld 168 F2
Badavanich Highld 156 D2
Badbury Swindon 38 F1
Badby Northants 52 D3
Badcall Highld 166 D4
Badcaul Highld 162 E4
Baddeley Green Stoke 75 D6
Baddesley Clinton Warks 51 B7
Baddesley Clinton Hall Warks 51 B7
Baddesley Ensor Warks 63 E6
Baddidarach Highld 162 B4
Baddoch Aberds 149 F7
Baddock Highld 157 D8
Badenscoth Aberds 160 E4
Badenyon Aberds 150 C2
Badger Shrops 61 E7
Badger's Mount Kent 29 C5
Badgeworth Glos 37 C6
Badgworth Som 23 D5
Badicaul Highld 155 H3
Badingham Suff 57 C7
Badlesmere Kent 30 D4
Badlipster Highld 169 E7
Badluarach Highld 162 E3
Badminton S Glos 37 F5
Badnaban Highld 162 B4
Badninish Highld 164 E4
Badrallach Highld 162 E4
Badsey Worcs 51 E5
Badshot Lea Sur 27 E6
Badsworth W Yorks 89 C5
Badwell Ash Suff 56 C3
Bae Colwyn = Colwyn Bay Conwy 83 D8
Bag Enderby Lincs 79 B6
Bagby N Yorks 102 F2
Bagendon Glos 37 D7
Bagh a Chaisteil = Castlebay W Isles 171 L2
Bagh Mor W Isles 170 E4
Bagh Shiarabhagh W Isles 171 K3
Baghasdal W Isles 171 J3
Bagillt Flint 73 B6
Baginton Warks 51 B8
Baglan Neath 33 E8
Bagley Shrops 60 B4
Bagnall Staffs 75 D6
Bagnor W Berks 26 C2
Bagshot Sur 27 C7
Bagshot Wilts 25 C8
Bagthorpe Norf 80 D3
Bagthorpe Notts 76 D4
Bagworth Leics 63 D8
Bagwy Llydiart Hereford 35 B8
Bail Ard Bhuirgh W Isles 172 C7
Bail Uachdraich W Isles 170 D4
Baildon W Yorks 94 F4
Baile W Isles 173 K2
Baile a Mhanaich W Isles 170 E3
Baile Ailein W Isles 172 F5
Baile an Truiseil W Isles 172 C6
Baile Boidheach Argyll 128 C2
Baile Glas W Isles 170 E4
Baile Mhartainn W Isles 170 C3
Baile Mhic Phail W Isles 170 C4
Baile Mor Argyll 136 F3
Baile Mor W Isles 170 D3
Baile na Creige W Isles 171 K2
Baile nan Cailleach W Isles 170 E3
Baile Raghaill W Isles 170 C3
Bailebeag Highld 147 C8
Baileyhead Cumb 108 B5
Bailiesward Aberds 159 F8
Baillieston Glasgow 121 C6
Bail'lochdrach W Isles 170 E4
Bail'Ur Tholastaidh W Isles 172 D8
Bainbridge N Yorks 100 E4
Bainsford Falk 133 F7
Bainshole Aberds 160 E3
Bainton E Yorks 97 D5
Bainton P'boro 65 D7
Bairnkine Borders 116 C2
Baker Street Thurrock 42 F2
Baker's End Herts 41 C6
Bakewell Derbys 76 C2
Bala = Y Bala Gwyn 72 F3
Balachuirn Highld 153 E6
Balavil Highld 148 D3
Balbeg Highld 147 B7
Balbeg Highld 157 F5
Balbeggie Perth 134 B3
Balbithan Aberds 151 C6
Balbithan Ho. Aberds 151 C7
Balblair Highld 157 C8
Balblair Highld 164 E2
Balby S Yorks 89 D6
Balchladich Highld 166 F2
Balchraggan Highld 157 F6
Balchraggan Highld 157 E6
Balchrick Highld 166 D3
Balchrystie Fife 135 D6
Balcladaich Highld 147 B5
Balcombe W Sus 28 F4
Balcombe Lane W Sus 28 F4
Balcomie Fife 135 C8
Balcurvie Fife 134 D5
Baldersby N Yorks 95 B6
Baldersby St James N Yorks 95 B6
Balderstone Lancs 93 F6
Balderton Ches 73 C7
Balderton Notts 77 D8
Baldhu Corn 3 B6
Baldinnie Fife 135 C6
Baldock Herts 54 F3
Baldovie Dundee 142 F4
Baldrine I o M 84 D4
Baldslow E Sus 18 D4
Baldwin I o M 84 D3
Baldwinholme Cumb 108 D3
Baldwin's Gate Staffs 74 E4
Bale Norf 81 D6
Balearn Aberds 161 C7
Balemartine Argyll 136 F1
Balephuil Argyll 136 F1
Balerno Edin 122 C4
Balevullin Argyll 136 F1

Balfield Angus 143 C5
Balfour Orkney 176 E3
Balfron Stirl 132 F4
Balfron Station Stirl 132 F4
Balgaveny Aberds 160 D3
Balgavies Angus 143 D5
Balgonar Fife 134 E2
Balgove Aberds 160 E5
Balgowan Highld 148 E2
Balgown Highld 152 C4
Balgrochan E Dunb 121 B6
Balgy Highld 155 E4
Balhaldie Stirl 133 D7
Balhalgardy Aberds 151 B6
Balham London 28 B3
Balhary Perth 142 E2
Baliasta Shetland 174 C8
Baligill Highld 168 C3
Balintore Angus 142 D2
Balintore Highld 158 B2
Balintraid Highld 157 B8
Balk N Yorks 102 F2
Balkeerie Angus 142 E3
Balkemback Angus 142 F3
Balkholme E Yorks 89 B8
Balkissock S Ayrs 104 A5
Ball Shrops 60 B3
Ball Haye Green Staffs 75 D6
Ball Hill Hants 26 C2
Ballabeg I o M 84 E2
Ballacannel I o M 84 D4
Ballachulish Highld 138 D4
Ballajora I o M 84 C4
Ballaleigh I o M 84 D3
Ballamodha I o M 84 E2
Ballantrae S Ayrs 104 A4
Ballaquine I o M 84 D4
Ballards Gore Essex 43 E5
Ballasalla I o M 84 C3
Ballasalla I o M 84 E2
Ballater Aberds 150 E2
Ballaugh I o M 84 C3
Ballaveare I o M 84 E3
Ballcorach Moray 149 B7
Ballechin Perth 141 D6
Balleigh Highld 164 F4
Ballencrieff E Loth 123 B7
Ballentoul Perth 141 C5
Ballidon Derbys 76 D2
Balliemore Argyll 129 B5
Balliemore Argyll 130 C4
Ballikinrain Stirl 132 F4
Ballimeanoch Argyll 131 D6
Ballimore Argyll 128 B4
Ballimore Stirl 132 C4
Ballinaby Argyll 126 C2
Ballindean Perth 134 B4
Ballingdon Suff 56 E2
Ballinger Common Bucks 40 D2
Ballingham Hereford 49 F7
Ballingry Fife 134 E3
Ballinlick Perth 141 E6
Ballinluig Perth 141 D6
Ballintuim Perth 141 D8
Balloch Angus 142 D3
Balloch Highld 157 E8
Balloch N Lnrk 121 B7
Balloch W Dunb 132 F2
Ballochan Aberds 150 E4
Ballochford Moray 159 F7
Ballochmorrie S Ayrs 112 F2
Balls Cross W Sus 16 B3
Balls Green Essex 43 B6
Ballygown Argyll 137 D5
Ballygrant Argyll 126 C3
Ballyhaugh Argyll 136 C2
Balmacara Highld 155 H4
Balmacara Square Highld 155 H4
Balmaclellan Dumfries 106 B3
Balmacneil Perth 141 D6
Balmacqueen Highld 152 B5
Balmae Dumfries 106 E3
Balmaha Stirl 132 E3
Balmalcolm Fife 134 D5
Balmeanach Highld 153 E6
Balmedie Aberds 151 C8
Balmer Heath Shrops 73 F8
Balmerino Fife 135 B5
Balmerlawn Hants 14 D4
Balmichael N Ayrs 119 C6
Balmirmer Angus 143 F5
Balmoral Castle and Gardens Aberds 149 E8
Balmore Highld 153 E3
Balmore Highld 156 F4
Balmore Highld 158 E2
Balmore Perth 141 D6
Balmule Fife 134 F4
Balmullo Fife 135 B6
Balmungie Highld 157 D8
Balnaboth Angus 142 C3
Balnabruaich Highld 157 C8
Balnabruich Highld 165 B8
Balnacoil Highld 165 C5
Balnacra Highld 155 F5
Balnafoich Highld 157 F7
Balnagall Highld 165 F5
Balnaguard Perth 141 D6
Balnahard Argyll 127 C2
Balnahard Argyll 137 E5
Balnain Highld 157 F5
Balnakeil Highld 167 C5
Balnaknock Highld 152 C5
Balnapaling Highld 157 C8
Balne N Yorks 89 C6
Balochroy Argyll 128 E2
Balone Fife 135 C6
Balornock Glasgow 121 C6
Balquharn Perth 141 F7
Balquhidder Stirl 132 B4
Balsall W Mid 51 B7
Balsall Common W Mid 51 B7
Balsall Heath W Mid 62 F4
Balscott Oxon 51 E8
Balsham Cambs 55 D6
Baltasound Shetland 174 C8
Balterley Staffs 74 D4
Baltersan Dumfries 105 C8
Balthangie Aberds 160 C5
Baltonsborough Som 23 F7
Balvaird Highld 157 D6
Balvicar Argyll 130 D3
Balvraid Highld 145 B8
Balvraid Highld 158 F2
Bamber Bridge Lancs 86 B3
Bambers Green Essex 42 B1
Bamburgh Northumb 125 F7
Bamburgh Castle Northumb 125 F7
Bamff Perth 142 D2
Bamford Derbys 88 F3
Bamford Gtr Man 87 C6
Bampton Cumb 99 C7
Bampton Devon 10 B4
Bampton Oxon 38 D3
Bampton Grange Cumb 99 C7
Banavie Highld 139 B5
Banbury Oxon 52 E2
Bancffosfelen Carms 33 C5
Banchory Aberds 151 E5
Banchory-Devenick Aberds 151 D8
Bancycapel Carms 33 C5
Bancyfelin Carms 32 C4
Bancyffordd Carms 46 F3
Bandirran Perth 142 F2
Banff Aberds 160 B3
Bangor Gwyn 83 D5
Bangor-is-y-coed Wrex 73 E7
Bangor on Dee Racecourse Wrex 73 E7
Banham Norf 68 F3
Banham Zoo, Diss Norf 68 F3
Bank Hants 14 D3
Bank Newton N Yorks 94 D2
Bank Street Worcs 49 C8
Bankend Dumfries 107 C7
Bankfoot Perth 141 F7
Bankglen E Ayrs 113 C6
Bankhead Aberdeen 151 C7
Bankhead Aberds 151 D5
Banknock Falk 121 B7
Banks Cumb 109 C5
Banks Lancs 85 B4
Bankshill Dumfries 114 F4
Banningham Norf 81 E8
Banniskirk Ho. Highld 169 D6
Bannister Green Essex 42 B2
Bannockburn Stirl 133 E7
Banstead Sur 28 D3
Bantham Devon 6 E4
Banton N Lnrk 121 B7
Banwell N Som 23 D5
Banyard's Green Suff 57 B6
Bapchild Kent 30 C3
Bar Hill Cambs 54 C4
Barabhas W Isles 172 D6
Barabhas Iarach W Isles 172 D6
Barabhas Uarach W Isles 172 C6
Barachandroman Argyll 130 C2
Barassie S Ayrs 120 F3
Baravullin Argyll 130 B4
Barbaraville Highld 157 B8
Barber Booth Derbys 88 F2
Barbieston S Ayrs 112 C4
Barbon Cumb 99 F8
Barbridge Ches 74 D3
Barbrook Devon 21 E6
Barby Northants 52 B3
Barcaldine Argyll 138 E3
Barcaldine Sea Life Centre Argyll 130 A5
Barcheston Warks 51 F7
Barcombe E Sus 17 C8
Barcombe Cross E Sus 17 C8
Barden N Yorks 101 E6
Barden Scale N Yorks 94 D3
Bardennoch Dumfries 113 E5
Bardfield Saling Essex 42 B2
Bardister Shetland 174 F5
Bardney Lincs 78 C4
Bardon Leics 63 C8
Bardon Mill Northumb 109 C7
Bardowie E Dunb 121 B5
Bardrainney Invclyd 120 B3
Bardsea Cumb 92 B3
Bardsey W Yorks 95 E6
Bardwell Suff 56 B3
Bare Lancs 92 C4
Barfad Argyll 128 D3
Barford Norf 68 D4
Barford Warks 51 C7
Barford St John Oxon 52 F2
Barford St Martin Wilts 25 F5
Barford St Michael Oxon 52 F2
Barfrestone Kent 31 D6
Bargod = Bargoed Caerph 35 E5
Bargoed = Bargod Caerph 35 E5
Bargrennan Dumfries 105 B7
Barham Cambs 54 B2
Barham Kent 31 D6
Barham Suff 56 D5
Barharrow Dumfries 106 D3
Barhill Dumfries 106 C5
Barholm Lincs 65 C7
Barkby Leics 64 D3
Barkestone-le-Vale Leics 77 F7
Barkham Wokingham 27 C5
Barking London 41 F7
Barking Suff 56 D4
Barking Tye Suff 56 D4
Barkingside London 41 F7
Barkisland W Yorks 87 C8
Barkston Lincs 78 E2
Barkston N Yorks 95 F7
Barkway Herts 54 F4
Barlaston Staffs 75 F5
Barlavington W Sus 16 C3
Barlborough Derbys 76 B4
Barlby N Yorks 96 F2
Barlestone Leics 63 D8
Barley Herts 54 F4
Barley Lancs 93 E8
Barley Mow T & W 111 D5
Barleythorpe Rutland 64 D5
Barling Essex 43 F5
Barlow Derbys 76 B3
Barlow N Yorks 89 B7
Barlow T & W 110 C4
Barmby Moor E Yorks 96 E3
Barmby on the Marsh E Yorks 89 B7
Barmer Norf 80 D4
Barmoor Castle Northumb 125 F5
Barmoor Lane End Northumb 125 F6
Barmouth = Abermaw Gwyn 58 C3
Barmpton Darl 101 C8
Barmston E Yorks 97 D7
Barnack P'boro 65 D7
Barnacle Warks 63 F7
Barnard Castle Durham 101 C5
Barnard Gate Oxon 38 C4
Barnardiston Suff 55 E8
Barnbarroch Dumfries 106 D5
Barnburgh S Yorks 89 D5
Barnby Suff 69 F7
Barnby Dun S Yorks 89 D7
Barnby in the Willows Notts 77 D8
Barnby Moor Notts 89 F7
Barnes Street Kent 29 E7
Barnet London 41 E5
Barnetby le Wold N Lincs 90 D4
Barney Norf 81 D5
Barnham Suff 56 B2
Barnham W Sus 16 D3
Barnham Broom Norf 68 D3
Barnhead Angus 143 D6
Barnhill Ches 73 D8
Barnhill Dundee 142 F4
Barnhill Moray 158 D5
Barnhills Dumfries 104 B3
Barningham Durham 101 C5
Barningham Suff 56 B3
Barnoldby le Beck NE Lincs 91 D6
Barnoldswick Lancs 93 E8
Barns Green W Sus 16 B5
Barnsley Glos 37 D7
Barnsley S Yorks 88 D4
Barnstaple Devon 20 F4
Barnston Essex 42 C2
Barnston Mers 85 F3
Barnstone Notts 77 F7
Barnt Green Worcs 50 B5
Barnton Ches 74 B3
Barnton Edin 122 B4
Barnwell All Saints Northants 65 F7
Barnwell St Andrew Northants 65 F7
Barnwood Glos 37 C5
Barochreal Argyll 130 C4
Barons Cross Hereford 49 D6
Barr S Ayrs 112 E2
Barra Airport W Isles 171 K2
Barra Castle Aberds 151 B6
Barrachan Dumfries 105 E7
Barrack Aberds 161 D5
Barraglom W Isles 172 E4
Barrahormid Argyll 128 B2
Barran Argyll 130 C4
Barrapol Argyll 136 F1
Barras Aberds 151 F7
Barras Cumb 100 C3
Barrasford Northumb 110 B2
Barravullin Argyll 130 E4
Barregarrow I o M 84 D3
Barrhead E Renf 120 D4
Barrhill S Ayrs 112 F2
Barrington Cambs 54 E4
Barrington Som 11 C8
Barripper Corn 2 C5
Barrmill N Ayrs 120 D3
Barrock Highld 169 B7
Barrock Ho. Highld 169 C7
Barrow Lancs 93 F7
Barrow Rutland 65 C5
Barrow Suff 55 C8
Barrow Green Kent 30 C3
Barrow Gurney N Som 23 C7
Barrow Haven N Lincs 90 B4
Barrow-in-Furness Cumb 92 C2
Barrow Island Cumb 92 C1
Barrow Nook Lancs 86 D2
Barrow Street Wilts 24 F3
Barrow upon Humber N Lincs 90 B4
Barrow upon Soar Leics 64 C2
Barrow upon Trent Derbys 63 B7
Barroway Drove Norf 67 D5
Barrowburn Northumb 116 C4
Barrowby Lincs 77 F8
Barrowcliff N Yorks 103 F8
Barrowden Rutland 65 D6
Barrowford Lancs 93 F8
Barrows Green Ches 74 D3
Barrows Green Cumb 99 F7
Barrow's Green Mers 86 F3
Barry Angus 143 F5
Barry = Y Barri V Glam 22 C3
Barry Island V Glam 22 C3
Barsby Leics 64 C3
Barsham Suff 69 F6
Barston W Mid 51 B7
Bartestree Hereford 49 E7
Barthol Chapel Aberds 160 E5
Barthomley Ches 74 D4
Bartley Hants 14 C4
Bartley Green W Mid 62 F4
Bartlow Cambs 55 E6
Barton Cambs 54 D5
Barton Ches 73 D8
Barton Glos 37 B8
Barton Lancs 85 D4
Barton Lancs 92 F5
Barton N Yorks 101 D7
Barton Oxon 39 D5
Barton Torbay 7 C7
Barton Warks 51 D6
Barton Bendish Norf 67 D7
Barton Hartshorn Bucks 52 F4
Barton in Fabis Notts 76 F5
Barton in the Beans Leics 63 D7
Barton-le-Clay Beds 53 F8
Barton-le-Street N Yorks 96 B3
Barton-le-Willows N Yorks 96 C3
Barton Mills Suff 55 B8
Barton on Sea Hants 14 E3
Barton on the Heath Warks 51 F7
Barton St David Som 23 F7
Barton Seagrave Northants 53 B6
Barton Stacey Hants 26 E2
Barton Turf Norf 69 B6
Barton-under-Needwood Staffs 63 C5
Barton-upon-Humber N Lincs 90 B4
Barton Waterside N Lincs 90 B4
Barugh S Yorks 88 D4
Barway Cambs 55 B6
Barwell Leics 63 E8
Barwick Herts 41 C6
Barwick Som 12 C3
Barwick in Elmet W Yorks 95 F6
Baschurch Shrops 60 B4
Bascote Warks 52 C2
Basford Green Staffs 75 D6
Bashall Eaves Lancs 93 E6
Bashley Hants 14 E3
Basildon Essex 42 F3
Basingstoke Hants 26 D4
Baslow Derbys 76 B2
Bason Bridge Som 22 E5
Bassaleg Newport 35 F6
Bassenthwaite Cumb 108 F2
Bassett Soton 14 C5
Bassingbourn Cambs 54 E4
Bassingfield Notts 77 F6
Bassingham Lincs 78 C2
Bassingthorpe Lincs 65 B6
Basta Shetland 174 D7
Baston Lincs 65 C8
Bastwick Norf 69 C7
Baswick Steer E Yorks 97 E6
Batchworth Heath Herts 40 E3
Batcombe Dorset 12 D4
Batcombe Som 23 F8
Bate Heath Ches 74 B3
Bateman's, Burwash E Sus 18 C3
Batford Herts 40 C4
Bath Bath 24 C2
Bath Abbey Bath 24 C2
Bath Racecourse Bath 24 C2
Bathampton Bath 24 C2
Bathealton Som 11 B5
Batheaston Bath 24 C2
Bathford Bath 24 C2
Bathgate W Loth 122 C2
Bathley Notts 77 D7
Bathpool Corn 5 B7
Bathpool Som 11 B7
Bathville W Loth 122 C2
Batley W Yorks 88 B3
Batsford Glos 51 F6
Battersby N Yorks 102 D3
Battersea London 28 B3
Battisborough Cross Devon 6 E3
Battisford Suff 56 D4
Battisford Tye Suff 56 D4
Battle E Sus 18 D4
Battle Powys 48 F2
Battle Abbey E Sus 18 D4
Battledown Glos 37 B6
Battlefield Shrops 60 C5
Battlesbridge Essex 42 E3
Battlesden Beds 40 B2
Battlesea Green Suff 57 B6
Battleton Som 10 B4
Battram Leics 63 D8
Battramsley Hants 14 E4
Baughton Worcs 50 E3
Baughurst Hants 26 D3
Baulking Oxon 38 E3
Baumber Lincs 78 B5
Baunton Glos 37 D7
Baverstock Wilts 24 F5
Bawburgh Norf 68 D4
Bawdeswell Norf 81 E6
Bawdrip Som 22 F5
Bawdsey Suff 57 E7
Bawtry S Yorks 89 E7
Baxenden Lancs 87 B5
Baxterley Warks 63 E6
Baybridge Hants 15 B6
Baycliff Cumb 92 B2
Baydon Wilts 25 B7
Bayford Herts 41 D6
Bayford Som 12 B5
Bayles Cumb 109 E7
Baylham Suff 56 D5
Baynard's Green Oxon 39 B5
Bayston Hill Shrops 60 D4
Baythorn End Essex 55 E8
Bayton Worcs 49 B8
Beach Highld 138 D1
Beachampton Bucks 53 F5
Beachamwell Norf 67 D7
Beachans Moray 158 E4
Beacharr Argyll 118 B3
Beachborough Kent 19 B8
Beachley Glos 36 E2
Beacon Devon 11 D6
Beacon End Essex 43 B5
Beacon Hill Sur 27 F6
Beacon's Bottom Bucks 39 E7
Beaconsfield Bucks 40 F2
Beacrabhaic W Isles 173 J4
Beadlam N Yorks 102 F4
Beadlow Beds 54 F2
Beadnell Northumb 117 B8
Beaford Devon 9 C7
Beal Northumb 125 E6
Beal N Yorks 89 B6
Beale Park, Goring W Berks 26 B4
Beamhurst Staffs 75 F7
Beaminster Dorset 12 D2
Beamish Durham 110 D5
Beamish Open Air Museum, Stanley Durham 110 D5
Beamsley N Yorks 94 D3
Bean Kent 29 B6
Beanacre Wilts 24 C4
Beanley Northumb 117 C6
Beaquoy Orkney 176 D2
Bear Cross Bmouth 13 E8
Beardwood Blkburn 86 B4
Beare Green Sur 28 E2
Bearley Warks 51 C6
Bearnus Argyll 136 D4
Bearpark Durham 110 E5
Bearsbridge Northumb 109 D7
Bearsden E Dunb 120 B5
Bearsted Kent 29 D8
Bearstone Shrops 74 F4
Bearwood Hereford 49 D5
Bearwood Poole 13 E8
Bearwood W Mid 62 F4
Beattock Dumfries 114 D3
Beauchamp Roding Essex 42 C1
Beauchief S Yorks 88 F4
Beaufort Bl Gwent 35 C5
Beaufort Castle Highld 157 E6
Beaulieu Hants 14 D4
Beauly Highld 157 E6
Beaumaris Anglesey 83 D6
Beaumaris Castle Anglesey 83 D6
Beaumont Cumb 108 D3
Beaumont Essex 43 B7
Beaumont Hill Darl 101 C7
Beausale Warks 51 B7
Beauworth Hants 15 B6
Beaworthy Devon 9 E6
Beazley End Essex 42 B3
Bebington Mers 85 F4
Bebside Northumb 117 F8
Beccles Suff 69 E7
Becconsall Lancs 86 B2
Beck Foot Cumb 99 E8
Beck Hole N Yorks 103 D6
Beck Row Suff 55 B7
Beck Side Cumb 98 F4
Beckbury Shrops 61 D7
Beckenham London 28 C4
Beckermet Cumb 98 D2
Beckfoot Cumb 98 D3
Beckfoot Cumb 107 E7
Beckford Worcs 50 F4
Beckhampton Wilts 25 C5
Beckingham Lincs 77 D8
Beckingham Notts 89 F8
Beckington Som 24 D3
Beckley E Sus 19 C5
Beckley Hants 14 E3
Beckley Oxon 39 C5
Beckton London 41 F7
Beckwithshaw N Yorks 95 D5
Becontree London 41 F7
Bed-y-coedwr Gwyn 71 E8
Bedale N Yorks 101 F7
Bedburn Durham 110 F4
Bedchester Dorset 13 C6
Beddau Rhondda 34 F4
Beddgelert Gwyn 71 C6
Beddingham E Sus 17 D8
Beddington London 28 C4
Bedfield Suff 57 C6
Bedford Beds 53 D8
Bedgebury Pinetum Kent 18 B4
Bedham W Sus 16 B4
Bedhampton Hants 15 D8
Bedingfield Suff 57 C5
Bedlam N Yorks 95 C5
Bedlington Northumb 117 F8
Bedlington Station Northumb 117 F8
Bedlinog M Tydf 34 D4
Bedminster Bristol 23 B7
Bedmond Herts 40 D3
Bednall Staffs 62 C3
Bedrule Borders 116 C2
Bedstone Shrops 49 B5
Bedwas Caerph 35 F5
Bedworth Warks 63 F7
Bedworth Heath Warks 63 F7
Beeby Leics 64 D3
Beech Hants 26 F4
Beech Staffs 75 F5
Beech Hill Gtr Man 86 D3
Beech Hill W Berks 26 C4
Beechingstoke Wilts 25 D5
Beedon W Berks 26 B2
Beeford E Yorks 97 D7
Beeley Derbys 76 C2
Beelsby NE Lincs 91 D6
Beenham W Berks 26 C3
Beeny Corn 8 E3
Beer Devon 11 F7
Beer Hackett Dorset 12 C3
Beercrocombe Som 11 B8
Beesands Devon 7 E6
Beesby Lincs 91 F8
Beeson Devon 7 E6
Beeston Beds 54 E2
Beeston Ches 74 D2
Beeston Norf 68 C2
Beeston Notts 76 F5
Beeston W Yorks 95 F5
Beeston Castle Ches 74 D2
Beeston Regis Norf 81 C7
Beeswing Dumfries 107 C5
Beetham Cumb 92 B4
Beetley Norf 68 C2
Begbroke Oxon 38 C4
Begelly Pembs 32 D2
Beggar's Bush Powys 48 C4
Beguildy Powys 48 B3
Beighton Norf 69 D6
Beighton S Yorks 88 F5
Beighton Hill Derbys 76 D2
Beith N Ayrs 120 D3
Bekesbourne Kent 31 D5
Bekonscot Model Village, Beaconsfield Bucks 40 C2
Belaugh Norf 69 C5
Belbroughton Worcs 50 B4
Belchamp Otten Essex 56 E2
Belchamp St Paul Essex 55 E8
Belchamp Walter Essex 56 E2
Belchford Lincs 79 B5
Belford Northumb 125 F7
Belhaven E Loth 124 B2
Belhelvie Aberds 151 C8
Belhinnie Aberds 150 B3
Bell Bar Herts 41 D5
Bell Busk N Yorks 94 D2
Bell End Worcs 50 B4
Bell o'th'Hill Ches 74 E2
Bellabeg Aberds 150 C2
Bellamore S Ayrs 112 F2
Bellanoch Argyll 128 A2
Bellaty Angus 142 D2
Belleau Lincs 79 B7
Bellehiglash Moray 159 F5
Bellerby N Yorks 101 E6
Bellever Devon 6 B4
Belliehill Angus 143 C5
Bellingdon Bucks 40 D2
Bellingham Northumb 116 F4
Belloch Argyll 118 C3
Bellochantuy Argyll 118 C3
Bells Yew Green E Sus 18 B3
Bellsbank E Ayrs 112 D4
Bellshill N Lnrk 121 C7
Bellshill Northumb 125 F7
Bellspool Borders 122 F4
Bellsquarry W Loth 122 C3
Belmaduthy Highld 157 D7
Belmesthorpe Rutland 65 C7
Belmont Blkburn 86 C4
Belmont London 28 C3
Belmont S Ayrs 112 B3
Belmont Shetland 174 C7
Belnacraig Aberds 150 C2
Belowda Corn 4 C4
Belper Derbys 76 E3
Belper Lane End Derbys 76 E3
Belsay Northumb 110 B4
Belsay Hall Northumb 110 B3
Belses Borders 115 B8
Belsford Devon 7 D5
Belstead Suff 56 E5
Belston S Ayrs 112 B3
Belstone Devon 9 E8
Belthorn Lancs 86 B5
Beltinge Kent 31 C5
Beltoft N Lincs 90 D2
Belton Leics 63 B8
Belton Lincs 78 F2
Belton N Lincs 89 D8
Belton Norf 69 D7
Belton House, Grantham Lincs 78 F2
Belton in Rutland Rutland 64 D5
Beltring Kent 29 E7
Belts of Collonach Aberds 151 E5
Belvedere London 29 B5
Belvoir Leics 77 F8
Belvoir Leics 77 F8
Bembridge I o W 15 F7
Bemersyde Borders 123 F8
Bemerton Wilts 25 F6
Bempton E Yorks 97 B7
Ben Alder Lodge Highld 140 B2
Ben Armine Lodge Highld 164 C4
Ben Casgro W Isles 172 F7
Benacre Suff 69 F8
Benbecula Airport W Isles 170 E3
Benbuie Dumfries 113 E7
Benderloch Argyll 130 B5
Bendronaig Lodge Highld 155 G6
Benenden Kent 18 B5
Benfield Dumfries 105 C7
Bengate Norf 69 B6
Bengeworth Worcs 50 E5
Benhall Green Suff 57 C7
Benhall Street Suff 57 C7
Benholm Aberds 143 C8
Beningbrough N Yorks 95 D8
Beningbrough Hall N Yorks 95 D8
Benington Herts 41 B5
Benington Lincs 79 E6
Benllech Anglesey 82 C5
Benmore Argyll 129 B6
Benmore Stirl 132 B3
Benmore Lodge Highld 163 C7
Bennacott Corn 8 E4
Bennan N Ayrs 119 D6
Benniworth Lincs 91 F6
Benover Kent 29 E8
Bensham T & W 110 C5
Benslie N Ayrs 120 E3
Benson Oxon 39 E6
Bent Aberds 143 B6
Bent Gate Lancs 87 B5
Benthall Northumb 117 B8
Benthall Shrops 61 D6
Bentham Glos 37 C6
Benthoul Aberdeen 151 D7
Bentlawnt Shrops 60 D3
Bentley E Yorks 97 F6
Bentley Hants 27 E5
Bentley Suff 56 F5
Bentley S Yorks 89 D6
Bentley Warks 63 E6
Bentley Worcs 50 C4
Bentley Heath W Mid 51 B6
Benton Devon 21 F5
Bentpath Dumfries 115 E6
Bents W Loth 122 C2
Bentworth Hants 26 E4
Benvie Dundee 142 F3
Benwick Cambs 66 E3
Beoley Worcs 51 C5
Beoraidbeg Highld 145 D6
Bepton W Sus 16 C2
Berden Essex 41 B7
Bere Alston Devon 6 C2
Bere Ferrers Devon 6 C2
Bere Regis Dorset 13 E6
Berepper Corn 3 D5
Bergh Apton Norf 69 D6
Berinsfield Oxon 39 E5
Berkeley Glos 36 E3
Berkhamsted Herts 40 D2
Berkley Som 24 E3
Berkswell W Mid 51 B7
Bermondsey London 28 B4
Bernera Highld 155 H4
Bernice Argyll 129 A6
Bernisdale Highld 152 D5
Berrick Salome Oxon 39 E6
Berriedale Highld 165 B8
Berrier Cumb 99 B5
Berriew Powys 59 D8
Berrington Northumb 125 E6
Berrington Shrops 60 D5
Berrow Som 22 D5
Berrow Green Worcs 50 D2
Berry Down Cross Devon 20 E4
Berry Hill Glos 36 C2
Berry Hill Pembs 45 E2
Berry Pomeroy Devon 7 C6
Berryhillock Moray 160 B2
Berrynarbor Devon 20 E4
Bersham Wrex 73 E7
Berstane Orkney 176 E3
Berwick E Sus 18 E2
Berwick Bassett Wilts 25 B5
Berwick Hill Northumb 110 B4
Berwick St James Wilts 25 F5
Berwick St John Wilts 13 B7
Berwick St Leonard Wilts 24 F4
Berwick-upon-Tweed Northumb 125 D5
Bescar Lancs 85 C4
Besford Worcs 50 E4
Bessacarr S Yorks 89 D7
Bessels Leigh Oxon 38 D4
Bessingby E Yorks 97 C7
Bessingham Norf 81 D7
Bestbeech Hill E Sus 18 B3
Besthorpe Norf 68 E3
Besthorpe Notts 77 C8
Bestwood Nottingham 77 E5
Bestwood Village Notts 77 E5
Beswick E Yorks 97 E6
Betchworth Sur 28 E3
Beth Shalom Holocaust Centre, Laxton Notts 77 C7
Bethania Ceredig 46 C4
Bethania Gwyn 83 F6
Bethania Gwyn 71 C8
Bethel Anglesey 82 D3
Bethel Gwyn 82 E5
Bethel Gwyn 72 F3
Bethersden Kent 30 E3
Bethesda Gwyn 83 E6
Bethesda Pembs 32 C1
Bethlehem Carms 33 B7
Bethnal Green London 41 F6
Betley Staffs 74 E4
Betsham Kent 29 B7
Betteshanger Kent 31 D7
Bettiscombe Dorset 11 E8
Bettisfield Wrex 73 F8
Betton Shrops 60 D3
Betton Shrops 74 F3
Bettws Bridgend 34 F3
Bettws Mon 35 C6
Bettws Newport 35 E6
Bettws Cedewain Powys 59 E8
Bettws Gwerfil Goch Denb 72 E4
Bettws Ifan Ceredig 46 E2
Bettws Newydd Mon 35 D7
Bettws-y-crwyn Shrops 60 F2
Bettyhill Highld 168 C2
Betws Carms 33 C7
Betws Bledrws Ceredig 46 D4
Betws-Garmon Gwyn 82 F5
Betws-y-Coed Conwy 83 F7
Betws-yn-Rhos Conwy 72 B3
Beulah Ceredig 45 E4
Beulah Powys 47 D8
Bevendean Brighton 17 D7
Bevercotes Notts 77 B6
Beverley E Yorks 97 F6
Beverley Minster E Yorks 97 F6
Beverley Racecourse E Yorks 97 E6
Beverston Glos 37 E5
Bevington Glos 36 E3
Bewaldeth Cumb 108 F2
Bewcastle Cumb 109 B5
Bewdley Worcs 50 B2
Bewerley N Yorks 94 C4
Bewholme E Yorks 97 D7
Bexhill E Sus 18 E4
Bexley London 29 B5
Bexleyheath London 29 B5
Bexwell Norf 67 D6
Beyton Suff 56 C3
Bhaltos W Isles 172 E3
Bhatarsaigh W Isles 171 L2
Bibury Glos 37 D8
Bicester Oxon 39 B5
Bickenhall Som 11 C7
Bickenhill W Mid 63 F5
Bicker Lincs 78 F5
Bickershaw Gtr Man 86 D4
Bickerstaffe Lancs 86 D2
Bickerton Ches 74 D2
Bickerton N Yorks 95 D7
Bickington Devon 7 B5
Bickington Devon 20 F4
Bickleigh Devon 10 D4
Bickleigh Devon 6 C3
Bickleton Devon 20 F4
Bickley London 28 C5
Bickley Moss Ches 74 E2
Bicknacre Essex 42 D3
Bicknoller Som 22 F3
Bicknor Kent 30 D2
Bickton Hants 14 C2
Bicton Shrops 60 C4
Bicton Shrops 60 F2
Bicton Park Gardens Devon 11 F5
Bidborough Kent 29 E6
Biddenden Kent 19 B5
Biddenham Beds 53 E8
Biddestone Wilts 24 B3
Biddisham Som 23 D5
Biddlesden Bucks 52 E4
Biddlestone Northumb 117 D5
Biddulph Staffs 75 D5
Biddulph Moor Staffs 75 D6
Bideford Devon 9 B6
Bidford-on-Avon Warks 51 D6
Bidston Mers 85 E3
Bielby E Yorks 96 E3
Bieldside Aberdeen 151 D7
Bierley I o W 15 G6
Bierley W Yorks 94 F4
Bierton Bucks 39 C8
Big Pit National Mining Museum, Blaenavon Torf 35 D6
Big Sand Highld 154 C3
Bigbury Devon 6 E4
Bigbury on Sea Devon 6 E4
Bigby Lincs 90 D4
Biggar Cumb 92 C1
Biggar S Lnrk 122 F3
Biggin Derbys 75 D8
Biggin Derbys 76 E2
Biggin N Yorks 95 F8
Biggin Hill London 28 D5
Biggings Shetland 175 G3
Biggleswade Beds 54 E2
Bighouse Highld 168 C3
Bighton Hants 26 F4
Bignor W Sus 16 C3
Bigton Shetland 175 L5
Bilberry Corn 4 C5
Bilborough Nottingham 76 E5
Bilbrook Som 22 E2
Bilbrough N Yorks 95 E8
Bilbster Highld 169 D7
Bildershaw Durham 101 B7
Bildeston Suff 56 E3
Billericay Essex 42 E2
Billesdon Leics 64 D4
Billesley Warks 51 D6
Billingborough Lincs 78 F4
Billinge Mers 86 D3
Billingford Norf 81 E6
Billingham Stockton 102 B2
Billinghay Lincs 78 D4
Billingley S Yorks 88 D5
Billingshurst W Sus 16 B4
Billingsley Shrops 61 F7
Billington Beds 40 B2
Billington Lancs 93 F7
Billockby Norf 69 C7
Billown Motor Racing Circuit I o M 84 F2
Billy Row Durham 110 F4
Bilsborrow Lancs 92 F5
Bilsby Lincs 79 B7
Bilsham W Sus 16 D3
Bilsington Kent 19 B7
Bilson Green Glos 36 C3
Bilsthorpe Notts 77 C6
Bilsthorpe Moor Notts 77 D6
Bilston Midloth 123 C5
Bilston W Mid 62 E3
Bilstone Leics 63 D7

Bilting Kent 30 E4
Bilton E Yorks 97 F7
Bilton Northumb 117 C8
Bilton Warks 52 B2
Bilton in Ainsty N Yorks 95 E7
Bimbister Orkney 176 E2
Binbrook Lincs 91 E6
Binchester Blocks Durham 110 F5
Bincombe Dorset 12 F4
Bindal Highld 165 F6
Binegar Som 23 E8
Binfield Brack 27 B6
Binfield Heath Oxon 26 B5
Bingfield Northumb 110 B2
Bingham Notts 77 F7
Bingley W Yorks 94 F4
Bings Heath Shrops 60 C5
Binham Norf 81 D5
Binley Hants 26 D2
Binley W Mid 51 B8
Binley Woods Warks 51 B8
Binniehill Falk 121 B8
Binsoe N Yorks 94 B5
Binstead I o W 15 E6
Binsted Hants 27 E5
Binton Warks 51 D6
Bintree Norf 81 E6
Binweston Shrops 60 D3
Birch Essex 43 C5
Birch Gtr Man 87 D6
Birch Green Essex 43 C5
Birch Heath Ches 74 C2
Birch Hill Ches 74 B2
Birch Vale Derbys 87 F8
Bircham Newton Norf 80 D3
Bircham Tofts Norf 80 D3
Birchanger Essex 41 B8
Birchencliffe W Yorks 88 C2
Bircher Hereford 49 C6
Birchfield Highld 149 B5
Birchgrove Cardiff 22 B3
Birchgrove Swansea 33 E8
Birchington Kent 31 C6
Birchmoor Warks 63 D6
Birchover Derbys 76 C2
Birchwood Lincs 78 C2
Birchwood Warr 86 E4
Bircotes Notts 89 E7
Birdbrook Essex 55 E8
Birdforth N Yorks 95 B7
Birdham W Sus 16 E2
Birdholme Derbys 76 C3
Birdingbury Warks 52 C2
Birdland Park, Bourton-on-the-Water Glos 38 B1
Birdlip Glos 37 C6
Birds Edge W Yorks 88 D3
Birdsall N Yorks 96 C4
Birdsgreen Shrops 61 F7
Birdsmoor Gate Dorset 11 D8
Birdston E Dunb 121 B6
Birdwell S Yorks 88 D4
Birdwood Glos 36 C4
Birgham Borders 124 F3
Birkby N Yorks 101 D8
Birkdale Mers 85 C4
Birkenhead Mers 85 F4
Birkenhills Aberds 160 D4
Birkenshaw N Lnrk 121 C6
Birkenshaw W Yorks 88 B3
Birkhall Aberds 150 E2
Birkhill Angus 142 F3
Birkhill Dumfries 114 C5
Birkholme Lincs 65 B6
Birkin N Yorks 89 B6
Birley Hereford 49 D6
Birling Kent 29 C7
Birling Northumb 117 D8
Birling Gap E Sus 18 F2
Birlingham Worcs 50 E4
Birmingham W Mid 62 F4
Birmingham Botanical Gardens W Mid 62 F4
Birmingham International Airport W Mid 63 F5
Birmingham Museum and Art Gallery W Mid 62 F4
Birmingham Museum of Science and Technology W Mid 62 F4
Birnam Perth 141 E7
Birse Aberds 150 E4
Birsemore Aberds 150 E4
Birstall Leics 64 D2
Birstall W Yorks 88 B3
Birstwith N Yorks 94 D5
Birthorpe Lincs 78 F4
Birtley Hereford 49 C5
Birtley Northumb 109 B8
Birtley T & W 111 D5
Birts Street Worcs 50 F2
Bisbrooke Rutland 65 E5
Biscathorpe Lincs 91 F6
Biscot Luton 40 B3
Bish Mill Devon 10 B2
Bisham Windsor 39 F8
Bishampton Worcs 50 D4
Bishop Auckland Durham 101 B7
Bishop Burton E Yorks 97 F5
Bishop Middleham Durham 111 F6
Bishop Monkton N Yorks 95 C6
Bishop Norton Lincs 90 E3
Bishop Sutton Bath 23 D7
Bishop Thornton N Yorks 95 C5
Bishop Wilton E Yorks 96 D3
Bishopbridge Lincs 90 E4
Bishopbriggs E Dunb 121 C6
Bishopmill Moray 159 C6
Bishops Cannings Wilts 24 C5
Bishop's Castle Shrops 60 F3
Bishop's Caundle Dorset 12 C4
Bishop's Cleeve Glos 37 B6
Bishops Frome Hereford 49 E8
Bishop's Green Essex 42 C2
Bishop's Hull Som 11 B7
Bishop's Itchington Warks 51 D8
Bishops Lydeard Som 11 B6
Bishops Nympton Devon 10 B2
Bishop's Offley Staffs 61 B7
Bishop's Stortford Herts 41 B7
Bishop's Sutton Hants 26 F4
Bishop's Tachbrook Warks 51 C8
Bishops Tawton Devon 20 F4
Bishop's Waltham Hants 15 C6
Bishop's Wood Staffs 62 D2
Bishopsbourne Kent 31 D5
Bishopsteignton Devon 7 B7
Bishopstoke Hants 15 C5
Bishopston Swansea 33 F6
Bishopstone Bucks 39 C8
Bishopstone E Sus 17 D8
Bishopstone Hereford 49 E6
Bishopstone Swindon 38 F2
Bishopstone Wilts 13 B8
Bishopstrow Wilts 24 E3
Bishopswood Som 11 C7
Bishopsworth Bristol 23 C7
Bishopthorpe York 95 E8
Bishopton Darl 102 B1
Bishopton Dumfries 105 E8
Bishopton N Yorks 95 B6
Bishopton Renfs 120 B4
Bishopton Warks 51 D6
Bishton Newport 35 F7
Bisley Glos 37 D6
Bisley Sur 27 D7
Bispham Blkpool 92 E3
Bispham Green Lancs 86 C2
Bissoe Corn 3 B6
Bisterne Close Hants 14 D3
Bitchfield Lincs 65 B6
Bittadon Devon 20 E4
Bittaford Devon 6 D4
Bittering Norf 68 C2
Bitterley Shrops 49 B7
Bitterne Soton 15 C5
Bitteswell Leics 64 F2
Bitton S Glos 23 C8
Bix Oxon 39 F7
Bixter Shetland 175 H5
Blaby Leics 64 E2
Black Bourton Oxon 38 D2
Black Callerton T & W 110 C4
Black Clauchrie S Ayrs 112 F2
Black Corries Lodge Highld 139 D6
Black Crofts Argyll 130 B5
Black Dog Devon 10 D3
Black Heddon Northumb 110 B3
Black Lane Gtr Man 87 D5
Black Marsh Shrops 60 E3
Black Mount Argyll 139 E6
Black Notley Essex 42 B3
Black Pill Swansea 33 E7
Black Tar Pembs 44 E4
Black Torrington Devon 9 D6
Blackacre Dumfries 114 E3
Blackadder West Borders 124 D4
Blackawton Devon 7 D6
Blackborough Devon 11 D5
Blackborough End Norf 67 C6
Blackboys E Sus 18 C2
Blackbrook Derbys 76 E3
Blackbrook Mers 86 E3
Blackbrook Staffs 74 F4
Blackburn Aberds 160 E2
Blackburn Aberds 151 C7
Blackburn Blkburn 86 B4
Blackburn W Loth 122 C2
Blackcraig Dumfries 113 F7
Blackden Heath Ches 74 B4
Blackdog Aberds 151 C8
Blackfell T & W 111 D5
Blackfield Hants 14 D5
Blackford Cumb 108 C3
Blackford Perth 133 D7
Blackford Som 23 E6
Blackford Som 12 B4
Blackfordby Leics 63 C7
Blackgang I o W 15 G5
Blackgang Chine Fantasy I o W 15 G5
Blackhall Colliery Durham 111 F7
Blackhall Mill T & W 110 D4
Blackhall Rocks Durham 111 F7
Blackham E Sus 29 F5
Blackhaugh Borders 123 F7
Blackheath Essex 43 B6
Blackheath Suff 57 B8
Blackheath Sur 27 E8
Blackheath W Mid 62 F3
Blackhill Aberds 161 D7
Blackhill Aberds 161 C7
Blackhill Highld 152 D4
Blackhills Highld 158 D3
Blackhills Moray 159 D6
Blackhorse S Glos 23 B8
Blackland Wilts 24 C5
Blacklaw Aberds 160 C3
Blackley Gtr Man 87 D6
Blacklunans Perth 142 C1
Blackmill Bridgend 34 F3
Blackmoor Hants 27 F5
Blackmoor Gate Devon 21 E5
Blackmore Essex 42 D2
Blackmore End Essex 55 F8
Blackmore End Herts 40 C4
Blackness Falk 122 B3
Blacknest Hants 27 E5
Blacko Lancs 93 E8
Blackpool Blkpool 92 F3
Blackpool Devon 7 E6
Blackpool Pembs 32 C1
Blackpool Airport Lancs 92 F3
Blackpool Gate Cumb 108 B5
Blackpool Pleasure Beach Blkpool 92 F3
Blackpool Sea Life Centre Blkpool 92 F3
Blackpool Tower Blkpool 92 F3
Blackpool Zoo Park Blkpool 92 F3
Blackridge W Loth 121 C8
Blackrock Argyll 126 C3
Blackrock Mon 35 C6
Blackrod Gtr Man 86 C4
Blackshaw Dumfries 107 C7
Blackshaw Head W Yorks 87 B7
Blacksmith's Green Suff 56 C5
Blackstone W Sus 17 C6
Blackthorn Oxon 39 C6
Blackthorpe Suff 56 C3
Blacktoft E Yorks 90 B2
Blacktop Aberdeen 151 D7
Blacktown Newport 35 F6
Blackwall Tunnel London 41 F6
Blackwater Corn 3 B6
Blackwater Hants 27 D6
Blackwater I o W 15 F6
Blackwaterfoot N Ayrs 119 D5
Blackwell Darl 101 C7
Blackwell Derbys 75 B8
Blackwell Derbys 76 D4
Blackwell Warks 51 E7
Blackwell Worcs 50 B4
Blackwell W Sus 28 F4
Blackwood S Lnrk 121 E7
Blackwood = Coed Duon Caerph 35 E5
Blackwood Hill Staffs 75 D6
Blacon Ches 73 C7
Bladnoch Dumfries 105 D8
Bladon Oxon 38 C4
Blaen-gwynfi Neath 34 E2
Blaen-waun Carms 32 B3
Blaen-y-coed Carms 32 B4
Blaen-y-Cwm Denb 72 F4
Blaen-y-Cwm Gwyn 71 E8
Blaen-y-cwm Powys 59 B7
Blaenannerch Ceredig 45 E4
Blaenau Ffestiniog Gwyn 71 C8
Blaenavon Torf 35 D6
Blaencelyn Ceredig 46 D2
Blaendyryn Powys 47 F8
Blaenffos Pembs 45 F3
Blaengarw Bridgend 34 E3
Blaengwrach Neath 34 D2
Blaenpennal Ceredig 46 C5
Blaenplwyf Ceredig 46 B4
Blaenporth Ceredig 45 E4
Blaenrhondda Rhondda 34 D3
Blaenycwm Ceredig 47 B7
Blagdon N Som 23 D7
Blagdon Torbay 7 C6
Blagdon Hill Som 11 C7
Blagill Cumb 109 E7
Blaguegate Lancs 86 D2
Blaich Highld 138 B4
Blain Highld 137 B7
Blaina Bl Gwent 35 D6
Blair Atholl Perth 141 C5
Blair Castle, Blair Atholl Perth 141 C5
Blair Drummond Stirl 133 E6
Blair Drummond Safari Park, Dunblane Stirl 133 E6
Blairbeg N Ayrs 119 C7
Blairdaff Aberds 151 C5
Blairglas Argyll 129 B8
Blairgowrie Perth 142 E1
Blairhall Fife 134 F2
Blairingone Perth 133 E8
Blairland N Ayrs 120 E3
Blairlogie Stirl 133 E7
Blairlomond Argyll 131 F7
Blairmore Argyll 129 B6
Blairnamarrow Moray 149 C8
Blairquhosh Stirl 132 F4
Blair's Ferry Argyll 128 D4
Blairskaith E Dunb 121 B5
Blaisdon Glos 36 C4
Blakebrook Worcs 50 B3
Blakedown Worcs 50 B3
Blakelaw Borders 124 F3
Blakeley Staffs 62 E2
Blakeley Lane Staffs 75 E6
Blakemere Hereford 49 E5
Blakeney Glos 36 D3
Blakeney Norf 81 C6
Blakeney Point NNR Norf 81 C6
Blakenhall Ches 74 E4
Blakenhall W Mid 62 E3
Blakeshall Worcs 62 F2
Blakesley Northants 52 D4
Blanchland Northumb 110 D2
Bland Hill N Yorks 94 D5
Blandford Forum Dorset 13 D6
Blandford St Mary Dorset 13 D6
Blanefield Stirl 121 B5
Blankney Lincs 78 C3
Blantyre S Lnrk 121 D6
Blar a'Chaorainn Highld 139 C5
Blaran Argyll 130 D4
Blarghour Argyll 131 D5
Blarmachfoldach Highld 138 C4
Blarnalearoch Highld 163 E5
Blashford Hants 14 D2
Blaston Leics 64 E5
Blatherwycke Northants 65 E6
Blawith Cumb 98 F4
Blaxhall Suff 57 D7
Blaxton S Yorks 89 D7
Blaydon T & W 110 C4
Bleadon N Som 22 D5
Bleak Hey Nook Gtr Man 87 D8
Blean Kent 30 C5
Bleasby Lincs 90 F5
Bleasby Notts 77 E7
Bleasdale Lancs 93 E5
Bleatarn Cumb 100 C2
Blebocraigs Fife 135 C6
Bleddfa Powys 48 C4
Bledington Glos 38 B2
Bledlow Bucks 39 D7
Bledlow Ridge Bucks 39 E7
Blegbie E Loth 123 C7
Blencarn Cumb 109 F6
Blencogo Cumb 107 E8
Blendworth Hants 15 C8
Blenheim Palace, Woodstock Oxon 38 C4
Blenheim Park Norf 80 D4
Blennerhasset Cumb 107 E8
Blervie Castle Moray 158 D4
Bletchingdon Oxon 39 C5
Bletchingley Sur 28 D4
Bletchley M Keynes 53 F6
Bletchley Shrops 74 F3
Bletherston Pembs 32 B1
Bletsoe Beds 53 D8
Blewbury Oxon 39 F5
Blickling Norf 81 E7
Blickling Hall, Aylsham Norf 81 E7
Blidworth Notts 77 D5
Blindburn Northumb 116 C4
Blindcrake Cumb 107 F8
Blindley Heath Sur 28 E4
Blisland Corn 5 B6
Bliss Gate Worcs 50 B2
Blissford Hants 14 C2
Blisworth Northants 52 D5
Blithbury Staffs 62 B4
Blitterlees Cumb 107 D8
Blockley Glos 51 F6
Blofield Norf 69 D6
Blofield Heath Norf 69 C6
Blo'Norton Norf 56 B4
Bloomfield Borders 115 B8
Blore Staffs 75 E8
Blount's Green Staffs 75 F7
Blowick Mers 85 C4
Bloxham Oxon 52 F2
Bloxholm Lincs 78 D3
Bloxwich W Mid 62 D3
Bloxworth Dorset 13 E6
Blubberhouses N Yorks 94 D4
Blue Anchor Som 22 E2
Blue Anchor Swansea 33 E6
Blue Planet Aquarium Ches 73 B8
Blue Row Essex 43 C6
Blundeston Suff 69 E8
Blunham Beds 54 D2
Blunsdon St Andrew Swindon 37 F8
Bluntington Worcs 50 B3
Bluntisham Cambs 54 B4
Blunts Corn 5 C8
Blyborough Lincs 90 E3
Blyford Suff 57 B8
Blymhill Staffs 62 C2
Blyth Notts 89 F7
Blyth Northumb 117 F9
Blyth Bridge Borders 122 E4
Blythburgh Suff 57 B8
Blythe Borders 123 E8
Blythe Bridge Staffs 75 E6
Blyton Lincs 90 E2
Boarhills Fife 135 C7
Boarhunt Hants 15 D7
Boars Head Gtr Man 86 D3
Boars Hill Oxon 38 D4
Boarshead E Sus 18 B2
Boarstall Bucks 39 C6
Boasley Cross Devon 9 E6
Boat of Garten Highld 148 C5
Boath Highld 157 B6
Bobbing Kent 30 C2
Bobbington Staffs 62 E2
Bobbingworth Essex 41 D8
Bocaddon Corn 5 D6
Bochastle Stirl 132 D5
Bocking Essex 42 B3
Bocking Churchstreet Essex 42 B3
Boddam Aberds 161 D8
Boddam Shetland 175 M5
Boddington Glos 37 B5
Bodedern Anglesey 82 C3
Bodelwyddan Denb 72 B4
Bodenham Hereford 49 D7
Bodenham Wilts 14 B2
Bodenham Arboretum and Earth Centre Worcs 62 F2
Bodenham Moor Hereford 49 D7
Bodermid Gwyn 70 E2
Bodewryd Anglesey 82 B3
Bodfari Denb 72 B4
Bodffordd Anglesey 82 D4
Bodham Norf 81 C7
Bodiam E Sus 18 C4
Bodiam Castle E Sus 18 C4
Bodicote Oxon 52 F2
Bodieve Corn 4 B4
Bodinnick Corn 5 D6
Bodle Street Green E Sus 18 D3
Bodmin Corn 5 C5
Bodnant Garden, Colwyn Bay Conwy 83 D8
Bodney Norf 67 E8
Bodorgan Anglesey 82 E3
Bodsham Kent 30 E5
Boduan Gwyn 70 D4
Bodymoor Heath Warks 63 E5
Bogallan Highld 157 D7
Bogbrae Aberds 161 E7
Bogend Borders 124 E3
Bogend S Ayrs 120 F3
Boghall W Loth 122 C2
Boghead S Lnrk 121 E7
Bogmoor Moray 159 C7
Bogniebrae Aberds 160 D2
Bognor Regis W Sus 16 E3
Bograxie Aberds 151 C6
Bogside N Lnrk 121 D8
Bogton Aberds 160 C3
Bogue Dumfries 113 F6
Bohenie Highld 147 F5
Bohortha Corn 3 C7
Bohuntine Highld 147 F5
Boirseam W Isles 173 K3
Bojewyan Corn 2 C2
Bolam Durham 101 B6
Bolam Northumb 117 F6
Bolberry Devon 6 F4
Bold Heath Mers 86 F3
Boldon T & W 111 C6
Boldon Colliery T & W 111 C6
Boldre Hants 14 E4
Boldron Durham 101 C5
Bole Notts 89 F8
Bolehill Derbys 76 D2
Boleside Borders 123 F7
Bolham Devon 10 C4
Bolham Water Devon 11 C6
Bolingey Corn 4 D2
Bollington Ches 75 B6
Bollington Cross Ches 75 B6
Bolney W Sus 17 B6
Bolnhurst Beds 53 D8
Bolshan Angus 143 D6
Bolsover Derbys 76 B4
Bolsterstone S Yorks 88 E3
Bolstone Hereford 49 F7
Boltby N Yorks 102 F2
Bolter End Bucks 39 E7
Bolton Cumb 99 B8
Bolton E Loth 123 B8
Bolton E Yorks 96 D3
Bolton Gtr Man 86 D5
Bolton Northumb 117 C7
Bolton Abbey N Yorks 94 D3
Bolton Abbey, Skipton N Yorks 94 D3
Bolton Bridge N Yorks 94 D3
Bolton-by-Bowland Lancs 93 E7
Bolton Castle, Leyburn N Yorks 101 E5
Bolton le Sands Lancs 92 C4
Bolton Low Houses Cumb 108 E2
Bolton-on-Swale N Yorks 101 E7
Bolton Percy N Yorks 95 E8
Bolton Town End Lancs 92 C4
Bolton upon Dearne S Yorks 89 D5
Boltonfellend Cumb 108 C4
Boltongate Cumb 108 E2
Bolventor Corn 5 B6
Bomere Heath Shrops 60 C4
Bon-y-maen Swansea 33 E7
Bonar Bridge Highld 164 E3
Bonawe Argyll 131 B6
Bonby N Lincs 90 C4
Boncath Pembs 45 F4
Bonchester Bridge Borders 115 C8
Bonchurch I o W 15 G6
Bondleigh Devon 9 D8
Bonehill Devon 6 B5
Bonehill Staffs 63 D5
Bo'ness Falk 133 F8
Bonhill W Dunb 120 B3
Boningale Shrops 62 D2
Bonjedward Borders 116 B2
Bonkle N Lnrk 121 D8
Bonnavoulin Highld 137 C6
Bonnington Edin 122 C4
Bonnington Kent 19 B7
Bonnybank Fife 135 D5
Bonnybridge Falk 133 F7
Bonnykelly Aberds 161 C5
Bonnyrigg and Lasswade Midloth 123 C6
Bonnyton Aberds 160 E3
Bonnyton Angus 142 F3
Bonnyton Angus 143 D6
Bonsall Derbys 76 D2
Bonskeid House Perth 141 C5
Bont Mon 35 C7
Bont-Dolgadfan Powys 59 D5
Bont-goch Ceredig 58 F3
Bont-newydd Conwy 72 B4
Bont Newydd Gwyn 71 C8
Bont Newydd Gwyn 71 E8
Bontddu Gwyn 58 C3
Bonthorpe Lincs 79 B7
Bontnewydd Ceredig 46 C5
Bontnewydd Gwyn 82 F4
Bontuchel Denb 72 D4
Bonvilston V Glam 22 B2
Booker Bucks 39 E8
Boon Borders 123 E8
Boosbeck Redcar 102 C4
Boot Cumb 98 D3
Boot Street Suff 57 E6
Booth W Yorks 87 B8
Booth Wood W Yorks 87 C8
Boothby Graffoe Lincs 78 D2
Boothby Pagnell Lincs 78 F2
Boothen Stoke 75 E5
Boothferry E Yorks 89 B8
Boothville Northants 53 C5
Bootle Cumb 98 F3
Bootle Mers 85 E4
Booton Norf 81 E7
Boquhan Stirl 132 F4
Boraston Shrops 49 B8
Borden Kent 30 C2
Borden W Sus 16 B2
Bordley N Yorks 94 C2
Bordon Hants 27 F6
Bordon Camp Hants 27 F5
Boreham Essex 42 D3
Boreham Wilts 24 E3
Boreham Street E Sus 18 D3
Borehamwood Herts 40 E4
Boreland Dumfries 114 E4
Boreland Stirl 140 F2
Borgh W Isles 171 K2
Borgh W Isles 173 K2
Borghastan W Isles 172 D5
Borgie Highld 167 D8
Borgue Dumfries 106 E3
Borgue Highld 165 B8
Borley Essex 56 E2
Bornais W Isles 171 H3
Bornesketaig Highld 152 B4
Borness Dumfries 106 E3
Borough Green Kent 29 D7
Boroughbridge N Yorks 95 C6
Borras Head Wrex 73 D7
Borreraig Highld 152 D2
Borrobol Lodge Highld 165 B5
Borrowash Derbys 76 F4
Borrowby N Yorks 102 F2
Borrowdale Cumb 98 C4
Borrowfield Aberds 151 E7
Borth Ceredig 58 E3
Borth-y-Gest Gwyn 71 D6
Borthwickbrae Borders 115 C7
Borthwickshiels Borders 115 C7
Borve Highld 152 E5
Borve Lodge W Isles 173 J3
Borwick Lancs 92 B5
Bosavern Corn 2 C2
Bosbury Hereford 49 E8
Boscastle Corn 8 E3
Boscombe Bmouth 14 E2
Boscombe Wilts 25 F7
Boscoppa Corn 4 D5
Bosham W Sus 16 D2
Bosherston Pembs 44 F4
Boskenna Corn 2 D3
Bosley Ches 75 C6
Bossall N Yorks 96 C3
Bossiney Corn 8 F2
Bossingham Kent 31 E5
Bossington Som 21 E7
Bostock Green Ches 74 C3
Boston Lincs 79 E6
Boston Long Hedges Lincs 79 E6
Boston Spa W Yorks 95 E7
Boston West Lincs 79 E5
Boswinger Corn 3 B8
Botallack Corn 2 C2
Botany Bay London 41 E5
Botcherby Cumb 108 D4
Botcheston Leics 63 D8
Botesdale Suff 56 B4
Bothal Northumb 117 F8
Bothamsall Notts 77 B6
Bothel Cumb 107 F8
Bothenhampton Dorset 12 E2
Bothwell S Lnrk 121 D7
Botley Bucks 40 D2
Botley Hants 15 C6
Botley Oxon 38 D4
Botolph Claydon Bucks 39 B7
Botolphs W Sus 17 D5
Bottacks Highld 157 C5
Bottesford Leics 77 F8
Bottesford N Lincs 90 D2
Bottisham Cambs 55 C6
Bottlesford Wilts 25 D6
Bottom Boat W Yorks 88 B4
Bottom House Staffs 75 D7
Bottom of Hutton Lancs 86 B2
Bottom o'th'Moor Gtr Man 86 C4
Bottomcraig Fife 135 B5
Botusfleming Corn 6 C2
Botwnnog Gwyn 70 D3
Bough Beech Kent 29 E5
Boughrood Powys 48 F3
Boughspring Glos 36 E2
Boughton Norf 67 D6
Boughton Notts 77 C6
Boughton Northants 53 C5
Boughton Aluph Kent 30 E4
Boughton Lees Kent 30 E4
Boughton Malherbe Kent 30 E2
Boughton Monchelsea Kent 29 D8
Boughton Street Kent 30 D4
Boulby Redcar 103 C5
Boulden Shrops 60 F5
Boulmer Northumb 117 C8
Boulston Pembs 44 D4
Boultenstone Aberds 150 C3
Boultham Lincs 78 C2
Bourn Cambs 54 D4
Bourne Lincs 65 B7
Bourne End Beds 53 E7
Bourne End Bucks 40 F1
Bourne End Herts 40 D3
Bournemouth Bmouth 13 E8
Bournemouth International Airport Dorset 14 E2
Bournes Green Glos 37 D6
Bournes Green Sthend 43 F5
Bournheath Worcs 50 B4
Bournmoor Durham 111 D6
Bournville W Mid 62 F4
Bourton Dorset 24 F2
Bourton N Som 23 C5
Bourton Oxon 38 F2
Bourton Shrops 61 E5
Bourton on Dunsmore Warks 52 B2
Bourton on the Hill Glos 51 F6
Bourton-on-the-Water Glos 38 B1
Bousd Argyll 136 B3
Boustead Hill Cumb 108 D2
Bouth Cumb 99 F5
Bouthwaite N Yorks 94 B4
Boveney Bucks 27 B7
Boverton V Glam 21 C8
Bovey Tracey Devon 7 B6
Bovingdon Herts 40 D3
Bovingdon Green Bucks 39 F8
Bovingdon Green Herts 40 D3
Bovinger Essex 41 D8
Bovington Camp Dorset 13 F6
Bow Borders 123 E7
Bow Devon 10 D2
Bow Orkney 176 G2
Bow Brickhill M Keynes 53 F7
Bow of Fife Fife 134 C5
Bow Street Ceredig 58 F3
Bowbank Durham 100 B4
Bowburn Durham 111 F6
Bowcombe I o W 15 F5
Bowd Devon 11 E6
Bowden Borders 123 F8
Bowden Devon 7 E6
Bowden Hill Wilts 24 C4
Bowderdale Cumb 100 D1
Bowdon Gtr Man 87 F5
Bower Northumb 116 F3
Bower Hinton Som 12 C2
Bowerchalke Wilts 13 B8
Bowerhill Wilts 24 C4
Bowermadden Highld 169 C7
Bowers Gifford Essex 42 F3
Bowershall Fife 134 E2
Bowertower Highld 169 C7
Bowes Durham 100 C4
Bowgreave Lancs 92 E4
Bowgreen Gtr Man 87 F5
Bowhill Borders 115 B7
Bowhouse Dumfries 107 C7
Bowland Bridge Cumb 99 F6
Bowley Hereford 49 D7
Bowlhead Green Sur 27 F7
Bowling W Dunb 120 B4
Bowling W Yorks 94 F4
Bowling Bank Wrex 73 E7
Bowling Green Worcs 50 D3
Bowmanstead Cumb 99 E5
Bowmore Argyll 126 D3
Bowness-on-Solway Cumb 108 C2
Bowness-on-Windermere Cumb 99 E6
Bowood House and Gardens, Calne Wilts 24 C4
Bowsden Northumb 125 E5
Bowside Lodge Highld 168 C3
Bowston Cumb 99 E6
Bowthorpe Norf 68 D4
Box Glos 37 D5
Box Wilts 24 C3
Box End Beds 53 E8
Boxbush Glos 36 C4
Boxford Suff 56 E3
Boxford W Berks 26 B2
Boxgrove W Sus 16 D3
Boxley Kent 29 D8
Boxmoor Herts 40 D3
Boxted Essex 56 F4
Boxted Suff 56 D2
Boxted Cross Essex 56 F4
Boxted Heath Essex 56 F4
Boxworth Cambs 54 C4
Boxworth End Cambs 54 C4
Boyden Gate Kent 31 C6
Boylestone Derbys 75 F8
Boyndie Aberds 160 B3
Boynton E Yorks 97 C7
Boysack Angus 143 E6
Boyton Corn 8 E5
Boyton Suff 57 E7
Boyton Wilts 24 F4
Boyton Cross Essex 42 D2
Boyton End Suff 55 E8
Bozeat Northants 53 D7
Braaid I o M 84 E3
Braal Castle Highld 169 C6
Brabling Green Suff 57 C6
Brabourne Kent 30 E4
Brabourne Lees Kent 30 E4
Brabster Highld 169 C8
Bracadale Highld 153 F4
Bracara Highld 145 D7
Braceborough Lincs 65 C7
Bracebridge Lincs 78 C2
Bracebridge Heath Lincs 78 C2
Bracebridge Low Fields Lincs 78 C2
Braceby Lincs 78 F3
Bracewell Lancs 93 E8
Brackenfield Derbys 76 D3
Brackenthwaite Cumb 108 E2
Brackenthwaite N Yorks 95 D5
Brackletter Highld 146 F4
Brackley Argyll 118 B4
Brackley Northants 52 F3
Brackloch Highld 163 B5
Bracknell Brack 27 C6
Braco Perth 133 D7
Bracobrae Moray 160 C2
Bracon Ash Norf 68 E4
Bracorina Highld 145 D7
Bradbourne Derbys 76 D2
Bradbury Durham 101 B8
Bradda I o M 84 F1
Bradden Northants 52 E4
Braddock Corn 5 C6
Bradeley Stoke 75 D5
Bradenham Bucks 39 E8
Bradenham Norf 68 D2
Bradenstoke Wilts 24 B5
Bradfield Essex 56 F5
Bradfield Norf 81 D8
Bradfield W Berks 26 B4
Bradfield Combust Suff 56 D2
Bradfield Green Ches 74 D3
Bradfield Heath Essex 43 B7
Bradfield St Clare Suff 56 D3
Bradfield St George Suff 56 C3
Bradford Corn 5 B6
Bradford Derbys 76 C2
Bradford Devon 9 D6
Bradford Northumb 125 F7
Bradford W Yorks 94 F4
Bradford Abbas Dorset 12 C3
Bradford Cathedral W Yorks 94 F4
Bradford Industrial Museum W Yorks 94 F4
Bradford Leigh Wilts 24 C3
Bradford-on-Avon Wilts 24 C3
Bradford on Tone Som 11 B6
Bradford Peverell Dorset 12 E4
Brading I o W 15 F7
Bradley Derbys 76 E2
Bradley Hants 26 E4
Bradley NE Lincs 91 D6
Bradley Staffs 62 C2
Bradley W Mid 62 E3
Bradley W Yorks 88 B2
Bradley Green Worcs 50 C4
Bradley in the Moors Staffs 75 E7
Bradlow Hereford 50 F2
Bradmore Notts 77 F5
Bradmore W Mid 62 E2
Bradninch Devon 10 D5
Bradnop Staffs 75 D7
Bradpole Dorset 12 E2
Bradshaw Gtr Man 86 C5
Bradshaw W Yorks 87 C8
Bradstone Devon 9 F5
Bradwall Green Ches 74 C4
Bradway S Yorks 88 F4
Bradwell Derbys 88 F2
Bradwell Essex 42 B4
Bradwell M Keynes 53 F6
Bradwell Norf 69 D8
Bradwell Staffs 74 E5
Bradwell Grove Oxon 38 D2
Bradwell on Sea Essex 43 D6
Bradwell Waterside Essex 43 D5
Bradworthy Devon 8 C5
Bradworthy Cross Devon 8 C5
Brae Dumfries 107 B5
Brae Highld 154 B4
Brae Highld 163 D8
Brae Shetland 174 G5
Brae of Achnahaird Highld 162 C4
Brae Roy Lodge Highld 147 E6
Braeantra Highld 157 B6
Braedownie Angus 142 B2
Braefield Highld 156 F5
Braegrum Perth 134 B2
Braehead Dumfries 105 D8
Braehead Orkney 176 F4
Braehead Orkney 176 B3
Braehead S Lnrk 121 F8
Braehead S Lnrk 122 D2
Braehead of Lunan Angus 143 D6
Braehoulland Shetland 174 F4
Braehungie Highld 169 F6
Braelangwell Lodge Highld 164 E2
Braemar Aberds 149 E7
Braemore Highld 169 F5
Braemore Highld 156 B2
Braes of Enzie Moray 159 D7
Braeside Invclyd 129 C7
Braeswick Orkney 176 C5
Braewick Shetland 175 H5
Brafferton Darl 101 B7
Brafferton N Yorks 95 B7
Brafield-on-the-Green Northants 53 D6
Bragar W Isles 172 D5
Bragbury End Herts 41 B5
Bragleenmore Argyll 130 C5
Braichmelyn Gwyn 83 E6
Braid Edin 122 C5
Braides Lancs 92 D4
Braidley N Yorks 101 F5
Braidwood S Lnrk 121 E8

Burnham Bucks 40 F2
Burnham N Lincs 90 C4
Burnham Deepdale Norf 80 C4
Burnham Green Herts 41 C5
Burnham Market Norf 80 C4
Burnham Norton Norf 80 C4
Burnham-on-Crouch Essex 43 E5
Burnham-on-Sea Som 22 E5
Burnham Overy Staithe Norf 80 C4
Burnham Overy Town Norf 80 C4
Burnham Thorpe Norf 80 C4
Burnhead Dumfries 113 E8
Burnhead S Ayrs 112 D2
Burnhervie Aberds 151 C6
Burnhill Green Staffs 61 D7
Burnhope Durham 110 E4
Burnhouse N Ayrs 120 D3
Burniston N Yorks 103 E8
Burnlee W Yorks 88 D2
Burnley Lancs 93 F8
Burnley Lane Lancs 93 F8
Burnmouth Borders 125 C5
Burnopfield Durham 110 D4
Burnsall N Yorks 94 C3
Burnside Angus 143 D5
Burnside E Ayrs 113 C5
Burnside Fife 134 D3
Burnside Shetland 174 F4
Burnside S Lnrk 121 C6
Burnside W Loth 122 B3
Burnside of Duntrune Angus 142 F4
Burnswark Dumfries 107 B8
Burnt Heath Derbys 76 B2
Burnt Houses Durham 101 B6
Burnt Yates N Yorks 95 C5
Burntcommon Sur 27 D8
Burnthouse Corn 3 C6
Burntisland Fife 134 F4
Burnton E Ayrs 112 D4
Burntwood Staffs 62 D4
Burnwynd Edin 122 C4
Burpham Sur 27 D8
Burpham W Sus 16 D4
Burradon Northumb 117 D5
Burradon T & W 111 B5
Burrafirth Shetland 174 B8
Burraland Shetland 174 F5
Burraland Shetland 175 J4
Burras Corn 3 C5
Burravoe Shetland 174 G5
Burravoe Shetland 174 F7
Burray Village Orkney 176 G3
Burrells Cumb 100 C1
Burrelton Perth 142 F2
Burridge Devon 20 F4
Burridge Hants 15 C6
Burrill N Yorks 101 F7
Burringham N Lincs 90 D2
Burrington Devon 9 C8
Burrington Hereford 49 B6
Burrington N Som 23 D6
Burrough Green Cambs 55 D7
Burrough on the Hill Leics 64 C4
Burrow-bridge Som 11 B8
Burrowhill Sur 27 C7
Burry Swansea 33 E5
Burry Green Swansea 33 E5
Burry Port = Porth Tywyn Carms 33 D5
Burscough Lancs 86 C2
Burscough Bridge Lancs 86 C2
Bursea E Yorks 96 F4
Burshill E Yorks 97 E6
Bursledon Hants 15 D5
Burslem Stoke 75 E5
Burstall Suff 56 E4
Burstock Dorset 12 D2
Burston Norf 68 F4
Burston Staffs 75 F6
Burstow Sur 28 E4
Burstwick E Yorks 91 B6
Burtersett N Yorks 100 F3
Burtle Som 23 E5
Burton Ches 73 B7
Burton Ches 74 C2
Burton Dorset 14 E2
Burton Lincs 78 B2
Burton Northumb 125 F7
Burton Pembs 44 E4
Burton Som 22 E3
Burton Wilts 24 B3
Burton Agnes E Yorks 97 C7
Burton Bradstock Dorset 12 F2
Burton Dassett Warks 51 D8
Burton Fleming E Yorks 97 B6
Burton Green W Mid 51 B7
Burton Green Wrex 73 D7
Burton Hastings Warks 63 E8
Burton-in-Kendal Cumb 92 B5
Burton in Lonsdale N Yorks 93 B6
Burton Joyce Notts 77 E6
Burton Latimer Northants 53 B7
Burton Lazars Leics 64 C4
Burton-le-Coggles Lincs 65 B6
Burton Leonard N Yorks 95 C6
Burton on the Wolds Leics 64 B2
Burton Overy Leics 64 E3
Burton Pedwardine Lincs 78 E4
Burton Pidsea E Yorks 97 F8
Burton Salmon N Yorks 89 B5
Burton Stather N Lincs 90 C2
Burton upon Stather N Lincs 90 C2
Burton upon Trent Staffs 63 B6
Burtonwood Warr 86 E3
Burwardsley Ches 74 D2
Burwarton Shrops 61 F6
Burwash E Sus 18 C3
Burwash Common E Sus 18 C3
Burwash Weald E Sus 18 C3
Burwell Cambs 55 C6
Burwell Lincs 79 B6
Burwen Anglesey 82 B4
Burwick Orkney 176 H3
Bury Cambs 66 F2
Bury Gtr Man 87 C6
Bury Som 10 B4
Bury W Sus 16 C4
Bury Green Herts 41 B7
Bury St Edmunds Suff 56 C2
Burythorpe N Yorks 96 C3
Busby E Renf 121 D5
Buscot Oxon 38 E2
Bush Bank Hereford 49 D6
Bush Crathie Aberds 149 E8
Bush Green Norf 68 F5
Bushbury W Mid 62 D3
Bushby Leics 64 D3
Bushey Herts 40 E4
Bushey Heath Herts 40 E4
Bushley Worcs 50 F3
Bushton Wilts 25 B5
Buslingthorpe Lincs 90 F4
Busta Shetland 174 G5
Butcher's Cross E Sus 18 C2
Butcher's Pasture Essex 42 B2
Butcombe N Som 23 C7
Butetown Cardiff 22 B3
Butleigh Som 23 F7
Butleigh Wootton Som 23 F7
Butler's Cross Bucks 39 D8
Butler's End Warks 63 F6
Butlers Marston Warks 51 E8
Butley Suff 57 D7
Butley High Corner Suff 57 E7
Butt Green Ches 74 D3
Butterburn Cumb 109 B6
Buttercrambe N Yorks 96 D3
Butterknowle Durham 101 B6
Butterleigh Devon 10 D4
Buttermere Cumb 98 C3
Buttermere Wilts 25 C8
Buttershaw W Yorks 88 B2
Butterstone Perth 141 E7
Butterton Staffs 75 D7
Butterwick Durham 102 B1
Butterwick Lincs 79 E6
Butterwick N Yorks 96 B3
Butterwick N Yorks 97 B5
Buttington Powys 60 D2
Buttonoak Shrops 50 B2
Butt's Green Hants 14 B4
Buttsash Hants 14 D5
Buxhall Suff 56 D4
Buxhall Fen Street Suff 56 D4
Buxley Borders 124 D4
Buxted E Sus 17 B8
Buxton Derbys 75 B7
Buxton Norf 81 E8
Buxworth Derbys 87 F8
Bwcle = Buckley Flint 73 C6
Bwlch Powys 35 B5
Bwlch-Llan Ceredig 46 D4
Bwlch-y-cibau Powys 59 C8
Bwlch-y-fadfa Ceredig 46 E3
Bwlch-y-ffridd Powys 59 E7
Bwlch-y-sarnau Powys 48 B2
Bwlchgwyn Wrex 73 D6
Bwlchnewydd Carms 32 B4
Bwlchtocyn Gwyn 70 E4
Bwlchyddar Powys 59 B8
Bwlchygroes Pembs 45 F4
Byermoor T & W 110 D4
Byers Green Durham 110 F5
Byfield Northants 52 D3
Byfleet Sur 27 C8
Byford Hereford 49 E5
Bygrave Herts 54 F3
Byker T & W 111 C5
Bylchau Conwy 72 C3
Byley Ches 74 C4
Bynea Carms 33 E6
Byrness Northumb 116 D3
Bythorn Cambs 53 B8
Byton Hereford 49 C5
Byworth W Sus 16 B3

C

Cabharstadh W Isles 172 F6
Cablea Perth 141 F6
Cabourne Lincs 90 D5
Cabrach Argyll 127 F2
Cabrach Moray 150 B2
Cabrich Highld 157 E6
Cabus Lancs 92 E4
Cackle Street E Sus 17 B8
Cadbury Devon 10 D4
Cadbury Barton Devon 9 C8
Cadbury World, Bournville W Mid 62 F4
Cadder E Dunb 121 B6
Caddington Beds 40 C3
Caddonfoot Borders 123 F7
Cade Street E Sus 18 C3
Cadeby Leics 63 D8
Cadeby S Yorks 89 D6
Cadeleigh Devon 10 D4
Cadgwith Corn 3 E6
Cadham Fife 134 D4
Cadishead Gtr Man 86 E5
Cadle Swansea 33 E7
Cadley Lancs 92 F5
Cadley Wilts 25 D7
Cadley Wilts 25 C7
Cadmore End Bucks 39 E7
Cadnam Hants 14 C3
Cadney N Lincs 90 D4
Cadole Flint 73 C6
Cadoxton V Glam 22 C3
Cadoxton-Juxta-Neath Neath 34 E1
Cadshaw Blkburn 86 C5
Cadwell Park Motor Racing Circuit Lincs 91 F6
Cadzow S Lnrk 121 D7
Caeathro Gwyn 82 E4
Caehopkin Powys 34 C2
Caenby Lincs 90 F4
Caenby Corner Lincs 90 F3
Cae'r-bryn Carms 33 C6
Caer Llan Mon 36 D1
Caerau Bridgend 34 E2
Caerau Cardiff 22 B3
Caerdeon Gwyn 58 C3
Caerdydd = Cardiff Cardiff 22 B3
Caerfarchell Pembs 44 C2
Caerffili = Caerphilly Caerph 35 F5
Caerfyrddin = Carmarthen Carms 33 B5
Caergeiliog Anglesey 82 D3
Caergwrle Flint 73 D7
Caergybi = Holyhead Anglesey 82 C2
Caerleon = Caerllion Newport 35 E7
Caerllion = Caerleon Newport 35 E7
Caernarfon Gwyn 82 E4
Caernarfon Castle Gwyn 82 E4
Caerphilly = Caerffili Caerph 35 F5
Caersws Powys 59 E7
Caerwedros Ceredig 46 D2
Caerwent Mon 36 E1
Caerwych Gwyn 71 D7
Caerwys Flint 72 B5
Caethle Gwyn 58 E3
Caim Anglesey 83 C6
Caio Carms 47 F5
Cairinis W Isles 170 D4
Cairisiadar W Isles 172 E3
Cairminis W Isles 173 K3
Cairnbaan Argyll 128 A3
Cairnbanno Ho. Aberds 160 D5
Cairnborrow Aberds 159 E8
Cairnbrogie Aberds 151 B7
Cairnbulg Castle Aberds 161 B7
Cairncross Angus 142 B4
Cairncross Borders 124 C4
Cairndow Argyll 131 D7
Cairness Aberds 161 B7
Cairneyhill Fife 134 F2
Cairnfield Ho. Moray 159 C8
Cairngaan Dumfries 104 F5
Cairngarroch Dumfries 104 E4
Cairnhill Aberds 160 E3
Cairnie Aberds 159 E8
Cairnie Aberds 151 D7
Cairnorrie Aberds 161 D5
Cairnpark Aberds 151 C7
Cairnryan Dumfries 104 C4
Cairnton Orkney 176 F2
Caister-on-Sea Norf 69 C8
Caistor Lincs 90 D5
Caistor St Edmund Norf 68 D5
Caistron Northumb 117 D5
Caitha Bowland Borders 123 E7
Caithness Glass, Perth Perth 134 B2
Calais Street Suff 56 F3
Calanais W Isles 172 E5
Calbost W Isles 172 G7
Calbourne I o W 14 F5
Calceby Lincs 79 B6
Calcot Row W Berks 26 B4
Calcott Kent 31 C5
Caldback Shetland 174 C8
Caldbeck Cumb 108 F3
Caldbergh N Yorks 101 F5
Caldecote Cambs 54 D4
Caldecote Cambs 65 F8
Caldecote Herts 54 F3
Caldecote Northants 52 D4
Caldecott Northants 53 C7
Caldecott Oxon 38 E4
Caldecott Rutland 65 E5
Calder Bridge Cumb 98 D2
Calder Hall Cumb 98 D2
Calder Mains Highld 169 D5
Calder Vale Lancs 92 E5
Calderbank N Lnrk 121 C7
Calderbrook Gtr Man 87 C7
Caldercruix N Lnrk 121 C8
Caldermill S Lnrk 121 E6
Calderwood S Lnrk 121 D6
Caldhame Angus 142 E4
Caldicot Mon 36 F1
Caldwell Derbys 63 C6
Caldwell N Yorks 101 C6
Caldy Mers 85 F3
Caledrhydiau Ceredig 46 D3
Calfsound Orkney 176 C4
Calgary Argyll 136 C4
Califer Moray 158 D4
California Falk 122 B2
California Norf 69 C8
Calke Derbys 63 B7
Callakille Highld 155 E2
Callaly Northumb 117 D6
Callander Stirl 132 D5
Callaughton Shrops 61 E6
Callestick Corn 4 D2
Calligarry Highld 145 C6
Callington Corn 5 C8
Callow Hereford 49 F6
Callow End Worcs 50 E3
Callow Hill Wilts 37 F7
Callow Hill Worcs 50 B2
Callows Grave Worcs 49 C7
Calmore Hants 14 C4
Calmsden Glos 37 D7
Calne Wilts 24 B5
Calow Derbys 76 B4
Calshot Hants 15 D5
Calstock Corn 6 C2
Calstone Wellington Wilts 24 C5
Calthorpe Norf 81 D7
Calthwaite Cumb 108 E4
Calton N Yorks 94 D2
Calton Staffs 75 D8
Calveley Ches 74 D2
Calver Derbys 76 B2
Calver Hill Hereford 49 E5
Calverhall Shrops 74 F3
Calverleigh Devon 10 C4
Calverley W Yorks 94 F5
Calvert Bucks 39 B6
Calverton M Keynes 53 F5
Calverton Notts 77 E6
Calvine Perth 141 C5
Calvo Cumb 107 D8
Cam Glos 36 E4
Camas-luinie Highld 146 B2
Camasnacroise Highld 138 D2
Camastianavaig Highld 153 F6
Camasunary Highld 153 H6
Camault Muir Highld 157 E6
Camb Shetland 174 D7
Camber E Sus 19 D6
Camberley Sur 27 C6
Camberwell London 28 B4
Camblesforth N Yorks 89 B7
Cambo Northumb 117 F6
Cambois Northumb 117 F9
Camborne Corn 3 B5
Cambourne Cambs 54 D4
Cambridge Cambs 55 D5
Cambridge Glos 36 D4
Cambridge Airport Cambs 55 D5
Cambridge Town Sthend 43 F5
Cambus Clack 133 E7
Cambusavie Farm Highld 164 E4
Cambusbarron Stirl 133 E6
Cambuskenneth Stirl 133 E7
Cambuslang S Lnrk 121 C6
Cambusmore Lodge Highld 164 E4
Camden London 41 F5
Camelford Corn 8 F3
Camelot Theme Park, Chorley Lancs 86 C3
Camelsdale W Sus 27 F6
Camerory Highld 158 F4
Camer's Green Worcs 50 F2
Camerton Bath 23 D8
Camerton Cumb 107 F7
Camerton E Yorks 91 B6
Camghouran Perth 140 D2
Cammachmore Aberds 151 E8
Cammeringham Lincs 90 F3
Camore Highld 164 E4
Camp Hill Warks 63 E7
Campbeltown Argyll 118 D4
Campbeltown Airport Argyll 118 D3
Camperdown T & W 111 B5
Campmuir Perth 142 F2
Campsall S Yorks 89 C6
Campsey Ash Suff 57 D7
Campton Beds 54 F2
Camptown Borders 116 C2
Camrose Pembs 44 C4
Camserney Perth 141 E5
Camster Highld 169 E7
Camuschoirk Highld 138 C1
Camuscross Highld 145 B6
Camusnagaul Highld 138 B4
Camusnagaul Highld 162 F4
Camusrory Highld 145 D8
Camusteel Highld 155 F3
Camusterrach Highld 155 F3
Camusvrachan Perth 140 E3
Canada Hants 14 C3
Canadia E Sus 18 D4
Canal Side S Yorks 89 C7
Candacraig Ho. Aberds 150 C2
Candlesby Lincs 79 C7
Candy Mill S Lnrk 122 E3
Cane End Oxon 26 B4
Canewdon Essex 42 E4
Canford Bottom Dorset 13 D8
Canford Cliffs Poole 13 F8
Canford Magna Poole 13 E8
Canham's Green Suff 56 C4
Canholes Derbys 75 B7
Canisbay Highld 169 B8
Cann Dorset 13 B6
Cann Common Dorset 13 B6
Cannard's Grave Som 23 E8
Cannich Highld 156 F4
Cannington Som 22 F4
Cannock Staffs 62 D3
Cannock Wood Staffs 62 C4
Canon Bridge Hereford 49 E6
Canon Frome Hereford 49 E8
Canon Pyon Hereford 49 E6
Canonbie Dumfries 108 B3
Canons Ashby Northants 52 D3
Canonstown Corn 2 C4
Canterbury Kent 30 D5
Canterbury Cathedral Kent 30 D5
Canterbury Tales Kent 30 D5
Cantley Norf 69 D6
Cantley S Yorks 89 D7
Cantlop Shrops 60 D5
Canton Cardiff 22 B3
Cantraybruich Highld 157 E8
Cantraydoune Highld 157 E8
Cantraywood Highld 157 E8
Cantsfield Lancs 93 B6
Canvey Island Essex 42 F3
Canwick Lincs 78 C2
Canworthy Water Corn 8 E4
Caol Highld 139 B5
Caol Ila Argyll 126 B4
Caolas Argyll 136 F2
Caolas Scalpaigh W Isles 173 J5
Caolas Stocinis W Isles 173 J4
Capel Sur 28 E2
Capel Bangor Ceredig 58 F3
Capel Betws Lleucu Ceredig 46 D5
Capel Carmel Gwyn 70 E2
Capel Coch Anglesey 82 C4
Capel Curig Conwy 83 F7
Capel Cynon Ceredig 46 E2
Capel Dewi Ceredig 46 E3
Capel Dewi Ceredig 58 F3
Capel Dewi Carms 33 B5
Capel Garmon Conwy 83 F8
Capel-gwyn Anglesey 82 D3
Capel Gwyn Carms 33 B5
Capel Gwynfe Carms 33 B8
Capel Hendre Carms 33 C6
Capel Hermon Gwyn 71 E8
Capel Isaac Carms 33 B6
Capel Iwan Carms 45 F4
Capel le Ferne Kent 31 F6
Capel Llanilltern Cardiff 34 F4
Capel Mawr Anglesey 82 D4
Capel St Andrew Suff 57 E7
Capel St Mary Suff 56 F4
Capel Seion Ceredig 46 B5
Capel Tygwydd Ceredig 45 E4
Capel Uchaf Gwyn 70 C5
Capel-y-graig Gwyn 82 E5
Capelulo Conwy 83 D7
Capenhurst Ches 73 B7
Capernwray Lancs 92 B5
Capheaton Northumb 117 F6
Cappercleuch Borders 115 B5
Capplegill Dumfries 114 D4
Capton Devon 7 D6
Caputh Perth 141 F7
Car Colston Notts 77 E7
Carbis Bay Corn 2 C4
Carbost Highld 153 F4
Carbost Highld 152 E5
Carbrook S Yorks 88 F4
Carbrooke Norf 68 D2
Carburton Notts 77 B6
Carcant Borders 123 D6
Carcary Angus 143 D6
Carclaze Corn 4 D5
Carcroft S Yorks 89 C6
Cardenden Fife 134 E4
Cardeston Shrops 60 C3
Cardiff = Caerdydd Cardiff 22 B3
Cardiff Bay Barrage Cardiff 22 B3
Cardiff Castle Cardiff 22 B3
Cardiff International Airport V Glam 22 C2
Cardigan = Aberteifi Ceredig 45 E3
Cardington Beds 53 E8
Cardington Shrops 60 E5
Cardinham Corn 5 C6
Cardonald Glasgow 120 C5
Cardow Moray 159 E5
Cardrona Borders 123 F6
Cardross Argyll 120 B3
Cardurnock Cumb 107 D8
Careby Lincs 65 C7
Careston Castle Angus 143 D5
Carew Pembs 32 D1
Carew Cheriton Pembs 32 D1
Carew Newton Pembs 32 D1
Carey Hereford 49 F7
Carfrae E Loth 123 C8
Cargenbridge Dumfries 107 B6
Cargill Perth 142 F1
Cargo Cumb 108 D3
Cargreen Corn 6 C2
Carham Northumb 124 F4
Carhampton Som 22 E2
Carharrack Corn 3 B6
Carie Perth 140 F3
Carie Perth 140 D3
Carines Corn 4 D2
Carisbrooke I o W 15 F5
Carisbrooke Castle I o W 15 F5
Cark Cumb 92 B3
Carlabhagh W Isles 172 D5
Carland Cross Corn 4 D3
Carlby Lincs 65 C7
Carlecotes S Yorks 88 D2
Carlesmoor N Yorks 94 B4
Carleton Cumb 99 B7
Carleton Cumb 108 D4
Carleton Lancs 92 F3
Carleton N Yorks 94 E2
Carleton Forehoe Norf 68 D3
Carleton Rode Norf 68 E4
Carlin How Redcar 103 C5
Carlingcott Bath 23 D8
Carlisle Cumb 108 D4
Carlisle Airport Cumb 108 C4
Carlisle Cathedral Cumb 108 D3
Carlisle Racecourse Cumb 108 D3
Carlops Borders 122 D4
Carlton Beds 53 D7
Carlton Cambs 55 D7
Carlton Leics 63 D7
Carlton Notts 77 E6
Carlton N Yorks 102 F4
Carlton N Yorks 89 B7
Carlton N Yorks 101 F5
Carlton N Yorks 101 C6
Carlton Stockton 102 B1
Carlton Suff 57 C7
Carlton S Yorks 88 C4
Carlton W Yorks 88 B4
Carlton Colville Suff 69 F8
Carlton Curlieu Leics 64 E3
Carlton Husthwaite N Yorks 95 B7
Carlton in Cleveland N Yorks 102 D3
Carlton in Lindrick Notts 89 F6
Carlton le Moorland Lincs 78 D2
Carlton Miniott N Yorks 102 F1
Carlton on Trent Notts 77 C7
Carlton Scroop Lincs 78 E2
Carluke S Lnrk 121 D8
Carmarthen = Caerfyrddin Carms 33 B5
Carmel Anglesey 82 C3
Carmel Carms 33 C6
Carmel Flint 73 B5
Carmel Guern 16
Carmel Gwyn 82 F4
Carmont Aberds 151 F7
Carmunnock Glasgow 121 D6
Carmyle Glasgow 121 C6
Carmyllie Angus 143 E5
Carn-gorm Highld 146 B2
Carnaby E Yorks 97 C7
Carnach Highld 162 E4
Carnach Highld 146 B3
Carnach W Isles 173 J5
Carnachy Highld 168 D2
Càrnais W Isles 172 E3
Carnbee Fife 135 D7
Carnbo Perth 134 D2
Carnbrea Corn 3 B5
Carnduff S Lnrk 121 E6
Carnduncan Argyll 126 C2
Carne Corn 3 C8
Carnforth Lancs 92 B4
Carnhedryn Pembs 44 C3
Carnhell Green Corn 2 C5
Carnkie Corn 3 C6
Carnkie Corn 3 C5
Carno Powys 59 E6
Carnoch Highld 156 F4
Carnoch Highld 156 D3
Carnock Fife 134 F2
Carnon Downs Corn 3 B6
Carnousie Aberds 160 C3
Carnoustie Angus 143 F5
Carnwath S Lnrk 122 E2
Carnyorth Corn 2 C2
Carperby N Yorks 101 F5
Carpley Green N Yorks 100 F4
Carr S Yorks 89 E6
Carr Hill T & W 111 C5
Carradale Argyll 118 C5
Carragraich W Isles 173 J4
Carrbridge Highld 148 B5
Carrefour Selous Jersey 17
Carreg-wen Pembs 45 E4
Carreglefn Anglesey 82 C3
Carrick Argyll 128 B4
Carrick Fife 135 B6
Carrick Castle Argyll 129 A6
Carrick Ho. Orkney 176 C4
Carriden Falk 134 F2
Carrington Gtr Man 86 E5
Carrington Lincs 79 D6
Carrington Midloth 123 C6
Carrog Conwy 71 C8
Carrog Denb 72 E5
Carron Falk 133 F7
Carron Moray 159 E6
Carron Bridge N Lnrk 133 F6
Carronbridge Dumfries 113 E8
Carrshield Northumb 109 E8
Carrutherstown Dumfries 107 B8
Carrville Durham 111 E6
Carsaig Argyll 137 F6
Carsaig Argyll 128 B2
Carscreugh Dumfries 105 D6
Carse Gray Angus 142 D4
Carse Ho. Argyll 128 D2
Carsegowan Dumfries 105 D8
Carseriggan Dumfries 105 C7
Carsethorn Dumfries 107 D6
Carshalton London 28 C3
Carsington Derbys 76 D2
Carskiey Argyll 118 F3
Carsluith Dumfries 105 D8
Carsphairn Dumfries 113 E5
Carstairs S Lnrk 122 E2
Carstairs Junction S Lnrk 122 E2
Carswell Marsh Oxon 38 E3
Carter's Clay Hants 14 B4
Carterton Oxon 38 D2
Carterway Heads Northumb 110 D3
Carthew Corn 4 D5
Carthorpe N Yorks 101 F8
Cartington Northumb 117 D6
Cartland S Lnrk 121 E8
Cartmel Cumb 92 B3
Cartmel Fell Cumb 99 F6
Cartmel Racecourse Cumb 92 B3
Carway Carms 33 D5
Cary Fitzpaine Som 12 B3
Cas-gwent = Chepstow Mon 36 E2
Cascob Powys 48 C4
Cashlie Perth 140 E1
Cashmere Visitor Centre, Elgin Moray 159 E6
Cashmoor Dorset 13 C7
Casnewydd = Newport Newport 35 F7
Cassey Compton Glos 37 C7
Cassington Oxon 38 C4
Cassop Durham 111 F6
Castell Denb 72 C5
Castell Coch Cardiff 35 F5
Castell-Howell Ceredig 46 E3
Castell-Nedd = Neath Neath 33 E8
Castell Newydd Emlyn = Newcastle Emlyn Carms 46 E2
Castell-y-bwch Torf 35 E6
Castellau Rhondda 34 F4
Casterton Cumb 93 B6
Castle Acre Norf 67 C8
Castle Ashby Northants 53 D6
Castle Bolton N Yorks 101 E5
Castle Bromwich W Mid 62 F5
Castle Bytham Lincs 65 C6
Castle Caereinion Powys 59 D8
Castle Camps Cambs 55 E7
Castle Carrock Cumb 108 D5
Castle Cary Som 23 F8
Castle Combe Wilts 24 B3
Castle Combe Motor Racing Circuit Wilts 24 B3
Castle Donington Leics 63 B8
Castle Douglas Dumfries 106 C4
Castle Drogo, Exeter Devon 10 E2
Castle Eaton Swindon 37 E8
Castle Eden Durham 111 F7
Castle Forbes Aberds 150 C5
Castle Frome Hereford 49 E8
Castle Green Sur 27 C7
Castle Gresley Derbys 63 C6
Castle Heaton Northumb 124 E5
Castle Hedingham Essex 55 F8
Castle Hill Kent 29 E7
Castle Howard, Malton N Yorks 96 B3
Castle Huntly Perth 134 B5
Castle Kennedy Dumfries 104 D5
Castle O'er Dumfries 115 E5
Castle Pulverbatch Shrops 60 D4
Castle Rising Norf 67 B6
Castle Stuart Highld 157 E8
Castlebay = Bagh a Chaisteil W Isles 171 L2
Castlebythe Pembs 32 B1
Castlecary N Lnrk 121 B7
Castlecraig Highld 158 C2
Castlefairn Dumfries 113 F7
Castleford W Yorks 88 B5
Castlehill Borders 122 F5
Castlehill Highld 169 C6
Castlehill W Dunb 120 B3
Castlemaddy Dumfries 113 F5
Castlemartin Pembs 44 F4
Castlemilk Dumfries 107 B8
Castlemilk Glasgow 121 D6
Castlemorris Pembs 44 B4
Castlemorton Worcs 50 F2
Castleside Durham 110 E3
Castlethorpe M Keynes 53 E6
Castleton Angus 142 E3
Castleton Argyll 128 B3
Castleton Derbys 88 F2
Castleton Gtr Man 87 C6
Castleton Newport 35 F6
Castleton N Yorks 102 D4
Castletown Ches 73 D8
Castletown Highld 169 C6
Castletown Highld 157 E8
Castletown I o M 84 F2
Castletown T & W 111 D6
Castleweary Borders 115 D7
Castley N Yorks 95 E5
Caston Norf 68 E2
Castor P'boro 65 E8
Catacol N Ayrs 119 B6
Catbrain S Glos 36 F2
Catbrook Mon 36 D2
Catchall Corn 2 D3
Catchems Corner W Mid 51 B7
Catchgate Durham 110 D4
Catcleugh Northumb 116 D3
Catcliffe S Yorks 88 F5
Catcott Som 23 F5
Caterham Sur 28 D4
Catfield Norf 69 B6
Catfirth Shetland 175 H6
Catford London 28 B4
Catforth Lancs 92 F4
Cathays Cardiff 22 B3
Cathcart Glasgow 121 C5
Cathedine Powys 35 B5
Catherington Hants 15 C7
Catherton Shrops 49 B8
Catlodge Highld 148 E2
Catlowdy Cumb 108 B4
Catmore W Berks 38 F4
Caton Lancs 92 C5
Caton Green Lancs 92 C5
Catrine E Ayrs 113 B5
Cat's Ash Newport 35 E7
Catsfield E Sus 18 D4
Catshill Worcs 50 B4
Cattal N Yorks 95 D7
Cattawade Suff 56 F5
Catterall Lancs 92 E4
Catterick N Yorks 101 E7
Catterick Bridge N Yorks 101 E7
Catterick Garrison N Yorks 101 E6
Catterick Racecourse N Yorks 101 E7
Catterlen Cumb 108 F4
Catterline Aberds 143 B8
Catterton N Yorks 95 E8
Catthorpe Leics 52 B3
Cattistock Dorset 12 E3
Catton Northumb 109 D8
Catton N Yorks 95 B6
Catwick E Yorks 97 E7
Catworth Cambs 53 B8
Caudlesprings Norf 68 D2
Caudwell's Mill, Matlock Derbys 76 C2
Caulcott Oxon 39 B5
Cauldcots Angus 143 E6
Cauldhame Stirl 132 E5
Cauldmill Borders 115 C8
Cauldon Staffs 75 E7
Caulkerbush Dumfries 107 D6
Caulside Dumfries 115 F7
Caunsall Worcs 62 F2
Caunton Notts 77 D7
Causeway End Dumfries 105 C8
Causeway Foot W Yorks 94 F3
Causeway-head Stirl 133 E6
Causewayend S Lnrk 122 F3
Causewayhead Cumb 107 D8
Causey Park Bridge Northumb 117 E7
Causeyend Aberds 151 C8
Cautley Cumb 100 E1
Cavendish Suff 56 E2
Cavendish Bridge Leics 63 B8
Cavenham Suff 55 C8
Caversfield Oxon 39 B5
Caversham Reading 26 B5
Caverswall Staffs 75 E6
Cavil E Yorks 96 F3
Cawdor Highld 158 D2
Cawdor Castle and Gardens Highld 158 E2
Cawkwell Lincs 79 B5
Cawood N Yorks 95 F8
Cawsand Corn 6 D2
Cawston Norf 81 E7
Cawthorne S Yorks 88 D3
Cawthorpe Lincs 65 B7
Cawton N Yorks 96 B2
Caxton Cambs 54 D4
Caynham Shrops 49 B7
Caythorpe Lincs 78 E2
Caythorpe Notts 77 E6
Cayton N Yorks 103 F8
Ceann a Bhaigh W Isles 170 D3
Ceann a Deas Loch Baghasdail W Isles 171 J3
Ceann Shiphoirt W Isles 172 G5
Ceann Tarabhaigh W Isles 172 G5
Ceannacroc Lodge Highld 146 C5
Cearsiadair W Isles 172 F6
Cefn Berain Conwy 72 C3
Cefn-brith Conwy 72 D3
Cefn Canol Powys 73 F6
Cefn-coch Conwy 83 E8
Cefn Coch Powys 59 B8
Cefn-coed-y-cymmer M Tydf 34 D4
Cefn Cribbwr Bridgend 34 F2
Cefn Cross Bridgend 34 F2
Cefn-ddwysarn Gwyn 72 F3
Cefn Einion Shrops 60 F2
Cefn-gorwydd Powys 47 E8
Cefn-mawr Wrex 73 E6
Cefn-y-bedd Flint 73 D7
Cefn-y-pant Carms 32 B2
Cefneithin Carms 33 C6
Cei-bach Ceredig 46 D3
Ceinewydd = New Quay Ceredig 46 D2
Ceint Anglesey 82 D4
Cellan Ceredig 46 E5
Cellarhead Staffs 75 E6
Cemaes Anglesey 82 B3
Cemmaes Powys 58 D5
Cemmaes Road Powys 58 D5
Cenarth Carms 45 E4
Cenin Gwyn 71 C5
Central Invclyd 129 C7
Ceos W Isles 172 F6
Ceres Fife 135 C6
Cerne Abbas Dorset 12 D4
Cerney Wick Glos 37 E7
Cerrigceinwen Anglesey 82 D4
Cerrigydrudion Conwy 72 E3
Cessford Borders 116 B3
Ceunant Gwyn 82 E5
Chaceley Glos 50 F3
Chacewater Corn 3 B6
Chackmore Bucks 52 F4
Chacombe Northants 52 E2
Chad Valley W Mid 62 F4
Chadderton Gtr Man 87 D7
Chadderton Fold Gtr Man 87 D6
Chaddesden Derby 76 F3
Chaddesley Corbett Worcs 50 B3
Chaddleworth W Berks 26 B2
Chadlington Oxon 38 B3
Chadshunt Warks 51 D8
Chadwell Leics 64 B4
Chadwell St Mary Thurrock 29 B7

Coed Ystumgwern Gwyn 71 E6
Coedely Rhondda 34 F4
Coedkernew Newport 35 F6
Coedpoeth Wrex 73 D6
Coedway Powys 60 C3
Coelbren Powys 34 C2
Coffinswell Devon 7 C6
Cofton Hackett Worcs 50 B5
Cogan V Glam 22 B3
Cogenhoe Northants 53 C6
Cogges Oxon 38 D3
Coggeshall Essex 42 B4
Coggeshall Hamlet Essex 42 B4
Coggins Mill E Sus 18 C2
Coig Peighinnean W Isles 172 B8
Coig Peighinnean Bhuirgh W Isles 172 C7
Coignafearn Lodge Highld 148 C2
Coilacriech Aberds 150 E2
Coilantogle Stirl 132 D4
Coilleag W Isles 171 J3
Coillore Highld 153 F4
Coity Bridgend 34 F3
Col W Isles 172 D7
Col Uarach W Isles 172 E7
Colaboll Highld 164 C2
Colan Corn 4 C3
Colaton Raleigh Devon 11 F5
Colbost Highld 152 E3
Colburn N Yorks 101 E6
Colby Cumb 100 B1
Colby I o M 84 E2
Colby Norf 81 D8
Colchester Essex 43 B6
Colchester Zoo Essex 43 B5
Colcot V Glam 22 C3
Cold Ash W Berks 26 C3
Cold Ashby Northants 52 B4
Cold Ashton S Glos 24 B2
Cold Aston Glos 37 C8
Cold Blow Pembs 32 C2
Cold Brayfield M Keynes 53 D7
Cold Hanworth Lincs 90 F4
Cold Harbour Lincs 78 F2
Cold Hatton Telford 61 B6
Cold Hesledon Durham 111 E7
Cold Higham Northants 52 D4
Cold Kirby N Yorks 102 F3
Cold Newton Leics 64 D4
Cold Northcott Corn 8 F4
Cold Norton Essex 42 D4
Cold Overton Leics 64 C5
Coldbackie Highld 167 D8
Coldbeck Cumb 100 D2
Coldblow London 29 B6
Coldean Brighton 17 D7
Coldeast Devon 7 B6
Colden W Yorks 87 B7
Colden Common Hants 15 B5
Coldfair Green Suff 57 C8
Coldham Cambs 66 D4
Coldharbour Glos 36 D2
Coldharbour Kent 29 D6
Coldharbour Sur 28 E2
Coldingham Borders 124 C5
Coldrain Perth 134 D2
Coldred Kent 31 E6
Coldridge Devon 9 D8
Coldstream Angus 142 F3
Coldstream Borders 124 F4
Coldwaltham W Sus 16 C4
Coldwells Aberds 161 D8
Coldwells Croft Aberds 150 B4
Coldyeld Shrops 60 E3
Cole Som 23 F8
Cole Green Herts 41 C5
Cole Henley Hants 26 D2
Colebatch Shrops 60 F3
Colebrook Devon 10 D5
Colebrooke Devon 10 E2
Coleby Lincs 78 C2
Coleby N Lincs 90 C2
Coleford Devon 10 D2
Coleford Glos 36 C2
Coleford Som 23 E8
Colehill Dorset 13 D8
Coleman's Hatch E Sus 29 F5
Colemere Shrops 73 F8
Colemore Hants 26 F5
Coleorton Leics 63 C8
Colerne Wilts 24 B3
Cole's Green Suff 57 C6
Coles Green Suff 56 E4
Colesbourne Glos 37 C6
Colesden Beds 54 D2
Coleshill Bucks 40 E2
Coleshill Oxon 38 E2
Coleshill Warks 63 F6
Colestocks Devon 11 D5
Colgate W Sus 28 F3
Colgrain Argyll 129 B8
Colinsburgh Fife 135 D6
Colinton Edin 122 C5
Colintraive Argyll 129 C5
Colkirk Norf 80 E5
Collace Perth 142 F2
Collafirth Shetland 174 G6
Collaton St Mary Torbay 7 D6
College Milton S Lnrk 121 D6
Collessie Fife 134 C4
Collier Row London 41 E8
Collier Street Kent 29 E8
Collier's End Herts 41 B6
Collier's Green Kent 18 B4
Colliery Row T & W 111 E6
Collieston Aberds 161 F7
Collin Dumfries 107 B7
Collingbourne Ducis Wilts 25 D7
Collingbourne Kingston Wilts 25 D7
Collingham Notts 77 C8
Collingham W Yorks 95 E6
Collington Hereford 49 C8
Collingtree Northants 53 D5
Collins Green Warr 86 E3
Colliston Angus 143 E6
Collycroft Warks 63 F7
Collynie Aberds 160 E5
Collyweston Northants 65 D6
Colmonell S Ayrs 104 A5
Colmworth Beds 54 D2
Coln Rogers Glos 37 D7
Coln St Aldwyn's Glos 37 D8
Coln St Dennis Glos 37 C7
Colnabaichin Aberds 149 D8
Colnbrook Slough 27 B8
Colne Cambs 54 B4
Colne Lancs 93 E8
Colne Edge Lancs 93 E8
Colne Engaine Essex 56 F2
Colney Norf 68 D4
Colney Heath Herts 41 D5
Colney Street Herts 40 D4
Colpy Aberds 160 E3
Colquhar Borders 123 E6
Colsterdale N Yorks 101 F6
Colsterworth Lincs 65 B6
Colston Bassett Notts 77 F6
Coltfield Moray 158 C5
Colthouse Cumb 99 E5
Coltishall Norf 69 C5
Coltness N Lnrk 121 D8
Colton Cumb 99 F5
Colton Norf 68 D4
Colton N Yorks 95 E8
Colton Staffs 62 B4
Colton W Yorks 95 F6
Colva Powys 48 D4
Colvend Dumfries 107 D5
Colvister Shetland 174 D7
Colwall Green Hereford 50 E2
Colwall Stone Hereford 50 E2
Colwell Northumb 110 B2
Colwich Staffs 62 B4
Colwick Notts 77 E6
Colwinston V Glam 21 B8
Colworth W Sus 16 D3
Colwyn Bay = Bae Colwyn Conwy 83 D8
Colyford Devon 11 E7
Colyton Devon 11 E7
Combe Hereford 48 C5
Combe Oxon 38 C4
Combe W Berks 25 C8
Combe Common Sur 27 F7
Combe Down Bath 24 C2
Combe Florey Som 22 F3
Combe Hay Bath 24 D2
Combe Martin Devon 20 E4
Combe Moor Hereford 49 C5
Combe Raleigh Devon 11 D6
Combe St Nicholas Som 11 C8
Combeinteignhead Devon 7 B7
Comberbach Ches 74 B3
Comberton Cambs 54 D4
Comberton Hereford 49 C6
Combpyne Devon 11 E7
Combridge Staffs 75 F7
Combrook Warks 51 D8
Combs Derbys 75 B7
Combs Suff 56 D4
Combs Ford Suff 56 D4
Combwich Som 22 E4
Comers Aberds 151 D5
Comins Coch Ceredig 58 F3
Commercial End Cambs 55 C6
Commins Capel Betws Ceredig 46 D5
Commins Coch Powys 58 D5
Common Edge Blkpool 92 F3
Common Side Derbys 76 B3
Commondale N Yorks 102 C4
Commonmoor Corn 5 C7
Commonside Ches 74 B2
Compstall Gtr Man 87 E7
Compton Devon 7 C6
Compton Hants 15 B5
Compton Sur 27 E6
Compton Sur 27 E7
Compton W Berks 26 B3
Compton Wilts 25 D6
Compton W Sus 15 C8
Compton Abbas Dorset 13 C6
Compton Abdale Glos 37 C7
Compton Acres Poole 13 F8
Compton Bassett Wilts 24 B5
Compton Beauchamp Oxon 38 F2
Compton Bishop Som 23 D5
Compton Chamberlayne Wilts 13 B8
Compton Dando Bath 23 C8
Compton Dundon Som 23 F6
Compton Martin Bath 23 D7
Compton Pauncefoot Som 12 B4
Compton Valence Dorset 12 E3
Comrie Fife 134 F2
Comrie Perth 133 B6
Conaglen House Highld 138 C4
Conchra Argyll 129 B5
Concraigie Perth 141 E8
Conder Green Lancs 92 D4
Conderton Worcs 50 F4
Condicote Glos 38 B1
Condorrat N Lnrk 121 B7
Condover Shrops 60 D4
Coney Weston Suff 56 B3
Coneyhurst W Sus 16 B5
Coneysthorpe N Yorks 96 B3
Coneythorpe N Yorks 95 D6
Conford Hants 27 F6
Congash Highld 149 B6
Congdon's Shop Corn 5 B7
Congerstone Leics 63 D7
Congham Norf 80 E3
Congl-y-wal Gwyn 71 C8
Congleton Ches 75 C5
Congresbury N Som 23 C6
Congreve Staffs 62 C3
Conicavel Moray 158 D3
Coningsby Lincs 78 D5
Conington Cambs 65 F8
Conington Cambs 54 C4
Conisbrough S Yorks 89 E6
Conisby Argyll 126 C2
Conisholme Lincs 91 E8
Coniston Cumb 99 E5
Coniston E Yorks 97 F7
Coniston Cold N Yorks 94 D2
Conistone N Yorks 94 C2
Connah's Quay Flint 73 C6
Connel Argyll 130 B5
Connel Park E Ayrs 113 C6
Connor Downs Corn 2 C4
Conon Bridge Highld 157 D6
Conon House Highld 157 D6
Cononley N Yorks 94 E2
Conordan Highld 153 F6
Consall Staffs 75 E6
Consett Durham 110 D4
Constable Burton N Yorks 101 E6
Constantine Corn 3 D6
Constantine Bay Corn 4 B3
Contin Highld 157 D5
Contlaw Aberdeen 151 D7
Conwy Conwy 83 D7
Conwy Castle Conwy 83 D7
Conyer Kent 30 C3
Conyers Green Suff 56 C2
Cooden E Sus 18 E4
Cooil I o M 84 E3
Cookbury Devon 9 D6
Cookham Windsor 40 F1
Cookham Dean Windsor 40 F1
Cookham Rise Windsor 40 F1
Cookhill Worcs 51 D5
Cookley Suff 57 B7
Cookley Worcs 62 F2
Cookley Green Oxon 39 E6
Cookney Aberds 151 E7
Cookridge W Yorks 95 E5
Cooksbridge E Sus 17 C8
Cooksmill Green Essex 42 D2
Coolham W Sus 16 B5
Cooling Medway 29 B8
Coombe Corn 8 C4
Coombe Corn 4 D4
Coombe Hants 15 B7
Coombe Wilts 25 D6
Coombe Bissett Wilts 14 B2
Coombe Hill Glos 37 B5
Coombe Keynes Dorset 13 F6
Coombes W Sus 17 D5
Coopersale Common Essex 41 D7
Cootham W Sus 16 C4
Copdock Suff 56 E5
Copford Green Essex 43 B5
Copgrove N Yorks 95 C6
Copister Shetland 174 F6
Cople Beds 54 E2
Copley Durham 101 B5
Coplow Dale Derbys 75 B8
Copmanthorpe York 95 E8
Coppathorne Corn 8 D4
Coppenhall Staffs 62 C3
Coppenhall Moss Ches 74 D4
Copperhouse Corn 2 C4
Coppingford Cambs 65 F8
Copplestone Devon 10 D2
Coppull Lancs 86 C3
Coppull Moor Lancs 86 C3
Copsale W Sus 17 B5
Copshaw Holm = Newcastleton Borders 115 F7
Copster Green Lancs 93 F6
Copston Magna Warks 63 F8
Copt Heath W Mid 51 B6
Copt Hewick N Yorks 95 B6
Copt Oak Leics 63 C8
Copthorne Shrops 60 C4
Copthorne W Sus 28 F4
Copy's Green Norf 80 D5
Copythorne Hants 14 C4
Corbets Tey London 42 F1
Corbridge Northumb 110 C2
Corby Northants 65 F5
Corby Glen Lincs 65 B6
Cordon N Ayrs 119 C7
Coreley Shrops 49 B8
Cores End Bucks 40 F2
Corfe Som 11 C7
Corfe Castle Dorset 13 F7
Corfe Castle Dorset 13 F7
Corfe Mullen Dorset 13 E7
Corfton Shrops 60 F4
Corgarff Aberds 149 D8
Corhampton Hants 15 B7
Corlae Dumfries 113 E6
Corley Warks 63 F7
Corley Ash Warks 63 F6
Corley Moor Warks 63 F6
Cornaa I o M 84 D4
Cornabus Argyll 126 E3
Cornel Conwy 83 E7
Corner Row Lancs 92 F4
Corney Cumb 98 E3
Cornforth Durham 111 F6
Cornhill Aberds 160 C2
Cornhill-on-Tweed Northumb 124 F4
Cornholme W Yorks 87 B7
Cornish Cyder Farm, Truro Corn 4 D2
Cornish Hall End Essex 55 F7
Cornquoy Orkney 176 G4
Cornsay Durham 110 E4
Cornsay Colliery Durham 110 E4
Corntown Highld 157 D6
Corntown V Glam 21 B8
Cornwell Oxon 38 B2
Cornwood Devon 6 D4
Cornworthy Devon 7 D6
Corpach Highld 138 B4
Corpusty Norf 81 D7
Corran Highld 138 C4
Corran Highld 145 C8
Corranbuie Argyll 128 D3
Corrany I o M 84 D4
Corrie N Ayrs 119 B7
Corrie Common Dumfries 114 F5
Corriecravie N Ayrs 119 D6
Corriemoillie Highld 156 C4
Corriemulzie Lodge Highld 163 E7
Corrievarkie Lodge Perth 140 B2
Corrievorrie Highld 148 B3
Corrimony Highld 156 F4
Corringham Lincs 90 E2
Corringham Thurrock 42 F3
Corris Gwyn 58 D4
Corris Uchaf Gwyn 58 D4
Corrour Shooting Lodge Highld 139 C8
Corrow Argyll 131 E7
Corry Highld 155 H2
Corry of Ardnagrask Highld 157 E6
Corrykinloch Highld 163 B7
Corrymuckloch Perth 141 F5
Corrynachenchy Argyll 137 D7
Cors-y-Gedol Gwyn 71 E6
Corsback Highld 169 B7
Corscombe Dorset 12 D3
Corse Aberds 160 D3
Corse Glos 36 B4
Corse Lawn Worcs 50 F3
Corse of Kinnoir Aberds 160 D2
Corsewall Dumfries 104 C4
Corsham Wilts 24 B3
Corsindae Aberds 151 D5
Corsley Wilts 24 E3
Corsley Heath Wilts 24 E3
Corsock Dumfries 106 B4
Corston Bath 23 C8
Corston Wilts 37 F6
Corstorphine Edin 122 B4
Cortachy Angus 142 D3
Corton Suff 69 E8
Corton Wilts 24 E4
Corton Denham Som 12 B4
Coruanan Lodge Highld 138 C4
Corunna W Isles 170 D4
Corwen Denb 72 E4
Coryton Devon 9 F6
Coryton Thurrock 42 F3
Cosby Leics 64 E2
Coseley W Mid 62 E3
Cosgrove Northants 53 E5
Cosham Ptsmth 15 D7
Cosheston Pembs 32 D1
Cossall Notts 76 E4
Cossington Leics 64 C3
Cossington Som 23 E5
Costa Orkney 176 D2
Costessey Norf 68 C4
Costock Notts 64 B2
Coston Leics 64 B5
Cote Oxon 38 D3
Cotebrook Ches 74 C2
Cotehele House Corn 6 C2
Cotehill Cumb 108 D4
Cotes Cumb 99 F6
Cotes Leics 64 B2
Cotes Staffs 74 F5
Cotesbach Leics 64 F2
Cotgrave Notts 77 F6
Cothall Aberds 151 C7
Cotham Notts 77 E7
Cothelstone Som 22 F3
Cotherstone Durham 101 C5
Cothill Oxon 38 E4
Cotleigh Devon 11 D7
Cotmanhay Derbys 76 E4
Cotmaton Devon 11 F6
Coton Cambs 54 D5
Coton Northants 52 B4
Coton Staffs 62 B2
Coton Staffs 75 F6
Coton Clanford Staffs 62 B2
Coton Hill Shrops 60 C4
Coton Hill Staffs 75 F6
Coton in the Elms Derbys 63 C6
Cotswold Wild Life Park, Burford Oxon 38 D2
Cott Devon 7 C5
Cottam E Yorks 97 C5
Cottam Lancs 92 F5
Cottam Notts 77 B8
Cottartown Highld 158 F4
Cottenham Cambs 54 C5
Cotterdale N Yorks 100 E3
Cottered Herts 41 B6
Cotteridge W Mid 50 B5
Cotterstock Northants 65 E7
Cottesbrooke Northants 52 B5
Cottesmore Rutland 65 C6
Cotteylands Devon 10 C4
Cottingham E Yorks 97 F6
Cottingham Northants 64 E5
Cottingley W Yorks 94 F4
Cottisford Oxon 52 F3
Cotton Staffs 75 E7
Cotton Suff 56 C4
Cotton End Beds 53 E8
Cottown Aberds 150 B4
Cottown Aberds 151 C6
Cottown Aberds 160 D5
Cotwalton Staffs 75 F6
Couch's Mill Corn 5 D6
Coughton Hereford 36 B2
Coughton Warks 51 C5
Coulaghailtro Argyll 128 D2
Coulags Highld 155 F5
Coulby Newham M'bro 102 C3
Coulderton Cumb 98 D1
Coulin Highld 155 E6
Coull Aberds 150 D4
Coull Argyll 126 C2
Coulport Argyll 129 B7
Coulsdon London 28 D3
Coulston Wilts 24 D4
Coulter S Lnrk 122 F3
Coulton N Yorks 96 B2
Cound Shrops 61 D5
Coundon Durham 101 B7
Coundon W Mid 63 F7
Coundon Grange Durham 101 B7
Countersett N Yorks 100 F4
Countess Wilts 25 E6
Countess Wear Devon 10 F4
Countesthorpe Leics 64 E2
Countisbury Devon 21 E6
County Oak W Sus 28 F3
Coup Green Lancs 86 B3
Coupar Angus Perth 142 E2
Coupland Northumb 124 F5
Cour Argyll 118 B5
Courance Dumfries 114 E3
Court-at-Street Kent 19 B7
Court Henry Carms 33 B6
Courteenhall Northants 53 D5
Courtsend Essex 43 E6
Courtway Som 22 F4
Cousland Midloth 123 C6
Cousley Wood E Sus 18 B3
Cove Argyll 129 B7
Cove Borders 124 B3
Cove Devon 10 C4
Cove Hants 27 D6
Cove Highld 162 E2
Cove Bay Aberdeen 151 D8
Cove Bottom Suff 57 B8
Covehithe Suff 69 F8
Coven Staffs 62 D3
Coveney Cambs 66 F4
Covenham St Bartholomew Lincs 91 E7
Covenham St Mary Lincs 91 E7
Coventry W Mid 51 B8
Coventry Airport Warks 51 B8
Coventry Cathedral W Mid 51 B8
Coverack Corn 3 E6
Coverham N Yorks 101 F6
Covesea Moray 159 B5
Covington Cambs 53 B8
Covington S Lnrk 122 F2
Cow Ark Lancs 93 E6
Cowan Bridge Lancs 93 B6
Cowbeech E Sus 18 D3
Cowbit Lincs 66 C2
Cowbridge Lincs 79 E6
Cowbridge Som 21 E8
Cowbridge = Y Bont-Faen V Glam 21 B8
Cowdale Derbys 75 B7
Cowden Kent 29 E5
Cowdenbeath Fife 134 E3
Cowdenburn Borders 122 D5
Cowers Lane Derbys 76 E3
Cowes I o W 15 E5
Cowesby N Yorks 102 F2
Cowfold W Sus 17 B6
Cowgill Cumb 100 F2
Cowie Aberds 151 F7
Cowie Stirl 133 F7
Cowley Devon 10 E4
Cowley Glos 37 C6
Cowley London 40 F3
Cowley Oxon 39 D5
Cowleymoor Devon 10 C4
Cowling Lancs 86 C3
Cowling N Yorks 94 E2
Cowling N Yorks 101 F7
Cowlinge Suff 55 D8
Cowpe Lancs 87 B6
Cowpen Northumb 117 F8
Cowpen Bewley Stockton 102 B2
Cowplain Hants 15 C7
Cowshill Durham 109 E8
Cowslip Green N Som 23 C6
Cowstrandburn Fife 134 E2
Cowthorpe N Yorks 95 D7
Cox Common Suff 69 F6
Cox Green Windsor 27 B6
Cox Moor Notts 76 D5
Coxbank Ches 74 E3
Coxbench Derbys 76 E3
Coxford Norf 80 E4
Coxford Soton 14 C4
Coxheath Kent 29 D8
Coxhill Kent 31 E6
Coxhoe Durham 111 F6
Coxley Som 23 E7
Coxwold N Yorks 95 B8
Coychurch Bridgend 21 B8
Coylton S Ayrs 112 B4
Coylumbridge Highld 148 C5
Coynach Aberds 150 D3
Coynachie Aberds 159 F8
Coytrahen Bridgend 34 F2
Crabadon Devon 7 D5
Crabbs Cross Worcs 50 C5
Crabtree W Sus 17 B6
Crackenthorpe Cumb 100 B1
Crackington Haven Corn 8 E3
Crackley Warks 51 B7
Crackleybank Shrops 61 C7
Crackpot N Yorks 100 E4
Cracoe N Yorks 94 C2
Craddock Devon 11 C5
Cradhlastadh W Isles 172 E3
Cradley Hereford 50 E2
Cradley Heath W Mid 62 F3
Crafthole Corn 5 D8
Cragg Vale W Yorks 87 B8
Craggan Highld 149 B6
Craggie Highld 165 C5
Craggie Highld 157 F8
Craghead Durham 110 D5
Crai Powys 34 B2
Craibstone Moray 159 D8
Craichie Angus 143 E5
Craig Dumfries 106 B3
Craig Dumfries 106 C3
Craig Highld 155 F6
Craig Castle Aberds 150 B3
Craig-cefn-parc Swansea 33 D7
Craig Penllyn V Glam 21 B8
Craig-y-don Conwy 83 C7
Craig-y-nos Powys 34 C2
Craiganor Lodge Perth 140 D3
Craigdam Aberds 160 E5
Craigdarroch Dumfries 113 E7
Craigdarroch Highld 156 D5
Craigdhu Highld 156 E5
Craigearn Aberds 151 C6
Craigellachie Moray 159 E6
Craigencross Dumfries 104 C4
Craigend Perth 134 B3
Craigend Stirl 133 F6
Craigendive Argyll 129 B5
Craigendoran Argyll 129 B8
Craigends Renfs 120 C4
Craigens Argyll 126 C2
Craigens E Ayrs 113 C5
Craighat Stirl 132 F3
Craighead Fife 135 D8
Craighlaw Mains Dumfries 105 C7
Craighouse Argyll 127 F3
Craigie Aberds 151 C8
Craigie Dundee 142 F4
Craigie Perth 134 B3
Craigie Perth 141 E8
Craigie S Ayrs 120 F4
Craigiefield Orkney 176 E3
Craigielaw E Loth 123 B7
Craiglockhart Edin 122 B5
Craigmalloch E Ayrs 112 E4
Craigmaud Aberds 161 C5
Craigmillar Edin 123 B5
Craigmore Argyll 129 D6
Craignant Shrops 73 F6
Craigneuk N Lnrk 121 D7
Craigneuk N Lnrk 121 C7
Craignure Argyll 130 B3
Craigo Angus 143 C6
Craigow Perth 134 D2
Craigrothie Fife 135 C5
Craigroy Moray 158 D5
Craigruie Stirl 132 B3
Craigston Castle Aberds 160 C4
Craigton Aberdeen 151 D7
Craigton Angus 142 D3
Craigton Angus 143 F5
Craigton Highld 164 E3
Craigtown Highld 168 D3
Craik Borders 115 D6
Crail Fife 135 D8
Crailing Borders 116 B2
Crailinghall Borders 116 B2
Craiselound N Lincs 89 E8
Crakehill N Yorks 95 B7
Crakemarsh Staffs 75 F7
Crambe N Yorks 96 C3
Cramlington Northumb 111 B5
Cramond Edin 122 B4
Cramond Bridge Edin 122 B4
Cranage Ches 74 C4
Cranberry Staffs 74 F5
Cranborne Dorset 13 C8
Cranbourne Brack 27 B7
Cranbrook Kent 18 B4
Cranbrook Common Kent 18 B4
Crane Moor S Yorks 88 D4
Crane's Corner Norf 68 C2
Cranfield Beds 53 E7
Cranford London 28 B2
Cranford St Andrew Northants 53 B7
Cranford St John Northants 53 B7
Cranham Glos 37 C5
Cranham London 42 F1
Crank Mers 86 E3
Crank Wood Gtr Man 86 D4
Cranleigh Sur 27 F8
Cranley Suff 57 B5
Cranmer Green Suff 56 B4
Cranmore I o W 14 F4
Cranna Aberds 160 C3
Crannich Argyll 137 D6
Crannoch Moray 159 D8
Cranoe Leics 64 E4
Cransford Suff 57 C7
Cranshaws Borders 124 C2
Cranstal I o M 84 B4
Crantock Corn 4 C2
Cranwell Lincs 78 E3
Cranwich Norf 67 E7
Cranworth Norf 68 D2
Craobh Haven Argyll 130 E3
Crapstone Devon 6 C3
Crarae Argyll 131 F5
Crask Inn Highld 164 B2
Crask of Aigas Highld 157 E5
Craskins Aberds 150 D4
Craster Northumb 117 C8
Craswall Hereford 48 F4
Craffield Suff 57 B7
Crathes Aberds 151 E6
Crathes Castle and Gardens Aberds 151 E6
Crathie Aberds 149 E8
Crathie Highld 147 E8
Crathorne N Yorks 102 D2
Craven Arms Shrops 60 F4
Crawcrook T & W 110 C4
Crawford Lancs 86 D2
Crawford S Lnrk 114 B2
Crawfordjohn S Lnrk 113 B8
Crawick Dumfries 113 C7
Crawley Hants 26 F2
Crawley Oxon 38 C3
Crawley W Sus 28 F3
Crawley Down W Sus 28 F4
Crawleyside Durham 110 E2
Crawshawbooth Lancs 87 B6
Crawton Aberds 143 B8
Cray N Yorks 94 B2
Cray Perth 141 C8
Crayford London 29 B6
Crayke N Yorks 95 B8
Crays Hill Essex 42 E3
Cray's Pond Oxon 39 F6
Creacombe Devon 10 C3
Creag Ghoraidh W Isles 170 F3
Creagan Argyll 138 E3
Creaguaineach Lodge Highld 139 C7
Creaksea Essex 43 E5
Creaton Northants 52 B5
Creca Dumfries 108 B2
Credenhill Hereford 49 E6
Crediton Devon 10 D3
Creebridge Dumfries 105 C8
Creech Heathfield Som 11 B7
Creech St Michael Som 11 B7
Creed Corn 3 B8
Creekmouth London 41 F7
Creeting Bottoms Suff 56 D5
Creeting St Mary Suff 56 D4
Creeton Lincs 65 B7
Creetown Dumfries 105 D8
Creg-ny-Baa I o M 84 D3
Creggans Argyll 131 E6
Cregneash I o M 84 F1
Cregrina Powys 48 D3
Creich Fife 134 B5
Creigiau Cardiff 34 F4
Cremyll Corn 6 D2
Creslow Bucks 39 B8
Cressage Shrops 61 D5
Cressbrook Derbys 75 B8
Cresselly Pembs 32 D1
Cressing Essex 42 B3
Cresswell Northumb 117 E8
Cresswell Staffs 75 F6
Cresswell Quay Pembs 32 D1
Creswell Derbys 76 B5
Cretingham Suff 57 C6
Cretshengan Argyll 128 D2
Crewe Ches 73 D8
Crewe Ches 74 D4
Crewgreen Powys 60 C3
Crewkerne Som 12 D2
Crianlarich Stirl 132 B2
Cribyn Ceredig 46 D4
Criccieth Gwyn 71 D5
Crich Derbys 76 D3
Crichie Aberds 161 D6
Crichton Midloth 123 C6
Crick Mon 36 E1
Crick Northants 52 B3
Crickadarn Powys 48 E2
Cricket Malherbie Som 11 C8
Cricket St Thomas Som 11 D8
Crickheath Shrops 60 B2
Crickhowell Powys 35 C6
Cricklade Wilts 37 E8
Cricklewood London 41 F5
Cridling Stubbs N Yorks 89 B6
Crieff Perth 133 B7
Crieff Visitors' Centre Perth 133 B7
Criggion Powys 60 C2
Crigglestone W Yorks 88 C4
Crimond Aberds 161 C7
Crimonmogate Aberds 161 C7
Crimplesham Norf 67 D6
Crinan Argyll 128 A2
Cringleford Norf 68 D4
Cringles W Yorks 94 E3
Crinow Pembs 32 C2
Cripplesease Corn 2 C4
Cripplestyle Dorset 13 C8
Cripp's Corner E Sus 18 C4
Croasdale Cumb 98 C2
Crock Street Som 11 C8
Crockenhill Kent 29 C6
Crockernwell Devon 10 E2
Crockerton Wilts 24 E3
Crocketford or Ninemile Bar Dumfries 106 B5
Crockey Hill York 96 E2
Crockham Hill Kent 28 D5
Crockleford Heath Essex 43 B6
Crockness Orkney 176 G2
Croes-goch Pembs 44 B3
Croes-lan Ceredig 46 E2
Croes-y-mwyalch Torf 35 E7
Croeserw Neath 34 E2
Croesor Gwyn 71 C7
Croesyceiliog Carms 33 C5
Croesyceiliog Torf 35 E7
Croesywaun Gwyn 82 F5
Croft Leics 64 E2
Croft Lincs 79 C8
Croft Pembs 45 E3
Croft Warr 86 E4
Croft Motor Racing Circuit N Yorks 101 D7
Croft-on-Tees N Yorks 101 D7
Croftamie Stirl 132 F3
Croftmalloch W Loth 122 C2
Crofton Wilts 25 C7
Crofton W Yorks 88 C4
Crofts of Benachielt Highld 169 F6
Crofts of Haddo Aberds 160 E5
Crofts of Inverthernie Aberds 160 D4
Crofts of Meikle Ardo Aberds 161 D5
Crofty Swansea 33 E6
Croggan Argyll 130 C3
Croglin Cumb 109 E5
Croich Highld 164 E1
Crois Dughaill W Isles 171 H3
Cromarty Highld 157 C8
Cromblet Aberds 160 E4
Cromdale Highld 149 B6
Cromer Herts 41 B5
Cromer Norf 81 C8
Cromford Derbys 76 D2
Cromhall S Glos 36 E3
Cromhall Common S Glos 36 F3
Cromor W Isles 172 F7
Cromra Highld 147 E8
Cromwell Notts 77 C7
Cronberry E Ayrs 113 B6
Crondall Hants 27 E5
Cronk-y-Voddy I o M 84 D3
Cronton Mers 86 F2
Crook Cumb 99 E6
Crook Durham 110 F4
Crook of Devon Perth 134 D2
Crookedholm E Ayrs 120 F4
Crookes S Yorks 88 F4
Crookham Northumb 124 F5
Crookham W Berks 26 C3
Crookham Village Hants 27 D5
Crookhaugh Borders 114 B4
Crookhouse Borders 116 B3
Crooklands Cumb 99 F7
Croome Park, Pershore Worcs 50 E3
Cropredy Oxon 52 E2
Cropston Leics 64 C2
Cropthorne Worcs 50 E4
Cropton N Yorks 103 F5
Cropwell Bishop Notts 77 F6
Cropwell Butler Notts 77 F6
Cros W Isles 172 B8
Crosbost W Isles 172 F6
Crosby Cumb 107 F7
Crosby I o M 84 E3
Crosby N Lincs 90 C2
Crosby Garrett Cumb 100 D2
Crosby Ravensworth Cumb 99 C8
Crosby Villa Cumb 107 F7
Croscombe Som 23 E7
Cross Som 23 D6
Cross Ash Mon 35 C8
Cross-at-Hand Kent 29 E8
Cross Green Devon 9 F5
Cross Green Suff 56 D3
Cross Green Suff 56 D2
Cross Green Warks 51 D8
Cross Hands Carms 33 C6
Cross-hands Carms 32 B2
Cross Hands Pembs 32 C1
Cross Hill Derbys 76 E4
Cross Houses Shrops 60 D5
Cross in Hand E Sus 18 C2
Cross in Hand Leics 64 F2
Cross Inn Ceredig 46 D2
Cross Inn Ceredig 46 C4
Cross Inn Rhondda 34 F4
Cross Keys Kent 29 D6
Cross Lane Head Shrops 61 E7
Cross Lanes Corn 3 D5
Cross Lanes N Yorks 95 C8
Cross Lanes Wrex 73 E7
Cross Oak Powys 35 B5
Cross of Jackston Aberds 160 E4
Cross o'th'hands Derbys 76 E2
Cross Street Suff 57 B5
Crossaig Argyll 118 A5
Crossal Highld 153 F5
Crossapol Argyll 136 F1
Crossburn Falk 121 B8
Crossbush W Sus 16 D4
Crosscanonby Cumb 107 F7
Crossdale Street Norf 81 D8
Crossens Mers 85 C4
Crossflatts W Yorks 94 E4
Crossford Fife 134 F2
Crossford S Lnrk 121 E8
Crossgate Lincs 66 B2
Crossgatehall E Loth 123 C6
Crossgates Fife 134 F3
Crossgates Powys 48 C2
Crossgill Lancs 93 C5
Crosshill E Ayrs 112 B4
Crosshill Fife 134 E3
Crosshill S Ayrs 112 D3
Crosshouse E Ayrs 120 F3
Crossings Cumb 108 B5
Crosskeys Caerph 35 E6
Crosskirk Highld 168 B5
Crosslanes Shrops 60 C3
Crosslee Borders 115 C6
Crosslee Renfs 120 C4
Crossmichael Dumfries 106 C4

D

Drefach Carms 46 F2
Drefach Carms 33 C6
Drefelin Carms 46 F2
Dreghorn N Ayrs 120 F3
Drellingore Kent 31 E6
Drem E Loth 123 B8
Dresden Stoke 75 E6
Dreumasdal W Isles 170 G3
Drewsteignton Devon 10 E2
Driby Lincs 79 B6
Driffield E Yorks 97 D6
Driffield Glos 37 E7
Drigg Cumb 98 E2
Drighlington W Yorks 88 B3
Drimnin Highld 137 C6
Drimpton Dorset 12 D2
Drimsynie Argyll 131 E7
Drinisiadar W Isles 173 J4
Drinkstone Suff 56 C3
Drinkstone Green Suff 56 C3
Drishaig Argyll 131 D7
Drissaig Argyll 130 D5
Drochil Borders 122 E4
Drointon Staffs 62 B4
Droitwich Spa Worcs 50 C3
Droman Highld 166 D3
Dron Perth 134 C3
Dronfield Derbys 76 B3
Dronfield Woodhouse Derbys 76 B3
Drongan E Ayrs 112 C4
Dronley Angus 142 F3
Droxford Hants 15 C7
Droylsden Gtr Man 87 E7
Druid Denb 72 E4
Druidston Pembs 44 D3
Druimarbin Highld 138 B4
Druimavuic Argyll 138 E4
Druimdrishaig Argyll 128 C2
Druimindarroch Highld 145 E6
Druimyeon More Argyll 118 A3
Drum Argyll 128 C4
Drum Perth 134 D2
Drumbeg Highld 166 F3
Drumblade Aberds 160 D2
Drumblair Aberds 160 D3
Drumbuie Dumfries 113 F5
Drumbuie Highld 155 G3
Drumburgh Cumb 108 D2
Drumburn Dumfries 107 C6
Drumchapel Glasgow 120 B5
Drumchardine Highld 157 E6
Drumchork Highld 162 F2
Drumclog S Lnrk 121 F6
Drumderfit Highld 157 D7
Drumeldrie Fife 135 D6
Drumelzier Borders 122 F4
Drumfearn Highld 145 B6
Drumgask Highld 148 E2
Drumgley Angus 142 D4
Drumguish Highld 148 E3
Drumin Moray 159 F5
Drumlasie Aberds 150 D5
Drumlemble Argyll 118 E3
Drumligair Aberds 151 C8
Drumlithie Aberds 151 F6
Drummoddie Dumfries 105 E7
Drummond Highld 157 C7
Drummore Dumfries 104 F5
Drummuir Moray 159 E7
Drummuir Castle Moray 159 E7
Drumnadrochit Highld 147 B8
Drumnagorrach Moray 160 C2
Drumoak Aberds 151 E6
Drumpark Dumfries 107 A5
Drumphail Dumfries 105 C6
Drumrash Dumfries 106 B3
Drumrunie Highld 163 D5
Drums Aberds 151 B8
Drumsallie Highld 138 B3
Drumstinchall Dumfries 107 D5
Drumsturdy Angus 142 F4
Drumtochty Castle Aberds 143 B6
Drumtroddan Dumfries 105 E7
Drumuie Highld 152 E5
Drumuillie Highld 148 B5
Drumvaich Stirl 133 D5
Drumwhindle Aberds 161 E6
Drunkendub Angus 143 E6
Drury Flint 73 C6
Drury Square Norf 68 C2
Drusillas Park, Polegate E Sus 18 E2
Dry Doddington Lincs 77 E8
Dry Drayton Cambs 54 C4
Drybeck Cumb 100 C1
Drybridge Moray 159 C8
Drybridge N Ayrs 120 F3
Drybrook Glos 36 C3
Dryburgh Borders 123 F8
Dryhope Borders 115 B5
Drylaw Edin 122 B5
Drym Corn 2 C5
Drymen Stirl 132 F3
Drymuir Aberds 161 D6
Drynoch Highld 153 F5
Dryslwyn Carms 33 B6
Dryton Shrops 61 D5
Dubford Aberds 160 B5
Dubton Angus 143 D5
Duchally Highld 163 C7
Duchlage Argyll 129 B8
Duck Corner Suff 57 E7
Duckington Ches 73 D8
Ducklington Oxon 38 D3
Duckmanton Derbys 76 B4
Duck's Cross Beds 54 D2
Duddenhoe End Essex 55 F5
Duddingston Edin 123 B5
Duddington Northants 65 D6
Duddleswell E Sus 17 B8
Duddo Northumb 124 E5
Duddon Ches 74 C2
Duddon Bridge Cumb 98 F4
Dudleston Shrops 73 F7
Dudleston Heath Shrops 73 F7
Dudley T & W 111 B5
Dudley W Mid 62 E3
Dudley Port W Mid 62 E3
Dudley Zoological Gardens W Mid 62 E3
Duffield Derbys 76 E3
Duffryn Newport 35 F6
Duffryn Neath 34 E2
Dufftown Moray 159 F7
Duffus Moray 159 C5
Dufton Cumb 100 B1
Duggleby N Yorks 96 C4
Duirinish Highld 155 G3
Duisdalemore Highld 145 B7
Duisky Highld 138 B4
Dukestown Bl Gwent 35 C5
Dukinfield Gtr Man 87 E7
Dulas Anglesey 82 C4
Dulcote Som 23 E7
Dulford Devon 11 D5
Dull Perth 141 E5
Dullatur N Lnrk 121 B7
Dullingham Cambs 55 D7
Dulnain Bridge Highld 149 B5
Duloe Beds 54 C2
Duloe Corn 5 D7
Dulsie Highld 158 E3
Dulverton Som 10 B4
Dulwich London 28 B4
Dumbarton W Dunb 120 B3
Dumbleton Glos 50 F5
Dumcrieff Dumfries 114 D4
Dumfries Dumfries 107 B6
Dumgoyne Stirl 132 F4
Dummer Hants 26 E3
Dumpford W Sus 16 B2
Dumpton Kent 31 C7
Dun Angus 143 D6
Dun Charlabhaigh W Isles 172 D4
Dunain Ho. Highld 157 E7
Dunalastair Perth 140 D4
Dunan Highld 153 G6
Dunans Argyll 129 A5
Dunball Som 22 E5
Dunbar E Loth 124 B2
Dunbeath Highld 165 B8
Dunbeg Argyll 130 B4
Dunblane Stirl 133 D6
Dunbog Fife 134 C4
Duncanston Aberds 150 B4
Duncanston Highld 157 D6
Dunchurch Warks 52 B2
Duncote Northants 52 D4
Duncow Dumfries 114 F2
Duncraggan Stirl 132 D4
Duncrievie Perth 134 D3
Duncton W Sus 16 C3
Dundas Ho. Orkney 176 H3
Dundee Dundee 142 F4
Dundee Airport Dundee 135 B5
Dundeugh Dumfries 113 F5
Dundon Som 23 F6
Dundonald S Ayrs 120 F3
Dundonnell Highld 162 F4
Dundonnell Hotel Highld 162 F4
Dundonnell House Highld 163 F5
Dundraw Cumb 108 E2
Dundreggan Highld 147 C6
Dundreggan Lodge Highld 147 C6
Dundrennan Dumfries 106 E4
Dundry N Som 23 C7
Dunecht Aberds 151 D6
Dunfermline Fife 134 F2
Dunfield Glos 37 E8
Dunford Bridge S Yorks 88 D2
Dungworth S Yorks 88 F3
Dunham Notts 77 B8
Dunham Massey Gtr Man 86 F5
Dunham-on-the-Hill Ches 73 B8
Dunham Town Gtr Man 86 F5
Dunhampton Worcs 50 C3
Dunholme Lincs 78 B3
Dunino Fife 135 C7
Dunipace Falk 133 F7
Dunira Perth 133 B6
Dunkeld Perth 141 E7
Dunkerton Bath 24 D2
Dunkeswell Devon 11 D6
Dunkeswick N Yorks 95 E6
Dunkirk Kent 30 D4
Dunkirk Norf 81 E8
Dunk's Green Kent 29 D7
Dunlappie Angus 143 C5
Dunley Hants 26 D2
Dunley Worcs 50 C2
Dunlichity Lodge Highld 157 F7
Dunlop E Ayrs 120 E4
Dunmaglass Lodge Highld 147 B8
Dunmore Argyll 128 D2
Dunmore Falk 133 F7
Dunnet Highld 169 B7
Dunnichen Angus 143 E5
Dunninald Angus 143 D7
Dunning Perth 134 C2
Dunnington E Yorks 97 D7
Dunnington Warks 51 D5
Dunnington York 96 D2
Dunnockshaw Lancs 87 B6
Dunollie Argyll 130 B4
Dunoon Argyll 129 C6
Dunragit Dumfries 105 D5
Dunrobin Castle Museum & Gardens Highld 165 D5
Dunrostan Argyll 128 B2
Duns Borders 124 D3
Duns Tew Oxon 38 D4
Dunsby Lincs 65 B8
Dunscore Dumfries 113 F8
Dunscroft S Yorks 89 D7
Dunsdale Redcar 102 C4
Dunsden Green Oxon 26 B5
Dunsfold Sur 27 F8
Dunsford Devon 10 F3
Dunshalt Fife 134 C4
Dunshillock Aberds 161 D6
Dunskey Ho. Dumfries 104 D4
Dunsley N Yorks 103 C6
Dunsmore Bucks 40 D1
Dunsop Bridge Lancs 93 D6
Dunstable Beds 40 B3
Dunstall Staffs 63 B5
Dunstall Common Worcs 50 E3
Dunstall Green Suff 55 C8
Dunstan Northumb 117 C8
Dunstan Steads Northumb 117 B8
Dunster Som 21 E8
Dunster Castle, Minehead Som 21 E8
Dunston Lincs 78 C3
Dunston Norf 68 D5
Dunston Staffs 62 C3
Dunston T & W 110 C5
Dunsville S Yorks 89 D7
Dunswell E Yorks 97 F6
Dunsyre S Lnrk 122 E3
Dunterton Devon 5 B8
Duntisbourne Abbots Glos 37 D6
Duntisbourne Leer Glos 37 D6
Duntisbourne Rouse Glos 37 D6
Duntish Dorset 12 D4
Duntocher W Dunb 120 B4
Dunton Beds 54 E3
Dunton Bucks 39 B8
Dunton Norf 80 D4
Dunton Bassett Leics 64 E2
Dunton Green Kent 29 D6
Dunton Wayletts Essex 42 E2
Duntulm Highld 152 B5
Dunure S Ayrs 112 C2
Dunvant Swansea 33 E6
Dunvegan Highld 152 E3
Dunvegan Castle Highld 152 E3
Dunwich Suff 57 B8
Dunwood Staffs 75 D6
Dupplin Castle Perth 134 C2
Durdar Cumb 108 D4
Durgates E Sus 18 B3
Durham Durham 111 E5
Durham Cathedral Durham 111 E5
Durham Tees Valley Airport Stockton 102 C1
Durisdeer Dumfries 113 D8
Durisdeermill Dumfries 113 D8
Durkar W Yorks 88 C4
Durleigh Som 22 F4
Durley Hants 15 C6
Durley Wilts 25 C7
Durnamuck Highld 162 E4
Durness Highld 167 C6
Durno Aberds 151 B6
Duror Highld 138 D3
Durran Argyll 131 E5
Durran Highld 169 C6
Durrington Wilts 25 E6
Durrington W Sus 16 D5
Dursley Glos 36 E4
Durston Som 11 B7
Durweston Dorset 13 D6
Dury Shetland 175 G6
Duston Northants 52 C5
Duthil Highld 148 B5
Dutlas Powys 48 B4
Duton Hill Essex 42 B2
Dutson Corn 8 F5
Dutton Ches 74 B2
Duxford Cambs 55 E5
Duxford Oxon 38 E3
Duxford Airfield (Imperial War Museum), Sawston Cambs 55 E5
Dwygyfylchi Conwy 83 D7
Dwyran Anglesey 82 E4
Dyce Aberdeen 151 C7
Dye House Northumb 110 D2
Dyffryn Bridgend 34 E2
Dyffryn Carms 32 B4
Dyffryn Pembs 44 B4
Dyffryn Ardudwy Gwyn 71 E6
Dyffryn Castell Ceredig 58 F4
Dyffryn Ceidrych Carms 33 B8
Dyffryn Cellwen Neath 34 D2
Dyke Lincs 65 B8
Dyke Moray 158 D3
Dykehead Angus 142 C3
Dykehead N Lnrk 121 D8
Dykehead Stirl 132 E4
Dykelands Aberds 143 C7
Dykends Angus 142 D2
Dykeside Aberds 160 D4
Dykesmains N Ayrs 120 E2
Dylife Powys 59 E5
Dymchurch Kent 19 C7
Dymock Glos 50 F2
Dyrham S Glos 24 B2
Dyrham Park S Glos 24 B2
Dysart Fife 134 E5
Dyserth Denb 72 B4

E

Eachwick Northumb 110 B4
Eadar Dha Fhadhail W Isles 172 E3
Eagland Hill Lancs 92 E4
Eagle Lincs 77 C8
Eagle Barnsdale Lincs 77 C8
Eagle Moor Lincs 77 C8
Eaglescliffe Stockton 102 C2
Eaglesfield Cumb 98 B2
Eaglesfield Dumfries 108 B2
Eaglesham E Renf 121 D5
Eaglethorpe Northants 65 E7
Eairy I o M 84 E2
Eakley Lanes M Keynes 53 D6
Eakring Notts 77 C6
Ealand N Lincs 89 C8
Ealing London 40 F4
Eals Northumb 109 D6
Eamont Bridge Cumb 99 B7
Earby Lancs 94 E2
Earcroft Blkburn 86 B4
Eardington Shrops 61 E7
Eardisland Hereford 49 D6
Eardisley Hereford 48 E5
Eardiston Shrops 60 B3
Eardiston Worcs 49 C8
Earith Cambs 54 B4
Earl Shilton Leics 63 E8
Earl Soham Suff 57 C6
Earl Sterndale Derbys 75 C7
Earl Stonham Suff 56 D5
Earle Northumb 117 B5
Earley Wokingham 27 B5
Earlham Norf 68 D5
Earlish Highld 152 C4
Earls Barton Northants 53 C6
Earls Colne Essex 42 B4
Earl's Croome Worcs 50 E3
Earl's Green Suff 56 C4
Earlsdon W Mid 51 B8
Earlsferry Fife 135 E6
Earlsfield Lincs 78 F2
Earlsford Aberds 160 E5
Earlsheaton W Yorks 88 B3
Earlsmill Moray 158 D3
Earlston Borders 123 F8
Earlston E Ayrs 120 F4
Earlswood Mon 36 E1
Earlswood Sur 28 E3
Earlswood Warks 51 B6
Earnley W Sus 16 E2
Earsairidh W Isles 171 L3
Earsdon T & W 111 B6
Earsham Norf 69 F6
Earswick York 96 D2
Eartham W Sus 16 D3
Easby N Yorks 102 D3
Easby N Yorks 101 D6
Easdale Argyll 130 D3
Easebourne W Sus 16 B2
Easenhall Warks 52 B2
Eashing Sur 27 E7
Easington Bucks 39 C6
Easington Durham 111 E7
Easington E Yorks 91 C7
Easington Northumb 125 F7
Easington Oxon 52 F2
Easington Oxon 39 E6
Easington Redcar 103 C5
Easington Colliery Durham 111 E7
Easington Lane T & W 111 E6
Easingwold N Yorks 95 C8
Easole Street Kent 31 D6
Eassie Angus 142 E3
East Aberthaw V Glam 22 C2
East Adderbury Oxon 52 F2
East Allington Devon 7 E5
East Anstey Devon 10 B3
East Appleton N Yorks 101 E7
East Ardsley W Yorks 88 B4
East Ashling W Sus 16 D2
East Auchronie Aberds 151 D7
East Ayton N Yorks 103 F7
East Bank Bl Gwent 35 D6
East Barkwith Lincs 91 F5
East Barming Kent 29 D8
East Barnby N Yorks 103 C6
East Barnet London 41 E5
East Barns E Loth 124 B3
East Barsham Norf 80 D5
East Beckham Norf 81 D7
East Bedfont London 27 B8
East Bergholt Suff 56 F4
East Bilney Norf 68 C2
East Blatchington E Sus 17 D8
East Boldre Hants 14 D4
East Brent Som 22 D5
East Bridgford Notts 77 E6
East Buckland Devon 21 F5
East Budleigh Devon 11 F5
East Burrafirth Shetland 175 H5
East Burton Dorset 13 F6
East Butsfield Durham 110 E4
East Butterwick N Lincs 90 D2
East Cairnbeg Aberds 143 B7
East Calder W Loth 122 C3
East Carleton Norf 68 D4
East Carlton Northants 64 F5
East Carlton W Yorks 94 E5
East Chaldon Dorset 13 F5
East Challow Oxon 38 F3
East Chiltington E Sus 17 C7
East Chinnock Som 12 C2
East Chisenbury Wilts 25 D6
East Clandon Sur 27 D8
East Claydon Bucks 39 B7
East Clyne Highld 165 D6
East Coker Som 12 C3
East Combe Som 22 F3
East Common N Yorks 96 F2
East Compton Som 23 E8
East Cottingwith E Yorks 96 E3
East Cowes I o W 15 E6
East Cowick E Yorks 89 B7
East Cowton N Yorks 101 D8
East Cramlington Northumb 111 B5
East Cranmore Som 23 E8
East Creech Dorset 13 F7
East Croachy Highld 148 B2
East Croftmore Highld 149 C5
East Curthwaite Cumb 108 E3
East Dean E Sus 18 F2
East Dean Hants 14 B3
East Dean W Sus 16 C3
East Down Devon 20 E5
East Drayton Notts 77 B7
East Ella Hull 90 B4
East End Dorset 13 E7
East End E Yorks 91 B6
East End Hants 14 E4
East End Hants 15 B7
East End Hants 26 C2
East End Herts 41 B7
East End Kent 18 B5
East End N Som 23 B6
East End Oxon 38 C3
East Farleigh Kent 29 D8
East Farndon Northants 64 F4
East Ferry Lincs 90 E2
East Fortune E Loth 123 B8
East Garston W Berks 25 B8
East Ginge Oxon 38 F4
East Goscote Leics 64 C3
East Grafton Wilts 25 C7
East Grimstead Wilts 14 B3
East Grinstead W Sus 28 F4
East Guldeford E Sus 19 C6
East Haddon Northants 52 C4
East Hagbourne Oxon 39 F5
East Halton N Lincs 90 C5
East Ham London 41 F7
East Hanney Oxon 38 E4
East Hanningfield Essex 42 D3
East Hardwick W Yorks 89 C5
East Harling Norf 68 F2
East Harlsey N Yorks 102 E2
East Harnham Wilts 14 B2
East Harptree Bath 23 D7
East Hartford Northumb 111 B5
East Harting W Sus 15 C8
East Hatley Cambs 54 D3
East Hauxwell N Yorks 101 E6
East Haven Angus 143 F5
East Heckington Lincs 78 E4
East Hedleyhope Durham 110 E4
East Hendred Oxon 38 F4
East Herrington T & W 111 D6
East Heslerton N Yorks 96 B5
East Hoathly E Sus 18 D2
East Horrington Som 23 E7
East Horsley Sur 27 D8
East Horton Northumb 125 F6
East Huntspill Som 22 E5
East Hyde Beds 40 C4
East Ilkerton Devon 21 E6
East Ilsley W Berks 38 F4
East Keal Lincs 79 C6
East Kennett Wilts 25 C6
East Keswick W Yorks 95 E6
East Kilbride S Lnrk 121 D6
East Kirkby Lincs 79 C6
East Knapton N Yorks 96 B4
East Knighton Dorset 13 F6
East Knoyle Wilts 24 F3
East Kyloe Northumb 125 F6
East Lambrook Som 12 C2
East Lamington Highld 157 B8
East Langdon Kent 31 E7
East Langton Leics 64 E4
East Langwell Highld 164 D4
East Lavant W Sus 16 D2
East Lavington W Sus 16 C3
East Layton N Yorks 101 D6
East Leake Notts 64 B2
East Learmouth Northumb 124 F4
East Leigh Devon 9 D8
East Lexham Norf 67 C8
East Lilburn Northumb 117 B6
East Linton E Loth 123 B8
East Liss Hants 15 B8
East Looe Corn 5 D7
East Lound N Lincs 89 E8
East Lulworth Dorset 13 F6
East Lutton N Yorks 96 C5
East Lydford Som 23 F7
East Mains Aberds 151 E5
East Malling Kent 29 D8
East March Angus 142 F4
East Marden W Sus 16 C2
East Markham Notts 77 B7
East Marton N Yorks 94 D2
East Meon Hants 15 B7
East Mere Devon 10 C4
East Mersea Essex 43 C6
East Mey Highld 169 B8
East Molesey Sur 28 C2
East Morden Dorset 13 E7
East Morton W Yorks 94 E3
East Ness N Yorks 96 B2
East Newton E Yorks 97 F8
East Norton Leics 64 D4
East Nynehead Som 11 B6
East Oakley Hants 26 D3
East Ogwell Devon 7 B6
East Orchard Dorset 13 C6
East Ord Northumb 125 D5
East Panson Devon 9 E5
East Peckham Kent 29 E7
East Pennard Som 23 F7
East Perry Cambs 54 C2
East Portlemouth Devon 6 F5
East Prawle Devon 7 F5
East Preston W Sus 16 D4
East Putford Devon 9 C5
East Quantoxhead Som 22 E3
East Rainton T & W 111 E6
East Ravendale NE Lincs 91 E6
East Raynham Norf 80 E4
East Rhidorroch Lodge Highld 163 E6
East Rigton W Yorks 95 E6
East Rounton N Yorks 102 D2
East Row N Yorks 103 C6
East Rudham Norf 80 E4
East Runton Norf 81 C7
East Ruston Norf 69 B6
East Saltoun E Loth 123 C7
East Sleekburn Northumb 117 F8
East Somerton Norf 69 C7
East Stockwith Lincs 89 E8
East Stoke Dorset 13 F6
East Stoke Notts 77 E7
East Stour Dorset 13 B6
East Stourmouth Kent 31 C6
East Stowford Devon 9 B8
East Stratton Hants 26 F3
East Studdal Kent 31 E7
East Suisnish Highld 153 F6
East Taphouse Corn 5 C6
East-the-Water Devon 9 B6
East Thirston Northumb 117 E7
East Tilbury Thurrock 29 B7
East Tisted Hants 26 F5
East Torrington Lincs 90 F5
East Tuddenham Norf 68 C3
East Tytherley Hants 14 B3
East Tytherton Wilts 24 B4
East Village Devon 10 D3
East Wall Shrops 60 E5
East Walton Norf 67 C7
East Wellow Hants 14 B4
East Wemyss Fife 134 E5
East Whitburn W Loth 122 C2
East Williamston Pembs 32 D1
East Winch Norf 67 C6
East Winterslow Wilts 25 F7
East Wittering W Sus 15 E8
East Witton N Yorks 101 F6
East Woodburn Northumb 116 F5
East Woodhay Hants 26 C2
East Worldham Hants 26 F5
East Worlington Devon 10 C2
East Worthing W Sus 17 D5
Eastbourne E Sus 18 F3
Eastbridge Suff 57 C8
Eastburn W Yorks 94 E3
Eastbury Herts 40 E3
Eastbury W Berks 25 B8
Eastby N Yorks 94 D3
Eastchurch Kent 30 B3
Eastcombe Glos 37 D5
Eastcote London 40 F4
Eastcote Northants 52 D4
Eastcote W Mid 51 B6
Eastcott Corn 8 C4
Eastcott Wilts 24 D5
Eastcourt Wilts 37 E6
Eastcourt Wilts 25 C7
Easter Ardross Highld 157 B7
Easter Balmoral Aberds 149 E8
Easter Boleskine Highld 147 B8
Easter Compton S Glos 36 F2
Easter Cringate Stirl 133 F6
Easter Davoch Aberds 150 D3
Easter Earshaig Dumfries 114 D3
Easter Fearn Highld 164 F3
Easter Galcantray Highld 158 E2
Easter Howgate Midloth 122 C5
Easter Howlaws Borders 124 E3
Easter Kinkell Highld 157 D6
Easter Lednathie Angus 142 C3
Easter Milton Highld 158 D3
Easter Moniack Highld 157 E6
Easter Ord Aberds 151 D7
Easter Quarff Shetland 175 K6
Easter Rhynd Perth 134 C3
Easter Row Stirl 133 E6
Easter Silverford Aberds 160 B4
Easter Skeld Shetland 175 J5
Easter Whyntie Aberds 160 B3
Eastergate W Sus 16 D3
Easterhouse Glasgow 121 C6
Eastern Green W Mid 63 F6
Easterton Wilts 24 D5
Eastertown Som 22 D5
Eastertown of Auchleuchries Aberds 161 E7
Eastfield N Lnrk 121 C8
Eastfield N Yorks 103 F8
Eastfield Hall Northumb 117 D8
Eastgate Durham 110 F2
Eastgate Norf 81 E7
Eastham Mers 85 F4
Eastham Ferry Mers 85 F4
Easthampstead Brack 27 C6
Eastheath Wokingham 27 C6
Easthope Shrops 61 E5
Easthorpe Essex 43 B5
Easthorpe Leics 77 F8
Easthorpe Notts 77 D7
Easthouses Midloth 123 C6
Eastington Devon 10 D2
Eastington Glos 36 D4
Eastington Glos 37 C8
Eastleach Martin Glos 38 D2
Eastleach Turville Glos 38 D1
Eastleigh Devon 9 B6
Eastleigh Hants 14 C5
Eastling Kent 30 D3
Eastmoor Derbys 76 B3
Eastmoor Norf 67 D7
Eastney Ptsmth 15 E7
Eastnor Hereford 50 F2
Eastoft N Lincs 90 C2
Eastoke Hants 15 E8
Easton Cambs 54 B2
Easton Cumb 108 D2
Easton Cumb 108 B4
Easton Devon 10 F2
Easton Dorset 12 G4
Easton Hants 26 F3
Easton Lincs 65 B6
Easton Norf 68 C4
Easton Som 23 E7
Easton Suff 57 D6
Easton Wilts 24 B3
Easton Grey Wilts 37 F5
Easton-in-Gordano N Som 23 B7
Easton Maudit Northants 53 D6
Easton on the Hill Northants 65 D7
Easton Royal Wilts 25 C7
Eastpark Dumfries 107 C7
Eastrea Cambs 66 E2
Eastriggs Dumfries 108 C2
Eastrington E Yorks 89 B8
Eastry Kent 31 D7
Eastville Bristol 23 B8
Eastville Lincs 79 D7
Eastwell Leics 64 B4
Eastwick Herts 41 C7
Eastwick Shetland 174 F5
Eastwood Notts 76 E4
Eastwood Sthend 42 F4
Eastwood W Yorks 87 B7
Eathorpe Warks 51 C8
Eaton Ches 74 C2
Eaton Ches 75 C5
Eaton Leics 64 B4
Eaton Norf 68 D5
Eaton Notts 77 B7
Eaton Oxon 38 D4
Eaton Shrops 60 F3
Eaton Shrops 60 F5
Eaton Bishop Hereford 49 F6
Eaton Bray Beds 40 B2
Eaton Constantine Shrops 61 D5
Eaton Green Beds 40 B2
Eaton Hastings Oxon 38 E2
Eaton on Tern Shrops 61 B6
Eaton Socon Cambs 54 D2
Eavestone N Yorks 94 C5
Ebberston N Yorks 103 F6
Ebbesbourne Wake Wilts 13 B7
Ebbw Vale = Glyn Ebwy Bl Gwent 35 D5
Ebchester Durham 110 D4
Ebford Devon 10 F4
Ebley Glos 37 D5
Ebnal Ches 73 E8
Ebrington Glos 51 E6
Ecchinswell Hants 26 D2
Ecclaw Borders 124 C3
Ecclefechan Dumfries 107 B8
Eccles Borders 124 E3
Eccles Gtr Man 87 E5
Eccles Kent 29 C8
Eccles on Sea Norf 69 B7
Eccles Road Norf 68 E3
Ecclesall S Yorks 88 F4
Ecclesfield S Yorks 88 E4
Ecclesgreig Aberds 143 C7
Eccleshall Staffs 62 B2
Eccleshill W Yorks 94 F4
Ecclesmachan W Loth 122 B3
Eccleston Ches 73 C8
Eccleston Lancs 86 C3
Eccleston Mers 86 E2
Eccleston Park Mers 86 E2
Eccup W Yorks 95 E5
Echt Aberds 151 D6
Eckford Borders 116 B3
Eckington Derbys 76 B4
Eckington Worcs 50 E4
Ecton Northants 53 C6
Edale Derbys 88 F2
Edburton W Sus 17 C6
Edderside Cumb 107 E7
Edderton Highld 164 F4
Eddistone Devon 8 B4
Eddleston Borders 122 E5
Eden Camp Museum, Malton N Yorks 96 B3
Eden Park London 28 C4
Edenbridge Kent 28 E5
Edenfield Lancs 87 C5
Edenhall Cumb 109 F5
Edenham Lincs 65 B7
Edensor Derbys 76 C2
Edentaggart Argyll 129 A8
Edenthorpe S Yorks 89 D7
Edentown Cumb 108 D3
Ederline Argyll 130 E4
Edern Gwyn 70 D3
Edgarley Som 23 F7
Edgbaston W Mid 62 F4
Edgcott Bucks 39 B6
Edgcott Som 21 F7
Edge Shrops 60 D3
Edge End Glos 36 C2
Edge Green Ches 73 D8
Edge Hill Mers 85 F4
Edgebolton Shrops 61 B5
Edgefield Norf 81 D6
Edgefield Street Norf 81 D6
Edgeside Lancs 87 B6
Edgeworth Glos 37 D6
Edgmond Telford 61 C7
Edgmond Marsh Telford 61 B7
Edgton Shrops 60 F3
Edgware London 40 E4
Edgworth Blkburn 86 C5
Edinample Stirl 132 B4
Edinbane Highld 152 D4
Edinburgh Edin 123 B5
Edinburgh Airport Edin 122 B4
Edinburgh Castle Edin 123 B5
Edinburgh Crystal Visitor Centre, Penicuik Midloth 122 C5
Edinburgh Zoo Edin 122 B5
Edingale Staffs 63 C6
Edingight Ho. Moray 160 C2
Edingley Notts 77 D6
Edingthorpe Norf 69 A6
Edingthorpe Green Norf 69 A6
Edington Som 23 F5
Edington Wilts 24 D4
Edintore Moray 159 E8
Edith Weston Rutland 65 D6
Edithmead Som 22 E5
Edlesborough Bucks 40 C2
Edlingham Northumb 117 D7
Edlington Lincs 78 B5
Edmondsham Dorset 13 C8
Edmondsley Durham 110 E5
Edmondthorpe Leics 65 C5
Edmonstone Orkney 176 D4
Edmonton London 41 E6
Edmundbyers Durham 110 D3
Ednam Borders 124 F3
Ednaston Derbys 76 E2
Edradynate Perth 141 D5
Edrom Borders 124 D4
Edstaston Shrops 74 F2
Edstone Warks 51 C6
Edvin Loach Hereford 49 D8
Edwalton Notts 77 F5
Edwardstone Suff 56 E3
Edwinsford Carms 46 F5
Edwinstowe Notts 77 C6
Edworth Beds 54 E3
Edwyn Ralph Hereford 49 D8
Edzell Angus 143 C5
Efail Isaf Rhondda 34 F4
Efailnewydd Gwyn 70 D4
Efailwen Carms 32 B2
Efenechtyd Denb 72 D5
Effingham Sur 28 D2
Effirth Shetland 175 H5
Efford Devon 10 D3
Egdon Worcs 50 D4
Egerton Gtr Man 86 C5
Egerton Kent 30 E3
Egerton Forstal Kent 30 E2
Eggborough N Yorks 89 B6
Eggbuckland Plym 6 D3
Eggington Beds 40 B2
Egginton Derbys 63 B6
Egglescliffe Stockton 102 C2
Eggleston Durham 100 B4
Egham Sur 27 B8
Egleton Rutland 65 D5
Eglingham Northumb 117 C7
Egloshayle Corn 4 B5
Egloskerry Corn 8 F4
Eglwys-Brewis V Glam 22 C2
Eglwys Cross Wrex 73 E8
Eglwys Fach Ceredig 58 E3
Eglwysbach Conwy 83 D8
Eglwyswen Pembs 45 F3
Eglwyswrw Pembs 45 F3
Egmanton Notts 77 C7
Egremont Cumb 98 C2
Egremont Mers 85 E4
Egton N Yorks 103 D6
Egton Bridge N Yorks 103 D6
Eight Ash Green Essex 43 B5
Eignaig Highld 138 E1
Eil Highld 148 C4
Eilanreach Highld 145 B8
Eilean Darach Highld 163 F5
Eileanach Lodge Highld 157 C6
Einacleite W Isles 172 F4
Eisgean W Isles 173 G6
Eisingrug Gwyn 71 D7
Elan Village Powys 47 C8
Elberton S Glos 36 F3
Elburton Plym 6 D3
Elcho Perth 134 B3
Elcombe Swindon 37 F8
Eldernell Cambs 66 E3
Eldersfield Worcs 50 F3
Elderslie Renfs 120 C4
Eldon Durham 101 B7
Eldrick S Ayrs 112 F2
Eldroth N Yorks 93 C7
Eldwick W Yorks 94 E4
Elfhowe Cumb 99 E6
Elford Northumb 125 F7
Elford Staffs 63 C5
Elgin Moray 159 C6
Elgol Highld 153 H6
Elham Kent 31 E5
Elie Fife 135 D6
Elim Anglesey 82 C3
Eling Hants 14 C4
Elishader Highld 152 C6
Elishaw Northumb 116 E4
Elkesley Notts 77 B6
Elkstone Glos 37 C6
Ellan Highld 148 B4

F

G

H

Hardwicke Hereford 48 E4
Hardy's Green Essex 43 B5
Hare Green Essex 43 B6
Hare Hatch Wokingham 27 B6
Hare Street Herts 41 B6
Hareby Lincs 79 C6
Hareden Lancs 93 D6
Harefield London 40 E3
Harehills W Yorks 95 F6
Harehope Northumb 117 B6
Haresceugh Cumb 109 E6
Harescombe Glos 37 C5
Haresfield Glos 37 C5
Hareshaw N Lnrk 121 C8
Hareshaw Head Northumb 116 F4
Harewood W Yorks 95 E6
Harewood End Hereford 36 B2
Harewood House, Wetherby W Yorks 95 E6
Harford Carms 46 E5
Harford Devon 6 D4
Hargate Norf 68 E4
Hargatewall Derbys 75 B8
Hargrave Ches 73 C8
Hargrave Northants 53 B8
Hargrave Suff 55 D8
Harker Cumb 108 C3
Harkland Shetland 174 E6
Harkstead Suff 57 F5
Harlaston Staffs 63 C6
Harlaw Ho. Aberds 151 B6
Harlaxton Lincs 77 F8
Harle Syke Lancs 93 F8
Harlech Gwyn 71 D6
Harlech Castle Gwyn 71 D6
Harlequin Notts 77 F6
Harlescott Shrops 60 C5
Harlesden London 41 F5
Harleston Devon 7 E5
Harleston Norf 68 F5
Harleston Suff 56 D4
Harlestone Northants 52 C5
Harley Shrops 61 D5
Harley S Yorks 88 E4
Harleyholm S Lnrk 122 F2
Harlington Beds 53 F8
Harlington London 27 B8
Harlington S Yorks 89 D5
Harlosh Highld 153 E3
Harlow Essex 41 C7
Harlow Carr RHS Garden, Harrogate N Yorks 95 D5
Harlow Hill Northumb 110 C3
Harlow Hill N Yorks 95 D5
Harlthorpe E Yorks 96 F3
Harlton Cambs 54 D4
Harman's Cross Dorset 13 F7
Harmby N Yorks 101 F6
Harmer Green Herts 41 C5
Harmer Hill Shrops 60 B4
Harmondsworth London 27 B8
Harmston Lincs 78 C2
Harnham Northumb 110 B3
Harnhill Glos 37 D7
Harold Hill London 41 E8
Harold Wood London 41 E8
Haroldston West Pembs 44 D3
Haroldswick Shetland 174 B8
Harome N Yorks 102 F4
Harpenden Herts 40 C4
Harpford Devon 11 E5
Harpham E Yorks 97 C6
Harpley Norf 80 E3
Harpley Worcs 49 C8
Harpole Northants 52 C4
Harpsdale Highld 169 D6
Harpsden Oxon 39 F7
Harpswell Lincs 90 F3
Harpur Hill Derbys 75 B7
Harpurhey Gtr Man 87 D6
Harraby Cumb 108 D4
Harrapool Highld 155 H2
Harrier Shetland 175 J1
Harrietfield Perth 133 B8
Harrietsham Kent 30 D2
Harrington Cumb 98 B1
Harrington Lincs 79 B6
Harrington Northants 64 F4
Harringworth Northants 65 E6
Harris Highld 144 D3
Harris Museum, Preston Lancs 86 B3
Harrogate N Yorks 95 D6
Harrold Beds 53 D7
Harrow London 40 F4
Harrow on the Hill London 40 F4
Harrow Street Suff 56 F3
Harrow Weald London 40 E4
Harrowbarrow Corn 5 C8
Harrowden Beds 53 E8
Harrowgate Hill Darl 101 C7
Harston Cambs 54 D5
Harston Leics 77 F8
Harswell E Yorks 96 E4
Hart Hrtlpl 111 F7
Hart Common Gtr Man 86 D4
Hart Hill Luton 40 B4
Hart Station Hrtlpl 111 F7
Hartburn Northumb 117 F6
Hartburn Stockton 102 C2
Hartest Suff 56 D2
Hartfield E Sus 29 F5
Hartford Cambs 54 B3
Hartford Ches 74 B3
Hartford End Essex 42 C2
Hartfordbridge Hants 27 D5
Hartforth N Yorks 101 D6
Harthill Ches 74 D2
Harthill N Lnrk 122 C2
Harthill S Yorks 89 F5
Hartington Derbys 75 C8
Hartland Devon 8 B4
Hartlebury Worcs 50 B3
Hartlepool Hrtlpl 111 F8
Hartlepool's Maritime Experience Hrtlpl 111 F8
Hartley Cumb 100 D2
Hartley Kent 29 C7
Hartley Kent 18 B4
Hartley Northumb 111 B6
Hartley Westpall Hants 26 D4
Hartley Wintney Hants 27 D5
Hartlip Kent 30 C2
Hartoft End N Yorks 103 E5
Harton N Yorks 96 C3
Harton Shrops 60 F4
Harton T & W 111 C6
Hartpury Glos 36 B4
Hartshead W Yorks 88 B2
Hartshill Warks 63 E7
Hartshorne Derbys 63 B7
Hartsop Cumb 99 C6
Hartwell Northants 53 D5
Hartwood N Lnrk 121 D8
Harvieston Stirl 132 F4
Harvington Worcs 51 E5
Harvington Cross Worcs 51 E5
Harwell Oxon 38 F4
Harwich Essex 57 F6
Harwood Durham 109 F8
Harwood Gtr Man 86 C5
Harwood Dale N Yorks 103 E7
Harworth Notts 89 E7
Hasbury W Mid 62 F3
Hascombe Sur 27 E7
Haselbech Northants 52 B5
Haselbury Plucknett Som 12 C2
Haseley Warks 51 C7
Haselor Warks 51 D6
Hasfield Glos 37 B5
Hasguard Pembs 44 E3
Haskayne Lancs 85 D4
Hasketon Suff 57 D6
Hasland Derbys 76 C3
Haslemere Sur 27 F7
Haslingden Lancs 87 B5
Haslingfield Cambs 54 D5
Haslington Ches 74 D4
Hassall Ches 74 D4
Hassall Green Ches 74 D4
Hassell Street Kent 30 E4
Hassendean Borders 115 B8
Hassingham Norf 69 D6
Hassocks W Sus 17 C6
Hassop Derbys 76 B2
Hastigrow Highld 169 C7
Hastingleigh Kent 30 E4
Hastings E Sus 18 E5
Hastings Castle E Sus 18 D5
Hastings Sea Life Centre E Sus 18 E5
Hastingwood Essex 41 D7
Hastoe Herts 40 D2
Haswell Durham 111 E6
Haswell Plough Durham 111 E6
Hatch Beds 54 E2
Hatch Hants 26 D4
Hatch Wilts 13 B7
Hatch Beauchamp Som 11 B8
Hatch End London 40 E4
Hatch Green Som 11 C8
Hatchet Gate Hants 14 D4
Hatching Green Herts 40 C4
Hatchmere Ches 74 B2
Hatcliffe NE Lincs 91 D6
Hatfield Hereford 49 D7
Hatfield Herts 41 D5
Hatfield S Yorks 89 D7
Hatfield Worcs 50 D3
Hatfield Broad Oak Essex 41 C8
Hatfield Garden Village Herts 41 D5
Hatfield Heath Essex 41 C8
Hatfield House Herts 41 D5
Hatfield Hyde Herts 41 C5
Hatfield Peverel Essex 42 C3
Hatfield Woodhouse S Yorks 89 D7
Hatford Oxon 38 E3
Hatherden Hants 25 D8
Hatherleigh Devon 9 D7
Hathern Leics 63 B8
Hatherop Glos 38 D1
Hathersage Derbys 88 F3
Hathershaw Gtr Man 87 D7
Hatherton Ches 74 E3
Hatherton Staffs 62 C3
Hatley St George Cambs 54 D3
Hatt Corn 5 C8
Hattingley Hants 26 F4
Hatton Aberds 161 E7
Hatton Derbys 63 B6
Hatton Lincs 78 B4
Hatton Shrops 60 E4
Hatton Warks 51 C7
Hatton Warr 86 F3
Hatton Castle Aberds 160 D4
Hatton Country World Warks 51 C7
Hatton Heath Ches 73 C8
Hatton of Fintray Aberds 151 C7
Hattoncrook Aberds 151 B7
Haugh E Ayrs 112 B4
Haugh Gtr Man 87 C7
Haugh Lincs 79 B7
Haugh Head Northumb 117 B6
Haugh of Glass Moray 159 F8
Haugh of Urr Dumfries 106 C5
Haugham Lincs 91 F7
Haughley Suff 56 C4
Haughley Green Suff 56 C4
Haughs of Clinterty Aberdeen 151 C7
Haughton Notts 77 B6
Haughton Shrops 61 E6
Haughton Shrops 60 B3
Haughton Shrops 61 C5
Haughton Shrops 61 D7
Haughton Staffs 62 B2
Haughton Castle Northumb 110 B2
Haughton Green Gtr Man 87 E7
Haughton Le Skerne Darl 101 C8
Haughton Moss Ches 74 D2
Haultwick Herts 41 B6
Haunn Argyll 136 D4
Haunn W Isles 171 J3
Haunton Staffs 63 C6
Hauxley Northumb 117 D8
Hauxton Cambs 54 D5
Havant Hants 15 D8
Haven Hereford 49 D6
Haven Bank Lincs 78 D5
Haven Side E Yorks 91 B5
Havenstreet I o W 15 E6
Havercroft W Yorks 88 C4
Haverfordwest = Hwlffordd Pembs 44 D4
Haverhill Suff 55 E7
Haverigg Cumb 92 B1
Havering-atte-Bower London 41 E8
Haveringland Norf 81 E7
Haversham M Keynes 53 E6
Haverthwaite Cumb 99 F5
Haverton Hill Stockton 102 B2
Hawarden = Penarlâg Flint 73 C7
Hawcoat Cumb 92 B2
Hawen Ceredig 46 E2
Hawes N Yorks 100 F3
Hawes Side Blkpool 92 F3
Hawes'Green Norf 68 E5
Hawford Worcs 50 C3
Hawick Borders 115 C8
Hawk Green Gtr Man 87 F7
Hawkchurch Devon 11 D8
Hawkedon Suff 55 D8
Hawkenbury Kent 30 E2
Hawkenbury Kent 18 B2
Hawkeridge Wilts 24 D3
Hawkerland Devon 11 F5
Hawkes End W Mid 63 F7
Hawkesbury S Glos 36 F4
Hawkesbury Warks 63 F7
Hawkesbury Upton S Glos 36 F4
Hawkhill Northumb 117 C8
Hawkhurst Kent 18 B4
Hawkinge Kent 31 F6
Hawkley Hants 15 B8
Hawkridge Som 21 F7
Hawkshead Cumb 99 E5
Hawkshead Hill Cumb 99 E5
Hawksland S Lnrk 121 F8
Hawkswick N Yorks 94 B2
Hawksworth Notts 77 E7
Hawksworth W Yorks 94 E4
Hawksworth W Yorks 95 F5
Hawkwell Essex 42 E4
Hawley Hants 27 D6
Hawley Kent 29 B6
Hawling Glos 37 B7
Hawnby N Yorks 102 F3
Haworth W Yorks 94 F3
Hawstead Suff 56 D2
Hawthorn Durham 111 E7
Hawthorn Rhondda 35 F5
Hawthorn Wilts 24 C3
Hawthorn Hill Brack 27 B6
Hawthorn Hill Lincs 78 D5
Hawthorpe Lincs 65 B7
Hawton Notts 77 D7
Haxby York 96 D2
Haxey N Lincs 89 D8
Hay Green Norf 66 C5
Hay-on-Wye = Y Gelli Gandryll Powys 48 E4
Hay Street Herts 41 B6
Haydock Mers 86 E3
Haydock Park Racecourse Mers 86 E3
Haydon Dorset 12 C4
Haydon Bridge Northumb 109 C8
Haydon Wick Swindon 37 F8
Haye Corn 5 C8
Hayes London 28 C5
Hayes London 40 F4
Hayfield Derbys 87 F8
Hayfield Fife 134 E4
Hayhill E Ayrs 112 C4
Hayhillock Angus 143 E5
Hayle Corn 2 C4
Haynes Beds 53 E8
Haynes Church End Beds 53 E8
Hayscastle Pembs 44 C3
Hayscastle Cross Pembs 44 C4
Hayshead Angus 143 E6
Hayton Aberdeen 151 D8
Hayton Cumb 107 E8
Hayton Cumb 108 D5
Hayton E Yorks 96 E4
Hayton Notts 89 F8
Hayton's Bent Shrops 60 F5
Haytor Vale Devon 7 B5
Haywards Heath W Sus 17 B7
Haywood S Yorks 89 C6
Haywood Oaks Notts 77 D6
Hazel Grove Gtr Man 87 F7
Hazel Street Kent 18 B3
Hazelbank S Lnrk 121 E8
Hazelbury Bryan Dorset 12 D5
Hazeley Hants 26 D5
Hazelhurst Gtr Man 87 D7
Hazelslade Staffs 62 C4
Hazelton Glos 37 C7
Hazelton Walls Fife 134 B5
Hazelwood Derbys 76 E3
Hazlemere Bucks 40 E1
Hazlerigg T & W 110 B5
Hazlewood N Yorks 94 D3
Hazon Northumb 117 D7
Heacham Norf 80 D2
Head of Muir Falk 133 F7
Headbourne Worthy Hants 26 F2
Headbrook Hereford 48 D5
Headcorn Kent 30 E2
Headingley W Yorks 95 F5
Headington Oxon 39 D5
Headlam Durham 101 C6
Headless Cross Worcs 50 C5
Headley Hants 26 C3
Headley Hants 27 F6
Headley Sur 28 D3
Headon Notts 77 B7
Heads S Lnrk 121 E7
Heads Nook Cumb 108 D4
Heage Derbys 76 D3
Healaugh N Yorks 95 E7
Healaugh N Yorks 101 E5
Heald Green Gtr Man 87 F6
Heale Devon 20 E5
Heale Som 23 E8
Healey Gtr Man 87 C6
Healey Northumb 110 D3
Healey N Yorks 101 F6
Healing NE Lincs 91 C6
Heamoor Corn 2 C3
Heanish Argyll 136 F2
Heanor Derbys 76 E4
Heanton Punchardon Devon 20 F4
Heapham Lincs 90 F2
Heart of the National Forest Leics 63 C7
Hearthstane Borders 114 B4
Heasley Mill Devon 21 F6
Heast Highld 145 B6
Heath Cardiff 22 B3
Heath Derbys 76 C4
Heath and Reach Beds 40 B2
Heath End Hants 26 C3
Heath End Sur 27 E6
Heath End Warks 51 C7
Heath Hayes Staffs 62 C4
Heath Hill Shrops 61 C7
Heath House Som 23 E6
Heath Town W Mid 62 E3
Heathcote Derbys 75 C8
Heather Leics 63 C7
Heatherfield Highld 153 E5
Heathfield Devon 7 B6
Heathfield E Sus 18 C2
Heathfield Som 11 B6
Heathhall Dumfries 107 B6
Heathstock Devon 11 D7
Heathton Shrops 62 E2
Heatley Warr 86 F5
Heaton Lancs 92 C4
Heaton Staffs 75 C6
Heaton T & W 111 C5
Heaton W Yorks 94 F4
Heaton Moor Gtr Man 87 E6
Heaverham Kent 29 D6
Heaviley Gtr Man 87 F7
Heavitree Devon 10 E4
Hebburn T & W 111 C6
Hebden N Yorks 94 C3
Hebden Bridge W Yorks 87 B7
Hebron Anglesey 82 C4
Hebron Carms 32 B2
Hebron Northumb 117 F7
Heck Dumfries 114 F3
Heckfield Hants 26 C5
Heckfield Green Suff 57 B5
Heckfordbridge Essex 43 B5
Heckington Lincs 78 E4
Heckmondwike W Yorks 88 B3
Heddington Wilts 24 C4
Heddle Orkney 176 E2
Heddon-on-the-Wall Northumb 110 C4
Hedenham Norf 69 E6
Hedge End Hants 15 C5
Hedgerley Bucks 40 F2
Hedging Som 11 B8
Hedley on the Hill Northumb 110 D3
Hednesford Staffs 62 C4
Hedon E Yorks 91 B5
Hedsor Bucks 40 F2
Hedworth T & W 111 C6
Heeley City Farm, Sheffield S Yorks 88 F4
Hegdon Hill Hereford 49 D7
Heggerscales Cumb 100 C3
Heglibister Shetland 175 H5
Heighington Darl 101 B7
Heighington Lincs 78 C3
Heights of Brae Highld 157 C6
Heights of Kinlochewe Highld 154 D6
Heilam Highld 167 C6
Heiton Borders 124 F3
Hele Devon 20 E4
Hele Devon 10 D4
Helensburgh Argyll 129 B7
Helford Corn 3 D6
Helford Passage Corn 3 D6
Helhoughton Norf 80 E4
Helions Bumpstead Essex 55 E7
Hellaby S Yorks 89 E6
Helland Corn 5 B5
Hellesdon Norf 68 C5
Hellidon Northants 52 D3
Hellifield N Yorks 93 D8
Hellingly E Sus 18 D2
Hellington Norf 69 D6
Hellister Shetland 175 J5
Helm Northumb 117 E7
Helmdon Northants 52 E3
Helmingham Suff 57 D5
Helmington Row Durham 110 F4
Helmsdale Highld 165 C7
Helmshore Lancs 87 B5
Helmsley N Yorks 102 F4
Helperby N Yorks 95 C7
Helperthorpe N Yorks 97 B5
Helpringham Lincs 78 E4
Helpston P'boro 65 D8
Helsby Ches 73 B8
Helsey Lincs 79 B8
Helston Corn 3 D5
Helstone Corn 8 F2
Helton Cumb 99 B7
Helwith Bridge N Yorks 93 C8
Hemblington Norf 69 C6
Hemel Hempstead Herts 40 D3
Hemingbrough N Yorks 96 F2
Hemingby Lincs 78 B5
Hemingford Abbots Cambs 54 B3
Hemingford Grey Cambs 54 B3
Hemingstone Suff 57 D5
Hemington Leics 63 B8
Hemington Northants 65 F7
Hemington Som 24 D2
Hemley Suff 57 E6
Hemlington M'bro 102 C3
Hemp Green Suff 57 C7
Hempholme E Yorks 97 D6
Hempnall Norf 68 E5
Hempnall Green Norf 68 E5
Hempriggs House Highld 169 E8
Hempstead Essex 55 F7
Hempstead Medway 29 C8
Hempstead Norf 81 D7
Hempstead Norf 69 B7
Hempsted Glos 37 C5
Hempton Norf 80 E5
Hempton Oxon 52 F2
Hemsby Norf 69 C7
Hemswell Lincs 90 E3
Hemswell Cliff Lincs 90 F3
Hemsworth W Yorks 88 C5
Hemyock Devon 11 C6
Hen-feddau fawr Pembs 45 F4
Henbury Bristol 23 B7
Henbury Ches 75 B5
Hendon London 41 F5
Hendon T & W 111 D7
Hendre Flint 73 C5
Hendre-ddu Conwy 83 E8
Hendreforgan Rhondda 34 F3
Hendy Carms 33 D6
Heneglwys Anglesey 82 D4
Henfield W Sus 17 C6
Henford Devon 9 E5
Henghurst Kent 19 B6
Hengoed Caerph 35 E5
Hengoed Powys 48 D4
Hengoed Shrops 73 F6
Hengrave Suff 56 C2
Henham Essex 41 B8
Heniarth Powys 59 D8
Henlade Som 11 B7
Henley Shrops 49 B7
Henley Som 23 F6
Henley Suff 57 D5
Henley W Sus 16 B2
Henley-in-Arden Warks 51 C6
Henley-on-Thames Oxon 39 F7
Henley's Down E Sus 18 D4
Henllan Ceredig 46 E2
Henllan Denb 72 C4
Henllan Amgoed Carms 32 B2
Henllys Torf 35 E6
Henlow Beds 54 F2
Hennock Devon 10 F3
Henny Street Essex 56 F2
Henryd Conwy 83 D7
Henry's Moat Pembs 32 B1
Hensall N Yorks 89 B6
Henshaw Northumb 109 C7
Hensingham Cumb 98 C1
Henstead Suff 69 F7
Henstridge Som 12 C5
Henstridge Ash Som 12 B5
Henstridge Marsh Som 12 B5
Henton Oxon 39 D7
Henton Som 23 E6
Henwood Corn 5 B7
Heogan Shetland 175 J6
Heol-las Swansea 33 E7
Heol Senni Powys 34 B3
Heol-y-Cyw Bridgend 34 F3
Hepburn Northumb 117 B6
Hepple Northumb 117 D5
Hepscott Northumb 117 F8
Heptonstall W Yorks 87 B7
Hepworth Suff 56 B3
Hepworth W Yorks 88 D2
Herbrandston Pembs 44 E3
Hereford Hereford 49 E7
Hereford Cathedral Hereford 49 F7
Hereford Racecourse Hereford 49 E7
Heriot Borders 123 D6
Heritage Motor Centre, Gaydon Warks 51 D8
Hermiston Edin 122 B4
Hermitage Borders 115 E8
Hermitage Dorset 12 D4
Hermitage W Berks 26 B3
Hermitage W Sus 15 D8
Hermon Anglesey 82 E3
Hermon Carms 46 F2
Hermon Carms 33 B7
Hermon Pembs 45 F4
Herne Kent 31 C5
Herne Bay Kent 31 C5
Herner Devon 9 B7
Hernhill Kent 30 C4
Herodsfoot Corn 5 C7
Herongate Essex 42 E2
Heronsford S Ayrs 104 A5
Herriard Hants 26 E4
Herringfleet Suff 69 E7
Herringswell Suff 55 B8
Hersden Kent 31 C6
Hersham Corn 8 D4
Hersham Sur 28 C2
Herstmonceux E Sus 18 D3
Herston Orkney 176 G3
Hertford Herts 41 C6
Hertford Heath Herts 41 C6
Hertingfordbury Herts 41 C6
Hesket Newmarket Cumb 108 F3
Hesketh Bank Lancs 86 B2
Hesketh Lane Lancs 93 E6
Heskin Green Lancs 86 C3
Hesleden Durham 111 F7
Hesleyside Northumb 116 F4
Heslington York 96 D2
Hessay York 95 D8
Hessenford Corn 5 D8
Hessett Suff 56 C3
Hessle E Yorks 90 B4
Hest Bank Lancs 92 C4
Heston London 28 B2
Hestwall Orkney 176 E1
Heswall Mers 85 F3
Hethe Oxon 39 B5
Hethersett Norf 68 D4
Hethersgill Cumb 108 C4
Hethpool Northumb 116 B4
Hett Durham 111 F5
Hetton N Yorks 94 D2
Hetton-le-Hole T & W 111 E6
Hetton Steads Northumb 125 F6
Heugh Northumb 110 B3
Heugh-head Aberds 150 C2
Heveningham Suff 57 B7
Hever Kent 29 E5
Hever Castle and Gardens Kent 29 E5
Heversham Cumb 99 F6
Hevingham Norf 81 E7
Hewas Water Corn 3 B8
Hewelsfield Glos 36 D2
Hewish N Som 23 C6
Hewish Som 12 D2
Heworth York 96 D2
Hexham Northumb 110 C2
Hexham Abbey Northumb 110 C2
Hexham Racecourse Northumb 110 C2
Hextable Kent 29 B6
Hexton Herts 54 F2
Hexworthy Devon 6 B4
Hey Lancs 93 E8
Heybridge Essex 42 E2
Heybridge Essex 42 D4
Heybridge Basin Essex 42 D4
Heybrook Bay Devon 6 E3
Heydon Cambs 54 E5
Heydon Norf 81 E7
Heydour Lincs 78 F3
Heylipol Argyll 136 F1
Heylor Shetland 174 E4
Heysham Lancs 92 C4
Heyshott W Sus 16 C2
Heyside Gtr Man 87 D7
Heytesbury Wilts 24 E4
Heythrop Oxon 38 B3
Heywood Gtr Man 87 C6
Heywood Wilts 24 D3
Hibaldstow N Lincs 90 D3
Hickleton S Yorks 89 D5
Hickling Norf 69 B7
Hickling Notts 64 B3
Hickling Green Norf 69 B7
Hickling Heath Norf 69 B7
Hickstead W Sus 17 B6
Hidcote Boyce Glos 51 E6
Hidcote Manor Garden, Moreton-in-Marsh Glos 51 E6
High Ackworth W Yorks 88 C5
High Angerton Northumb 117 F6
High Bankhill Cumb 109 E5
High Barnes T & W 111 D6
High Beach Essex 41 E7
High Bentham N Yorks 93 C6
High Bickington Devon 9 B8
High Birkwith N Yorks 93 B7
High Blantyre S Lnrk 121 D6
High Bonnybridge Falk 121 B8
High Bradfield S Yorks 88 E3
High Bray Devon 21 F5
High Brooms Kent 29 E6
High Bullen Devon 9 B7
High Buston Northumb 117 D8
High Callerton Northumb 110 B4
High Catton E Yorks 96 D3
High Cogges Oxon 38 D3
High Coniscliffe Darl 101 C7
High Cross Hants 15 B8
High Cross Herts 41 C6
High Easter Essex 42 C2
High Eggborough N Yorks 89 B6
High Ellington N Yorks 101 F6
High Ercall Telford 61 C5
High Etherley Durham 101 B6
High Garrett Essex 42 B3
High Grange Durham 110 F4
High Green Norf 68 D4
High Green S Yorks 88 E4
High Green Worcs 50 E3
High Halden Kent 19 B5
High Halstow Medway 29 B8
High Ham Som 23 F6
High Harrington Cumb 98 B2
High Hatton Shrops 61 B6
High Hawsker N Yorks 103 D7
High Hesket Cumb 108 E4
High Hesleden Durham 111 F7
High Hoyland S Yorks 88 C3
High Hunsley E Yorks 97 F5
High Hurstwood E Sus 17 B8
High Hutton N Yorks 96 C3
High Ireby Cumb 108 F2
High Kelling Norf 81 C7
High Kilburn N Yorks 95 B8
High Lands Durham 101 B6
High Lane Gtr Man 87 F7
High Lane Hereford 49 C8
High Laver Essex 41 D8
High Legh Ches 86 F5
High Leven Stockton 102 C2
High Littleton Bath 23 D8
High Lorton Cumb 98 B3
High Marishes N Yorks 96 B4
High Marnham Notts 77 B8
High Melton S Yorks 89 D6
High Mickley Northumb 110 C3
High Mindork Dumfries 105 D7
High Moorland Visitor Centre, Princetown Devon 6 B3
High Newton Cumb 99 F6
High Newton-by-the-Sea Northumb 117 B8
High Nibthwaite Cumb 98 F4
High Offley Staffs 61 B7
High Ongar Essex 42 D1
High Onn Staffs 62 C2
High Roding Essex 42 C2
High Row Cumb 108 F3
High Salvington W Sus 16 D5
High Sellafield Cumb 98 D2
High Shaw N Yorks 100 E3
High Spen T & W 110 D4
High Stoop Durham 110 E4
High Street Corn 4 D4
High Street Kent 18 B4
High Street Suff 57 D8
High Street Suff 57 B8
High Street Suff 56 E2
High Street Green Suff 56 D4
High Throston Hrtlpl 111 F7
High Toynton Lincs 79 C5
High Trewhitt Northumb 117 D6
High Valleyfield Fife 134 F2
High Westwood Durham 110 D4
High Wray Cumb 99 E5
High Wych Herts 41 C7
High Wycombe Bucks 40 E1
Higham Derbys 76 D3
Higham Kent 29 B8
Higham Lancs 93 F8
Higham Suff 56 F4
Higham Suff 55 C8
Higham Dykes Northumb 110 B4
Higham Ferrers Northants 53 C7
Higham Gobion Beds 54 F2
Higham on the Hill Leics 63 E7
Higham Wood Kent 29 E6
Highampton Devon 9 D6
Highbridge Highld 146 F4
Highbridge Som 22 E5
Highbrook W Sus 28 F4
Highburton W Yorks 88 C2
Highbury Som 23 E8
Highclere Hants 26 C2
Highcliffe Dorset 14 E3
Higher Ansty Dorset 13 D5
Higher Ashton Devon 10 F3
Higher Ballam Lancs 92 F3
Higher Bartle Lancs 92 F5
Higher Boscaswell Corn 2 C2
Higher Burwardsley Ches 74 D2
Higher Clovelly Devon 8 B5
Higher End Gtr Man 86 D3
Higher Kinnerton Flint 73 C7
Higher Penwortham Lancs 86 B3
Higher Town Scilly 2 E4
Higher Walreddon Devon 6 B2
Higher Walton Lancs 86 B3
Higher Walton Warr 86 F3
Higher Wheelton Lancs 86 B4
Higher Whitley Ches 86 F4
Higher Wincham Ches 74 B3
Higher Wych Ches 73 E8
Highfield E Yorks 96 F3
Highfield Gtr Man 86 D5
Highfield N Ayrs 120 D3
Highfield Oxon 39 B5
Highfield S Yorks 88 F4
Highfield T & W 110 D4
Highfields Cambs 54 D4
Highfields Northumb 125 D5
Highgate London 41 F5
Highland Folk Museum, Aultlairie Highld 148 E3
Highland Folk Museum, Kingussie Highld 148 D3
Highlane Ches 75 C5
Highlane Derbys 88 F5
Highlaws Cumb 107 E8
Highleadon Glos 36 B4
Highleigh W Sus 16 E2
Highley Shrops 61 F7
Highmoor Cross Oxon 39 F7
Highmoor Hill Mon 36 F1
Highnam Glos 36 C4
Highnam Green Glos 36 B4
Highsted Kent 30 C3
Highstreet Green Essex 55 F8
Hightae Dumfries 107 B7
Hightown Ches 75 C5
Hightown Mers 85 D4
Hightown Green Suff 56 D3
Highway Wilts 24 B5
Highweek Devon 7 B6
Highworth Swindon 38 E2
Hilborough Norf 67 D8
Hilcote Derbys 76 D4
Hilcott Wilts 25 D6
Hilden Park Kent 29 E6
Hildenborough Kent 29 E6
Hildersham Cambs 55 E6
Hilderstone Staffs 75 F6
Hilderthorpe E Yorks 97 C7
Hilfield Dorset 12 D4
Hilgay Norf 67 E6
Hill Pembs 32 D2
Hill S Glos 36 E3
Hill W Mid 62 E5
Hill Brow W Sus 15 B8
Hill Dale Lancs 86 C2
Hill Dyke Lincs 79 E6
Hill End Durham 110 F3
Hill End Fife 134 E2
Hill End N Yorks 94 D3
Hill Head Hants 15 D6
Hill Head Northumb 110 C2
Hill Mountain Pembs 44 E4
Hill of Beath Fife 134 E3
Hill of Fearn Highld 158 B2
Hill of Mountblairy Aberds 160 C3
Hill Ridware Staffs 62 C4
Hill Top Durham 100 B4
Hill Top Hants 14 D5
Hill Top W Mid 62 E3
Hill Top W Yorks 88 C4
Hill Top, Sawrey Cumb 99 E5
Hill View Dorset 13 E7
Hillam N Yorks 89 B6
Hillbeck Cumb 100 C2
Hillborough Kent 31 C6
Hillbrae Aberds 151 B6
Hillbrae Aberds 160 D3
Hillbutts Dorset 13 D7
Hillclifflane Derbys 76 E2
Hillcommon Som 11 B6
Hillend Fife 134 F3
Hillerton Devon 10 E2
Hillesden Bucks 39 B6
Hillesley Glos 36 F4
Hillfarance Som 11 B6
Hillhead Aberds 160 E2
Hillhead Devon 7 D7
Hillhead S Ayrs 112 C4
Hillhead of Auchentumb Aberds 161 C6
Hillhead of Cocklaw Aberds 161 D7
Hillhouse Borders 123 D8
Hilliclay Highld 169 C6
Hillier Gardens and Arboretum Hants 14 B4
Hillingdon London 40 F3
Hillington Glasgow 120 C5
Hillington Norf 80 E3
Hillmorton Warks 52 B3
Hillockhead Aberds 150 C3
Hillockhead Aberds 150 D2
Hillside Aberds 151 E8
Hillside Angus 143 C7
Hillside Mers 85 C4
Hillside Orkney 176 G3
Hillside Shetland 175 G6
Hillswick Shetland 174 F4
Hillway I o W 15 F7
Hillwell Shetland 175 M5
Hilmarton Wilts 24 B5
Hilperton Wilts 24 D3
Hilsea Ptsmth 15 D7
Hilston E Yorks 97 F8
Hilton Aberds 161 E6
Hilton Cambs 54 C3
Hilton Cumb 100 B2
Hilton Derbys 76 F2
Hilton Dorset 13 D5
Hilton Durham 101 B6
Hilton Highld 164 F4
Hilton Shrops 61 E7
Hilton Stockton 102 C2
Hilton of Cadboll Highld 158 B2
Himbleton Worcs 50 D4
Himley Staffs 62 E2
Hincaster Cumb 99 F7
Hinckley Leics 63 E8
Hinderclay Suff 56 B4
Hinderton Ches 73 B7
Hinderwell N Yorks 103 C5
Hindford Shrops 73 F7
Hindhead Sur 27 F6
Hindley Gtr Man 86 D4
Hindley Green Gtr Man 86 D4
Hindlip Worcs 50 D3
Hindolveston Norf 81 E6
Hindon Wilts 24 F4
Hindringham Norf 81 D5
Hingham Norf 68 D3
Hinstock Shrops 61 B6
Hintlesham Suff 56 E4
Hinton Hants 14 E3
Hinton Hereford 48 F5
Hinton Northants 52 D3

I

L

Little Harrowden Northants 53 B6
Little Haseley Oxon 39 D6
Little Hatfield E Yorks 97 E7
Little Hautbois Norf 81 E8
Little Haven Pembs 44 D3
Little Hay Staffs 62 D5
Little Hayfield Derbys 87 F8
Little Haywood Staffs 62 B4
Little Heath W Mid 63 F7
Little Hereford Hereford 49 C7
Little Horkesley Essex 56 F3
Little Horsted E Sus 17 C8
Little Horton W Yorks 94 F4
Little Horwood Bucks 53 F5
Little Houghton Northants 53 D6
Little Houghton S Yorks 88 D5
Little Hucklow Derbys 75 B8
Little Hulton Gtr Man 86 D5
Little Humber E Yorks 91 B5
Little Hungerford W Berks 26 B3
Little Irchester Northants 53 C7
Little Kimble Bucks 39 D8
Little Kineton Warks 51 D8
Little Kingshill Bucks 40 E1
Little Langdale Cumb 99 D5
Little Langford Wilts 25 F5
Little Laver Essex 41 D8
Little Leigh Ches 74 B3
Little Leighs Essex 42 C3
Little Lever Gtr Man 87 D5
Little London Bucks 39 C6
Little London E Sus 18 D2
Little London Hants 25 E8
Little London Hants 26 D4
Little London Lincs 66 B2
Little London Lincs 66 B4
Little London Norf 81 E7
Little London Powys 59 F7
Little Longstone Derbys 75 B8
Little Lynturk Aberds 150 C4
Little Malvern Worcs 50 E2
Little Maplestead Essex 56 F2
Little Marcle Hereford 49 F8
Little Marlow Bucks 40 F1
Little Marsden Lancs 93 F8
Little Massingham Norf 80 E3
Little Melton Norf 68 D4
Little Mill Mon 35 D7
Little Milton Oxon 39 D6
Little Missenden Bucks 40 E2
Little Musgrave Cumb 100 C2
Little Ness Shrops 60 C4
Little Neston Ches 73 B6
Little Newcastle Pembs 44 C4
Little Newsham Durham 101 C6
Little Oakley Essex 43 B8
Little Oakley Northants 65 F5
Little Orton Cumb 108 D3
Little Ouseburn N Yorks 95 C7
Little Paxton Cambs 54 C2
Little Petherick Corn 4 B4
Little Pitlurg Moray 159 E8
Little Plumpton Lancs 92 F3
Little Plumstead Norf 69 C6
Little Ponton Lincs 78 F2
Little Raveley Cambs 54 B3
Little Reedness E Yorks 90 B2
Little Ribston N Yorks 95 D6
Little Rissington Glos 38 C1
Little Ryburgh Norf 81 E5
Little Ryle Northumb 117 C6
Little Salkeld Cumb 109 F5
Little Sampford Essex 55 F7
Little Sandhurst Brack 27 C6
Little Saxham Suff 55 C8
Little Scatwell Highld 156 D4
Little Sessay N Yorks 95 B7
Little Shelford Cambs 54 D5
Little Singleton Lancs 92 F3
Little Skillymarno Aberds 161 C6
Little Smeaton N Yorks 89 C6
Little Snoring Norf 81 D5
Little Sodbury S Glos 36 F4
Little Somborne Hants 25 F8
Little Somerford Wilts 37 F6
Little Stainforth N Yorks 93 C8
Little Stainton Darl 101 B8
Little Stanney Ches 73 B8
Little Staughton Beds 54 C2
Little Steeping Lincs 79 C7
Little Stoke Staffs 75 F6
Little Stonham Suff 56 C5
Little Stretton Leics 64 D3
Little Stretton Shrops 60 E4
Little Strickland Cumb 99 C7
Little Stukeley Cambs 54 B3
Little Sutton Ches 73 B7
Little Tew Oxon 38 B3
Little Thetford Cambs 55 B6
Little Thirkleby N Yorks 95 B7
Little Thurlow Suff 55 D7
Little Thurrock Thurrock 29 B7
Little Torboll Highld 164 E4
Little Torrington Devon 9 C6
Little Totham Essex 42 C4
Little Toux Aberds 160 C2
Little Town Cumb 98 C4
Little Town Lancs 93 F6
Little Urswick Cumb 92 B2
Little Wakering Essex 43 F5
Little Walden Essex 55 E6
Little Waldingfield Suff 56 E3
Little Walsingham Norf 80 D5
Little Waltham Essex 42 C3
Little Warley Essex 42 E2
Little Weighton E Yorks 97 F5
Little Weldon Northants 65 F6
Little Welnetham Suff 56 C2
Little Wenlock Telford 61 D6
Little Whittingham Green Suff 57 B6
Little Wilbraham Cambs 55 D6
Little Wishford Wilts 25 F5
Little Witley Worcs 50 C2
Little Wittenham Oxon 39 E5
Little Wolford Warks 51 F7
Little Wratting Suff 55 E7
Little Wymington Beds 53 C7
Little Wymondley Herts 41 B5
Little Wyrley Staffs 62 D4
Little Yeldham Essex 55 F8
Littlebeck N Yorks 103 D6
Littleborough Gtr Man 87 C7
Littleborough Notts 90 F2
Littlebourne Kent 31 D6
Littlebredy Dorset 12 F3
Littlebury Essex 55 F6
Littlebury Green Essex 55 F5
Littledean Glos 36 C3
Littleferry Highld 165 E5
Littleham Devon 10 F5
Littleham Devon 9 B6
Littlehampton W Sus 16 D4
Littlehempston Devon 7 C6
Littlehoughton Northumb 117 C8
Littlemill Aberds 150 E2
Littlemill E Ayrs 112 C4
Littlemill Highld 158 D3
Littlemill Northumb 117 C8
Littlemoor Dorset 12 F4
Littlemore Oxon 39 D5
Littleover Derby 76 F3
Littleport Cambs 67 F5
Littlestone on Sea Kent 19 C7
Littlethorpe Leics 64 E2
Littlethorpe N Yorks 95 C6
Littleton Ches 73 C8
Littleton Hants 26 F2
Littleton Perth 142 F2
Littleton Som 23 F6
Littleton Sur 27 C8
Littleton Sur 27 E7
Littleton Drew Wilts 37 F5
Littleton-on-Severn S Glos 36 F2
Littleton Pannell Wilts 24 D5
Littletown Durham 111 E6
Littlewick Green Windsor 27 B6
Littleworth Beds 53 E8
Littleworth Glos 37 D5
Littleworth Oxon 38 E3
Littleworth Staffs 62 C4
Littleworth Worcs 50 D3
Litton Derbys 75 B8
Litton N Yorks 94 B2
Litton Som 23 D7
Litton Cheney Dorset 12 E3
Liurbost W Isles 172 F6
Liverpool Mers 85 E4
Liverpool Cathedral (C of E) Mers 85 F4
Liverpool Cathedral (RC) Mers 85 E4
Liverpool John Lennon Airport Mers 86 F2
Liversedge W Yorks 88 B3
Liverton Devon 7 B6
Liverton Redcar 103 C5
Livingston W Loth 122 C3
Livingston Village W Loth 122 C3
Lixwm Flint 73 B5
Lizard Corn 3 E6
Llaingoch Anglesey 82 C2
Llaithddu Powys 59 F7
Llan Powys 59 D5
Llan Ffestiniog Gwyn 71 C8
Llan-y-pwll Wrex 73 D7
Llanaber Gwyn 58 C3
Llanaelhaearn Gwyn 70 C4
Llanafan Ceredig 47 B5
Llanafan-fawr Powys 47 D8
Llanallgo Anglesey 82 C4
Llanandras = Presteigne Powys 48 C5
Llanarmon Gwyn 70 D5
Llanarmon Dyffryn Ceiriog Wrex 73 F5
Llanarmon-yn-Ial Denb 73 D5
Llanarth Ceredig 46 D3
Llanarth Mon 35 C7
Llanarthne Carms 33 B6
Llanasa Flint 85 F2
Llanbabo Anglesey 82 C3
Llanbadarn Fawr Ceredig 58 F3
Llanbadarn Fynydd Powys 48 B3
Llanbadarn-y-Garreg Powys 48 E3
Llanbadoc Mon 35 E7
Llanbadrig Anglesey 82 B3
Llanbeder Newport 35 E7
Llanbedr Gwyn 71 E6
Llanbedr Powys 48 E3
Llanbedr Powys 35 B6
Llanbedr-Dyffryn-Clwyd Denb 72 D5
Llanbedr Pont Steffan = Lampeter Ceredig 46 E4
Llanbedr-y-cennin Conwy 83 E7
Llanbedrgoch Anglesey 82 C5
Llanbedrog Gwyn 70 D4
Llanberis Gwyn 83 E5
Llanbethêry V Glam 22 C2
Llanbister Powys 48 B3
Llanblethian V Glam 21 B8
Llanboidy Carms 32 B3
Llanbradach Caerph 35 E5
Llanbrynmair Powys 59 D5
Llancarfan V Glam 22 B2
Llancayo Mon 35 D7
Llancloudy Hereford 36 B1
Llancynfelyn Ceredig 58 E3
Llandaff Cardiff 22 B3
Llandanwg Gwyn 71 E6
Llandarcy Neath 33 E8
Llandawke Carms 32 C3
Llanddaniel Fab Anglesey 82 D4
Llanddarog Carms 33 C6
Llanddeiniol Ceredig 46 B4
Llanddeiniolen Gwyn 82 E5
Llandderfel Gwyn 72 F3
Llanddeusant Anglesey 82 C3
Llanddeusant Carms 34 B1
Llanddew Powys 48 F2
Llanddewi Swansea 33 F5
Llanddewi-Brefi Ceredig 47 D5
Llanddewi Rhydderch Mon 35 C7
Llanddewi Velfrey Pembs 32 C2
Llanddewi'r Cwm Powys 48 E2
Llanddoged Conwy 83 E8
Llanddona Anglesey 83 D5
Llanddowror Carms 32 C3
Llanddulas Conwy 72 B3
Llanddwywe Gwyn 71 E6
Llanddyfynan Anglesey 82 D5
Llandefaelog Fach Powys 48 F2
Llandefaelog-tre'r-graig Powys 35 B5
Llandefalle Powys 48 F3
Llandegai Gwyn 83 D5
Llandegfan Anglesey 83 D5
Llandegla Denb 73 D5
Llandegley Powys 48 C3
Llandegveth Mon 35 E7
Llandegwning Gwyn 70 D3
Llandeilo Carms 33 B7
Llandeilo Graban Powys 48 E2
Llandeilo'r Fan Powys 47 F7
Llandeloy Pembs 44 C3
Llandenny Mon 35 D8
Llandevenny Mon 35 F8
Llandewednock Corn 3 E6
Llandewi Ystradenny Powys 48 C3
Llandinabo Hereford 36 B2
Llandinam Powys 59 F7
Llandissilio Pembs 32 B2
Llandogo Mon 36 D2
Llandough V Glam 21 B8
Llandough V Glam 22 B3
Llandovery = Llanymddyfri Carms 47 F6
Llandow V Glam 21 B8
Llandre Ceredig 58 F3
Llandre Carms 47 E5
Llandrillo Denb 72 F4
Llandrillo-yn-Rhos Conwy 83 C8
Llandrindod = Llandrindod Wells Powys 48 C2
Llandrindod Wells = Llandrindod Powys 48 C2
Llandrinio Powys 60 C2
Llandudno Conwy 83 C7
Llandudno Junction = Cyffordd Llandudno Conwy 83 D7
Llandwrog Gwyn 82 F4
Llandybie Carms 33 C7
Llandyfaelog Carms 33 C5
Llandyfan Carms 33 C7
Llandyfriog Ceredig 46 E2
Llandyfrydog Anglesey 82 C4
Llandygwydd Ceredig 45 E4
Llandynan Denb 73 E5
Llandyrnog Denb 72 C5
Llandysilio Powys 60 C2
Llandyssil Powys 59 E8
Llandysul Ceredig 46 E3
Llanedeyrn Cardiff 35 F6
Llanedi Carms 33 D6
Llaneglwys Powys 48 F2
Llanegryn Gwyn 58 D2
Llanegwad Carms 33 B6
Llaneilian Anglesey 82 B4
Llanelian-yn-Rhos Conwy 83 D8
Llanelidan Denb 72 D5
Llanelieu Powys 48 F3
Llanellen Mon 35 C7
Llanelli Carms 33 E6
Llanelltyd Gwyn 58 C4
Llanelly Mon 35 C6
Llanelly Hill Mon 35 C6
Llanelwedd Powys 48 D2
Llanelwy = St Asaph Denb 72 B4
Llanenddwyn Gwyn 71 E6
Llanengan Gwyn 70 E3
Llanerchymedd Anglesey 82 C4
Llanerfyl Powys 59 D7
Llanfachraeth Anglesey 82 C3
Llanfachreth Gwyn 71 E8
Llanfaelog Anglesey 82 D3
Llanfaelrhys Gwyn 70 E3
Llanfaenor Mon 35 C8
Llanfaes Anglesey 83 D6
Llanfaes Powys 34 B4
Llanfaethlu Anglesey 82 C3
Llanfaglan Gwyn 82 E4
Llanfair Gwyn 71 E6
Llanfair-ar-y-bryn Carms 47 F7
Llanfair Caereinion Powys 59 D8
Llanfair Clydogau Ceredig 46 D5
Llanfair-Dyffryn-Clwyd Denb 72 D5
Llanfair Kilgheddin Mon 35 D7
Llanfair-Nant-Gwyn Pembs 45 F3
Llanfair Talhaiarn Conwy 72 B3
Llanfair Waterdine Shrops 48 B4
Llanfair-ym-Muallt = Builth Wells Powys 48 D2
Llanfairfechan Conwy 83 D6
Llanfairpwll-gwyngyll Anglesey 82 D5
Llanfairyneubwll Anglesey 82 D3
Llanfairynghornwy Anglesey 82 B3
Llanfallteg Carms 32 C2
Llanfaredd Powys 48 D2
Llanfarian Ceredig 46 B4
Llanfechain Powys 59 B8
Llanfechan Powys 47 D8
Llanfechell Anglesey 82 B3
Llanfendigaid Gwyn 58 D2
Llanferres Denb 73 C5
Llanfflewyn Anglesey 82 C3
Llanfihangel-ar-arth Carms 46 F3
Llanfihangel-Crucorney Mon 35 B7
Llanfihangel Glyn Myfyr Conwy 72 E3
Llanfihangel Nant Bran Powys 47 F8
Llanfihangel-nant-Melan Powys 48 D3
Llanfihangel Rhydithon Powys 48 C3
Llanfihangel Rogiet Mon 35 F8
Llanfihangel Tal-y-llyn Powys 35 B5
Llanfihangel-uwch-Gwili Carms 33 B5
Llanfihangel-y-Creuddyn Ceredig 47 B5
Llanfihangel-y-pennant Gwyn 71 C6
Llanfihangel-y-pennant Gwyn 58 D3
Llanfihangel-y-traethau Gwyn 71 D6
Llanfihangel-yn-Ngwynfa Powys 59 C7
Llanfihangel yn Nhowyn Anglesey 82 D3
Llanfilo Powys 48 F3
Llanfoist Mon 35 C6
Llanfor Gwyn 72 F3
Llanfrechfa Torf 35 E7
Llanfrothen Gwyn 71 C7
Llanfrynach Powys 34 B4
Llanfwrog Anglesey 82 C3
Llanfwrog Denb 72 D5
Llanfyllin Powys 59 C8
Llanfynydd Carms 33 B6
Llanfynydd Flint 73 D6
Llanfyrnach Pembs 45 F4
Llangadfan Powys 59 C7
Llangadog Carms 33 B8
Llangadwaladr Anglesey 82 E3
Llangadwaladr Powys 73 F5
Llangaffo Anglesey 82 E4
Llangain Carms 32 C4
Llangammarch Wells Powys 47 E8
Llangan V Glam 21 B8
Llangarron Hereford 36 B2
Llangasty Talyllyn Powys 35 B5
Llangathen Carms 33 B6
Llangattock Powys 35 C6
Llangattock Lingoed Mon 35 B7
Llangattock nigh Usk Mon 35 D7
Llangattock-Vibon-Avel Mon 36 C1
Llangedwyn Powys 59 B8
Llangefni Anglesey 82 D4
Llangeinor Bridgend 34 F3
Llangeitho Ceredig 46 D5
Llangeler Carms 46 F2
Llangelynin Gwyn 58 D2
Llangendeirne Carms 33 C5
Llangennech Carms 33 D6
Llangennith Swansea 33 E5
Llangenny Powys 35 C6
Llangernyw Conwy 83 E8
Llangian Gwyn 70 E3
Llanglydwen Carms 32 B2
Llangoed Anglesey 83 D6
Llangoedmor Ceredig 45 E3
Llangollen Denb 73 E6
Llangolman Pembs 32 B2
Llangors Powys 35 B5
Llangovan Mon 36 D1
Llangower Gwyn 72 F3
Llangrannog Ceredig 46 D2
Llangristiolus Anglesey 82 D4
Llangrove Hereford 36 C2
Llangua Mon 35 B7
Llangunllo Powys 48 B4
Llangunnor Carms 33 C5
Llangurig Powys 47 B8
Llangwm Conwy 72 E3
Llangwm Mon 35 D8
Llangwm Pembs 44 E4
Llangwnnadl Gwyn 70 D3
Llangwyfan Denb 72 C5
Llangwyfan-isaf Anglesey 82 E3
Llangwyllog Anglesey 82 D4
Llangwyryfon Ceredig 46 B4
Llangybi Ceredig 46 D5
Llangybi Gwyn 70 C5
Llangybi Mon 35 E7
Llangyfelach Swansea 33 E7
Llangynhafal Denb 72 C5
Llangynidr Powys 35 C5
Llangynin Carms 32 C3
Llangynog Carms 32 C4
Llangynog Powys 59 B7
Llangynwyd Bridgend 34 F2
Llanhamlach Powys 34 B4
Llanharan Rhondda 34 F4
Llanharry Rhondda 34 F4
Llanhennock Mon 35 E7
Llanhiledd = Llanhilleth Bl Gwent 35 D6
Llanhilleth = Llanhiledd Bl Gwent 35 D6
Llanidloes Powys 59 F6
Llaniestyn Gwyn 70 D3
Llanifyny Powys 59 F5
Llanigon Powys 48 F4
Llanilar Ceredig 46 B5
Llanilid Rhondda 34 F3
Llanilltud Fawr = Llantwit Major V Glam 21 C8
Llanishen Cardiff 35 F5
Llanishen Mon 36 D1
Llanllawddog Carms 33 B5
Llanllechid Gwyn 83 E6
Llanllowell Mon 35 E7
Llanllugan Powys 59 D7
Llanllwch Carms 32 C4
Llanllwchaiarn Powys 59 E8
Llanllwni Carms 46 F3
Llanllyfni Gwyn 82 F4
Llanmadoc Swansea 33 E5
Llanmaes V Glam 21 C8
Llanmartin Newport 35 F7
Llanmihangel V Glam 21 B8
Llanmorlais Swansea 33 E6
Llannefydd Conwy 72 B3
Llannon Carms 33 D6
Llannor Gwyn 70 D4
Llanon Ceredig 46 C4
Llanover Mon 35 D7
Llanpumsaint Carms 33 B5
Llanreithan Pembs 44 C3
Llanrhaeadr Denb 72 C4
Llanrhaeadr-ym-Mochnant Powys 59 B8
Llanrhian Pembs 44 B3
Llanrhidian Swansea 33 E5
Llanrhos Conwy 83 C7
Llanrhyddlad Anglesey 82 C3
Llanrhystud Ceredig 46 C4
Llanrosser Hereford 48 F4
Llanrothal Hereford 36 C1
Llanrug Gwyn 82 E5
Llanrumney Cardiff 35 F6
Llanrwst Conwy 83 E8
Llansadurnen Carms 32 C3
Llansadwrn Anglesey 83 D5
Llansadwrn Carms 47 F5
Llansaint Carms 32 D4
Llansamlet Swansea 33 E7
Llansannan Conwy 72 C3
Llansannor V Glam 21 B8
Llansantffraed Ceredig 46 C4
Llansantffraed Powys 35 B5
Llansantffraed Cwmdeuddwr Powys 47 C8
Llansantffraed-in-Elvel Powys 48 D2
Llansantffraid-ym-Mechain Powys 60 B2
Llansawel Carms 46 F5
Llansilin Powys 60 B2
Llansoy Mon 35 D8
Llanspyddid Powys 34 B4
Llanstadwell Pembs 44 E4
Llansteffan Carms 32 C4
Llanstephan Powys 48 E3
Llantarnam Torf 35 E7
Llanteg Pembs 32 C2
Llanthony Mon 35 B6
Llantilio Crossenny Mon 35 C7
Llantilio Pertholey Mon 35 C7
Llantood Pembs 45 E3
Llantrisant Anglesey 82 C3
Llantrisant Mon 35 E7
Llantrisant Rhondda 34 F4
Llantrithyd V Glam 22 B2
Llantwit Fardre Rhondda 34 F4
Llantwit Major = Llanilltud Fawr V Glam 21 C8
Llanuwchllyn Gwyn 72 F2
Llanvaches Newport 35 E8
Llanvair Discoed Mon 35 E8
Llanvapley Mon 35 C7
Llanvetherine Mon 35 C7
Llanveynoe Hereford 48 F5
Llanvihangel Gobion Mon 35 D7
Llanvihangel-Ystern-Llewern Mon 35 C8
Llanwarne Hereford 36 B2
Llanwddyn Powys 59 C7
Llanwenog Ceredig 46 E3
Llanwern Newport 35 F7
Llanwinio Carms 32 B3
Llanwnda Gwyn 82 F4
Llanwnda Pembs 44 B4
Llanwnnen Ceredig 46 E4
Llanwnog Powys 59 E7
Llanwrda Carms 47 F6
Llanwrin Powys 58 D4
Llanwrthwl Powys 47 C8
Llanwrtud = Llanwrtyd Wells Powys 47 E7
Llanwrtyd Powys 47 E7
Llanwrtyd Wells = Llanwrtud Powys 47 E7
Llanwyddelan Powys 59 D7
Llanyblodwel Shrops 60 B2
Llanybri Carms 32 C4
Llanybydder Carms 46 E4
Llanycefn Pembs 32 B1
Llanychaer Pembs 44 B4
Llanycil Gwyn 72 F3
Llanycrwys Carms 46 E5
Llanymawddwy Gwyn 59 C6
Llanymddyfri = Llandovery Carms 47 F6
Llanymynech Powys 60 B2
Llanynghenedl Anglesey 82 C3
Llanynys Denb 72 C5
Llanyre Powys 48 C2
Llanystumdwy Gwyn 71 D5
Llanywern Powys 35 B5
Llawhaden Pembs 32 C1
Llawnt Shrops 73 F6
Llawr Dref Gwyn 70 E3
Llawryglyn Powys 59 E6
Llay Wrex 73 D7
Llechcynfarwy Anglesey 82 C3
Llecheiddior Gwyn 71 C5
Llechfaen Powys 34 B4
Llechryd Caerph 35 D5
Llechryd Ceredig 45 E4
Llechrydau Powys 73 F6
Llechwedd Slate Caverns, Blaenau Ffestiniog Gwyn 71 C8
Lledrod Ceredig 46 B5
Llenmerewig Powys 59 E8
Llethrid Swansea 33 E6
Llidiad Nenog Carms 46 F4
Llidiardau Gwyn 72 F2
Llidiart-y-parc Denb 72 E5
Llithfaen Gwyn 70 C4
Llong Flint 73 C6
Llowes Powys 48 E3
Llundain-fach Ceredig 46 D4
Llwydcoed Rhondda 34 D3
Llwyn Shrops 60 F2
Llwyn-du Mon 35 C6
Llwyn-hendy Carms 33 E6
Llwyn-têg Carms 33 D6
Llwyn-y-brain Carms 32 C2
Llwyn-y-groes Ceredig 46 D4
Llwyncelyn Ceredig 46 D3
Llwyndafydd Ceredig 46 D2
Llwynderw Powys 60 D2
Llwyndyrys Gwyn 70 C4
Llwyngwril Gwyn 58 D2
Llwynmawr Wrex 73 F6
Llwynypia Rhondda 34 E3
Llynclys Shrops 60 B2
Llynfaes Anglesey 82 D4
Llys-y-frân Pembs 32 B1
Llysfaen Conwy 83 D8
Llyswen Powys 48 F3
Llysworney V Glam 21 B8
Llywel Powys 47 F7
Loan Falk 122 B2
Loanend Northumb 124 D5
Loanhead Midloth 123 C5
Loans S Ayrs 120 F3
Loans of Tullich Highld 158 B2
Lobb Devon 20 F3
Loch a Charnain W Isles 170 F4
Loch a'Ghainmhich W Isles 172 F5
Loch Baghasdail = Lochboisdale W Isles 171 J3
Loch Choire Lodge Highld 167 F8
Loch Euphoirt W Isles 170 D4
Loch Head Dumfries 105 E7
Loch Loyal Lodge Highld 167 E8
Loch nam Madadh = Lochmaddy W Isles 170 D5
Loch Ness Monster Exhibition, Drumnadrochit Highld 157 F6
Loch Sgioport W Isles 170 G4
Lochailort Highld 145 E7
Lochaline Highld 137 D7
Lochanhully Highld 148 B5
Lochans Dumfries 104 D4
Locharbriggs Dumfries 114 F2
Lochassynt Lodge Highld 163 B5
Lochavich Ho. Argyll 130 D5
Lochawe Argyll 131 C7
Lochboisdale = Loch Baghasdail W Isles 171 J3
Lochbuie Argyll 137 F7
Lochcarron Highld 155 G4
Lochdhu Highld 168 E5
Lochdochart House Stirl 132 B3
Lochdon Argyll 130 B3
Lochdrum Highld 156 B3
Lochead Argyll 128 C2
Lochearnhead Stirl 132 B4
Lochee Dundee 142 F3
Lochend Highld 157 F6
Lochend Highld 169 C7
Locherben Dumfries 114 E2
Lochfoot Dumfries 107 B5
Lochgair Argyll 128 A4
Lochgarthside Highld 147 C8
Lochgelly Fife 134 E3
Lochgilphead Argyll 128 B3
Lochgoilhead Argyll 131 E8
Lochhill Moray 159 C6
Lochindorb Lodge Highld 158 F3
Lochinver Highld 162 B4
Lochlane Perth 133 B7
Lochluichart Highld 156 C4
Lochmaben Dumfries 114 F3
Lochmaddy = Loch nam Madadh W Isles 170 D5
Lochmore Cottage Highld 169 E5
Lochmore Lodge Highld 166 F4
Lochore Fife 134 E3
Lochportain W Isles 170 C5
Lochranza N Ayrs 119 A6
Lochs Crofts Moray 159 C7
Lochside Aberds 143 C7
Lochside Highld 167 D6
Lochside Highld 168 F3
Lochside Highld 158 D2
Lochslin Highld 165 F5
Lochstack Lodge Highld 166 E4
Lochton Aberds 151 E6
Lochty Angus 143 C5
Lochty Fife 135 D7
Lochty Perth 134 B2
Lochuisge Highld 138 D1
Lochurr Dumfries 113 F7
Lochwinnoch Renfs 120 D3
Lochwood Dumfries 114 E3
Lochyside Highld 139 B5
Lockengate Corn 4 C5
Lockerbie Dumfries 114 F4
Lockeridge Wilts 25 C6
Lockerley Hants 14 B3
Locking N Som 23 D5
Lockinge Oxon 38 F4
Lockington E Yorks 97 E5
Lockington Leics 63 B8
Lockleywood Shrops 61 B6
Locks Heath Hants 15 D6
Lockton N Yorks 103 E6
Lockwood W Yorks 88 C2
Locomotion Museum, Shildon Durham 101 B7
Loddington Leics 64 D4
Loddington Northants 53 B6
Loddiswell Devon 6 E5
Loddon Norf 69 E6
Lode Cambs 55 C6
Loders Dorset 12 E2
Lodsworth W Sus 16 B3
Lofthouse N Yorks 94 B4
Lofthouse W Yorks 88 B4
Loftus Redcar 103 C5
Logan E Ayrs 113 B5
Logan Mains Dumfries 104 E4
Loganlea W Loth 122 C2
Loggerheads Staffs 74 F4
Logie Angus 143 C6
Logie Fife 135 B6
Logie Moray 158 D4
Logie Coldstone Aberds 150 D3
Logie Hill Highld 157 B8
Logie Newton Aberds 160 E3
Logie Pert Angus 143 C6
Logiealmond Lodge Perth 141 F6
Logierait Perth 141 D6
Login Carms 32 B2
Lolworth Cambs 54 C4
Lonbain Highld 155 E2
Londesborough E Yorks 96 E4
London, City of = City of London London 41 F6
London City Airport London 41 F7
London Colney Herts 40 D4
London Gatwick Airport W Sus 28 E3
London Heathrow Airport London 27 B8
London Luton Airport Luton 40 B4
London Stansted Airport Essex 41 B8
London Zoo London 41 F5
Londonderry N Yorks 101 F8
Londonthorpe Lincs 78 F2
Londubh Highld 154 B4
Lonemore Highld 164 F4
Long Ashton N Som 23 B7
Long Bennington Lincs 77 E8
Long Bredy Dorset 12 E3
Long Buckby Northants 52 C4
Long Clawson Leics 64 B4
Long Common Hants 15 C6
Long Compton Staffs 62 B2
Long Compton Warks 51 F7
Long Crendon Bucks 39 D6
Long Crichel Dorset 13 C7
Long Ditton Sur 28 C2
Long Drax N Yorks 89 B7
Long Duckmanton Derbys 76 B4
Long Eaton Derbys 76 F4
Long Green Worcs 50 F3
Long Hanborough Oxon 38 C4
Long Itchington Warks 52 C2
Long Lawford Warks 52 B2
Long Load Som 12 B2
Long Marston Herts 40 C1
Long Marston N Yorks 95 D8
Long Marston Warks 51 E6
Long Marton Cumb 100 B1
Long Melford Suff 56 E2
Long Newnton Glos 37 E6
Long Newton E Loth 123 C8
Long Preston N Yorks 93 D8
Long Riston E Yorks 97 E7
Long Sight Gtr Man 87 D7
Long Stratton Norf 68 E4
Long Street M Keynes 53 E5
Long Sutton Hants 26 E5
Long Sutton Lincs 66 B4
Long Sutton Som 12 B2
Long Thurlow Suff 56 C4
Long Whatton Leics 63 B8
Long Wittenham Oxon 39 E5
Longbar N Ayrs 120 D3
Longbenton T & W 111 C5
Longborough Glos 38 B1
Longbridge Warks 51 C7
Longbridge W Mid 50 B5
Longbridge Deverill Wilts 24 E3
Longburton Dorset 12 C4
Longcliffe Derbys 76 D2
Longcot Oxon 38 E2
Longcroft Falk 121 B7
Longden Shrops 60 D4
Longdon Staffs 62 C4
Longdon Worcs 50 F3
Longdon Green Staffs 62 C4
Longdon on Tern Telford 61 C6
Longdown Devon 10 E3
Longdowns Corn 3 C6
Longfield Kent 29 C7
Longfield Shetland 175 M5
Longford Derbys 76 F2
Longford Glos 37 B5
Longford London 27 B8
Longford Shrops 74 F3
Longford Telford 61 C7
Longford W Mid 63 F7
Longfordlane Derbys 76 F2
Longforgan Perth 134 B5
Longformacus Borders 124 D2
Longframlington Northumb 117 D7
Longham Dorset 13 E8
Longham Norf 68 C2
Longhaven Aberds 161 E8
Longhill Aberds 161 C6
Longhirst Northumb 117 F8
Longhope Glos 36 C3
Longhope Orkney 176 G2
Longhorsley Northumb 117 E7
Longhoughton Northumb 117 C8
Longlane Derbys 76 F2
Longlane W Berks 26 B2
Longleat, Warminster Wilts 24 E3
Longlevens Glos 37 B5
Longley W Yorks 88 D2
Longley Green Worcs 50 D2
Longmanhill Aberds 160 B4
Longmoor Camp Hants 27 F5
Longmorn Moray 159 D6
Longnewton Borders 115 B8
Longnewton Stockton 102 C1
Longney Glos 36 C4
Longniddry E Loth 123 B7
Longnor Shrops 60 D4
Longnor Staffs 75 C7
Longparish Hants 26 E2
Longport Stoke 75 E5
Longridge Lancs 93 F6
Longridge Staffs 62 C3
Longridge W Loth 122 C2
Longriggend N Lnrk 121 B8
Longsdon Staffs 75 D6
Longshaw Gtr Man 86 D3
Longside Aberds 161 D7
Longstanton Cambs 54 C4
Longstock Hants 25 F8
Longstone Pembs 32 D2
Longstowe Cambs 54 D4
Longthorpe P'boro 65 E8
Longthwaite Cumb 99 B6
Longton Lancs 86 B2
Longton Stoke 75 E6
Longtown Cumb 108 C3
Longtown Hereford 35 B7
Longview Mers 86 E2
Longville in the Dale Shrops 60 E5
Longwick Bucks 39 D7
Longwitton Northumb 117 F6
Longwood Shrops 61 D6
Longworth Oxon 38 E3
Longyester E Loth 123 C8
Lonmay Aberds 161 C7
Lonmore Highld 152 E3
Looe Corn 5 D7
Loose Kent 29 D8
Loosley Row Bucks 39 D8
Lopcombe Corner Wilts 25 F7
Lopen Som 12 C2
Loppington Shrops 60 B4
Lopwell Devon 6 C2
Lorbottle Northumb 117 D6
Lorbottle Hall Northumb 117 D6
Lord's Cricket Ground London 41 F5
Lornty Perth 142 E1
Loscoe Derbys 76 E4
Losgaintir W Isles 173 J3
Lossiemouth Moray 159 B6
Lossit Argyll 126 D1
Lostford Shrops 74 F3
Lostock Gralam Ches 74 B3
Lostock Green Ches 74 B3
Lostock Hall Lancs 86 B3
Lostock Junction Gtr Man 86 D4
Lostwithiel Corn 5 D6
Loth Orkney 176 C5
Lothbeg Highld 165 C6
Lothersdale N Yorks 94 E2
Lothmore Highld 165 C6
Loudwater Bucks 40 E2

M

Murra Orkney 176 F1
Murrayfield Edin 122 B5
Murrayfield Stadium Edin 123 B5
Murrays Motorcycle Museum I o M 84 D3
Murrow Cambs 66 D3
Mursley Bucks 39 B8
Murthill Angus 142 D4
Murthly Perth 141 F7
Murton Cumb 100 B2
Murton Durham 111 E6
Murton Northumb 125 E5
Murton York 96 D2
Musbury Devon 11 E7
Muscoates N Yorks 102 F4
Musdale Argyll 130 C5
Museum of Childhood, Bethnal Green London 41 F6
Museum of the Broads, Sutton Norf 69 B6
Musselburgh E Loth 123 B6
Musselburgh Racecourse E Loth 123 B6
Muston Leics 77 F8
Muston N Yorks 97 B6
Mustow Green Worcs 50 B3
Mutehill Dumfries 106 E3
Mutford Suff 69 F7
Muthill Perth 133 C7
Mutterton Devon 10 D5
Muxton Telford 61 C7
Mybster Highld 169 D6
Myddfai Carms 34 B1
Myddle Shrops 60 B4
Mydroilyn Ceredig 46 D3
Myerscough Lancs 92 F4
Mylor Bridge Corn 3 C7
Mynachlog-ddu Pembs 45 F3
Myndtown Shrops 60 F3
Mynydd Bach Ceredig 47 B6
Mynydd-bach Mon 36 E1
Mynydd Bodafon Anglesey 82 C4
Mynydd-isa Flint 73 C6
Mynyddygarreg Carms 33 D5
Mynytho Gwyn 70 D4
Myrebird Aberds 151 E6
Myrelandhorn Highld 169 D7
Myreside Perth 134 B4
Myrtle Hill Carms 47 F6
Mytchett Sur 27 D6
Mytholm W Yorks 87 B7
Mytholmroyd W Yorks 87 B8
Myton-on-Swale N Yorks 95 C7
Mytton Shrops 60 C4

N

Na Gearrannan W Isles 172 D4
Naast Highld 154 B4
Naburn York 95 E8
Nackington Kent 31 D5
Nacton Suff 57 E6
Nafferton E Yorks 97 D6
Nailbridge Glos 36 C3
Nailsbourne Som 11 B7
Nailsea N Som 23 B6
Nailstone Leics 63 D8
Nailsworth Glos 37 E5
Nairn Highld 158 D2
Nalderswood Sur 28 E3
Nancegollan Corn 2 C5
Nancledra Corn 2 C3
Nanhoron Gwyn 70 D3
Nannau Gwyn 71 E8
Nannerch Flint 73 C5
Nanpantan Leics 64 C2
Nanpean Corn 4 D4
Nanstallon Corn 4 C5
Nant-ddu Powys 34 C4
Nant-glas Powys 47 C8
Nant Peris Gwyn 83 F6
Nant Uchaf Denb 72 D4
Nant-y-Bai Carms 47 E6
Nant-y-cafn Neath 34 D2
Nant-y-derry Mon 35 D7
Nant-y-ffin Carms 46 F4
Nant-y-moel Bridgend 34 E3
Nant-y-pandy Conwy 83 D6
Nanternis Ceredig 46 D2
Nantgaredig Carms 33 B5
Nantgarw Rhondda 35 F5
Nantglyn Denb 72 C4
Nantgwyn Powys 47 B8
Nantlle Gwyn 82 F5
Nantmawr Shrops 60 B2
Nantmel Powys 48 C2
Nantmor Gwyn 71 C7
Nantwich Ches 74 D3
Nantycaws Carms 33 C5
Nantyffyllon Bridgend 34 E2
Nantyglo Bl Gwent 35 C5
Naphill Bucks 39 E8
Nappa N Yorks 93 D8
Napton on the Hill Warks 52 C2
Narberth = Arberth Pembs 32 C2
Narborough Leics 64 E2
Narborough Norf 67 C7
Nasareth Gwyn 82 F4
Naseby Northants 52 B4
Nash Bucks 53 F5
Nash Hereford 48 C5
Nash Newport 35 F7
Nash Shrops 49 B8
Nash Lee Bucks 39 D8
Nassington Northants 65 E7
Nasty Herts 41 B6
Nateby Cumb 100 D2
Nateby Lancs 92 E4
National Agricultural Centre, Stoneleigh Warks 51 B8
National Botanic Garden of Wales Carms 33 C6
National Cycle Collection, Llandrindod Wells Powys 48 C2
National Exhibition Centre, Birmingham W Mid 63 F5
National Fishing Heritage Centre, Grimsby NE Lincs 91 D6
National Gallery London 41 F5
National Hockey Stadium M Keynes 87 E6
National Ice Centre Nottingham 77 F5
National Maritime Museum London 28 B4
National Maritime Museum, Falmouth Corn 4 F3
National Motor Museum, Beaulieu Hants 14 D4
National Museum of Photography, Bradford W Yorks 94 F4
National Museum of Wales Cardiff 22 B3
National Portrait Gallery (See National Gallery) London 41 F5
National Railway Museum York 95 D8
National Seal Sanctuary, Gweek Corn 3 D6
National Space Science Centre Leics 64 D2
National Squash Centre Gtr Man 87 E6
Natland Cumb 99 F7
Natural History Museum London 28 B3
Natureland Seal Sanctuary, Skegness Lincs 79 C8
Naughton Suff 56 E4
Naunton Glos 37 B8
Naunton Worcs 50 F3
Naunton Beauchamp Worcs 50 D4
Navenby Lincs 78 D2
Navestock Heath Essex 41 E8
Navestock Side Essex 42 E1
Navidale Highld 165 C7
Nawton N Yorks 102 F4
Nayland Suff 56 F3
Nazeing Essex 41 D7
Neacroft Hants 14 E2
Neal's Green Warks 63 F7
Neap Shetland 175 H7
Near Sawrey Cumb 99 E5
Neasham Darl 101 C8
Neath = Castell-Nedd Neath 33 E8
Neath Abbey Neath 33 E8
Neatishead Norf 69 B6
Nebo Anglesey 82 B4
Nebo Ceredig 46 C4
Nebo Conwy 83 F8
Nebo Gwyn 82 F4
Necton Norf 67 D8
Nedd Highld 166 F3
Nedderton Northumb 117 F8
Nedging Tye Suff 56 E4
Needham Norf 68 F5
Needham Market Suff 56 D4
Needingworth Cambs 54 B4
Needwood Staffs 63 B5
Neen Savage Shrops 49 B8
Neen Sollars Shrops 49 B8
Neenton Shrops 61 F6
Nefyn Gwyn 70 C4
Neilston E Renf 120 D4
Neinthirion Powys 59 D6
Neithrop Oxon 52 E2
Nelly Andrews Green Powys 60 D2
Nelson Caerph 35 E5
Nelson Lancs 93 F8
Nelson Village Northumb 111 B5
Nemphlar S Lnrk 121 E8
Nempnett Thrubwell Bath 23 C7
Nene Terrace Lincs 66 D2
Nenthall Cumb 109 E7
Nenthead Cumb 109 E7
Nenthorn Borders 124 F2
Nerabus Argyll 126 D2
Nercwys Flint 73 C6
Nerston S Lnrk 121 D6
Nesbit Northumb 125 F5
Ness Ches 73 B7
Ness Gardens, Connah's Quay Ches 73 B7
Nesscliffe Shrops 60 C3
Neston Ches 73 B6
Neston Wilts 24 C3
Nether Alderley Ches 74 B5
Nether Blainslie Borders 123 E8
Nether Booth Derbys 88 F2
Nether Broughton Leics 64 B3
Nether Burrow Lancs 93 B6
Nether Cerne Dorset 12 E4
Nether Compton Dorset 12 C3
Nether Crimond Aberds 151 B7
Nether Dalgliesh Borders 115 D5
Nether Dallachy Moray 159 C7
Nether Exe Devon 10 D4
Nether Glasslaw Aberds 161 C5
Nether Handwick Angus 142 E3
Nether Haugh S Yorks 88 E5
Nether Heage Derbys 76 D3
Nether Heyford Northants 52 D4
Nether Hindhope Borders 116 C3
Nether Howecleuch S Lnrk 114 C3
Nether Kellet Lancs 92 C5
Nether Kinmundy Aberds 161 D7
Nether Langwith Notts 76 B5
Nether Leask Aberds 161 E7
Nether Lenshie Aberds 160 D3
Nether Monynut Borders 124 C3
Nether Padley Derbys 76 B2
Nether Park Aberds 161 C7
Nether Poppleton York 95 D8
Nether Silton N Yorks 102 E2
Nether Stowey Som 22 F3
Nether Urquhart Fife 134 D3
Nether Wallop Hants 25 F8
Nether Wasdale Cumb 98 D3
Nether Whitacre Warks 63 E6
Nether Worton Oxon 52 F2
Netheravon Wilts 25 E6
Netherbrae Aberds 160 C4
Netherbrough Orkney 176 E2
Netherburn S Lnrk 121 E8
Netherbury Dorset 12 E2
Netherby Cumb 108 B3
Netherby N Yorks 95 E6
Nethercote Warks 52 C3
Nethercott Devon 20 F3
Netherend Glos 36 D2
Netherfield E Sus 18 D4
Netherhampton Wilts 14 B2
Netherlaw Dumfries 106 E4
Netherley Aberds 151 E7
Netherley Mers 86 F2
Nethermill Dumfries 114 F3
Nethermuir Aberds 161 D6
Netherplace E Renf 120 D5
Netherseal Derbys 63 C6
Netherthird E Ayrs 113 C5
Netherthong W Yorks 88 D2
Netherthorpe S Yorks 89 F6
Netherton Angus 143 D5
Netherton Devon 7 B6
Netherton Hants 25 D8
Netherton Mers 85 D4
Netherton Northumb 117 D5
Netherton Oxon 38 E4
Netherton Perth 141 D8
Netherton Stirl 121 B5
Netherton W Mid 62 F3
Netherton Worcs 50 E4
Netherton W Yorks 88 C2
Netherton W Yorks 88 C3
Nethertown Cumb 98 D1
Nethertown Highld 169 B8
Netherwitton Northumb 117 E7
Netherwood E Ayrs 113 B6
Nethy Bridge Highld 149 B6
Netley Hants 15 D5
Netley Marsh Hants 14 C4
Netteswell Essex 41 C7
Nettlebed Oxon 39 F7
Nettlebridge Som 23 E8
Nettlecombe Dorset 12 E3
Nettleden Herts 40 C3
Nettleham Lincs 78 B3
Nettlestead Kent 29 D7
Nettlestead Green Kent 29 D7
Nettlestone I o W 15 E7
Nettlesworth Durham 111 E5
Nettleton Lincs 90 D5
Nettleton Wilts 24 B3
Neuadd Carms 33 B7
Nevendon Essex 42 E3
Nevern Pembs 45 E2
Nevis Range Ski Centre, Torlundy Highld 139 B5
New Abbey Dumfries 107 C6
New Aberdour Aberds 161 B5
New Addington London 28 C4
New Alresford Hants 26 F3
New Alyth Perth 142 E2
New Arley Warks 63 F6
New Ash Green Kent 29 C7
New Barn Kent 29 C7
New Barnetby N Lincs 90 C4
New Barton Northants 53 C6
New Bewick Northumb 117 B6
New-bigging Angus 142 E2
New Bilton Warks 52 B2
New Bolingbroke Lincs 79 D6
New Boultham Lincs 78 B2
New Bradwell M Keynes 53 E6
New Brancepeth Durham 110 E5
New Bridge Wrex 73 E6
New Brighton Flint 73 C6
New Brighton Mers 85 E4
New Brinsley Notts 76 D4
New Broughton Wrex 73 D7
New Buckenham Norf 68 E3
New Byth Aberds 160 C5
New Catton Norf 68 C5
New Cheriton Hants 15 B6
New Costessey Norf 68 C4
New Cowper Cumb 107 E8
New Cross Ceredig 46 B5
New Cross London 28 B4
New Cumnock E Ayrs 113 C6
New Deer Aberds 161 D5
New Delaval Northumb 111 B5
New Duston Northants 52 C5
New Earswick York 96 D2
New Edlington S Yorks 89 E6
New Elgin Moray 159 C6
New Ellerby E Yorks 97 F7
New Eltham London 28 B5
New End Worcs 51 D5
New Farnley W Yorks 94 F5
New Ferry Mers 85 F4
New Fryston W Yorks 89 B5
New Galloway Dumfries 106 B3
New Gilston Fife 135 D6
New Grimsby Scilly 2 E3
New Hainford Norf 68 C5
New Hartley Northumb 111 B6
New Haw Sur 27 C8
New Hedges Pembs 32 D2
New Herrington T & W 111 D6
New Hinksey Oxon 39 D5
New Holkham Norf 80 D4
New Holland N Lincs 90 B4
New Houghton Derbys 76 C4
New Houghton Norf 80 E3
New Houses N Yorks 93 B8
New Humberstone Leicester 64 D3
New Hutton Cumb 99 E7
New Hythe Kent 29 D8
New Inn Carms 46 F3
New Inn Mon 36 D1
New Inn Pembs 45 F2
New Inn Torf 35 E7
New Invention Shrops 48 B4
New Invention W Mid 62 D3
New Kelso Highld 155 F5
New Kingston Notts 64 B2
New Lanark S Lnrk 121 E8
New Lanark Village & Visitor Centre, Lanark S Lnrk 121 E8
New Lane Lancs 86 C2
New Lane End Warr 86 E4
New Leake Lincs 79 D7
New Leeds Aberds 161 C6
New Longton Lancs 86 B3
New Luce Dumfries 105 C5
New Malden London 28 C3
New Marske Redcar 102 B4
New Marton Shrops 73 F7
New Micklefield W Yorks 95 F7
New Mill Aberds 151 F6
New Mill Herts 40 C2
New Mill Wilts 25 C6
New Mill W Yorks 88 D2
New Mills Ches 87 F5
New Mills Corn 4 D3
New Mills Derbys 87 F7
New Mills Powys 59 D7
New Milton Hants 14 E3
New Moat Pembs 32 B1
New Ollerton Notts 77 C6
New Oscott W Mid 62 E4
New Park N Yorks 95 D5
New Pitsligo Aberds 161 C5
New Pleasurewood Hills Leisure Park, Lowestoft Suff 69 E8
New Polzeath Corn 4 B4
New Quay = Ceinewydd Ceredig 46 D2
New Rackheath Norf 69 C5
New Radnor Powys 48 C4
New Rent Cumb 108 F4
New Ridley Northumb 110 D3
New Road Side N Yorks 94 E2
New Romney Kent 19 C7
New Rossington S Yorks 89 E7
New Row Ceredig 47 B6
New Row Lancs 93 F6
New Row N Yorks 102 C4
New Sarum Wilts 25 F6
New Silksworth T & W 111 D6
New Stevenston N Lnrk 121 D7
New Street Staffs 75 D7
New Street Lane Shrops 74 F3
New Swanage Dorset 13 F8
New Totley S Yorks 76 B3
New Town E Loth 123 B7
New Tredegar = Tredegar Newydd Caerph 35 D5
New Trows S Lnrk 121 F8
New Ulva Argyll 128 B2
New Walsoken Cambs 66 D4
New Waltham NE Lincs 91 D6
New Whittington Derbys 76 B3
New Wimpole Cambs 54 E4
New Winton E Loth 123 B7
New Yatt Oxon 38 C3
New York Lincs 78 D5
New York N Yorks 94 C4
Newall W Yorks 94 E4
Newark Orkney 176 B6
Newark P'boro 66 D2
Newark Castle Notts 77 D7
Newark-on-Trent Notts 77 D7
Newarthill N Lnrk 121 D7
Newbarns Cumb 92 B2
Newbattle Midloth 123 C6
Newbiggin Cumb 98 E2
Newbiggin Cumb 92 C2
Newbiggin Cumb 99 B6
Newbiggin Cumb 109 E5
Newbiggin Cumb 99 B8
Newbiggin Durham 100 B4
Newbiggin N Yorks 100 E4
Newbiggin N Yorks 100 F4
Newbiggin-by-the-Sea Northumb 117 F9
Newbiggin-on-Lune Cumb 100 D2
Newbigging Angus 142 F4
Newbigging Angus 142 F4
Newbigging S Lnrk 122 E3
Newbold Derbys 76 B3
Newbold Leics 63 C8
Newbold on Avon Warks 52 B2
Newbold on Stour Warks 51 E7
Newbold Pacey Warks 51 D7
Newbold Verdon Leics 63 D8
Newborough Anglesey 82 E4
Newborough P'boro 66 D2
Newborough Staffs 62 B5
Newbottle Northants 52 F3
Newbottle T & W 111 D6
Newbourne Suff 57 E6
Newbridge Caerph 35 E6
Newbridge Ceredig 46 D4
Newbridge Corn 2 C3
Newbridge Corn 5 C8
Newbridge Dumfries 107 B6
Newbridge Edin 122 B4
Newbridge Hants 14 C3
Newbridge I o W 14 F5
Newbridge Pembs 44 B4
Newbridge Green Worcs 50 F3
Newbridge-on-Usk Mon 35 E7
Newbridge on Wye Powys 48 D2
Newbrough Northumb 109 C8
Newbuildings Devon 10 D2
Newburgh Aberds 151 B8
Newburgh Aberds 161 C6
Newburgh Borders 115 C6
Newburgh Fife 134 C4
Newburgh Lancs 86 C2
Newburn T & W 110 C4
Newbury W Berks 26 C2
Newbury Park London 41 F7
Newbury Racecourse W Berks 26 C2
Newby Cumb 99 B7
Newby Lancs 93 E8
Newby N Yorks 93 B7
Newby N Yorks 102 C3
Newby N Yorks 103 E8
Newby Bridge Cumb 99 F5
Newby East Cumb 108 D4
Newby Hall, Ripon N Yorks 95 C6
Newby West Cumb 108 D3
Newby Wiske N Yorks 102 F1
Newcastle Mon 35 C8
Newcastle Shrops 60 F2
Newcastle Discovery T & W 110 C5
Newcastle Emlyn = Castell Newydd Emlyn Carms 46 E2
Newcastle International Airport T & W 110 B4
Newcastle Racecourse T & W 110 B5
Newcastle-under-Lyme Staffs 74 E5
Newcastle Upon Tyne T & W 110 C5
Newcastleton = Copshaw Holm Borders 115 F7
Newchapel Pembs 45 F4
Newchapel Powys 59 F6
Newchapel Staffs 75 D5
Newchapel Sur 28 E4
Newchurch Carms 32 B4
Newchurch I o W 15 F6
Newchurch Kent 19 B7
Newchurch Lancs 93 F8
Newchurch Mon 36 E1
Newchurch Powys 48 D4
Newchurch Staffs 62 B5
Newcott Devon 11 D7
Newcraighall Edin 123 B6
Newdigate Sur 28 E2
Newell Green Brack 27 B6
Newenden Kent 18 C5
Newent Glos 36 B4
Newerne Glos 36 D3
Newfield Durham 110 F5
Newfield Highld 157 B8
Newford Scilly 2 E4
Newfound Hants 26 D3
Newgale Pembs 44 C3
Newgate Norf 81 C6
Newgate Street Herts 41 D6
Newhall Ches 74 E3
Newhall Derbys 63 B6
Newhall House Highld 157 C7
Newhall Point Highld 157 C8
Newham Northumb 117 B7
Newham Hall Northumb 117 B7
Newhaven Derbys 75 D8
Newhaven Edin 123 B5
Newhaven E Sus 17 D8
Newhey Gtr Man 87 C7
Newholm N Yorks 103 C6
Newhouse N Lnrk 121 C7
Newick E Sus 17 B8
Newingreen Kent 19 B8
Newington Kent 30 C2
Newington Kent 19 B8
Newington Kent 31 C7
Newington Notts 89 E7
Newington Oxon 39 E6
Newington Shrops 60 F4
Newland Glos 36 D2
Newland Hull 97 F6
Newland N Yorks 89 B7
Newland Worcs 50 E2
Newlandrig Midloth 123 C6
Newlands Borders 115 E8
Newlands Highld 157 E8
Newlands Moray 159 D7
Newlands Northumb 110 D3
Newland's Corner Sur 27 E8
Newlands of Geise Highld 169 C5
Newlands of Tynet Moray 159 C7
Newlands Park Anglesey 82 C2
Newlandsmuir S Lnrk 121 D6
Newlot Orkney 176 E4
Newlyn Corn 2 D3
Newmachar Aberds 151 C7
Newmains N Lnrk 121 D8
Newmarket Suff 55 C7
Newmarket W Isles 172 E7
Newmarket Racecourse Suff 55 C7
Newmill Borders 115 C7
Newmill Corn 2 C3
Newmill Moray 159 D8
Newmill of Inshewan Angus 142 C4
Newmills of Boyne Aberds 160 C2
Newmiln Perth 141 F8
Newmilns E Ayrs 120 F5
Newnham Cambs 54 D5
Newnham Glos 36 C3
Newnham Hants 26 D5
Newnham Herts 54 F3
Newnham Kent 30 D3
Newnham Northants 52 D3
Newnham Bridge Worcs 49 C8
Newpark Fife 135 C6
Newport Devon 20 F4
Newport E Yorks 96 F4
Newport Essex 55 F6
Newport Highld 165 B8
Newport I o W 15 F6
Newport Norf 69 C8
Newport Telford 61 C7
Newport = Casnewydd Newport 35 F7
Newport = Trefdraeth Pembs 45 F2
Newport Museum & Art Gallery Newport 35 F7
Newport-on-Tay Fife 135 B6
Newport Pagnell M Keynes 53 E6
Newpound Common W Sus 16 B4
Newquay Corn 4 C3
Newquay Airport Corn 4 C3
Newquay Sea Life Centre Corn 4 C3
Newsbank Ches 74 C5
Newseat Aberds 160 E4
Newseat Aberds 161 D7
Newsham Northumb 111 B6
Newsham N Yorks 101 C6
Newsham N Yorks 102 F1
Newsholme E Yorks 89 B8
Newsholme Lancs 93 D8
Newsome W Yorks 88 C2
Newstead Borders 123 F8
Newstead Notts 76 D5
Newstead Northumb 117 B7
Newstead Abbey, Kirkby in Ashfield Notts 76 D5
Newthorpe N Yorks 95 F7
Newton Argyll 131 F6
Newton Borders 116 B2
Newton Bridgend 21 B7
Newton Cambs 54 E5
Newton Cambs 66 C4
Newton Cardiff 22 B4
Newton Ches 74 D2
Newton Ches 73 C8
Newton Ches 74 B2
Newton Cumb 92 B2
Newton Derbys 76 D4
Newton Dorset 13 C5
Newton Dumfries 114 E4
Newton Dumfries 108 B2
Newton Gtr Man 87 E7
Newton Hereford 48 F5
Newton Hereford 49 D7
Newton Highld 157 C8
Newton Highld 166 F4
Newton Highld 169 E8
Newton Highld 157 E8
Newton Lancs 92 F4
Newton Lancs 93 D6
Newton Lancs 93 B5
Newton Lincs 78 F3
Newton Moray 159 C5
Newton Norf 67 C8
Newton Notts 77 E6
Newton Northants 65 F5
Newton Northumb 110 C3
Newton Perth 141 F5
Newton S Lnrk 121 C6
Newton S Lnrk 122 F2
Newton Staffs 62 B4
Newton Suff 56 E3
Newton Swansea 33 F7
Newton S Yorks 89 D6
Newton Warks 52 B3
Newton Wilts 14 B3
Newton W Loth 122 B3
Newton Abbot Devon 7 B6
Newton Abbot Racecourse Devon 7 B6
Newton Arlosh Cumb 107 D8
Newton Aycliffe Durham 101 B7
Newton Bewley Hrtlpl 102 B2
Newton Blossomville M Keynes 53 D7
Newton Bromswold Northants 53 C7
Newton Burgoland Leics 63 D7
Newton by Toft Lincs 90 F4
Newton Ferrers Devon 6 E3
Newton Flotman Norf 68 E5
Newton Hall Northumb 110 C3
Newton Harcourt Leics 64 E3
Newton Heath Gtr Man 87 D6
Newton Ho. Aberds 151 B5
Newton Kyme N Yorks 95 E7
Newton-le-Willows Mers 86 E3
Newton-le-Willows N Yorks 101 F7
Newton Longville Bucks 53 F6
Newton Mearns E Renf 120 D5
Newton Morrell N Yorks 101 D7
Newton Mulgrave N Yorks 103 C5
Newton of Ardtoe Highld 145 F6
Newton of Balcanquhal Perth 134 C3
Newton of Falkland Fife 134 D4
Newton on Ayr S Ayrs 112 B3
Newton on Ouse N Yorks 95 D8
Newton-on-Rawcliffe N Yorks 103 E6
Newton-on-the-Moor Northumb 117 D7
Newton on Trent Lincs 77 B8
Newton Park Argyll 129 D6
Newton Poppleford Devon 11 F5
Newton Purcell Oxon 52 F4
Newton Regis Warks 63 D6
Newton Reigny Cumb 108 F4
Newton St Cyres Devon 10 E3
Newton St Faith Norf 68 C5
Newton St Loe Bath 24 C2
Newton St Petrock Devon 9 C6
Newton Solney Derbys 63 B6
Newton Stacey Hants 26 E2
Newton Stewart Dumfries 105 C8
Newton Tony Wilts 25 E7
Newton Tracey Devon 9 B7
Newton under Roseberry Redcar 102 C3
Newton upon Derwent E Yorks 96 E3
Newton Valence Hants 26 F5
Newtonairds Dumfries 113 F8
Newtongrange Midloth 123 C6
Newtonhill Aberds 151 E8
Newtonhill Highld 157 E6
Newtonmill Angus 143 C6
Newtonmore Highld 148 E3
Newtown Argyll 131 E6
Newtown Ches 74 B2
Newtown Corn 3 D6
Newtown Cumb 107 E7
Newtown Cumb 108 C5
Newtown Derbys 87 F7
Newtown Devon 10 B2
Newtown Glos 36 D3
Newtown Glos 50 F4
Newtown Hants 14 C3
Newtown Hants 14 B4
Newtown Hants 15 C7
Newtown Hants 26 C2
Newtown Hants 15 C6
Newtown Hants 15 D5
Newtown Hereford 49 E8
Newtown Highld 147 D6
Newtown I o M 84 E3
Newtown I o W 14 E5
Newtown Northumb 117 D6
Newtown Northumb 117 B6
Newtown Northumb 125 F5
Newtown Poole 13 E8
Newtown Shrops 73 F8
Newtown Staffs 75 C6
Newtown Staffs 75 C7
Newtown Wilts 13 B7
Newtown = Y Drenewydd Powys 59 E8
Newtown Linford Leics 64 D2
Newtown St Boswells Borders 123 F8
Newtown Unthank Leics 63 D8
Newtyle Angus 142 E2
Neyland Pembs 44 E4
Niarbyl I o M 84 E2
Nibley S Glos 36 F3
Nibley Green Glos 36 E4
Nibon Shetland 174 F5
Nicholashayne Devon 11 C6
Nicholaston Swansea 33 F6
Nidd N Yorks 95 C6
Nigg Aberdeen 151 D8
Nigg Highld 158 B2
Nigg Ferry Highld 157 C8
Nightcott Som 10 B3
Nilig Denb 72 D4
Nine Ashes Essex 42 D1
Nine Mile Burn Midloth 122 D4
Nine Wells Pembs 44 C2
Ninebanks Northumb 109 D7
Ninfield E Sus 18 D4
Ningwood I o W 14 F4
Nisbet Borders 116 B2
Nisthouse Orkney 176 E2
Nisthouse Shetland 175 G7
Niton I o W 15 G6
Nitshill Glasgow 120 C5
No Man's Heath Ches 74 E2
No Man's Heath Warks 63 D6
Noak Hill London 41 E8
Noblethorpe S Yorks 88 D3
Nobottle Northants 52 C4
Nocton Lincs 78 C3
Noke Oxon 39 C5
Nolton Pembs 44 D3
Nolton Haven Pembs 44 D3
Nomansland Devon 10 C3
Nomansland Wilts 14 C3
Noneley Shrops 60 B4
Nonikiln Highld 157 B7
Nonington Kent 31 D6
Noonsbrough Shetland 175 H4
Norbreck Blkpool 92 E3
Norbridge Hereford 50 E2
Norbury Ches 74 E2
Norbury Derbys 75 E8
Norbury Shrops 60 E3
Norbury Staffs 61 B7
Nordelph Norf 67 D5
Norden Gtr Man 87 C6
Norden Heath Dorset 13 F7
Nordley Shrops 61 E6
Norham Northumb 124 E5
Norley Ches 74 B2
Norleywood Hants 14 E4
Norman Cross Cambs 65 E8
Normanby N Lincs 90 C2
Normanby N Yorks 103 F5
Normanby Redcar 102 C3
Normanby-by-Spital Lincs 90 F4
Normanby by Stow Lincs 90 F2
Normanby le Wold Lincs 90 E5
Normandy Sur 27 D7
Norman's Bay E Sus 18 E3
Norman's Green Devon 11 D5
Normanstone Suff 69 E8
Normanton Derby 76 F3
Normanton Leics 77 E8
Normanton Lincs 78 E2
Normanton Notts 77 D7
Normanton Rutland 65 D6
Normanton W Yorks 88 B4
Normanton le Heath Leics 63 C7
Normanton on Soar Notts 64 B2
Normanton-on-the-Wolds Notts 77 F6
Normanton on Trent Notts 77 C7
Normoss Lancs 92 F3
Norney Sur 27 E7
Norrington Common Wilts 24 C3
Norris Green Mers 85 E4
Norris Hill Leics 63 C7
North Anston S Yorks 89 F6
North Aston Oxon 38 B4
North Baddesley Hants 14 C4
North Ballachulish Highld 138 C4
North Barrow Som 12 B4
North Barsham Norf 80 D5
North Benfleet Essex 42 F3
North Bersted W Sus 16 D3
North Berwick E Loth 135 F7
North Boarhunt Hants 15 C7
North Bovey Devon 10 F2
North Bradley Wilts 24 D3
North Brentor Devon 9 F6
North Brewham Som 24 F2
North Buckland Devon 20 E3
North Burlingham Norf 69 C6
North Cadbury Som 12 B4
North Cairn Dumfries 104 B3
North Carlton Lincs 78 B2
North Carrine Argyll 118 F3
North Cave E Yorks 96 F4
North Cerney Glos 37 D7
North Charford Wilts 14 C2
North Charlton Northumb 117 B7
North Cheriton Som 12 B4
North Cliff E Yorks 97 E8
North Cliffe E Yorks 96 F4
North Clifton Notts 77 B8
North Cockerington Lincs 91 E7
North Coker Som 12 C3
North Collafirth Shetland 174 E5
North Common E Sus 17 B7
North Connel Argyll 130 B5
North Cornelly Bridgend 34 F2
North Cotes Lincs 91 D7
North Cove Suff 69 F7
North Cowton N Yorks 101 D7
North Crawley M Keynes 53 E7
North Cray London 29 B5
North Creake Norf 80 D4
North Curry Som 11 B8
North Dalton E Yorks 96 D5
North Dawn Orkney 176 F3
North Deighton N Yorks 95 D6
North Duffield N Yorks 96 F2
North Elkington Lincs 91 E6
North Elmham Norf 81 E5
North Elmshall W Yorks 89 C5
North End Bucks 39 B8
North End E Yorks 97 F8
North End Essex 42 C2
North End Hants 26 C2

O

P

S

Seend Wilts 24 C4
Seend Cleeve Wilts 24 C4
Seer Green Bucks 40 E2
Seething Norf 69 E6
Sefton Mers 85 D4
Seghill Northumb 111 B5
Seifton Shrops 60 F4
Seighford Staffs 62 B2
Seilebost W Isles 173 J3
Seion Gwyn 82 E5
Seisdon Staffs 62 E2
Seisiadar W Isles 172 E8
Selattyn Shrops 73 F6
Selborne Hants 26 F5
Selby N Yorks 96 F2
Selham W Sus 16 B3
Selhurst London 28 C4
Selkirk Borders 115 B7
Selkirk Glass Borders 115 B7
Sellack Hereford 36 B2
Sellafirth Shetland 174 D7
Sellibister Orkney 176 B6
Sellindge Kent 19 B7
Sellindge Lees Kent 19 B8
Selling Kent 30 D4
Sells Green Wilts 24 C4
Selly Oak W Mid 62 F4
Selmeston E Sus 18 E2
Selsdon London 28 C4
Selsey W Sus 16 E2
Selsfield Common W Sus 28 F4
Selsted Kent 31 E6
Selston Notts 76 D4
Selworthy Som 21 E8
Semblister Shetland 175 H5
Semer Suff 56 E3
Semington Wilts 24 C3
Semley Wilts 13 B6
Send Sur 27 D8
Send Marsh Sur 27 D8
Senghenydd Caerph 35 E5
Sennen Corn 2 D2
Sennen Cove Corn 2 D2
Sennybridge = Pont Senni Powys 34 B3
Serlby Notts 89 F7
Sessay N Yorks 95 B7
Setchey Norf 67 C6
Setley Hants 14 D4
Setter Shetland 175 H5
Setter Shetland 174 E6
Setter Shetland 175 J7
Settiscarth Orkney 176 E2
Settle N Yorks 93 C8
Settrington N Yorks 96 B4
Seven Kings London 41 F7
Seven Sisters Neath 34 D2
Sevenhampton Glos 37 B7
Sevenoaks Kent 29 D6
Sevenoaks Weald Kent 29 D6
Severn Beach S Glos 36 F2
Severn Bridges Visitor Centre S Glos 36 F2
Severn Stoke Worcs 50 E3
Severn Valley Railway Worcs 50 B2
Severnhampton Swindon 38 E2
Sevington Kent 30 E4
Sewards End Essex 55 F6
Sewardstone Essex 41 E6
Sewardstonebury Essex 41 E6
Sewerby E Yorks 97 C7
Sewerby Hall and Gardens, Bridlington E Yorks 97 C8
Seworgan Corn 3 C6
Sewstern Leics 65 B5
Sezincote Glos 51 F6
Sgarasta Mhor W Isles 173 J3
Sgiogarstaigh W Isles 172 B8
Shabbington Bucks 39 D6
Shackerstone Leics 63 D7
Shackleford Sur 27 E7
Shade W Yorks 87 B7
Shadforth Durham 111 E6
Shadingfield Suff 69 F7
Shadoxhurst Kent 19 B6
Shadsworth Blkburn 86 B5
Shadwell Norf 68 F2
Shadwell W Yorks 95 F6
Shaftesbury Dorset 13 B6
Shafton S Yorks 88 C4
Shakespeare's Birthplace, Stratford-upon-Avon Warks 51 D6
Shalbourne Wilts 25 C8
Shalcombe I o W 14 F4
Shalden Hants 26 E4
Shaldon Devon 7 B7
Shalfleet I o W 14 F5
Shalford Essex 42 B3
Shalford Sur 27 E8
Shalford Green Essex 42 B3
Shallowford Devon 21 E6
Shalmsford Street Kent 30 D4
Shalstone Bucks 52 F4
Shamley Green Sur 27 E8
Shandon Argyll 129 B7
Shandwick Highld 158 B2
Shangton Leics 64 E4
Shankhouse Northumb 111 B5
Shanklin I o W 15 F6
Shanklin Chine I o W 15 F6
Shanquhar Aberds 160 E2
Shanzie Perth 142 D2
Shap Cumb 99 C7
Shapwick Dorset 13 D7
Shapwick Som 23 F6
Shardlow Derbys 76 F4
Shareshill Staffs 62 D3
Sharlston W Yorks 88 C4
Sharlston Common W Yorks 88 C4
Sharnbrook Beds 53 D7
Sharnford Leics 63 E8
Sharoe Green Lancs 92 F5
Sharow N Yorks 95 B6
Sharp Street Norf 69 B6
Sharpenhoe Beds 53 F8
Sharperton Northumb 117 D5
Sharpness Glos 36 D3
Sharpthorne W Sus 28 F4
Sharrington Norf 81 D6
Shatterford Worcs 61 F7
Shaugh Prior Devon 6 C3
Shavington Ches 74 D4
Shaw Gtr Man 87 D7
Shaw W Berks 26 C2
Shaw Wilts 24 C3
Shaw Green Lancs 86 C3
Shaw Mills N Yorks 95 C5
Shawbury Shrops 61 B5
Shawdon Hall Northumb 117 C6
Shawell Leics 64 F2
Shawford Hants 15 B5
Shawforth Lancs 87 B6
Shawhead Dumfries 107 B5
Shawhill Dumfries 108 C2
Shawton S Lnrk 121 E6
Shawtonhill S Lnrk 121 E6
Shear Cross Wilts 24 E3
Shearington Dumfries 107 C7
Shearsby Leics 64 E3
Shebbear Devon 9 D6
Shebdon Staffs 61 B7
Shebster Highld 168 C5
Sheddens E Renf 121 D5
Shedfield Hants 15 C6
Sheen Staffs 75 C8
Sheepscar W Yorks 95 F6
Sheepscombe Glos 37 C5
Sheepstor Devon 6 C3
Sheepwash Devon 9 D6
Sheepway N Som 23 B6
Sheepy Magna Leics 63 D7
Sheepy Parva Leics 63 D7
Sheering Essex 41 C8
Sheerness Kent 30 B3
Sheet Hants 15 B8
Sheffield S Yorks 88 F4
Sheffield Bottom W Berks 26 C4
Sheffield Green E Sus 17 B8
Sheffield Park, Uckfield E Sus 17 B8
Shefford Beds 54 F2
Shefford Woodlands W Berks 25 B8
Sheigra Highld 166 C3
Sheinton Shrops 61 D6
Shelderton Shrops 49 B6
Sheldon Derbys 75 C8
Sheldon Devon 11 D6
Sheldon W Mid 63 F5
Sheldwich Kent 30 D4
Shelf W Yorks 88 B2
Shelfanger Norf 68 F4
Shelfield Warks 51 C6
Shelfield W Mid 62 D4
Shelford Notts 77 E6
Shellacres Northumb 124 E4
Shelley Essex 42 D1
Shelley Suff 56 F4
Shelley W Yorks 88 C3
Shellingford Oxon 38 E3
Shellow Bowells Essex 42 D2
Shelsley Beauchamp Worcs 50 C2
Shelsley Walsh Worcs 50 C2
Shelthorpe Leics 64 C2
Shelton Beds 53 C8
Shelton Norf 68 E5
Shelton Notts 77 E7
Shelton Shrops 60 C4
Shelton Green Norf 68 E5
Shelve Shrops 60 E3
Shelwick Hereford 49 E7
Shenfield Essex 42 E2
Shenington Oxon 51 E8
Shenley Herts 40 D4
Shenley Brook End M Keynes 53 F6
Shenley Church End M Keynes 53 F6
Shenleybury Herts 40 D4
Shenmore Hereford 49 F5
Shennanton Dumfries 105 C7
Shenstone Staffs 62 D5
Shenstone Worcs 50 B3
Shenton Leics 63 D7
Shenval Highld 147 B7
Shenval Moray 149 B8
Shepeau Stow Lincs 66 C3
Shephall Herts 41 B5
Shepherd's Green Oxon 39 F7
Shepherd's Port Norf 80 D2
Shepherdswell Kent 31 E6
Shepley W Yorks 88 D2
Shepperdine S Glos 36 E3
Shepperton Sur 27 C8
Shepreth Cambs 54 E4
Shepshed Leics 63 C8
Shepton Beauchamp Som 12 C2
Shepton Mallet Som 23 E8
Shepton Montague Som 23 F8
Shepway Kent 29 D8
Sheraton Durham 111 F7
Sherborne Dorset 12 C4
Sherborne Glos 38 C1
Sherborne St John Hants 26 D4
Sherbourne Warks 51 C7
Sherburn Durham 111 E6
Sherburn N Yorks 97 B5
Sherburn Hill Durham 111 E6
Sherburn in Elmet N Yorks 95 F7
Shere Sur 27 E8
Shereford Norf 80 E4
Sherfield English Hants 14 B3
Sherfield on Loddon Hants 26 D4
Sherford Devon 7 E5
Sheriff Hutton N Yorks 96 C2
Sheriffhales Shrops 61 C7
Sheringham Norf 81 C7
Sherington M Keynes 53 E6
Shernal Green Worcs 50 C4
Shernborne Norf 80 D3
Sherrington Wilts 24 F4
Sherston Wilts 37 F5
Sherwood Green Devon 9 B7
Shettleston Glasgow 121 C6
Shevington Gtr Man 86 D3
Shevington Moor Gtr Man 86 C3
Shevington Vale Gtr Man 86 D3
Sheviock Corn 5 D8
Shide I o W 15 F5
Shiel Bridge Highld 146 C2
Shieldaig Highld 155 E4
Shieldaig Highld 154 C4
Shieldhill Dumfries 114 F3
Shieldhill Falk 121 B8
Shieldhill S Lnrk 122 E3
Shielfoot Highld 137 B7
Shielhill Angus 142 D4
Shielhill Invclyd 129 C7
Shifford Oxon 38 D3
Shifnal Shrops 61 D7
Shilbottle Northumb 117 D7
Shildon Durham 101 B7
Shillingford Devon 10 B4
Shillingford Oxon 39 E5
Shillingford St George Devon 10 F4
Shillingstone Dorset 13 C6
Shillington Beds 54 F2
Shillmoor Northumb 116 D4
Shilton Oxon 38 D2
Shilton Warks 63 F8
Shilvington Northumb 117 F7
Shimpling Norf 68 F4
Shimpling Suff 56 D2
Shimpling Street Suff 56 D2
Shincliffe Durham 111 E5
Shiney Row T & W 111 D6
Shinfield Wokingham 26 C5
Shingham Norf 67 D7
Shingle Street Suff 57 E7
Shinner's Bridge Devon 7 C5
Shinness Highld 164 C2
Shipbourne Kent 29 D6
Shipdham Norf 68 D2
Shipham Som 23 D6
Shiphay Torbay 7 C6
Shiplake Oxon 27 B5
Shipley Derbys 76 E4
Shipley Northumb 117 C7
Shipley Shrops 62 E2
Shipley W Sus 16 B5
Shipley W Yorks 94 F4
Shipley Shiels Northumb 116 E3
Shipmeadow Suff 69 F6
Shippea Hill Station Cambs 67 F6
Shippon Oxon 38 E4
Shipston-on-Stour Warks 51 E7
Shipton Glos 37 C7
Shipton N Yorks 95 D8
Shipton Shrops 61 E5
Shipton Bellinger Hants 25 E7
Shipton Gorge Dorset 12 E2
Shipton Green W Sus 16 D2
Shipton Moyne Glos 37 F5
Shipton on Cherwell Oxon 38 C4
Shipton Solers Glos 37 C7
Shipton-under-Wychwood Oxon 38 C2
Shiptonthorpe E Yorks 96 E4
Shirburn Oxon 39 E6
Shirdley Hill Lancs 85 C4
Shire Horse Centre, Stratford-upon-Avon Warks 51 D7
Shirebrook Derbys 76 C5
Shiregreen S Yorks 88 E4
Shirehampton Bristol 23 B7
Shiremoor T & W 111 B6
Shirenewton Mon 36 E1
Shireoaks Notts 89 F6
Shirkoak Kent 19 B6
Shirl Heath Hereford 49 D6
Shirland Derbys 76 D3
Shirley Derbys 76 E2
Shirley London 28 C4
Shirley Soton 14 C5
Shirley W Mid 51 B6
Shirrell Heath Hants 15 C6
Shirwell Devon 20 F4
Shirwell Cross Devon 20 F4
Shiskine N Ayrs 119 D6
Shobdon Hereford 49 C6
Shobnall Staffs 63 B6
Shobrooke Devon 10 D3
Shoby Leics 64 C3
Shocklach Ches 73 E8
Shoeburyness Sthend 43 F5
Sholden Kent 31 D7
Sholing Soton 14 C5
Shoot Hill Shrops 60 C4
Shop Corn 8 C4
Shop Corn 4 B3
Shop Corner Suff 57 F6
Shore Mill Highld 157 C8
Shoreditch London 41 F6
Shoreham Kent 29 C6
Shoreham Airport W Sus 17 D6
Shoreham-By-Sea W Sus 17 D6
Shoresdean Northumb 125 E5
Shoreswood Northumb 124 E5
Shoreton Highld 157 C7
Shorncote Glos 37 E7
Shorne Kent 29 B7
Short Heath W Mid 62 D3
Shortacombe Devon 9 F7
Shortgate E Sus 17 C8
Shortlanesend Corn 3 B7
Shortlees E Ayrs 120 F4
Shortstown Beds 53 E8
Shorwell I o W 15 F5
Shoscombe Bath 24 D2
Shotatton Shrops 60 B3
Shotesham Norf 69 E5
Shotgate Essex 42 E3
Shotley Suff 57 F6
Shotley Bridge Durham 110 D3
Shotley Gate Suff 57 F6
Shotleyfield Northumb 110 D3
Shottenden Kent 30 D4
Shottermill Sur 27 F6
Shottery Warks 51 D6
Shotteswell Warks 52 E2
Shottisham Suff 57 E7
Shottle Derbys 76 E3
Shottlegate Derbys 76 E3
Shotton Durham 111 F7
Shotton Flint 73 C7
Shotton Northumb 124 F4
Shotton Colliery Durham 111 E6
Shotts N Lnrk 121 C8
Shotwick Ches 73 B7
Shouldham Norf 67 D6
Shouldham Thorpe Norf 67 D6
Shoulton Worcs 50 D3
Shover's Green E Sus 18 B3
Shrawardine Shrops 60 C4
Shrawley Worcs 50 C3
Shrewley Common Warks 51 C7
Shrewsbury Shrops 60 C4
Shrewton Wilts 25 E5
Shripney W Sus 16 D3
Shrivenham Oxon 38 F2
Shropham Norf 68 E2
Shrub End Essex 43 B5
Shucknall Hereford 49 E7
Shudy Camps Cambs 55 E7
Shulishadermor Highld 153 E5
Shurdington Glos 37 C6
Shurlock Row Windsor 27 B6
Shurrery Highld 168 D5
Shurrery Lodge Highld 168 D5
Shurton Som 22 E4
Shustoke Warks 63 E6
Shute Devon 11 E7
Shute Devon 10 D3
Shutford Oxon 51 E8
Shuthonger Glos 50 F3
Shutlanger Northants 52 D5
Shuttington Warks 63 D6
Shuttlewood Derbys 76 B4
Siabost bho Dheas W Isles 172 D5
Siabost bho Thuath W Isles 172 D5
Siadar W Isles 172 C6
Siadar Iarach W Isles 172 C6
Siadar Uarach W Isles 172 C6
Sibbaldbie Dumfries 114 F4
Sibbertoft Northants 64 F3
Sibdon Carwood Shrops 60 F4
Sibford Ferris Oxon 51 F8
Sibford Gower Oxon 51 F8
Sible Hedingham Essex 55 F8
Sibsey Lincs 79 D6
Sibson Cambs 65 E7
Sibson Leics 63 D7
Sibthorpe Notts 77 E7
Sibton Suff 57 C7
Sibton Green Suff 57 B7
Sicklesmere Suff 56 C2
Sicklinghall N Yorks 95 E6
Sid Devon 11 F6
Sidbury Devon 11 E6
Sidbury Shrops 61 F6
Sidcot N Som 23 D6
Sidcup London 29 B5
Siddick Cumb 107 F7
Siddington Ches 74 B5
Siddington Glos 37 E7
Sidemoor Worcs 50 B4
Sidestrand Norf 81 D8
Sidford Devon 11 E6
Sidlesham W Sus 16 E2
Sidley E Sus 18 E4
Sidlow Sur 28 E3
Sidmouth Devon 11 F6
Sigford Devon 7 B5
Sigglesthorne E Yorks 97 E7
Sighthill Edin 122 B4
Sigingstone V Glam 21 B8
Signet Oxon 38 C2
Silchester Hants 26 C4
Sildinis W Isles 172 G5
Sileby Leics 64 C2
Silecroft Cumb 98 F3
Silfield Norf 68 E4
Silian Ceredig 46 D4
Silk Willoughby Lincs 78 E3
Silkstone S Yorks 88 D3
Silkstone Common S Yorks 88 D3
Silloth Cumb 107 D8
Sills Northumb 116 D4
Sillyearn Moray 160 C2
Siloh Carms 47 F6
Silpho N Yorks 103 E7
Silsden W Yorks 94 E3
Silsoe Beds 53 F8
Silver End Essex 42 C4
Silverburn Midloth 122 C5
Silverdale Lancs 92 B4
Silverdale Staffs 74 E5
Silvergate Norf 81 E7
Silverhill E Sus 18 D4
Silverley's Green Suff 57 B6
Silverstone Northants 52 E4
Silverstone Motor Racing Circuit Northants 52 E4
Silverton Devon 10 D4
Silvington Shrops 49 B8
Silwick Shetland 175 J4
Simmondley Derbys 87 E8
Simonburn Northumb 109 B8
Simonsbath Som 21 F6
Simonstone Lancs 93 F7
Simprim Borders 124 E4
Simpson M Keynes 53 F6
Simpson Cross Pembs 44 D3
Sinclair's Hill Borders 124 D4
Sinclairston E Ayrs 112 C4
Sinderby N Yorks 101 F8
Sinderhope Northumb 109 D8
Sindlesham Wokingham 27 C5
Singdean Borders 115 D8
Singleborough Bucks 53 F5
Singleton Lancs 92 F3
Singleton W Sus 16 C2
Singlewell Kent 29 B7
Sinkhurst Green Kent 30 E2
Sinnahard Aberds 150 C3
Sinnington N Yorks 103 F5
Sinton Green Worcs 50 C3
Sipson London 27 B8
Sirhowy Bl Gwent 35 C5
Sisland Norf 69 E6
Sissinghurst Kent 18 B4
Sissinghurst, Cranbrook Kent 18 B5
Sisterpath Borders 124 E3
Siston S Glos 23 B8
Sithney Corn 2 D5
Sittingbourne Kent 30 C2
Six Ashes Staffs 61 F7
Six Hills Leics 64 B3
Six Mile Bottom Cambs 55 D6
Sixhills Lincs 91 F5
Sixpenny Handley Dorset 13 C7
Sizewell Suff 57 C8
Skail Highld 168 E2
Skaill Orkney 176 E1
Skaill Orkney 176 E3
Skaill Orkney 176 F4
Skara Brae Orkney 176 E1
Skares E Ayrs 113 C5
Skateraw E Loth 124 B3
Skaw Shetland 174 G7
Skeabost Highld 152 E5
Skeabrae Orkney 176 D1
Skeeby N Yorks 101 D7
Skeffington Leics 64 D4
Skeffling E Yorks 91 C7
Skegby Notts 76 C4
Skegness Lincs 79 C8
Skelberry Shetland 175 M5
Skelbo Highld 164 E4
Skelbrooke S Yorks 89 C6
Skeldyke Lincs 79 F6
Skellingthorpe Lincs 78 B2
Skellister Shetland 175 H6
Skellow S Yorks 89 C6
Skelmanthorpe W Yorks 88 C3
Skelmersdale Lancs 86 D2
Skelmonae Aberds 161 E5
Skelmorlie N Ayrs 129 D6
Skelmuir Aberds 161 D6
Skelpick Highld 168 D2
Skelton Cumb 108 F4
Skelton E Yorks 89 B8
Skelton N Yorks 101 D5
Skelton Redcar 102 C4
Skelton York 95 D8
Skelton-on-Ure N Yorks 95 C6
Skelwick Orkney 176 B3
Skelwith Bridge Cumb 99 D5
Skendleby Lincs 79 C7
Skene Ho. Aberds 151 D6
Skenfrith Mon 36 B1
Skerne E Yorks 97 D6
Skeroblingarry Argyll 118 D4
Skerray Highld 167 C8
Skerton Lancs 92 C4
Sketchley Leics 63 E8
Sketty Swansea 33 E7
Skewen Neath 33 E8
Skewsby N Yorks 96 B2
Skeyton Norf 81 E8
Skiag Bridge Highld 163 B6
Skibo Castle Highld 164 F4
Skidbrooke Lincs 91 E8
Skidbrooke North End Lincs 91 E8
Skidby E Yorks 97 F6
Skilgate Som 10 B4
Skillington Lincs 65 B5
Skinburness Cumb 107 D8
Skinflats Falk 133 F8
Skinidin Highld 152 E3
Skinnet Highld 167 C7
Skinningrove Redcar 103 B5
Skipness Argyll 128 E3
Skippool Lancs 92 E3
Skipsea E Yorks 97 D7
Skipsea Brough E Yorks 97 D7
Skipton N Yorks 94 D2
Skipton-on-Swale N Yorks 95 B6
Skipwith N Yorks 96 F2
Skirbeck Lincs 79 E6
Skirbeck Quarter Lincs 79 E6
Skirlaugh E Yorks 97 F7
Skirling Borders 122 F3
Skirmett Bucks 39 F7
Skirpenbeck E Yorks 96 D3
Skirwith Cumb 109 F6
Skirza Highld 169 C8
Skulamus Highld 155 H2
Skullomie Highld 167 C8
Skyborry Green Shrops 48 B4
Skye of Curr Highld 149 B5
Skyreholme N Yorks 94 C3
Slackhall Derbys 87 F8
Slackhead Moray 159 C8
Slad Glos 37 D5
Slade Devon 20 E4
Slade Pembs 44 D4
Slade Green London 29 B6
Slaggyford Northumb 109 D6
Slaidburn Lancs 93 D7
Slaithwaite W Yorks 87 C8
Slaley Northumb 110 D2
Slamannan Falk 121 B8
Slapton Bucks 40 B2
Slapton Devon 7 E6
Slapton Northants 52 E4
Slatepit Dale Derbys 76 C3
Slattocks Gtr Man 87 D6
Slaugham W Sus 17 B6
Slaughterford Wilts 24 B3
Slawston Leics 64 E4
Sleaford Hants 27 F6
Sleaford Lincs 78 E3
Sleagill Cumb 99 C7
Sleapford Telford 61 C6
Sledge Green Worcs 50 F3
Sledmere E Yorks 96 C5
Sleightholme Durham 100 C4
Sleights N Yorks 103 D6
Slepe Dorset 13 E7
Slickly Highld 169 C7
Sliddery N Ayrs 119 D6
Sligachan Hotel Highld 153 G5
Slimbridge Glos 36 D4
Slimbridge Wildfowl & Wetlands Centre, Frampton on Severn Glos 36 D4
Slindon Staffs 74 F5
Slindon W Sus 16 D3
Slinfold W Sus 28 F2
Sling Gwyn 83 E6
Slingsby N Yorks 96 B2
Slioch Aberds 160 E2
Slip End Beds 40 C3
Slip End Herts 54 F3
Slipton Northants 53 B7
Slitting Mill Staffs 62 C4
Slochd Highld 148 B4
Slockavullin Argyll 130 F4
Sloley Norf 81 E8
Sloothby Lincs 79 B7
Slough Slough 27 B7
Slough Green W Sus 17 B6
Sluggan Highld 148 B4
Slumbay Highld 155 G4
Slyfield Sur 27 D7
Slyne Lancs 92 C4
Smailholm Borders 124 F2
Small Dole W Sus 17 C6
Small Hythe Kent 19 B5
Smallbridge Gtr Man 87 C7
Smallburgh Norf 69 B6
Smallburn Aberds 161 D7
Smallburn E Ayrs 113 B6
Smalley Derbys 76 E4
Smallfield Sur 28 E4
Smallridge Devon 11 D8
Smannell Hants 25 E8
Smardale Cumb 100 D2
Smarden Kent 30 E2
Smarden Bell Kent 30 E2
Smeeth Kent 19 B7
Smeeton Westerby Leics 64 E3
Smercleit W Isles 171 J3
Smerral Highld 169 F6
Smethwick W Mid 62 F4
Smirisary Highld 145 F6
Smisby Derbys 63 C7
Smith Green Lancs 92 D4
Smithfield Cumb 108 C4
Smithincott Devon 11 C5
Smith's Green Essex 42 B1
Smithstown Highld 154 C3
Smithton Highld 157 E8
Smithy Green Ches 74 B4
Smockington Leics 63 F8
Smoogro Orkney 176 F2
Smythe's Green Essex 43 C5
Snaefell Mountain Railway I o M 84 D4
Snaigow House Perth 141 E7
Snailbeach Shrops 60 D3
Snailwell Cambs 55 C7
Snainton N Yorks 103 F7
Snaith E Yorks 89 B7
Snape N Yorks 101 F7
Snape Suff 57 D7
Snape Green Lancs 85 C4
Snarestone Leics 63 D7
Snarford Lincs 90 F4
Snargate Kent 19 C6
Snave Kent 19 C7
Snead Powys 60 E3
Sneath Common Norf 68 F4
Sneaton N Yorks 103 D6
Sneatonthorpe N Yorks 103 D7
Snelland Lincs 90 F4
Snelston Derbys 75 E8
Snetterton Motor Racing Circuit Norf 68 F3
Snettisham Norf 80 D2
Snibston Discovery Park, Coalville Leics 63 C8
Sniseabhal W Isles 171 G3
Snitter Northumb 117 D6
Snitterby Lincs 90 E3
Snitterfield Warks 51 D7
Snitton Shrops 49 B7
Snodhill Hereford 48 E5
Snodland Kent 29 C7
Snowden Hill S Yorks 88 D3
Snowdon Mountain Railway, Llanberis Gwyn 83 F6
Snowdown Kent 31 D6
Snowshill Glos 51 F5
Snowshill Manor Glos 51 F5
Snydale W Yorks 88 C5
Soar Anglesey 82 D3
Soar Carms 33 B7
Soar Devon 6 F5
Soar-y-Mynydd Ceredig 47 D6
Soberton Hants 15 C7
Soberton Heath Hants 15 C7
Sockbridge Cumb 99 B7
Sockburn Darl 101 D8
Soham Cambs 55 B6
Soham Cotes Cambs 55 B6
Solas W Isles 170 C4
Soldon Cross Devon 8 C5
Soldridge Hants 26 F4
Sole Street Kent 29 C7
Sole Street Kent 30 E4
Solihull W Mid 51 B6
Sollers Dilwyn Hereford 49 D6
Sollers Hope Hereford 49 F8
Sollom Lancs 86 C2
Solva Pembs 44 C2
Somerby Leics 64 C4
Somerby Lincs 90 D4
Somercotes Derbys 76 D4
Somerford Dorset 14 E2
Somerford Keynes Glos 37 E7
Somerley W Sus 16 E2
Somerleyton Suff 69 E7
Somersal Herbert Derbys 75 F8
Somersby Lincs 79 B6
Somersham Cambs 54 B4
Somersham Suff 56 E4
Somerton Oxon 38 B4
Somerton Som 12 B2
Sompting W Sus 17 D5
Sonning Wokingham 27 B5
Sonning Common Oxon 39 F7
Sonning Eye Oxon 27 B5
Sontley Wrex 73 E7
Sopley Hants 14 E2
Sopwell Herts 40 D4
Sopworth Wilts 37 F5
Sorbie Dumfries 105 E8
Sordale Highld 169 C6
Sorisdale Argyll 136 B3
Sorn E Ayrs 113 B5
Sornhill E Ayrs 120 F5
Sortat Highld 169 C7
Sotby Lincs 78 B5
Sots Hole Lincs 78 C4
Sotterley Suff 69 F7
Soudley Shrops 61 B7
Soughton Flint 73 C6
Soulbury Bucks 40 B1
Soulby Cumb 100 C2
Souldern Oxon 52 F3
Souldrop Beds 53 C7
Sound Ches 74 E3
Sound Shetland 175 H5
Sound Shetland 175 J6
Sound Heath Ches 74 E3
Soundwell S Glos 23 B8
Sourhope Borders 116 B4
Sourin Orkney 176 C3
Sourton Devon 9 E7
Soutergate Cumb 98 F4
South Acre Norf 67 C8
South Allington Devon 7 F5
South Alloa Falk 133 E7
South Ambersham W Sus 16 B3
South Anston S Yorks 89 F6
South Ascot Windsor 27 C7
South Ballachulish Highld 138 D4
South Balloch S Ayrs 112 E3
South Bank Redcar 102 B3
South Barrow Som 12 B4
South Beach Gwyn 70 D4
South Benfleet Essex 42 F3
South Bersted W Sus 16 D3
South Brent Devon 6 C4
South Brewham Som 24 F2
South Broomhill Northumb 117 E8
South Burlingham Norf 69 D6
South Cadbury Som 12 B4
South Cairn Dumfries 104 C3
South Carlton Lincs 78 B2
South Cave E Yorks 96 F5
South Cerney Glos 37 E7
South Chard Som 11 D8
South Charlton Northumb 117 B7
South Cheriton Som 12 B4
South Cliffe E Yorks 96 F4
South Clifton Notts 77 B8
South Cockerington Lincs 91 F7
South Cornelly Bridgend 34 F2
South Cove Suff 69 F7
South Creagan Argyll 138 E3
South Creake Norf 80 D4
South Croxton Leics 64 C3
South Croydon London 28 C4
South Dalton E Yorks 97 E5
South Darenth Kent 29 C6
South Duffield N Yorks 96 F2
South Elkington Lincs 91 F6
South Elmsall W Yorks 89 C5
South End Bucks 40 B1
South End Cumb 92 C2
South End N Lincs 90 B5
South Erradale Highld 154 C3
South Fambridge Essex 42 E4
South Fawley W Berks 38 F3
South Ferriby N Lincs 90 B3
South Garth Shetland 174 D7
South Garvan Highld 138 B3
South Glendale W Isles 171 J3
South Godstone Sur 28 E4
South Gorley Hants 14 C2
South Green Essex 42 E2
South Green Kent 30 C2
South-haa Shetland 174 E5
South Ham Hants 26 D4
South Hanningfield Essex 42 E3
South Harting W Sus 15 C8
South Hatfield Herts 41 D5
South Hayling Hants 15 E8
South Hazelrigg Northumb 125 F6
South Heath Bucks 40 D2
South Heighton E Sus 17 D8
South Hetton Durham 111 E6
South Hiendley W Yorks 88 C4
South Hill Corn 5 B8
South Hinksey Oxon 39 D5
South Hole Devon 8 B4
South Holme N Yorks 96 B2
South Holmwood Sur 28 E2
South Hornchurch London 41 F8
South Hykeham Lincs 78 C2
South Hylton T & W 111 D6
South Kelsey Lincs 90 E4
South Kessock Highld 157 E7
South Killingholme N Lincs 91 C5
South Kilvington N Yorks 102 F2
South Kilworth Leics 64 F3
South Kirkby W Yorks 88 C5
South Kirkton Aberds 151 D6
South Kiscadale N Ayrs 119 D7
South Kyme Lincs 78 E4
South Lancing W Sus 17 D5
South Leigh Oxon 38 D3
South Leverton Notts 89 F8
South Littleton Worcs 51 E5
South Lopham Norf 68 F3
South Luffenham Rutland 65 D6
South Malling E Sus 17 C8
South Marston Swindon 38 F1
South Middleton Northumb 117 B5
South Milford N Yorks 95 F7
South Millbrex Aberds 160 D5
South Milton Devon 6 E5
South Mimms Herts 41 D5
South Molton Devon 10 B2
South Moreton Oxon 39 F5
South Mundham W Sus 16 D2
South Muskham Notts 77 D7
South Newbald E Yorks 96 F5
South Newington Oxon 52 F2
South Newton Wilts 25 F5
South Normanton Derbys 76 D4
South Norwood London 28 C4
South Nutfield Sur 28 E4
South Ockendon Thurrock 42 F1
South Ormsby Lincs 79 B6
South Otterington N Yorks 102 F1
South Owersby Lincs 90 E4
South Oxhey Herts 40 E4
South Perrott Dorset 12 D2
South Petherton Som 12 C2
South Petherwin Corn 8 F5
South Pickenham Norf 67 D8
South Pool Devon 7 E5
South Port Argyll 131 C6
South Radworthy Devon 21 F6
South Rauceby Lincs 78 E3
South Raynham Norf 80 E4
South Reston Lincs 91 F8
South Runcton Norf 67 D6
South Scarle Notts 77 C8
South Shian Argyll 138 E3
South Shields T & W 111 C6
South Shields Museum T & W 111 C6
South Shore Blkpool 92 F3
South Somercotes Lincs 91 E8
South Stainley N Yorks 95 C6
South Stainmore Cumb 100 C3
South Stifford Thurrock 29 B7
South Stoke Oxon 39 F5
South Stoke W Sus 16 D4
South Street E Sus 17 C7
South Street London 28 D5
South Street Kent 30 C5
South Street Kent 30 D4
South Tawton Devon 9 E8
South Thoresby Lincs 79 B7
South Tidworth Wilts 25 E7
South Town Hants 26 F4
South View Hants 26 D4
South Walsham Norf 69 C6
South Warnborough Hants 26 E5
South Weald Essex 42 E1
South Weston Oxon 39 E7

South Wheatley Corn 8 E4
South Wheatley Notts 89 F8
South Whiteness Shetland 175 J5
South Widcombe Bath 23 D7
South Wigston Leics 64 E2
South Willingham Lincs 91 F5
South Wingfield Derbys 76 D3
South Witham Lincs 65 C6
South Wonston Hants 26 F2
South Woodham Ferrers Essex 42 E4
South Wootton Norf 67 B6
South Wraxall Wilts 24 C3
South Zeal Devon 9 E8
Southall London 40 F4
Southam Glos 37 B6
Southam Warks 52 C2
Southampton Soton 14 C5
Southampton International Airport Hants 15 C5
Southborough Kent 29 E6
Southbourne Bmouth 14 E2
Southbourne W Sus 15 D8
Southburgh Norf 68 D2
Southburn E Yorks 97 D5
Southchurch Sthend 43 F5
Southcott Wilts 25 D6
Southcourt Bucks 39 C8
Southdean Borders 116 D2
Southdene Mers 86 E2
Southease E Sus 17 D8
Southend Argyll 118 F3
Southend W Berks 26 B3
Southend Wilts 25 B6
Southend Airport Essex 42 F4
Southend-on-Sea Sthend 42 F4
Southend Sea Life Centre Essex 42 E4
Southernden Kent 30 E2
Southerndown V Glam 21 B7
Southerness Dumfries 107 D6
Southery Norf 67 E6
Southfield Northumb 111 B5
Southfleet Kent 29 B7
Southgate Ceredig 46 B4
Southgate London 41 E5
Southgate Norf 81 E7
Southgate Swansea 33 F6
Southill Beds 54 E2
Southleigh Devon 11 E7
Southminster Essex 43 E5
Southmoor Oxon 38 E3
Southoe Cambs 54 C2
Southolt Suff 57 C5
Southorpe P'boro 65 D7
Southowram W Yorks 88 B2
Southport Mers 85 C4
Southpunds Shetland 175 L6
Southrepps Norf 81 D8
Southrey Lincs 78 C4
Southrop Glos 38 D1
Southrope Hants 26 E4
Southsea Ptsmth 15 E7
Southstoke Bath 24 C2
Southtown Norf 69 D8
Southtown Orkney 176 G3
Southwaite Cumb 108 E4
Southwark London 28 B4
Southwater W Sus 17 B5
Southwater Street W Sus 17 B5
Southway Som 23 E7
Southwell Dorset 12 G4
Southwell Notts 77 D6
Southwell Minster Notts 77 D7
Southwell Racecourse Notts 77 D7
Southwick Hants 15 D7
Southwick Northants 65 E7
Southwick T & W 111 D6
Southwick Wilts 24 D3
Southwick W Sus 17 D6
Southwold Suff 57 B9
Southwood Norf 69 D6
Southwood Som 23 F7
Soval Lodge W Isles 172 F6
Sowber Gate N Yorks 102 F1
Sowerby N Yorks 102 F2
Sowerby W Yorks 87 B8
Sowerby Bridge W Yorks 87 B8
Sowerby Row Cumb 108 F3
Sowood W Yorks 87 C8
Sowton Devon 10 E4
Soyal Highld 164 E2
Spa Common Norf 81 D8
Spacey Houses N Yorks 95 D6
Spadeadam Farm Cumb 109 B5
Spalding Lincs 66 B2
Spaldington E Yorks 96 F3
Spaldwick Cambs 54 B2
Spalford Notts 77 C8
Spanby Lincs 78 F3
Sparham Norf 68 C3
Spark Bridge Cumb 99 F5
Sparkford Som 12 B4
Sparkhill W Mid 62 F4
Sparkwell Devon 6 D3
Sparrow Green Norf 68 C2
Sparrowpit Derbys 87 F8
Sparsholt Hants 26 F2
Sparsholt Oxon 38 F3
Spartylea Northumb 109 E8
Spaunton N Yorks 103 F5
Spaxton Som 22 F4
Spean Bridge Highld 146 F5
Spear Hill W Sus 16 C5
Speen Bucks 39 E8
Speen W Berks 26 C2
Speeton N Yorks 97 B7
Speke Mers 86 F2
Speke Hall Mers 86 F2
Speldhurst Kent 29 E6
Spellbrook Herts 41 C7
Spelsbury Oxon 38 B3
Spelter Bridgend 34 E2
Spencers Wood Wokingham 26 C5
Spennithorne N Yorks 101 F6
Spennymoor Durham 111 F5
Spetchley Worcs 50 D3
Spetisbury Dorset 13 D7
Spexhall Suff 69 F6
Spey Bay Moray 159 C7
Speybridge Highld 149 B6
Speyview Moray 159 E6
Spilsby Lincs 79 C7
Spindlestone Northumb 125 F7
Spinkhill Derbys 76 B4
Spinningdale Highld 164 F3
Spirit of the West, St Columb Major Corn 4 C4
Spirthill Wilts 24 B4
Spital Hill S Yorks 89 E7
Spital in the Street Lincs 90 F3
Spitfire and Hurricane Memorial, Manston Kent 31 C7
Spithurst E Sus 17 C8
Spittal Dumfries 105 D7
Spittal E Loth 123 B7
Spittal Highld 169 D6
Spittal Northumb 125 D6
Spittal Pembs 44 C4
Spittal Stirl 132 F4
Spittal of Glenmuick Aberds 150 F2
Spittal of Glenshee Perth 141 B8
Spittalfield Perth 141 E8
Spixworth Norf 68 C5
Splayne's Green E Sus 17 B8
Spofforth N Yorks 95 D6
Spon End W Mid 51 B8
Spon Green Flint 73 C6
Spondon Derby 76 F4
Spooner Row Norf 68 E3
Sporle Norf 67 C8
Spott E Loth 124 B2
Spratton Northants 52 B5
Spreakley Sur 27 E6
Spreyton Devon 9 E8
Spridlington Lincs 90 F4
Spring Vale S Yorks 88 D3
Spring Valley I o M 84 E3
Springburn Glasgow 121 C6
Springfield Dumfries 108 C3
Springfield Essex 42 D3
Springfield Fife 134 C5
Springfield Moray 158 D4
Springfield W Mid 62 F4
Springhill Staffs 62 D3
Springholm Dumfries 106 C5
Springkell Dumfries 108 B2
Springside N Ayrs 120 F3
Springthorpe Lincs 90 F2
Springwell T & W 111 D5
Sproatley E Yorks 97 F7
Sproston Green Ches 74 C4
Sprotbrough S Yorks 89 D6
Sproughton Suff 56 E5
Sprouston Borders 124 F3
Sprowston Norf 68 C5
Sproxton Leics 65 B5
Sproxton N Yorks 102 F4
Spurstow Ches 74 D2
Spynie Moray 159 C6
Squires Gate Blkpool 92 F3
Srannda W Isles 173 K3
Sronphadruig Lodge Perth 140 B4
SS Great Britain Bristol 23 B7
Stableford Shrops 61 E7
Stableford Staffs 74 F5
Stacey Bank S Yorks 88 E3
Stackhouse N Yorks 93 C8
Stackpole Pembs 44 F4
Staddiscombe Devon 6 D3
Staddlethorpe E Yorks 90 B2
Stadhampton Oxon 39 E6
Stadhlaigearraidh W Isles 170 G3
Staffield Cumb 108 E5
Staffin Highld 152 C5
Stafford Staffs 62 B3
Stagsden Beds 53 E7
Stainburn Cumb 98 B2
Stainburn N Yorks 94 E5
Stainby Lincs 65 B6
Staincross S Yorks 88 C4
Staindrop Durham 101 B6
Staines Sur 27 B8
Stainfield Lincs 65 B7
Stainfield Lincs 78 B4
Stainforth N Yorks 93 C8
Stainforth S Yorks 89 C7
Staining Lancs 92 F3
Stainland W Yorks 87 C8
Stainsacre N Yorks 103 D7
Stainsby Derbys 76 C4
Stainton Cumb 99 F7
Stainton Cumb 99 B6
Stainton Durham 101 C5
Stainton M'bro 102 C2
Stainton N Yorks 101 E6
Stainton S Yorks 89 E6
Stainton by Langworth Lincs 78 B3
Stainton le Vale Lincs 91 E5
Stainton with Adgarley Cumb 92 B2
Staintondale N Yorks 103 E7
Stair Cumb 98 B4
Stair E Ayrs 112 B4
Stairhaven Dumfries 105 D6
Staithes N Yorks 103 C5
Stake Pool Lancs 92 E4
Stakeford Northumb 117 F8
Stalbridge Dorset 12 C5
Stalbridge Weston Dorset 12 C5
Stalham Norf 69 B6
Stalham Green Norf 69 B6
Stalisfield Green Kent 30 D3
Stalling Busk N Yorks 100 F4
Stallingborough NE Lincs 91 C5
Stalmine Lancs 92 E3
Stalybridge Gtr Man 87 E7
Stambourne Essex 55 F8
Stambourne Green Essex 55 F8
Stamford Lincs 65 D7
Stamford Bridge Ches 73 C8
Stamford Bridge E Yorks 96 D3
Stamfordham Northumb 110 B3
Stanah Cumb 99 C5
Stanborough Herts 41 C5
Stanbridge Beds 40 B2
Stanbridge Dorset 13 D8
Stanbrook Worcs 50 E3
Stanbury W Yorks 94 F3
Stand Gtr Man 87 D5
Stand N Lnrk 121 C7
Standburn Falk 122 B2
Standeford Staffs 62 D3
Standen Kent 30 E2
Standen, East Grinstead W Sus 28 F4
Standford Hants 27 F6
Standingstone Cumb 107 F7
Standish Gtr Man 86 C3
Standlake Oxon 38 D3
Standon Hants 14 B5
Standon Herts 41 B6
Standon Staffs 74 F5
Stane N Lnrk 121 D8
Stanfield Norf 80 E5
Stanford Beds 54 E2
Stanford Kent 19 B8
Stanford Bishop Hereford 49 D8
Stanford Bridge Worcs 50 C2
Stanford Dingley W Berks 26 B3
Stanford in the Vale Oxon 38 E3
Stanford-le-Hope Thurrock 42 F2
Stanford on Avon Northants 52 B3
Stanford on Soar Notts 64 B2
Stanford on Teme Worcs 50 C2
Stanford Rivers Essex 41 D8
Stanfree Derbys 76 B4
Stanghow Redcar 102 C4
Stanground P'boro 66 E2
Stanhoe Norf 80 D4
Stanhope Borders 114 B4
Stanhope Durham 110 F2
Stanion Northants 65 F6
Stanley Derbys 76 E4
Stanley Durham 110 D4
Stanley Lancs 86 D2
Stanley Perth 141 F8
Stanley Staffs 75 D6
Stanley W Yorks 88 B4
Stanley Common Derbys 76 E4
Stanley Gate Lancs 86 D2
Stanley Hill Hereford 49 E8
Stanlow Ches 73 B8
Stanmer Brighton 17 D7
Stanmore London 40 E4
Stanmore Hants 15 B5
Stanmore W Berks 26 B2
Stannergate Dundee 142 F4
Stanningley W Yorks 94 F5
Stannington Northumb 110 B5
Stannington S Yorks 88 F4
Stansbatch Hereford 48 C5
Stansfield Suff 55 D8
Stanstead Suff 56 E2
Stanstead Abbotts Herts 41 C6
Stansted Kent 29 C7
Stansted Mountfitchet Essex 41 B8
Stanton Glos 51 F5
Stanton Mon 35 B7
Stanton Northumb 117 F7
Stanton Staffs 75 E8
Stanton Suff 56 B3
Stanton by Bridge Derbys 63 B7
Stanton-by-Dale Derbys 76 F4
Stanton Drew Bath 23 C7
Stanton Fitzwarren Swindon 38 E1
Stanton Harcourt Oxon 38 D4
Stanton Hill Notts 76 C4
Stanton in Peak Derbys 76 C2
Stanton Lacy Shrops 49 B6
Stanton Long Shrops 61 E5
Stanton-on-the-Wolds Notts 77 F6
Stanton Prior Bath 23 C8
Stanton St Bernard Wilts 25 C5
Stanton St John Oxon 39 D5
Stanton St Quintin Wilts 24 B4
Stanton Street Suff 56 C3
Stanton under Bardon Leics 63 C8
Stanton upon Hine Heath Shrops 61 B5
Stanton Wick Bath 23 C8
Stanwardine in the Fields Shrops 60 B4
Stanwardine in the Wood Shrops 60 B4
Stanway Essex 43 B5
Stanway Glos 51 F5
Stanway Green Suff 57 B6
Stanwell Sur 27 B8
Stanwell Moor Sur 27 B8
Stanwick Northants 53 B7
Stanwick-St-John N Yorks 101 C6
Stanwix Cumb 108 D4
Stanydale Shetland 175 H4
Staoinebrig W Isles 171 G3
Stape N Yorks 103 E5
Stapehill Dorset 13 D8
Stapeley Ches 74 E3
Stapeley Water Gardens, Nantwich Ches 74 D3
Stapenhill Staffs 63 B6
Staple Kent 31 D6
Staple Som 22 E3
Staple Cross E Sus 18 C4
Staple Fitzpaine Som 11 C7
Staplefield W Sus 17 B6
Stapleford Cambs 55 D5
Stapleford Herts 41 C6
Stapleford Leics 64 C5
Stapleford Lincs 77 D8
Stapleford Notts 76 F4
Stapleford Wilts 25 F5
Stapleford Abbotts Essex 41 E8
Stapleford Tawney Essex 41 E8
Staplegrove Som 11 B7
Staplehay Som 11 B7
Staplehurst Kent 29 E8
Staplers I o W 15 F6
Stapleton Bristol 23 B8
Stapleton Cumb 108 B5
Stapleton Hereford 48 C5
Stapleton Leics 63 E8
Stapleton N Yorks 101 C7
Stapleton Shrops 60 D4
Stapleton Som 12 B2
Stapley Som 11 C6
Staploe Beds 54 C2
Staplow Hereford 49 E8
Star Fife 134 D5
Star Pembs 45 F4
Star Som 23 D6
Stara Orkney 176 D1
Starbeck N Yorks 95 D6
Starbotton N Yorks 94 B2
Starcross Devon 10 F4
Stareton Warks 51 B8
Starkholmes Derbys 76 D3
Starlings Green Essex 55 F5
Starston Norf 68 F5
Startforth Durham 101 C5
Startley Wilts 37 F6
Stathe Som 11 B8
Stathern Leics 77 F7
Station Town Durham 111 F7
Staughton Green Cambs 54 C2
Staughton Highway Cambs 54 C2
Staunton Glos 36 C2
Staunton Glos 36 B4
Staunton in the Vale Notts 77 E8
Staunton on Arrow Hereford 49 C5
Staunton on Wye Hereford 49 E5
Staveley Cumb 99 F5
Staveley Cumb 99 E6
Staveley Derbys 76 B4
Staveley N Yorks 95 C6
Staverton Devon 7 C5
Staverton Glos 37 B5
Staverton Northants 52 C3
Staverton Wilts 24 C3
Staverton Bridge Glos 37 B5
Stawell Som 23 F5
Staxigoe Highld 169 D8
Staxton N Yorks 97 B6
Staylittle Powys 59 E5
Staynall Lancs 92 E3
Staythorpe Notts 77 D7
Stean N Yorks 94 B3
Stearsby N Yorks 96 B2
Steart Som 22 E4
Stebbing Essex 42 B2
Stebbing Green Essex 42 B2
Stedham W Sus 16 B2
Steele Road Borders 115 E8
Steen's Bridge Hereford 49 D7
Steep Hants 15 B8
Steep Marsh Hants 15 B8
Steeple Dorset 13 F7
Steeple Essex 43 D5
Steeple Ashton Wilts 24 D4
Steeple Aston Oxon 38 B4
Steeple Barton Oxon 38 B4
Steeple Bumpstead Essex 55 E7
Steeple Claydon Bucks 39 B6
Steeple Gidding Cambs 65 F8
Steeple Langford Wilts 24 F5
Steeple Morden Cambs 54 E3
Steeton W Yorks 94 E3
Stein Highld 152 D3
Steinmanhill Aberds 160 D4
Stelling Minnis Kent 30 E5
Stemster Highld 169 C6
Stemster Ho. Highld 169 C6
Stenalees Corn 4 D5
Stenhousemuir Falk 133 F7
Stenigot Lincs 91 F6
Stenness Shetland 174 F4
Stenscholl Highld 152 C5
Stenso Orkney 176 D2
Stenson Derbys 63 B7
Stenton E Loth 124 B2
Stenton Fife 134 E4
Stenwith Lincs 77 F8
Stepaside Pembs 32 D2
Stepping Hill Gtr Man 87 F7
Steppingley Beds 53 F8
Stepps N Lnrk 121 C6
Sterndale Moor Derbys 75 C8
Sternfield Suff 57 C7
Sterridge Devon 20 E4
Stert Wilts 24 D5
Stetchworth Cambs 55 D7
Stevenage Herts 41 B5
Stevenston N Ayrs 120 E2
Steventon Hants 26 E3
Steventon Oxon 38 E4
Stevington Beds 53 D7
Stewartby Beds 53 E8
Stewarton Argyll 118 E3
Stewarton E Ayrs 120 E4
Stewkley Bucks 40 B1
Stewton Lincs 91 F7
Steyne Cross I o W 15 F7
Steyning W Sus 17 C5
Steynton Pembs 44 E4
Stibb Corn 8 C4
Stibb Cross Devon 9 C6
Stibb Green Wilts 25 C7
Stibbard Norf 81 E5
Stibbington Cambs 65 E7
Stichill Borders 124 F3
Sticker Corn 4 D4
Stickford Lincs 79 D6
Sticklepath Devon 9 E8
Stickney Lincs 79 D6
Stiffkey Norf 81 C5
Stifford's Bridge Hereford 50 E2
Stillingfleet N Yorks 95 E8
Stillington N Yorks 95 C8
Stillington Stockton 102 B1
Stilton Cambs 65 F8
Stinchcombe Glos 36 E4
Stinsford Dorset 12 E5
Stirchley Telford 61 D7
Stirkoke Ho. Highld 169 D8
Stirling Aberds 161 D8
Stirling Stirl 133 E6
Stirling Castle Stirl 133 E6
Stisted Essex 42 B3
Stithians Corn 3 C6
Stittenham Highld 157 B7
Stivichall W Mid 51 B8
Stixwould Lincs 78 C4
Stoak Ches 73 B8
Stobieside S Lnrk 121 F6
Stobo Borders 122 F4
Stoborough Dorset 13 F7
Stoborough Green Dorset 13 F7
Stobshiel E Loth 123 C7
Stobswood Northumb 117 E8
Stock Essex 42 E2
Stock Green Worcs 50 D4
Stock Wood Worcs 50 D5
Stockbridge Hants 25 F8
Stockbury Kent 30 C2
Stockcross W Berks 26 C2
Stockdalewath Cumb 108 E3
Stockerston Leics 64 E5
Stockheath Hants 15 D8
Stockiemuir Stirl 132 F4
Stocking Pelham Herts 41 B7
Stockingford Warks 63 E7
Stockland Devon 11 D7
Stockland Bristol Som 22 E4
Stockleigh English Devon 10 D3
Stockleigh Pomeroy Devon 10 D3
Stockley Wilts 24 C5
Stocklinch Som 11 C8
Stockport Gtr Man 87 E6
Stocksbridge S Yorks 88 E3
Stocksfield Northumb 110 C3
Stockton Hereford 49 C7
Stockton Norf 69 E6
Stockton Shrops 60 D2
Stockton Shrops 61 E7
Stockton Warks 52 C2
Stockton Wilts 24 F4
Stockton Heath Warr 86 F4
Stockton-on-Tees Stockton 102 C2
Stockton on Teme Worcs 50 C2
Stockton on the Forest York 96 D2
Stockwood Park Museum, Luton Luton 40 C3
Stodmarsh Kent 31 C6
Stody Norf 81 D6
Stoer Highld 162 B4
Stoford Som 12 C3
Stoford Wilts 25 F5
Stogumber Som 22 F2
Stogursey Som 22 E4
Stoke Devon 8 B4
Stoke Hants 26 D2
Stoke Hants 15 D8
Stoke Medway 30 B2
Stoke Suff 57 E5
Stoke Abbott Dorset 12 D2
Stoke Albany Northants 64 F5
Stoke Ash Suff 56 B5
Stoke Bardolph Notts 77 E6
Stoke Bliss Worcs 49 C8
Stoke Bruerne Northants 52 E5
Stoke by Clare Suff 55 E8
Stoke-by-Nayland Suff 56 F3
Stoke Canon Devon 10 E4
Stoke Charity Hants 26 F2
Stoke Climsland Corn 5 B8
Stoke D'Abernon Sur 28 D2
Stoke Doyle Northants 65 F7
Stoke Dry Rutland 65 E5
Stoke Farthing Wilts 13 B8
Stoke Ferry Norf 67 E7
Stoke Fleming Devon 7 E6
Stoke Gabriel Devon 7 D6
Stoke Gifford S Glos 23 B8
Stoke Golding Leics 63 E7
Stoke Goldington M Keynes 53 E6
Stoke Green Bucks 40 F2
Stoke Hammond Bucks 40 B1
Stoke Heath Shrops 61 B6
Stoke Holy Cross Norf 68 D5
Stoke Lacy Hereford 49 E8
Stoke Lyne Oxon 39 B5
Stoke Mandeville Bucks 39 C8
Stoke Newington London 41 F6
Stoke on Tern Shrops 61 B6
Stoke-on-Trent Stoke 75 E5
Stoke Orchard Glos 37 B6
Stoke Poges Bucks 40 F2
Stoke Prior Hereford 49 D7
Stoke Prior Worcs 50 C4
Stoke Rivers Devon 20 F5
Stoke Rochford Lincs 65 B6
Stoke Row Oxon 39 F6
Stoke St Gregory Som 11 B8
Stoke St Mary Som 11 B7
Stoke St Michael Som 23 E8
Stoke St Milborough Shrops 61 F5
Stoke sub Hamdon Som 12 C2
Stoke Talmage Oxon 39 E6
Stoke Trister Som 12 B5
Stoke Wake Dorset 13 D5
Stokeford Dorset 13 F6
Stokeham Notts 77 B7
Stokeinteignhead Devon 7 B7
Stokenchurch Bucks 39 E7
Stokenham Devon 7 E6
Stokesay Shrops 60 F4
Stokesby Norf 69 C7
Stokesley N Yorks 102 D3
Stolford Som 22 E4
Ston Easton Som 23 D8
Stondon Massey Essex 42 D1
Stone Bucks 39 C7
Stone Glos 36 E3
Stone Kent 19 C6
Stone Kent 29 B6
Stone Staffs 75 F6
Stone S Yorks 89 F6
Stone Worcs 50 B3
Stone Allerton Som 23 D6
Stone Bridge Corner P'boro 66 D2
Stone Chair W Yorks 88 B2
Stone Cross E Sus 18 E3
Stone Cross Kent 31 D7
Stone-edge Batch N Som 23 B6
Stone House Cumb 100 F2
Stone Street Kent 29 D6
Stone Street Suff 56 F3
Stone Street Suff 69 F6
Stonebroom Derbys 76 D4
Stoneferry Hull 97 F7
Stonefield S Lnrk 121 D6
Stonegate E Sus 18 C3
Stonegate N Yorks 103 D5
Stonegrave N Yorks 96 B2
Stonehaugh Northumb 109 B7
Stonehaven Aberds 151 F7
Stonehenge, Amesbury Wilts 25 E6
Stonehouse Glos 37 D5
Stonehouse Northumb 109 D6
Stonehouse S Lnrk 121 E7
Stoneleigh Warks 51 B8
Stonely Cambs 54 C2
Stoner Hill Hants 15 B8
Stone's Green Essex 43 B7
Stonesby Leics 64 B5
Stonesfield Oxon 38 C3
Stonethwaite Cumb 98 C4
Stoney Cross Hants 14 C3
Stoney Middleton Derbys 76 B2
Stoney Stanton Leics 63 E8
Stoney Stoke Som 24 F2
Stoney Stratton Som 23 F8
Stoney Stretton Shrops 60 D3
Stoneybreck Shetland 175 L3
Stoneyburn W Loth 122 C2
Stoneygate Aberds 161 E7
Stoneygate Leicester 64 D3
Stoneyhills Essex 43 E5
Stoneykirk Dumfries 104 D4
Stoneywood Aberdeen 151 C7
Stoneywood Falk 133 F6
Stonganess Shetland 174 C7
Stonham Aspal Suff 56 D5
Stonnall Staffs 62 D4
Stonor Oxon 39 F7
Stonton Wyville Leics 64 E4
Stony Cross Hereford 50 E2
Stony Stratford M Keynes 53 E5
Stonyfield Highld 157 B7
Stoodleigh Devon 10 C4
Stopes S Yorks 88 F3
Stopham W Sus 16 C4
Stopsley Luton 40 B4
Stores Corner Suff 57 E7
Storeton Mers 85 F4
Stornoway W Isles 172 E7
Stornoway Airport W Isles 172 E7
Storridge Hereford 50 E2
Storrington W Sus 16 C4
Storrs Cumb 99 E5
Storth Cumb 99 F6
Storwood E Yorks 96 E3
Stotfield Moray 159 B6
Stotfold Beds 54 F3
Stottesdon Shrops 61 F6
Stoughton Leics 64 D3
Stoughton Sur 27 D7
Stoughton W Sus 16 C2
Stoul Highld 145 D7
Stoulton Worcs 50 E4
Stour Provost Dorset 13 B5
Stour Row Dorset 13 B6
Stourbridge W Mid 62 F3
Stourhead Garden Wilts 24 F2
Stourpaine Dorset 13 D6
Stourport on Severn Worcs 50 B3
Stourton Staffs 62 F2
Stourton Warks 51 F7
Stourton Wilts 24 F2
Stourton Caundle Dorset 12 C5
Stove Orkney 176 C5
Stove Shetland 175 L6
Stoven Suff 69 F7
Stow Borders 123 E7
Stow Lincs 90 F2
Stow Lincs 78 F3
Stow Bardolph Norf 67 D6
Stow Bedon Norf 68 E2
Stow cum Quy Cambs 55 C6
Stow Longa Cambs 54 B2
Stow Maries Essex 42 E4
Stow-on-the-Wold Glos 38 B1
Stowbridge Norf 67 D6
Stowe Shrops 48 B5
Stowe-by-Chartley Staffs 62 B4
Stowe Green Glos 36 D2
Stowe House and Gardens, Buckingham Bucks 52 F4
Stowell Som 12 B4
Stowford Devon 9 F6
Stowlangtoft Suff 56 C3
Stowmarket Suff 56 D4
Stowting Kent 30 E5
Stowupland Suff 56 D4
Straad Argyll 129 D5
Strachan Aberds 151 E5
Stradbroke Suff 57 B6
Stradishall Suff 55 D8
Stradsett Norf 67 D6
Stragglethorpe Lincs 78 D2
Straid S Ayrs 112 E1
Straith Dumfries 113 F8
Straiton Edin 123 C5
Straiton S Ayrs 112 D3
Straloch Aberds 151 B7
Straloch Perth 141 C7
Stramshall Staffs 75 F7
Strang I o M 84 E3
Stranraer Dumfries 104 C4
Stratfield Mortimer W Berks 26 C4
Stratfield Saye Hants 26 C4
Stratfield Turgis Hants 26 D4
Stratford London 41 F6
Stratford Racecourse Warks 51 D6
Stratford St Andrew Suff 57 C7
Stratford St Mary Suff 56 F4
Stratford Sub Castle Wilts 25 F6
Stratford Tony Wilts 13 B8
Stratford-upon-Avon Warks 51 D6
Strath Highld 169 D7
Strath Highld 154 C3
Strathan Highld 146 E2
Strathan Highld 167 C7
Strathan Highld 162 B4
Strathaven S Lnrk 121 E7
Strathblane Stirl 121 B5
Strathcanaird Highld 163 D5
Strathcarron Highld 155 F5
Strathcoil Argyll 130 B2
Strathdon Aberds 150 C2
Strathellie Aberds 161 B7
Strathkinness Fife 135 C6
Strathmashie House Highld 147 E8
Strathmiglo Fife 134 C4
Strathmore Lodge Highld 169 E6
Strathpeffer Highld 157 D5
Strathrannoch Highld 156 B4
Strathtay Perth 141 D6
Strathvaich Lodge Highld 156 B4
Strathwhillan N Ayrs 119 C7
Strathy Highld 168 C3
Strathyre Stirl 132 C4
Stratton Corn 8 D4
Stratton Dorset 12 E4
Stratton Glos 37 D7
Stratton Audley Oxon 39 B6
Stratton on the Fosse Som 23 D8
Stratton St Margaret Swindon 38 F1
Stratton St Michael Norf 68 E5
Stratton Strawless Norf 81 E8
Stravithie Fife 135 C7
Streat E Sus 17 C7
Streatham London 28 B4
Streatley Beds 40 B3
Streatley W Berks 39 F5
Street Lancs 92 D5
Street N Yorks 103 D5
Street Som 23 F6
Street Dinas Shrops 73 F7
Street End Kent 30 D5
Street End W Sus 16 E2
Street Gate T & W 110 D5
Street Lydan Wrex 73 F8
Streethay Staffs 62 C5
Streetlam N Yorks 101 E8
Streetly W Mid 62 E4
Streetly End Cambs 55 E7
Strefford Shrops 60 F4
Strelley Notts 76 E5
Strensall York 96 C2
Stretcholt Som 22 E4
Strete Devon 7 E6
Stretford Gtr Man 87 E6
Strethall Essex 55 F5
Stretham Cambs 55 B6
Strettington W Sus 16 D2
Stretton Ches 73 D8
Stretton Derbys 76 C3
Stretton Rutland 65 C6
Stretton Staffs 62 C2
Stretton Staffs 63 B6
Stretton Warr 86 F4
Stretton Grandison Hereford 49 E8
Stretton-on-Dunsmore Warks 52 B2
Stretton-on-Fosse Warks 51 F7
Stretton Sugwas Hereford 49 E6
Stretton under Fosse Warks 63 F8
Stretton Westwood Shrops 61 E5
Strichen Aberds 161 C6
Strines Gtr Man 87 F7
Stringston Som 22 E3
Strixton Northants 53 C7
Stroat Glos 36 E2
Stromeferry Highld 155 G4
Stromemore Highld 155 G4
Stromness Orkney 176 F1
Stronaba Highld 146 F5
Stronachlachar Stirl 132 C3
Stronchreggan Highld 138 B4
Stronchrubie Highld 163 C6
Strone Argyll 129 B6
Strone Highld 147 B8
Strone Highld 146 F4
Strone Invclyd 129 C7
Stronmilchan Argyll 131 C7
Stronsay Airport Orkney 176 D5
Strontian Highld 138 C2
Strood Medway 29 C8
Strood Green Sur 28 E3
Strood Green W Sus 16 B4
Strood Green W Sus 28 F2
Stroud Glos 37 D5
Stroud Hants 15 B8
Stroud Green Essex 42 E4
Stroxton Lincs 78 F2
Struan Highld 153 F4
Struan Perth 141 C5
Strubby Lincs 91 F8
Strumpshaw Norf 69 D6
Strutherhill S Lnrk 121 E7
Struy Highld 156 F4
Stryt-issa Wrex 73 E6
Stuartfield Aberds 161 D6
Stub Place Cumb 98 E2
Stubbington Hants 15 D6
Stubbins Lancs 87 C5
Stubbs Cross Kent 19 B6
Stubb's Green Norf 69 E5
Stubbs Green Norf 69 E6
Stubhampton Dorset 13 C7
Stubton Lincs 77 E8
Stuckgowan Argyll 132 D2
Stuckton Hants 14 C2
Stud Green Windsor 27 B6
Studham Beds 40 C3
Studland Dorset 13 F8
Studley Warks 51 C5
Studley Wilts 24 B4
Studley Roger N Yorks 95 B5
Stump Cross Essex 55 E6
Stuntney Cambs 55 B6
Sturbridge Staffs 74 F5
Sturmer Essex 55 E7
Sturminster Marshall Dorset 13 D7
Sturminster Newton Dorset 13 C5
Sturry Kent 31 C5
Sturton N Lincs 90 D3
Sturton by Stow Lincs 90 F2
Sturton le Steeple Notts 89 F8
Stuston Suff 56 B5
Stutton N Yorks 95 E7
Stutton Suff 57 F5
Styal Ches 87 F6
Styrrup Notts 89 E7
Suainebost W Isles 172 B8
Suardail W Isles 172 E7
Succoth Aberds 159 F8
Succoth Argyll 131 E8
Suckley Worcs 50 D2
Suckquoy Orkney 176 H3
Sudborough Northants 65 F6
Sudbourne Suff 57 D8
Sudbrook Lincs 78 E2
Sudbrook Mon 36 F2
Sudbrooke Lincs 78 B3
Sudbury Derbys 75 F8
Sudbury London 40 F4
Sudbury Suff 56 E2
Suddie Highld 157 D7
Sudeley Castle and Gardens Glos 37 B7
Sudgrove Glos 37 D6
Suffield Norf 81 D8
Suffield N Yorks 103 E7
Sugnall Staffs 74 F4
Suladale Highld 152 D4
Sulaisiadar W Isles 172 E8
Sulby I o M 84 C3
Sulgrave Northants 52 E3
Sulham W Berks 26 B4
Sulhamstead W Berks 26 C4
Sulland Orkney 176 B4
Sullington W Sus 16 C4
Sullom Shetland 174 F5
Sullom Voe Oil Terminal Shetland 174 F5

Sully V Glam 22 C3
Sumburgh Shetland 175 N6
Sumburgh Airport Shetland 175 M5
Summer Bridge N Yorks 94 C5
Summer-house Darl 101 C7
Summercourt Corn 4 D3
Summerfield Norf 80 D3
Summergangs Hull 97 F7
Summerleaze Mon 35 F8
Summerlee Heritage Centre, Coatbridge N Lnrk 121 C7
Summersdale W Sus 16 D2
Summerseat Gtr Man 87 C5
Summertown Oxon 39 D5
Summit Gtr Man 87 D7
Sunbury-on-Thames Sur 28 C2
Sundaywell Dumfries 113 F8
Sunderland Argyll 126 C2
Sunderland Cumb 107 F8
Sunderland T & W 111 D6
Sunderland Bridge Durham 111 F5
Sundhope Borders 115 B6
Sundon Park Luton 40 B3
Sundown Adventure Land, Rampton Notts 77 B7
Sundridge Kent 29 D5
Sunipol Argyll 136 C4
Sunk Island E Yorks 91 C6
Sunningdale Windsor 27 C7
Sunninghill Windsor 27 C7
Sunningwell Oxon 38 D4
Sunniside Durham 110 F4
Sunniside T & W 110 D5
Sunnyhurst Blkburn 86 B4
Sunnylaw Stirl 133 E6
Sunnyside W Sus 28 F4
Sunton Wilts 25 D7
Surbiton London 28 C2
Surby I o M 84 E2
Surfleet Lincs 66 B2
Surfleet Seas End Lincs 66 B2
Surlingham Norf 69 D6
Sustead Norf 81 D7
Susworth Lincs 90 D2
Sutcombe Devon 8 C5
Suton Norf 68 E3
Sutors of Cromarty Highld 158 C2
Sutterby Lincs 79 B6
Sutterton Lincs 79 F5
Sutton Beds 54 E3
Sutton Cambs 54 B5
Sutton London 28 C3
Sutton Kent 31 E7
Sutton Mers 86 E3
Sutton Norf 69 B6
Sutton Notts 77 F7
Sutton Notts 89 F7
Sutton N Yorks 89 B5
Sutton Oxon 38 D4
Sutton P'boro 65 E7
Sutton Shrops 61 F7
Sutton Shrops 74 F3
Sutton Som 23 F8
Sutton Staffs 61 B7
Sutton Suff 57 E7
Sutton Sur 27 E8
Sutton S Yorks 89 C6
Sutton W Sus 16 C3
Sutton at Hone Kent 29 B6
Sutton Bassett Northants 64 E4
Sutton Benger Wilts 24 B4
Sutton Bonington Notts 64 B2
Sutton Bridge Lincs 66 B4
Sutton Cheney Leics 63 D8
Sutton Coldfield W Mid 62 E5
Sutton Courtenay Oxon 39 E5
Sutton Crosses Lincs 66 B4
Sutton Grange N Yorks 95 B5
Sutton Green Sur 27 D8
Sutton Howgrave N Yorks 95 B6
Sutton In Ashfield Notts 76 D4
Sutton-in-Craven N Yorks 94 E3
Sutton in the Elms Leics 64 E2
Sutton Ings Hull 97 F7
Sutton Lane Ends Ches 75 B6
Sutton Leach Mers 86 E3
Sutton Maddock Shrops 61 D7
Sutton Mallet Som 23 F5
Sutton Mandeville Wilts 13 B7
Sutton Manor Mers 86 E3
Sutton Montis Som 12 B4
Sutton on Hull Hull 97 F7
Sutton on Sea Lincs 91 F9
Sutton-on-the-Forest N Yorks 95 C8
Sutton on the Hill Derbys 76 F2
Sutton on Trent Notts 77 C7
Sutton St Edmund Lincs 66 C3
Sutton St James Lincs 66 C3
Sutton St Nicholas Hereford 49 E7
Sutton Scarsdale Derbys 76 C4
Sutton Scotney Hants 26 F2
Sutton under Brailes Warks 51 F8
Sutton-under-Whitestonecliffe N Yorks 102 F2
Sutton upon Derwent E Yorks 96 E3
Sutton Valence Kent 30 E2
Sutton Veny Wilts 24 E3
Sutton Waldron Dorset 13 C6
Sutton Weaver Ches 74 B2
Sutton Wick Bath 23 D7
Swaby Lincs 79 B6
Swadlincote Derbys 63 C7
Swaffham Norf 67 D8
Swaffham Bulbeck Cambs 55 C6
Swaffham Prior Cambs 55 C6
Swafield Norf 81 D8
Swainby N Yorks 102 D2
Swainshill Hereford 49 E6
Swainsthorpe Norf 68 D5
Swainswick Bath 24 C2
Swalcliffe Oxon 51 F8
Swalecliffe Kent 30 C5
Swallow Lincs 91 D5
Swallowcliffe Wilts 13 B7
Swallowfield Wokingham 26 C5
Swallownest S Yorks 89 F5
Swallows Cross Essex 42 E2
Swan Green Ches 74 B4
Swan Green Suff 57 B6
Swanage Dorset 13 G8
Swanage Railway Dorset 13 G8
Swanbister Orkney 176 F2
Swanbourne Bucks 39 B8
Swanland E Yorks 90 B3
Swanley Kent 29 C6
Swanley Village Kent 29 C6
Swanmore Hants 15 C6
Swannery, Abbotsbury Dorset 12 F3
Swannington Leics 63 C8
Swannington Norf 68 C4
Swanscombe Kent 29 B7
Swansea = Abertawe Swansea 33 E7
Swanton Abbott Norf 81 E8
Swanton Morley Norf 68 C3
Swanton Novers Norf 81 D6
Swanton Street Kent 30 D2
Swanwick Derbys 76 D4
Swanwick Hants 15 D6
Swarby Lincs 78 E3
Swardeston Norf 68 D5
Swarister Shetland 174 E7
Swarkestone Derbys 63 B7
Swarland Northumb 117 D7
Swarland Estate Northumb 117 D7
Swarthmoor Cumb 92 B2
Swathwick Derbys 76 C3
Swaton Lincs 78 F4
Swavesey Cambs 54 C4
Sway Hants 14 E3
Swayfield Lincs 65 B6
Swaythling Soton 14 C5
Sweet Green Worcs 49 C8
Sweetham Devon 10 E3
Sweethouse Corn 5 C5
Sweffling Suff 57 C7
Swepstone Leics 63 C7
Swerford Oxon 51 F8
Swettenham Ches 74 C5
Swetton N Yorks 94 B4
Swffryd Bl Gwent 35 E6
Swiftsden E Sus 18 C4
Swilland Suff 57 D5
Swillington W Yorks 95 F6
Swimbridge Devon 9 B8
Swimbridge Newland Devon 20 F5
Swinbrook Oxon 38 C2
Swinderby Lincs 77 C8
Swindon Glos 37 B6
Swindon Staffs 62 E2
Swindon Swindon 38 F1
Swine E Yorks 97 F7
Swinefleet E Yorks 89 B8
Swineshead Beds 53 C8
Swineshead Lincs 78 E5
Swineshead Bridge Lincs 78 E5
Swiney Highld 169 F7
Swinford Leics 52 B3
Swinford Oxon 38 D4
Swingate Notts 76 E5
Swingfield Minnis Kent 31 E6
Swingfield St Kent 31 E6
Swinhoe Northumb 117 B8
Swinhope Lincs 91 E6
Swining Shetland 174 G6
Swinithwaite N Yorks 101 F5
Swinnow Moor W Yorks 94 F5
Swinscoe Staffs 75 E8
Swinside Hall Borders 116 C3
Swinstead Lincs 65 B7
Swinton Borders 124 E4
Swinton Gtr Man 87 D5
Swinton N Yorks 94 B5
Swinton N Yorks 96 B3
Swinton S Yorks 88 E5
Swintonmill Borders 124 E4
Swithland Leics 64 C2
Swordale Highld 157 C6
Swordland Highld 145 D7
Swordly Highld 168 C2
Sworton Heath Ches 86 F4
Swydd-ffynnon Ceredig 47 C5
Swynnerton Staffs 75 F5
Swyre Dorset 12 F3
Sychtyn Powys 59 D6
Syde Glos 37 C6
Sydenham London 28 B4
Sydenham Oxon 39 D7
Sydenham Damerel Devon 6 B2
Syderstone Norf 80 D4
Sydling St Nicholas Dorset 12 E4
Sydmonton Hants 26 D2
Syerston Notts 77 E7
Syke Gtr Man 87 C6
Sykehouse S Yorks 89 C7
Sykes Lancs 93 D6
Syleham Suff 57 B6
Sylen Carms 33 D6
Symbister Shetland 175 G7
Symington S Ayrs 120 F3
Symington S Lnrk 122 F2
Symonds Yat Hereford 36 C2
Symondsbury Dorset 12 E2
Synod Inn Ceredig 46 D3
Syon Park & House London 28 B2
Syre Highld 167 E8
Syreford Glos 37 B7
Syresham Northants 52 E4
Syston Leics 64 C3
Syston Lincs 78 E2
Sytchampton Worcs 50 C3
Sywell Northants 53 C6

T

Taagan Highld 154 D6
Tàbost W Isles 172 B8
Tabost W Isles 172 G6
Tackley Oxon 38 B4
Tacleit W Isles 172 E4
Tacolneston Norf 68 E4
Tadcaster N Yorks 95 E7
Taddington Derbys 75 B8
Taddiport Devon 9 C6
Tadley Hants 26 C4
Tadlow Beds 54 E3
Tadmarton Oxon 51 F8
Tadworth Sur 28 D3
Tafarn-y-gelyn Denb 73 C5
Tafarnau-bach Bl Gwent 35 C5
Taff's Well Rhondda 35 F5
Tafolwern Powys 59 D5
Tai Conwy 83 E7
Tai-bach Powys 59 B8
Tai-mawr Conwy 72 E3
Tai-Ucha Denb 72 D4
Taibach Neath 34 F1
Taigh a Ghearraidh W Isles 170 C3
Tain Highld 164 F4
Tain Highld 169 C7
Tainant Wrex 73 E6
Tainlon Gwyn 82 F4
Tai'r-Bull Powys 34 B3
Tairbeart = Tarbert W Isles 173 H4
Tairgwaith Neath 33 C8
Takeley Essex 42 B1
Takeley Street Essex 41 B8
Tal-sarn Ceredig 46 D4
Tal-y-bont Ceredig 58 F3
Tal-y-Bont Conwy 83 E7
Tal-y-bont Gwyn 83 D6
Tal-y-bont Gwyn 71 E6
Tal-y-cafn Conwy 83 D7
Tal-y-llyn Gwyn 58 D4
Tal-y-wern Powys 58 D5
Talachddu Powys 48 F2
Talacre Flint 85 F2
Talardd Gwyn 59 B5
Talaton Devon 11 E5
Talbenny Pembs 44 D3
Talbot Green Rhondda 34 F4
Talbot Village Poole 13 E8
Tale Devon 11 D5
Talerddig Powys 59 D6
Talgarreg Ceredig 46 D3
Talgarth Powys 48 F3
Talisker Highld 153 F4
Talke Staffs 74 D5
Talkin Cumb 109 D5
Talla Linnfoots Borders 114 B4
Talladale Highld 154 C5
Tallarn Green Wrex 73 E8
Tallentire Cumb 107 F8
Talley Carms 46 F5
Tallington Lincs 65 D7
Talmine Highld 167 C7
Talog Carms 32 B4
Talsarn Carms 34 B1
Talsarnau Gwyn 71 D7
Talskiddy Corn 4 C4
Talwrn Anglesey 82 D4
Talwrn Wrex 73 E6
Talybont-on-Usk Powys 35 B5
Talygarn Rhondda 34 F4
Talyllyn Powys 35 B5
Talysarn Gwyn 82 F4
Talywain Torf 35 D6
Tame Bridge N Yorks 102 D3
Tamerton Foliot Plym 6 C2
Tamworth Staffs 63 D6
Tan Hinon Powys 59 F5
Tan-lan Conwy 83 E7
Tan-lan Gwyn 71 C7
Tan-y-bwlch Gwyn 71 C7
Tan-y-fron Conwy 72 C3
Tan-y-graig Anglesey 82 D5
Tan-y-graig Gwyn 70 D4
Tan-y-groes Ceredig 45 E4
Tan-y-pistyll Powys 59 B7
Tan-yr-allt Gwyn 82 F4
Tandem W Yorks 88 C2
Tanden Kent 19 B6
Tandridge Sur 28 D4
Tanerdy Carms 33 B5
Tanfield Durham 110 D4
Tanfield Lea Durham 110 D4
Tangasdal W Isles 171 L2
Tangiers Pembs 44 D4
Tangley Hants 25 D8
Tanglwst Carms 46 F2
Tangmere W Sus 16 D3
Tangwick Shetland 174 F4
Tank Museum, Bovington Dorset 13 F6
Tankersley S Yorks 88 D4
Tankerton Kent 30 C5
Tannach Highld 169 E8
Tannachie Aberds 151 F6
Tannadice Angus 142 D4
Tannington Suff 57 C6
Tansley Derbys 76 D3
Tansley Knoll Derbys 76 C3
Tansor Northants 65 E7
Tantobie Durham 110 D4
Tanton N Yorks 102 C3
Tanworth-in-Arden Warks 51 B6
Tanygrisiau Gwyn 71 C7
Tanyrhydiau Ceredig 47 C6
Taobh a Chaolais W Isles 171 J3
Taobh a Thuath Loch Aineort W Isles 171 H3
Taobh a Tuath Loch Baghasdail W Isles 171 H3
Taobh a'Ghlinne W Isles 172 G6
Taobh Tuath W Isles 173 K2
Taplow Bucks 40 F2
Tapton Derbys 76 B3
Tarbat Ho. Highld 157 B8
Tarbert Argyll 127 D4
Tarbert Argyll 128 D3
Tarbert Argyll 118 A3
Tarbert = Tairbeart W Isles 173 H4
Tarbet Argyll 132 D2
Tarbet Highld 166 E3
Tarbet Highld 145 D7
Tarbock Green Mers 86 F2
Tarbolton S Ayrs 112 B4
Tarbrax S Lnrk 122 D3
Tardebigge Worcs 50 C5
Tarfside Angus 142 B4
Tarland Aberds 150 D3
Tarleton Lancs 86 B2
Tarlogie Highld 164 F4
Tarlscough Lancs 86 C2
Tarlton Glos 37 E6
Tarnbrook Lancs 93 D5
Tarporley Ches 74 C2
Tarr Som 22 F3
Tarrant Crawford Dorset 13 D7
Tarrant Gunville Dorset 13 C7
Tarrant Hinton Dorset 13 C7
Tarrant Keyneston Dorset 13 D7
Tarrant Launceston Dorset 13 D7
Tarrant Monkton Dorset 13 D7
Tarrant Rawston Dorset 13 D7
Tarrant Rushton Dorset 13 D7
Tarrel Highld 165 F5
Tarring Neville E Sus 17 D8
Tarrington Hereford 49 E8
Tarsappie Perth 134 B3
Tarskavaig Highld 145 C5
Tarves Aberds 161 E5
Tarvie Highld 156 D5
Tarvie Perth 141 C7
Tarvin Ches 73 C8
Tasburgh Norf 68 E5
Tasley Shrops 61 E6
Taston Oxon 38 B3
Tate Gallery London 28 B3
Tate Gallery, Albert Dock Mers 85 F4
Tate Modern London 28 B4
Tate St Ives Corn 2 B4
Tatenhill Staffs 63 B6
Tathall End M Keynes 53 E6
Tatham Lancs 93 C6
Tathwell Lincs 91 F7
Tatling End Bucks 40 F3
Tatsfield Sur 28 D5
Tattenhall Ches 73 D8
Tattenhoe M Keynes 53 F6
Tatterford Norf 80 E4
Tattersett Norf 80 D4
Tattershall Lincs 78 D5
Tattershall Bridge Lincs 78 D4
Tattershall Thorpe Lincs 78 D5
Tattingstone Suff 56 F5
Tatton House, Knutsford Ches 86 F5
Tatworth Som 11 D8
Taunton Som 11 B7
Taunton Racecourse Som 11 B7
Taverham Norf 68 C4
Tavernspite Pembs 32 C2
Tavistock Devon 6 B2
Taw Green Devon 9 E8
Tawstock Devon 9 B7
Taxal Derbys 75 B7
Tay Bridge Dundee 135 B6
Tayinloan Argyll 118 B3
Taymouth Castle Perth 140 E4
Taynish Argyll 128 B2
Taynton Glos 36 B4
Taynton Oxon 38 C2
Taynuilt Argyll 131 B6
Tayport Fife 135 B6
Tayvallich Argyll 128 B2
Tealby Lincs 91 E5
Tealing Angus 142 F4
Teangue Highld 145 C6
Teanna Mhachair W Isles 170 D3
Tebay Cumb 99 D8
Tebworth Beds 40 B2
Tedburn St Mary Devon 10 E3
Teddington Glos 50 F4
Teddington London 28 B2
Tedstone Delamere Hereford 49 D8
Tedstone Wafre Hereford 49 D8
Teeton Northants 52 B4
Teffont Evias Wilts 24 F4
Teffont Magna Wilts 24 F4
Tegryn Pembs 45 F4
Teigh Rutland 65 C5
Teigncombe Devon 9 F8
Teigngrace Devon 7 B6
Teignmouth Devon 7 B7
Telford Telford 61 D6
Telham E Sus 18 D4
Tellisford Som 24 D3
Telscombe E Sus 17 D8
Telscombe Cliffs E Sus 17 D7
Templand Dumfries 114 F3
Temple Corn 5 B6
Temple Glasgow 120 C5
Temple Midloth 123 D6
Temple Balsall W Mid 51 B7
Temple Bar Ceredig 46 D4
Temple Bar Carms 33 C6
Temple Cloud Bath 23 D8
Temple Combe Som 12 B5
Temple Ewell Kent 31 E6
Temple Grafton Warks 51 D6
Temple Guiting Glos 37 B7
Temple Herdewyke Warks 51 D8
Temple Hirst N Yorks 89 B7
Temple Normanton Derbys 76 C4
Temple Sowerby Cumb 99 B8
Templehall Fife 134 E4
Templeton Devon 10 C3
Templeton Pembs 32 C2
Templeton Bridge Devon 10 C3
Templetown Durham 110 D4
Tempsford Beds 54 D2
Ten Mile Bank Norf 67 E6
Tenbury Wells Worcs 49 C7
Tenby = Dinbych-y-Pysgod Pembs 32 D2
Tendring Essex 43 B7
Tendring Green Essex 43 B7
Tenston Orkney 176 E1
Tenterden Kent 19 B5
Terling Essex 42 C3
Ternhill Shrops 74 F3
Terregles Banks Dumfries 107 B6
Terrick Bucks 39 D8
Terrington N Yorks 96 B2
Terrington St Clement Norf 66 C5
Terrington St John Norf 66 C5
Teston Kent 29 D8
Testwood Hants 14 C4
Tetbury Glos 37 E5
Tetbury Upton Glos 37 E5
Tetchill Shrops 73 F7
Tetcott Devon 8 E5
Tetford Lincs 79 B6
Tetney Lincs 91 D7
Tetney Lock Lincs 91 D7
Tetsworth Oxon 39 D6
Tettenhall W Mid 62 E2
Teuchan Aberds 161 E7
Teversal Notts 76 C4
Teversham Cambs 55 D5
Teviothead Borders 115 D7
Tewel Aberds 151 F7
Tewin Herts 41 C5
Tewkesbury Glos 50 F3
Tewkesbury Abbey Glos 50 F3
Teynham Kent 30 C3
Thackthwaite Cumb 98 B3
Thainston Aberds 143 B6
Thakeham W Sus 16 C5
Thame Oxon 39 D7
Thames Ditton Sur 28 C2
Thames Haven Thurrock 42 F3
Thamesmead London 41 F7
Thanington Kent 30 D5
Thankerton S Lnrk 122 F2
Tharston Norf 68 E4
Thatcham W Berks 26 C3
Thatto Heath Mers 86 E3
Thaxted Essex 55 F7
The Aird Highld 152 D5
The All England Jumping Course, Hickstead W Sus 17 C6
The Arms Norf 67 E8
The Bage Hereford 48 E4
The Balloch Perth 133 C7
The Barony Orkney 176 D1
The Bluebell Railway, Sheffield Park E Sus 17 B8
The Bog Shrops 60 E3
The Bourne Sur 27 E6
The Braes Highld 153 F6
The Broad Hereford 49 C6
The Burrell Collection Glasgow 121 C5
The Butts Som 24 E2
The Camp Glos 37 D6
The Camp Herts 40 D4
The Chequer Wrex 73 E8
The City Bucks 39 E7
The Common Wilts 25 F7
The Craigs Highld 164 E1
The Cronk I o M 84 C3
The Dell Suff 69 E7
The Den N Ayrs 120 D3
The Dinosaur Museum, Dorchester Dorset 12 E4
The Eals Northumb 116 F3
The Eaves Glos 36 D3
The Flatt Cumb 109 B5
The Four Alls Shrops 74 F3
The Friars, Aylesford Kent 29 D8
The Garths Shetland 174 B8
The Green Cumb 98 F3
The Green Wilts 24 F3
The Grove Dumfries 107 B6
The Hall Shetland 174 D8
The Haven W Sus 27 F8
The Heath Norf 81 E7
The Heath Suff 56 F5
The Hill Cumb 98 F3
The Howe Cumb 99 F6
The Howe I o M 84 F1
The Hundred Hereford 49 C7
The Lee Bucks 40 D2
The Lhen I o M 84 B3
The Living RainForest W Berks 26 B3
The Long Man of Wilmington E Sus 18 E2
The Lost Gardens of Heligan, Mevagissey Corn 4 E4
The Lowry, Salford Gtr Man 87 E6
The Marsh Powys 60 E3
The Marsh Wilts 37 F7
The Middles Durham 110 D5
The Moor Kent 18 C4
The Moors Centre, Danby N Yorks 103 D5
The Mumbles = Y Mwmbwls Swansea 33 F7
The Murray S Lnrk 121 D6
The National Archives, Kew London 28 B3
The National Tramway Museum, Crich Derbys 76 D3
The Needles Old Battery I o W 14 F3
The Neuk Aberds 151 E6
The Oval Bath 24 C2
The Oval Cricket Ground London 28 B4
The Oxford Story, Oxford Oxon 39 D5
The Pole of Itlaw Aberds 160 C3
The Quarry Glos 36 E4
The Rhos Pembs 32 C1
The Rock Telford 61 D6
The Ryde Herts 41 D5
The Sands Sur 27 E6
The Stocks Kent 19 C6
The Tales of Robin Hood Nottingham 77 E5
The Throat Wokingham 27 C6
The Tutankhamun Exhibition, Dorchester Dorset 12 E4
The Vauld Hereford 49 E7
The Vyne Hants 26 D4
The World of Beatrix Potter, Bowness-on-Windermere Cumb 99 E6
The Wyke Shrops 61 D7
Theakston N Yorks 101 F8
Thealby N Lincs 90 C2
Theale Som 23 E6
Theale W Berks 26 B4
Thearne E Yorks 97 F6
Theberton Suff 57 C8
Theddingworth Leics 64 F3
Theddlethorpe All Saints Lincs 91 F8
Theddlethorpe St Helen Lincs 91 F8
Thelbridge Barton Devon 10 C2
Thelnetham Suff 56 B4
Thelveton Norf 68 F4
Thelwall Warr 86 F4
Themelthorpe Norf 81 E6
Thenford Northants 52 E3
Therfield Herts 54 F4
Thetford Lincs 65 C8
Thetford Norf 67 F8
Theydon Bois Essex 41 E7
Thickwood Wilts 24 B3
Thimbleby Lincs 78 C5
Thimbleby N Yorks 102 E2
Thingwall Mers 85 F3
Thirdpart N Ayrs 119 B8
Thirlby N Yorks 102 F2
Thirlestane Borders 123 E8
Thirn N Yorks 101 F7
Thirsk N Yorks 102 F2
Thirsk Racecourse N Yorks 102 F2
Thirtleby E Yorks 97 F7
Thistleton Lancs 92 F4
Thistleton Rutland 65 C6
Thistley Green Suff 55 B7
Thixendale N Yorks 96 C4
Thockrington Northumb 110 B2
Tholomas Drove Cambs 66 D3
Tholthorpe N Yorks 95 C7
Thomas Chapel Pembs 32 D2
Thomas Close Cumb 108 E4
Thomastown Aberds 160 E2
Thompson Norf 68 E2
Thomshill Moray 159 D6
Thong Kent 29 B7
Thongsbridge W Yorks 88 D2
Thoralby N Yorks 101 F5
Thoresway Lincs 91 E5
Thorganby Lincs 91 E6
Thorganby N Yorks 96 E2
Thorgill N Yorks 103 E5
Thorington Suff 57 B8
Thorington Street Suff 56 F4
Thorlby N Yorks 94 D2
Thorley Herts 41 C7
Thorley Street Herts 41 C7
Thorley Street I o W 14 F4
Thormanby N Yorks 95 B7
Thornaby on Tees Stockton 102 C2
Thornage Norf 81 D6
Thornborough Bucks 52 F5
Thornborough N Yorks 95 B5
Thornbury Devon 9 D6
Thornbury Hereford 49 D8
Thornbury S Glos 36 E3
Thornbury W Yorks 94 F4
Thornby Northants 52 B4
Thorncliffe Staffs 75 D7
Thorncombe Dorset 11 D8
Thorncombe Dorset 13 D6
Thorncombe Street Sur 27 E8
Thorncote Green Beds 54 E2
Thorncross I o W 14 F5
Thorndon Suff 56 C5
Thorndon Cross Devon 9 E7
Thorne S Yorks 89 C7
Thorne St Margaret Som 11 B5
Thorner W Yorks 95 E6
Thorney Notts 77 B8
Thorney P'boro 66 D2
Thorney Crofts E Yorks 91 B6
Thorney Green Suff 56 C4
Thorney Hill Hants 14 E2
Thorney Toll Cambs 66 D3
Thornfalcon Som 11 B7
Thornford Dorset 12 C4
Thorngumbald E Yorks 91 B6
Thornham Norf 80 C3
Thornham Magna Suff 56 B5
Thornham Parva Suff 56 B5
Thornhaugh P'boro 65 D7
Thornhill Caerph 35 F5
Thornhill Cumb 98 D2
Thornhill Derbys 88 F2
Thornhill Dumfries 113 E8
Thornhill Soton 15 C5
Thornhill Stirl 133 E5
Thornhill W Yorks 88 C3
Thornhill Edge W Yorks 88 C3
Thornhill Lees W Yorks 88 C3
Thornholme E Yorks 97 C7
Thornley Durham 110 F4
Thornley Durham 111 F6
Thornliebank E Renf 120 D5
Thorns Suff 55 D8
Thorns Green Ches 87 F5
Thornsett Derbys 87 F8
Thornthwaite Cumb 98 B4
Thornthwaite N Yorks 94 D4
Thornton Angus 142 E3
Thornton Bucks 53 F5
Thornton E Yorks 96 E3
Thornton Fife 134 E4
Thornton Lancs 92 E3
Thornton Leics 63 D8
Thornton Lincs 78 C5
Thornton Mers 85 D4
Thornton M'bro 102 C2
Thornton Northumb 125 E5
Thornton Pembs 44 E4
Thornton W Yorks 94 F4
Thornton Curtis N Lincs 90 C4
Thornton Heath London 28 C4
Thornton Hough Mers 85 F4
Thornton in Craven N Yorks 94 E2
Thornton-le-Beans N Yorks 102 E1
Thornton-le-Clay N Yorks 96 C2
Thornton-le-Dale N Yorks 103 F6
Thornton le Moor Lincs 90 E4
Thornton-le-Moor N Yorks 102 F1
Thornton-le-Moors Ches 73 B8
Thornton-le-Street N Yorks 102 F2
Thornton Rust N Yorks 100 F4
Thornton Steward N Yorks 101 F6
Thornton Watlass N Yorks 101 F7
Thorntonhall S Lnrk 121 D5
Thorntonloch E Loth 124 B3
Thorntonpark Northumb 124 E5
Thornwood Common Essex 41 D7
Thornydykes Borders 124 E2
Thoroton Notts 77 E7
Thorp Arch W Yorks 95 E7
Thorpe Derbys 75 D8
Thorpe E Yorks 97 E5
Thorpe Lincs 91 F8
Thorpe Norf 69 E7
Thorpe Notts 77 E7
Thorpe N Yorks 94 C3
Thorpe Sur 27 C8
Thorpe Abbotts Norf 57 B5
Thorpe Acre Leics 64 B2
Thorpe Arnold Leics 64 B4
Thorpe Audlin W Yorks 89 C5
Thorpe Bassett N Yorks 96 B4
Thorpe Bay Sthend 43 F5
Thorpe by Water Rutland 65 E5
Thorpe Common Suff 57 F6
Thorpe Constantine Staffs 63 D6
Thorpe Culvert Lincs 79 C7
Thorpe End Norf 69 C5
Thorpe Fendykes Lincs 79 C7
Thorpe Green Essex 43 B7
Thorpe Green Suff 56 D3
Thorpe Hesley S Yorks 88 E4
Thorpe in Balne S Yorks 89 C6
Thorpe in the Fallows Lincs 90 F3
Thorpe Langton Leics 64 E4
Thorpe Larches Durham 102 B1
Thorpe-le-Soken Essex 43 B7
Thorpe le Street E Yorks 96 E4
Thorpe Malsor Northants 53 B6
Thorpe Mandeville Northants 52 E3
Thorpe Market Norf 81 D8
Thorpe Marriot Norf 68 C4
Thorpe Morieux Suff 56 D3
Thorpe on the Hill Lincs 78 C2
Thorpe Park, Chertsey Sur 27 C8
Thorpe St Andrew Norf 69 D5
Thorpe St Peter Lincs 79 C7
Thorpe Salvin S Yorks 89 F6
Thorpe Satchville Leics 64 C4
Thorpe Thewles Stockton 102 B2
Thorpe Tilney Lincs 78 D4
Thorpe Underwood N Yorks 95 D7
Thorpe Waterville Northants 65 F7
Thorpe Willoughby N Yorks 95 F8
Thorpeness Suff 57 D8
Thorrington Essex 43 C6
Thorverton Devon 10 D4
Thrandeston Suff 56 B5
Thrapston Northants 53 B7
Thrashbush N Lnrk 121 C7
Threapland Cumb 107 F8
Threapland N Yorks 94 C2
Threapwood Ches 73 E8
Threapwood Staffs 75 E7
Threave Gardens Dumfries 106 C4
Three Ashes Hereford 36 B2
Three Bridges W Sus 28 F3
Three Burrows Corn 3 B6
Three Chimneys Kent 18 B5
Three Cocks Powys 48 F3
Three Counties Showground, Malvern Worcs 50 E2
Three Crosses Swansea 33 E6
Three Cups Corner E Sus 18 C3
Three Holes Norf 66 D5
Three Leg Cross E Sus 18 B3
Three Legged Cross Dorset 13 D8
Three Oaks E Sus 18 D5
Threehammer Common Norf 69 C6
Threekingham Lincs 78 F3
Threemile Cross Wokingham 26 C5
Threemilestone Corn 3 B6
Threemiletown W Loth 122 B3
Threlkeld Cumb 99 B5
Threshfield N Yorks 94 C2
Thrigby Norf 69 C7
Thringarth Durham 100 B4
Thringstone Leics 63 C8
Thrintoft N Yorks 101 E8
Thriplow Cambs 54 E5
Throckenholt Lincs 66 D3
Throcking Herts 54 F4
Throckley T & W 110 C4
Throckmorton Worcs 50 E4
Throphill Northumb 117 F7
Thropton Northumb 117 D6
Throsk Stirl 133 E7
Throwleigh Devon 9 E8
Throwley Kent 30 D3
Thrumpton Notts 76 F5
Thrumster Highld 169 E8
Thrunton Northumb 117 C6
Thrupp Glos 37 D5
Thrupp Oxon 38 C4
Thrushelton Devon 9 F6
Thrussington Leics 64 C3
Thruxton Hants 25 E7
Thruxton Hereford 49 F6
Thruxton Motor Racing Circuit Hants 25 E7
Thrybergh S Yorks 89 E5
Thulston Derbys 76 F4
Thundergay N Ayrs 119 B5
Thundersley Essex 42 F3
Thundridge Herts 41 C6
Thurcaston Leics 64 C2
Thurcroft S Yorks 89 F5
Thurgarton Norf 81 D7
Thurgarton Notts 77 E6
Thurgoland S Yorks 88 D3
Thurlaston Leics 64 E2
Thurlaston Warks 52 B2
Thurlbear Som 11 B7
Thurlby Lincs 65 C8
Thurlby Lincs 78 C2
Thurleigh Beds 53 D8
Thurlestone Devon 6 E4
Thurloxton Som 22 F4
Thurlstone S Yorks 88 D3
Thurlton Norf 69 E7
Thurlwood Ches 74 D5
Thurmaston Leics 64 D3
Thurnby Leics 64 D3
Thurne Norf 69 C7
Thurnham Kent 30 D2
Thurnham Lancs 92 D4

U

Upper Framilode Glos 36 C4
Upper Glenfintaig Highld 147 F5
Upper Gornal W Mid 62 E3
Upper Gravenhurst Beds 54 F2
Upper Green Mon 35 C7
Upper Green W Berks 25 C8
Upper Grove Common Hereford 36 B2
Upper Hackney Derbys 76 C2
Upper Hale Sur 27 E6
Upper Halistra Highld 152 D3
Upper Halling Medway 29 C7
Upper Hambleton Rutland 65 D6
Upper Hardres Court Kent 31 D5
Upper Hartfield E Sus 29 F5
Upper Haugh S Yorks 88 E5
Upper Heath Shrops 61 F5
Upper Hellesdon Norf 68 C5
Upper Helmsley N Yorks 96 D2
Upper Hergest Hereford 48 D4
Upper Heyford Northants 52 D4
Upper Heyford Oxon 38 B4
Upper Hill Hereford 49 D6
Upper Hopton W Yorks 88 C2
Upper Horsebridge E Sus 18 D2
Upper Hulme Staffs 75 C7
Upper Inglesham Swindon 38 E2
Upper Inverbrough Highld 158 F2
Upper Killay Swansea 33 E6
Upper Knockando Moray 159 E5
Upper Lambourn W Berks 38 F3
Upper Leigh Staffs 75 F7
Upper Lenie Highld 147 B8
Upper Lochton Aberds 151 E5
Upper Longdon Staffs 62 C4
Upper Lybster Highld 169 F7
Upper Lydbrook Glos 36 C3
Upper Maes-coed Hereford 48 F5
Upper Midway Derbys 63 B6
Upper Milovaig Highld 152 E2
Upper Minety Wilts 37 E7
Upper Mitton Worcs 50 B3
Upper North Dean Bucks 39 E8
Upper Obney Perth 141 F7
Upper Ollach Highld 153 F6
Upper Padley Derbys 76 B2
Upper Pollicott Bucks 39 C7
Upper Poppleton York 95 D8
Upper Quinton Warks 51 E6
Upper Ratley Hants 14 B4
Upper Rissington Glos 38 C2
Upper Rochford Worcs 49 C8
Upper Sandaig Highld 145 B7
Upper Sanday Orkney 176 F4
Upper Sapey Hereford 49 C8
Upper Seagry Wilts 37 F6
Upper Shelton Beds 53 E7
Upper Sheringham Norf 81 C7
Upper Skelmorlie N Ayrs 129 D7
Upper Slaughter Glos 38 B1
Upper Soudley Glos 36 C3
Upper Stondon Beds 54 F2
Upper Stowe Northants 52 D4
Upper Stratton Swindon 38 F1
Upper Street Hants 14 C2
Upper Street Norf 69 C6
Upper Street Norf 69 C6
Upper Street Suff 56 F5
Upper Strensham Worcs 50 F4
Upper Sundon Beds 40 B3
Upper Swell Glos 38 B1
Upper Tean Staffs 75 F7
Upper Tillyrie Perth 134 D3
Upper Tooting London 28 B3
Upper Tote Highld 152 D6
Upper Town N Som 23 C7
Upper Treverward Shrops 48 B4
Upper Tysoe Warks 51 E8
Upper Upham Wilts 25 B7
Upper Wardington Oxon 52 E2
Upper Weald M Keynes 53 F5
Upper Weedon Northants 52 D4
Upper Wield Hants 26 F4
Upper Winchendon Bucks 39 C7
Upper Witton W Mid 62 E4
Upper Woodend Aberds 151 C5
Upper Woodford Wilts 25 F6
Upper Wootton Hants 26 D3
Upper Wyche Worcs 50 E2
Upperby Cumb 108 D4
Uppermill Gtr Man 87 D7
Uppersound Shetland 175 J6
Upperthong W Yorks 88 D2
Upperthorpe N Lincs 89 D8
Upperton W Sus 16 B3
Uppertown Derbys 76 C3
Uppertown Highld 169 B8
Uppertown Orkney 176 G3
Uppingham Rutland 65 E5
Uppington Shrops 61 D6
Upsall N Yorks 102 F2
Upshire Essex 41 D7
Upstreet Kent 31 C6
Upthorpe Suff 56 B3
Upton Cambs 54 B2
Upton Ches 73 C8
Upton Corn 8 D4
Upton Dorset 12 F5
Upton Dorset 13 E7
Upton Hants 14 C4
Upton Hants 25 D8
Upton Leics 63 E7
Upton Lincs 90 F2
Upton Mers 85 F3
Upton Norf 69 C6
Upton Notts 77 D7
Upton Notts 77 B7
Upton Northants 52 C5
Upton Oxon 39 F5
Upton P'boro 65 D8
Upton Slough 27 B7
Upton Som 10 B4
Upton W Yorks 89 C5
Upton Bishop Hereford 36 B3
Upton Cheyney S Glos 23 C8
Upton Cressett Shrops 61 E6
Upton Cross Corn 5 B7
Upton Grey Hants 26 E4
Upton Hellions Devon 10 D3
Upton House Warks 51 E8
Upton Lovell Wilts 24 E4
Upton Magna Shrops 61 C5
Upton Noble Som 24 F2
Upton Pyne Devon 10 E4
Upton St Leonard's Glos 37 C5
Upton Scudamore Wilts 24 E3
Upton Snodsbury Worcs 50 D4
Upton upon Severn Worcs 50 E3
Upton Warren Worcs 50 C4
Upwaltham W Sus 16 C3
Upware Cambs 55 B6
Upwell Norf 66 D4
Upwey Dorset 12 F4
Upwood Cambs 66 F2
Uradale Shetland 175 K6
Urafirth Shetland 174 F5
Urchfont Wilts 24 D5
Urdimarsh Hereford 49 E7
Ure Shetland 174 F4
Ure Bank N Yorks 95 B6
Urgha W Isles 173 J4
Urishay Common Hereford 48 F5
Urlay Nook Stockton 102 C1
Urmston Gtr Man 87 E5
Urpeth Durham 110 D5
Urquhart Highld 157 D6
Urquhart Moray 159 C6
Urquhart Castle, Drumnadrochit Highld 147 B8
Urra N Yorks 102 D3
Urray Highld 157 D6
Ushaw Moor Durham 110 E5
Usk = Brynbuga Mon 35 D7
Usselby Lincs 90 E4
Usworth T & W 111 D6
Utkinton Ches 74 C2
Utley W Yorks 94 E3
Uton Devon 10 E3
Utterby Lincs 91 E7
Uttoxeter Staffs 75 F7
Uttoxeter Racecourse Staffs 75 F8
Uwchmynydd Gwyn 70 E2
Uxbridge London 40 F3
Uyeasound Shetland 174 C7
Uzmaston Pembs 44 D4

V

Valley Anglesey 82 D2
Valley Truckle Corn 8 F2
Valleyfield Dumfries 106 D3
Valsgarth Shetland 174 B8
Valtos Highld 152 C6
Van Powys 59 F6
Vange Essex 42 F3
Varteg Torf 35 D6
Vatten Highld 153 E3
Vaul Argyll 136 F2
Vaynor M Tydf 34 C4
Veensgarth Shetland 175 J6
Velindre Powys 48 F3
Vellow Som 22 F2
Veness Orkney 176 D4
Venn Green Devon 9 C5
Venn Ottery Devon 11 E5
Vennington Shrops 60 D3
Venny Tedburn Devon 10 E3
Ventnor I o W 15 G6
Ventnor Botanic Garden I o W 15 G6
Vernham Dean Hants 25 D8
Vernham Street Hants 25 D8
Vernolds Common Shrops 60 F4
Verwood Dorset 13 D8
Veryan Corn 3 C8
Vicarage Devon 11 F7
Vickerstown Cumb 92 C1
Victoria Corn 4 C4
Victoria S Yorks 88 D2
Victoria and Albert Museum London 28 B3
Vidlin Shetland 174 G6
Viewpark N Lnrk 121 C7
Vigo Village Kent 29 C7
Vinehall Street E Sus 18 C4
Vine's Cross E Sus 18 D2
Viney Hill Glos 36 D3
Virginia Water Sur 27 C8
Virginstow Devon 9 E5
Vobster Som 24 E2
Voe Shetland 175 G6
Voe Shetland 174 E5
Vowchurch Hereford 49 F5
Voxter Shetland 174 F5
Voy Orkney 176 E1

W

Wackerfield Durham 101 B6
Wacton Norf 68 E4
Wadbister Shetland 175 J6
Wadborough Worcs 50 E4
Waddesdon Bucks 39 C7
Waddesdon Manor, Aylesbury Bucks 39 C7
Waddingham Lincs 90 E3
Waddington Lancs 93 E7
Waddington Lincs 78 C2
Wadebridge Corn 4 B4
Wadeford Som 11 C8
Wadenhoe Northants 65 F7
Wadesmill Herts 41 C6
Wadhurst E Sus 18 B3
Wadshelf Derbys 76 B3
Wadsley S Yorks 88 E4
Wadsley Bridge S Yorks 88 E4
Wadworth S Yorks 89 E6
Waen Denb 72 C5
Waen Denb 72 C3
Waen Fach Powys 60 C2
Waen Goleugoed Denb 72 B4
Wag Highld 165 B7
Wainfleet All Saints Lincs 79 D7
Wainfleet Bank Lincs 79 D7
Wainfleet St Mary Lincs 79 D8
Wainfleet Tofts Lincs 79 D7
Wainhouse Corner Corn 8 E3
Wainscott Medway 29 B8
Wainstalls W Yorks 87 B8
Waitby Cumb 100 D2
Waithe Lincs 91 D6
Wake Lady Green N Yorks 102 E4
Wakefield W Yorks 88 B4
Wakehurst Place Garden, Crawley W Sus 28 F4
Wakerley Northants 65 E6
Wakes Colne Essex 42 B4
Walberswick Suff 57 B8
Walberton W Sus 16 D3
Walbottle T & W 110 C4
Walcot Lincs 78 F3
Walcot N Lincs 90 B2
Walcot Shrops 60 F3
Walcot Telford 61 C5
Walcot Swindon 38 F1
Walcot Green Norf 68 F4
Walcote Leics 64 F2
Walcote Warks 51 D6
Walcott Lincs 78 D4
Walcott Norf 69 A6
Walden N Yorks 101 F5
Walden Head N Yorks 100 F4
Walden Stubbs N Yorks 89 C6
Waldersey Cambs 66 D4
Walderslade Medway 29 C8
Walderton W Sus 15 C8
Walditch Dorset 12 E2
Waldley Derbys 75 F8
Waldridge Durham 111 D5
Waldringfield Suff 57 E6
Waldringfield Heath Suff 57 E6
Waldron E Sus 18 D2
Wales S Yorks 89 F5
Walesby Lincs 90 E5
Walesby Notts 77 B6
Walford Hereford 49 B5
Walford Hereford 36 B2
Walford Shrops 60 B4
Walford Heath Shrops 60 C4
Walgherton Ches 74 E3
Walgrave Northants 53 B6
Walhampton Hants 14 E4
Walk Mill Lancs 93 F8
Walkden Gtr Man 86 D5
Walker T & W 111 C5
Walker Art Gallery Mers 85 E4
Walker Barn Ches 75 B6
Walker Fold Lancs 93 E6
Walkerburn Borders 123 F6
Walkeringham Notts 89 E8
Walkerith Lincs 89 E8
Walkern Herts 41 B5
Walker's Green Hereford 49 E7
Walkerville N Yorks 101 E7
Walkford Dorset 14 E3
Walkhampton Devon 6 C3
Walkington E Yorks 97 F5
Walkley S Yorks 88 F4
Walkley Clogs, Hebden Bridge W Yorks 87 B3
Wall Northumb 110 C2
Wall Staffs 62 D5
Wall Bank Shrops 60 E5
Wall Heath W Mid 62 F2
Wall under Heywood Shrops 60 E5
Wallaceton Dumfries 113 F8
Wallacetown S Ayrs 112 D2
Wallacetown S Ayrs 112 B3
Wallands Park E Sus 17 C8
Wallasey Mers 85 E4
Wallcrouch E Sus 18 B3
Wallingford Oxon 39 F6
Wallington London 28 C3
Wallington Hants 15 D6
Wallington Herts 54 F3
Wallington House, Ponteland Northumb 117 F6
Wallis Pembs 32 B1
Walliswood Sur 28 F2
Walls Shetland 175 J4
Wallsend T & W 111 C5
Wallston V Glam 22 B3
Wallyford E Loth 123 B6
Walmer Kent 31 D7
Walmer Bridge Lancs 86 B2
Walmersley Gtr Man 87 C6
Walmley W Mid 62 E5
Walney Island Airport Cumb 92 B1
Walpole Suff 57 B7
Walpole Cross Keys Norf 66 C5
Walpole Highway Norf 66 C5
Walpole Marsh Norf 66 C4
Walpole St Andrew Norf 66 C5
Walpole St Peter Norf 66 C5
Walsall W Mid 62 E4
Walsall Arboretum W Mid 62 E4
Walsall Wood W Mid 62 D4
Walsden W Yorks 87 B7
Walsgrave on Sowe W Mid 63 F7
Walsham le Willows Suff 56 B3
Walshaw Gtr Man 87 C5
Walshford N Yorks 95 D7
Walsoken Cambs 66 C4
Walston S Lnrk 122 E3
Walsworth Herts 54 F3
Walters Ash Bucks 39 E8
Walterston V Glam 22 B2
Walterstone Hereford 35 B7
Waltham Kent 30 E5
Waltham NE Lincs 91 D6
Waltham Abbey Essex 41 D6
Waltham Chase Hants 15 C6
Waltham Cross Herts 41 D6
Waltham on the Wolds Leics 64 B5
Waltham St Lawrence Windsor 27 B6
Walthamstow London 41 F6
Walton Cumb 108 C5
Walton Derbys 76 C3
Walton Leics 64 F2
Walton Mers 85 E4
Walton M Keynes 53 F6
Walton P'boro 65 D8
Walton Powys 48 D4
Walton Som 23 F6
Walton Staffs 75 F5
Walton Suff 57 F6
Walton Telford 61 C5
Walton Warks 51 D7
Walton W Yorks 88 C4
Walton W Yorks 95 E7
Walton Cardiff Glos 50 F4
Walton East Pembs 32 B1
Walton Hall Warr 86 F4
Walton-in-Gordano N Som 23 B6
Walton-le-Dale Lancs 86 B3
Walton-on-Thames Sur 28 C2
Walton on the Hill Staffs 62 B3
Walton on the Hill Sur 28 D3
Walton-on-the-Naze Essex 43 B8
Walton on the Wolds Leics 64 C2
Walton-on-Trent Derbys 63 C6
Walton West Pembs 44 D3
Walwen Flint 73 B6
Walwick Northumb 110 B2
Walworth Darl 101 C7
Walworth Gate Darl 101 B7
Walwyn's Castle Pembs 44 D3
Wambrook Som 11 D7
Wanborough Sur 27 E7
Wanborough Swindon 38 F2
Wandsworth London 28 B3
Wangford Suff 57 B8
Wanlockhead Dumfries 113 C8
Wansford E Yorks 97 D6
Wansford P'boro 65 E7
Wanstead London 41 F7
Wanstrow Som 24 E2
Wanswell Glos 36 D3
Wantage Oxon 38 F3
Wapley S Glos 24 B2
Wappenbury Warks 51 C8
Wappenham Northants 52 E4
Warbleton E Sus 18 D3
Warblington Hants 15 D8
Warborough Oxon 39 E5
Warboys Cambs 66 F3
Warbreck Blkpool 92 F3
Warbstow Corn 8 E4
Warburton Gtr Man 86 F5
Warcop Cumb 100 C2
Ward End W Mid 62 F5
Ward Green Suff 56 C4
Warden Kent 30 B4
Warden Northumb 110 C2
Wardhill Orkney 176 D5
Wardington Oxon 52 E2
Wardlaw Borders 115 C5
Wardle Ches 74 D3
Wardle Gtr Man 87 C7
Wardley Rutland 64 D5
Wardlow Derbys 75 B8
Wardy Hill Cambs 66 F4
Ware Herts 41 C6
Ware Kent 31 C6
Wareham Dorset 13 F7
Warehorne Kent 19 B6
Waren Mill Northumb 125 F7
Warenford Northumb 117 B7
Warenton Northumb 125 F7
Wareside Herts 41 C6
Waresley Cambs 54 D3
Waresley Worcs 50 B3
Warfield Brack 27 B6
Warfleet Devon 7 D6
Wargrave Wokingham 27 B5
Warham Norf 80 C5
Warhill Gtr Man 87 E7
Wark Northumb 109 B8
Wark Northumb 124 F4
Warkleigh Devon 9 B8
Warkton Northants 53 B6
Warkworth Northants 52 E2
Warkworth Northumb 117 D8
Warlaby N Yorks 101 E8
Warland W Yorks 87 B7
Warleggan Corn 5 C6
Warlingham Sur 28 D4
Warmfield W Yorks 88 B4
Warmingham Ches 74 C4
Warmington Northants 65 E7
Warmington Warks 52 E2
Warminster Wilts 24 E3
Warmlake Kent 30 D2
Warmley S Glos 23 B8
Warmley Tower S Glos 23 B8
Warmonds Hill Northants 53 C7
Warmsworth S Yorks 89 D6
Warmwell Dorset 13 F5
Warndon Worcs 50 D3
Warnford Hants 15 B7
Warnham W Sus 28 F2
Warninglid W Sus 17 B6
Warren Ches 75 B5
Warren Pembs 44 F4
Warren Heath Suff 57 E6
Warren Row Windsor 39 F8
Warren Street Kent 30 D3
Warrington M Keynes 53 D6
Warrington Warr 86 F4
Warsash Hants 15 D5
Warslow Staffs 75 D7
Warter E Yorks 96 D4
Warthermarske N Yorks 94 B5
Warthill N Yorks 96 D2
Wartling E Sus 18 E3
Wartnaby Leics 64 B4
Warton Lancs 86 B2
Warton Lancs 92 B4
Warton Northumb 117 D6
Warton Warks 63 D6
Warwick Warks 51 C7
Warwick Bridge Cumb 108 D4
Warwick Castle Warks 51 C7
Warwick on Eden Cumb 108 D4
Warwick Racecourse Warks 51 C7
Wasbister Orkney 176 C2
Wasdale Head Cumb 98 D3
Wash Common W Berks 26 C2
Washaway Corn 4 C5
Washbourne Devon 7 D5
Washfield Devon 10 C4
Washfold N Yorks 101 D5
Washford Som 22 E2
Washford Pyne Devon 10 C3
Washingborough Lincs 78 B3
Washington T & W 111 D6
Washington W Sus 16 C5
Wasing W Berks 26 C3
Waskerley Durham 110 E3
Wasperton Warks 51 D7
Wasps Nest Lincs 78 C3
Wass N Yorks 95 B8
Watchet Som 22 E2
Watchfield Oxon 38 E2
Watchfield Som 22 E5
Watchgate Cumb 99 E7
Watchhill Cumb 107 E8
Watcombe Torbay 7 C7
Watendlath Cumb 98 C4
Water Devon 10 F2
Water Lancs 87 B6
Water End E Yorks 96 F3
Water End Herts 40 C3
Water End Herts 41 D5
Water Newton Cambs 65 E8
Water Orton Warks 63 E5
Water Stratford Bucks 52 F4
Water Yeat Cumb 98 F4
Waterbeach Cambs 55 C5
Waterbeck Dumfries 108 B2
Watercress Line (Mid Hants Railway), Alton Hants 26 F4
Waterden Norf 80 D4
Waterfall Staffs 75 D7
Waterfoot E Renf 121 D5
Waterfoot Lancs 87 B6
Waterford Hants 14 E4
Waterford Herts 41 C6
Waterhead Cumb 99 D5
Waterhead Dumfries 114 E4
Waterheads Borders 122 D5
Waterhouses Durham 110 E4
Waterhouses Staffs 75 D7
Wateringbury Kent 29 D7
Waterloo Gtr Man 87 D7
Waterloo Highld 155 H2
Waterloo Mers 85 E4
Waterloo N Lnrk 121 D8
Waterloo Norf 68 C5
Waterloo Perth 141 F7
Waterloo Poole 13 E8
Waterloo Shrops 74 F2
Waterloo Port Gwyn 82 E4
Waterlooville Hants 15 D7
Watermeetings S Lnrk 114 C2
Watermillock Cumb 99 B6
Watermouth Castle, Ilfracombe Devon 20 E4
Waterperry Oxon 39 D6
Waterrow Som 11 B5
Water's Nook Gtr Man 86 D4
Waters Upton Telford 61 C6
Watersfield W Sus 16 C4
Watershed Mill Visitor Centre, Settle N Yorks 93 C8
Waterside Aberds 161 F7
Waterside Blkburn 86 B5
Waterside Cumb 108 E2
Waterside E Ayrs 112 D4
Waterside E Ayrs 120 E4
Waterside E Dunb 121 B6
Waterside E Renf 120 D5
Waterstock Oxon 39 D6
Waterston Pembs 44 E4
Watford Herts 40 E4
Watford Northants 52 C4
Watford Gap W Mid 62 D5
Wath N Yorks 94 C4
Wath N Yorks 95 B6
Wath N Yorks 96 B2
Wath Brow Cumb 98 C2
Wath upon Dearne S Yorks 88 D5
Watley's End S Glos 36 F3
Watlington Norf 67 C6
Watlington Oxon 39 E6
Watnall Notts 76 E5
Watten Highld 169 D7
Wattisfield Suff 56 B4
Wattisham Suff 56 D4
Wattlesborough Heath Shrops 60 C3
Watton E Yorks 97 D6
Watton Norf 68 D2
Watton at Stone Herts 41 C6
Wattston N Lnrk 121 B7
Wattstown Rhondda 34 E4
Wauchan Highld 146 F2
Waulkmill Lodge Orkney 176 F2
Waun Powys 59 D5
Waun-y-clyn Carms 33 D5
Waunarlwydd Swansea 33 E7
Waunclunda Carms 47 F5
Waunfawr Gwyn 82 F5
Waungron Swansea 33 D6
Waunlwyd Bl Gwent 35 D5
Wavendon M Keynes 53 F7
Waverbridge Cumb 108 E2
Waverton Ches 73 C8
Waverton Cumb 108 E2
Wavertree Mers 85 F4
Wawne E Yorks 97 F6
Waxham Norf 69 B7
Waxholme E Yorks 91 B7
Way Kent 31 C7
Way Village Devon 10 C3
Wayfield Medway 29 C8
Wayford Som 12 D2
Waymills Shrops 74 E2
Wayne Green Mon 35 C8
Wdig = Goodwick Pembs 44 B4
Weachyburn Aberds 160 C3
Weald Oxon 38 D3
Weald and Downland Open Air Museum, Chichester W Sus 16 C2
Wealdstone London 40 F4
Weardley W Yorks 95 E5
Weare Som 23 D6
Weare Giffard Devon 9 B6
Wearhead Durham 109 F8
Weasdale Cumb 100 D1
Weasenham All Saints Norf 80 E4
Weasenham St Peter Norf 80 E4
Weatherhill Sur 28 E4
Weaverham Ches 74 B3
Weaverthorpe N Yorks 97 B5
Webheath Worcs 50 C5
Wedderlairs Aberds 161 E5
Wedderlie Borders 124 D2
Weddington Warks 63 E7
Wedgwood Visitor Centre, Barlaston Staffs 75 F6
Wedhampton Wilts 25 D5
Wedmore Som 23 E6
Wednesbury W Mid 62 E3
Wednesfield W Mid 62 D3
Weedon Bucks 39 C8
Weedon Bec Northants 52 D4
Weedon Lois Northants 52 E4
Weeford Staffs 62 D5
Week Devon 10 C2
Week St Mary Corn 8 E4
Weeke Hants 26 F2
Weekley Northants 65 F5
Weel E Yorks 97 F6
Weeley Essex 43 B7
Weeley Heath Essex 43 B7
Weem Perth 141 E5
Weeping Cross Staffs 62 B3
Weethley Gate Warks 51 D5
Weeting Norf 67 F7
Weeting Heath NNR Norf 67 F7
Weeton E Yorks 91 B7
Weeton Lancs 92 F3
Weeton N Yorks 95 E5
Weetwood Hall Northumb 117 B6
Weir Lancs 87 B6
Weir Quay Devon 6 C2
Welborne Norf 68 D3
Welbourn Lincs 78 D2
Welburn N Yorks 96 C3
Welburn N Yorks 102 F4
Welbury N Yorks 102 D1
Welby Lincs 78 F2
Welches Dam Cambs 66 F4
Welcombe Devon 8 C4
Weld Bank Lancs 86 C3
Weldon Northumb 117 E7
Welford Northants 64 F3
Welford W Berks 26 B2
Welford-on-Avon Warks 51 D6
Welham Leics 64 E4
Welham Notts 89 F8
Welham Green Herts 41 D5
Well Hants 27 E5
Well Lincs 79 B7
Well N Yorks 101 F7
Well End Bucks 40 F1
Well Heads W Yorks 94 F3
Well Hill Kent 29 C5
Well Town Devon 10 D4
Welland Worcs 50 E2
Wellbank Angus 142 F4
Welldale Dumfries 107 C8
Wellesbourne Warks 51 D7
Welling London 29 B5
Wellingborough Northants 53 C6
Wellingham Norf 80 E4
Wellingore Lincs 78 D2
Wellington Cumb 98 D2
Wellington Hereford 49 E6
Wellington Som 11 B6
Wellington Telford 61 C6
Wellington Heath Hereford 50 E2
Wellington Hill W Yorks 95 F6
Wellow Bath 24 D2
Wellow I o W 14 F4
Wellow Notts 77 C6
Wellpond Green Herts 41 B7
Wells Som 23 E7
Wells Cathedral Som 23 E7
Wells Green Ches 74 D3
Wells-Next-The-Sea Norf 80 C5
Wellsborough Leics 63 D7
Wellswood Torbay 7 C7
Wellwood Fife 134 F2
Welney Norf 66 E5
Welsh Bicknor Hereford 36 C2
Welsh End Shrops 74 F2
Welsh Frankton Shrops 73 F7
Welsh Highland Railway, Caernarfon Gwyn 82 E4
Welsh Highland Railway, Porthmadog Gwyn 71 D6
Welsh Hook Pembs 44 C4
Welsh National Velodrome Newport 35 F7
Welsh Newton Hereford 36 C1
Welsh St Donats V Glam 22 B2
Welshampton Shrops 73 F8
Welshpool = Y Trallwng Powys 60 D2
Welton Cumb 108 E3
Welton E Yorks 90 B3
Welton Lincs 78 B3
Welton Northants 52 C3
Welton Hill Lincs 90 F4
Welton le Marsh Lincs 79 C7
Welton le Wold Lincs 91 F6
Welwick E Yorks 91 B7
Welwyn Herts 41 C5
Welwyn Garden City Herts 41 C5
Wem Shrops 60 B5
Wembdon Som 22 F4
Wembley London 40 F4
Wembley Stadium London 40 F4
Wembury Devon 6 E3
Wembworthy Devon 9 D8
Wemyss Bay Invclyd 129 D6
Wenallt Ceredig 47 B5
Wenallt Gwyn 72 E3
Wendens Ambo Essex 55 F6
Wendlebury Oxon 39 C5
Wendling Norf 68 C2
Wendover Bucks 40 D1
Wendron Corn 3 C5
Wendy Cambs 54 E4
Wenfordbridge Corn 5 B5
Wenhaston Suff 57 B8
Wennington Cambs 54 B3
Wennington London 41 F8
Wennington Lancs 93 B6
Wensley Derbys 76 C2
Wensley N Yorks 101 F5
Wentbridge W Yorks 89 C5
Wentnor Shrops 60 E3
Wentworth Cambs 55 B5
Wentworth S Yorks 88 E4
Wenvoe V Glam 22 B3
Weobley Hereford 49 D6
Weobley Marsh Hereford 49 D6
Wereham Norf 67 D6
Wergs W Mid 62 D2
Wern Powys 59 C6
Wern Powys 60 C2
Wernffrwd Swansea 33 E6
Wernyrheolydd Mon 35 C7
Werrington Corn 8 F5
Werrington P'boro 65 D8
Werrington Staffs 75 E6
Wervin Ches 73 B8
Wesham Lancs 92 F4
Wessington Derbys 76 D3
West Acre Norf 67 C7
West Adderbury Oxon 52 F2
West Allerdean Northumb 125 E5
West Alvington Devon 6 E5
West Amesbury Wilts 25 E6
West Anstey Devon 10 B3
West Ashby Lincs 79 B5
West Ashling W Sus 16 D2
West Ashton Wilts 24 D3
West Auckland Durham 101 B6
West Ayton N Yorks 103 F7
West Bagborough Som 22 F3
West Barkwith Lincs 91 F5
West Barnby N Yorks 103 C6
West Barns E Loth 124 B2
West Barsham Norf 80 D5
West Bay Dorset 12 E2
West Beckham Norf 81 D7
West Bedfont Sur 27 B8
West Benhar N Lnrk 121 C8
West Bergholt Essex 43 B5
West Bexington Dorset 12 F3
West Bilney Norf 67 C7
West Blatchington Brighton 17 D6
West Bowling W Yorks 94 F4
West Bradford Lancs 93 E7
West Bradley Som 23 F7
West Bretton W Yorks 88 C3
West Bridgford Notts 77 F5
West Bromwich W Mid 62 E4
West Buckland Devon 21 F5
West Buckland Som 11 B6
West Burrafirth Shetland 175 H4
West Burton N Yorks 101 F5
West Burton W Sus 16 C3
West Butterwick N Lincs 90 D2
West Byfleet Sur 27 C8
West Caister Norf 69 C8
West Calder W Loth 122 C3
West Camel Som 12 B3
West Challow Oxon 38 F3
West Chelborough Dorset 12 D3
West Chevington Northumb 117 E8
West Chiltington W Sus 16 C4
West Chiltington Common W Sus 16 C4
West Chinnock Som 12 C2
West Chisenbury Wilts 25 D6
West Clandon Sur 27 D8
West Cliffe Kent 31 E7
West Clyne Highld 165 D5
West Clyth Highld 169 F7
West Coker Som 12 C3
West Compton Dorset 12 E3
West Compton Som 23 E7
West Cowick E Yorks 89 B7
West Cranmore Som 23 E8
West Cross Swansea 33 F7
West Cullery Aberds 151 D6
West Curry Corn 8 E4
West Curthwaite Cumb 108 E3
West Darlochan Argyll 118 D3
West Dean Wilts 14 B3
West Dean W Sus 16 C2
West Deeping Lincs 65 D8
West Derby Mers 85 E4
West Dereham Norf 67 D6
West Didsbury Gtr Man 87 E6
West Ditchburn Northumb 117 B7
West Down Devon 20 E4
West Drayton London 27 B8
West Drayton Notts 77 B7
West Ella E Yorks 90 B4
West End Beds 53 D7
West End E Yorks 96 F5
West End E Yorks 97 F7
West End Hants 15 C5
West End Lancs 86 B5
West End Norf 68 D2
West End Norf 69 C8
West End N Som 23 C6
West End N Yorks 94 D4
West End Oxon 38 D4
West End S Lnrk 122 E2
West End Suff 69 F7
West End Sur 27 C7
West End S Yorks 89 D7
West End Wilts 13 B7
West End Wilts 24 B4
West End W Sus 17 C6
West End Green Hants 26 C4
West Farleigh Kent 29 D8
West Felton Shrops 60 B3
West Fenton E Loth 135 F6
West Ferry Dundee 142 F4
West Firle E Sus 17 D8
West Ginge Oxon 38 F4
West Grafton Wilts 25 C7
West Green Hants 26 D5
West Greenskares Aberds 160 B4
West Grimstead Wilts 14 B3
West Grinstead W Sus 17 B5
West Haddlesey N Yorks 89 B6
West Haddon Northants 52 B4
West Hagbourne Oxon 39 F5
West Hagley Worcs 62 F3
West Hall Cumb 109 C5
West Hallam Derbys 76 E4
West Halton N Lincs 90 B3
West Ham London 41 F7
West Handley Derbys 76 B3
West Hanney Oxon 38 E4
West Hanningfield Essex 42 E3
West Hardwick W Yorks 88 C5
West Harnham Wilts 14 B2
West Harptree Bath 23 D7
West Hatch Som 11 B7
West Head Norf 67 D5
West Heath Ches 74 C5
West Heath Hants 27 D6
West Heath Hants 26 D3
West Helmsdale Highld 165 C7
West Hendred Oxon 38 F4
West Heslerton N Yorks 96 B5
West Hill Devon 11 E5
West Hill E Yorks 97 C7
West Hill N Som 23 B6
West Hoathly W Sus 28 F4
West Holme Dorset 13 F6

Winterbourne Gunner Wilts 25 F6
Winterbourne Steepleton Dorset 12 F4
Winterbourne Stoke Wilts 25 E5
Winterburn N Yorks 94 D2
Winteringham N Lincs 90 B3
Winterley Ches 74 D4
Wintersett W Yorks 88 C4
Wintershill Hants 15 C6
Winterton N Lincs 90 C3
Winterton-on-Sea Norf 69 C7
Winthorpe Lincs 79 C8
Winthorpe Notts 77 D8
Winton Bmouth 13 E8
Winton Cumb 100 C2
Winton N Yorks 102 E2
Wintringham N Yorks 96 B4
Winwick Cambs 65 F8
Winwick Northants 52 B4
Winwick Warr 86 E4
Wirksworth Derbys 76 D2
Wirksworth Moor Derbys 76 D3
Wirswall Ches 74 E2
Wisbech Cambs 66 D4
Wisbech St Mary Cambs 66 D4
Wisborough Green W Sus 16 B4
Wiseton Notts 89 F8
Wishaw N Lnrk 121 D7
Wishaw Warks 63 E5
Wisley Sur 27 D8
Wispington Lincs 78 B5
Wissenden Kent 30 E3
Wissett Suff 57 B7
Wistanstow Shrops 60 F4
Wistanswick Shrops 61 B6
Wistaston Ches 74 D3
Wistaston Green Ches 74 D3
Wiston Pembs 32 C1
Wiston S Lnrk 122 F2
Wiston W Sus 16 C5
Wistow Cambs 66 F2
Wistow N Yorks 95 F8
Wiswell Lancs 93 F7
Witcham Cambs 66 F4
Witchampton Dorset 13 D7
Witchford Cambs 55 B6
Witham Essex 42 C4
Witham Friary Som 24 E2
Witham on the Hill Lincs 65 C7
Withcall Lincs 91 F6
Withdean Brighton 17 D7
Witherenden Hill E Sus 18 C3
Witheridge Devon 10 C3
Witherley Leics 63 E7
Withern Lincs 91 F8
Withernsea E Yorks 91 B7
Withernwick E Yorks 97 E7
Withersdale Street Suff 69 F5
Withersfield Suff 55 E7
Witherslack Cumb 99 F6
Withiel Corn 4 C4
Withiel Florey Som 21 F8
Withington Glos 37 C7
Withington Gtr Man 87 E6
Withington Hereford 49 E7
Withington Shrops 61 C5
Withington Staffs 75 F7
Withington Green Ches 74 B5
Withleigh Devon 10 C4
Withnell Lancs 86 B4
Withybrook Warks 63 F8
Withycombe Som 22 E2
Withycombe Raleigh Devon 10 F5
Withyham E Sus 29 F5
Withypool Som 21 F7
Witley Sur 27 F7
Witnesham Suff 57 D5
Witney Oxon 38 C3
Wittering P'boro 65 D7
Wittersham Kent 19 C5
Witton Angus 143 B5
Witton Worcs 50 C3
Witton Bridge Norf 69 A6
Witton Gilbert Durham 110 E5
Witton-le-Wear Durham 110 F4
Witton Park Durham 110 F4
Wiveliscombe Som 11 B5
Wivelrod Hants 26 F4
Wivelsfield E Sus 17 B7
Wivelsfield Green E Sus 17 B7
Wivenhoe Essex 43 B6
Wivenhoe Cross Essex 43 B6
Wiveton Norf 81 C6
Wix Essex 43 B7
Wixford Warks 51 D5
Wixhill Shrops 61 B5
Wixoe Suff 55 E8
Woburn Beds 53 F7
Woburn Abbey, Woburn Beds 53 F7
Woburn Sands M Keynes 53 F7
Woburn Wild Animal Kingdom Beds 53 F7
Wokefield Park W Berks 26 C4
Woking Sur 27 D8
Wokingham Wokingham 27 C6
Wolborough Devon 7 B6
Wold Newton E Yorks 97 B6
Wold Newton NE Lincs 91 E6
Woldingham Sur 28 D4
Wolfclyde S Lnrk 122 F3
Wolferton Norf 67 B6
Wolfhill Perth 142 F1
Wolf's Castle Pembs 44 C4
Wolfsdale Pembs 44 C4
Woll Borders 115 B7
Wollaston Northants 53 C7
Wollaston Shrops 60 C3
Wollaton Nottingham 76 F5
Wollaton Hall Nottingham 76 F5
Wollerton Shrops 74 F3
Wollescote W Mid 62 F3
Wolsingham Durham 110 F3
Wolstanton Staffs 75 E5
Wolston Warks 52 B2
Wolvercote Oxon 38 D4
Wolverhampton W Mid 62 E3
Wolverhampton Racecourse W Mid 62 D3
Wolverley Shrops 73 F8
Wolverley Worcs 50 B3
Wolverton Hants 26 D3
Wolverton M Keynes 53 E6
Wolverton Warks 51 C7
Wolverton Common Hants 26 D3
Wolvesnewton Mon 36 E1
Wolvey Warks 63 F8
Wolviston Stockton 102 B2
Wombleton N Yorks 102 F4
Wombourne Staffs 62 E2
Wombwell S Yorks 88 D4
Womenswold Kent 31 D6
Womersley N Yorks 89 C6
Wonastow Mon 36 C1
Wonersh Sur 27 E8
Wonson Devon 9 F8
Wonston Hants 26 F2
Wooburn Bucks 40 F2
Wooburn Green Bucks 40 F2
Wood Dalling Norf 81 E6
Wood End Herts 41 B6
Wood End Warks 51 B6
Wood End Warks 63 E6
Wood Enderby Lincs 79 C5
Wood Field Sur 28 D2
Wood Green London 41 E6
Wood Green Animal Shelter, Godmanchester Cambs 54 C3
Wood Hayes W Mid 62 D3
Wood Lanes Ches 87 F7
Wood Norton Norf 81 E6
Wood Street Norf 69 B6
Wood Street Sur 27 D7
Wood Walton Cambs 66 F2
Woodacott Devon 9 D5
Woodale N Yorks 94 B3
Woodbank Argyll 118 E3
Woodbastwick Norf 69 C6
Woodbeck Notts 77 B7
Woodborough Notts 77 E6
Woodborough Wilts 25 D6
Woodbridge Dorset 12 C5
Woodbridge Suff 57 E6
Woodbury Devon 10 F5
Woodbury Salterton Devon 10 F5
Woodchester Glos 37 D5
Woodchurch Kent 19 B6
Woodchurch Mers 85 F3
Woodcombe Som 21 E8
Woodcote Oxon 39 F6
Woodcott Hants 26 D2
Woodcroft Glos 36 E2
Woodcutts Dorset 13 C7
Woodditton Cambs 55 D7
Woodeaton Oxon 39 C5
Woodend Cumb 98 E3
Woodend Northants 52 E4
Woodend W Sus 16 D2
Woodend Green Northants 52 E4
Woodfalls Wilts 14 B2
Woodfield Oxon 39 B5
Woodfield S Ayrs 112 B3
Woodford Corn 8 C4
Woodford Devon 7 D5
Woodford Glos 36 E3
Woodford London 41 E7
Woodford Gtr Man 87 F6
Woodford Northants 53 B7
Woodford Bridge London 41 E7
Woodford Halse Northants 52 D3
Woodgate Norf 68 C3
Woodgate W Mid 62 F3
Woodgate Worcs 50 C4
Woodgate W Sus 16 D3
Woodgreen Hants 14 C2
Woodhall Herts 41 C5
Woodhall Invclyd 120 B3
Woodhall N Yorks 100 E4
Woodhall Spa Lincs 78 C4
Woodham Sur 27 C8
Woodham Ferrers Essex 42 E3
Woodham Mortimer Essex 42 D4
Woodham Walter Essex 42 D4
Woodhaven Fife 135 B6
Woodhead Aberds 160 E4
Woodhey Gtr Man 87 C5
Woodhill Shrops 61 F7
Woodhorn Northumb 117 F8
Woodhouse Leics 64 C2
Woodhouse N Lincs 89 D8
Woodhouse S Yorks 88 F5
Woodhouse W Yorks 95 F5
Woodhouse W Yorks 88 B4
Woodhouse Eaves Leics 64 C2
Woodhouse Park Gtr Man 87 F6
Woodhouselee Midloth 122 C5
Woodhouselees Dumfries 108 B3
Woodhouses Staffs 63 C5
Woodhurst Cambs 54 B4
Woodingdean Brighton 17 D7
Woodkirk W Yorks 88 B3
Woodland Devon 7 C5
Woodland Durham 101 B5
Woodland Leisure Park, Dartmouth Devon 7 D6
Woodlands Aberds 151 E6
Woodlands Dorset 13 D8
Woodlands Hants 14 C4
Woodlands Highld 157 C6
Woodlands N Yorks 95 D6
Woodlands S Yorks 89 D6
Woodlands Park Windsor 27 B6
Woodlands St Mary W Berks 25 B8
Woodlane Staffs 62 B5
Woodleigh Devon 6 E5
Woodlesford W Yorks 88 B4
Woodley Gtr Man 87 E7
Woodley Wokingham 27 B5
Woodmancote Glos 36 E4
Woodmancote Glos 37 D7
Woodmancote Glos 37 B6
Woodmancote W Sus 15 D8
Woodmancote W Sus 17 C6
Woodmancott Hants 26 E3
Woodmansey E Yorks 97 F6
Woodmansterne Sur 28 D3
Woodminton Wilts 13 B8
Woodnesborough Kent 31 D7
Woodnewton Northants 65 E7
Woodplumpton Lancs 92 F5
Woodrising Norf 68 D2
Wood's Green E Sus 18 B3
Woodseaves Shrops 74 F3
Woodseaves Staffs 61 B7
Woodsend Wilts 25 B7
Woodsetts S Yorks 89 F6
Woodsford Dorset 13 E5
Woodside Aberdeen 151 D8
Woodside Aberds 161 D7
Woodside Brack 27 B7
Woodside Fife 135 D6
Woodside Hants 14 E4
Woodside Herts 41 D5
Woodside Perth 142 F2
Woodside Farm and Wildfowl Park, Luton Beds 40 C3
Woodside of Arbeadie Aberds 151 E6
Woodstock Oxon 38 C4
Woodstock Pembs 32 B1
Woodthorpe Derbys 76 B4
Woodthorpe Leics 64 C2
Woodthorpe Lincs 91 F8
Woodthorpe York 95 E8
Woodton Norf 69 E5
Woodtown Devon 9 B6
Woodtown Devon 9 B6
Woodvale Mers 85 C4
Woodville Derbys 63 C7
Woodyates Dorset 13 C8
Woofferton Shrops 49 C7
Wookey Som 23 E7
Wookey Hole Som 23 E7
Wookey Hole Caves & Papermill, Wells Som 23 E7
Wool Dorset 13 F6
Woolacombe Devon 20 E3
Woolage Green Kent 31 E6
Woolaston Glos 36 E2
Woolavington Som 22 E5
Woolbeding W Sus 16 B2
Wooldale W Yorks 88 D2
Wooler Northumb 117 B5
Woolfardisworthy Devon 8 B5
Woolfardisworthy Devon 10 D3
Woolfords Cottages S Lnrk 122 D3
Woolhampton W Berks 26 C3
Woolhope Hereford 49 F8
Woolhope Cockshoot Hereford 49 F8
Woolland Dorset 13 D5
Woollaton Devon 9 C6
Woolley Bath 24 C2
Woolley Cambs 54 B2
Woolley Corn 8 C4
Woolley Derbys 76 C3
Woolley W Yorks 88 C4
Woolmer Green Herts 41 C5
Woolmere Green Worcs 50 C4
Woolpit Suff 56 C3
Woolscott Warks 52 C2
Woolsington T & W 110 C4
Woolstanwood Ches 74 D3
Woolstaston Shrops 60 E4
Woolsthorpe Lincs 77 F8
Woolsthorpe Lincs 65 B6
Woolston Devon 6 E5
Woolston Shrops 60 F4
Woolston Shrops 60 B3
Woolston Soton 14 C5
Woolston Warr 86 F4
Woolstone M Keynes 53 F6
Woolstone Oxon 38 F2
Woolton Mers 86 F2
Woolton Hill Hants 26 C2
Woolverstone Suff 57 F5
Woolverton Som 24 D2
Woolwich London 28 B5
Woolwich Ferry London 28 B5
Woonton Hereford 49 D5
Wooperton Northumb 117 B6
Woore Shrops 74 E4
Wootten Green Suff 57 B6
Wootton Beds 53 E8
Wootton Hants 14 E3
Wootton Hereford 48 D5
Wootton Kent 31 E6
Wootton N Lincs 90 C4
Wootton Northants 53 D5
Wootton Oxon 38 C4
Wootton Oxon 38 D4
Wootton Shrops 49 B6
Wootton Shrops 60 B3
Wootton Staffs 62 B2
Wootton Staffs 75 E8
Wootton Bassett Wilts 37 F7
Wootton Bridge I o W 15 E6
Wootton Common I o W 15 E6
Wootton Courtenay Som 21 E8
Wootton Fitzpaine Dorset 11 E8
Wootton Rivers Wilts 25 C6
Wootton St Lawrence Hants 26 D3
Wootton Wawen Warks 51 C6
Worcester Worcs 50 D3
Worcester Cathedral Worcs 50 D3
Worcester Park London 28 C3
Worcester Racecourse Worcs 50 D3
Wordsley W Mid 62 F2
Worfield Shrops 61 E7
Work Orkney 176 E3
Workington Cumb 98 B1
Worksop Notts 77 B5
Worlaby N Lincs 90 C4
World of James Herriot N Yorks 102 F2
World's End W Berks 26 B2
Worle N Som 23 C5
Worleston Ches 74 D3
Worlingham Suff 69 F7
Worlington Suff 55 B7
Worlingworth Suff 57 C6
Wormald Green N Yorks 95 C6
Wormbridge Hereford 49 F6
Wormegay Norf 67 C6
Wormelow Tump Hereford 49 F6
Wormhill Derbys 75 B8
Wormingford Essex 56 F3
Worminghall Bucks 39 D6
Wormington Glos 50 F5
Worminster Som 23 E7
Wormit Fife 135 B5
Wormleighton Warks 52 D2
Wormley Herts 41 D6
Wormley Sur 27 F7
Wormley West End Herts 41 D6
Wormshill Kent 30 D2
Wormsley Hereford 49 E6
Worplesdon Sur 27 D7
Worrall S Yorks 88 E4
Worsbrough S Yorks 88 D4
Worsbrough Common S Yorks 88 D4
Worsley Gtr Man 86 D5
Worstead Norf 69 B6
Worsthorne Lancs 93 F8
Worston Lancs 93 E7
Worswell Devon 6 E3
Worth Kent 31 D7
Worth W Sus 28 F4
Worth Matravers Dorset 13 G7
Wortham Suff 56 B4
Worthen Shrops 60 D3
Worthenbury Wrex 73 E8
Worthing Norf 68 C2
Worthing W Sus 16 D5
Worthington Leics 63 B8
Worting Hants 26 D4
Wortley S Yorks 88 E4
Wortley W Yorks 95 F5
Worton N Yorks 100 E4
Worton Wilts 24 D4
Wortwell Norf 69 F5
Wotherton Shrops 60 D2
Wotter Devon 6 C3
Wotton Sur 28 E2
Wotton-under-Edge Glos 36 E4
Wotton Underwood Bucks 39 C6
Woughton on the Green M Keynes 53 F6
Wouldham Kent 29 C8
Wrabness Essex 57 F5
Wrafton Devon 20 F3
Wragby Lincs 78 B4
Wragby W Yorks 88 C5
Wragholme Lincs 91 E7
Wramplingham Norf 68 D4
Wrangbrook W Yorks 89 C5
Wrangham Aberds 160 E3
Wrangle Lincs 79 D7
Wrangle Bank Lincs 79 D7
Wrangle Lowgate Lincs 79 D7
Wrangway Som 11 C6
Wrantage Som 11 B8
Wrawby N Lincs 90 D4
Wraxall Dorset 12 D3
Wraxall N Som 23 B6
Wraxall Som 23 F8
Wray Lancs 93 C6
Wraysbury Windsor 27 B8
Wrayton Lancs 93 B6
Wrea Green Lancs 92 F3
Wreay Cumb 99 B6
Wreay Cumb 108 E4
Wrecclesham Sur 27 E6
Wrecsam = Wrexham Wrex 73 D7
Wrekenton T & W 111 D5
Wrelton N Yorks 103 F5
Wrenbury Ches 74 E2
Wrench Green N Yorks 103 F7
Wreningham Norf 68 E4
Wrentham Suff 69 F7
Wrenthorpe W Yorks 88 B4
Wrentnall Shrops 60 D4
Wressle E Yorks 96 F3
Wressle N Lincs 90 D3
Wrestlingworth Beds 54 E3
Wretham Norf 68 F2
Wretton Norf 67 E6
Wrexham = Wrecsam Wrex 73 D7
Wrexham Industrial Estate Wrex 73 E7
Wribbenhall Worcs 50 B2
Wrightington Bar Lancs 86 C3
Wrinehill Staffs 74 E4
Wrington N Som 23 C6
Writhlington Bath 24 D2
Writtle Essex 42 D2
Wrockwardine Telford 61 C6
Wroot N Lincs 89 D8
Wrotham Kent 29 D7
Wrotham Heath Kent 29 D7
Wroughton Swindon 37 F8
Wroxall I o W 15 G6
Wroxall Warks 51 B7
Wroxeter Shrops 61 D5
Wroxham Norf 69 C6
Wroxham Barns, Hoveton Norf 69 B6
Wroxton Oxon 52 E2
Wyaston Derbys 75 E8
Wyberton Lincs 79 E6
Wyboston Beds 54 D2
Wybunbury Ches 74 E4
Wych Cross E Sus 28 F5
Wychbold Worcs 50 C4
Wyck Hants 27 F5
Wyck Rissington Glos 38 B1
Wycoller Lancs 94 F2
Wycomb Leics 64 B4
Wycombe Marsh Bucks 40 E1
Wyddial Herts 54 F4
Wye Kent 30 E4
Wyesham Mon 36 C2
Wyfordby Leics 64 C4
Wyke Dorset 13 B5
Wyke Shrops 61 D6
Wyke Sur 27 D7
Wyke W Yorks 88 B2
Wyke Regis Dorset 12 G4
Wykeham N Yorks 103 F7
Wykeham N Yorks 96 B4
Wyken W Mid 63 F7
Wykey Shrops 60 B3
Wylam Northumb 110 C4
Wylde Green W Mid 62 E5
Wyllie Caerph 35 E5
Wylye Wilts 24 F5
Wymering Ptsmth 15 D7
Wymeswold Leics 64 B3
Wymington Beds 53 C7
Wymondham Leics 65 C5
Wymondham Norf 68 D4
Wyndham Bridgend 34 E3
Wynford Eagle Dorset 12 E3
Wyng Orkney 176 G2
Wynyard Village Stockton 102 B2
Wyre Piddle Worcs 50 E4
Wysall Notts 64 B3
Wythall Worcs 51 B5
Wytham Oxon 38 D4
Wythburn Cumb 99 C5
Wythenshawe Gtr Man 87 F6
Wythop Mill Cumb 98 B3
Wyton Cambs 54 B3
Wyverstone Suff 56 C4
Wyverstone Street Suff 56 C4
Wyville Lincs 65 B5
Wyvis Lodge Highld 157 B5

Y

Y Bala = Bala Gwyn 72 F3
Y Barri = Barry V Glam 22 C3
Y Bont-Faen = Cowbridge V Glam 21 B8
Y Drenewydd = Newtown Powys 59 E8
Y Felinheli Gwyn 82 E5
Y Fenni = Abergavenny Mon 35 C6
Y Fflint = Flint Flint 73 B6
Y Ffôr Gwyn 70 D4
Y-Ffrith Denb 72 A4
Y Gelli Gandryll = Hay-on-Wye Powys 48 E4
Y Mwmbwls = The Mumbles Swansea 33 F7
Y Pîl = Pyle Bridgend 34 F2
Y Rhws = Rhoose V Glam 22 C2
Y Rhyl = Rhyl Denb 72 A4
Y Trallwng = Welshpool Powys 60 D2
Y Waun = Chirk Wrex 73 F6
Yaddlethorpe N Lincs 90 D2
Yafford I o W 14 F5
Yafforth N Yorks 101 E8
Yalding Kent 29 D7
Yanworth Glos 37 C7
Yapham E Yorks 96 D3
Yapton W Sus 16 D3
Yarburgh Lincs 91 E7
Yarcombe Devon 11 D7
Yard Som 22 F2
Yardley W Mid 62 F5
Yardley Gobion Northants 53 E5
Yardley Hastings Northants 53 D6
Yardro Powys 48 D4
Yarkhill Hereford 49 E8
Yarlet Staffs 62 B3
Yarlington Som 12 B4
Yarlside Cumb 92 C2
Yarm Stockton 102 C2
Yarmouth I o W 14 F4
Yarmouth Racecourse Norf 69 C8
Yarnbrook Wilts 24 D3
Yarnfield Staffs 75 F5
Yarnscombe Devon 9 B7
Yarnton Oxon 38 C4
Yarpole Hereford 49 C6
Yarrow Borders 115 B6
Yarrow Feus Borders 115 B6
Yarsop Hereford 49 E6
Yarwell Northants 65 E7
Yate S Glos 36 F4
Yateley Hants 27 C6
Yatesbury Wilts 25 B5
Yattendon W Berks 26 B3
Yatton Hereford 49 C6
Yatton N Som 23 C6
Yatton Keynell Wilts 24 B3
Yaverland I o W 15 F7
Yaxham Norf 68 C3
Yaxley Cambs 65 E8
Yaxley Suff 56 B5
Yazor Hereford 49 E6
Yeading London 40 F4
Yeadon W Yorks 94 E5
Yealand Conyers Lancs 92 B5
Yealand Redmayne Lancs 92 B5
Yealmpton Devon 6 D3
Yearby Redcar 102 B4
Yearsley N Yorks 95 B8
Yeaton Shrops 60 C4
Yeaveley Derbys 75 E8
Yedingham N Yorks 96 B4
Yeldon Beds 53 C8
Yelford Oxon 38 D3
Yelland Devon 20 F3
Yelling Cambs 54 C3
Yelvertoft Northants 52 B3
Yelverton Devon 6 C3
Yelverton Norf 69 D5
Yenston Som 12 B5
Yeo Mill Devon 10 B3
Yeoford Devon 10 E2
Yeolmbridge Corn 8 F5
Yeovil Som 12 C3
Yeovil Marsh Som 12 C3
Yeovilton Som 12 B3
Yerbeston Pembs 32 D1
Yesnaby Orkney 176 E1
Yetlington Northumb 117 D6
Yetminster Dorset 12 C3
Yettington Devon 11 F5
Yetts o'Muckhart Clack 134 D2
Yieldshields S Lnrk 121 D8
Yiewsley London 40 F3
Ynys-meudwy Neath 33 D8
Ynysboeth Rhondda 34 E4
Ynysddu Caerph 35 E5
Ynysgyfflog Gwyn 58 C3
Ynyshir Rhondda 34 E4
Ynyslas Ceredig 58 E3
Ynystawe Swansea 33 D7
Ynysybwl Rhondda 34 E4
Yockenthwaite N Yorks 94 B2
Yockleton Shrops 60 C3
Yokefleet E Yorks 90 B2
Yoker Glasgow 120 C5
Yonder Bognie Aberds 160 D2
York York 95 D8
York Castle Museum York 96 D2
York Minster York 96 D2
York Racecourse York 95 E8
York Town Sur 27 C6
Yorkletts Kent 30 C4
Yorkley Glos 36 D3
Yorkshire Museum York 95 D8
Yorkshire Sculpture Park, Wakefield W Yorks 88 C3
Yorton Shrops 60 B5
Youlgreave Derbys 76 C2
Youlstone Devon 8 C4
Youlthorpe E Yorks 96 D3
Youlton N Yorks 95 C7
Young Wood Lincs 78 B4
Young's End Essex 42 C3
Yoxall Staffs 62 C5
Yoxford Suff 57 C7
Yr Hôb = Hope Flint 73 D7
Yr Wyddgrug = Mold Flint 73 C6
Ysbyty-Cynfyn Ceredig 47 B6
Ysbyty Ifan Conwy 72 E2
Ysbyty Ystwyth Ceredig 47 B6
Ysceifiog Flint 73 B5
Yspitty Carms 33 E6
Ystalyfera Neath 34 D1
Ystrad Rhondda 34 E3
Ystrad Aeron Ceredig 46 D4
Ystrad-mynach Caerph 35 E5
Ystradfellte Powys 34 C3
Ystradffin Carms 47 E6
Ystradgynlais Powys 34 C1
Ystradmeurig Ceredig 47 C6
Ystradowen Carms 33 C8
Ystradowen V Glam 22 B2
Ystumtuen Ceredig 47 B6
Ythanbank Aberds 161 E6
Ythanwells Aberds 160 E3
Ythsie Aberds 161 E5

Z

Zeal Monachorum Devon 10 D2
Zeals Wilts 24 F2
Zelah Corn 4 D3
Zennor Corn 2 C3

www.philips-maps.co.uk

First published in 2007 by Philip's
a division of Octopus Publishing Group Ltd
www.octopusbooks.co.uk
2–4 Heron Quays
London E14 4JP
An Hachette Livre UK Company

www.philips-maps.co.uk

First edition 2007
First impression 2007

Cartography by Philip's

Data for the speed cameras provided by PocketGPSWorld.com Ltd.

Information for Tourist Attractions shown on the mapping supplied by VisitBritain

Information for National Parks, Areas of Outstanding Natural Beauty, National Trails and Country Parks in Wales supplied by the Countryside Council for Wales.

Information for National Parks, Areas of Outstanding Natural Beauty, National Trails and Country Parks in England supplied by the Countryside Agency. Data for Regional Parks, Long Distance Footpaths and Country Parks in Scotland provided by Scottish Natural Heritage.

Gaelic name forms used in the Western Isles provided by Comhairle nan Eilean.

Data for the National Nature Reserves in England provided by English Nature. Data for the National Nature Reserves in Wales provided by Countryside Council for Wales. Darparwyd data'n ymwneud â Gwarchodfeydd Natur Cenedlaethol Cymru gan Gyngor Cefn Gwlad Cymru.

Information on the location of National Nature Reserves in Scotland was provided by Scottish Natural Heritage.

Data for National Scenic Areas in Scotland provided by the Scottish Executive Office. Crown copyright material is reproduced with the permission of the Controller of HMSO and the Queen's Printer for Scotland. Licence number C02W0003960.

Printed in Italy by Rotolito

Photographic acknowledgments
Cover, page I and pages IV, VI, VIII top *imagebroker / Alamy.*

Page II *Justin Kase / Alamy* • Page III inset *Paul Springett / Alamy;* background *James Hughes* • Page IV left *Victor de Schwanberg / Alamy* • Page V *Environmental Transport Association* • Page VI left *Pixel / Alamy;* bottom *Justin Kase / Alamy* • Page VII inset *Environmental Transport Association;* background *James Hughes* • Page VIII bottom *Nick Kirk / Alamy*; inset *Environmental Transport Association*; Page IX *NPA Group (www.satmaps.com).*